American Writers
Before 1800

AMERICAN WRITERS BEFORE 1800

A Biographical and Critical Dictionary

Q–Z

EDITED BY James A. Levernier AND Douglas R. Wilmes

GREENWOOD PRESS
WESTPORT, CONNECTICUT
LONDON, ENGLAND

Library of Congress Cataloging in Publication Data
Main entry under title:

American writers before 1800.

Bibliography: p.
Includes index.
1. American literature—Colonial period, ca. 1600-
1775—History and criticism. 2. American literature—
Revolutionary period, 1775-1783—History and criticism.
3. American literature—1783-1850—History and criticism.
4. American literature—Colonial period, ca. 1600-1775—
Bio-bibliography. 5. Authors, American—18th century—
Biography. 6. Authors, American—To 1700—Biography.
I. Levernier, James A. II. Wilmes, Douglas R.
PS185.A4   810'.9'001   82-933
ISBN 0-313-24096-5 (lib. bdg. : v. 3)   AACR2

Library of Congress Catalog Card Number: 82-933
ISBN 0-313-22229-0 (set)
          0-313-23476-0 (vol. 1)
          0-313-23477-9 (vol. 2)
          0-313-24096-5 (vol. 3)

First published in 1983

Greenwood Press
A division of Congressional Information Service, Inc.
88 Post Road West
Westport, Connecticut 06881

Printed in the United States of America

10 9 8 7 6 5 4 3 2 1

In Memory of
Theodore Hornberger

Contents

Preface   *ix*

Acknowledgments   *xv*

Abbreviations   *xvii*

Biographical and Critical Dictionary   *3*

Appendixes

  A. *Year of Birth*   *1671*

  B. *Place of Birth*   *1687*

  C. *Principal Place(s) of Residence*   *1697*

  D. *Chronology*   *1709*

Index   *1725*

Preface

This book is designed to provide a convenient source of information about the lives and works of a large number (786) of early American writers. Each writer is discussed in an individual entry that includes primary and secondary bibliographical references, a brief biography, and a critical appraisal of the writer's works and significance. The entries are arranged alphabetically and are followed by appendixes (classifying the writers by date of birth, place of birth, and principal place of residence and presenting a chronology of important events from 1492 to 1800) and by a general index.

A noteworthy feature of this reference tool is its wide scope and broad principles of inclusion, enabling us to include entries on a variety of minor writers. Although we have also provided entries on the major writers of the period, which should prove useful and informative in their own right, we have recognized that treatments of authors such as William Bradford, Benjamin Franklin, Cotton Mather, and Edward Taylor are available in a variety of readily accessible reference formats. However, convenient accessibility of information does not prevail when one turns to the study of the many early American writers who are not well-known or highly valued in strictly literary terms but who are nevertheless worthy of our attention. As microform reproductions of practically all texts published in colonial and early national America are now available, the need for widely inclusive reference tools is all the more apparent. In an effort to meet this need, we have included entries on a large number of lesser-known writers, many of whom are discussed and evaluated here in some detail for the first time.

Students of early American culture will be aware of the vitality and scope of current scholarly interest in early American writing. It would be impossible to summarize briefly and fairly the development of this body of scholarship; a thorough survey would note the many biographies and works of criticism focusing on major writers, but it would also note the appearance of a number of anthologies and histories or interpretations founded in wide-ranging appreciations of the pluralism and multiplicity of early American writing. Works such as

The New England Mind by Perry Miller, the anthology of Puritan writing edited by Miller and Thomas H. Johnson, the anthologies of early American poetry edited by Harrison T. Meserole and Kenneth Silverman, the writings of Sacvan Bercovitch and Richard Beale Davis, and many other distinguished contributions have immeasurably broadened and deepened our knowledge of the substance and import of the lesser-known voices of early American culture.

In fact, our early literature has always—by its nature—demanded of its students an acquaintance with minor voices. In 1878, when Moses Coit Tyler wrote the preface to his pioneering literary history of the colonial period, he was careful to define his subject broadly, as inclusive of those "early authors whose writings, whether many or few, have any appreciable merit, or throw any helpful light upon the evolution of thought and of style in America, during those flourishing and indispensable days." The history of twentieth-century scholarship in early American studies has validated Tyler's approach, and this reference work is based upon a similar reluctance to define narrowly the matter of early American literature.

A reference tool's success is measured by its practical, utilitarian ability to perform the task for which it is designed. We have kept this principle firmly in mind when preparing these volumes, and it has informed two areas of our responsibility that merit particular explanation. These areas are the method by which we selected writers for inclusion and the format of the entries.

SELECTION OF ENTRIES

The writers included in *American Writers Before 1800* are not necessarily the 786 "best" writers of the period. We have not, in other words, selected writers by applying any original definition of literary quality. Such a methodology would have presupposed an ability to form a widely useful and acceptable objective definition of literary quality, which has important subjective components. Moreover, to apply such a definition to a project of this size would require encyclopedic knowledge, and the book would become in part an argument for the validity of the definition and for the accuracy of its application.

Therefore, the selection of writers for this volume was not based upon our individual and personal judgments of their merit. Rather, we have worked inductively from the evidence of a selection of anthologies, literary and cultural histories, and bibliographies of the period. In the first instance, writers have been included in these volumes by virtue of their appearance in secondary works likely to be read or used by scholars and students of early American literature. This array of writers—which we believe includes most writers of works with clearly significant literary merit—forms the backbone of the book. It has been expanded upon in two additional ways. First, in some areas we included some very minor figures in order to provide a representative coverage of certain subgenres, such as the Puritan elegy or early nature reportage. Second, we have sought the advice of experts in certain specialized fields, such as Quaker writing, German pietism, and black literature, to ascertain whether we had included significant and representative writers from those fields.

In examining the results of this process of selection, other scholars will undoubtedly discover sins of omission and commission. As a matter of individual judgment, one might wish for an entry on one writer at the expense of another. Stepping beyond the limits of this equation, we would regard the sin of omission as the more serious and the more to be regretted but also as an inevitable result of limitations of space and human fallibility. There are certainly many more early writers who deserve at least the kind of preliminary and limited discussion and evaluation that our format allows. On the other hand, we are not persuaded that we have included writers who are not worth even the brief discussion they have received in these volumes.

In every regard, our selection is founded upon a considered estimation of the practical uses to which this reference book may be put. We hope, for example, to have met the needs of readers of anthologies, histories, or critical analyses of early American literature who discover passing references to minor writers and want to obtain a sense of who those writers were and what they wrote. Our method of selection should ensure that these volumes will meet such needs in many cases. Furthermore, although the book has a literary bias, its scope is broad enough to accommodate the needs of many constituencies within the field of early American studies. Finally, practical considerations have led us to avoid any prescriptive limitation that might make the book less useful. We have not, for example, interpreted the meaning of "American writers" narrowly. The world of early America obviously had important transatlantic dimensions, and we have therefore included entries on a number of temporary residents or visitors to America who could not themselves be considered "American." In a few instances, we have included entries on writers who themselves never visited America but whose writings concern America and influenced, in some significant way, the development of an American literary heritage and cultural self-identity. In every case, we have asked whether or not the entry would benefit the student of early American culture; we have allowed no consideration to outweigh this central concern.

ENTRY FORMAT

In keeping with our intention to provide information on a variety of lesser-known writers, we have not scaled the length of the entries in proportion to the importance of the writer being discussed in a given entry. Although in some cases minor writers have received a relatively shorter treatment and major writers a relatively longer treatment, in general we have tried to maintain a fairly constant length. Thus a minor writer will often receive more attention than that writer might otherwise have gained, and a major writer less attention, on the principle that the reader may easily obtain further information and critical analyses of the major figures in early American literature. First references within each entry to other writers included in the book are indicated by cross-references (q.v.).

Each entry has been divided into four sections, which organize the content in a predictable and convenient manner:

Works: Each writer's major publications are listed in chronological order. Works are listed by short title, and each title is followed by the date of publication. Significant delays between composition and publication have been indicated when possible. Unpublished material is included where appropriate. In general, we have excluded writers whose work exists only in manuscript, but we have made a few exceptions to this rule where future publication of such material is expected. Although the focus of this book is not primarily bibliographical, we have attempted to ensure that these primary bibliographies are as complete and accurate as possible. In a very few instances, a complete listing of the writer's major publications has not been practicable; in these instances, the reader is directed to appropriate bibliographies or sources. Both American and European imprints are listed; in most cases, the titles will have been published in America, and texts may be obtained by using Charles Evans's *American Bibliography* or the *National Index of American Imprints Through 1800: The Short-Title Evans* (1969), by Clifford K. Shipton and James E. Mooney. Texts listed in these bibliographies may be read in microprint in the Early American Imprints Series. Further references to modern printings or reprintings are included in the "Works" or "Suggested Readings" sections of the entry as appropriate.

Biography: A brief summary of the salient features of the writer's life is included in the second section. In some instances, very little is known about the writer's biography, but in every instance, the entry provides an overview of the writer's life and social context within the limitations of present knowledge.

Critical Appraisal: The third section of the entry is devoted to a summary of the writer's work and a critical estimation of its value. Depending on the nature of the writing, the appraisal may place the writer's work into the context of intellectual, religious, social, or political history. This section of the entry is judgmental and offers opinions; however, an attempt has been made to present each writer in a positive light, without being misleadingly uncritical. Since a vast variety of writing is discussed in these volumes, the kinds of analyses made in the critical appraisals will necessarily vary. But in each case, the appraisal supplies a critical introduction to the writer and serves as a guide to further readings in the original texts.

Suggested Readings: The final section of each entry is devoted to a secondary bibliography. References to standard sources (such as the *Dictionary of American Biography* [DAB] and the *Dictionary of National Biography* [DNB]) are listed first in abbreviated form, followed by fuller references to other sources.

These suggested readings do not in any way pretend to be inclusive or exhaustive, and in the cases of major writers, they are highly selective. Their purpose is solely to direct the reader to sources that the authors of entries in these volumes found particularly useful or informative when they wrote their essays.

The entries in this book have been contributed by some 250 scholars of early American culture and literature. These volumes are thus a collective effort and do contain many voices and many points of view. The format has been designed to maintain a productive tension between the consistency of form required in a reference tool and the variety of content implicit in the individuality of the writers selected for inclusion and of the scholars who have interpreted and judged them.

James A. Levernier
Douglas R. Wilmes

Acknowledgments

In organizing and undertaking this project, we have incurred professional debts far too numerous to list in these acknowledgments. For their invaluable assistance in helping us review the entries to be included in these volumes and/or seek appropriate contributors, we are especially indebted to Ronald Bosco of the State University of New York at Albany; Hennig Cohen of the University of Pennsylvania; Michael Lofaro of the University of Tennessee; Pattie Cowell of Colorado State University; David S. Wilson of the University of California at Davis; Sacvan Bercovitch of Columbia University; Richard Beale Davis, late of the University of Tennessee; and Philip Barbour, late of the Early American Institute in Williamsburg, Virginia.

In addition, we wish to acknowledge a special debt of gratitude to the following individuals for their willingness to assume responsibilities well above and beyond the call of duty for entries that we requested them to research and write: Douglas M. Arnold of Yale University; Dorothy and Edmund Berkeley of Charlottesville, Virginia; Steven Kagle of Illinois State University; Daniel F. Littlefield, Jr., of Little Rock, Arkansas; Julian Mason of the University of North Carolina at Charlotte; David Minter of Emory University; Irving N. Rothman of the University of Houston; John Shields of Illinois State University; Frank Shuffelton of the University of Rochester; James Stephens of Marquette University; and Marion Barber Stowell of Milledgeville, Georgia.

We wish also to thank the editorial staff at Greenwood Press, particularly Cynthia Harris, Anne Kugielsky, Maureen Melino, Mildred Vasan, and James T. Sabin, for their strong commitment to this project, from its inception through to its publication, and for their patient and always helpful advice, commentary, and attention. In this capacity, we likewise wish to thank Mary DeVries for the painstaking attention she gave to copy-editing the completed manuscript. Our thanks also go to the many friends and colleagues, especially David Jauss, Mary De Jong, Frank Parks, Julian Wasserman, and Bruce Weigl, who gave us their tireless encouragement and support. To these individuals we owe an immeasurable debt; without their assistance and confidence we could not have completed this project.

In addition, we wish to thank the following institutions and their staffs for allowing us access to their resource materials and holdings: The Boston Public Library, The Newberry Library, and the libraries at Alliance College, Harvard University, Northwestern University, the Pennsylvania State University, Rice University, the University of Arkansas at Fayetteville, the University of Arkansas at Little Rock, the University of Connecticut, the University of Pennsylvania, Wesleyan University, Westminster College (New Wilmington, Pennsylvania), Yale University, and Youngstown State University. In this capacity, we wish to express particular gratitude to Shirley A. Snyder, librarian, and Eric R. Birdsall, associate director for academic affairs, both of the Pennsylvania State University, the Shenango Valley Campus.

Finally, we wish to thank the Donaghey Foundation and the faculty research committee at the University of Arkansas at Little Rock for a grant that helped defray expenses related to this project, and we wish to thank all of our contributors for their patience, cooperation, and support.

J.A.L. and D.R.W.

Abbreviations

BDAS	Clark A. Elliott, *Biographical Dictionary of American Science: The Seventeenth Through the Nineteenth Centuries* (Westport, Conn., 1979).
CCMC	Frederick Lewis Weis, *The Colonial Churches and the Colonial Clergy of the Middle and Southern Colonies, 1607-1776* (Lancaster, Mass., 1938).
CCMDG	Frederick Lewis Weis, *The Colonial Clergy of Maryland, Delaware and Georgia* (Lancaster, Mass., 1950).
CCNE	Frederick Lewis Weis, *The Colonial Clergy and the Colonial Churches of New England* (Lancaster, Mass., 1936).
CCV	Frederick Lewis Weis, *The Colonial Clergy of Virginia, North Carolina and South Carolina* (Boston, Mass., 1955).
DAB	*Dictionary of American Biography*, ed. Allen Johnson and Dumas Malone, 20 vols. (New York, 1928-37; Seven Supplements, 1944-1965).
DARB	Henry Warner Bowden, *Dictionary of American Religious Biography* (Westport, Conn., 1977).
Dexter	Franklin Bowditch Dexter, *Biographical Sketches of the Graduates of Yale College*, 6 vols. (New York, 1885-1912).
DNB	*The Dictionary of National Biography*, ed. Leslie Stephen and Sidney Lee, 21 vols. and 1 supplement (London, 1882-1900; Six Supplements, 1901-1950).
FCNEV	Harold S. Jantz, *The First Century of New England Verse* (Worcester, Mass., 1944; 1962; 1974).

LHUS   *Literary History of the United States*, ed. Robert E. Spiller et al., 2 vols. (New York, 1948; 4th ed., 1974).

NAW   *Notable American Women, 1607-1950: A Biographical Dictionary*, ed. Edward T. James et al., 3 vols. (1971-1980).

P   *Princetonians: A Biographical Dictionary* (Vol. 1: *1748-1768*, ed. James McLachlan; Vol. 2: *1769-1775* and Vol. 3: 1776-1783, ed. Richard A. Harrison, Princeton, N.J.).

Sibley-Shipton   John L. Sibley and Clifford K. Shipton, *Biographical Sketches of Those Who Attended Harvard College* (Vols. 1-3: 1642-1689, Boston, Mass., 1873; Vols. 4-17: 1690-1771, Boston, Mass., 1933-1975).

Sprague   *Annals of the American Pulpit*, ed. William B. Sprague, 9 vols. (New York, 1857-1869; 1969).

T$_1$ Moses Coit Tyler, *A History of American Literature During the Colonial Period, 1607-1765*, 2 vols. (New York, 1878; 1897; 1898).

T$_2$ Moses Coit Tyler, *The Literary History of the American Revolution, 1763-1783*, 2 vols. (New York, 1897).

JOURNALS AND PERIODICALS

AC   *American Collector*
AEST   *American Ethnological Society Transactions*
AGR   *American German Review*
AH   *American Heritage*
AHAAR   *American Historical Association Annual Report*
AHR   *American Historical Review*
AJHQ   *American Jewish Historical Quarterly*
AJP   *American Journal of Physics*
AL   *American Literature*
AM   *Atlantic Monthly*
AMH   *Annals of Medical History*
AmR   *American Review*
APSR   *American Political Science Review*
AQ   *American Quarterly*
AS   *American Speech*
ASJ   *Alchemical Society Journal*
BB   *Bulletin of Bibliography*
BC   *Baptist Courier*
BEM   *Blackwood's Edinburgh Magazine*
BFHA   *Bulletin of the Friends' Historical Association*
BHM   *Bulletin of the History of Medicine*
BHSP   *Bulletin of the Historical Society of Pennsylvania*

Biblioteca	*Biblioteca Sacra*
BJHH	*Bulletin of the Johns Hopkins Hospital*
BNYPL	*Bulletin of the New York Public Library*
Bookman	*The Bookman*
BPLQ	*Boston Public Library Quarterly*
BQ	*Baptist Quarterly*
BrHP	*Branch Historical Papers*
BRPR	*Biblical Repertory and Princeton Review*
BSMHC	*Bulletin of the Society of Medical History of Chicago*
BSP	*Bostonian Society Publications*
BSPNEA	*Bulletin of the Society for the Preservation of New England Antiquities*
CanHR	*Canadian Historical Review*
CanL	*Canadian Literature*
CGHS	*Collections of the Georgia Historical Society*
CH	*Church History*
CHer	*Choir Herald*
CHR	*Catholic Historical Review*
CHSB	*Connecticut Historical Society Bulletin*
CHSC	*Connecticut Historical Society Collections*
CJ	*Classical Journal*
CLAJ	*College Language Association Journal*
CM	*The Connecticut Magazine*
CMaineHS	*Collections of the Maine Historical Society*
CMHS	*Collections of the Massachusetts Historical Society*
CNHamHS	*Collections of the New Hampshire Historical Society*
CNYHS	*Collections of the New York Historical Society*
CR	*Church Review*
CRevAS	*Canadian Review of American Studies*
CS	*Christian Spectator*
CUQ	*Columbia University Quarterly*
DAI	*Dissertation Abstracts International*
DalR	*Dalhousie Review*
DBR	*De Bow's Review*
DedHR	*Dedham Historical Review*
DiaN	*Dialect Notes*
DN	*Delaware Notes*
EAL	*Early American Literature*
ECS	*Eighteenth-Century Studies*
EIHC	*Essex Institute Historical Collections*
EN	*Essex Naturalist*
ES	*Economic Studies*
ESQ	*Emerson Society Quarterly*
ESRS	*Emporia State Research Studies*

EUQ	*Emory University Quarterly*
GHQ	*Georgia Historical Quarterly*
GHR	*Georgia Historical Review*
HER	*Harvard Educational Review*
HGM	*Harvard Graduates' Magazine*
Historian	*The Historian*
HL	*Historica Linguistica*
HLB	*Harvard Library Bulletin*
HLQ	*Huntington Library Quarterly*
HM	*The Historical Magazine*
HMagPEC	*Historical Magazine of the Protestant Episcopal Church*
HTR	*Harvard Theological Review*
HTS	*Harvard Theological Studies*
HudR	*Hudson Review*
HumLov	*Humanistica Lovaniensia: Journal of Neo-Latin Studies* (Louvain, Belgium)
IHSP	*Ipswich Historical Society Publications*
IUS	*Indiana University Studies*
JA	*Jahrbuch für Ameríkastudien*
JAH	*Journal of American History*
JAmS	*Journal of American Studies*
JD	*Journal of Documentation*
JHI	*Journal of the History of Ideas*
JHS	*Johns Hopkins University Studies in History and Political Science*
JLH	*Journal of Library History*
JNH	*Journal of Negro History*
JPH	*Journal of Presbyterian History*
JPHS	*Journal of the Presbyterian Historical Society*
JQ	*Journalism Quarterly*
JR	*Journal of Religion*
JRUL	*Journal of the Rutgers University Library*
JSAH	*Journal of the Society of Architectural Historians*
JSBNH	*Journal of the Society for the Bibliography of Natural History*
JSCBHS	*Journal of the South Carolina Baptist Historical Society*
JSH	*Journal of Southern History*
JSR	*Jackson State Review* (Mississippi)
Judaism	*Judaism: A Quarterly Journal of Jewish Life and Thought*
LCR	*Lutheran Church Review*
MagA	*The Magazine of Art*
MagH	*Magazine of History*
MdHM	*Maryland Historical Magazine*
MH	*Methodist History*
MHSP	*Memoirs of the Historical Society of Pennsylvania*

MichH	*Michigan History*
MiH	*Minnesota History*
MLN	*Modern Language Notes*
MQ	*Mississippi Quarterly*
MR	*Massachusetts Review*
MusQ	*Musical Quarterly*
MVHR	*Mississippi Valley Historical Review*
Nation	*The Nation*
NCarF	*North Carolina Folklore*
NCF	*Nineteenth-Century Fiction*
NCHR	*North Carolina Historical Review*
NEG	*New England Galaxy*
NEHGR	*New England Historical and Genealogical Review*
NEM	*New England Magazine*
NEQ	*New England Quarterly*
NHB	*Negro History Bulletin*
NHR	*Narragansett Historical Review*
NJHSC	*New Jersey Historical Society Collections*
NJHSP	*New Jersey Historical Society Proceedings*
N&Q	*Notes and Queries*
NYGBR	*New York Genealogical and Biographical Review*
NYH	*New York History*
NYHSQ	*New York Historical Society Quarterly*
NYTBR	*New York Times Book Review*
OC	*Open Court*
OCHSC	*Old Colony Historical Society Collections*
OHSQ	*Oregon Historical Society Quarterly*
OntHSPR	*Ontario Historical Society Papers and Records*
PAAS	*Proceedings of the American Antiquarian Society*
PAH	*Perspectives in American History*
PAHS	*Papers of the Albemarle Historical Society*
PAJHS	*Publications of the American Jewish Historical Society*
PAPS	*Proceedings of the American Philosophical Society*
PBosS	*Proceedings of the Bostonian Society*
PBSA	*Papers of the Bibliographical Society of America*
PCSM	*Publications of the Colonial Society of Massachusetts*
PennH	*Pennsylvania History*
Phaedrus	*Phaedrus: An International Journal of Children's Literature Research*
Phylon	*Phylon: The Atlanta University Review of Race and Culture*
PIHS	*Publications of the Ipswich Historical Society*
PM	*Presbyterian Magazine*
PMHB	*Pennsylvania Magazine of History and Biography*
PMHS	*Proceedings of the Massachusetts Historical Society*

PMichA	*Papers of the Michigan Academy of Sciences, Arts, and Letters*
PMLA	*PMLA: Publications of the Modern Language Association of America*
PMPJ	*Philadelphia Medical and Physical Journal*
PNHCHS	*Papers of the New Haven Colony Historical Society*
PNYHS	*Proceedings of the New York Historical Society*
PQ	*Philological Quarterly*
PRev	*Princeton Review*
PSR	*Political Science Review*
PULC	*Princeton University Library Chronicle*
PWASA	*Proceedings of the Wisconsin Academy of Sciences and Arts*
PWHS	*Proceedings of the Wesley Historical Society*
QH	*Quaker History*
QMIMS	*Quarterly Magazine of the International Musical Society*
QQ	*Queen's Quarterly*
RACHSP	*Records of the American Catholic Historical Society of Philadelphia*
RALS	*Resources for American Literary Study*
RIH	*Rhode Island History*
RIHSC	*Rhode Island Historical Society Collections*
RP	*Register of Pennsylvania*
RS	*Research Studies* (Pullman, Washington)
RSCHS	*Records of the Scottish Church History Society*
SAQ	*South Atlantic Quarterly*
SatR	*Saturday Review*
SB	*Studies in Bibliography: Papers of the Bibliographical Society of the University of Virginia*
SCBHSP	*South Central Baptist Historical Society Proceedings*
SCHM	*South Carolina Historical Magazine*
SChR	*Scottish Church Review*
SCLR	*South Carolina Law Review*
SCM	*South Carolina Magazine*
SCN	*Seventeenth-Century Notes*
SEJ	*Southern Economic Journal*
Serif	*The Serif* (Kent, Ohio)
SF	*Social Forces*
Signs	*Signs: Journal of Women in Culture and Society*
SLitI	*Studies in the Literary Imagination*
SLJ	*Southern Literary Journal*
SLL	*Studies in Language and Literature*
SoPR	*Southern Presbyterian Review*
SP	*Studies in Philology*
SRC	*Studies in Religion and Culture*
SS	*Scandinavian Studies*

SSS	*Studies in the Social Sciences*
TA	*Theatre Annual*
TAAS	*Transactions of the American Antiquarian Society*
TAPS	*Transactions of the American Philosophical Society*
TCSM	*Transactions of the Colonial Society of Massachusetts*
TennSL	*Tennessee Studies in Literature*
ThS	*Theatre Survey*
TMHS	*Transactions of the Moravian Historical Society*
TQHGM	*Tyler's Quarterly Historical and Genealogical Magazine*
TR	*Texas Review*
TRSC	*Transactions of the Royal Society of Canada*
UCC	*University of California Chronicles*
UMS	*University of Missouri Studies*
USCHM	*United States Catholic Historical Magazine*
VC	*Virginia Cavalcade*
VELM	*Virginia Evangelical and Literary Magazine*
VMHB	*Virginia Magazine of History and Biography*
VMM	*Virginia Medical Monthly*
WHQ	*Western Historical Quarterly*
WL	*Woodstock Letters*
WMH	*Wisconsin Magazine of History*
WMQ	*William and Mary Quarterly*
WPHM	*Western Pennsylvania Historical Magazine*
YR	*Yale Review*
YULG	*Yale University Library Gazette*

Biographical and Critical Dictionary

— Q ——————————

JOSIAH QUINCY, JR. (1744-1775)

Works: *Observations on the Act of Parliament* (1774); *Reports of Cases Argued...Between 1761 and 1772* (1865); *Journal of Josiah Quincy, Jr., 1773* (1916); *Journal of Josiah Quincy, Jun., During His Voyage and Residence in England* (w. 1774-1775; pub. 1917).

Biography: Josiah Quincy, Jr., the son of Col. Josiah Quincy (1709-1774), was born in Boston on Feb. 23, 1744. After graduating from Harvard in 1763, he entered the law office of Oxenbridge Thacher (q.v.) and when his teacher died in 1765 took over his practice. During his early days as a lawyer, he compiled most of the manuscript notes of cases later published as *Reports of Cases* (1865).

In 1767, under the pseudonym "Hyperion," he published the first of his many newspaper pieces attacking British colonial policies. Despite his strong patriot views and the evident danger to his thriving political and legal careers, however, he joined with John Adams (q.v.) in the successful defense of the soldiers accused of the Boston Massacre in 1770.

After a brief respite from his political activities, he returned to the public scene with more political letters (under a variety of pseudonyms). But on Feb. 8, 1773, because of his failing health, he was forced to sail to Charleston, S.C., planning an overland return. He returned in May to find a fresh controversy surrounding the Thomas Hutchinson (q.v.)-Peter Oliver (q.v.) correspondence, which had recently been made public, and he entered the fray with a new series of letters under the suggestive name of "Marchmont Nedham."

In 1774 the Boston Port Act led him to his fullest and most impressive contribution to the pamphlet wars of the early 1770s: *Observations on the Act of Parliament*. This lengthy essay provided a learned and vehement denunciation of colonial policy as well as a full and interesting exposition of the Real Whig fear of standing armies. According to his prefatory letter, it also brought a threat on his life.

Josiah Quincy, Jr.'s eloquent defense of colonial interests was not unappreciated by his fellow patriots, and on Sept. 28, 1774, he quietly sailed to Eng. on a political mission. He carried letters to English supporters and to Benjamin Franklin (q.v.), tested the political winds of Eng., and even met with Lord North himself, all of which he reported at length in his correspondence and journal. Despite his rapidly failing health, he thought that a first-hand report of his conversations was needed in Boston, and on Mar. 4 he sailed back to the colonies. He died within sight of land but before hearing that the fighting he had long predicted had already begun.

Critical Appraisal: Despite his filiopietistic excesses, Josiah Quincy's (1772-1864) praise for his father in his *Memoir. . .of Josiah Quincy, Jr.* seems justified. Despite his constant ill health, Josiah Quincy, Jr., was a staunch and gifted supporter of the patriots and one evidently prepared very early to endure a revolution. His Real Whig principles are central to every piece he wrote, and his correspondence reveals a man for whom such views were a matter of undeviating principle.

His most substantial work, and the one that attracted him the greatest notoriety, was *Observations on the Act of Parliament Commonly Called the Boston Port-Bill; with Thoughts on Civil Society and Standing Armies* (1774), occasioned by the closure of Boston harbor following the Boston Tea Party. Josiah Quincy, Jr., as might be expected, saw the actions of the Sons of Liberty (with whom he was long associated) as an understandable *reaction* to the repression of a corrupt and conspiratorial colonial ministry. Besides, as he commonsensically observed, the punishment fell on the innocent along with the guilty and was far too stringent for the crime.

In elaborating this position, he undoubtedly said no more than every patriot thought and many had already said. What distinguishes his expositon of the issues, though, is his thoroughness, the clear logic of his argument, and the wealth of legal and historical precedent he could marshal for the patriots' defense. In his lively and forceful rhetoric, he revealed himself as one of the truest heirs of the English Commonwealth men, as when he observed how in all ages, complaints against oppressors have "been denominated sedition and faction; and to turn upon tyrants, treason and rebellion. But tyrants are rebels against the first laws of Heaven and Society:—to oppose their ravages is an instinct of nature— the inspiration of God in the heart of man."

One of the most interesting features of his lengthy essay is its extended attack on standing armies—another staple of the Real Whigs. The Boston Port Bill and the standing army are not unrelated issues for him, as he proved through numerous historical examples, and not just because soldiers stood ready to enforce Parliament's wishes. The bill itself could result only from a Parliament and customs officers who did not themselves feel the consequences of their laws. Justice, as Josiah Quincy, Jr., observed, depends on the shared perception of the laws' consequences, and a distant Parliament, corrupt customs officers, and a professional army are all unlikely to feel the ill effects of their own actions.

Josiah Quincy, Jr.'s journals reveal that his intense freeholder convictions and support for concerted action against Eng. were not just a public posture. His trip in 1773 allowed him to assess the resolve of the southern and middle colonies while forming valuable friendships with southern leaders. Although he worried about "those Zealots for Liberty, who are Enslavers of Negroes" and found his new acquaintances strangely uncivilized, he also found "the whole body almost of this people...averse to the claims and assumptions of [Parliament]." This first journal is by no means dominated by political entries, however; he also described his efforts as a poet, extolled the virtues of Laurence Sterne, attended horse races and visited courtrooms, and mused on the evils of slavery.

The second journal, which ends shortly before his death, is similarly rich in its variety, but more obviously marked by the pressure of events. This journal, in fact, offers an excellent sample of the more-or-less private views of a patriot on the eve of the Revolution and does so in the context of a close look at his English adversaries and allies.

The *Observations on the Act of Parliament* and the two journals reveal a man of keen intelligence and wide-ranging knowledge and above all a man of unswerving political convictions. Had he lived longer, he undoubtedly would have served as an effective spokesman for the independent colonies. As it stands, however, he is an almost forgotten patriot.

Suggested Readings: DAB; Sibley-Shipton (XV, 479-491); T$_2$. *See also* Robert A. McCaughey, *Josiah Quincy, 1772-1864* (1974), pp. 6-10; George H. Nash III, "From Radicalism to Revolution: The Political Career of Josiah Quincy, Jr.," PAAS, 79 (1969), 253-290; Josiah Quincy, *Memoir of the Life of Josiah Quincy, Jr.* (1825, 1874); Peter Shaw, *American Patriots and the Rituals of Revolution* (1981), pp. 153-174. Quincy's journals are printed in PMHS, 49 (1915-1916), 424-481, and PMHS, 50 (1916-1917), 433-496.

Barry R. Bell
Washington State University

R

JAMES RALPH (c. 1705-1762)

Works: *Night: A Poem* (1727); *The Tempest* (1727); *The Muses' Address to the King: An Ode* (1728); *Sawney. A Heroic Poem Occasion'd by the Dunciad. Together with a Critique on That Poem Addressed to Mr. T—D, Mr. M—R, Mr. Eu—n, &c.* (1728); *Touch-Stone: Or, Historical, Critical, Political, Philosophical, or Theological Essays on the Reigning Diversions of the Town* (1728); *Zeuma: Or, The Love of Liberty. A Poem. In Three Books* (1728); *Clarinda: Or, The Fair Libertine. A Poem in Four Cantos* (published anonymously; 1729); *The Loss of Liberty: Or, Fall of Rome* (1729); *The Fashionable Lady; Or, Harlequin's Opera. In the Manner of a Rehearsal* (1730); *The Fall of the Earl of Essex* (1731); *The Cornish Squire. Done from the French by Sir John Vanbrugh* (1733); *Critical Review of Publick Buildings, Statues and Ornaments in and About London and Westminster* (1734); *The Court-Secret: A Melancholy Truth. Now First Translated from the Original Arabic. By an Adept in the Oriental Tongues* (1741); *The Groans of Germany* (1741); *The Affecting Case of the Queen of Hungary* (1742); *The Ax Laid to the Root of Christian Priestcraft* (1742); *The Other Side of the Question* (1742); *Case of Our Present Theatrical Disputes, Fairly Stated* (1743); *A Critical History of Administration of Sr. Robert Walpole* (1743); *A Defence of the People* (coauthored with Chesterfield; 1743); *History of England* (in fascicules, 1744-1749; in two vols., 1749); *Of the Use and Abuse of Parliaments: In Two Discourses* (1744); *The Case of Authors by Profession or Trade, Stated* (1758); *The Case of the Late Resignation Set in a True Light* (1761); *The Right Honourable Annuitant Vindicated; with a Word or Two in Favour of the Other Great Man, in Case of His Resignation* (1761).

Biography: James Ralph was probably born in Philadelphia, Penn., sometime around 1705. He married there and a daughter was born there in 1724. The same year, he accompanied his friend Benjamin Franklin (q.v.) to London, later working as a teacher in Berkshire. In 1728 he returned to London, where he supported himself as a writer for the rest of his life.

He first tried poetry (1728-1729), next playwriting, and then theatre management with Henry Fielding at the Little Theatre in the Haymarket (1730-1736). More successfully, he also tried journalism, taking over the *Weekly Register* (1731-1735) and also writing for the *Daily Courant* (1731-1735). Quitting the pro-Walpole papers in 1735, he wrote for the opposition in *The Universal Spectator* and *Common Sense*. Ralph worked closely with Fielding on the latter's new opposition paper, *The Champion*, founded in 1739, and took over its editorsip in 1741. In 1743 he founded *Old England: Or, The Constitutional Journal*, and in 1747 accepted the editorship of the *Remembrancer*, the new journal of the faction of Prince Frederick. After the prince's death in 1751, he became editor in 1753 of *The Protester*, which spoke for the duke of Bedford's faction. However, when Newcastle granted Ralph a pension, he retired from journalism, although he continued to review political and historical works for the *Monthly Review* until 1758. In 1761 he was about to edit a journal for Lord Bute's new ministry but was too ill to assume his duties.

Critical Appraisal: James Ralph is most notable for the profusion and diversity of his publications. In addition to writing prolifically and editing for journals, he wrote several works of greater interest today than his journalism, as well as a massive two-volume history of Eng. from 1660 on and a fourteen-volume edition of parliamentary debates.

After Ralph published *Sawney. A Heroic Poem* (1728) defending the Dunces, Alexander Pope devoted two lines and an obituary to Ralph in his revised *Dunciad* (1729). No one, not even Ralph, questioned Pope's judgment, and Ralph turned to the drama. All of his plays are adaptations of existing dramas. *The Fashionable Lady* (1730) is the most interesting of them, especially for its portrayal of a young American in Eng.

Touch-Stone; Or...Essays on the Reigning Diversions of the Town (1728) and *Clarinda: Or, The Fair Libertine* (1729) are both of sociological interest for their depictions of the pleasures and entertainments of the time, and his *Critical Review of the Publick Buildings, Statues and Ornaments in and About London and Westminster* was, according to his biographer J. B. Shipley, "the first work to ask Londoners to consider the beauty and magnificences, the appearance of their entire city."

Later in his life, he wrote two critical works on the state of the literary profession: *Case of Our Present Theatrical Disputes* (1743) and *The Case of Authors by Profession or Trade* (1758). They, too, are primarily of sociological interest.

The literary and perhaps the political twists and turns of Ralph's career occurred, J. B. Shipley suggested, because "unfortunately for his peace of mind, he pretended to a genius that was not his." But he was the first American to earn a living by his pen in Br., and as Benjamin Franklin wrote, "He became a pretty good Prose Writer."

Suggested Readings: DAB; T_1. See also Anthony Graham-White, "A British Contribution to the Bicentennial; A Note on James Ralph," ThS, 17 (1976), 217-219;

Robert W. Kenny, "James Ralph: An Eighteenth-Century Philadelphian in Grub Street," PMHB, 64 (1940), 218-242; John Burke Shipley, "James Ralph: Pretender to Genius" (Ph.D. diss., Columbia Univ., 1963).

Anthony Graham-White
University of Illinois at Chicago Circle

DAVID RAMSAY (1749-1815)

Works: *Sermon on Tea* (1774); *Address to the Freemen* (1778); *Oration on the Advantages* (1778); *History of the Revolution of South Carolina* (1785); *Dissertation on the Manner* (1789); *History of the American Revolution* (1789); *Observations* (1789); *Dissertation on the Means* (1790); *Oration Delivered on the Anniversary* (1794); *Sketch of the Soil* (1796); *Oration on the Death* (1800); *Review of Medicine* (1801); *Oration on the Cession* (1804); *Life of George Washington* (1807); *History of South Carolina* (1809); *Memoirs of the Life* (1811); *Chronological Table* (1811); *Eulogium* (1813); *History of the Independent* (1815); *History of the United States* (1816-1817); *Universal History* (1819).

Biography: The youngest son of an immigrant who farmed in the backcountry, Lancaster County, Pa., David Ramsay was born on Apr. 2, 1749. Despite his humble birth, he attended the College of New Jersey (now Princeton University), where he took a B.A. in 1765. In 1770 he entered the Medical School, Philadelphia, where he earned an M.B. (1773) and later an M.D. (in absentia, 1780). With help from Dr. Benjamin Rush (q.v.), his teacher and lifelong friend, Ramsay migrated in 1774 to a busy practice at Charleston, S.C. There he wrote occasionally on medical topics and was immediately active in civic affairs. He married first (1775) Sabina Ellis, a local heiress who died in 1776; then (1783) Frances Witherspoon of N.J., who died the next year; and finally (1787) Martha Laurens, daughter of the well-known Carolina merchant planter Henry Laurens. She died in 1811.

An ardent Whig and a nationalist, Dr. Ramsay was a surgeon in the colonial militia, served in the S.C. Assembly and as a member of the Privy Council, was imprisoned by the British during the Revolution, and was elected to the Continental Congress. He ended his political career in the 1790s as president of the Senate of his state. After the Revolution, Ramsay put to use his intimate knowledge of the event by writing history, which engaged his leisure time for the rest of his life. On May 6, 1815, Dr. Ramsay, best known as a scholar, was shot in the streets of Charleston by a former mental patient. He died two days later.

Critical Appraisal: Once referred to as "the American historian" and "the father of American history," David Ramsay at the dawn of the twentieth century abruptly became a name familiar only to scholars. It is probably significant that harsh criticism of his works came at a time when the "Imperial interpretation" of the colonial era flourished. Ramsay's specialty, the American Revolution, was then viewed by many as an unfortunate incident plotted by designing men who needed an excuse to found an independent nation. Never one of great moment in Eng. because of his American orientation, his reputation at home plummeted when he was attacked in 1901 by O. G. Libby in an article in *The American Historical Review* titled "Ramsay as a Plagiarist." Libby, and others who followed, claimed correctly that Ramsay had played fast and loose with the *Annual Register*, a contemporary London publication that regularly summarized the events of the Revolution.

In defense of Ramsay, it must be pointed out that he wrote without the benefits of training or long-term perspective and at a time when the canons of scholarship were not as rigid as they later became. Moreover, the instances that have been uncovered where he copied without attribution or quotation marks are few when compared with the entire body of his work, which ran to thousands of pages. Ramsay was more than simply a compiler. The materials for his three major works—*The History of the Revolution of South Carolina* (1785), *The History of the American Revolution* (1789), and *The History of South Carolina* (1809)—were collected from a variety of reputable sources and digested over a lengthy period in the light of his personal experience. As he pointed out in the preface to his most lasting achievement, the two-volume, 717-page *History of the American Revolution*, his membership in Congress allowed him to consult all official documents of the U.S.

Ramsay had great respect for documentary evidence. Robert L. Brunhouse, who edited selections from his writings in 1965, said that *The History of the Revolution of South Carolina* "floated in a sea of documents." In his book on the American Revolution, Ramsay placed the documents between chapters, where they were less intrusive.

In the 1960s, a more favorable assessment of Ramsay's Whiggish interpretation of colonial and Revolutionary America helped stimulate a modest revival of interest in his work. It was pointed out by several historians that the doctor displayed a laudatory concern for motivation, treated a broad variety of social and diplomatic, as well as political, issues, and never suggested "devil theories" in lieu of thoughtful explanations for events. Although it is true that Ramsay boasted of his impartiality and contempt for "passion, prejudice and party-spirit," he did not always maintain a disinterested attitude. His idea that history was useful only for the lessons it taught, his veneration of responsible representative government, and his own suffering in the Revolution led him to view British pre-Revolutionary policy in America with scorn and to make unsubstantiated attacks on certain English officers. His analysis of the advantages and disadvantages of the American Revolution was brilliant, but his characterization in the same volume of Whigs as "the young, the ardent, the ambitious, and the enterprising" and Tories as "the phlegmatic, the timid, the interested, and those who wanted decision" makes light of some of his claims to impartiality.

Minor works after 1800 by Ramsay that have merit include his *Life of George Washington* (1807), eulogistic in style, and a pamphlet titled *A Review of Im-*

provements, Progress and State of Medicine in the XVIIIth Century (1801), which has been praised as "probably the first serious attempt in medical historiography in this country."

Suggested Readings: DAB; P; T$_2$. *See also* Robert L. Brunhouse, ed., *David Ramsay, 1749-1815, Selections from His Writings*, TAPS, New Series, 55, pt. 4 (1965); Josephine Fitts, "David Ramsay, South Carolinean Physician and Historian" (Thesis, Columbia Univ., 1936); Robert Y. Hayne, "Biographical Memoir of David Ramsay, M.D.," *Analectic Magazine*, 6 (1815), 204-224; Orin G. Libby, "Ramsay as a Plagiarist," AHR, 7 (1901-1902), 697-703; Page Smith, "David Ramsay and the Causes of the American Revolution," WMQ, 17 (1960), 51-77; Joseph I. Waring, *A History of Medicine in South Carolina, 1670-1825* (1964), pp. 279-299; Carnes Weeks, "David Ramsay, Physician, Patriot, and Historian," AMH, New Series, 1 (1929), 600-607.

A. R. Riggs
McGill University

WILLIAM RAND (1700-1779)

Works: *Ministers Must Preach Christ* (1736); *The Minister's Duty* (1739); *The Ministers of Christ* (1741); *Ministers Should Have a Sincere and Ardent Love* (1742); *The Late Religious Commotions* (1743); *Ministers Exhorted* (1749); *The Superiour Dignity* (1756); *Gospel-Ministers* (1757).

Biography: William Rand was born at Charlestown, Mass., on Mar. 24, 1700, the son of William Rand, a weaver, and Persis (Pierce, Shepherd) Rand. Receiving a B.A. and an M.A. from Harvard College in 1721, Rand was ordained to the Congregational ministry at Sunderland, Mass., on May 20, 1724. Soon after that, he married Bridget Cook, of nearby Hadley. Although Sunderland was a small frontier town, Rand found himself involved in some major new developments in American religion. In 1727 young Jonathan Edwards (q.v.) was ordained at Northampton, Mass., about a dozen miles south of Sunderland. The great Frontier Revival of 1734-1735 began in Edwards's congregation, from which it spread widely through the Connecticut Valley. In the fall of 1734, Rand got into difficulties with his congregation for advancing "Arminian" doctrines of justification, but he recanted his views, under pressure, the following spring. On May 30, 1735, Edwards wrote that there was "an exceeding alienation at Sunderland, between the minister and many of the people," but that "it all vanished at once" when Sunderland experienced revival that spring, "and the people are universally united in hearty affection to their minister." Nevertheless, when the more general Great Awakening, championed by Edwards, reached New Eng. in 1740-1743, Rand emerged as a leader of the Old Light opposition to it. Rand's congregation took a different view: in a slap at him, the town voted, on Dec. 6, 1742, "that we are inclined to allow travelling preachers to preach among us." On Jul. 25, 1745, Rand was dismissed. He was installed as minister of the

Congregational Church at Kingston, Mass., on Sept. 12, 1746. This was a happy match, since the Kingston congregation opposed itinerant preachers and had dismissed its previous minister, Thaddeus Maccarty, for his New Light sympathies. Rand continued to serve at Kingston until his death, Mar. 14, 1779.

Critical Appraisal: William Rand published a convention sermon (1757) and six ordination sermons. Clifford K. Shipton took note of a thesis of tolerance to which Rand in his sermons "returned time and again: it is the duty of every man to discard all doctrinal inheritance and to arrive at the truth for himself." That way of putting it makes Rand sound less dogmatic and more tolerant than he actually was. Far from calling for "all doctrinal inheritance" to be discarded, Rand affirmed the supreme and continuing authority of biblical doctrines, and his sermons were largely devoted to exposition of the Bible. What Rand strongly objected to was ascribing to human statements of Christian doctrine—such as creeds, confessions of faith, and catechisms—authority rivaling that of the Bible. Rand upheld the right of every Christian to learn Christian doctrine directly from the Bible, without the mediation of human authorities. In *The Minister's Duty*, Rand wrote: "We ought (at least) to teach our Children to distinguish between their Bibles and their Catechisms." In *Gospel-Ministers*, he declared that "none of us should act towards others, as if *we had dominion over their faith.*"

In *Ministers Should Have a Sincere and Ardent Love*, Rand made a number of oblique references to the turmoil of the Great Awakening. Expounding a number of texts from II Corinthians, Rand commended Paul for the affection he continued to have for the people of Corinth, despite the efforts of false prophets to undermine his ministry there. "And this is not a Case peculiar to the apostolick Age.... Many of the faithful Ministers of Christ in this Land, are at this Day groaning under this Burden." Rand exhorted the candidate for ordination: "And...don't flatter Persons into an Opinion of their being in a State of Grace, when there is not sufficient Evidence of it.... By such a Method...you might perhaps make your self very *popular*, but this would be greatly offensive to Christ, as well as injurious to Souls."

Jonathan Edwards's New Haven sermon, *The Distinguishing Marks of a Work of the Spirit of God*, defending the Great Awakening, was published late in 1741, with a long Preface by William Cooper (q.v.). *The Late Religious Commotions* is an anonymous reply to Edwards and Cooper, ascribed to "a *Lover* of Truth and Peace." The structure of this reply, whose very title expresses a negative attitude toward the Great Awakening, parallels that of the work that it is criticizing: a Preface replying point by point to Cooper's Preface precedes a similar response to the main body of Edwards's sermon. In both parts of the reply, it is argued that the excesses and abuses accompanying the recent religious upheaval weigh against Edwards's view of it as truly a work of God's Spirit. Such phenomena as "crying out,—falling down, —Twitchings and convulsive Motions—Foamings and Frothings,—Trances and Visions and Revelations—Exhorters,—Censoriousness, —Pharisaism, &c" are not the fruits of the Spirit promised in the Scriptures.

It is *notorious*, that among many of the great Zealots for the Times, there hath been and is a Spirit *diametrically* opposite to the Spirit of Christianity: A *Spirit* of Censoriousness, Reviling, Clamour, Insolence, Spite, and Malice. . . if they are under the *Dominion* of Pride, Uncharitableness, and Passion, they belong not to the Number of *New-Creatures*: They are yet carnal.

The critic argued that the late religious commotions have their basic origin in human factors, especially human imagination and the spirit of enthusiasm: it is not necessary to point to either God or Satan as their cause. Near the end of his Preface, the critic called for ministers to lay aside "the Use of Party Names, as *Arminians* and Antinomians"; later, he ignored his own injunction, when he criticized those whose religion is "a Mixture of *Enthusiasm* and *Antinomianism*."

Henry Martyn Dexter, in his "Bibliography of Congregationalism" (1880), curiously listed *The Late Religious Commotions* twice, once with Charles Chauncy (q.v.) as the author (entry 3134, author's name in brackets) and once with Rand as the author (entry 3130, author's name *not* in brackets!). For many years, critical opinion was divided about whether Rand or Chauncy wrote this book, with no other alternatives suggested. But Edwin Gaustad has demonstrated convincingly that Chauncy could not have written it. In itself, that does not prove that Rand wrote it, and Gaustad preferred to regard its authorship as anonymous. Giving weight to Rand's claim are inscriptions made in three copies of the book by early owners naming Rand as the author, including one inscription that is definitely in an eighteenth-century hand. C. C. Goen, who once listed Chauncy as the author, changed his mind and wrote, in a later book, that "more recent evidence. . . points to his friend William Rand." Gaustad noted a reference in *The Late Religious Commotions* to "them in Boston," indicating that the author lived outside of Boston, and also a passage in the book justifying Arminianism; both of these points are compatible with Rand's authorship. Rand's delicate position in 1743, as a minister at odds with his congregation over his attitude toward the Great Awakening, would have been a good reason for publishing this tract anonymously.

Rand is most significant as a leader of the Old Light opposition to the Great Awakening, but his place in history has been overshadowed by the greater importance of Chauncy as an Old Light leader and also by the lack of absolute certainty about whether Rand wrote *The Late Religious Commotions*.

Suggested Readings: CCNE; Sibley-Shipton (V, 549-553). *See also* "Description of Kingston," CMHS, 2nd ser., 3 (1846), 211; Henry Martyn Dexter, *The Congregationalism of the Last Three Hundred Years* (1880), Appendix, p. 138; Jonathan Edwards, *The Great Awakening*, ed. C. C. Goen (1972), pp. 17-18, 22-23, 64, 102-103, 119, 153, 158 (for Edwards's sermon, *The Distinguishing Marks*, see pp. 52-60, 213-288); Edwin S. Gaustad, "Charles Chauncy and the Great Awakening: A Survey and Bibliography," PBSA, 45 (1951), 129-131; idem, *The Great Awakening in New England* (1957), p. 165; C. C. Goen, *Revivalism and Separatism in New England, 1740-1800* (1962), p. 331; Theophilus Packard, Jr., *A History of Churches and Ministers, and of Franklin Associa-*

tion, *in Franklin County, Mass.* (1854), pp. 368-371; Florence O. Rand, *Genealogy of the Rand Family* (1898), p. 28; John Montague Smith, *History of the Town of Sunderland, Massachusetts* (1899), pp. 60-62; Ezra Stiles, *Extracts from the Itineraries,* ed. Franklin Bowditch Dexter (1916), pp. 240, 255; H. W. Taft, "Address," *History and Proceedings of the Pocumtuck Valley Association* (1890), I, 194-195.

Richard Frothingham
University of Arkansas at Little Rock

EDMUND RANDOLPH (1753-1813)

Works: *An Oration in Commemoration of the Founders of William and Mary College* (1771); *A Letter . . . on the Federal Constitution* (1787); *Germanicus* (1794); *A Vindication of Mr. Randolph's Resignation* (1795); *A Political Truth* (1796); *History of Virginia* (1970).

Biography: Edmund Jenings (or *Jennings*) Randolph, first attorney general of the U.S., was born at Tazewell Hall, near Williamsburg, Va., on Aug. 10, 1753, to John and Ariana Jenings Randolph. John Randolph, his brother Peyton, and their father, Sir John Randolph, had been king's attorneys in Va.. Mrs. Randolph's father, Edmund Jenings, was formerly king's attorney of Md. Randolph, therefore, grew up meeting the important men of the period and went on to attend the College of William and Mary, followed by the study of law under his father's direction.

At the outbreak of the Revolutionary War, John Randolph proved to be a Loyalist and followed Lord Dunmore to Eng. in Aug. 1775, leaving Edmund, who had just begun his legal practice, to live with Peyton Randolph. With letters of introduction from prominent Virginians in hand, Randolph arrived in Cambridge during the siege of Boston in Aug. 1775. There he was appointed by Gen. George Washington (q.v.) to be his aide-de-camp. In 1776, shortly after the death of Peyton Randolph, Edmund returned to Williamsburg, where he served as the youngest member of Va.'s constitutional convention. In that year, he was also elected mayor of Williamsburg, became Va.'s first attorney general, and married Elizabeth Nicholas, daughter of state treasurer Robert Carter Nicholas (q.v.).

Randolph was elected to the Continental Congress in the spring in 1779. In 1786 he defeated Richard Henry Lee (q.v.) and Theodoric Bland (q.v.) in a race for governor of Va. He then headed Va.'s delegation to the Annapolis Convention and served as a delegate to the federal Constitutional Convention in 1787, to which it is believed he engineered Washington's membership. He presented the so-called Virginia Plan and served on the committee of detail, which was charged with drawing up a first draft of a constitution. Along with George Mason (q.v.), he refused to sign the final draft, however, since he was opposed to what he believed was a dangerous concentration of power in the executive branch, and published his criticisms in *A Letter...on the Federal Constitution* in 1787. But when the time came for Va.'s vote in 1788, he joined James Madison (q.v.) and John Marshall in their support for the Constitution, stating his overriding fear of a broken Union should Va. refuse to ratify. He then served as leader of the committee to codify Va.'s laws.

Randolph's old friend, George Washington, appointed him as the country's first attorney general in Sept. 1789. He ably fulfilled his duties, remaining neutral in cabinet wrangles between Thomas Jefferson (q.v.) and Alexander Hamilton (q.v.) in spite of his own reservations concerning the constitutionality of the Bank of the United States. Upon Jefferson's retirement from the office of secretary of state, Randolph accepted the post (for which Jefferson had urged him) on Jan. 2, 1794. He found himself inheriting the difficult task of keeping the U.S. neutral in the Anglo-French conflict then being waged. Both sides were pressuring the Americans for support, and Hamilton's interference was contributing to tensions. Randolph rid himself of French minister Edmond Charles Genêt, but refused to turn him over to the French government for arrest. He approved Gouverneur Morris's (q.v.) recall from Fr. and his replacement by James Monroe. He insisted on America's neutrality in dealing with Fauchet, Genêt's successor, and felt compelled to order Monroe to cool what he thought were the envoy's blatant pro-French sentiments.

Closer to home, but more difficult to control, were Hamilton's pro-British machinations. Br. had violated American neutrality and had failed to live up to several agreements of the 1783 peace treaty, including the return of two western forts and all captured black slaves. Washington ordered a special envoy sent to London. Randolph opposed Hamilton for obvious reasons and vetoed John Jay's (q.v.) appointment unless Jay should resign his position on the Supreme Court. Still, Hamilton prevailed in at least getting Jay's appointment over Randolph's initial objections. Jay was sent to London with his orders coming from Hamilton, rather than Randolph, who was especially opposed to a proposed commercial treaty with Br. Randolph was backed by both Washington and the Senate when Jay returned with a treaty including an article banning the U.S. exports of molasses, sugar, coffee, cocoa, and cotton and providing for the seizure of American ships exporting these products.

Meanwhile, Monroe was attempting to convince Fr. of America's neutrality while being kept ignorant of Jay's activities in Eng. Virtually the only success of American diplomacy at this time was the Treaty of San Lorenzo with Sp., which allowed free navigation of the Mississippi River (including use of the vital port of New Orleans) and recognized America's southern boundaries in the Gulf Coast region.

What little hold Randolph had maintained abruptly came to an end when George Hammond, the British minister to the U.S., revealed an intercepted memorandum from Claude Fauchet to Fr. Fauchet had supposedly implied that Randolph had indicated his support for Fr. and could be bought. Humiliated by Washington's inquiry of his conduct, Randolph resigned on Aug. 19, 1795.

Fauchet denied any attack on Randolph's honor, and Randolph himself wrote *A Vindication of Mr. Randolph's Resignation*. The charges of solicitation of bribes were never proved.

Back in Richmond, Randolph returned to an esteemed legal practice, but found much of his time spent in untangling and defending his complicated financial affairs, called into question by his enemies. Questioning and investigations of these affairs continued until 1809. He again returned to the public eye in 1807 as senior counsel for Aaron Burr in his treason trial. He spent his leisure time writing a history of Va., most of which was lost in a fire. The remainder was kept in the Virginia Historical Society archives and was finally published in 1970. Elizabeth Randolph died in 1810 and Edmund followed on Sept. 12, 1813, in Clarke County, having suffered from a hereditary paralytical condition for some time. He had fathered three daughters and a son, Peyton, who was in turn father of Edmund Randolph (1819-1861), Calif. lawyer and historian.

Critical Appraisal: Among the first writings of Edmund Randolph that have survived is his *Oration in Commemoration of the Founders of William and Mary College*, delivered while he was a student at William and Mary in 1771. It is a short, but nonetheless long-winded, dense document, written in the nature of a very dense, yet stretched, metaphor, full of Classical and contemporary allusions. It may be viewed perhaps as a bit of eighteenth-century schoolboy rhetoric, guaranteed to please the masters with its baroque form and intricate content, among which one may find thanks to King William and Queen Mary for their beneficence in establishing the college, a paean to Bishop Berkeley (q.v.), and an appeal for temperance among the students.

Randolph's next major writing in public life is his *A Letter . . . on the Federal Constitution*. He felt obliged, in 1787, to explain why he was opposed to the draft of the Constitution recently completed. This he did cogently in the *Letter*, putting forth his views about how it might best be amended by presenting what was known as the Virginia Plan.

Germanicus was written as a series of thirteen letters in response to those who opposed Washington's actions during the Whiskey Rebellion. He saw the rebellion as a grave danger to the Republic by organized "democratic" or "popular" societies and discussed the differences between the rights of individuals and those of groups, favoring the former. He raised here the question of what a government can or should do with a group that cloaks itself with constitutional rights more easily to effect its goal of subverting (as Randolph saw it) the very government and constitution that allows it to do so. Randolph pointed to the excesses of both Jacobins and counterrevolutionaries in Fr. to illustrate the potential for danger he saw extant in America at this time.

A Vindication of Mr. Randolph's Resignation is a long and painful document to read. The utter sincerity and hurt present in Randolph's belief that Washington had so little faith and trust in him is poignant. Randolph, in this piece, addressed the president and recounted the great lengths to which he had gone to enlist Fauchet's help in clearing his name. Randolph's biographer, Moncure Conway, raised several counterpoints to Jefferson's criticisms and argued against Col. Pickering's account of Washington's reaction to the book. Conway also cited Madison and Jefferson (both of whom knew Randolph well, but neither of whom was a close friend or admirer) to the effect that anyone who knew Randolph, enemies included, knew that the charges against him were absurd and, moreover, that the *Vindication* was, therefore, all the more embarrassing. Conway's conclusion was that Randolph was Washington's scapegoat and that the president could do nothing to save Randolph's reputation without casting suspicion on himself. Enemies of Randolph seized on the pamphlet, and in 1796 two parodies of it were published. The first, written by William Cobbett (q.v.), editor of *Bone to Gnaw*, was titled *A New Year's Gift to the Democrats, or Observations on a Pamphlet, Entitled "A Vindication of Mr. Randolph's Resignation," by Peter Porcupine*. The second was a poem titled *The Traitor Detected, or An Examination of Mr. Randolph's Vindication*.

Political Truth, which Randolph published in 1796, is subtitled "Animadversions on the Past and Present State of Public Affairs; with an Inquiry into the Truth of the Charges Preferred Against Mr. Randolph." He did expand on the *Vindication* here, but, more important, he presented his views of political truth, including the state of relations between what he saw as a corrupt Old World and the new America and the damage already wrought in the new nation by those who capitalized on the vagueness of the Constitution.

In 1970, Randolph's *History of Virginia* (or, rather, what was left of it) was edited and presented by Arthur H. Shaffer and published by the University Press of Virginia. Written after Randolph's retreat from politics, it is, stated Shaffer, not so much a "definite history" of the colony as it is a "historical essay" that testifies "to a concerted effort to arrive at an understanding of what Randolph regarded as the genius of Virginia's political system." Randolph viewed Virginian history as an evolutionary and logical progression. True to his sense of seeing the good in the golden mean, he characterized Virginians as free from both "the fanaticism and hypocrisy of Cromwell" and "the poison of the licentiousness of the second Charles"; true to his Virginian bias, he saw the Revolution as springing about solely from Virginian grievances and the natural leaders of the Revolution and the new nation (including some of his sometime enemies such as Washington and Patrick Henry) as coming quite naturally from Va.

Suggested Readings: DAB; LHUS. *See also* D. R. Anderson, "Edmund Randolph" in *The American Secretaries of State and Their Diplomacy*, ed. Samuel F. Bemis (1928), II, 95-159; Irving Brent, "Edmund Randolph, Not Guilty!" WMQ, 7 (1950), 179-198; John G. Clifford, "A Muddy Middle of the Road: The Politics of Edmund Randolph, 1790-1795," VMHB, 80 (1972), 286-311; Moncure D. Conway, *Omitted Chapters of History Disclosed in the Life and Papers of Edmund Randolph* (1888); Hamilton J. Eckenrode, *The Randolphs: The Story of a Virginia Family* (1946); "Edmund Randolph on the British Treaty," AHR, 12 (1907), 587-599; "Edmund Randolph's Essay on the Revolutionary History of Virginia (1774-1782)," VMHB, 43 (1935), 115-138; 44 (1936), 35-50; 45 (1937), 46-47; Charles F. Hobson, "The Early Career of Edmund

Randolph: 1753-89" (Ph.D. diss., Emory Univ., 1974); John J. Reardon, *Edmund Randolph: A Biography* (1975).

Randal Owen
St. Mary's Dominican College

GRINDALL RAWSON (1659-1715)

Works: *Sampwulteatiae Quinnuppekom-Pauaenin* (1689; translation of *The Sincere Convert* by Thomas Shepard); *Nashauaniltne Meninnuck* (1691; translation of *Milk for Babes* by John Cotton); *Visit to the Several Plantations of Indians in the Province of Massachusetts Bay* (translator, with Samuel Danforth; pub. in Nicholas Noyes, *New England's Duty*, pp. 89-99; 1698); *A Confession of Faith* (translated into Indian language as *Wunnamptomoe Sampooaont Wussampoowontamum*; 1699); "To the Learned and Reverend Mr. Cotton Mather" (pub. in Cotton Mather, *Magnalia Christi Americana* [1702] I, 9); *Miles Christianus* (1703); *The Necessity of a Speedy and Thorough Reformation* (1709); "Upon the Death of. . .John Saffin Junior" (in John Saffin, ms. commonplace book, Rhode Island Historical Society).

Biography: Grindall Rawson was born in Boston on Jan. 23, 1659, the son of Edward Rawson, secretary of the Massachusetts Bay colony. In 1675 Rawson entered Harvard College, where his classmates included Cotton Mather (q.v.) and Urian Oakes (q.v.). After receiving the B.A. in 1678, he studied theology in preparation for entering the ministry. In 1680 he was called as pastor of the church of Mendon, Mass., where he remained until his death on Feb. 6, 1715. In 1683 he married Susanna Wilson, the granddaughter of the famous John Wilson (q.v.). The couple had eleven children.

While living in the frontier village of Mendon, Rawson devoted himself to the conversion of the Indians to Christianity. He mastered the Indian language, preached to them in their language, and began translating Puritan works for the Indians. In 1689 Rawson, with Samuel Danforth (q.v.), was chosen by the commissioners of the New England Company to visit the Indians of outlying districts and to write a report on the state of Christianity among the Indians. This report, though lacking in details, was for many years the best account of missionary efforts in New Eng. Rawson himself served as a missionary to the Indians of Nantucket during the winter of 1708. Back in Mendon, he tutored Benjamin Larnell, a brilliant Indian student who entered Harvard in 1710 but who died while still a student.

Rawson rejected offers to ministries in larger towns and preferred to remain in Mendon, where he was a popular pastor. Rawson continued to catechize children and preach to small groups in his parishioners' homes until his death. He was remembered for his strict observance of the Sabbath, his devotion to his duties, and his concern for the Indians.

Critical Appraisal: Grindall Rawson's sermons follow the usual pattern of doctrine and application. *The Necessity of a Speedy and Thorough Reformation* contains an excellent explanation of the jeremiad, since Rawson used types to explain covenant theology and the duties of a chosen people. His poems likewise follow typical Puritan patterns and forms of expression. "Upon the Death of. . . Mr. John Saffin Junior" is a rhyming elegy that mixes biblical and Classical allusions. "To. . . Cotton Mather" is an anagram prefaced to Mather's *Magnalia Christi Americana* in which Rawson praised Mather's skill in writing a monument to the founders of New Eng. Rawson's translations of the works of earlier Puritans into the language of the Mass. Indians were a major contribution to Puritan missionary efforts.

Suggested Readings: CCNE; FCNEV; Sibley-Shipton (III, 159-168). *See also* William Kellaway, *The New England Company, 1649-1776* (1961); David Levin, *Cotton Mather* (1978), pp. 24-25, 42-43, 55; Cotton Mather, *Just Commemorations* (1715); idem, Preface, *Magnalia Christi Americana* (1702), II, 31, 439; Harrison T. Meserole, *Seventeenth-Century American Poetry* (1968), pp. 476-479; Samuel Sewall, *The Diary of Samuel Sewall*, ed. M. Halsey Thomas (1973); Kenneth Silverman, *Colonial American Poetry* (1968), pp. 31-45, 121-132; Kenneth Silverman, ed., *Selected Letters of Cotton Mather* (1971), p. 127; Frederick L. Weis, "The New England Company of 1649 and its Missionary Enterprises," PCSM, 38 (1959), 134-218.

Cheryl Rivers
Manhattanville College

THOMAS REESE (1742-1796)

Works: *An Essay on the Influence of Religion in Civil Society* (1788); *The Character of Haman* (1791); *Death the Christian's Gain* (1791); *Steadfastness in Religion, Recommended* (1793).

Biography: A respected minister and learned essayist, Thomas Reese was born in Pa. in 1742. In early youth, he moved to Mecklenburg County, N.C., and received a sound Classical education at the academy of Rev. Joseph Alexander and Mr. Benedict. His studies gained him admission to Princeton, where he graduated in 1768. Licensed to preach in 1773, Reese moved to S.C. and accepted the pastoral charge of Salem Presbyterian Church at Black River. For almost two decades, Reese served Salem as minister, master of a Classical school, teacher of a school for slaves, and even physician. During this time, he ably refuted, at the request of influential Presbyterians, an abolitionist sermon by Rev. W. C. Davis. But the revolutionary upheavals, which intensified after the British occupation of Charleston in 1780, interrupted Reese's duties. After two members of his congregation were murdered by a Tory, the patriot Reese fled to N.C., returning to Salem in 1782. These violent experiences influenced Reese's best-known work, the 1788 *Essay*, for which he was recognized by a doctor of divinity degree from Princeton, the first ever conferred upon a Carolinian. Because of ill health and a controversy over hymnology, Reese left Salem in 1792 and became pastor of the Hopewell-Keowee and Carmel congregations in the Pendleton District of S.C. Among his elders at Hopewell-Keowee (later the Old Stone Church) were Revolutionary War heroes Gen. Andrew Pickens and Gen. Robert Anderson. Reese died in 1796 in the Pendleton District, honored by his congregations as a man of scholarship, ability, and piety.

Critical Appraisal: Excepting the city of Charleston, colonial S.C. was largely a frontier—often subject to social turmoil and outbreaks of lawlessness, often devoid of the stabilizing influences of religion and law. In this context, Thomas Reese deserves credit for maintaining the Classical virtues of the American Enlightenment and for promoting the social influence of a benevolent Christianity. His small body of published work reveals a writer of erudition, persistent logic, and vigorous but restrained rhetoric. He wrote as a patriot without fanaticism, as a theological rationalist within a context of Christian orthodoxy. In a time and place of extremes, Reese emerged as a defender of education, reason, and order.

From his relatively isolated residences, Reese published only three sermons. The notoriety, however limited, accompanying his 1788 *Essay* led to the solicitation and publishing in 1791 of two sermons in *The American Preacher* of N.J. A third sermon was published in Philadelphia in 1793. Accounts of Reese's sermons stress both the logic of his arguments and the emotional conviction of his delivery. His knowledge of theology, history, and the arts was evident to his audiences. Doctrinally, Reese apparently absorbed little of the New Light evangelicalism of Presbyterians such as Pa.'s Gilbert Tennent (q.v.) and William Tennent II (q.v.) and Va.'s Samuel Davies (q.v.). Rather, he combined the piety of the Great Awakening with an emphasis on reason and practical morality. Reese avoided the militant enthusiasm of many colonial dissenters in favor of a more restrained but sincere support of his religion and his country.

Reese's most ambitious work, and the one most deserving of renewed attention, is his *Essay on the Influence of Religion in Civil Society*. This eighty-seven-page pamphlet was published in Charleston in 1788 and reprinted in the Philadelphia *American Museum* in 1790. In this work, Reese argued that Christian belief is the only effective antidote to the recurrent social problem of lawlessness. Proposing Christianity as the foundation of individual morality and social order, Reese confronted the increasing secularism of the Enlightenment and the anticlericalism of many Deists. With allusions to diverse authorities such as Aristotle, Homer, Montesquieu, and Locke, Reese exhibited his own learning and stressed the stabilizing value of education. Reese began the essay with a fundamental propositon: the neglect of religion causes immorality and resultant lawlessness; men are motivated by desire and aversion; therefore, only religion can offer rewards and punishments powerful enough to control the actions of men. Reese then confronted contemporary Deistic and materialistic moral theories with an orthodox affirmation of human fallibility. The idea of "self-love" as a moral precept is attacked as unreliable and vulnerable to man's "furious impulse to present gratification." Confronting natural or intuitive morality, Reese rejected the "moral sense" as uncertain. Convinced of the inadequacy of law and social morality, Reese then proposed Christianity as the only sure moral foundation. In words characteristic of his rationalist leaning, Reese portrayed God as underlying the "vast and complicated machine of the universe," as the source for "all beauty, order, and harmony." He then explained the Christian moral precepts of benevolence, justice, and moderation, stressing behavior rather than abstract doctrine, and recalling the Christian rationalism of Benjamin Franklin (q.v.) and Thomas Jefferson (q.v.). Reese affirmed Christianity as a "natural religion," essential to good citizenship, and proposed its support by public taxes, the education of ministers, and the encouragement of religion in the frontier. Lamenting the "barbarian" state of much of the backcountry, Reese closed by linking the success of the new nation to the piety and morality of its citizens. The *Essay* is a clearly expressed, logically developed argument that confirms Reese's position as a minor but accomplished contributor to the development of American political and religious ideals.

Suggested Readings: CCV; P; Sprague (III, 331-332). *See also* George Howe, *History of the Presbyterian Church in South Carolina* (1870), I, 411-412, 492-493, 593, 636-639; David Ramsay, *History of South Carolina* (1809), II, 505-507; R. W. Simpson, *History of the Old Pendleton District* (1913), pp. 33-34, 87-90; J. R. Witherspoon, "Memoirs of the Late Rev'd Thomas Reese," SoPR, 6 (1853), 116-120.

Tony J. Owens
Daniel International Corporation
Greenville, South Carolina

JAMES REID (fl. 1768-1769)

Works: "The Religion of the Bible and Religion of K[ing] W[illiam] County Compared" (pub. in R. B. Davis, ed., *The Colonial Virginia Satirist: Mid-Eighteenth-Century Commentaries on Politics, Religion, and Society*, TAPS, New Series, 57, pt. 1 (1967), 43-74; four essays in the *Virginia Gazette* (Purdie and and Dixon): Dec. 15, 1768; Jan. 29, Mar. 16, 30, 1768; and verse: Sept. 15, Oct. 27, Nov. 3, 10, 17, Dec. 1, 29, 1768; Mar. 16, 1769.

Biography: Recorded evidences concerning James Reid's birthdate and place of nativity and the time and place of his death are not known. Internal evidence in his long prose satire shows that he was a Scot, probably was born in Edinburgh and educated in the university in that city, and was a personal friend of the Scottish blind poet Thomas Blacklock. This same work also suggests that he was a tutor, perhaps indentured, in the family of Col. Robert Ruffin. Records regarding Ruffin suggest that Reid moved with him from Mayfield, near Petersburg,

Va., to Sweet Hall, an estate on the Pamunkey River in King William County during the winter of 1768-1769, and datelines of Reid's published pieces in the *Virginia Gazette* establish the fact of the remove beyond question. Although at certain places in his writing he appears to be Presbyterian, at others he seems to suggest low-church Anglican attitudes. The King William records of the period were for the most part destroyed. Therefore we know nothing of his life after 1769.

Critical Appraisal: James Reid's known work, taken all together and printed from manuscript or reprinted from the *Virginia Gazette*, forms an impressive body of writing. "The Religion of the Bible and Religion of K[ing] W[illiam] County Compared" is a long prose satire of thirty-four chapters that comments devastatingly on the local rural society in which he lived. It is of course moral, and it sees the world of William Byrd of Westover (q.v.) and Thomas Jefferson (q.v.) at its worst. The upper-class plantation owners are "Ass-queers [Esquires]" who worship wealth, practice miscegenation, and exhibit the qualities of overweening pride, extravagant gluttony, inordinate love of horse and dog and minuet, and above all arrogance. He attacked the established church, a tyrannical Grand Jury, and the self-perpetuating class of esquires. In his criticisms, he paralleled Jefferson, although he lacked the ultimate faith in human nature that the great native of the colony had.

Reid wrote with verve, erudition, and eloquence. He showed an intimate acquaintance with the French language and literature of his day, Pope and Addison and several of the British libertarian writers, and the Classics. He also gave a picture of social life at parish church and private ball. He pointed out that the Va. gentleman knows more of law than he does of Scripture.

The newspaper essays are concerned with biblical interpretation, the question of a future state, and his contemporaries' careless use of language. The linguistic essay will probably prove to be the most interesting today. All four are well argued.

The verse is conventional in form but personal in content. "To My Pen" (Sept. 15, 1768) spells out his ideas about the proper function and content of poetry, in pentameter couplets. A second "To My Pen" answers a critic in an earlier issue of the *Gazette* who ridiculed Reid's allegedly ineffective moral verse. The ridicule is returned with interest. In other poems, he is more playful, as in one lamenting the loss of a young lady's favorite bird to a cruel cat. A kindred piece is a mock elegy perhaps inspired by the same incident but departing from his usual heroic couplet by using octosyllabics in six five-line stanzas.

Then came two playful occasional poems on love, the first a poem of paradoxes, the second "A Play upon the Words FIRE, ICE, SNOW." "A Billet Doux in the Modern Taste," slightly mocking in tone, follows soon after. Quite different is the beautiful "Ode on Christmas Day 1768," twelve stanzas of six-line octosyllabics rhyming *aabcddc*. His last known verse, however, "To Ignorance," is a bitter meditation of considerable length. Presumably autobiographical, it is among the better southern poems of the years before independence.

Politics and political rights were never Reid's major themes. He was concerned almost solely with what men were and what their relation to their God was. Like Samuel Davies (q.v.) in earlier decades, he was part of a tradition that finally flowered in the twentieth century in the South's pervasive exploration of the individual in relation to his immediate society, his cosmos, and his God. Reid is closer in temper to William Faulkner and Robert Penn Warren than he is to Thomas Jefferson.

Suggested Readings: Robert Bain et al., ed., *Southern Writers: A Biographical Dictionary* (1980), pp. 380-381; Richard Beale Davis, *A Colonial Southern Bookshelf: Reading in the Eighteenth Century* (1979); idem, *Intellectual Life in the Colonial South, 1585-1763* (1978), I, 309-312; III, 1375-1376, 1470-1487; idem, Introduction and Notes, *The Colonial Virginia Satirist*, TAPS, New Series, 57, pt. 1 (1967), 5-16, 43-74; idem, *Literature and Society in Early Virginia, 1608-1840* (1973), pp. 168-191; Kenneth Silverman, ed., *Literature in America: The Founding of a Nation* (1971), pp. 220, 253-259.

Richard Beale Davis
University of Tennessee, Knoxville

SAMUEL RELF (1776-1823)

Works: *Infidelity; Or, The Victims of Sentiment* (1797); *Philadelphia Gazette* (editor; 1797-1823); *The Remarkable Narrative of Cordelia Krats* (1846); *Remarkable Narrative of the Female Hermit* (1849).

Biography: Samuel Relf was born in Va. in 1776 and later moved with his mother to Philadelphia. Relf began his career as a journalist with the *National Gazette* and eventually moved to the *Philadelphia Gazette*. As a journalist, Relf was known as an able writer and as a Federalist of the Washington school. Relf published his novel *Infidelity; Or, The Victims of Sentiment* in Philadelphia in 1797. Also in 1797 Relf became editor and proprietor of the *Philadelphia Gazette*, after its previous owner Anarew Brown died in a fire. When Relf later bought out the Brown family's interest in the *Gazette*, the paper became known as *Relf's Gazette*. Relf died unexpectedly on Feb. 14, 1823, as a result of complications from a broken arm suffered in a fall on the ice. He was survived by his wife, four sons, and a daughter.

Critical Appraisal: Samuel Relf's exploration of the theme of excess sensibility and his use of an epistolary narrative make *Infidelity* a conventional early American novel. Relf's craft, however, lent sophistication to these elements. For instance, his exploration of the effects of sensibility was complicated by the interchange that Relf developed between character and environment. The wild, picturesque nature of *Infidelity* provides both setting and occasion for the characters' exercises in sensibility. Although many early American novelists used the epistolary technique, few exploited its potential as a device for character revelation as Relf did.

Excess sensibility is the principle mechanism of the plot. Caroline Franks, the distressed wife of a disinterested husband, relishes the sensations that her admirer's declarations of love afford her. Caroline's indulgence of her sensibility propels the series of tragic events that lead to the denouement. Caroline's jealous husband sees his wife and her lover, Charles Alfred, together with another pair of lovers and commits suicide in despair over his wife's illicit attraction. After hearing of her husband's death, Caroline first goes mad and then dies, a victim of her overwrought sensibility. Caroline's admirer, Charles Alfred, dies in a duel with her outraged brother Courtney, when he refused to shoot at Courtney. Only the happy union of Fanny Alfred and Henry Wellsford, whose love triumphs over parental opposition, mitigates the effects of this series of deaths.

Although Relf pointedly condemned excess sensibility, his novel invited reader as well as character to savor the heightened sensations of love and melancholy, to respond to nature's pleasing wilderness. Warnings like Caroline's lament over her heightened sensibility punctuate the novel: "But ah, I am weak of mind, and even criminally susceptible! Sentiment will finally destroy me!" However, Caroline's marital predicament, Relf's allusions to the sentimental tradition, and the role the reader plays in the novel all undermine the effects of these warnings. The barrenness of Caroline's marriage creates sympathy for a relationship that will free her emotions. Also Relf allows Charles to invoke that chaste model from Laurence Sterne, Yorick, in characterizing his love. Finally, the novel itself, especially the extended descriptions of the characters' feelings, asks the reader to partake of their sensations—to experience the stinging melancholy of Caroline's oppressive marriage as well as the heady elixir of Charles's illicit love.

Relf's use of nature as setting and occasion for the characters' sensations distinguishes his novel from much early American fiction and calls to mind the role that nature plays in the Gothic novel. For instance, at moments of crisis, the heroines Caroline and Fanny retreat from the world to find outlet for their feelings in nature's wilderness, where their rocky bower exists to feed their feelings: "a purling stream, which runs from the precipice and buries itself in an unforeseen basan [sic] below, creates prattling music congenial to the solemn aspect of the scene and to a mind tempered for melancholic meditation." Sanctioned by Relf, Caroline and Fanny are romantics who see in nature the emotions of the self. Relf's use of nature to awaken appropriate emotions makes setting as well as character and plot an agent in the development of the novel.

The use of the letters for character revelation marks Relf's maturity as an artist. Unlike Enos Hitchcock (q.v.) or to a lesser extent William Hill Brown (q.v.), Relf gave his letter writers their own voice and style, for example, the voice of Caroline's extravagant sensibility, "Oh hide me, hide me, from the censuring world! Hide me, if possible, from myself!" or the voice of Maria's studied advice, "how desirable it is to acquire a mind patient in suffering, and a soul indignant of complaint." Perhaps more significantly, Relf used the characters' letters to reveal attitudes of which they are not aware. Caroline's description of her meeting with Charles—"his eyes. . . of the blackest hue, initially sparkling with feeling"—reveals to the reader, if not to Caroline, that her sensations have already been awakened by her husband's new visitor.

The novellas *Cordelia Krats* and the *Female Hermit*, attributed to Relf by Lyle Wright, both appear to be nineteenth-century reprint collections of earlier fiction. The *Female Hermit*, another exploration of excess sensibility, tells of a woman whose "idolotrous love" for her young suitor isolates her first from her brother and then from the world, after her brother accidently kills the suitor in a hunting accident.

Samuel Relf's achievement as a writer is limited by the sentimental fiction that he chose to write. Within the framework of a sentimental novel, though, Relf displayed considerable craft in his handling of characterization and in his use of setting as environment rather than as backdrop. As a result of this craftsmanship, *Infidelity* points to the maturity that the American novel would soon obtain.

Suggested Readings: Herbert Ross Brown, *The Sentimental Novel in America: 1798-1860* (1940), pp. 36-37, 77-78, 83-85; Kenneth John Meyer, "Social Class and Family Structure: Attitudes Revealed by the Earliest American Novels, 1789-1815" (Ph.D. diss., Univ. of Minn., 1965), pp. 136-139; Henri Petter, *The Early American Novel* (1971), pp. 267-271.

David M. Craig
Clarkson College

RICHARD RICH (fl. 1609-1610)

Works: *Newes from Virginia* (1610; rep., 1865, 1874, 1937).

Biography: Richard Rich is one of many now unidentifiable British authors of contemporary works on the American colonies. The *Dictionary of National Biography* speculates about who he was, but all of its guesses have been found untenable by scholars. Rich may have been the illegitimate son of Baron Richard Rich or, as Wesley F. Craven suggested in his facsimile edition of *Newes from Virginia*, one of the Hampshire Riches who flourished in London for two centuries and were often called "Richard." The *Dictionary of American Biography* refers to Richard Rich as "Robert Rich." All we know is that Rich was a self-described "blunt and plaine" soldier who traveled to the New World with Sir George Summers's fleet in 1609, probably on the famous *Sea Venture*. He experienced the storm that separated the ship from its fleet and, on Jul. 28, drove it onto the Bermuda shore. The survival of all 150 men on board, and their 42 weeks of comparatively pleasant living in that new paradise, moved Rich to write his poem *Newes from Virginia*, the theme of which is the "lost Flocke Triumphant."

Critical Appraisal: Richard Rich's *Newes*, a poem of twenty-two eight-line stanzas, is of historical, rather than literary, interest. It tells again the well-known and exciting story of one episode in the early history of Va. It may have been one of the travelogs that inspired Shakespeare's *The Tempest*, a similar drama of Divine Providence, rancor in paradise, and the ultimate salvation or renewal granted to men of youth, vigor, and self-confidence. The poem provides as well some valuable information on, or corroboration of, the details of Va.'s first settlement. We learn from it much about daily life in both the Bermudas and Va., and Rich gave accurate accounts of the population and its communal activities. *Newes from Virginia* seems to have played a role in Va.'s subsequent good fortune; two fleets left for the colony soon after its publication.

As Rich put it in his preface, the poem is a blunt man's very "rude" attempt to avoid the excess and dilation that to "the writing of prose is allowed." Although of uneven quality, the poem, he assures us, is "an honest verse," not a feigned or fictive work of mere advertising. Such an assurance seemed necessary, no doubt, in view of the flood of promotional literature sponsored by the Virginia Company during the first decade of the seventeenth century. Rich's narrative is very different from a work like Robert Johnson's (q.v.) *Nova Britannia* (1609) or Robert Gray's (q.v.) *A Good Speed to Virginia* (1609), both polished rhetorical pieces. His is a "fabulous" story, telling as it does the epic tale of men in struggle with the fierce God Neptune, who "gan to frowne" and, like a proud horse, "would throwe his ryder downe." The *Sea Venture* was literally thrown onto the rocks, and the men were forced to coexist, like characters in Homer, with monstrous tortoises, hogs, and wild birds, until they could build the now famous vessels *Patience* and *Deliverance*, which would take them to Va. On arrival, they brought joy to the English colonists, who were "oppres't with greife / and discontent of minde," and who became more "distracted and forlorne" as they heard tales of adventure, fear, and "pale death." The heroes of this myth are, of course, Sir Thomas Gates and Capt. Christopher Newport, as well as Lord De La Warr (Thomas West [q.v.]), who later brought supplies. As villains, the sea and the godless monsters of Bermuda serve very well. The dramatic scene is both Bermuda, "Iland of Devils," and Va., a new Eden "where none before hath stood." Rich promised all would-be adventurers, therefore, that God had proved his interest in the British settlement of America, because "To glorifie the Lord 'tis done / and to no other end." The poem's last nine stanzas describe prosaically the delights of Va. and the terms on which any one may join the 800 heroes already there. These efforts are made to combat the scandal and false reports spread so successfully in recent years by those opposed to British expansionism. *Newes from Virginia*, frankly a fable, has a certain charm and humor that must have appealed to many readers whose imaginations were little stimulated by other works promoting Va.

Suggested Readings: DAB; DNB. *See also* Howard Mumford Jones, *O Strange New World: American Culture: The Formative Years* (1964), pp. 188-190; H. C. Porter, *The Inconstant Savage: England and the North American Indian* (1979), pp. 280-309.

James Stephens
Marquette University

JOHN RICHARDSON (1647-1696)

Works: "An Homo Sit Causa Libera Suarum Actionum?" (w. 1666; pub. in 1669 in *Quaestiones in Philosophia Discutiendae*); *An Almanack...for...*

1670 (1670); *The Necessity of a Well Experienced Souldiery* (w. 1675; pub. 1679).

Biography: The eldest son of a Boston merchant tailor, John Richardson was born in Dec. 1647. He graduated from Harvard College in 1666 and later joined his classmate Joseph Browne as a tutor and fellow. Noteworthy graduates such as Edward Taylor (q.v.), Samuel Sewall (q.v.), and Samuel Danforth (q.v.) attended the college during his residence. He was ordained as the minister of the Congregational Church in Newbury on Oct. 20, 1675, and about this time married his wife, Mary, who bore him five children. Richardson carried out his ministerial duties at Newbury until 1694, when he contracted a lingering illness that brought about his death in 1696.

Richardson's life is punctuated by two incidents that suggest he was a man of both humor and enlightenment. In a poem from his 1670 *Almanack*, he poked gentle fun at superstitious farmers; his humorous portrait provoked a defensive retort in verse from the poet-farmer Samuel Bailey. Harold Jantz recorded that, despite Bailey's attempt to censure the young poet (still a fellow at Harvard), Richardson's joke continued to be, for the students at the college, "excruciatingly funny for the rest of the century." In Jun. 1675, a year and a half after the people of Newbury had begun construction of his house but some four months before his ordination, Richardson preached *The Necessity of a Well Experienced Souldiery*, a sermon advocating a call to arms on the eve of King Philip's War (1675-1678). The sermon is interesting, not just because of its vehement militancy, but especially because Richardson displayed a familiarity with scientific method and practical reason that refused to entertain any path to the resolution of difficulties but a planned, rational one.

Critical Appraisal: John Richardson's Latin poem, which asks "How can man be the free cause of his own actions?" is a Commencement exercise of the sort required from graduating Harvard students during the seventeenth century. Modern students will find Richardson's *Almanack* poem and sermon of greater interest. Richardson's 1670 *An Almanack of Coelestial Motions* first presents a detailed description of the year's eclipses and charts mapping the movements of heavenly bodies, all replete with the dates of elections—this last reflecting the Puritan spirit of democracy. But the focus of attention in this slender volume is on his concluding poem, "The Country-man's Apocrypha."

This fascinating poem is arranged into thirty-six lines of iambic pentameter couplets in which the poet poked fun at rustic superstition. He opened with this arresting couplet: "If stars do Rule the World, then never fancy / What's told from them is wrought by Nigromancy." The light, feminine endings of these lines underscore their ludicrous hyperbole, which he followed with this unflattering portrait of farmers: "Th' admiring Rusticks faith will shrink perhaps, / Hearing the Tidings of such After-claps." Richardson next titilated his readers with several fantastic events that result as a consequence of unsympathetic astrological movements. These movements cause the very constellations seemingly to play havoc with one another, "Trees walking with their Roots towards the Sky," and

"Men not a few, with Swines heads." These remarkable pictures seem inspired by an emblem book (for example, Francis Quarles's immensely popular *Emblems* of 1635). At one point, Richardson asserted, "The Moon is habitable, some averre; / And that some Creatures have their Dwelling there." Has this poet herein created the first bit of American science fiction?

At any rate, it is easy to grasp why Harvard undergraduates had such great fun reading Richardson's poem. Written five years later, *The Necessity of a Well Experienced Souldiery* is, by contrast, starkly sobering. Conceived as a response to the growing hostility of the Wampanoag Indians and their allies, led by Metacom (King Philip), the sermon forcefully develops the doctrine that "It is the great Duty and Prudence of those in Supream Power and Authority, to Order that their People be Trained up and Experienced in the Military Arts." Throughout, Richardson called on the example of David's courage and acumen in training his men, particularly in the use of the enemy's weapons. At one crucially fervent point, Richardson claimed that "Warr is an Ordinance appoynted by God for subduing and destroying the Churches enemies here upon Earth." This position is understandable when one realizes that the homes and lives of Richardson and his congregation were in peril of extinction. It is ironic, nevertheless, that in the midst of all of this impassioned rhetoric resounds a voice of reason and practicality. Although the sermon is regrettably repetitious, it offers enlightened observations such as "Art [that is, skill] or science is altogether vain which may not admit of a practicall part" and "But we in these dayes have no promise of such a miraculous and immediate assistance [as in biblical times]; God works now by men and meanes, not by miracles." Such remarks seem to predict the Age of Reason. The discovery of a man with such an affable sense of humor, who can also confront the most severe vicissitudes of life in the wilderness with sane judgment schooled by a scientific approach to logical thought, causes one to deplore so brief a list of extant works.

Suggested Readings: CCNE; FCNEV; Sibley-Shipton (II, 210-213); Sprague (I, 130). *See also* Perry Miller and Thomas H. Johnson, eds., *The Puritans: A Sourcebook of Their Writings* (1963), I, 24n; II, 732; Samuel Eliot Morison, *Harvard College in the Seventeenth Century* (1936), I, 137n, 178n, 220; II, 398, 405, 603, 649; idem, *The Intellectual Life in Colonial New England* (1936), p. 111; Marion Barber Stowell, *Early American Almanacs* (1977), pp. 46, 64.

John C. Shields
Illinois State University

JAMES RIVINGTON (1724-1802)

Works: Affirmation of newspaper policies and content (1773); prospectus for publishing newspaper (1773); *Rivington's New-York Gazetteer, or the Connecticut, New Jersey, Hudson's River and Quebec Weekly Advertiser* (publisher and editor; 1773-1775); various almanacs and pamphlets (1774-1783); declaration of liberty of the press (1775); resolution to conform to the Association (1775); *Rivington's New-York Gazette* (publisher and editor; 1777); *Rivington's New York Loyal Gazette* (publisher and editor; 1777); *Royal Gazette* (publisher and editor; 1777-1783); *Rivington's New York Gazette, and Universal Advertiser* (publisher and editor; 1783).

Biography: Born in London in 1724, James Rivington was a member of a book publishing family that provided him with a good education. He helped an older brother with the publishing business after his father's death in 1742 and in 1756 began a partnership in London with James Fletcher, Jr. That company was declared bankrupt in Jan. 1760, however, reportedly because of Rivington's gambling weaknesses at the racetrack and lawsuits against him for pirating books. In the autumn of 1760, Rivington immigrated with his family to N.Y., where he opened a bookstore. For a few years, he was involved in book stores in Philadelphia and Boston as well, but after 1765 he confined his business largely to N.Y.

In 1769, shortly after his first wife died, Rivington married Elizabeth Van Horne, widow of a wealthy merchant. He developed a printing business in addition to his bookselling and acquired considerable property, including 1,000 acres in the Mohawk Valley. In the spring of 1773, Rivington entered the newspaper publishing business with his *Rivington's New-York Gazetteer*. The well-edited paper was financially successful from the beginning, although its circulation was confined largely to the N.Y. area.

An affable, witty, and intelligent man, Rivington appears to have been popular in N.Y. until the outbreak of the American Revolution. His publishing of Tory tracts (both pamphlets and newspaper items) got him into trouble with the patriot element—although he initially published tracts for both sides. Rivington was hanged in effigy at New Brunswick in the spring of 1775. He later apologized to the public for any offense he may have caused; however, rioters pillaged his shop and forced him to take refuge aboard British vessels in N.Y. harbor. After signing the Association, Rivington was allowed to return to his business and family. He continued to print Tory as well as patriot pamphlets, however, and on Nov. 27, 1775, Rivington's press was destroyed by a group of Sons of Liberty.

Rivington took his wife and children to London in Jan. 1776 and did not return until Sept. 1777, when N.Y. was occupied by British troops. In Oct., he resumed publication of the *Gazette*, later changing the name briefly to *Rivington's New York Loyal Gazette* and then to the *Royal Gazette*. The *Royal Gazette* had a strong pro-British slant and earned Rivington a reputation as the "best hated of all Tory editors." The *Royal Gazette* was published until the withdrawal of British troops from the city on Nov. 25, 1783.

Subsequent editions appeared as *Rivington's New York Gazette and Universal Advertiser*. But the old Sons of Liberty element still harassed Rivington, and he sold his printing stock in Jan. 1784. He continued to operate as a bookseller and stationer for awhile, but disappeared from the public eye. His wife died in 1795, and Rivington spent some time in debtors' prison between 1797 and 1801. He died in 1802—ironically, on Jul. 4.

Critical Appraisal: James Rivington, according to Philip Freneau (q.v.), was "The INVENTOR, as well as the PRINTER of Lies!" Such was the view of his N.Y. newspaper taken by the patriot element during and after the American Revolution. Yet Rivington was in the forefront of those advocating impartiality and freedom of the press during the early stages of the American Revolution. His contributions to writing in America were made more through his policies and principles than through his actual writings.

As is the case with most newspaper editors of Rivington's time, it is difficult to pinpoint which articles in his newspaper he wrote himself. However, it is clear that he wrote his newspaper prospectus and policies in the spring of 1773, as well as some other notices published in the newspaper in the two years following. Such writings as can be attributed definitely to Rivington are models of clarity and show a flair for style.

In the first issue of his *New York Gazette* in Apr. 1773, Rivington made it clear that he intended to publish no partisan sheet, but would make his paper "as generally useful and amusing as possible." He said that no personal satire or "acrimonious censures on any society or class of men, shall ever stain this paper."

Furthermore, Rivington promised to publish an account of every new performance in the state of arts and sciences "deem'd worthy of notice" as well as essays on morality, decorum, and other literary topics. Nor would women be overlooked. "They shall be assiduously made acquainted with the publications which immediately tend to their improvement, and such particulars as may be worthy of their notice shall be industrously [sic] inserted," he wrote.

Rivington's policy of impartiality caused him little trouble until the events following the Boston Tea Party in Dec. 1773. During the year following, he published letters and pamphlets from both Tory and patriot viewpoints, but he became embroiled in an argument with Isaac Sears, leader of the most radical and violent of the patriot factions. In the Dec. 8, 1774, issue of the *Gazette*, Rivington noted that any gentleman of any party wishing to comment on American affairs "may depend upon having free access to the press of James Rivington."

Most of the letters printed in early 1775 were of the Tory persuasion. Items picked up from newspapers elsewhere, however, usually had a patriot slant. On Feb. 16 Rivington wrote that no attempt had been made to convict him of partiality, but that his crime "is neither more or less, than the keeping a free press...for if this newspaper is not impartial, it is the fault of his correspondents." He said that it was his fixed determination "to live and die a free, and 'An Impartial Printer.' "

When Rivington was hanged in effigy by patriots at New Brunswick, N.J., in the spring of 1775, the editor took advantage of the act to publish a woodcut of the hanging in his *Gazette*. This is considered the first true attempt to illustrate a news story in an American newspaper. In the same issue, Rivington affirmed again that his press "has been open to publication from all parties."

A short time later, nonetheless, Rivington's shop was pillaged, and he took refuge aboard a British vessel in N.Y. harbor. In a written request to the Continental Congress that he be allowed to return to his business and family, Rivington made an eloquent plea for the right to print under the liberty of the press according to the laws of Eng. On Jun. 7, 1775, the N.Y. Congress issued a proclamation noting that Rivington had published a handbill declaring his intention to adhere to the Association and had asked the pardon of the public. When he returned to his house and family, Rivington carried no further opinionated letters in his newspaper, although he did continue to print both Tory and patriot pamphlets. In late Nov. 1775, a group of Sons of Liberty destroyed his press, causing Rivington and his family to flee to Eng. in Jan. 1776.

When Rivington returned to N.Y. and resumed publication of his newspaper in the autumn of 1777, the city was under occupation by British troops. He soon changed the name of the newspaper to the *Royal Gazette* and carried news on the war primarily from the Tory viewpoint. The newspaper became known as "Rivington's Lying Gazette" among patriots throughout the colonies. Although Rivington did exaggerate on occasion and certainly reported anything that reflected badly on the patriot cause, he also admitted that many of his news items were based on hearsay, and he periodically carried such stories under the heading "RUMOURS."

Rivington's newspaper did not long survive the withdrawal of British troops from N.Y. in Nov. 1783, and he no longer appeared in public print. The tragedy was not only a personal one, but a blow to American journalism. For Rivington, in the policies announced in 1773 and adhered to for awhile thereafter, had much to offer concerning both the content of newspapers and the impartiality of editors.

Suggested Readings: DAB; DNB; T$_2$. *See also* Bernard Bailyn, *Pamphlets of the American Revolution, 1750-1776* (1965); Leroy Hewlett, "James Rivington, Loyalist Printer, Publisher, and Bookseller of the American Revolution" (Ph.D. diss., Univ. of Michigan, 1958); Charles Hildeburn, *Sketches of Printers and Printing in Colonial New York* (1895); Frederic Hudson, *Journalism in the United States, 1690-1872* (1873); Robert M. Ours, "James Rivington: Another Viewpoint" in *Newsletters to Newspapers*, eds. Donovan H. Bond and W. Reynolds McLeod (1977).

Robert M. Ours
West Virginia University

SPENCER ROANE (1762-1822)

Works: Open letter to Gov. Edmund Randolph against new Constitution (pub. in *Virginia Gazette*; 1788); *Kamper* vs. *Hawkins* opinion (1793); "An Interesting Case" (pub. in Richmond *Enquirer*; 1816); "Amphictyon" articles (pub. in Richmond *Enquirer*; 1819); "Hampden" articles (pub. in Richmond *Enquirer*; 1819); "Algernon Sidney" articles (pub. in Richmond *Enquirer*; 1821).

Biography: One of the leading advocates of the right of states to resist encroachments of the national government in the early years of the Republic was Judge Spencer Roane, a member of the planter class whose family roots in Va. dated to 1664. Roane was born Apr. 4, 1762, second son of William and Elizabeth Roane, in Essex County, Va. He was educated at the College of William and Mary, where he studied law under George Wythe and was active in Phi Beta Kappa Society.

Roane was elected to the Va. House of Delegates in 1783 and served in the Va. Senate from 1785 to 1789. He was named a judge of the General Court in 1789 and served on the Supreme Court of Appeals of Va. from Apr. 1795 to Apr. 1822.

Judge Roane led the battle to maintain state rights through both his position on the bench and through articles published in the Richmond *Enquirer*, which was edited by his cousin Thomas Ritchie. Many of his articles were written in response to decisions by U.S. Supreme Court Chief Justice John Marshall and were published under the pseudonyms "Amphictyon," "Hampden," and "Algernon Sidney." In his later years, Roane carried on an extensive correspondence concerning state rights with Thomas Jefferson (q.v.), James Madison (q.v.), and James Barbour.

Roane married the daughter of Patrick Henry, Anne, and had four sons and three daughters. Anne died in 1799, and Roane never remarried. Spencer Roane died Sept. 4, 1822, at age 60.

Critical Appraisal: Spencer Roane came to maturity during the Revolutionary period and knew many of the Va. leaders intimately. At William and Mary, he roomed at one time with Richard Henry Lee (q.v.) and studied law under George Wythe. Later, he married a daughter of Patrick Henry. It is not surprising that his writings concerned liberty and that he was primarily concerned with state rights. However, he carried his theory of state rights beyond that of most of his compatriots in the early national period.

Roane's first published work was an open letter to Governor Edmund Randolph (q.v.) in the *Virginia Gazette* of Feb. 13, 1788, attacking the governor for inconsistency in supporting the new Constitution. Roane asked how Randolph could accept a constitution "which is to beget a monarch or an aristocracy."

While a judge of the Va. General Court in 1793, Roane helped set the principle of judicial review in Va. with his opinion in *Kamper* vs. *Hawkins*. He wrote that the people were the only sovereign power, that they had established as fundamental law the constitutional charter that alone gave authority to the legislature. Each state was a distinct sovereignty, its officials responsible to the people generally and frequently—but ultimately beholden only to a higher power, reason. The principle of state judicial review of legislative action would maintain such a course of reason. However, he did not consider the relationship of the

people of Va. to their state government as being the same as the relationship of
the people of Va. to the national government.

Roane's first article of note in the Richmond *Enquirer* appeared Feb. 1, 1816,
under the title "An Interesting Case." In it, he replied to the decision of U.S.
Supreme Court Chief Justice John Marshall in the case of *Martin* vs. *Hunter's
Lessee*. Although written in a clear fashion, the article was lengthy and was not
aimed at the people as much as at judges, lawyers, and legislators. Roane wrote
that a law of the general government must be proved to be constitutional—not the
other way around—and said that could be done only by showing the power to
pass a particular law had been granted in the Constitution.

His most famous writings, the "Amphictyon" and "Hampden" articles, appeared in the Richmond *Enquirer* in 1819 in response to Chief Justice Marshall's
decision in *McCulloch* vs. *Maryland*. "Amphictyon" argued on Mar. 30 and
Apr. 2 that two principles in the decision appeared to endanger the very existence
of state rights. They were the denial that the powers of the federal government
were delegated by the states and the doctrine of implied power. Roane argued
that the states, not the people of the U.S., had created the Union. He reiterated
his belief in the strict construction of the Constitution. "Amphictyon" called on
the Va. legislature to take note of the decision and to do its duty (passing
resolutions against unconstitutional laws, endeavoring to convince the public of
the baneful effects of usurped powers, and endeavoring to unite and combine the
moral force of the states against such usurpation).

The arguments were continued in a series of four articles, signed "Hampden,"
that appeared in the Richmond *Enquirer* in Jun. These articles were addressed
directly to his fellow citizens, to make them aware of the usurpations of the U.S.
Supreme Court against state rights. Roane said he meant to invoke no Revolutionary or insurrectionary measures, but claimed only that the people should
understand the questions involved. He hoped the force of public opinion would
calmly rectify the evil, but added,

> I have no sanguine presages of success. Such is the torpor of the public
> mind, and such the temper of the present times, that we can count on
> nothing with certainty. It would require more than the pen of Junius, and
> all the patriotism of Hampden, to rouse our people from the fatal coma
> which has fallen upon them.

In May and Jun. 1821, in response to the U.S. Supreme Court decision in
Cohens vs. *Virginia* (that the court had the power to review the acts of a state
judiciary body), Roane once again appealed to the people to take note of the
usurpations as he saw them. This time he used the pseudonym "Algernon Sidney." Although his writing in 1821 was more emotionally intense than in the
"Amphictyon" and "Hampden" articles three years earlier, he still did not anticipate his work would be effective.

Throughout, Roane's writings were lengthy and legalistic, but they also were
clearly written and well constructed. If they did not appeal to the public, they

certainly must have made interesting reading for legislators, judges, and lawyers. He presented, with much legal precedent and proof as he saw it, a viewpoint that was fated to be a minority one. It was a viewpoint that lent itself to demagogic appeals, but such was not the case in the calm, reasoned writings of Spencer Roane.

Suggested Readings: DAB. *See also* William E. Dodd, "Chief Justice Marshall and Virginia," AHR, 12 (1907), 776-787; Clyde Christian Gelbach, "Spencer Roane of Virginia, 1762-1822" (Ph.D. diss., Univ. of Pittsburgh, 1955); Gerald Gunther, ed., *John Marshall's Defense of McCulloch v. Maryland* (1969), pp. 52-77, 106-154.

Robert M. Ours
West Virginia University

PHILEMON ROBBINS (1709-1781)

Works: *A Plain Narrative* (1747); *A Sermon Preached at the Ordination of . . . Chandler Robbins* (1760); *A Sermon Preached at the Ordination of . . . Ammi-Ruhamah Robbins* (1762).

Biography: Philemon Robbins was born in Cambridge, Mass., in 1709 and died in 1781, having been pastor of the Branford, Conn., church for nearly fifty years. He graduated from Harvard College in 1729, and was ordained at Branford on Feb. 7, 1732. Robbins married Hannah Foote; they had at least two sons, both of whom became successful ministers.

Critical Appraisal: In the sermons preached at the ordinations of his two sons, Philemon Robbins charged each gently and lovingly to do God's work as "ambassadors for Christ" or as "a shepherd feeding his sheep and lambs." Like ambassadors who must know, honor, love, and be faithful to their prince, the minister must similarly perform Christ's work. As Christ's minister, "he should feed his flocks by example," by praying for his flock and instructing them in doctrine.

In *A Plain Narrative of the Proceedings of the Reverend Association and Consociation of New-Haven County*, he recorded the six-year conflict between the Association and himself that arose over the question of whether or not he acted in a "disorderly" fashion when he accepted an invitation to preach at the Baptist meeting house in Wallingford, Conn., without the consent of the minister Samuel Whittelsey, Sr. He was expelled from the Council and was brought before it repeatedly in later years to answer charges stemming from the original incident. With the exception of a few who saw an opportunity to voice their dissatisfaction with him by adding more charges, his congregation finally voted in 1745 to remove themselves from the government of the Association and strongly declared their support for Robbins. There follows a postscript about the authority and law of the governing body that is in agreement with Robbins's handling of the situation.

Suggested Readings: CCNE; DAB; Sibley-Shipton (VIII, 616-627). *See also* Edwin Scott Gaustad, *The Great Awakening in New England* (1957); *Appleton's Cyclopaedia of American Biography*, vol. V (1888).

Peggy McCormack
Loyola University of New Orleans

J. ROBINSON (fl. 1792)

Works: *The Yorker's Stratagem; or, Banana's Wedding* (1792).

Biography: Almost nothing is known about J. Robinson, not even his first name. Like many actors of his day who performed on the American stage, he was probably born in Eng. and came to America in search of work. The setting and the dialog of Robinson's only published play, *The Yorker's Stratagem*, suggest that Robinson probably sojourned for a time in the West Indies, possibly in Jamaica. A member of the Old American Company, he may have gone to the West Indies during the Revolutionary War along with other actors and actresses with British backgrounds. The only extant records about Robinson's association with the Old American Company concern his activities during the years 1791 and 1792. In Sept. of 1791, a "Mr. Robinson" is listed as having participated in a dramatic recitation of the first act of *Hamlet* at Corre's Assembly Room in New York City. In Oct. of that year, Robinson is also mentioned as having performed the part of "Brush" in *The Clandestine Marriage*. Just how often Robinson's *The Yorker's Stratagem* was performed is uncertain, but it did play at least twice, and the title page of the play claims that it was received "with universal applause." No information has yet come to light about Robinson's whereabouts or activities after 1792.

Critical Appraisal: Like many of his contemporaries who acted in the American theater during the last decades of the eighteenth century, J. Robinson decided to try his hand at writing a play. The product of his efforts was *The Yorker's Stratagem; or, Banana's Wedding*, "a farce in two acts." According to a prefatory note by Robinson, "The Author of the following little Piece is sensible of its numerous defects—it was got up in a hurry, and under many disadvantages. The very flattering marks of approbation, however, with which it was received, together with the pressing importunities of many friends, have led him to suppose that a publication of it would not be unpleasing."

The Yorker's Stratagem was one of many short dramatic productions written during the late eighteenth century and intended for use in conjunction with other short plays as an evening of light diversion. For the most part devoid of any hidden social or moral messages, the main purpose of the play was simple entertainment, and as such it succeeds quite well. The main plot of the play centers around the efforts of a rich New Yorker, who arrives in the West Indies disguised as a fop named Amant, to win the love of a woman named Sophia, who is carefully guarded by a parsimonious and vindictive man named Fingercash. A subplot involves the efforts of a Jamaican woman named Mrs. Banana to marry off her son Banana to Fingercash's daughter, Louisa. Banana, however, would rather marry a Jamaican girl named Priscilla, and Louisa would much prefer to marry Ledger, Fingercash's bookkeeper and, as it turns out, an old friend of Amant. Through a series of contrived but nonetheless humorous manipulations, the various characters in the play eventually marry whom they wish, and the evil Fingercash is roundly punished for his selfishness and corruption.

As various commentators on *The Yorker's Stratagem* have pointed out, the highpoints of the play include its lively dialog, which is much enhanced by Robinson's skillful use of American, English, French, and even Jamaican dialects; its variety of characters; and its adroit use of dramatic formula as a means of creating farce. The weaknesses in the play, on the other hand, include the fact that the interchange between the main plot and the subplot tends to divide itself too much into the two halves of the play as well as the fact that the drama is almost totally devoid of any moral or even social commentary. Robinson himself played the part of Banana, and this no doubt helped contribute to the "universal applause" which the play received when it was performed in New York. *The Yorker's Stratagem* has also received recognition as one of the first American plays to introduce black characters on the stage, even though Robinson does treat these characters with a patronizing condescension and fails to develop or comment on the moral ramifications of eighteenth-century social restrictions against interracial marriages such as that proposed between Banana and Louisa. Nonetheless, the play accomplished well what it set out to do. According to Walter J. Meserve, "Robinson managed to include in his farce a number of the characterizations which would be popular in American farces for the next several decades," and as a consequence, *The Yorker's Stratagem* was, during its time, "one of the brightest American farces to appear on the New York stage."

Suggested Readings: J. N. Ireland, *Records of the New York Stage from 1750 to 1860* (1866; rep., 1966), I, 85-93; Walter J. Meserve, *An Emerging Entertainment: The Drama of the American People to 1828* (1977), pp. 134-135; George C. Odell, *Annals of the New York Stage* (1927), I, 291-292, 294; Arthur Hobson Quinn, *A History of the American Drama from the Beginning to the Civil War* (1923), pp. 131-132, 294.

James A. Levernier
University of Arkansas at Little Rock

JOHN ROGERS (1630-1684)

Works: "Upon Mrs. Anne Bradstreet Her Poems, &c." (prefatory poem to the 1678 edition of Anne Bradstreet's *Several Poems*), pp. xii-xiv.

Biography: John Rogers was born in Coggeshall, Essex, Eng., on Jan. 23, 1630. His parents were the Rev. Nathaniel Rogers and Margaret (Crane) Rogers.

In 1636, during the Great Migration, Rogers accompanied his parents to Ipswich, Mass., where the family settled. During his youth, Rogers is said to have suffered from indecision and depression. Distressed by his son's behavior, the elder Rogers, upon his death in 1655, left his son less than would normally have been his legacy: "To my son John, to prevent expectation of a double portion, I have not so bequeathed; he hath never been by any labor serviceable to his brethren, but hath been upheld by their labor and pain, while he hath been determining his way, therefore I give and bequeath to him an equal portion with his other brethren."

Despite his father's early concerns, Rogers eventually proved more than "serviceable." After studying both theology and medicine, Rogers was graduated from Harvard College in 1649. He then began preaching at Ipswich, where he assisted William Hubbard (q.v.) and Thomas Cobbett (q.v.) in the pulpit and where he also practiced medicine. There is no record that Rogers was ever formally ordained, and in 1681 he apparently gave up preaching to devote full attention to his medical practice. After the resignation of Leonard Hoar (q.v.) in 1677, Rogers was offered the opportunity to succeed Hoar as president of Harvard, but he declined the offer. In 1682, however, after the death of Urian Oakes (q.v.), Rogers was again selected as the corporation's choice for president; Rogers accepted it, becoming Harvard's fifth president after Increase Mather (q.v.) declined the position. Although he showed every sign of being an excellent president, Rogers's term of office was cut short by his sudden and unexpected death on July 2, 1684, the day following commencement, at the very end of a total eclipse of the sun.

Cotton Mather (q.v.) wrote about John Rogers, "He was One of so sweet a Temper that the Title of *Delicae humani Generis* might have on that Score been given him; and his real *Piety* set off with the Accomplishments of a *Gentleman*, as a Gem set in *Gold*." The father of only one child, Rogers was married to Elizabeth (Denison) Rogers, the daughter of Major-General Daniel Denison and his wife Patience (Dudley) Denison, the daughter of Governor Thomas Dudley (q.v.) and the niece of Anne Bradstreet (q.v.).

Critical Appraisal: Although as president of Harvard College, John Rogers held one of the most distinguished positions in all of early New Eng., it is less for his work as a Harvard administrator than for his relationship with the poems of his aunt-by-marriage Anne Bradstreet that he is remembered today. The author of the longest and the best of the prefatory poems in the 1678 edition of Anne Bradstreet's *Several Poems*, Rogers is generally considered to have been the Bradstreet family's choice of a posthumous editor for Bradstreet's works. The choice was both logical and wise. As a member through marriage of the Bradstreet family, Rogers was in a position to sort through the "*Poems found amongst her* [Bradstreet's] *Papers after her Death*," poems which she "never meant should come to publick view," and select those works which illustrated the author's talents at their best and yet were not so personal or self-revealing that they might prove too intimate for publication and a possible embarrassment to the family.

Among the eighteen new poems that Rogers selected for inclusion in Bradstreet's *Several Poems* were "Contemplations," "The Author to Her Book," and several elegies Bradstreet wrote in memory of deceased relatives. Although it cannot be determined with any certainty that Rogers had total access to all of Bradstreet's verse, it seems likely that he overlooked poems such as the one on the burning of her house as possibly too sensitive for "publick view." In any event, the poems that Rogers did decide to publish are among Bradstreet's finest. They greatly expanded her canon of works, and they formed a fitting tribute to the author whose poetry, Rogers claimed, left him "welt'ring in delight."

Although readers of Bradstreet's *Several Poems* will probably never know for certain just how carefully the editor may or may not have transcribed the Bradstreet manuscripts and to what extent, if any, he himself revised them, evidence suggests that for Rogers the editing of the Bradstreet materials was an act of love. Internal suggestions within Rogers's "Upon Mrs. Anne Bradstreet Her Poems, &c." have led Bradstreet biographers to conclude that Rogers had probably long been familiar with Bradstreet and her poems, possibly even as early as his student days at Harvard, and that Bradstreet herself may have read and been honored by Rogers's poetic tribute to her. The two poets may even have had the opportunity to discuss their poetry together or at least to have exchanged manuscripts: "Madam, twice through the Muses' grove I walked, / Under your blissful bowers, I shrouding there... / Methought I was upon Mount Hiblas' top, / There where I might those fragrant flowers lop, / When did sweet odors flow, and honey spangles drop." Highly effusive in its praise of Bradstreet ("Nature with art, so closely did combine, / I thought I saw the Muses treble trine, / Which proved your lonely Muse superior to the nine."), Rogers's poem has been acclaimed "the best of the prefatory poems," and its final couplet ("I'll please my self, though I my self disgrace, / What errors here be found, are in Errata's place.") has prompted one Bradstreet biographer to conclude that Rogers's editing of the Bradstreet manuscripts was probably conducted quite carefully. According to Elizabeth Wade White, the existence of "an actual page of *errata*... in the 'Prince' copy" of Bradstreet's *Several Poems* "at the Boston Public Library" suggests that Rogers was "telling us, in the couplet at the end of his poem, that he had carefully proofread the text, in his capacity as editor, and insisted on the inclusion of an *errata*-leaf before the book was bound." As a poet, then, Rogers produced a memorable poem about one of seventeenth-century America's most celebrated poets, and as an editor, he may very well have performed a truly invaluable service for American literature.

Suggested Readings: CCNE; FCNEV; Sibley-Shipton (I, 166-171); Sprague (I, 146-148); T_1. *See also* John Harvard Ellis, ed., *The Works of Anne Bradstreet* (1897), pp. v, xlii, 93-96; Joseph R. McElrath, Jr. and Allan Robb, eds., *The Complete Works of Anne Bradstreet* (1981), pp. xi-xlii; Samuel Eliot Morison, *History of Harvard During the*

Seventeenth Century (1935), II, 415-445; Ann Stanford, *Anne Bradstreet: The Worldly Puritan* (1970), pp. 100, 121-124; Elizabeth Wade White, *Anne Bradstreet: "The Tenth Muse"* (1971), pp. 360-366.

James A. Levernier
University of Arkansas at Little Rock

JOHN ROGERS (1648-1721)

Works: *An Impartial Relation* (1701); *An Epistle to the Churches of Christ, Call'd Quakers* (1705); *A Mid-Night-Cry from the Temple of God* (1705); *An Epistle Sent from God to the World* (1718); *The Book of the Revelation of Jesus Christ* (1720); *An Answer to a Book Intituled, The Lord's Day Proved to Be the Christian Sabbath* (1721); *John Rogers a Servant of Jesus Christ*, 3rd ed. (1754).

Biography: Born in Milford, Conn., John Rogers moved with his family in 1660 to New London, where his father became the second richest man in Conn. In the early 1670s, Rogers came under the influence of the Seventh-Day Baptist Church of Newport, R.I., and converted members of his family and neighbors to that sect. Further Bible study persuaded him that Saturday had not been established as a Christian Sabbath, so he parted company with the Baptists and founded the sect that came to be known as the Rogerenes. Convinced of his sainthood, Rogers ostentatiously bore witness to his faith, preaching, condemning the Congregationalists, and working on the Sabbath—on one Sunday attempting to sell goods from a wheelbarrow he had pushed into the Congregational meeting. He defiantly accepted persecution for his beliefs, contending that Christ had died for his servants, who should be prepared to suffer for their master. He served a total of fifteen years in prison and might have been incarcerated longer had not local support prevented the colonial authorities from carrying out their designs. Rogers died of smallpox in New London on Oct. 17, 1721.

Critical Appraisal: John Rogers's writings blended elements from left-wing English Protestants such as the Quakers, the Puritan predecessors of the Congregationalists and Presbyterians, and the Baptists. His closest affinity was with the Quakers, a fact recognized in New London, where his followers were referred to as Rogerene Quakers.

Epistle to the Churches set forth his major ideas. In agreement with the Quakers, he wrote of the light within, variously described as the Holy Spirit or Christ, that existed in the saint and directed his actions. Consequently, the saint lived without sin. The Calvinist element in Rogers was the belief that the light was found only in the elect, not in all people as the Quakers maintained. He observed that the Quakers did not sufficiently refer to Scripture, for they did not accept the sacraments of adult baptism and the Lord's Supper mandated by the Bible.

Rogers was a literalist who held that Christians should follow the Bible's commands but reject what was not expressly required. The two sacraments were required, but Sabbath regulations to make Sunday a day of pious rest were not. He denied that the Bible made Sunday the Sabbath. Saturday was the Jewish Sabbath, but by applying a typological analysis similar to that used by Roger Williams (q.v.), he argued that Christians were released from Jewish practices: with the coming of Christ the day of rest became a symbol of the eternal sinless rest of the believer's soul.

In *John Rogers*, the author examined the relationship of the Christian with the state. Christ's arrival broke the alliance between church and state. The chosen people could no longer use secular means to aid the state in punishing evildoers. God alone would avenge wrong. Christians ought not to participate in government in any form save the payment of taxes, nor should they utilize the courts or offer oaths. Their pacifism prohibited them from going to war and even from serving on guard duty. Rogers, in passages reminiscent of Menno Simmons's variety of Anabaptism, wrote that an adversary relationship existed between church and state, for government would punish Christians for their beliefs, but the Christian could not resist state power. Some opponents of the New Eng. Way developed comprehensive doctrines advocating the separation of church and state. Rogers did not, perhaps because of his belief in the antagonism between the believer and the government. Like most dissenters, he agitated only for toleration of his beliefs, although he did not expect his desire to be honored.

Rogers's vision of the church was stark, as presented in *John Rogers* and *An Answer*. Worship, he found, need not occur at a special time in a special edifice. Public prayers could not be justified by Scripture. The only requirement for the church was that the minister have had a conversion experience. A cleric, no matter how well educated and well versed in Scripture, taught only dead works, because he lacked the understanding of the Word provided by the experience. Rogers, then, prefigured supporters of the Great Awakening who similarly stressed the role of the converted ministry rather than the authority of the institutional church. Rogers, indeed, was a harsh critic of Conn.'s Congregational Church, branding it the Red Beast of the Book of Revelation, which deceived church members and destroyed rather than saved souls.

A self-taught theologian, Rogers was not a systematic thinker. His manner of expression was imprecise; often Rogers ineffectually imitated the style and imagery of the King James Bible. Occasionally vitriolic, his prose was usually uninspiring and redundant. Rogers's method of exposition was exegetical, with Bible verses connected by commentary. His largest work, in fact, was a verse-by-verse exegesis of Revelation. Rogers is significant as a representative of that group of common people who took to heart the Reformation doctrine of the priesthood of believers.

Suggested Readings: CCNE; DAB. *See also* John R. Bolles and Anna B. Williams, *The Rogerenes: Some Hitherto Unpublished Annals Belonging to the Colonial History of Connecticut* (1904); Ellen Starr Brinton, "The Rogerenes," NEQ, 16 (1943),

3-19; William G. McLoughlin, *New England Dissent, 1630-1833: The Baptists and the Separation of Church and State* (1971), I, 249-252.

Robert Brunkow
Santa Barbara, California

ROBERT ROGERS (c. 1727-1795)

Works: *Journals of Major Robert Rogers* (1765); *A Concise Account of North America* (1765); *Ponteach: or the Savages of America* (1766).

Biography: Born in Methuen, Mass., sometime between 1727 and 1731, Robert Rogers grew up in the frontier environment of N.H., where he learned the skills of hunting, trading, and scouting. At the age of fifteen, Rogers began a career as a professional scout and Indian fighter, in which capacities he soon distinguished himself for his bravery and bravado. During the Seven Years' War, Rogers commanded an independent company of colonial soldiers known as "Rogers' Rangers." He was present at most of the major battles of the conflict, including the Siege of Crown Point in 1759, where he put an end to the hostilities of the Saint Francis Indians by raiding their camp in a surprise attack. Such tactics quickly elevated Roberts to the level of a folk hero, both in America and Great Britain.

After the war, Rogers traveled west and fought against Pontiac at the famous Siege of Detroit. He also served a brief tenure as gov. of Mackinac Island. It was at this time that he commissioned Jonathan Carver (q.v.) to explore the territories of what is today Wis. and Minn. Later, Rogers was forced to relinquish his position as gov. because of questionable dealings with the Indians and the French. After an extended trial Rogers was acquitted for lack of sufficient evidence to convict him. His reputation, however, was somewhat sullied by the incident, and for a time Rogers sought refuge in Eng. Unable to find employment in Eng., Rogers soon returned to North America, but with the coming of the American Revolution his involvement with the British drew upon him the suspicion of General George Washington (q.v.), who had him imprisoned on charges of espionage. Fleeing again to Eng., Rogers died in London in 1795, alone and forgotten.

Critical Appraisal: While few frontier heroes had either the time or the inclination to read and write literature, Robert Rogers's literary accomplishments are not to be gainsaid. Throughout his career as Indian fighter and professional soldier, Rogers kept meticulous journals about what he saw and what he did. Published in London in 1765, the *Journals of Major Robert Rogers* and a companion volume, *A Concise Account of North America*, provide one of the earliest and most accurate descriptions of the interior of North America before it was settled by Europeans.

An astute chronicler of human events and a skilled observer of natural phenomena, Rogers incorporated into his *Journals* history and information on topics ranging from variations in the lifestyles of the natives to detailed accounts of the flora and fauna he encountered while traversing the wilderness. Not beyond embellishing his narratives for the sake of dramatic effect, Rogers possessed a flair for adventure writing, and his *Journals* make for lively reading. Like an epic with Rogers himself the epic hero, the *Journals* are replete with episodes and battles reminiscent of the *Odyssey* and *Aeneid*, works to which Rogers's *Journals* have been compared and which Rogers deliberately echoed in order to emphasize the importance which he placed on the British settlement of North America and on his own role in that settlement. Widely read and circulated, the *Journals* made Rogers into an international celebrity and a forerunner of such legendary American heroes as Daniel Boone and Davy Crockett. Kenneth Roberts recognized this fact when he wrote *Northwest Passage* (1937), an historical novel based loosely on the adventures of Major Rogers.

Rogers's most ambitious literary endeavor, *Ponteach: or the Savages of America*, also stemmed from his American experiences. A play in five acts, *Ponteach* was based on the historical attempts of the Algonquin chief Pontiac to form an Indian confederacy that would halt the spread of white civilization west of the Great Lakes. To the literary and cultural historian, the play merits attention for its sensitive and, for the times, unusual portrayal of the plight of the Indian during the middle of the eighteenth century. Although Rogers is critical of Indian ways, he places the primary blame for the Pontiac rebellion on the unscrupulous dealings of white mercenaries who wantonly provoked the Indians into warfare. Like many American plays of the period, *Ponteach* suffers from a trite plot and melodramatic excess, but while it was never produced during Rogers's lifetime, the play inaugurated a series of dramatic productions by American playwrights on the subject of the Indian and deserves more critical attention than it has received.

Suggested Readings: DAB; T$_2$. *See also* John R. Cuneo, *Robert Rogers of the Rangers* (1959); Albert Keiser, *The Indian in American Literature* (1933), pp. 66-69; Montrose Moses, ed., *Representative Plays by American Dramatists* (1918), I, 111-114; Roy Harvey Pearce, *Savagism and Civilization* (1965), pp. 170-171; Arthur Hobson Quinn, *A History of American Drama from the Beginning to the Civil War* (1923), pp. 28-29; Richard Slotkin, *Regeneration Through Violence* (1973), passim.

James A. Levernier
University of Arkansas at Little Rock

JOHN ROLFE (c. 1585-1622)

Works: *A True Relation of the State of Virginia in 1616* (w. 1616; rep., 1839, 1848, 1951, 1971, 1972).

Biography: No hard evidence exists about who John Rolfe was or where he was born. Tradition has it that he was the John Rolf born in Norfolk, Eng., in

1585, one of twins. Every school child knows Rolfe, however, as the man who saved Va. by importing W. Ind. tobacco seed, crossing it with the local tobacco, and producing a commodity that took over the English market. In 1614 his marriage to Pocahontas, daughter of Powhatan, brought peace to the colony. Rolfe gained another measure of fame by helping to inspire Shakespeare's *The Tempest*. In 1608 he and his party were stranded in Bermuda, where they remained for many months. Reports from that strange land filled the poet's imagination with visions of a "brave new world."

Rolfe's first wife died in Va. shortly after their arrival in 1610. For two years, he occupied himself with experiments on the "esteemed weed," which he loved both for itself and for the economic stability it would bring to the colony. Rolfe was no doubt delighted when tobacco became noted in Eng. as a cure for nearly all ailments, including the "pox." His marriage to Pocahontas in 1614 came after nearly a year of close friendship, during which the beautiful young girl impressed Rolfe with her earnest desire to learn about Christianity. "Her own incitements," he also acknowledged, "were stirring me up." Moreover, Pocahontas was a prisoner of the English during her courtship and was freed when she took the Christian name Rebecca, renounced her heathen "idolatry," and married one of the colony's most prominent and pious citizens.

For his part, Rolfe agonized over the decision to marry an unbeliever. According to Ralph Hamor's *True Discourse of the Present State of Virginia* (1615), source for much personal information about Rolfe, Pocahontas touched off a "mighty war" in his heart. After much pious discussion with himself, we are told, Rolfe married the princess to save both his own soul and the colony. King James was reportedly annoyed by the marriage, but the Indians celebrated it with eight years of peace, and the grateful Virginia Company awarded Pocahontas an annuity. Rolfe became secretary and recorder general of the colony. In 1615 the Rolfes had a son, Thomas, and, in 1616, the family traveled to Eng., where Mrs. Rolfe was treated as royalty. She died there the same year. In 1617 Rolfe returned to Va., leaving the sickly Thomas to be raised in Eng. Two years later, he married Jane Pierce; a girl was born to them in 1621, the same year in which Rolfe was appointed to the Council of State and in which, "sicke in body," he made out his will. He died in 1622, possibly (and ironically) in an Indian massacre.

Critical Appraisal: *A True Relation* (1616) was composed during Rolfe's visit to Eng. It exists in three separate versions, addressed to King James, the earl of Pembroke, and Sir Robert Rich. A political document, this letter seeks to prevent the collapse of the nearly bankrupt Va. colony by persuading both concerned merchants and the warring factions of shareholders of Va.'s good climate, fertile soil, and rich potential. Rolfe, whose wife's social success had made him the man of the moment, seized the opportunity to revive faith in the colony and assure its short-term support from the king.

A True Relation describes the initial ten years of the first permanent settlement in the U.S. Because Samuel Purchas (q.v.) published his own altered version of the letter in his popular *Pilgrimage* (1617), it was not reprinted until 1839, when it appeared in the *Southern Literary Messenger*. In 1848 it was published by the *Virginia Historical Register* as an item of interest to adorers of Pocahontas, Va.'s "guardian angel." A thorough, annotated edition of the Pembroke letter was published in 1951 by the University of Virginia Press, which issued a revised edition in 1971.

Rolfe's defense of the colony mixes commercial pragmatism with moral and religious fervor. The fertility and "plentifull increase" in crop yields, for example, testify to God's benign concern for the colony; only "incredulous worldlinges" could disagree. Although two years of aristocratic government had ended in mismanagement and rancor, a new monarchical organization promised, and had delivered, new towns, growth in the profits and variety of crops, and peace with the Indians. In this paradise, every man can sit "under his *figtree* in safety, gathering and reaping the fruites of their labors with much joy and comfort." A detailed description of the crops and great natural resources of Va. follows, and the letter concludes with a passionate plea for a chance to use Va. further for the work of God: that is, to convert the savages to Christianity. Va.'s English supporters, Rolfe argued, are a "*peculier people* marked and chosen by the *finger* of God." Although he lacked literary gifts, Rolfe wrote from experience and, in 1616, was again well-placed to save his beloved Va.

Suggested Readings: DAB; DNB; LHUS. *See also* Philip L. Barbour, *The Three Worlds of Captain John Smith* (1964); Alexander Brown, *The Genesis of the United States*, 2 vols. (1890); John E. Cooke, *Virginia: A History of the People* (1903; rep., 1973); Wesley F. Craven, *Dissolution of the Virginia Company* (1932): Virginius Dabney, *Virginia: The New Dominion* (1971); Ralph Hamor, *A True Discourse of the Present State of Virginia* (1615; rep., 1860); Susan M. Kingsbury, ed., *Records of the Virginia Company of London* (1906-1935), III, 70-73, 241-248; John Smith, *The General Historie of Virginia* (1624); William Stith, *The History of the First Discovery and Settlement of Virginia* (1865).

James Stephens
Marquette University

AQUILA ROSE (1695-1723)

Works: *Poems on Several Occasions* (1740).

Biography: Aquila Rose was born in Eng. in 1695. We know nothing of his youth, although Elias Bockett in his elegy on Rose told us that some misfortune "Forc'd him to quit his former peaceful ways / And prove his fortune o'er a foamy sea." After a tour of Mediterranean ports of undetermined length, Rose arrived in Philadelphia some time before 1717, where illness forced him to remain. He soon became a friend of James Logan (q.v.) and secured a position as compositor in Andrew Bradford's (q.v.) printing shop. In 1722 Rose was appointed clerk of the Provincial Assembly and was granted the right to operate a ferry over the Schuylkill River. In either Jun. or Aug. of 1723 (Bockett and Samuel Keimer (q.v.), author of another elegy, differed, although Rose's son agreed with Bockett on the Jun. date), Rose slipped while retrieving a boat from the river and, as Bockett related, "wading thro' the chilling flood / A cold ill humour mingled with his blood." He died shortly thereafter, leaving a wife and two sons.

Critical Appraisal: Aquila Rose has been chiefly remembered as the subject of elegies by Bockett and Keimer—the latter memorable for Benjamin Franklin's (q.v.) account of its composition (Keimer apparently composed the lines as he set them) and for its quality ("perhaps the worst elegy ever written," according to the *Cambridge History of American Literature*). We should also note, however, that Rose's collection of poems, edited by his son and printed by Franklin, was the first volume of native poetry published in Pa. and that his verse is not without some merit.

George Duyckinck thought that the poems "display skill and ease in versification," an opinion shared by F. H. Williams: "That he is something more than a mere rhymester is shown not only by his mastery of the English couplet, but by sudden gleams of imagination which bespeak true insight and inspiration." Williams must also admit, however, that Rose is "only tolerable." Ellis Oberholtzer took a somewhat harsher stance: the verse "does not attest very highly to Rose's character as a poet, or to the critical sense of the people of that age in Philadelphia by whom it was so cordially admired." Perhaps the fairest estimate of Rose's ability is that by George Genzmer: "Rose's poems are the work of a cultured amateur, the best versifier in English that Philadelphia could show before the younger Thomas Godfrey (q.v.)."

Rose's canon includes two translations of Ovid's elegies; poems addressed to Richard Hill, to the memory of Rose's sister, and "To His Companion at Sea"; verse occasioned by William Keith's Indian treaty of 1717; a poem "On the Death of his Friend's much Lov'd child"; three holiday pieces written for the newspaper carriers; and an uncertain number of poems that his son suggested were borrowed by friends "who have forgot to return them."

The poems to Hill and Keith chiefly reflect contemporary poetic idiom and reveal little originality or energy. At times Rose slipped into similar poetic clichés in his translations of Ovid: "The fatal Day had almost lost its Light, / Vail'd by the Curtains of Sable Night." Rose seems to have been more effective when he chose a personal subject, such as the death of his sister or the memory of days spent at sea: "The gen'rous wine imparts a heat / To raise and quicken every sense. / No thoughts of death our bliss defeat, / Nor steal away our innocence" ("To His Companion at Sea"). The threat of imminent death shadowed life in colonial Pa., as it did Rose's poems: "Her Virgin Youth was past unknown to Strife / Each fleeting hour as if the last in life" ("To the Memory of His Sister"). Rose responded to this fear both with songs to transient pleasures, such as those afforded by wine at sea, and with reminiscence of lost innocence, perhaps a recollection of happier days in Eng.: "How far remov'd is this our western shore, / From those dear lands our fathers knew before" (New Year's Day Carrier's Verse, 1720). This sense of nostalgia and lost innocence certainly forms one major strain in American literature. We can only regret that Rose, like his contemporary Henry Brooke (q.v.), did not live to write into his maturity and move past these youthful sentiments and minor poems.

Suggested Readings: DAB; T₁. *See also* Francis Howard Williams, "Pennsylvania Poets of the Provincial Period," PMHB, 17 (1893), 5-10; Evert and George Duyckinck, *Cyclopaedia of American Literature* (1855), I, 97-99.

Timothy K. Conley
Bradley University

JAMES ROSIER (1575-1635)

Works: "A True Relation of the Most Prosperous Voyage Made. . . by Captain George Weymouth, in the Discovery of the Land of Virginia" (1605; rep. in part in *Purchas His Pilgrimes*, 1625, and Louis B. Wright, ed., *The Elizabethans' America*, 1965; rep. in full, 1843, 1860, 1887).

Biography: James Rosier is known to have been born in Eng. in 1575 and to have died in 1635. He took an M.A. at Cambridge in 1596 and, in 1605, traveled with Capt. Weymouth to the coast of Maine. Although Rosier claimed also to have accompanied Bartholomew Gosnold on his voyage to New Eng. in 1602, recent historians are certain that he did not. Samuel Purchas (q.v.), who attributed John Brereton's (q.v.) *Briefe and True Relation* (1602), an account of the Gosnold journey, to Rosier, printed it in his *Pilgrimes* in 1625, thus perpetuating the error. Rosier may well have been eager to establish a Catholic colony in New Eng., having apparently converted to that religion in 1602. Sir Thomas Arundell, an investor in the voyage of 1605 and a leading Catholic, may have appointed Rosier to write this report on prospective locations for such a settlement.

Critical Appraisal: *A True Relation* is a direct and readable, although circumspect, work. James Rosier was charged with narrating events of the Weymouth journey and describing the natural advantages to be found in America. The obvious aim is to coax the wealthy to invest money and the adventurous to invest their lives in further expeditions and long-term settlements. To prevent others from charting and claiming the territory and, perhaps, to disguise his plans for a Catholic colony, Rosier was unwilling to give many useful details. Enchanted with the locale, however, he described each day as a feast of new sensations: fresh water, elegant harbors, splendid tobacco, and the Penobscot Indians, " all very civil and merry." Seeking to gain friendship, the twenty-nine Englishmen on the trip first were courteous and then used a trick with magnetism to "cause them to imagine some power in us." The Indians are beautiful, inventive, intelligent people with remarkably fine table manners and great skill in the manual arts. Their language, many samples of which Rosier included, has recently been analyzed by Philip L. Barbour in an unpublished manuscript on deposit at the Institute of Early American History and Culture, Williamsburg, Va. Their religion, which Rosier described fully, can be distracting; ceremonies "of idolatry" commonly involve two hours or more of stamping and bellowing.

Rosier told also of a ten-mile expedition up the St. George River, finer than any river to be found in Europe. No man minded the labor of rowing, so pleasant and alluring was this new paradise, a land surely preserved for a nation "professing Christ." Before returning, the voyagers captured "with exceeding kind usage" five Indians and two canoes for display in Eng. Rosier, so certain of direction by the "Omnipotent Disposer" and desirous only to promote the public good by "promulgating God's holy church," wrote with inspiration and infectious zeal.

Suggested Readings: DNB; LHUS. *See also* Henry S. Burrage, *Early English and French Voyages* (1906); *Oxford Companion to American Literature* (1941); David Beers Quinn, *England and the Discovery of America: 1481-1620* (1974), pp. 389-391.

James Stephens
Marquette University

JOSEPH ROWLANDSON (c. 1631-1678)

Works: *The Possibility of God's Forsaking a People* (1682).

Biography: Joseph Rowlandson seems to have been born in Eng. about 1631 or 1632 and to have immigrated with his family to Ipswich, Mass., about 1638. He was the sole graduate of Harvard College in 1652. A year before graduation, he was involved in a little escapade in his home town of Ipswich. He had written a now obscure, anonymous, satirical insult of the Ipswich court, partly in rhyme and partly in prose. The authorities succeeded in identifying the culprit and sentenced him to be fined and publicly whipped. Whether or not the sentence was carried out is unknown, but Rowlandson submitted an abject apology.

In 1654, still unordained, Rowlandson settled in the frontier town of Lancaster, thirty-five miles west of Boston, as the town's first minister. Eventually ordained in 1660, Rowlandson in the meantime had married (in 1656) Mary (White) Rowlandson (q.v.), the daughter of the town's wealthiest landholder, by whom he had four children. Town records show some disputes with parishioners in the early years, but by 1672 his reputation was such that he was called upon to help settle the controversy raging around the formation of the Old South Church in Boston.

When Lancaster fell to the Indians in Feb. 1676, Rowlandson was not present. Whether or not the town had received word of the warning given by the Christian Indian James Quanopohit to Daniel Gookin (q.v.) is unclear, but Rowlandson and his wife's brother-in-law had been sent by the town to Boston to plead with the Mass. Council for help against the impending attack. Rowlandson declined service in an army gathered to pursue the Indians, who held captive his wife and children, in order to devote his time to appealing to the Mass. Council to arrange for the ransom of his family. The ransom of his wife was effected in May of that year.

As King Philip's War came to an end, Rowlandson accepted a position as minister to the town of Wethersfield, Conn. He died there in Nov. 1678, in possession of an unusually large library. His last sermon was published as a memorial, along with his wife's narrative of her captivity.

Critical Appraisal: Except for his youthful satire and consequent apology, Joseph Rowlandson's only known work is his final sermon, a competent if undistinguished example of a Puritan sermon. In the course of his argument, which has to do with the withdrawal of divine favor from a church or commonwealth hitherto "visibly near & dear to him," Rowlandson did at moments rise to a somberly baleful eloquence. Otherwise the sermon is of interest only because it displays some of the theological and spiritual underpinnings of his wife's captivity narrative. Although it contained no explicit references to the events of King Philip's War, Rowlandson's jeremiad provides a basis for interpretation of national calamity similar to that found in his wife's narrative and in Puritan histories of the period. In the early editions, the sermon was preceded by an introduction signed "B. W." (almost certainly Benjamin Woodbridge [q.v.], minister at Windsor, Conn., whose brother John Woodbridge [q.v.] had recently succeeded Rowlandson at Wethersfield). According to "B. W.", Rowlandson was "known amongst the Churches in the Wilderness," but his fame, such as it was, was soon to be eclipsed by that of his wife.

Suggested Readings: CCNE; FCNEV; Sibley-Shipton (I, 311-321). *See also* Adams and Stiles, *The History of Ancient Wethersfield, Connecticut* (1877); Abijah P. Marvin, *History of the Town of Lancaster, Massachusetts* (1879); Henry Stedman Nourse, "Brief Historical and Genealogical Sketches of Earliest Proprietors and Pioneers of Lancaster, Massachusetts" (unpublished); idem, *The Early Records of Lancaster, Massachusetts, 1643-1725* (1884); Marion Fuller Safford, *The Story of Colonial Lancaster* (1937); John Eliot Thayer and Henry Stedman Nourse, eds., *A Narrative of the Captivity and Restoration of Mrs. Mary Rowlandson* (1903); Almira Larkin White, *Genealogy of the Descendants of John White of Wenham, Massachusetts* (1900); Joseph Willard, *Topographical and Historical Sketches of the Town of Lancaster* (1835).

Robert K. Diebold
Husson College

MARY ROWLANDSON (c. 1635/1638-after 1678)

Works: *The Soveraignty and Goodness of God* [or *A True History of the Captivity and Restoration of Mrs. Mary Rowlandson*] (1682).

Biography: Mary Rowlandson was probably born in South Petherton in Somerset, Eng., between 1635 and 1638. Her father, John White (b. 1602), immigrated to Salem, Mass., in 1638 and was followed by the rest of the family a year later. The family soon moved from Salem to Wenham, where, according to a note in the town records, the Whites lived "for a long space of time...in ye woods from ye meanes [of grace]." By 1653 the family was in Lancaster, of which her father (identified as the wealthiest landowner in the area) was an incorporator. In 1656 Mary White married Joseph Rowlandson (q.v.), the town's first minister. She bore four children, one of whom died in infancy. She and the remaining three children were taken captive in Feb. 1676, when Lancaster was besieged by Indians during King Philip's War. The youngest child, a girl aged six, died in her mother's arms in captivity. The other two either escaped or were eventually ransomed. Mary herself was ransomed in May, the ransom negotiations themselves signaling the disintegration of the Indian confederacy and the end of the war. During her three months of captivity, she lived mainly with Weetamoo, a squaw sachem of the Pocassets, and her husband, Quanopen, a sachem of the Narragansetts and one of the leaders of the attack on Lancaster. Her narrative records conversations with King Philip among others.

After her ransom, Rowlandson joined her husband in Boston, where they lived for about a year, aided by the generosity of friends. In the spring of 1677, the Rowlandsons moved to Wethersfield, Conn., where Joseph had obtained a position as minister. Internal evidence suggests that Rowlandson's narrative of her captivity was written in Wethersfield in either 1677 or 1678. Her husband died in Nov. of the latter year. She last appears in the town records of Wethersfield in 1679, when she was granted a sum of money to pay for her husband's funeral. Although Rowlandson was probably still alive in 1682, when her narrative was published, there is no known historical record of her after 1679. The date and place of her death are therefore uncertain.

Critical Appraisal: Mary Rowlandson's account of her experiences has won general acclaim as probably the best of the captivity narratives. From its vivid opening to its eloquent conclusion, the narrative is always lively and often moving. It may well be the most readable work produced in seventeenth-century Puritan America. It went through more early editions (at least four) than any other American book of its time, thereby outstripping the works of Anne Bradstreet (q.v.) and the Puritan divines, and it continues to be the most reprinted of all of the captivity narratives.

Besides being readable, the Rowlandson narrative is for a number of reasons a very interesting and significant document. Its first-hand accounts of experiences with virtually all of the Indian leaders in King Philip's War have incalculable value for historians, and its descriptions of Indian living conditions and attitudes in the spring of 1676 are of interest both to anthropologists and general readers. In addition, the narrative is probably as good a reflection of the seventeenth-century New Eng. mind working on an extended concrete experience as is available anywhere. In her role as a Puritan minister's wife, Rowlandson was in contact with the thought of the educated elite, yet in possession of only a limited education herself. The narrative displays a genuine grasp of the New Eng.

Puritan way of understanding experience in the light of biblical typology, yet also displays popular prejudices often at odds with official Puritan policy.

In contrast to virtually all of the later captivity narratives, the Rowlandson narrative is remarkable for its coherence and depth. The extensive use of biblical quotations (as well as the absorption of biblical imagery into Rowlandson's own prose) does more than establish her credentials for piety: it converts her experience into symbolic drama. No other captivity narrative has such a steady and comprehensive view of itself as a story of profound religious experience. From the assault on Lancaster, through the shared experience of the Indians' perpetual quest of food and shelter, to the monetary assistance of friends in Boston, every detail contributes to the unfolding of one or another of the narrative's major themes. Even the narrative's division into twenty "removes"—the stages of her journey—contributes ultimately to her final theme: the "stillness" she learned in the wilderness, where divine power was manifested to her through the forces of Satan.

To be sure, Rowlandson's interpretation of her experience is often as narrow as it is profound. She is severely restricted in her capacity to understand her Indian captors, for example. Yet within her limitations, she is an honest and faithful recorder of events and humanly responsive to them. Her narrative has permanent literary and historical value.

Suggested Readings: DAB; LHUS; NAW. *See also* Douglas Leach, "The 'Whens' of Mary Rowlandson's Captivity," NEQ, 34 (1961), 352-363; Henry Stedman Nourse, "Mrs. Mary Rowlandson's Removes," PAAS, 2nd ser., 12 (1899), 401-409; Roy Harvey Pearce, "The Significance of the Captivity Narrative," AL, 19 (1947), 1-20; Richard H. Slotkin, *Regeneration Through Violence* (1973); John Eliot Thayer and Henry Stedman Nourse, eds., *A Narrative of the Captivity and Restoration of Mrs. Mary Rowlandson* (1903); R.W.G. Vail, "Indian Captives in New England," PMHS, 68 (1952), 113-131; Richard VanDerBeets, "The Indian Captivity Narrative as Ritual," AL, 43 (1972), 548-562; Almira White, *Genealogy of the Descendants of John White of Wenham, Massachusetts* (1900).

Robert K. Diebold

Husson College

SUSANNA HASWELL ROWSON (1762-1824)

Works: Fiction: *Victoria* (1786); *The Test of Honour* (1789); *The Inquisitor* (1793); *Charlotte Temple* (1794); *The Fille de Chambre* (1794); *Mentoria* (1794); *Trials of the Human Heart* (1795); *Reuben and Rachel* (1798); *Sarah* (1813); *Charlotte's Daughter* (1828).

Pedagogical Works: *An Abridgement of Universal Geography* (1805); *A Spelling Dictionary* (1807); *A Present for Young Ladies* (1811); *Youth's First Step in Geography* (1818); *Biblical Dialogues Between a Father and His Family* (1822); *Exercises in History, Chronology, and Biography* (1822).

Poetry: *Poems on Various Subjects* (1788); *A Trip to Parnassus* (1788); *Miscellaneous Poems* (1804).

Drama: *Slaves in Algiers* (1794); *The Volunteers* (1795).

Songs: "I Never Will Be Married" (1790-1820); "American, Commerce and Freedom" (1794); "A Soldier Is the Noblest Name" (1794); "Independent and Free" (1796); "In Vain Is the Verdure of Spring" (1797-1798); "The Little Sailor Boy" (1798); "Captn Truxton or Huzza! for the Constellation" (1799); "Truxton's Victory" (1799); "A Dirge" (1800); "Kiss the Brim and Bid It Pass" (1802); "Will Not Dare Not Tell" (1802); "Orphan Nosegay Girl" (1803-1806); "How Cold and Piercing Blows the Wind" (1809); "He Is Not Worth the Trouble" (c. 1813); "I'd Rather Be Excus'd" (1814-1815); "Soft as Yon Silver Ray That Sleeps" (1814-1825); "The Columbian Sailor" (c. 1816); "Come Strike the Silver String" (1817-1823); "National Song for the 4th of July" (c. 1818); "Will You Rise My Belov'd" (1818-1825); "Charity" (1820); "Peace and Holy Love" (1820); "Where Can Peace of Mind Be Found" (1821); "Child of Mortality" (1824).

Biography: Susanna (Haswell) Rowson was born in Portsmouth, Eng., in 1762. The daughter of a British Royal Navy officer, she spent her childhood in the colony of Mass. until the Revolutionary War, when colonists forced the family to remove to Eng. To support herself, Susanna Haswell became a governess and started writing novels. In 1786 she married William Rowson, with whom she joined a provincial theater company. In 1793 they joined the company of Thomas Wignell, who brought them to America, where Susanna Rowson performed in Philadelphia, Baltimore, and Boston. While acting, she wrote plays and song lyrics as well as novels. In 1797 she abruptly quit the theater and turned to a new career in education. For the next twenty-five years, she was the respectable headmistress of her own "Young Ladies' Academy," writing textbooks and school materials in addition to novels, magazine essays, and poems. She died in 1824, highly respected by her pupils and friends.

Critical Appraisal: Susanna (Haswell) Rowson is best known as the author of the novel *Charlotte Temple*. Published in Eng. in 1791 and in this country in 1794, it became by the middle of the nineteenth century the most frequently published novel in America. By 1905 it had appeared in over 200 editions. The popularity of this seduction tale has been variously attributed to the novel's "foundation in fact," to its compact and careful plot construction, to its blend of strict narration and dialog, and to its underlying message of forgiveness for the "fallen woman." *Charlotte Temple* is the story of a young English schoolgirl seduced by a young army officer, Montraville, and carried off to America. When Montraville delays in marrying Charlotte, he in turn falls prey to the evil ways of a false friend who persuades him of Charlotte's infidelity, causing Montraville to abandon her and marry another. Charlotte gives birth to a girl child and then suffers the death fated to all such heroines in seduction novels after 1800. Both characterization and structure in this work show a degree of sophistication. The supposed villain is himself as victimized as the heroine, and one of the real villains is a woman who never repents though she pays heavily for her crimes. A single subplot is introduced in medias res, and the whole story unfolds rapidly. The paperback edition today serves as a still-readable introduction to early American fiction.

The preface to *Charlotte Temple* states Rowson's concern for the education of young women, a consistent theme in all of her writings. Other themes are the superiority of the middle class, women's reliance upon a community of women, America as a haven of peace and democracy, and the author's hatred of violence and tyranny in any form. These themes appeared repeatedly in Rowson's other novels as well as in her plays, textbooks, and songs.

Rowson's years in the theater included collaboration with many immigrant musicians in writing songs for musical dramas that served as popular American entertainment after the Revolution. Rowson's lyrics show a strong sense of rhythm, an easy rhyme, a mild humor, and an acquaintance with the life of the sea. Only one of Rowson's plays exists in complete form today. *Slaves in Algiers*, performed in Philadelphia in 1794 and in Baltimore in 1795, presents an unlikely plot that catered to popular current interest in the Algerian regime then terrorizing American ships by taking captives for slavery and ransom. The feminist songs and dialog in this play led to a vicious critical attack on Rowson in 1795 by the English political satirist William Cobbett (q.v.).

Rowson's novels express a concern for women that was fifty years ahead of her time. The novels attack myths and stereotypes of women and replace them with a view of woman as separate but equal to man and capable of great achievement. All but her first novels contain heroines of good sense; they suffer from inexperience at the start but they successfully encounter physical and moral dangers. Only two of her earliest novels, *Victoria* and *Charlotte Temple*, written when Rowson was young, imitative, and in need of money, contain heroines who fall victim to men and circumstances because of their extreme sensibility. All of her heroines have "a delicate nature," but only in these two works are they complete victims.

In addition to their feminism, Rowson's works hold other interest for a modern reader. *Rebecca, or The Fille de Chambre* holds autobiographical interest for its descriptions of Rowson's childhood voyage to America and events during the Revolutionary War. *Trials of the Human Heart* exemplifies the episodic novel popular in Eng. in an earlier period. More episodic and less successful than *Rebecca, Trials of the Human Heart* strains reader credibility with its bizarre recognition scenes and arbitrary deaths, the sheer number of events that befall the heroine, and the cover of its poorly handled epistolary format. This picaresque account of sixteen years of the life of Meriel Howard creates little interest in the repeatedly victimized but ever saintly heroine. The loosely knit structure contrasts sharply with the far more successful *Charlotte Temple*.

Reuben and Rachel, Rowson's next novel, illustrates an unusual didactic effort, as it appends historical information, most of it accurate, to a typically romantic plot in order to serve its author's stated purpose of awakening in the minds of young women "a curiosity that might lead them to the attentive perusal of history in general, but more especially to the history of their native country." Although the novel covers a span of 250 years in at least six countries, it is less complex than *Trials of the Human Heart* and presents a systematic plot. The main character, Rachel Dudley, is a prototype of the American girl; she shows initiative and takes action on her own. Other characters succeed in holding reader interest, but the dialog grows tiresome.

Rowson's last novel, *Sarah*, relates a much simpler story, heavily autobiographical, about an ill-made marriage that leaves the heroine perpetually unhappy. A strong and independent woman, the main character speaks out poignantly on marriage and the role of wife. Both characterization and dialog help this novel succeed, and the epistolary format, handled more realistically than in *Trials of the Human Heart*, made it an effective serial for the *Boston Weekly Magazine* where it first appeared.

Rowson's textbooks and other writings derived from her schools show that her loyalty to Eng. and the English people remained strong despite her admiration for her adopted country. They also reflect her continuing concern for the formal education of young women and her desire to raise women's expectations of themselves. In *A Present for Young Ladies* Rowson collected poems and dialogs she had written for her students to read aloud at her Academy's annual "exhibition." The collection demonstrates that Rowson instilled into her students a firm belief in a sound education, a replacement of frivolity with judgment, a sense of filial duty, and an appreciation for fields of study such as geography and navigation usually reserved for boys. Included in *A Present* is an essay for use in Rowson's classrooms entitled "Female Biography," a series of biographies of women in ancient and recent history who developed and exercised their intellectual abilities in ways that might inspire the reader.

Rowson's least examined writings, her columns in the *Boston Weekly Magazine*, restate in essay form many of the themes found in her fiction: filial duty, the responsibility of parents to educate both sons and daughters carefully, and the need for careful selection of reading matter, especially novels.

As America's first woman of letters, Rowson lived during the beginning of the new nation whose philosophies, politics, music, and literature are reflected in her writings and her colorful career. Her active and productive life invites biography and critical study.

Suggested Readings: DAB; DNB; LHUS; NAW. *See also* Elias Nason, *A Memoir of Mrs. Susanna Rowson* (1870); Henri Petter, *The Early American Novel* (1971); R.W.G. Vail, "A Bibliographical Study," (1870) PAAS, 42 (1932), 47-160. A new edition of *Charlotte Temple* has been published by Clara and Rudolf Kirk" (1964).

Patricia L. Parker
Salem State College

ROWLAND RUGELEY (c. 1735-1776)

Works: *Miscellaneous Poems and Translations from La Fontaine and Others* (1763).

Biography: Thorough, reliable information about Rowland Rugeley has yet to appear in print. A careful search of colonial records kept in the S.C. Department of Archives and History might provide the basis for a worthwhile study of one of the earliest writers of belle-lettres in the South. Rugeley's exact year of birth is uncertain but is believed to have been 1735. He immigrated from Eng. to S.C. sometime around 1766, before which he published a volume of *Miscellaneous Poems and Translations from La Fontaine and Others* and made frequent contributions to the British periodicals.

Local records indicate that in 1766 Rugeley purchased a large tract of land on the banks of the Ashley River near Charleston. A contemporary diary describes him as a "merchant" and mentions that he had three brothers and three sisters, also of Charleston. Rugeley perhaps was writing local-color verse as early as 1757, but his name does not appear prominently in the history of S.C. until 1774. He was then elected to the Provincial Congress, to represent "the District between the Broad and Saludy Rivers," an upstate area now in Richland and Lexington Counties. Rugeley died of unknown causes during the autumn of 1776, possibly from the same epidemic of illness that killed his wife and youngest child a few weeks later. A death notice in the *South-Carolina and American General Gazette* states that he was an honest man and a jovial companion whose poetry was "very generally admired" and entitled him to "some Rank in the Literary World."

Critical Appraisal: Only a handful of copies of Rowland Rugeley's *Miscellaneous Poems* are known to be extant. On the basis of this lone published work, John Trumbull (q.v.), in a letter to Mathew Carey (q.v.), Jun. 4, 1780, pronounced Rugeley "a poet certainly superior to Evans." Trumbull continued: "He published a volume worth preserving; and since that, a travestie of the fourth book of Virgil, which for delicacy and true humor is superior to Cotton's."

Trumbull's reference to the fourth book of Virgil concerns one of the earliest known publications of a literary work in S.C. *The Story of Aeneas and Dido Burlesqued* presents a perplexing bibliographical problem. The work was first advertised in Robert Wells's *South-Carolina and American General Gazette*, Apr. 22, 1774 ("Lately Published...by a Gentleman of South-Carolina"). Joseph Sabin's original entry for *Aeneas and Dido* attributes authorship to Rugeley; however, in his corrected citation, he noted: "Wegelin...attributes to Rugeley on the authority of the inscription in the NYP. copy written by a former owner....However, in the obituary of Robert Wells printed in the 'Gentleman's Magazine,' vol. 64, pt. 2, 1794, p. 677, it is stated that 'Mr. W. was a man of letters, and a poet, evinced by a travestie of Virgil, which he wrote and published while at Charles-Town.'" The matter is confused yet further by Charles Evans's entry, which is introduced under "Virgil," with the author cited as "Rowland Rugeley [Robert Wells]," suggesting that Wells adopted a pseudonym. A 1774 Philadelphia reprint provides no further clues, bearing on its title page: "By a Gentleman of South-Carolina."

An earlier collection of poems, possibly composed by Rugeley, never has been discovered. Proposals for printing by subscription "A Collection of Poems, on Various Subjects" were advertised by Robert Wells and other Charleston merchants in the *South-Carolina Gazette*, Aug. 25, 1757. The advertisement describes the proposed collection as follows:

> The Books will contain, as near as can be computed, Six Sheets, printed on a fine new Type, as the Specimen annexed. The Price to Subscribers will be Two Dollars. One thereof to be paid at subscribing, the other on Delivery of the Book sewed in blue or marble paper. No more will be printed than are subscribed for. The work will be put to Press as soon as a sufficient Number of Subscriptions are obtained.

Appended to this advertisement is a specimen of a poem titled "Indico," which is not among the verses printed in Rugeley's collection and, apparently, was never published in its entirety elsewhere. The plan to publish this early collection of poems seems to have been abandoned. A letter from one "Agricola" in the *South-Carolina Gazette*, Dec. 1, 1758, alludes to "an Extract of the Poem Indico mentioned in your Gazette about Twelve Months ago; which can't be published 'till Subscriptions arrive from London, expected in the Spring, those here not amounting to the Expence of the Press."

By the latter part of 1759, it seems that Wells had abandoned the project altogether, apparently turning it over to Peter Timothy, Charleston's only other printer. Timothy announced in the *South-Carolina Gazette*, Nov. 3, 1759: "The Poem on Indico, for which subscriptions have been on foot above two years, being in our hands, will be put to press as soon as possible. Those gentlemen who had subscription papers, are requested to send them to the printer hereof, who also will take in subscriptions for the author." In the absence of any subsequent advertisement announcing publication, however, it seems very unlikely that this collection of poems ever was published. Hence Rugeley's reputation as an American writer rests almost solely on "Indico."

Suggested Readings: Hennig Cohen, *The South Carolina Gazette* (1953), pp. 209-211; J. A. Leo Lemay, "Sixty-eight Additional Writers of the Colonial South" in *A Bibliographical Guide to the Study of Southern Literature* (1969), ed. Louis D. Rubin, Jr., p. 349 (for references to Rugeley in the *South Carolina Historical and Genealogical Magazine*); James A. Levernier, "Rowland Rugeley" in *Southern Writers: A Biographical Dictionary*, ed., Robert Bain, Joseph M. Flora, and Louis D. Rubin, Jr. (1979), p. 389.

Christopher Gould
Southwestern Oklahoma State University
and James A. Levernier
University of Arkansas at Little Rock

GEORGE RUGGLE (1575-1622)

Works: *Ignoramus* (1615); *A Note of the Shipping, Men, and Provisions Sent to Virginia, by the Treasurer and Company in the Year 1619* (1619);

Another Note of the Shipping, Men, and Provisions Sent to Virginia . . . in the Year 1619 (1619); *A Declaration of the State of the Colonie and Affaires in Virginia* (1620); *A Treatise of the Art of Making Silke* (translator; by John Bonoeil; 1622); *Club Law* (n.d.); *Re Vera, or Verily* (n.d.).

Biography: George Ruggle, playwright and advisor to the Virginia Company, was born in Lavenham, Suffolk, Eng., and baptized on Nov. 3, 1575. He attended Lavenham Grammar School and matriculated from St. John's College, Cambridge, on Jun. 2, 1589. He then studied on scholarship at Trinity College and graduated B.A. in 1593 and M.A. in 1597. He was elected fellow of Clare Hall the following year and held that position until 1620. Ruggle's most notable literary achievement is his Latin comedy *Ignoramus*, which was first staged before James I at Clare Hall on Mar. 8, 1615. Ruggle is known to have written two other plays, *Club Law* and *Re Vera, or Verily*, although only the former is known to be extant. While at Clare, Ruggle became acquainted with Nicholas Ferrar during the latter's student days. When Sir Edwin Sandys, treasurer of the Virginia Company, sought to promote colonization efforts and "confute certain scandalous reports" in 1619, he requested Ruggle's assistance, apparently through Ferrar, then secretary of the Company. Ruggle anonymously wrote two pamphlets in 1619 and prepared a similar work the following year. These pamphlets were published in London, where Ruggle remained, resigning his fellowship and probably becoming a private tutor to the sons of Toby Palavicino. Ruggle most likely performed one additional service for the Virginia Company, again at the request of Ferrar. In 1622 he translated from the French John Bonoeil's treatise on sericulture. This work was also published in London, in 1622, the year of Ruggle's death. Although he never traveled to America, George Ruggle's interest in the Virginia Company extended to his will, in which he bequeathed 100 pounds for the Christian education of "the Infidells children" in Va.

Critical Appraisal: George Ruggle's authorship of the three pamphlets and translation of the sericulture treatise stand as his contribution to the colonization of Va. The significance of these writings can best be perceived when placed within the context of the history of early colonial Va. From the outset, the Va. colony was beset by squabbles over ownership of land and disagreements concerning which products should be planted. These problems were usually attributable to the ineffective government installed by the Virginia Company in London. Official control of the colony during its first decade was erratic and, according to John Rolfe (q.v.), writing in 1617, the colony was faced with "envie, dissentions and jarrs . . . [that] *choaked* the *seedes* and *blasted* the *fruits* of all mens labors." As a result, it had become increasingly difficult to entice Englishmen to immigrate to the new colony, and the very future of the colonial enterprise was threatened. In 1618 Governor Samuel Argall, an ineffective leader who tended to resolve conflicts of interest in his own favor, was replaced by the colonists with George Yeardly. But it was not until 1619, with the appointment of Sir Edwin Sandys as treasurer of the company and thus colonial governor, that serious reform began to take effect. By broadening Va.'s economic base through diversifying industry and agriculture, Sandys made enough progress to publicize the new prosperity of the colony. Thus Ruggle was commissioned to write three promotional tracts on the colony in the hope of inducing investment in the company and immigration to the colony. As a result of the changes instituted by Sandys and his successor Henry Wriothesely, earl of Southampton, the population of Va. had risen from slightly under 400 in 1617 to 3,500 in 1622. Of Ruggle's three tracts, one is published in *Force's Collection of Historical Tracts* and merits examination.

In his *Declaration of the State of the Colonie*, Ruggle explained that his purpose was "to remove that unworthy aspersion" that arose "by Letters from thence, and by rumours here at home" that "sought unjustly to staine and blemish that Countrey, as being barren and unprofitable." Ruggle countered these rumors by explaining how the colony was "rich, spacious, and well watered" and by offering a number of hyperbolic comparisons, such as: "The Wines, Fruit, and Salt of *France* and *Spaine*; The Silkes of *Persia* and *Italie*, will be found also in *Virginia*, and in no kinde of worth inferior." In addition, Ruggle promoted the colony by describing the type of person who had already immigrated and by enumerating the benefits they had accrued: "There have been also sundry persons of good quality, much commended for sufficiency, industry and honesty, provided and sent to take charge and government of those people." They are also described as having a number of shares of land "to hold and enjoy to him and his Heires." Furthermore, Ruggle made it clear that the weak colonial government and its often unjust system of laws were a part of the past: "The Governour is so restrained to a Counseil ioyned with him, that hee can doe wrong to no man, who may not have speedy remedy." Ruggle then summarized the state of the colony as one characterized by "alacritie and cheerefulnesse" in a land "abounding with all Gods naturall blessings." Appended to each tract was a list of the investors and amounts invested and statistics on the number of passengers who had arrived on each ship that year. Considering the means of communication at this time, it is reasonable to assume that Ruggle's three tracts of 1619-1620 played no small role in promoting the reformed Va. colony.

Ruggle's fourth publication, the translation of the sericulture treatise, was also useful to the colony. James I had a marked interest in silkworm cultivation and encouraged its development in Va. The early attempts were unsuccessful and other, more pressing problems of government and the economy came to overshadow the effort. When Sandys assumed control of the colony, however, his interest in diversifying the economy extended into the revitalization of the silk industry. Also, renewed attention to sericulture, a project to which the king was devoted, could only be in the colony's interest, since James I had repeatedly threatened to revoke the Virginia Company's patent because of its management problems. In 1620 the company brought several skilled silkworm breeders from Fr. to the colony, including John Bonoeil. Bonoeil's treatise on sericulture contained detailed if pseudoscientific advice that, according to historian Alden Vaughan, may well have been largely responsible for the failure of the colonial silk enterprise. Copies of this treatise, which Ruggle apparently translated, were sent to every colonist family in Va., on order of the company, so that each household could learn to cultivate a variety of fruit trees as well as wine and silk. These efforts at sericulture continued during the next few years, but never with any notable success. Yet Ruggle's contribution to the Va. colony was important, as Nicholas Ferrar acknowledged in his eulogy:

> he was a man second to none in knowledge of all manner of humanity.... All which good parts he had for these last three yeares, wholly almost spent and exercised in Virginia Buisinesses, having (besides continually assistinge his Brothers and himselfe with Counsell and all manner of helpe in these places) written sundry treatises for the benefitt of the Plantation, and in pticular the worke so highly commended by Sir Edwin Sandys, concerninge the Government of Virginia, but such was his modestie that he would by no meanes suffer it to be known duringe his life.

Suggested Readings: DNB. *See also* Gerald Eades Bentley, *The Jacobean and Caroline Stage* (1956), V, 1027-1028; Charles E. Hatch, Jr., "Mulberry Trees and Silkworms: Sericulture in Early Virginia," VMHB, 65 (1957), 3-61; Edward D. Neill, "George Ruggle, Author of Some Early Publications upon the Virginia Colony," NEHGR, 29 (1875), 296-297; idem, *History of the Virginia Company of London* (1869, 1968), pp. 362-363; Alden T. Vaughan, *American Genesis* (1975).

Francis J. Bosha
Adyama Gakuin University
Tokyo, Japan

BENJAMIN RUSH (1745-1813)

Works: *De Coctione Ciborum in Ventriculo* (1768); *Dissertation on the Spasmodic Asthma of Children* (1770); *Syllabus of a Course of Lectures on Chemistry* (1770; rev., 1773; fac. rep., 1954); *Sermons to Gentlemen upon Temperance and Exercise* (1772); *Experiments and Observations on the Mineral Waters* (1773); *Upon Slave-Keeping* (1773); *A Vindication* (1773); *The Natural History of Medicine Among the Indians* (1774); *The Present Government of Pennsylvania* (1777); *New Method of Inoculating for the Smallpox* (1781); *The Effects of Spirituous Liquors* (1784); *The Present Test-Law of Pennsylvania* (1784); *The Influence of Physical Causes upon the Moral Faculty* (1786); *Thoughts upon Female Education* (1787); *The Manners of the German Inhabitants of Pennsylvania* (1789); *Medical Inquiries and Observations*, 2 vols. (1789, 1793), vol. 3 (1794), vol. 4 (1796), 2d rev. ed. (1805); *The Injustice and Impolicy of Punishing Murder by Death* (1792); *The Sugar Maple-Tree of the United States* (1792); *The Bilious Remitting Yellow Fever* (1794); *Essays, Literary, Moral and Philosophical* (1798), 2d ed. (1806); *Three Lectures upon Animal Life* (1799);

George W. Corner, ed., *Autobiography* (w. 1800; pub. 1948); *The Life and Character of Christopher Ludwick* (1801); *Six Introductory Lectures to...the Institutes and Practice of Medicine* (1801); *Sixteen Introductory Lectures...the Institutes and Practices of Medicine* (1811); *Medical Inquiries and Observations upon the Diseases of the Mind* (1812), 2d ed. (1818); Lyman H. Butterfield, ed., *Letters* (1951); *My Dearest Julia: The Loveletters of Dr. Benjamin Rush to Julia Stockton* (1979).

Biography: Benjamin Rush was born in Byberry, near Philadelphia, Pa., in 1745. He received an A.B. in 1760 from the College of New Jersey (now Princeton University), served a medical apprenticeship from 1761 to 1766, and completed his medical studies in Edinburgh between 1766 and 1768. There he became a disciple of the renowned William Cullen. Rush interned in London, where he met Benjamin Franklin (q.v.), and returned to Philadelphia in 1769.

A man of great energy and diverse interests, Rush began to practice his profession, to teach chemistry at the College of Philadelphia, write, and engage in medical controversy. By 1774 his practice was well established, and he had probably published more on medical matters than any other American physician. He also wrote the first American textbook on chemistry. An early and zealous supporter of independence, Rush came to know John Adams (q.v.), George Washington (q.v.), Thomas Jefferson (q.v.), and Thomas Paine (q.v.) (whose book *Common Sense* was given its title by Rush). He was a delegate to the First Provincial Conference, a member of the Second Continental Congress, and a signer of the Declaration of Independence. Appointed to the medical department of the Revolutionary army in 1777, Rush resigned the next year over disagreements with the department's director, Dr. Shipman. The discovery that Rush had written an anonymous letter critical of Gen. Washington effectively ended his political career.

After the war, Rush returned to his increasingly demanding professional duties as practicing physician, teacher, and writer but continued to the end of his life to pursue a number of humanitarian reforms. He played a large role in the founding of Dickinson College in 1783 and remained active in its affairs. He was also a founder or charter member of the American Philosophical Society, the Philadelphia Dispensary, and many organizations devoted to single issues such as temperance, penal reform, and education. Made a professor of medicine at the new University of Pennsylvania medical school in 1792, Rush became the most influential teacher of medicine of his time. He died in 1813 at the age of 86.

Critical Appraisal: Well known during his lifetime as a patriot, reformer, humanitarian doctor, and educator, Benjamin Rush participated widely and vigorously in the life of his time through his professional pursuits and numerous other activities. He wrote constantly on a variety of subjects and was often involved in controversy over his forthrightly expressed and at times extreme opinions.

As a medical man, Rush became a prominent figure, recognized as an inspiring teacher, a devoted practicing physician, and a prolific author of medical lectures and treatises. Although he was honored by European royalty for his work during the severe yellow fever epidemic of 1793 and revered throughout the nineteenth century, Rush was criticized with equal fervor for his strong commitment to bleeding and purging as the appropriate treatment for all disease. In his recommendations for public health, however, he was an early advocate of improved sanitation, the alleviating of crowding, and good diet. The enlightened measures he urged in the treatment of insanity—the establishing of special hospitals, for example—led the American Psychiatric Association to describe him as the "father of American psychiatry."

The first medical figure to achieve a literary reputation, Rush ranged widely over all aspects of medicine, usually setting forth his topic in a clear, systematic, and highly readable fashion. Invariably his approach was didactic: he was a strong and usually stubborn partisan of a number of ideas from Cullen's theory of disease to the new method of smallpox inoculation. Today he is most appealing in lectures that are both commonsensical and high minded such as *Duties of a Physician* and *The Vices and Virtues of Physicians*, which mix counsels of humanity and responsibility toward patients with advice to purchase farm land. Among his more ambitious medical writings, Rush's *Account of the Bilious Remitting Yellow Fever* stands out as an impressive, vividly detailed narrative of the Philadelphia epidemic of 1793. Had he written nothing else, his pioneering work *Medical Inquiries and Observations upon the Diseases of the Mind* would have assured him a place in American medical history. It remained alone in the field for seventy-one years.

Rush's essays on nonmedical subjects reveal a lively intellectual engagement with issues of social polity and morality. A religious and idealistic spirit led him to protest against slavery and capital punishment and to favor free education from elementary school to college. Concerning the benefits of his various proposals, Rush was characteristically enthusiastic. He wrote that universal education, among other effects, would result in the disappearance of "the profane and indecent language which assaults our ears in every street." As well as the hortatory and the philosophical, Rush provided a descriptive record of his culture in essays on subjects such as the manufacture of saltpeter, the German inhabitants of Pa., and the sugar maple tree.

Although Rush was too impolitic and uncompromising to have the successful political career that he envisioned as a young Revolutionary, he was highly valued by many of the chief political men of his era. Upon Rush's death, Jefferson stated that "a better man than Rush could not have left us, more benevolent, more learned, of finer genius, or more honest." John Adams similarly remarked that he knew "of no character living or dead, who has done more real good in America." Modern medicine has discarded much of the content of Rush's practice, but he remains a historically significant figure, a respected and influential man during his lifetime, who can still be recognized as an admirable example of professional dedication and societal accomplishment.

Suggested Readings: BDAS; DAB; LHUS; P; T$_2$. *See also* Carl Binger, *Revolu-*

tionary Doctor (1966); Norman Dain, *Concepts of Insanity in the United States, 1789-1865* (1964); Donald J. D'Elia, *Benjamin Rush: Philosopher of the American Revolution* (1974); Nathan G. Goodman, *Benjamin Rush: Physician and Citizen* (1934); David Freeman Hawke, *Benjamin Rush: Revolutionary Gadfly* (1971); James Hendrie Lloyd, *Benjamin Rush and His Critics* (1930); Wyndham Miles, "Benjamin Rush, Chemist," *Chymia*, 4 (1953), 37-77; Winthrop and Frances Neilson, *Verdict for the Doctor: The Case of Benjamin Rush* (1958); Richard H. Shyrock, *Benjamin Rush from the Perspective of the Twentieth Century* (1946).

Louise K. Barnett
Rutgers University

DANIEL RUSSELL (1642-1679)

Works: *An Almanack of Coelestiall Motions* (1671).

Biography: Daniel Russell, minister and author of an almanac, was born in 1642 in Charlestown, Mass. He attended Harvard and took a B.A. in 1669. In 1675, after having obtained an M.A., he was elected a fellow of the college. Later in 1675 he was probably serving as an assistant minister in New London, Conn., since he was on record as one of the town's new residents. He married Mehetabell Willis, known as Mabel, in 1676, and two years later received a call from the church of his youth at Charlestown. However, Russell died of smallpox before he could accept his call. In his will, he left 1,000 acres of land to Harvard.

Critical Appraisal: Harrison T. Meserole observed of almanac verse, of which Daniel Russell composed some of the best, that it "probably reached consistently a broader audience than any other type of seventeenth-century American verse." Indeed, the almanac took the place of the newspaper and was the most widely disseminated publication issued from colonial presses, although unfortunately, like today's newspapers, it was quickly discarded for a new edition. One may safely assume, then, that Russell's *Almanack* enjoyed a large audience, if only for a brief time.

An Almanack of Coelestiall Motions for the Year of the Christian Aera, 1671 is a diminutive book of only about fifteen pages. It opens with a summary survey, projecting the year's solar and lunar eclipses. Then, beginning with the month of Mar. (the new year in the English colonies in America always began in Mar. until 1752), Russell provided twelve monthly tables enumerating celestial events on a daily basis. Each month's data was followed by an eight-line poem arranged into iambic pentameter couplets. Russell added on his last page "A Brief Geographicall Description of the World," dividing the earth into only these four parts: Europe, Asia, Africa, and America. Of course, this division was appropriate for 1671.

It is the poetry beneath each monthly table, however, that interests today's readers. Surprising for the time, as well as for the author, a Puritan minister, these tellurian verses lack any concrete Christian allusions but are literally filled with Classical, pagan ones. Many of the lines from these twelve poems, each designed to interpret a theme appropriate to its month, are delightfully pleasing and are written after the best pastoral tradition. In Mar. the sun or "The Starry Monarch" reanimates "with Celestial Fire" those whom stormy winter weather "caus'd t'expire." But in the warmer month of May, one discovers "Dame Tellus cloathed in a grass green coat, / By Flora's curious Needle-work well wrought," or as Russell explained in the next couplet: "for now the meads abound / with fragrant Roses, and with Lillies crown'd." Midsummer's Jul. brings forth "mighty Armies of Tall Blades. . .all Rank'd and Fil'd they stand / Ready for Battle." "Fierce Husbandmen" soon meet these "Armies" of grain who "being Victors lay them at their feet." Early autumn distends "The Noble vines with Grapes, the Grapes begin / To swell with Bacchus, which is Barell'd in." This last image denies outright notions that the Puritans were not given to strong drink.

For the month of Sept., Russell painted this seductive image of swains making off with newly ripened fruit: "Pomona's Daughters now at age, and dight / With pleasing Beauty, Lovers do invite / In multitudes: it's well if they escape / From each of these, without a cruel Rape." The rich sensuousness here recalls Spenser. When the month of Feb. comes, "the Worlds bright Torch, whose radiant Light / Dispels the gloomy Mists of black-fac'd Night: / The Twelve Herculean Labours of his Sphere, / Compleated hath, and Periodiz'd the Year." The analogy to Hercules and his twelve labors is appropriate, because the months of the year move somewhat arbitrarily, without certainty, just as the reader (listener) is never quite certain, while in the act of reading, whether Hercules will succeed; but at the same time all know that the year will run its course, despite the intermittent storms and calms, just as all know that Hercules will accomplish all twelve labors, despite his momentary setbacks and periods of ostensibly insurmountable difficulty.

Russell's twelve poems, each a delight in its own way, have been deservedly anthologized. They are significant, however, not just because of their playful gaiety. Russell's poems dissuade students of the colonial period from the notion that all Puritans were colorless and austere—indeed these florid poems come from the pen of a minister of the Gospel—and from the conclusion that all Puritans thought the Classical gods and goddesses to be "no better than harlots." Some, of course, were of this latter persuasion, including Edward Taylor (q.v.), but clearly not all.

Suggested Readings: CCNE; FCNEV; Sibley-Shipton (II, 284-287). *See also* Harrison T. Meserole, ed., *Seventeenth-Century American Poetry* (1968); Perry Miller and Thomas H. Johnson, eds., *The Puritans: A Sourcebook of Their Writings* (1938), II, 631, 633-635, 771; Marion Barber Stowell, *Early American Almanacs* (1977), pp. 41, 46, 238. Meserole and Miller and Johnson reprint the verse.

John C. Shields
Illinois State University

NOADIAH RUSSELL (1659-1713)

Works: *Cambridge Ephemeris, An Almanack* for 1684 (1684).

Biography: Born in New Haven, Conn., on July 22, 1659, the son of William and Sarah Davis Russell of New Haven, Conn., Noadiah Russell was left an orphan in early childhood, under the guardianship of Henry Glover. Russell received an M.A. from Harvard College in 1681, taught grammar school in Ipswich from 1683 to 1687, and received invitations from several churches to be their minister. Immediately after beginning his teaching career, he published his almanac. Settling in Middletown, Conn., he was ordained in 1688 and served his pastorate for twenty-nine years. His son William succeeded him, remaining in the same church for almost fifty years.

In 1690 Noadiah Russell married Mary Hamlin. Of their nine children, two (William and Daniel) graduated from Yale and became ministers. Russell helped to frame the Saybrook Platform and became a trustee of the newly established Yale College. President Ezra Stiles (q.v.) of Yale recorded in his diary that Russell was "little...in stature, pious & holy" and gave "good & holy counsel." Russell died in Middletown on Dec. 3, 1713.

Critical Appraisal: Noadiah Russell's principle contribution to the development of the American almanac was the introduction of the first full-page almanac illustration, a woodcut of King David with his harp. He also offered blatant scientific "facts" on the effects of thunder and lightning. For example, when a sleeping person is struck by lightning, "he dies with his eyes opened, the Reason is because it just wakes him and kills him before he can shut his eyes again." If, however, lightning should kill someone who is awake, "his eyes will be found to be shut, because it so amazes him that [he] winketh and dies before he can open his eyes again."

Aside from the first full-page illustration, Russell's almanac was not unusual. He quoted Genesis and Psalm 36 on his title page and included the conventional "Of the Eclipses," twelve calendar pages with topical tides prognostications, and two pages on "The Nature of the Twelve Signs." His tides information was expressed with extreme caution: for Jan. "tides will rise to a pretty great height"; for Feb., "continue (generally) indifferently high"; and for Aug., "The Tides... will be Indifferently high, as high (we think) as at the full, when the change [moon] comes they will be higher, and will continue to be so, for 3 or 4 dayes: (perhaps) till the 3 of the next month." "The Nature of the Twelve Signs" dealt with the humors appropriate to each sign, with relevant instructions for bleeding.

Russell's almanac reflected various aspects of contemporary scientific knowledge. Harvard College graduates apparently were still under the influence of Galen, and their expertise in meteorology was advanced to approximately the same extent.

Suggested Readings: CCNE; Sibley-Shipton (III, 216-222). *See also* Perry Miller and Thomas H. Johnson, eds., *The Puritans* (1963), II, 744-745; Marion Barber Stowell, *Early American Almanacs* (1977), pp. 50-51.

Marion Barber Stowell
Milledgeville, Georgia

S

JOHN SAFFIN (1626-1710)

Works: *A Brief and Candid Answer to a Late Printed Sheet, Entituled, the Selling of Joseph* (1701); *John Saffin, His Book* (1928).

Biography: A lawyer, merchant, and landowner, John Saffin was born in Exeter, Devonshire, Eng., on Nov. 22, 1626, and immigrated at age 7 or 8 to Scituate, Mass., as a ward of his mother's relatives. His parents were Simon Saffin (of a Somersetshire family) and Grace, daughter of John Garrett of Barnstable; apparently the mother outlived the father and married a man named Ellsworth. Saffin was a student in Charles Chauncy's (q.v.) school in Scituate but did not attend college; his legal training must have come through the Boston law firm of Foster and Hoar. He was elected selectman in 1653; the board of selectmen served as the chief administrative authority of a town. He was trading in Va. in 1654 and for a few years thereafter. He married Martha (born 1637), daughter of Thomas Willett, who later became the first mayor of N.Y., in Plymouth on Dec. 2, 1658, after which they moved to Boston. They had eight sons, some of whom died in infancy, his sons Simon and John (the second so named), and his wife dying in a smallpox epidemic in 1678. Three sons survived their mother. His son Thomas died in London on Jun. 18, 1687, and was buried in Stepney, Eng.; his last surviving son was buried on Oct. 15, 1687. On Jun. 4, 1680, Saffin married Elizabeth, widow of Peter Lidgett; she died on Nov. 1, 1687. In Mar. 1688 he moved to Bristol, Mass. (now R.I.), and on Nov. 16 married Rebecca, daughter of the Rev. Samuel Lee, whose youngest daughter became Cotton Mather's (q.v.) third wife. Saffin died Jul. 18, 1710; his widow married Rev. Joseph Baxter of Medfield on Jul. 26, 1712.

Wealth came through Saffin's numerous commercial enterprises, including the slave trade and landowning. His public life (including law suits) is well documented in records of Suffolk County (Boston) and of the First Church of Boston, which he joined in Nov. 1665. Three printed advertisements (Bristol 42, 68,

327) signed by him and others (including Simon Bradstreet, widowed husband of Anne Bradstreet [q.v.] and later governor) relate to the disposition of lands in Narragansett in 1678, 1686, and 1708. On Mar. 13, 1683, Saffin was appointed to a committee to draw up instructions for the deputies of the General Court; he himself was a deputy, 1684-1686. On May 20, 1686, he was appointed to a committee on the governmental charter and became the last speaker of the colonial House of Representatives in 1686. He was the first judge of the Inferior Court of Common Pleas for Bristol in 1692-1702 and annually was elected councilor from 1693 to 1699. His election in 1703 was vetoed by Governor Joseph Dudley (q.v.), largely because of the controversy with Samuel Sewall (q.v.) over slavery, although Dudley and Saffin had had difficulties before that. He was named judge of the Supreme Court at Plymouth on Aug. 1, 1701, and thus was sitting on the court when the case between him and his servant Adam came up in 1702.

Critical Appraisal: Saffin's answer to Samuel Sewall arose out of difficulties over a document signed by Saffin and his servant Adam on Nov. 15, 1694. In it Saffin agreed that he would "make free my s^d negro man named Adam to be fully at his own Dispose and Liberty as other free men are or ought to be according to all true Intents & purposes whatsoever," a date of freedom being set seven years hence. Adam was turned over to Thomas Shepherd of Bristol in 1694, who then bound him out to John Wilkins. Adam called for his freedom in 1701, and Saffin threatened to send him out of the province, which would have kept him a slave. Sewall published *The Selling of Joseph* in 1700 (reprinted in CMHS, VI, 16-20 notes), arguing that *"Joseph* was rightfully no more a Slave to his Brethren, than they were to him: and they had no more Authority to *Sell* him, than they had to *Slay* him." Against such arguments as the Christianizing of the pagan Negro, Sewall wrote, "Evil must not be done, that good may come of it." Saffin answered this position with *A Brief and Candid Answer to a Late Printed Sheet, Entituled, The Selling of Joseph. Whereunto Is Annexed, A True and Particular Narrative by Way of Vindication of the Author's Dealing with and Prosecution of His Negro Man Servant, for His Vile and Exorbitant Behaviour Towards His Master, and His Tenant Thomas Shepherd; Which Hath Been Wrongfully Represented to Their Prejudice and Defamation.* [(Evans 1022), reprinted in Moore, Appendix C, pp. 251-256, but without *A True and Particular Narrative*, which will be found in *Publications of the Colonial Society of Massachusetts*, I, 103-112.] Saffin attempted to counter each of Sewall's arguments by recourse to Scripture and the concept that God "ordained different degrees and orders of men, some to be High and Honourable, some to be Low and Despicable; some to be Monarchs, Kings, Princes and Governours, Masters and Commanders, others to be Subjects, and to be Commanded; Servants of sundry sorts and degrees, bound to obey; yea, some to be born Slaves, and so to remain during their lives." The argument that the Negro will be saved from paganism is repeated. But Saffin showed his bigotry in separating "men" from "Negroes" and his real concern when he noted that an owner who set his slaves free would "lose all the money they cost." An eight-line poem titled "The Negroes Character" employed words like "Cowardly," "Prone to Revenge," "Libidinous, Deceitful, False and Rude." Saffin's warning that manumission is impractical and potentially dangerous rings hollow alongside his clear wish to maintain the economic status quo.

Saffin's holograph commonplace book, owned by the Rhode Island Historical Society, was begun in 1665 and continued through 1708-1709; it is an octavo of 198 pages, some original pages now missing. It contains biographical notes, letters, notes on his reading, religious thoughts, medicinal cures, historical memoranda, pieces copied from various sources (for example, a poem by Sir Henry Wotton, maxims from Sir Philip Sidney's *Arcadia*), and poems, entered not in strictly chronological order, with the last several pages being much earlier random items. A few poems appear in two versions. Some of the poetry appeared in print before the 1928 publication of the notebook: "An Elegie on That Reverend Man of God Mr John Wilson," location unknown; anagram and ll. 1-4 printed in Cotton Mather's *Magnalia Christi Americana* (1702), I, 284 (variant); "An Elegie upon the Deplorable, or Rather Deplored Death of . . . Mr Jonathan Mitchel," location unknown; "Epitaph," 11. 49-60, printed in Nathaniel Morton's (q.v.) *New Englands Memoriall* (1669), p. 196; "To the Revd: Mr Wm Hubbard on His Exact History of New Englands Troubles," printed in Hubbard's (q.v.) A Narrative of the Troubles with the Indians (1677); "An Epitaph on the Honble John Leverett," location unknown; [elegy on Governor Josiah Winslow], location unknown, "An Elegy On the Late Deplorable Expiration of the Honorable Thomas Danforth," location unknown; [epitaph on his Son Thomas], not in commonplace book, printed in *The Spectator*, No. 518 (October 24, 1712), name given as "Thomas Sapper," in Daniel Lysons, *The Environs of London* (1796), IV, 639-640 (Addenda for Vol. III), with correct name, and in NEHGR, 4 (1850), 109-110, and in a seventeenth-century manuscript copy owned by James Osborn Collection, Yale University, shelf mark: P.B. VII/55, entitled "Stepney Churchyard" and dated Jun. 18, 1687; "A Memoriall of the Deplorable Death of . . . Revd: Mr Samuel Lee," printed in NHR, 4 (1885-86), 151-152. Daniel Lysons indicated the arms on the tombstone, partially from Saffin of Somersetshire: "three crescents jessant as many etoiles, impaling a lion rampant."

Although the contents of the commonplace book supply important information and give some sense of the man, it is the poetry that is of major significance and that demands Saffin be evaluated highly as a man of letters. Such kinds as elegies and epitaphs, love poems, verse letters, an epithalamion, encomia, and occasional pieces, satires and characters, acrostics and anagrams, philosophical verse and society verse are included in the fifty-five separate poems, indicating an unusual range for the times. These poems are supplemented by the verses in *A Brief and Candid Answer* and the tombstone epitaph, already cited. The public voice, as in "New England's Lamentation of Her Present State (1708/9)," is not different from that of others of the day, except that the poem in its telling description of the times and its satiric edge is superior. It is the private voice, as in ["Sweetly (my Dearest) I Left Thee Asleep"] and "A Lamentation on My Dear Son Simon," that comes to rival the poems of Anne Bradstreet as no others do. "A Character of a Pernicious Backbiter" is one of the strongest poems of the late seventeenth century in its wedding of language, stress, and sense; but perhaps it is Saffin's love lyrics, like "A Letter to His Dear Martha 1660," that will strike readers as the most memorable and heartfelt. Influence has been traced to Francis Quarles in "Sayle Gentle Pinnace"; Robert Herrick's opening poem in *Hesperides* may lie behind Saffin's opening poem on his book. Saffin's poetry has a plain style, employs nature as theme and domestic life as metaphor, and moves to sublimity and a "neo-Classicism" that was to dominate a few years later. Its usual meter is the heroic couplet.

Suggested Readings: FCNEV. *See also* Esther Bernon Carpenter, *South County Studies of Some Eighteenth-Century Persons, Places and Conditions in the Portion of Rhode Island Called Narragansett* (1924); William Bedford Clark, *"Caveat Emptor!: Judge Sewall vs. Slavery,"* SLitI, 9, no. 2 (1976), 19-30; CMHS, 5th ser., V (1878), VI (1879), and other volumes, passim; Jessie A. Coffee, "Arcadia to America: Sir Philip Sidney and John Saffin," AL, 45 (1973), 100-104; Norman S. Grabo, "The Profligate and the Puritan," N&Q, 9 (1962), 392-393; Caroline Hazard, ed., *John Saffin, His Book* (1928); Harrison T. Meserole, ed., *Seventeenth-Century American Poetry* (1968), pp. 193-195; George H. Moore, *Notes on the History of Slavery in Massachusetts* (1866, 1968); Alyce E. Sands, "Establishing John Saffin's Birthdate: A Biographical and Historical Problem," EAL, 2 (1967), 12-17; idem, "John Saffin: Seventeenth-Century American Citizen and Poet" (Ph.D. diss., Pa. State Univ., 1965); Kenneth Silverman, ed., *Colonial American Poetry* (1968); Lawrence W. Towner, "The Sewall-Saffin Dialogue on Slavery," WMQ, 21 (1964), 40-52; Brom Weber, "A Puritan Poem Regenerated: John Saffin's 'Sayle Gentle Pinnace,'" EAL, 3 (1968), 65-71.

John T. Shawcross
University of Kentucky

GURDON SALTONSTALL (1666-1724)

Works: *A Sermon Preached Before the General Assembly* (1697); *A Proclamation for a Fast* (1709); *A Proclamation Requiring All Judges and Other Law Officers to Suppress and Punish Immoralities and Irreligious Practices* (1715); *The State of the Mohegan Fields* (1715); *A Memorial to the General Assembly of Connecticut* (1716); *A Proclamation Concerning Smallpox* (1721); *A Proclamation for a Publick Thanksgiving* (1721).

Biography: Gurdon Saltonstall was born in Haverhill, Mass., on Mar. 27, 1666. He entered Harvard at 14, graduated in 1684, and became a minister at the Congregational Church of Christ in New London, Conn. He was married three times and fathered six girls and four boys. It was his custom to walk to the meeting house on the Sabbath followed by his wife, children, and household domestics in solemn procession joined by his son Gurdon's fourteen children and household. His namesake became a brigadier general in the Continental Army.

Saltonstall, a confidant of Governor Fitz-John Winthrop, was offered the governorship after Winthrop's death in 1707. With his acceptance came an experiment in the union of church and state in Conn.; he was the only minister to achieve such high office in colonial government. In 1711 his governorship was expanded to include a role as chief justice of the Superior Court. A founder of Yale University, Governor Saltonstall served for seventeen years, passing many measures to promote learning, piety, and order in the colony. In 1714 he received the largest land grant awarded to an individual in public office (2,000 acres).

Saltonstall died suddenly of apoplexy in New London in 1724 and was honored by Eliphalet Adams (q.v.) and by Cotton Mather (q.v.) in his *Decus ac Tutamen. A Brief Essay on the Blessings Enjoy'd by a People That Have Men of a Right Character Shining Among Them.*

Critical Appraisal: The works of Gurdon Saltonstall include many broadsides and public documents as well as sermons. He was known for his scholarly sermons, good judgment, and knowledge. His impact upon the ecclesiastical and governmental development of Conn. was influenced by Cotton Mather, who led the movement in Mass. to bring the church under greater control. Gurdon Saltonstall supported efforts to strengthen the church through town, county, and state meetings that eventually produced the Saybrook Platform passed by the General Assembly just after he became governor. A direct result of the movement for greater union of the independent churches was a meeting of the divines to discuss the formation of a college in Saybrook that was to be a forerunner of Yale University.

As governor, his writings involved the settlement of boundary disputes with the Mohegan Indians; financial aid for the Collegiate College and, later, Yale to promote learning, piety, and order through required collections in the churches; forced movement of the school's library from Saybrook to New Haven; authorization for searching peddlers' packs upon entering the colony during a smallpox epidemic; support of public morals and execution of punishment; and family discipline and government.

He successfully averted an attempt of the crown to revoke the Charter of Conn. because it was becoming too independent. Complaints had been made concerning the persecution of other religions in the colony, particularly the Church of England. The Episcopalians complained that double taxation required of them because they were not Congregationalists was designed to keep them poor. Baptist Rogerines were especially troublesome to Saltonstall, for they would interrupt services to dispute a point of controversy.

An example of Saltonstall's philosophy can be seen in his broadside *Proclamation Suppressing...Immoralities* (1715), where he excoriated the lack of family Bibles, neglect of attendance on Sabbath, tale bearing and defamation, contempt of authority both civil and ecclesiastical, and intemperance and acclaimed the necessity of catechizing family discipline and government. Another broadside on the education of children points out the necessity of punishment for lying, profane language, meeting of young people in evenings after Sabbath, and drunkenness. Saltonstall's style is authoritative and direct, and his use of the broadside recalls an important and popular part of the early colonists' reading.

Suggested Readings: CCNE; DAB; Sibley-Shipton (III, 277-286). *See also* Marguerite Allis, *Connecticut Trilogy* (1934), pp. 14, 148, 233, 259, 260, 262, 263; Maria Louise Green, *The Development of Religious Liberty in Connecticut* (1970), p. vi; Charles Edward Perry, *Founders and Leaders of Connecticut, 1633-1783* (1971), pp. 139-142; *Public Records of the Colony of Connecticut from October, 1706 to October, 1716* (1968), vols. V, VI.

Belle Harkrader Finocchio
University of Houston

NATHANIEL SALTONSTALL (c. 1639-1707)

Works: *The Present State of New-England with Respect to the Indian War* (doubtfully attributed; 1675); *A Continuation of the State of New-England* (doubtfully attributed; 1676); *A New and Further Narrative of the State of New-England* (doubtfully attributed; 1676).

Biography: Born in Ipswich, Mass., Nathaniel Saltonstall was the grandson of Sir Richard Saltonstall, a Cambridge-educated Puritan knight who was one of the original patentees and first associates of the Massachusetts Bay and Conn. colonies. Nathaniel's father, also named Richard, was a cofounder of Ipswich. Nathaniel was sent to Harvard College, from which he graduated in 1659, the first of seven successive generations of Saltonstalls to graduate from Harvard. At Harvard, Nathaniel was a "fellow commoner," a status granted to the sons of notable families willing to pay an extra charge; this status accorded him a number of privileges, including freedom from performing errands and the right to be called "*Mr*. Saltonstall."

After graduation, Saltonstall moved to Haverhill, where he took up residence on land owned by his father and proceeded to build "The Buttonwoods," which was to become the home of several generations of Saltonstalls. In 1663 he married Elizabeth Ward, the 16-year-old daughter of John Ward, Haverhill's pastor and Nathaniel's next-door neighbor. Saltonstall then proceeded to live the kind of life expected of the most prominent member of a small colonial village. He served his community as county commissioner, judge, town recorder and clerk of writs, deputy to the General Court, captain of the local militia, and so on.

Saltonstall's life interacted with three significant events in colonial history. In 1687, during the Andros controversy, he was for fifteen days placed under house arrest in Boston for refusing an appointment as "councillor" to the new Andros government. Previously identified as a Loyalist, Saltonstall had evidently joined the swell of colonial protest to the imposition of direct British rule. In 1692, during the witchcraft trials, he had himself removed as one of the judges in such cases. He is reported to have been "very much dissatisfied" with the proceedings. He appears to have been under much stress during this period, for a letter from Samuel Sewall (q.v.) to him indicates that Saltonstall had himself been accused of witchcraft by popular rumor and had also taken to excessive drinking. In 1697, after the Indian raid that had resulted in the captivity of the celebrated Hannah Dustin, Saltonstall was evidently accused of mismanaging the local militia. Nothing came of any of these charges, however, and Saltonstall continued to function in various official capacities. He died in Haverhill in 1707.

Critical Appraisal: Aside from various letters and court documents, Nathaniel Saltonstall is not known to be the author of any works other than the three historical tracts listed above, all of which date from King Philip's War. The title page of one of these tracts gives the author as "N. S." and another one identifies the author as "merchant of Boston." The idea that "N. S." was Nathaniel Saltonstall was first proposed by Samuel Drake in the nineteenth century and then repeated by Charles Lincoln in his 1913 edition of the tracts. It is, however, highly improbable that "N. S." was Nathaniel Saltonstall. First, it is difficult to see why a magistrate in Haverhill would identify himself as a "merchant of Boston," or why Saltonstall would want to conceal his identity in this way. Second, the tracts suggest life experiences different from those of Saltonstall. For example, one of the tracts contains a letter from the Barbados relevant to a black uprising there; it seems likely that the author of the tracts was indeed a merchant who had visited the Barbados, perhaps on several occasions, and was familiar with men and events there. Also, the tracts show considerable familiarity with men and events in Boston in 1675-1676, whereas Saltonstall is not known to have spent much time there during that period. Finally, although it is difficult to be certain, the tone and general attitude of the tracts do not correspond well with what is known of Saltonstall. Saltonstall's most recent biographer, Robert E. Moody (who gives "no credence" to the Drake-Lincoln attribution), said of Saltonstall's performance as judge that he was "firm and effective in law enforcement, and yet, where allowed discretion by law, humane and flexible." Saltonstall's letters generally reveal a calm and judicious temperament. Such is not the character of the author of the tracts.

The tracts, on the contrary, are bigoted, inaccurate, arrogant, and disposed to give credence to wild rumors. Much of the tract writer's information seems to be coming from the boastings of Capt. Samuel Mosely, one of the most troublesome and unlovable figures of the period. The tracts' reports of Mosely's derring-do and of Indian atrocities are generally not supported by other documents of the period. To the tract-writer's credit, some of the inaccuracies of the first tract are corrected in the second tract. Yet the tracts on the whole are so unreliable that the information in them cannot be trusted unless corroborated by other sources. The value of the tracts is that they probably reflect a state of mind commonly found in Boston during King Philip's War and help explain the conduct of the colonial armies and governments during that conflict.

Suggested Readings: Sibley-Shipton (II, 1-8). *See also* George Wingate Chase, *History of Haverhill, Massachusetts* (1861), pp. 47-661; Samuel G. Drake, *Old Indian Chronicle* (1867); Charles H. Lincoln, ed., *Narratives of the Indian Wars, 1675-1679* (1913), pp. 19-99; Robert E. Moody, *Records of the Magistrate's Court at Haverhill, Mass., Kept by Nathaniel Saltonstall, 1682-85*, PMHS, 79 (1967); idem, *The Saltonstall Papers, 1607-1815* (1972), I, 48-60, 163-279; Leverett Saltonstall, *Ancestors and Descendants of Sir Richard Saltonstall* (1897), pp. 106-121.

Robert K. Diebold
Husson College

EZRA SAMPSON (1749-1823)

Works: *A Sermon Preached at Roxbury-Camp* (1775); *The Ceasing and Failing* (1776); *A Discourse Delivered February 19, 1795* (1795); *A Sermon, on the Death of Miss Olive Soule* (w. 1795; pub. 1797); *The Beauties of the Bible* (1800); *The Sham-Patriot Unmasked* (1802); *The Youth's Companion, or An Historical Dictionary* (1804); *The Brief Remarker on the Ways of Man* (1818); *Remarks on Troubles of Our Own Making* (1821).

Biography: Ezra Sampson, eldest child of Uriah and Ann (White) Sampson, was born in Middleborough, Mass., on Feb. 12, 1749. After graduating from Yale in 1773 and studying theology, he was ordained on Feb. 15, 1775, as colleague pastor to the Rev. Jonathan Parker of the Congregational Church at Plympton, Mass. Voluntarily officiating as chaplain in the militia camp at Roxbury, he delivered the fast day sermon before Col. Cotton's regiment on Jul. 20, 1775. In the spring of 1776, he married Mary Bourne, by whom he was to have six children. When Rev. Parker died in Apr. of that year, Sampson assumed the Plympton pastorate and served with distinction until 1795, when he resigned due to "some change in his doctrinal views on the Trinity," a voice failure, a dizziness in the head, or some combination thereof. In the fall of the next year, he moved with his family to Hudson, N.Y., where he preached occasionally in the Presbyterian Church and became an elder in 1810. In addition, he was a founder and patron of the Hudson Academy. During 1801-1803 Sampson coedited a weekly newspaper, *The Balance*, with Harry Croswell, a Federalist journalist who in 1804 unsuccessfully defended a libel suit arising from his anti-Jefferson articles in the *Wasp*. In that year, Sampson moved to Hartford to edit the *Connecticut Courant*, returning to his family in Hudson in 1805 and continuing to contribute to the Hartford paper until 1817. In 1814 Sampson was appointed one of the judges of the Columbia County Court, but he soon resigned. His wife having died in 1812, he moved to New York City in 1820-1821 and lived with his son Joseph, a wealthy merchant. After a brief illness, he died on Dec. 12, 1823; the *New York Post* carried his obituary.

Critical Appraisal: Ezra Sampson's sermons, orthodox in theology and form, are typical of the New England plain style. His primary theme is God's direction of man's progress in this world, and his manner is humble and modest. Because of the simple fabric of his prose, Sampson gained special dramatic effects from an occasional flourish of rhetorical questions, an ending of unexpected self-reflection, or a sentimental conceit. Generally controlled and purposeful, Sampson's work belongs to a sermon tradition that relies more on sincerity of thought than on grandeur of phrasing.

After leaving the ministry, Sampson wrote educational, political, and moral essays. Two works intended for school use reflect his double commitment to spiritual and secular learning: *The Youth's Companion* (more of an encyclopedia than a dictionary) and *The Beauties of the Bible*. The latter, a selection of passages from the Old and New Testaments, opens with an essay urging that students use the simple, eloquent prose of the King James translation as a stylistic model. In the commentary after each selection, Sampson sometimes discusses the historical, social, and geographical context of the passage or its literary character, but since his primary aim is religious education, the typical commentary is a short sermon on vice, the value of prayer, miracles, God's justice, or the duties of a Christian. Charming and graceful in every line, Sampson's essays demonstrate the aesthetic and spiritual pleasure that he and his fellows derived from reading their favorite book.

The Sham-Patriot Unmasked, in five editions from 1802 to 1805, is a collection of twelve political, inspirational essays originally published in *The Balance* under the pseudonym "Historicus." Sampson argued throughout that an American public who have been educated in the lessons of history, are dedicated to virtue, and know a political shyster when they see one will prove to future generations that republicanism is a practicable form of government. Increasingly urgent and exhortatory, the essays rely on historical examples of men and governments that have failed by their own or the public's ignorance and deceit. Sampson used a more rhetorical and allusive style than in his sermons, although he continued to draw on everyday life for images: man, he said, "is either the *hammer* or the *anvil*...either smiting or being smitten; oppressing or being oppressed" (Essay VI).

The Brief Remarker on the Ways of Man (1818) is a collection of 106 moral essays from the *Connecticut Courant*. The essays range in subject from the evils of drink and gaming to the virtues of contentment, industry, and honesty. More than one-fourth discuss domestic relations: the benefits of marriage, the responsibilities of parenting, and the role of women. Never cynical or mocking and rarely recriminatory, Sampson maintained a paternal, conversational tone. Unlike the American imitators of Addison and Steele, he did not allude to contemporary persons or use fictionalized characters. He relied on proverbs, quotations from well-known authors, historical and fictional anecdotes, biblical stories, and Scripture. In the tradition of Samuel Johnson's *Rambler* essays but free of melancholy and Latinate vocabulary, *The Brief Remarker* advocates civil and ethical truisms with a confidence and optimism that anticipate the Transcendentalist essays of the next generations of American writers.

Suggested Readings: CCNE; Dexter (III, 501-504); Sprague (II, 122-125); T_2. *See also Appleton's Cyclopaedia of American Biography*, V, 382.

Roslyn L. Knutson
University of Arkansas at Little Rock

ROBERT SANDEMAN (1718-1771)

Works: *Letters on Theron and Aspasio* (1757); *An Epistolary Correspondence* (1762); *An Essay on Preaching* (1763); *Some Thoughts on Christianity* (1764); *Honour of Marriage* (1777); *Letters in Correspondence* (1851); *Discourse on Passages of Scripture* (1857).

Biography: Robert Sandeman was born in Perth, Scot., in 1718. In 1728 John Glas, a minister in the Established Church of Scotland, was expelled from the church for his belief that the deeds of Jesus Christ were sufficient to assure man's salvation "without a Deed or Thought on the Part of Man." Robert Sandeman, a Scottish linen maker and Glas's son-in-law, became an elder in the dissenting Glassite church in 1744. After defending the sect's views and establishing Glassite churches in Scot. and Eng., Sandeman came to Boston in 1764, where he became the American spokesman of Glassites (later known as Sandemanians). Although the colonial Glassite church was always small, never numbering more than 1,000, Sandeman founded congregations in Mass., N.H., and Conn. His writings systematized and confidently, even pompously, according to his detractors, defended the beliefs of John Glas. In the process, he angered leading New Eng. ministers, and by the time he died in Danbury, Conn., on April 2, 1771, Sandeman was widely known for his controversial writings.

Critical Appraisal: Robert Sandeman's writings clarified and defended the Glassite sect's belief in the separation of church and state, the prohibition of games of chance and college training, and the return to various primitive Christian practices. Most of his literary efforts, however, were directed toward a skillfully ordered defense of the doctrine of justification by faith. In *Some Thoughts on Christianity*, Sandeman explained the Glassite belief that man is saved by faith alone. The believer in what Sandeman called "the new idea of God" is "persuaded that God is already pleased in his beloved Son; that everything needful to recommend him to the divine favour, was completed by Jesus on the Cross." Man's joy at Christ's gift to him "leads him to love God and keep his commandments" in a continual expression of thanks to God for "the free gift of that righteousness." Man will be good, Sandeman reasoned, because he chooses to live in imitation of Christ. Sandeman's optimistic argument is impressive in its clarity and logic, but sometimes uncompelling in its simple faith. Thus in an annex to *Some Thoughts*, Sandeman less successfully adopted the persona of Jonathan the Jew, converted by faith and absolutely confident in his certain salvation: "I do not set out from conjectures to inquire after truth; but I set out with the light of undoubted truth, to observe what path it opens for me to walk in."

Sandeman's faith in the goodness that flows naturally from the believer met vigorous opposition from New Eng. clergy and laymen, as emotionally recorded in public letters with telling titles such as *A Full, Strong, and Clear Refutation of Mr. Sandeman's Pernicious Doctrines* (1765) and *Mr. Sandeman Refuted by an Old Woman* (1767). The controversy concerned the fear that Sandeman's beliefs would "lead men along in the direct road to destruction, with an elusive expectation of being saved by Christ's righteousness while they are not cleansed from their own sins," as Samuel Langdon claimed in *An Impartial Examination of Mr. Robert Sandeman's Letters* (1765). Clearly, the established New Eng. clergy, profoundly concerned with the wages of man's sins, did not share Sandeman's optimistic view of the strength of faith and Christian love. Yet almost as much anger was directed at Sandeman's manner as at his beliefs. Referring to Sandeman as "pecularly haughty," Langdon despaired of ever reasoning with him or "convincing him of any mistake." Similarly, an irate Boston minister who had been called a liar by a sect member wrote to Sandeman: "You own none as true Believers who are out of the pale of *your* Church." (*A Letter to Mr. Robert Sandeman*, 1766).

Sandeman's skillful rhetoric, dissenting beliefs, and inflammatory style put him at the center of a heated debate that established New Eng. ministers were apparently determined to win. In 1770, a year before his death, he was fined forty pounds as an "undesirable transient" in the town that he had made the center of a small but vocal dissenting sect.

Suggested Readings: CCNE; DAB; DNB; T$_2$. *See also* S. Austen Allibone, *A Critical Dictionary of English Literature and British and American Authors* (1870); A. L. Drummond and J. Bulloch, *The Scottish Church, 1688-1843* (1973).

Linda Palmer Young
University of California, Davis

GEORGE SANDYS (1578-1644)

Works: *A Relation of a Journey Begun Anno Dom. 1610* (1615); *Ovid's Mentamorphosis* (1626); *A Paraphrase upon the Psalms of David* (1636); *A Paraphrase upon the Divine Poems* (1638); *Christ's Passion* (translated from Grotius; 1640); *A Paraphrase upon the Song of Solomon* (1641, 1642); various Dutch and German editions; individual poems, R. B. Davis, ed., PBSA, 37 (1943), 215-222; idem, HLQ, 12 (1948), 105-111.

Biography: Born near York, Eng., the youngest son of Edwin, archbishop of York, George Sandys attended two Oxford colleges and the Inns of Court before he began his Mediterranean travels in 1610. Later a gentleman of the bedchamber to Charles I, he was an early friend of that sovereign. In 1621 he came to Jamestown, Va., as treasurer. On the voyage over and in the colony, he completed his translation of Ovid's *Metamorphoses* in heroic couplets. Returning to Br. in 1625, he published the first edition of the whole poem the following year. For a decade and a half, he was a gentleman attendant to the king, a member of the group of poets around Falkland and Ben Jonson, a principal figure in the Privy Council's Committee on the Plantations, and in 1640 or perhaps longer, the colony's agent in London. During the same period, he continued to write and publish verse, some of it touching on his experiences in the New World. His last years were spent in London and Oxfordshire and especially at Boxley in Kent with his niece and her husband Sir Francis Wyatt, who had been governor of the Va. colony in his time. He may be called Br.'s first colonial civil servant, an expert on the first colony. He died in 1644 and was buried near Wyatt in the church at Boxley Abbey.

Critical Appraisal: Although William Morrell (q.v.) briefly in New Eng. at the time Sandys was writing in Va. translated or paraphrased some Latin verses, he can hardly rival George Sandys as the first American poet writing in English. Sandys, whose prose travels to the Holy Land and Egypt resulted in the most popular travel book in G.B. throughout the century and whose scriptural paraphrases were reprinted several times in the seventeenth century, is best remembered historically and literarily for the translation of Ovid into tightly compressed heroic couplets. He was an adept and influential master of this metrical form and through it influenced Dryden and Pope and its lesser users for at least a century and a half. The learned and philosophical prose "Commentaries" in the 1632 folio edition have been called the greatest repository of allegorized myth in English. Later American poets were also aware of his Ovid, and with it began the Classical tradition in American verse and prose persistent to the midtwentieth century, especially in the South. That Sandys never after 1626 had America out of his mind is evident even when he translated Ovid's description of a storm at sea, and he compared Native Americans in their customs and appearance with primitive men in all of the known world. His verse is hardly secular even in the Ovid, but also it shares little in its form or tone with slightly later New Eng. Puritan poetry. The Christian context or subject matter is always treated within Anglican or Classical frames.

Suggested Readings: DAB; DNB; LHUS; T$_1$. See also Robert Bain et al., eds., *Southern Writers: A Biographical Dictionary* (1980); Douglas Bush, *Mythology and the Renaissance Tradition in English Poetry* (1932), pp. 32 ff.; R. B. Davis, "America in George Sandys' Ovid," WMQ, 4 (1947), 297-304; idem, "George Sandys," *Encyclopaedia Britannica* (1966), 19, 1004; idem, "*In Re* George Sandys' Ovid," SB, 8 (1956), 226-230; idem, *George Sandys, Poet-Adventurer* (1955); idem, *Intellectual Life in the Colonial South, 1585-1763*, vols. I and III (1978); idem, "The Literary Climate of Jamestown Under the Virginia Company, 1607-1624," in *Towards a New American*

Literary History: Essays in Honor of Arlin Turner, ed. Louis Budd et al. (1980), pp. 36-53; idem, "Sandys' *Song of Solomon*: Its Manuscript Versions and Their Circulation," *PBSA*, 50 (1956), 328-341; idem, "Volumes from George Sandys's Library Now in America," *VMHB*, 65 (1957), 450-477; idem [with Fredson Bowers], *George Sandys: A Bibliographical Catalogue of Printed Editions in England to 1700* (1950); Richard Hooper, ed., *The Poetical Works of George Sandys, Now First Collected. . .with Introd. and Notes*, 2 vols. (does not contain translation of Ovid; 1872); M. A. Rogers, "More Books from the Library of George Sandys," *VMHB*, 84 (1976), 362-364; Louis D. Rubin, ed., *A Bibliographical Guide to the Study of Southern Literature* (1969).

Richard Beale Davis
University of Tennessee, Knoxville

CHRISTOPHER SAUER I (1693-1758)

Works: Approximately 200 imprints produced by the Sauer press between 1739 and 1758, including: *Eine Ernstliche Ermahnung* (probably the first Sauer imprint and the first of many religious and political broadsides; 1739); *Der Hoch-Deutsche Americanische Calender* (a very popular almanac that appeared annually); *Zionitische Weyrauchshügel* (Sauer's first notable book, a hymnal of 800 pages printed for the Brotherhood at Ephrata; 1739); *Der Hoch-Deutsch Pensylvanische Geschichts-Schreiber* (first successful German newspaper in America, appearing quarterly in the beginning, then monthly, and in 1756 semimonthly; 1740); Lutheran translation of the Bible (first German Bible printed in America; 1743).

Biography: Christopher Sauer (surname also spelled *Saur* and *Sower*) is believed to have been born in the Palatinate in Ger. but was raised at Laasphe, a small town in Wittgenstein. Although his parents were members of the Reformed Church, he came under the direct influence of the Dunker Brethren during his formative years. Evidently, he never was a baptized member, but his close ties and religious loyalty remained with the Brethren throughout his life. He was married and had one son, Christopher.

In 1724 Sauer immigrated with his wife and 3-year-old son to Germantown, Pa. Less than two years later, the family moved to Lancaster County and began farming near Ephrata. In five years, Sauer sold his farm and returned to Germantown with his 10-year-old son, but his wife, who had meanwhile come under the spell of the highly mystical, eccentric, and charismatic Johann Conrad Beissel (q.v.), remained behind as Sister Marcella at the Ephrata Cloister. After fourteen long years, and at the urging of young Christopher, she left the cloister and returned to Germantown, where husband and wife were once again reconciled.

For approximately seven years following his return to Germantown, Sauer dabbled in numerous trades but found none of them completely satisfying. Finally, in 1738, he secured a printing press and started a publishing business that made him one of the best-known figures in colonial Pa. He died in 1758 and left the business to his son.

Critical Appraisal: Like so many early Pa. Germans, Christopher Sauer was imbued with the spirit of mystical pietism. Although he was a deeply religious man, he intensely disliked creeds, dogmas, and all other expressions of religious formalism. Although he was a compassionate and considerate individual, he had no tolerance for immorality, spiritual arrogance, and dishonesty. He was a man of prominence, but he advocated the simple life. Although he was a man of faith, he possessed a negative and acrimonious nature. He could be harsh and cruel, but he was a great humanitarian.

Again and again these contradictory characteristics were manifest in Sauer's writings and in his dealings with others. Editorials in the modern sense did not appear in his newspaper, but Sauer openly expressed his opinions in news articles, especially on religious and political matters.

In his selection of news items for print, he also revealed his obvious biases. For example, because he was so strongly opposed to slavery, his newspaper carried very few advertisements for runaway slaves. He is not remembered for the literary quality of his writings but for his conscious attempts to indoctrinate fellow Pa. Germans and to lure them to his side.

The vast majority of Sauer's writings, especially the broadsides and pamphlets, were religious. He constantly assailed the "incompetent" Lutheran and Reformed clergy and championed the rights of Indians and Pa. German religious minorities. Although he printed hymnals and other works for the Moravians and the Ephrata Brotherhood, he strongly opposed Nicholas Ludwig Count Von Zinzendorf's (q.v.) plan to unite all of the German sects and Beissel's efforts to proselytize unsuspecting individuals for his "heretical" communal society. On every hand, Sauer thought he saw hypocritical, dishonest, and immoral religious leaders, and he seized every opportunity to expose them.

At the outset, Sauer, like sectarians generally, was not inclined toward politics. However, the growing menace of war made him an increasingly vocal pacifist. He and Benjamin Franklin (q.v.) took opposite sides on matters of war and independence. To the bitter end, he defended the pacifist Quaker Assembly, while Franklin ridiculed him and the Quakers for being loyal to the king of Eng. For a time, he was a powerful political influence on both the denominational and the sectarian Pa. Germans, but war against the Indians and the British was inevitable. Eventually, the Lutheran and Reformed people abandoned the Quakers and took up arms. Sauer's following was thereby greatly reduced.

Perhaps the most appreciated product of Sauer's press was his almanac. It not only contained the calendar for each month but also the phases of the moon, information on the planets, the time of the rising and setting of the sun, announcements of important social and religious events, weather forecasts, religious admonitions, advice on many subjects, and a wealth of important lore. Sauer understood his constituency well and through this publication, better than through any other, was able to meet the literary needs of his readership.

Suggested Readings: DAB (*see* "Christopher Sower"). *See also* Preston A. Barba, "Christopher Sauer, Senior" in the "Deitsch Eck," *Allentown Morning Call* (Dec. 4, 11, and 18, 1943); Abraham H. Cassel, "The German Almanac of Christopher Sauer," *PMHB*, 6 (1882), 58-68; Edward H. Hocker, "The Sower Printing House of Colonial Times," *Pennsylvania German Society*, 53, pt. 2 (1948), 1-125; William R. Steckel, "Pietist in Colonial Pennsylvania: Christopher Sauer, Printer" (Ph.D. diss., Stanford Univ., 1949).

Willard Martin
The Pennsylvania State University

THOMAS SAVAGE (1640-1705)

Works: *An Account of the Late Action of New Englanders Against Canada* (1691).

Biography: In 1691 Maj. Thomas Savage wrote a letter to his brother in which he provided a first-hand account of an ill-fated expedition launched the previous year by Mass. troops against the French in Quebec. Little accurate biographical information has been gathered about the author of that account. Several sources (for instance, *The Oxford Companion to American Literature* and *The Reader's Encyclopedia of American Literature*) provide inaccurate biographical sketches, attributing to Thomas Savage, author of the *Account*, biographical information and dates actually belonging to an earlier Thomas Savage (1608-1682). The error undoubtedly arose because the two shared not only a common name but experience as majors in military expeditions sent out from Mass. The earlier Savage came to America from Eng. in 1635 and led an expedition against King Philip, chief of the Narragansetts, in 1675. The later Savage was third in command under Sir William Phips, later the first royal governor of Mass., in a failed expedition against Quebec in 1690.

Several accounts of this expedition exist, although Savage's role is rarely mentioned. Ill-conceived and poorly equipped, the expedition was apparently led by men with little military knowledge. The attack on the French was easily repelled, and the colonial troops returned to Boston much depleted by injuries, illness, and shipwrecks. The men were generally lauded for their bravery if not for their skill or success. Savage's account of the expedition provides a significant, apparently accurate, first-hand description of the ill-fated confrontation as well as a personal defense of the men who suffered through the defeat.

Critical Appraisal: During the disasterous expedition against French settlements in Can., the party led by Thomas Savage landed in a swell, lost its boats, and found itself marooned with insufficient ammunition. On his return to Mass., Savage wrote an account of the expedition to his brother in London. Notably defensive, Savage's letter suggests that he was eager to counter stories he thought would inevitably arise about the failed expedition. "As for News," he wrote, "here is very little, only about our Defeatment at Canada; and least some ill Tongues should abuse any with you, this will give you a brief Narrative of it."

His account vividly describes the plight of an expedition inadequately armed and with "not One Man for a Pilot." Although Savage's style is occasionally cumbersome, the letter is rich in detail: "We landed about 1200 Men, and as soon as we came ashore, at the side of the Beach, was a Swamp, where lay an Ambuscade of about 600 French, who gall'd us at our landing, but our Men running briskly on them, beat up their Ambuscade, and followed them a great way." Unfortunately, according to official documents that accompany the printing of the letter, Savage's men drove the French back to the fortress of the town, thus swelling the force awaiting the colonists there.

Savage's tone was notably defensive. Vague in assigning credit for decisions made on the mission, he emphasized the bravery of his men and anxiously explained tactical errors. According to his account, for instance, most of the ammunition carried ashore by the men was used to fight off the ambush, and promised backup ammunition was not forthcoming. The letter is, in sum, a defense of good men fighting in a poorly planned, inadequately backed, and ill-timed mission. Summaries of letters from other members of the expedition, printed with Savage's account, substantiate the difficulties and place the blame on the "unskillfulness, if not cowardice" of their officers. Savage, however, tried neither to pass the blame nor to place it on his superiors. Of Gen. Walley, he pointed out that "he is not guilty of what they charge him with; but there are some, who to make themselves Faultless, lay Fault upon him." Savage instead accepted the fate of the expedition, believing there "was a Providence of God" in it. His account offers a lively and detailed description of this colonial battle and an interesting defense of the honor of the soldiers involved.

Suggested Readings: William Kingsford, *The History of Canada*, vol. II (1888); Thomas Savage, *Account of New Englanders Against Canada* (printed in Hyatt's Photographic Reprints; 1691); Norah Story, ed., *The Oxford Companion to Canadian History and Literature* (1967).

Linda Palmer Young
University of California, Davis

JANET SCHAW (c. 1735-c. 1801)

Works: *Journal of a Lady of Quality; Being the Narrative of a Journey from Scotland to the West Indies, North Carolina, and Portugal, in the Years 1774 to 1776* (1921).

Biography: Besides what Janet Schaw revealed in her *Journal*, little else is known about this remarkable eighteenth-century traveler and observer. Her *Journal*—consisting of letters written to a friend in Scot. in the course of her travels aboard the *Jamaica Packet* and *Rebecca* to Antigua, St. Kitts, N.C., and Port.—

reveals that she was born at Lauriston, a suburb of Edinburgh, that she belonged to an aristocratic Scottish family, and that she was between 35 and 40 years of age when making the journey, which took place between 1774 and 1776. Her chief traveling companion was her brother Alexander; in addition, she was joined by three children of John Rutherford of N.C.—Fanny, John, and William—her maid, and her E. Ind. manservant. She apparently undertook the journey to escort the children to their parents and to visit a brother who was living in N.C. Evidence indicates that she never married.

Inferable from the text, of course, are many aspects of her personality and intellect. Thomas Clark stated that "she was not only an intelligent and keen observer, but also a shrewd judge of character. She availed herself of every opportunity to see the countries she visited and to meet people." Evangeline Walker Andrews and Charles McLean Andrews, her first editors and her first extollers, pointed to her quick wit, breadth of knowledge, warm-heartedness, and keen artistic eye to support their claim that what they found in the British Museum unheralded and untapped was truly a "treasure."

Critical Appraisal: The *Journal of a Lady of Quality*—part travel book, diary, and *belles lettres*—parallels the efforts of the prominent promotional tract writers of the time. Attention is, of course, paid to natural scenery, customs, and the people of the countries visited. As a stylist, Schaw could range from the sentimental novelist to the teller of expurgated goliardic tales, from rendering a romantic scene on the high seas to snickering over an indecent tale about a *menage à trois* aboard ship. Written as letters to her friends and dedicated to her brother Alexander, Schaw's *Journal* breaks down into four parts: the trip to the W. Ind., the stay at Antigua, her residence in N.C., and her "sojourn" in Port. What is remarkable about the book is the image of "Janet Schaw" that pervades the whole. In the first section, Schaw survives fierce storms and the fear of barbary pirates to give the reader a glimpse of sea life and exotic islands beneath the Tropic of Cancer. Schaw fully portrayed the local people in Antigua, their customs, and their way of life. Furthermore, in a digression on slaves, Schaw revealed a compassionate nature that drew her away from her role of detached observer and traveler. The third section, set in the area surrounding pre-Revolutionary War Wilmington, N.C., depicts Schaw stepping on ferocious alligators and risking tarring and feathering to get her strongly Loyalist letters off to her friend back home. After escaping a volatile Wilmington, Schaw sailed eastward to terminate her travel book abruptly with a brief stay in Lisbon. Dated "March 10, 1778," the manuscript of Schaw's *Journal* remained unpublished until 1921.

Suggested Readings: Evangeline Walker Andrews and Charles McLean Andrews, Introduction, in *Journal of a Lady of Quality*, by Janet Schaw (1921); Robert Bain, "Janet Schaw," in *Southern Writers: A Biographical Dictionary* (1979), ed. by Robert Bain, Joseph M. Flora, and Louis D. Rubin, Jr., pp. 400-401; Thomas D. Clark, *Travels in the Old South* (1956), pp. 279-280; Jay B. Hubbell, *The South in American Literature, 1607-1900* (1954), pp. 157-159, 958.

Dianna M. Parks
Cumberland, Maryland

MICHAEL SCHLATTER (1716-1790)

Works: *A True History of the Real Condition of the Destitute Congregations of Pennsylvania* (1752).

Biography: Michael Schlatter's background is impressive. He was born on July 14, 1716, in St. Gall, Switz., where his family enjoyed great prestige. His grandfather Schlatter was president of the St. Gall ministry, the Synod, and the theological college of the Reformed Church. His mother's family also had been prominent in the church. Schlatter attended the gymnasium and studied theology in St. Gall. After a brief period of study at the University of Leyden and possibly at Helmstadt, he became a private tutor. In 1744, having been previously ordained, he entered the ministry and served in Wigoldingen and Linschuehl in Switz. When officials of the Dutch Reformed Church sought a pastor to serve settlers of German Reformed background in Pa., he volunteered.

In 1746 Schlatter arrived in Philadelphia with instructions to visit congregations and bring their representatives together in an administrative organization. He carried out his duties energetically, traveling approximately 8,000 miles to German settlements primarily in Pa. but also in western N.J., western Md., and the Shenandoah Valley of Va. Where there were no congregations, he organized them, arranged them in charges, and tried to obtain pastors to serve them. In 1747 he convened four clergymen and twenty-eight elders of German Reformed congregations in what became known as the Coetus of Pa. This was his crowning achievement, for it was the first time that German Reformed pastors and people had ever assembled in America, and they continued to meet annually thereafter to deal with the church's problems.

When opposition to Schlatter's leadership developed, he left the Coetus in 1754 and became superintendent of the charity schools that were sponsored by the Society for the Promotion of the Knowledge of God among the Germans in America. Unfortunately for Schlatter, many German colonists interpreted the schools as attempts by English officials to destroy German culture, suspected Schlatter of complicity in the alleged scheme, and resisted their organization and maintenance. Consequently, he resigned his superintendency in late 1756.

Schlatter then became a military chaplain. He served with the Royal American Infantry of the British army at Louisbourg and probably at the Forks of the Ohio as well. In 1764 he was chaplain of the Second Pennsylvania Battalion. Because he refused to serve with the British in the War for American Independence, he was imprisoned, his house devastated, and many of his belongings destroyed. After the war, he lived quietly on a small farm at Chestnut Hill, not far from Philadelphia. He died on Oct. 31, 1790.

Critical Appraisal: Although Michael Schlatter wrote a catechism and a reader for schoolchildren (neither of which has survived), his best-known composition is his journal, which was published in Europe in 1751 and 1752 in Dutch, German, and English as *A True History of the Real Condition of the Destitute*

Congregations of Pennsylvania. His purpose was to obtain additional support for the German Reformed settlers in Pa. and neighboring provinces. The publication was successful, for it helped inspire Europeans to contribute financially and to volunteer for service in the American ministry.

More significant than the work's short-term effectiveness is what it reveals about its author and subject. Because Schlatter's papers are not extant—probably having been destroyed by the British troops in 1777—his published journal is one of the few surviving records of this important minister's activities and attitudes. Schlatter's tone, vocabulary, and contents suggest that he was inclined toward pietism. He seldom mentioned formal doctrinal creeds and frequently noted displays of emotion among the people to whom he preached and administered the sacraments. Concerning the situation among the German Reformed colonists, Schlatter described large numbers who lacked spiritual care and who were eager for preaching and the sacraments. He observed with obvious satisfaction that they received him favorably in every community that he visited. It was essential, Schlatter emphasized, that these people be provided with ministers because of the presence, especially in Pa., of so many sectarians who, he claimed, often misled them. For America's churchmen, such as the Lutheran pastor Henry Melchior Muhlenberg (q.v.), Schlatter demonstrated greater respect. He noted the good relationships that prevailed among the Lutheran and Reformed Church people in America, who frequently intermarried, and expressed the wish that they could get along as well in Ger. Schlatter was particularly concerned about the children. He noticed that German settlers lacked not only ministers but schoolmasters as well. Indeed, he claimed that German youth in Pa. could easily degenerate into heathens. He concluded his composition with an appeal for help in converting the Indians to whom, he reported, only a few English missionaries had tried to bring the Gospel of Christianity.

Other sources verify the accuracy of much of Schlatter's account. Nevertheless, several aspects must be used cautiously. He gave too little credit to the pioneer German Reformed minister John Philip Boehm (q.v.) for his work in organizing and serving numerous congregations, and Schlatter implied that he alone had established almost all of them. In his appeal for help, he exaggerated the German colonists' cultural destitution and failed to acknowledge not only the German Reformed congregations but also schools and presses that existed in Pa. before his arrival. Although his publication was received favorably in Europe, it produced a negative reaction in America that combined with other issues to undermine his influence among the German colonists.

Suggested Readings: CCMC; CCMDG; DAB; DARB. *See also* Joseph Henry Dubbs, *The Reformed Church in Pennsylvania* (1902); Charles H. Glatfelter, *Pastors and People: German Lutheran and Reformed Churches in the Pennsylvania Field, 1717-1793* (1980), pp. 117-119; James I. Good, *The History of the Reformed Church in the United States, 1725-1792* (1899); James I. Good and William J. Hinke, trans. and eds., *Minutes and Letters of the Coetus of the German Reformed Congregations in Pennsylvania, 1747-1792* (1903); Henry Harbaugh, *The Life of Rev. Michael Schlatter; with a Full Account of His Travel and Labors Among the Germans in Pennsylvania, New Jersey,*

Maryland, and Virginia (1857); William J. Hinke, *Ministers of the German Reformed Congregations in Pennsylvania and Other Colonies in the Eighteenth Century*, ed. George W. Richards (1951), pp. 37-47; Michael Schlatter, "Diary of the Rev. Michael Schlatter [*A True History*]," ed. William J. Hinke, JPHS, 3 (1905), 105-121, 158-176.

John B. Frantz

The Pennsylvania State University

JOB SCOTT (1751-1793)

Works: *The Baptism of Christ, A Gospel Ordinance* (1793); *Journal* (1797); *Five Letters* (1807); *On the Knowledge of the Lord* (1824); *Salvation by Christ* (1824); *Works*, 2 vols. (contains *Journal*; 1831); *Salvation by Christ; Epistolary Correspondence; A Treatise on Church Discipline; The Faith and Patience of the Saints; An Epistle of Tender Caution; On the Knowledge of the Lord; On Perseverence; Future Rewards and Punishments Maintained; The Baptism of Christ, A Gospel Ordinance; Remarks on an Essay upon Liberty and Necessity; An Epistle of Tender Caution Against Stumbling at the Faults of Others* (all 1834); *A Short Testimony* (n.d.); *Some Reflections in Verse* (n.d.).

Biography: Born in Providence, R.I., in 1751, Job Scott overcame a minimal formal education and "dissipation" in his late teens to become a respected traveling minister among the Quakers. Little is known of his life except as regards his religious activities. He taught school at Providence and later at Smithfield and at one time practiced medicine informally. In 1780 he married Eunice Anthony, who bore him six children. When he was 23, Scott began his public ministry, journeying to most of the New Eng. states, N.Y., Pa. (twice), and the southern states as far as Ga. Known for his teaching that vocal ministry must proceed from the *immediate* unction of the spirit, he often traveled to a meeting only to sit in silence, never feeling the necessity to speak rising within himself. In 1792 he sailed for Europe and attended and spoke at Quaker meetings in Eng., Wales, and Ire. In 1793 he contracted smallpox and died in Ballitore, Ire., at the age of 42.

Critical Appraisal: Job Scott is one of the best examples of a Friends traveling minister produced by the "quietistic" period of Quakerism. His prose style encompassed a range of possibilities from plain descriptive and argumentative passages to impassioned exhortations or jeremiads. He was not reluctant to write in modified short hymn stanzas, yet was also at home with typically Quaker stylistic components such as "queries" for the self-examination of the reader. His works contain preachments against standard Quaker targets such as war, colonial war taxes, frivolities of amusements, supposed necessity of water baptism, and corrupting influence of riches. Yet he always wrote with the zeal (and frequently with the skill) of the first-rank Quaker apologists.

Scott also wrote in essentially unorthodox ways regarding some aspects of

Christian doctrine. These beliefs are particularly evident in his *Journal* and *Salvation by Christ*, where Scott argued for an immediate, experimental religion characterized by personal victory over sin. In these writings, he utterly rejected the doctrines of imputed righteousness, predestination, and unconditional election espoused by Calvinists. Scott believed that he and his readers must identify with and, in a sense, "relive" the life of Christ to achieve salvation. On the one hand, he affirmed the "history of Christ's life, death, resurrection, ascension, and glory" but on the other expected "no final benefit from the death of Jesus, in any other way than through fellowship with him in his sufferings." In *Salvation by Christ*, he took an even more controversial position that attacked the doctrine of the Trinity and further amplified his view that Christ's sufferings were efficacious only as they were connected in some personal way with the sufferings of individual pilgrims either before or after the actual life of Jesus of Nazareth. Christ's righteousness, then, was never imputed to sinners nor forgiveness offered merely on Christ's account. Furthermore, the means of salvation were the same for all ages. Scott's views did not lead him to belief in universalism. On the contrary, he saw only a "remnant" successfully appropriating the power of Christ over sin and thus winning the rewards of heaven. His unorthodox positions were probably instrumental in preventing complete publication of his works until thirty-eight years after his death and after the great separation of Quakers into Hicksite and Orthodox branches (1827-1828). His works were then published by Hicksite Friends.

Scott was a mystic. The marks of his mysticism are on his view of salvation. They are also discovered in his behaviors as reported in his *Journal*. For example, he waited in silence for long periods before speaking in meetings, often not speaking at all, because he did not feel the "Key of David" to have "opened the door" to his speech. On one ministerial journey, he attended meetings for twenty days without speaking once. At such times, he thought himself in the "furnace of trial," a partaker of the sufferings of Christ. His *Journal* relates important dreams and visions that he believed were means by which God revealed truth to him. His final journey and eventual death were preceded by a prophetic vision that he recorded in both prose and verse. Rufus Jones has written an excellent account of the roots of Scott's mysticism, linking him with William Law and Jacob Boehme.

Job Scott was a product of a period of Quakerism that had shrugged off the burden of seventeenth-century Friends to evangelize the world and had instead concentrated on the problems within its own membership. He was a transitional figure in the development of Quaker thought. Many of his ideas, including his views on ministry, war, baptism, plain living, and so on, were foundational Friends' positions espoused by George Fox and other first-generation Quakers. On the other hand, his view of Christ and salvation anticipated the writings of modern liberal theologians.

Suggested Readings: DAB. *See also* Lucia K. Beamish, *Quaker Ministry, 1691 to 1834* (1967); Rufus Jones, *The Later Periods of Quakerism* (1921), I, 68-100, 288-312; idem, *Quakers in the American Colonies* (1910); Joseph Smith, *A Descriptive Catalogue* *of Friends' Books* (1867), II, 546-550, Supplement, p. 299; H. W. Wilbur, *Job Scott, an Eighteenth-Century Friend* (1911); Luella M. Wright, *the Literary Life of the Early Friends, 1650-1725* (1932).

Michael P. Graves
George Fox College

JOSHUA SCOTTOW (c. 1618-1698)

Works: *Old Men's Tears for Their Own Declensions* (1691); *A Narrative of the Planting of the Massachusets Colony Anno 1628* (1694).

Biography: Born in Eng., Joshua Scottow came to Boston in New Eng. with his widowed mother and elder brother Thomas sometime between 1630 and 1634. He was admitted to the Old (South) Church in 1639 and granted land along Muddy River that same year. He married in 1640, and the first of his seven children was born in 1641.

Scottow became a colonial merchant, dealing in waterfront lots in Boston, trading with Acadia (Quebec) to the north, investing in the fishing industry, and developing frontier settlements in the area around Scarborough, Maine. His most famous transaction was the purchase and resale of the condemned cargo of the *Charles of Oleron*, seized in 1661 by the Mass. authorities for allegedly smuggling French goods. Suit was brought before the General Court of the colony by Thomas Deane, one of the original owners, seeking damages. Although the suit was dismissed, the claim was brought up again (also without issue) before the royal commission that visited New Eng. in 1665.

Scottow continued to develop his Maine holdings until finally dispossessed by King Philip's War. He returned to Boston, continued in trade, and supported the older established interests of the town in colonial political and ecclesiastical affairs. Scottow evidently devoted himself to matters of church polity and discipline, because both of his published works are in some part responses to local church issues of the day and argue for the older system of church government. A successful merchant and a man of considerable wealth, he was also a devout supporter of the New Eng. orthodoxy.

Scottow died in 1698, survived by his wife and four children, three daughters and a son Thomas, who graduated from Harvard College in 1677. Scottow's career in Mass. spanned virtually the entire history of the colony in the seventeenth century, from the Great Migration to the reorganization of politics and trade under imperial control late in the 1690s. A member of a threatened class, Scottow became an interpreter of the divine mission of New Eng. in his two histories of the colony.

Critical Appraisal: As a writer, Joshua Scottow demonstrated both the intellectual strengths and eccentricities of the Mass. theocracy: a plain but colorful prose style, rich in biblical and Classical allusions, well-founded in Calvinist doctrine and in the system of scriptural exegesis as applied to New Eng. His two works are unparalleled examples (by a layman) of the jeremiad form that figured so largely in the development of American public language. Of the two, *A Narrative of the Planting* is in all respects the better, being an expansion and revision of the earlier volume. Both contrast the heroic stature and godly spirit of the founders with the profane, worldly, and apostacizing society of the 1680s and 1690s. (Scottow may have furnished the term for Perry Miller's well-known "declension thesis.")

Especially important is Scottow's recourse, at a critical period in colonial history, to the myth of New Eng. In writing his jeremiad-histories, Scottow recast the political and social events of the past sixty years into the form of a spiritual biography, the story of an elect nation in America, founded to one purpose, united by covenant and contract, called to one single destiny, and "animated as with one soul." Scottow celebrated the unanimity of the founding generation and offered their vision of providential design as a basis for a reconstituted communal enterprise in New Eng. In the face of increasing colonial diversity (social, economic, and religious), Scottow asserted New Eng.'s primary loyalty to a single set of common principles by proposing an ideology based on New Eng.'s special character as a simultaneously historical and spiritual society.

Scottow's jeremiads describe two New Engs. One is sunk in sin and beset by Indians, witches, Quakers, and the French, a society fallen off from the spiritual purity of its fathers. The other is prefigured in Scripture, preserved by God's special providence, a society representative of the nation of the elect, still guaranteed to triumph in anticipation of the apocalypse and in fulfillment of the millennial prophecies. Calling both of these entities "New-England" resolves the contradiction. Scottow mediated between opposite visions of his society by creating a symbolic "New England" that represents them both. When he wrote "That NEW-ENGLAND is not to be found in NEW-ENGLAND," Scottow's lament also contained a special promise: the very plenitude of symbolic language is itself proof of New Eng.'s destiny. Densely rhetorical, Scottow's prose abounds in scriptural types and figures that, when applied to New Eng., provide a system of reflected assurances. The signs of success are certain; the Puritan enterprise, already vindicated in Scripture, will inevitably be vindicated in fact.

Scottow's affirmation of the myth is strong enough to make him precisely invert the meaning of the lines of George Herbert he quoted in both works: *"Religion Stands on Tiptoe in our Land, / Ready to pass to the AMERICAN Strand."* Herbert's lines are from a poem on the vanity of human wishes; Scottow's inversion makes them an assertion of the new heavens, new earth, New World, and New Israel in America.

Suggested Readings: DNB; T₁. *See also* Bernard Bailyn, *The New England Merchants in the Seventeenth Century* (1955), pp. 122-123, 135, 138; Sacvan Bercovitch, *The American Jeremiad* (1978), pp. 79, 101, 105, 113; idem, *The Puritan Origins of the American Self* (1975), pp. 104-105, 115, 120, 132, 146, 226; "Memoir of Joshua Scottow," CMHS, 2nd ser., 4 (1816), 100-104; Perry Miller, *The New England Mind* (1953), pp.

46, 184, 263; "Sketch of Captain Joshua Scottow," PCSM, 10 (1906), 370-378. *A Narrative of the Planting of the Massachusets Colony* is reprinted in CMHS, 4th ser., 4 (1858), 279-332.

Paul Royster
Columbia University

SAMUEL SEABURY (1729-1796)

Works: *The Congress Canvassed* (1774); *Free Thoughts on the Proceedings of the Continental Congress* (1774); *A View of the Controversy Between Great-Britain and Her Colonies* (1774); *An Alarm to the Legislature of the Province of New-York* (1775); *A Discourse on Brotherly Love* (1777); *A Discourse on II. Tim. III. 16* (1777); *St. Peter's Exhortation to Fear God and Honor the King* (1777); *A Sermon Preached Before the Grand Lodge* (1783); *Bishop Seabury's Second Charge* (1786); *The Communion-Office* (1786); *A Sermon Delivered Before the Boston Episcopal Charitable Society* (1788); *The Duty of Considering Our Ways* (1789); *An Earnest Persuasive to Frequent Communion* (1789); *An Address to the Ministers and Congregations of the Presbyterian and Independent Persuasions* (1790); *A Discourse Delivered in St. John's Church in Portsmouth* (1791); *A Discourse Delivered Before the Triennial Convention of the Protestant Episcopal Church* (1792); *Discourses on Several Subjects*, 2 vols. (1793); *A Discourse Delivered Before an Assembly of Free and Accepted Masons* (1795); *Discourses on Several Important Subjects* (1798).

Biography: Born at Groton, Conn., in 1729, Samuel Seabury was the son of a Congregational ministerial candidate whose conversion to the Church of England and career as a SPG missionary gave the chief direction to Seabury's life. Immersed from childhood in an Episcopal atmosphere combining High Church and Puritan elements, he graduated from Yale in 1748, served a clerical apprenticeship as a catechist, and then studied medicine at Edinburgh in the year preceding his London ordination. A series of SPG missionary appointments followed, at New Brunswick, N.J., from 1753 to 1757; at Jamaica, N.Y., from 1757 to 1766; and at Westchester in the same colony, from 1766 to 1776. As a parish minister, Seabury was exceedingly conscientious—and notably less successful than his revered father. Never one to seek the limelight, he long resisted efforts to propel him onto a larger stage. But in 1774, spurred by the conviction that the Continental Congress aimed at independence, he suddenly assumed a leadership position. Combatting the patriot plot with his pen, he likewise took direct political action on a scale equal to that of any other N.Y. Loyalist. Oxford University rewarded him with a doctorate. Patriots harassed him, forcing him into exile in British-held New York City throughout the war years. In 1782-1783 Seabury was the principal agent in directing the Loyalist exodus to Nova Scotia. Plans to accompany it were altered when Conn.'s Episcopal clergy chose him as their bishop. Erastian considerations frustrating efforts to obtain consecration in Eng., he was raised to the episcopate by the hierarchy of Scot.'s Nonjuring Episcopal Church in 1784. In his diocese (which, after 1790, included R.I.), he labored energetically, traveling thousands of miles on systematic and often-repeated visitations while doing double duty as rector of his boyhood parish in New London. At the national level, he championed distinctive features of the High Church tradition and secured for a united Episcopal Church (1789) an organization and liturgy compatible with its interpretations. He died at New London in 1796.

Critical Appraisal: The writings of Samuel Seabury expressed concerns that stemmed directly from his clerical role. This orientation is obvious in his earliest publications: newspaper essays of 1755 championing Episcopal influence in the affairs of King's College, N.Y., and others of 1768-1769 censuring opponents of an American episcopate. Larger, abortive projects of the pre-Revolutionary years—notably a refutation of Jonathan Edwards's (q.v.) *Freedom of Will*—also displayed it in a straightforward fashion. The same goal, however, underlay his best-known and, seemingly, secular works, the four "A. W. Farmer" pamphlets of 1774-1775. The Loyalism that produced them was rooted in a conviction that independence would signal the destruction of the colonial Church of England.

"Probably no pamphlets more readable, none more witty and brilliant, none argumentatively more effective, were called forth on either side of the question during the whole controversy": so literary historian Moses Coit Tyler judged the series in 1897. The qualities he noted are related to Seabury's distinctive style, employed with special effectiveness in *Free Thoughts on the Proceedings of the Continental Congress*. Other Revolutionary-era writers—John Dickinson (q.v.), for example—posed as farmers but wrote an elaborate, legalistic prose. Seabury, however, had to hand a spare, direct, and sinewy style, developed in a constant effort to forge effective sermons for rural folk only mildly interested in his ministrations. In *Free Thoughts*—aimed especially at persuading N.Y.'s farmers to reject congressional modes of redressing American grievances—he added to this basic technique a close approximation of the countryman's own language, using homely expressions and figures of speech. Playing on rural distrust of the colony's metropolis, he argued that the Congress's plans for economic warfare would beggar farmers to the enrichment of townsmen. The power of Seabury's prose was shown by the intensity of the patriot response to *Free Thoughts*—numerous ceremonial burnings, widespread attempts to prevent its distribution, and refutations, the most ambitious by the young Alexander Hamilton (q.v.). Equally vigorous in style but much less significant in terms of impact was Seabury's second pamphlet, *The Congress Canvassed*, addressed to N.Y.'s merchants. Again he hewed closely to pocketbook arguments, emphasizing that the powers wielded by Revolutionary committees rendered property insecure. *A View of the Controversy*—his reply to Hamilton's strictures—suffered from a need to conform to an opponent's patterning of arguments. Still, it included passages of earthy, homespun rhetoric as lively as any in *Free Thoughts*. It set forth a plan for accommodating the Anglo-American dispute involving Parliament's grant to the colonies of "a fixed determinate constitution" that should mark a clear line between the quarreling parties' rights. The same idea appeared in *An Alarm to the Legislature of the Province of New-York*, a successful plea to negotiate apart from the Congress. All of these pamphlets of 1774-1775 exhibit a total concentration on the immediate situation, on the practical argument. Ideological speculation, indeed, any level of abstraction, apparently was distasteful to "A. W. Farmer."

As a wartime refugee in New York City, Seabury penned Loyalist newspaper essays for pay, his employers being the successive British commanders Sir William Howe and Sir Henry Clinton. Little is known of this work, and the assignment to him of particular items rests mainly on their stylistic resemblances to *Free Thoughts*. When American independence proved compatible with Episcopal interests, his published writings again openly displayed a clerical purpose. Mostly directed to his Conn. flock, they sought to "get this Church into better order before I die . . . and keep it so when I am gone." Chief among his goals was elevating the Eucharist to that position of central importance that Puritan-descended churchmen hitherto had accorded preaching. Seabury's efforts in this matter, which met with indifferent success, reflected his Scottish Nonjuring contacts. Producing a *Communion-Office* adapted from that of his consecrators, he argued his case in *An Earnest Persuasive to Frequent Communion* and again maintained it in three volumes of *Discourses*. A general exposition of High Church views, these collected sermons garnered a large audience, for lay readers frequently used them either in the original editions or a reprint. "A Majority of them," the Loyalist writer Jonathan Boucher (q.v.) declared, "are Equal to any in our Language." Boucher's description of the *Discourses'* language—"plain, clear, proper & strong"—recalls the prose of the "A. W. Farmer" pamphlets, as does his remark that "I no where know a Man, who can in so unassuming & unaffected a Manner, communicate such deep & important Information." Unified as regards their basic purpose, Samuel Seabury's writings likewise displayed a consistent style.

Suggested Readings: CCMC; CCNE; DAB; DARB; Dexter (II, 179-188); LHUS; Sprague (V, 149-154); T₂. *See also* Robert M. Calhoon, *The Loyalists in Revolutionary America, 1760-1781* (1973), pp. 244-252; J. M. Danson, "Seabury As a Preacher," SChR, 1 (1884), 654-666; Bruce E. Steiner, *Samuel Seabury, 1729-1796: A Study in the High Church Tradition* (1971); Clarence H. Vance, ed., *Letters of a Westchester Farmer* (1930).

Bruce E. Steiner
Ohio University

JOHN SECCOMB (1708-1792)

Works: *Father Abbey's Will* (c. 1731); *A Letter of Courtship to His Virtuous and Amiable Widow* (1731); *A Sermon Occasioned by the Death of . . . Abigail Belcher* (1772).

Biography: A Congregational clergyman, John Seccomb was born on Apr. 25, 1708, in Medford, Mass., the son of Peter and Hannah (Willis) Seccomb and grandson of Richard Seccomb who settled in Lynn about 1660. He graduated from Harvard College in 1728 and was ordained minister in Harvard, Mass., on Oct. 10, 1733. In 1739 there was a four-year revival of religion in his congregation that was stimulated by the Great Awakening and that manifested itself mainly in the fervent religiosity of the young people in his congregation. They became so enthusiastic in their zeal as to be unable to sleep, much to the amazement of their pastor. Seccomb was married on Mar. 10, 1737, to Mercy Williams, the daughter of the Rev. William Williams (q.v.) of Weston, and had four children. In 1757 she publicly accused him of misconduct; a church council acquitted him of all charges, but feeling he could no longer usefully serve as pastor, he asked to be dismissed. In 1763 Seccomb went to Nova Scotia to be minister at the Congregational Church at Chester, where he lived on a meager income until his death in Halifax on Oct. 27, 1792.

Critical Appraisal: John Seccomb's two poems, *Father Abbey's Will* and *A Letter of Courtship to His Virtuous and Amiable Widow* were written while he was a student at Harvard College. Although not great poetry, they are delightful in their humorous imagery of commonplace events. There is about them almost the cadence of nursery rhymes, although the satirical content is unquestionably adult, even racy. Seccomb poked fun at every flaw and awkward situation of man, from materialism to the dilemmas of youth and age and, of course, the problem of love. *Father Abbey's Will* was occasioned by the death of the spry, if aged, bedmaker and sweeper of his Harvard residence. Seccomb conjured up all of the possessions that the old caretaker might leave in his "estate" to his wife, all the while humorously mocking materialism. The poem opens with the speaker, Father Abbey, expressing his complete willingness to leave his entire estate—now that he will no longer need it—to the joy of his life, his wife, now that he will no longer have to live with her. There follows a recitation on all of the humble particulars of his "estate," from the almost full bottle of brandy to the slightly worn looking glass, complete with sly suggestions for uses of each.

In the companion poem *A Letter of Courtship to His Virtuous and Amiable Widow*, Seccomb dramatized the fictitious suit of another equally aged assistant sweeper to the new widow, Father Abbey's wife. The suitor professes a long-standing, unrequited love for the widow and appeals to her as the only relief from his now burning passion, insisting along the way that although silly youth might value the possession of one's teeth, he much preferred from his love a toothless smile and the assurance of not being bitten. The undeniable, almost Chaucerian charm of these two poems was a combination that proved to be a favorite with generations of New Englanders.

Unfortunately, John Seccomb did not publish again for many years, and his sense of humor seems to have deserted him. The passing of years, the raising of four children, his wife's public complaint against him, poverty, and the cold of Nova Scotia conspired to turn a witty and humorous, if not profound, poet into a stuffy, pompous lecturer. Theologically a traditional Calvinist, Seccomb published a sermon on the death of a friend's wife in 1772. It is decidedly reassuring in both its scriptural references and its basic doctrinal premise that a well-grounded hope and expectation of being with Christ in heaven immediately after death reconciles real Christians to the thought of departing this life and even begets in some an earnest desire to depart and be with Him.

Suggested Readings: CCNE; Sibley-Shipton (VIII, 481-490); T_1. *See also* Charles Brooks, *History of Medford* (1855); E. A. and G. L. Duyckinck, *Cyclopaedia of American Literature*, vol. I, (1855); H. S. Norse, *History of the Town of Harvard* (1889).

Peggy McCormack
Loyola University of New Orleans

JOSEPH SECCOMBE (1706-1760)

Works: *A Plain and Brief Rehearsal* (1740); *An Essay to Excite a Further Inquiry into...Sacred Singing* (1741); *Reflections on Hypocrisy* (1741); *Some Occasional Thoughts* (1742); *Business and Diversion...in the Fishing Season* (1743); *A Specimen of the Harmony of Wisdom and Felicity* (1743); "On the Death of...Benjamin Colman" (1747); *The Ways of Pleasure* (1762).

Biography: Joseph Seccombe—Indian missionary, poetaster, and author of several published sermons—was born on Jun. 14, 1706, in Boston. Seccombe's parents were poor, a fact that the young Seccombe never seems to have forgotten. He managed to attend Harvard through charity gifts and took a B.A. in 1731. Shortly thereafter, he was asked to participate in a mission of the Edinburgh Society for Propagating Christian Knowledge among the Indians. Having accepted this charge, he was later praised for his good conduct by Rev. Benjamin Colman (q.v.), with whom Seccombe carried on correspondence. In Dec. 1733, Seccombe and his associates Stephen Parker and Ebenezer Hinsdell were recalled to be ordained; Dr. Joseph Sewall (q.v.) preached the ordination sermon.

Seccombe ran into almost insurmountable difficulty on his mission to the Indians; not only did he have to convert them, but he also faced the more frustrating task of dissuading a large number who were professing Catholics. Seccombe's contest for the souls of these Indians was further complicated by a contingent of Jesuits occupying the same region who periodically threatened excommunication to any who adopted Seccombe's brand of Christianity. Seccombe's bout with the Jesuits for the souls of the Indians provoked great interest, even as far away as Eng., and brought him some degree of fame.

In Oct. 1737 Seccombe received a call from the congregation of Kingston, N.H. The following Jan., he married Mary Thuriel; the marriage, although childless, appears to have been happy. When Benjamin Colman died in 1747, Seccombe composed a sort of pastoral elegy, one of the first such attempts in America. In later life, Seccombe appears to have settled into the sedate routine of an Old Light, opposed to the fervor excited by George Whitefield (q.v.), the Great Awakener. His discourse *Business and Diversion...in the Fishing Season* (1743) is the first work on sports produced in America. Although Clifford Shipton concluded that Seccombe "had the worst social inferiority complex among the Harvard men of his generation," Seccombe produced sermons that, although sober, occasionally display an urbane wit and pleasant style. When he died on Sept. 15, 1760, he left a library of over 500 volumes.

Critical Appraisal: Joseph Seccombe's forté in letters lies with his prose, rather than with his one extant poem, "On the Death of...Benjamin Colman" (1747). But this little piece deserves attention, because it represents one of the first American attempts to write a pastoral elegy. Since Colman helped the younger Seccombe financially with his education, corresponded with him, and praised Seccombe for his successes with his Indian ministry, it is apropos that Seccombe, although he was 41, sign his name as "a young student." The "Argument" of the poem basically follows these lines: as Clericanor, a country Parson, and Tyro, a young student (Seccombe, perhaps) "who was supported...by the Doctor's Influence and Bounty," make their way toward town, they are beset by a thunderstorm and find shelter in a "Cott" belonging to Pastorella, "an ancient, pious Maiden supported...from a Bounty procur'd thence for Her and many other Poor by the Deceased." All three learn of Colman's death from Eusebius, "a virtuous Gentlemen from the Town." The poem clearly employs the obligatory pastoral names; after Eusebius's revelation, it also redounds with extensive lamentations for the deceased. Colman's "Bounty" to the poor is emphasized, perhaps supporting Shipton's claim that Seccombe felt inferior because of his own humble origins. Colman even showered his generosity on the literary arts: "More than Maecenas! many a Patron He / Procur'd the Muses, from beyond the Sea." Eusebius, for whose entry no preparation is made in the narrative, appears on the scene and tells of Colman's apotheosis, a common event in the Puritan funeral elegy: "I saw Him rise and tow'r towards the Stars, / With Thousands Seraphs on their flaming Cars! / When lo! a glorious Light shot beaming down, / Then spreading settled on the mourning Town." Eusebius then catalogs some admirers of Colman, including Mather Byles (q.v.), Charles Chauncy (q.v.), and Joseph Sewall. Although Seccombe definitely showed familiarity in this poem with the Classical demands of its genre, a more respectable contemporary performance in the pastoral mode may be found in "An Eclogue" by Joseph Green (q.v.).

As observed above, however, Seccombe is more successful in prose. With the exceptions of *Reflections on Hypocrisy* and *A Plain and Brief Rehersal*, his sermons resemble abbreviated treatises from the pen of a reserved and learned gentleman of culture. In these prose pieces, Seccombe made unobtrusive and helpful reference to figures such as Jerome, Ambrose, Tertullian, Livy, Herodotus, and even to John Locke. One, *A Specimen of the Harmony of Wisdom and Felicity*, strongly recommends prudence and discretion and seems actually to be a prescription for the achievement of the wisdom and happiness requisite to becoming a true gentleman.

Business and Diversion...in the Fishing Season, America's first published work on sports, opens appropriately with a quotation from Izaak Walton's *The Compleat Angler*. Seccombe adopted the equally fitting name of *Fluviatulis Piscator*, or fisher of rivers. In his "Dedication" honoring those who appreciate the art of angling, Seccombe stated that he derived any authority and credibility he may have had from the fact that both he and his audience had fished the same banks and then cleverly observed: "tho' I know this will be no Bait, I am fond of being esteemed, in the Affair of Fishing." The piece argues that fishing is "very friendly to Religion." After all, the Apostles were fishers of men, and Simon Peter once remarked, "I go a Fishing." At one crucial point, Seccombe made this supportive observation: "Every Thing calls for Labour, and Labour requires Rest." The argument then assumes the following structure: "the common Enterprizes of Life are not inconsistent with Piety towards God" and finally "Fishing is innocent [or "lawful" as he said later] as Business and Diversion."

A final "treatise" of interest is *Some Occasional Thoughts*, which deals with the overzealousness and even fanaticism excited by the enthusiasm of the Great Awakening. In the "Preface," Seccombe obtained support for his guarded position by quoting from Jonathan Edwards (q.v.), who had lamented the possible hypocrisy of overzealous claims of vision and fantastic dreams. But of particular interest to the literary student are Seccombe's reflections on imagination, to which he gave several pages. Excessive enthusiasm is attributed to an imagination functioning beyond, or outside, the control of the understanding. He identified the imagination as "a lower Power of human Nature, and at best but the Mirror of the Understanding, the Picture of Reality: Yet under Conduct of the Understanding, it's a very useful and powerful Faculty." Although Seccombe's analysis might have been extended, one may clearly observe that by 1742 the imagination was no longer "a dangerous Art" in America. Instead Seccombe recognized it as a powerful mental force, but one requiring control. Seccombe's contribution to America's history of literary aesthetics is, to be sure, modest, but his observations on the imagination and his attempt to construct a pastoral elegy should secure for him a permanent place in that history.

Suggested Readings: CCNE; Sibley-Shipton (IX, 87-96).

John C. Shields
Illinois State University

GERSHOM MENDEZ SEIXAS (1745-1816)

Works: *A Religious Discourse, Delivered...November 26, 1789* (1789); *A Discourse Delivered...the Ninth of May, 1798* (1798).

Biography: The "Patriot Jewish Minister of the American Revolution" was born in New York City, N.Y., on Jan. 14, 1745. His father, Isaac Mendez Seixas, was a successful merchant who had emigrated from Lisbon around 1730, and his mother, Rachel (Levy) Seixas, was also from an affluent trading family. Throughout his childhood and adolescence, however, Gershom Mendez Seixas was more interested in education and Jewish learning than in buying and selling. It was no surprise when in 1766 he was chosen to lead New York City's Spanish and Portuguese congregation, Shearith Israel. In 1768 he was formally installed as *hazzan*, a position he kept until his death.

Seixas was the first native-born Jewish minister in America, and he distinguished himself in that capacity. Although not a trained rabbinical scholar, he was the leader, authority, and judge for all of the Jews of N.Y. in matters of Hebrew language, literature, and law. Furthermore, he was the first Jewish circuit rider in America, and he occasionally traveled as far as Philadelphia in addition to regularly preaching around the N.Y. area. But Seixas was above all an American patriot who was proud that he was ignorant of the Spanish and Portuguese languages and conducted his services in English. The Revolutionary War was to test Seixas's convictions.

The Revolution split Seixas's family, congregation, and community. But unlike his largely Royalist Christian counterparts in the clergy, he was a committed supporter of independence. Through his efforts, Shearith Israel disbanded rather than exist under the British occupation of New York City, and in Aug. 1776 Seixas preached a farewell sermon, gathered up the Scrolls of the Law, and moved to Stratford, Conn., to wait out the war. Several of his congregation had fled to Philadelphia, however, and by 1780 they persuaded him to join them and found the congregation Mickve Israel. Seixas immediately became an influential member of Philadelphia society. Although strictly orthodox himself, he conducted unorthodox services, doing away with much of the Hebraic ritual, inviting Christian clergy to speak, and including blessings and prayers for America in the ceremonies. Because of his personal popularity and the unswerving patriotism of his congregation, Seixas successfully challenged the religious test that was at first included in Pa.'s new constitution.

Seixas continued his support for the new government when he returned to New York City in 1784. It is commonly believed that he served as one of fourteen clergy invited to preside at George Washington's (q.v.) inauguration, and he was one of the first ministers to heed the new president's call for a formal holiday of Thanksgiving. In 1784 he was appointed a trustee of Columbia College, an Episcopalian school, an honor he retained until 1814. He was also elected by the N.Y. State legislature to serve on the first Board of Regents for the new University of the State of New York. His interests in education and patriotism coincided in 1793 when he founded a Hebrew school in New York City so that Americans would no longer have to travel to Europe to study. The War of 1812 saw Seixas continue his support for the American cause.

In 1775 Seixas married Elkaleh Cohen, who bore him four children before her death in 1785. By his second wife, Hannah Manuel, whom he married in 1789, he had eleven more children. One of his sons, David G. Seixas, founded the Pennsylvania School for the Deaf and Dumb in 1820, and another, Joshua, became a professor of Hebrew at Andover School. Gershom Mendez Seixas died Jul. 2, 1816, in New York City, and he is buried in the cemetery of the now demolished Shearith Israel synagog in Chatham Square. Seixas collections are found at both the new Shearith Israel congregation and the American Jewish Historical Society.

Critical Appraisal: If the fame of Gershom Mendez Seixas had to rest upon his publications, it surely would be tenuous. Unlike the Christian clergy of the era, Seixas refrained from publishing treatises, disquisitions, homilies, and improvements. In fact, he published only two sermons, and both are undistinguished theologically or literarily. They are, however, historically important.

In 1789 Seixas preached a Thanksgiving Day sermon, "agreeable to the proclamation of the President of the United States." During the course of the sermon, he took issue with his Calvinist brethren and warned that "faith alone is insufficient to procure salvation, for we find the Almighty only had respect to Actions." Following a discussion of the ways men might please God, Seixas explained how God will reward the right actions of the Jews: the Hebrew people will again have a political nation of their own and "return to Zion." Modern Zionism traces its beginnings to this statement by Seixas. Within his discourse, however, the Zionist theme is insignificant. Seixas mentioned it because he was preaching about the duties of citizenship. His primary purpose was to bolster American nationalism. Seixas first sought to inspire gratitude in the Jews for the new nation, and he reminded his congregation that "the course and conclusion of the late war...the establishment of public liberty...the adoption of the new constitution are all blessing that demand our most grateful acknowledgments to the Supreme Ruler of the universe." Seixas also hoped to inculcate the duties of American citizenship. He closed his sermon with this injunction:

> It is necessary that we...behave in such a manner as to give strength and stability to the laws entered into by our representative; to consider the burden imposed on those who are appointed to act in the executive department; to contribute...to support that government which is founded upon the strictest principles of equal liberty and justice.

It is no coincidence that Seixas's other published sermon is printed "conformably to a Recommendation of the President of the United States." Although this discourse contains more traditional Jewish commentary than the Thanksgiving Day sermon, its purpose is also to support the American government. The members of Shearith Israel, observed Seixas, were fortunate to escape persecution. "It hath pleased God to have established us in this country where we possess every advantage that other citizens of these states enjoy," reminded Seixas, "and which is as much as we could in reason expect in this captivity." Consequently, the Jews owe the fledgling government their support.

The patriotic intent of both sermons is obvious. The allegiance of the Jews to the new government, the compliance of Seixas with the wishes of the new rulers, and the gratitude of the congregation for their acceptance suffuse these messages.

At a time when Jewish loyalties were suspect throughout the world, Seixas was clearly trying to allay such fears in the new Republic. He was not addressing only his congregation in these discourses. His intended audience was the Christian public, and the publication of these sermons was for the benefit of the Christian city, state, and nation.

Suggested Readings: DAB. *See also* David de Sola Pool, *Portraits Etched in Stone* (1952); *Encyclopedia Judaica* (1971), XIV, 1116-1117; *The Jewish Encyclopedia* (n.d.), XI, 159-161; Thomas Kessner, "Gershom Mendes Seixas," AJHQ, 58 (1969), 445-471; PAJHS, 27 (1920), 126-143; PAJHS, 35 (1939), 189-205; Ezra Stiles, *Ezra Stiles and the Jews* (1902).

John F. Schell
University of Arkansas at Little Rock

HENRICUS SELYNS (1636-1701)

Works: Henry C. Murphy, ed., selected poetry, *Anthology of New Netherland* (with Introduction by Murphy; 1865); E. T. Corwin, ed., Correspondence with the Classis of Amsterdam, 1660-1700, *Ecclesiastical Records of the State of New York* (1901-1916).

Biography: Henricus Selyns (Selijns), son of Jan Selijns Hendrickszoon and Janneken de Marees, was born in Amsterdam to a family long active in the Dutch Reformed Church. After being educated for the ministry at Leyden, Selyns, through the Classis, was called to serve at Breukelen (Brooklyn) by the Dutch West India Company, apparently because of his fluency in English. In Jul. 1660, just five months after his ordination, Selyns arrived in New Amsterdam to begin an agreed upon four-year term of office. His congregation, which then held services in a barn, numbered fewer than thirty persons, and problems in raising the promised 1,200 guilder salary immediately arose. By the time his contract expired, just before the colony fell to the English, Selyns's church had quadrupled in size. Upon his return to Europe, Selyns accepted a call to Waverveen, a poor village in the province of Utrecht. Twice during the 1670s, he declined calls to return to New Neth., choosing instead in 1675 to become a chaplain to the army. In 1681, however, Selyns agreed to return to N.Y., but not before having drawn up and notarized the terms and conditions of his service, including a guaranteed salary; free fuel and rent; and paid passage for himself, his wife (Machtelt Specht), and his children. The congregation to which he returned in 1682, although able to make Selyns more comfortable physically, was fraught with discord. To the Classis he wrote in 1685, "I lived in Abraham's bosom at Waverveen; but am sorrowful to live here among so many wild beasts and bulls of Bashan." From the people came the threat of the proselytizing Labadists (Quakers) who, Selyns believed, preached a dangerous enthusiasm that defied the church's authority. From the colonial government, beginning with the appointment of Governor Edmund Andros, came an attack on the individual church's right to call a minister of its choice. By 1692 Selyns had recorded the government's attempt to establish a kind of state church based on a quota system and designed to permit secular authorities to name and suspend ministers at will. This move Selyns opposed energetically, and in 1696, having applied for and been granted the first church charter in the colony, he became the head of an independent congregation. The expansion of the city ("growth. . .chiefly in houses and people and businesses, but not in piety and the conversion of sinners") and the frailty of old age brought the need for additional clergy. In 1699 the consistory sent the Rev. Gualterus du Bois to assist Selyns in his duties. He died in N.Y. in Jul. 1701, survived by his second wife, Margaretta de Riemer.

Critical Appraisal: Any history of the growth of the colony of N.Y., sacred or secular, owes a debt to Henricus Selyns's reports to his superiors in Amsterdam. His accounts are detailed and graphic records of economic hardships, of political and religious discord, of the constant menace of the Indians. These letters, furthermore, illuminate the character of their author as one who meets resistance with a reported "firmness, dignity and force of reasoning" as well as a ready wit and, when required, a barbed tongue. This last trait may have held particular appeal for Washington Irving, who reputedly possessed Selyns's manuscripts at the time he was writing his *Knickerbocker History*.

Henry C. Murphy's assessment of the nineteen "poetical effusions" he presented in his anthology of early Dutch poetry is roughly correct. Gleaned from a recovered bound manuscript volume of nearly 200 poems written in Dutch, Latin, and Greek, Selyns's contribution does not often stand "severe criticism. [The poems] are presented now only as interesting from the circumstances under which they were produced" and are offered as "proofs of culture and genius" as well as "a spirit of true humor." Selyns's occasional poems include a number of epitaphs, including a wry one for himself and one for Peter Stuyvesant that turns on a clever play on his name, a "Chronostic" demonstrating the power of the poet's punning, and several witty verses of social criticism. Among them are poems "On Mercenary and Unjust Bailiffs," "Of Scolding Wives and the Third Day Ague," and "Reasons for and Against Marrying Widows." Typical of Selyns's bluntness is his pronouncement "Upon the Bankruptcy of a Physician," where he claimed that such flagrant spending makes such people "rotten in the box and mouthy in the raiment."

Of greater interest and import is the Epithalamion that introduces Selyns's portion of the anthology. It bears only remote resemblance to the traditional marriage poem, for it is largely occupied with a poetic account of the Indian massacre of Esopus in 1663, meteoric phenomena, and citations of earthquakes, the latter, perhaps, helping to establish Selyns's contact with Cotton Mather (q.v.). In reality, the poem is two poems: one is a celebratory song; one is a lament for those slain. The result is a curious fusion of grief and well-wishing whose point of union is Cupid, deprived of his bow and demanding its return, a slender means of effecting coherence.

More of a piece is Selyns's prefatory poem to Mather's *Magnalia*, the only extended Latin verse in the series. Unlike some of the other introductory poems, Selyns's matches Mather's own theme and, while paying due respect to the church historian, consistently focuses on the marvelous development of "that wondrous waif Vesputio found." Abounding in allusions to the ancients (Strabo, Grotius, Lycurgus, Numa, Solon, Aeneas appear prominently), Selyns's tribute emphasizes God's mighty work in carrying order (civil government) to the wilderness, through Harvard, of bringing philosophy and science to this "exile-race," and in this "Age of Iron" conveying to doubters and miscreants the knowledge of God's awesome power. As surely as the *Magnalia* itself, Selyns's poem is designed "To Old World minds [to make] New World wonders known."

Suggested Readings: CCMC; DAB. *See also* E. T. Corwin et al., *A History of the Reformed Church. . .in the United States* (1894), pp. 50-52; Thomas DeWitt, "Introductory Note," CNYHS, 2nd ser., 1 (1841), 390-391; Joseph B. Felt, *The Ecclesiastical History of New England*, vol. 2 (1862); Harrison T. Meserole, *Seventeenth-Century American Poetry* (1968), pp. 429-432.

Cheryl Z. Oreovicz
Purdue University

ISAAC SENTER (1753-1799)

Works: Journal (w. 1775-1776; pub. 1846, 1938), facsimile of 1846 edn. (1969); "Remarks on Phthisis Pulmonalis," *Transactions of the College of Physicians of Philadelphia* (1795).

Biography: Born in 1753 in Londonderry, N.H., Isaac Senter studied medicine with the Scotch physician Thomas Moffat at Newport and joined the R.I. troops as a surgeon soon after the battle at Lexington. Assigned to Col. Benedict Arnold (q.v.), he participated in the 1775 American invasion of Quebec, during which he kept a journal. Retiring from the army and marrying in 1778, Senter became a physician in Cranston, R.I., also serving as its representative to the General Assembly from 1779 to 1780. Appointed surgeon and physician general to the state militia in 1780, he eventually moved his practice to Newport. His publications in medical journals won him recognition in both America and Europe. Senter was an honorary member of the Medical and Chirurgical Societies of Edinburgh and London, an honorary member of the Massachusetts Medical Society, and president of the Society of the Cincinnati of Rhode Island. He died on Dec. 20, 1799.

Critical Appraisal: Isaac Senter's journal of the Arnold invasion of Quebec via Maine, which begins at Cambridge on Sept. 13, 1775, is generally marked by what Kenneth Roberts termed "youthful erudition." With equal objectivity, Senter described incidents of dysentery and smallpox, places and living conditions, difficulties with leaky batteaux, and damage to provisions. The occasional jauntiness of the early entries all but vanishes as he noted the increasingly wretched condition of the troops. Yet he remained capable of admiring natural beauty and still punned that heavy rain had made the Dead River "live enough." But by Oct. 24, encountering rough water and treacherous mountains, Senter was recording "a direful howling wilderness not describable."

There is now dissension among the troops, Senter siding with those who choose to press on. Although they have John Montrésor's (q.v.) map to guide them to the Chaudiere River, they grope through "the most execrable bogmire" "with the terrible apprehension of famishing in this desert." At length the Americans encounter Canadian "inhabitants," and Senter quoted a speech Arnold delivered to local Indians to win support for the invasion. Arriving outside Quebec on Nov. 8, Senter recounted the long siege—the artillery fire, wounds, and smallpox—that preceded the night assault made under cover of a blizzard on Dec. 31.

Despite his usual scientific detachment, Senter wrote with a certain sense of history. Attached to the journal he "preserved in 'perpetuam rei memoriam' for future posterity" a note from Arnold declining Senter's offer to lead a company of men because Senter's medical skills would be needed (this is the only note of self-aggrandizement in the journal). He also interjected verse to enhance the epic scope of the attack. The final entry summarizes some five months; indeed, Justin H. Smith suggested that the entire journal was reconstructed from notes at a later date. Senter's military perspective is limited, his account of the critical assault second-hand. But having supervised the hospital during the attack, he provided a credible glimpse of the courage of the wounded Arnold, who defiantly refused to flee the hospital: "He ordered his pistols loaded, with a sword on his bed, &c., adding that he was determined to kill as many as possible if they came into the room."

The New Year's Eve assault failing, the siege of Quebec dragged on until May 6, when British reinforcements routed the Americans. Although Senter was among those who escaped, he commented bitterly on the "strange series of unaccountable misfortunes" that doomed the expedition and for which Senter faulted either the commanders for failing to report accurately on the army's condition or the Congress for failing to heed such warnings. He concluded with a cry of despair for "a once happy, but now convulsed and tottering country!"

Published in 1846 by the Historical Society of Pennsylvania, Isaac Senter's journal was reprinted by Kenneth Roberts in *March to Quebec* (1938), a compilation of documents Roberts used during the writing of his historical novel *Arundel* (1930). These documents supplement Senter's journal to provide a fuller view of a major event of the American Revolution, an adventure marked by tragedy and by extraordinary courage.

Suggested Readings: William Abatt, "A Neglected Name: Dr. Isaac Senter," AMH, 2 (1919), 381-383; Kenneth Roberts, comp., *March to Quebec* (Senter's journal; 1938), pp. 193-241; Justin H. Smith, *Arnold's March from Cambridge to Quebec* (1903), pp. 29-32.

Wesley T. Mott
University of Wisconsin at Madison

JOHN SERGEANT (1710-1749)

Works: *The Causes and Danger of Delusions in . . . Religion . . . with Particular Reference to . . . the Present Times* (1743); *A Letter . . . Containing . . . Proposal of a More Effectual Method for the Education of Indian Children* (1743).

Biography: John Sergeant was born in Newark, N.J., in 1710. Graduating from Yale in 1729, he continued his studies in theology and served as a tutor at Yale from 1731 to 1735. Invited by two clergymen to accept a mission to the small settlement of Housatonic Indians in Stockbridge, Mass., Sergeant readily accepted this call and in Jul. 1735 entered upon his lifelong missionary work. He was ordained to the Congregational ministry at Deerfield, Mass., in Aug. 1735. In the following year, a meeting house and a school were built for the Indians, and Sergeant evinced a special interest in the education of the children. One major project was the establishment of a boarding school that would give industrial training to the young women of the tribe as well as the men. This project was successfully completed shortly before Sergeant's untimely death in 1749. He was survived by his wife of ten years, Abigail Williams, half-sister of the founder of Williams College. One son, John, later served as a missionary to the Indians; a second son served as an officer in the Revolution.

Critical Appraisal: From 1735 until his death fourteen years later, John Sergeant lived among and gave educational and spiritual guidance to the Housatonic Indians of Stockbridge, Mass. He mastered their language to such a degree that the Indians said he spoke it better than they could themselves. He translated into the Indian dialect portions of the Bible, numerous prayers, and Isaac Watts's shorter catechism. His work was highly regarded by both the Housatonics and by the general community, and, in particular, he enjoyed the esteem and support of Governor Jonathan Belcher. In 1734 two of his works saw publication, a sermon and *A Letter*, the latter setting forth in detail his "Proposal of a More Effectual Method for the Education of Indian Children."

Suggested Readings: CCNE; DAB; Dexter (I, 395); Sprague (I, 388-394). *See also* Samuel Hopkins, *Historical Memoir Relating to the Housatunnuk Indians* (1753), reprinted in MagH, extra no. 17 (1911); E. F. Jones, *Stockbridge, Past and Present* (1854).

Robert Colbert
Louisiana State University in Shreveport

JONATHAN SEWALL (1728-1796)

Works: *The Association, etc., of the Delegates of the Colonies* (1774); *A Cure for the Spleen* (1775; reprinted as *The Americans Roused, in a Cure for the Spleen*, 1775).

Biography: Jonathan Sewall (also spelled *Sewell*) was born in Boston on Aug. 17, 1728, and educated at Harvard, graduating in 1748. He taught school at Salem but left in 1756 to train as a lawyer. In the early 1760s, he was an intimate of John Adams (q.v.) and other patriots but gradually became disenchanted with their views and accepted a series of crown appointments, culminating in a judgeship on the Vice-Admiralty Court. His close association with John Adams ended after his failure to dissuade Adams from attending the Philadelphia Congress.

Because of his public position and his sharp attacks on the patriot cause in Loyalist newspapers, he became an object of mob vengeance. His home in Cambridge was wrecked in Sept. 1774, and he moved into Boston; a few months later, he sailed with his family for Eng. In 1778-1779 he was officially banished and his property confiscated. While in Eng. he changed the spelling of his name to "Sewell" to make it consistent with Heraldry Office records. In 1786 he recrossed the Atlantic to settle in the newly formed Province of New Bruns., where he pursued his profession as a lawyer until his death on Sept. 26, 1796, at Saint John.

Critical Appraisal: As a writer, Jonathan Sewall was best known to his contemporaries as the author of many newspaper "letters" critical of patriot aims and supporting crown policy. Today, what remains is a satiric poem and a polemic drama. *The Association of the Delegates* (1774) is a verse travesty of the Association for Nonintercourse resolutions issued by the First Continental Congress in Oct. 1774. It follows the clauses of the original document closely in developing its subject, but insinuates satiric editorial commentary through the malicious views and blatant stupidity of its patriot narrator. The satirist's intention is to undermine the credibility of the document directly and indirectly by creating an unacceptable *persona*.

Many of the same issues appear again in *A Cure for the Spleen* (1775), a play that methodically raises all of the chief grievances of the American colonists and responds to them from the viewpoint of British policy. The scene is set in a tavern and involves a discussion between the intelligent Rev. Sharp; jolly Squire Bumper, the local magistrate; Mr. Trim, the barber; Mr. Graveairs, a deacon; Mr. Fillpot, an innkeeper; Mr. Brim, a Quaker; and Mr. Puff, a representative to the recent Congress at Philadelphia. As the discussion unfolds, the group divides into three categories: Sharp and Bumper are Loyalists who present and explain British policy; Trim, Graveairs, and Fillpot are ordinary men, sympathetic to colonial grievances but not fully aware of the wrong-headedness and seditious tendencies of American extremists; Brim and Puff are committed congressmen, but well meaning and open to reason. The burning political issues of the day are raised in conversation, one by one, and the sagacious Rev. Sharp quietly explains the truth of the matter and demonstrates the logic of British policy. The dramatic pattern involves the inevitable triumph of reason over human self-interest, ignorance, and irresponsibility. In the end, there is an impassioned outburst from Squire Bumper, expressing his fears on what could happen if the madness of civil war were loosed and appealing to the patriot-sympathizers to turn back while there is still time. Moved by Sharp's reason and Bumper's passion, all decide to abandon their false patriotism.

The Association and *A Cure* are not significant works of literature, but they are competently written and clear in their purpose. They provide a lively insight into a largely ignored set of attitudes toward the most critical period (1774-1776) of American social and political history.

Suggested Readings: DAB; Sibley-Shipton (XII, 306-325); T_2. *See also* Carol Berkin, *Jonathan Sewall: Odyssey of an American Loyalist* (1974); E. A. Jones, *The Loyalists of Massachusetts* (1930); J. W. Lawrence, *The Judges of New Brunswick and Their Time* (1907).

Thomas B. Vincent
Royal Military College of Canada

JONATHAN MITCHELL SEWALL (1748-1808)

Works: *War and Washington* (1779); *An Oration Delivered . . . on the Fourth of July, 1788* (1788); *A Versification of President Washington's Excellent Farewell-Address* (1798); *Eulogy on the Late General Washington* (1800); *Miscellaneous Poems* (1801).

Biography: Grand-nephew of diarist Samuel Sewall (q.v.), Jonathan Mitchell Sewall was born in Salem, Mass., early in 1748. Only his baptismal date (Mar. 27 of that year) is certain. His father, Mitchell Sewall, a 1718 graduate of Harvard and clerk of the inferior court at Salem, died in Oct. 1748. Jonathan was then adopted by his bachelor uncle, Stephen Sewall, who served as Mass. chief justice from 1752 to 1760. Jonathan's mother, Elizabeth (Prince) Sewall, died in 1758, and Stephen followed in 1760, leaving Jonathan alone. It is reported that he studied briefly at Harvard, but he did not graduate, and no record of his being there exists.

Sewall was employed for a time as a store clerk and then studied law in Portsmouth, N.H., under Judge John Pickering. Admitted to the bar, he was appointed in 1773 as register of probate in Grafton County, N.H.—a sparsely populated area lacking in lawyers—but no evidence exists that he took the position. Sewall enjoyed a successful legal career in Portsmouth, although often interrupted by illness, but he is best known for his avocation as a poet, chiefly of patriotic odes, and as an orator on various public occasions.

Sewall's writing first attracted public attention with the publication of his patriotic ballad *War and Washington*, written at the beginning of the Revolution and sung by patriots throughout the colonies. His output included many odes to George Washington (q.v.), three of which were presented publicly during the general's visit to Portsmouth in 1789. In addition to his *Versification of President Washington's Excellent Farewell-Address* (published anonymously in 1798), he wrote a *Eulogy on the Late General Washington* (delivered in St. John's Church,

Portsmouth, Dec. 31, 1799, and published in 1800). Also published anonymously was his Fourth of July address, delivered at Portsmouth's first Independence Day celebration in 1788.

Although Sewall was in demand during his lifetime as a public-spirited wit and orator at Federalist banquets (but never himself a political candidate), few of his speeches have survived him. His songs and poems, however, were widely (although often anonymously) published. A collection, *Miscellaneous Poems with Specimens from the Author's Manuscript Version of the Poems of Ossian*, published in Portsmouth in 1801, includes politically effusive and patriotic poems, lyrics, and odes, sprinkled with epilogs and epigrams. His "Epilogue to Cato," Addison's work, provided publisher Park Benjamin with a couplet (that Benjamin then paraphrased) for use as the motto for his newspaper, *New World*. Sewall is also credited with the authorship of several epitaphs in the burying grounds of Portsmouth. Sewall himself died in Portsmouth on Mar. 29, 1808. Reports indicate that he had become intemperate in his later years and that he died a bachelor, perhaps survived by a daughter.

Critical Appraisal: It is important to note that Jonathan Mitchell Sewall was essentially a political writer, writing in an era of Revolution and the creation of a new nation. He most often saw himself as a poet, however, and his politics, for good or ill, in effect color much of his poetry.

His *Oration Delivered. . .on the Fourth of July, 1788* is appropriately verbose and heavily rhetorical but well reasoned. Sewall defined the nature of independence by examining that of dependence—man's dependence on God and his dependence on other men. There is error in relying on or rebelling against either dependence in a fanatic fashion. Excessive dependence on God too often leads to self-righteousness and a hermitage from the world of men. He saw this as just as reprehensible as denial of God and overdependence on other men. Sewall cited man's dependence on others as two-fold: that of dependence on parents (born out of weakness in the face of the outside world) and on society, particularly its laws (arising from a need for protection from the wickedness in the world). He saw as natural and healthy a desire to rebel against such dependence. Speaking to the women in his audience, he conceded that "even" they desire independence after having promised to "obey" their husbands, but with a wink and a nudge told them that they really have and run everything despite their avowed obeisance. Sewall's message is that of the golden mean where love of liberty is concerned. Between the dilemma of anarchy and the harshness of British rule, he viewed the newly forged Constitution as this hoped-for mean.

The speech then brings up two noteworthy points. Sewall saw a need in the new Republic for the cultivation of "eloquence." Although frowning on the Puritans who saw the propagation of theaters as heinous, he alluded to eloquence—with its potential emphasis on truth and reality—as having a moral superiority over drama. He continued further on the subject of religious bigotry, closing with the still-timely: "We should be indulgent, even to the foibles of our brethren, especially when they appear to proceed from a zeal for religion—however ill-directed." Perhaps the low point of the oration is reached in the closing poem, dedicated to George Washington and entitled "Anniversary Ode on American Independence." This poem is but a foretaste of what is to come in *A Versification of President Washington's Farewell-Address.*

Sewall's introduction to this work is fatuously humble and self-contradictory. He explained that his motives for writing the poem are not that it should lead the reader to the original work and that verse may be "more easily retained in the memory," but that the poem might succeed in ways that the original failed. Yet, he asked, how could anyone better the master, Washington himself? Sewall certainly tried—in much more space than Washington's prose original occupied. Still, the reader is begged to indulge the author, for

> If, after all, his humble efforts should be generally condemned or disregarded; a consciousness of the purity of his intentions will be his consolation and support; and he shall think himself entitled to some small share of applause for his Patriotism, though he may justly forfeit the meed of Poetry.

Although one may wish Sewall's patriotism were but a quirk of his poetry, it returns in the prose *Eulogy.* It is only Sewall's anti-Deism that keeps him from comparing Washington to Christ, although he is safely compared to Moses, as in:

> Did he not waste the midnight lamp that we might enjoy repose? Yes! Countless nights while a whole Continent has been sunk in the balmy embraces of sleep like the Watchful Guardian of Israel, HIS eyes have neither slumbered, nor slept: but the morning sun has risen on his nocturnal labours for our safety!

Even the general's resignation of his military command after the war seems to Sewall an "August Spectacle! Glorious Example! For my own part, I never contemplate it, but each fibre vibrates with rapture, and the vital current trembles through every artery of my frame!" Such is the overall tone of the *Eulogy.* Sewall could not, it seems, end a speech without a poem, and here is the text of that which closes the *Eulogy*: "Oh, WASHINGTON! thy Country's boast and pride, / In ev'ry seene of woe, and peril try'd; / Thou se'est (though thron'd above yon starry spheres) / An Empire bleeding! and a world in tears!" In short, the *Eulogy* alone would be evidence enough to suspect Sewall, rather than Mason Locke Weems (q.v.), to be the source of that story about the hatchet and the cherry tree. Still, Sewall's work stands today as an example of intense patriotism born out of the struggle for independence, as well as the extreme depth to which that patriotism, coupled with sycophancy or, more kindly, hero worship, can descend in literature.

Suggested Readings: DAB; T_2. *See also* E. A. and G. L. Duyckinck, *Cyclopaedia of American Literature* (1855); Samuel Kettell, *Specimens of American Poetry* (1829), I, 198-200; A. H. Locke, *Portsmouth and Newcastle, N.H. Cemetery Inscriptions* (1907); A. N. Payson and Albert Leighton, *The Poets of Portsmouth* (1865).

Randal A. Owen
St. Mary's Dominican College

JOSEPH SEWALL (1688-1769)

Works: *Believers Invited* (1716); *The Certainty & Suddenness of Christ's Coming* (1716); *Desires That Joshua's Resolution May Be Revived* (1716); *The Character and Blessedness of the Upright* (1717); *Precious Treasure* (1717); *A Caveat Against Covetousness* (1718); *Sober-Mindedness* (1721); *Rulers Must Be Just* (1724); *The Duty of Every Man to Be Always Ready to Die* (1727); *The Duty of a People* (1727); *Jehovah* (1727); *Repentance the Sure Way to Escape Destruction* (1727); *He That Would Keep God's Commandments* (1728); *The Holy Spirit the Gift of God* (1728); *The Orphan's Best Legacy* (1730); *Christ Victorious* (1733); *When the Godly Cease* (1737); *Nineveh's Repentance and Deliverance* (1740); *All Flesh Is as Grass* (1741); *The Holy Spirit Convincing the World* (1741); *The First and Great Commandment* (1742); *God's People* (1742); *The Second Commandment* (1742); *The Thirsty Invited to Come* (1742); *The Lamb Slain* (1745); *A Tender Heart* (1756); *The Duty, Character and Reward of Christ's Faithful Servant* (1758); *A Sermon Preached at the Thursday-Lecture in Boston. . .on the Joyful News of the Reduction of Havannah* (1762); *The Character and Reward* (1763).

Biography: Joseph Sewall was destined from birth for a career of influence and power. His father, Judge Samuel Sewall (q.v.), was one of Boston's most respected citizens, and Joseph enjoyed all of the privileges the provincial town could offer. He graduated from Harvard in 1707 and five years later received a call from the congregation of Boston's Old South Church. The hand of his father, a deacon at the Old South, was evident in this appointment, for Sewall's conservative theological views varied greatly from those of Ebenezer Pemberton (q.v.), the church's senior pastor. Although Sewall was a protégé of the Mathers, and Pemberton was one of their leading opponents, this difference did not affect their relationship. Because of his position and family heritage, Sewall was invited to participate in the governing of Harvard College and in 1724 was offered its presidency, which he declined. After Cotton Mather's (q.v.) death, he became a leading, although moderate, spokesman for the clerical conservatives of Mass.; his influence in this role led to an honorary University of Glasgow doctorate in 1731. Throughout his career, the colony's General Assembly repeatedly asked Sewall's advice on ministerial candidates for vacant pulpits and on missionary work among the Indians. Although not an original thinker, he published many sermons and helped compile the works of his predecessor at the Old South, Samuel Willard (q.v.), into the massive *Body of Divinity*. Sewall was well paid and popular with the members of his congregation; both his moderate New Light views during the Great Awakening and his New Eng. patriotism reflected their sentiments. Long after his death, the Old South Church was popularly known as "Dr. Sewall's Meeting House."

Critical Appraisal: Joseph Sewall's many published sermons reveal the attributes that made him one of the most beloved and respected ministers of his age. Perhaps more than any of his contemporaries, Sewall was able to adapt the basic tenets of seventeenth-century Puritanism to an increasingly sophisticated provincial audience. From his ordination in 1712 to his death in 1769, he preached the same familiar message: man was indelibly scarred by original sin, and only through the knowledge of Christ and through good works could he hope for salvation in eternity. In sermons to his Old South congregation, public lectures, and election, ordination, and funeral addresses, Sewall repeated this theme again and again. This message had been Cotton Mather's central doctrine, but perhaps because Sewall was not as gifted as Mather, he was able to avoid the controversies that so troubled his mentor. Sewall tackled a much narrower range of issues than Mather, but as his reputation demonstrated, he was far more effective in adapting his message to his audience.

Throughout his career, Sewall applied theological doctrine to concrete events that held the attention of New Englanders. For example, when he preached at the funerals of his fellow pastor Ebenezer Pemberton and the powerful magistrate Wait Winthrop, he reminded listeners that they too shared the fate of these great men. Sewall, unlike many of his clerical colleagues, used these occasions not to praise the ministry and magistracy, but to emphasize the common religious duties of all New Englanders. When a young Bostonian was killed in a duel in 1717, Sewall presented in *The Character and Blessedness of the Upright* a catalog of sins to avoid, addressing this sermon primarily to the impetuous youth of the town. When an earthquake shook New Eng. in 1727, he enjoined his audience in *The Duty of a People* to "Stand in awe, and Sin not." This sermon, one of the last truly effective jeremiads of the eighteenth century, went through two printings, an indication of the responsive chord that it struck.

The success of Sewall's preaching, however, resulted as much from its style as from its messages. Early in his career, he became known as the "weeping minister." Although Perry Miller may have been correct in asserting that this sentimentality would have made earlier Puritan preachers like Thomas Hooker (q.v.) retch, there seems little doubt that Sewall's listeners found it moving. Sewall described the evils of sin and the terrors of hell with an eloquence unsurpassed in New Eng. before Jonathan Edwards (q.v.). Yet even more striking were his descriptions of the everlasting life that awaited Christ's saints. In sermons like *The Certainty & Suddenness of Christ's Coming* and *The Character and Blessedness of the Upright*, he counseled not to fear death, for it was only a sleep that would end on the glorious morning of resurrection. Sewall's ability to present the grave as a pleasant repose from the toils of the world was remarkable, and this message of confidence and optimism helps explain the warmth with which his sermons were received.

A final characteristic of Sewall's writings that may account for their popularity is his avoidance of many of the secular themes that consumed many of his fellow ministers. Unlike most of his peers, Sewall did not embroil himself in the clerical campaign for higher salaries and more respect for the pulpit. Even in 1721, when the Boston ministerial community rallied behind Cotton Mather's advocacy of smallpox inoculation, Sewall retained his aloofness and, as it turned out, his popularity as well. Sewall's social standing and personal wealth made issues like salary and prestige less meaningful to him than to his struggling colleagues in the country towns outside of Boston. He had the luxury to devote his preaching to the issues of life, death, and eternity. Yet as his success and the events of the Great Awakening demonstrated, his was a model most New Eng. ministers could have profitably emulated.

Suggested Readings: CCNE; Sibley-Shipton (V, 376-393); Sprague (I, 278-280). *See also* Perry Miller, *The New England Mind: From Colony to Province* (1953), pp. 270, 413, 482-484; Samuel Sewall, *The Diary of Samuel Sewall*, ed. Mark Van Doren (1927).

James W. Schmotter
Cornell University

SAMUEL SEWALL (1652-1730)

Works: *The Revolution in New-England Justified* (with Edward Rawson; 1691); *Mrs. Judith Hull* (1695); *Phaenomena Quaedam Apocalyptica* (1697); *Upon Mr. Samuel Willard* (1700); *The Selling of Joseph* (1700); *Talitha Cumi, or an Invitation to Women to Look after Their Inheritance in the Heavenly Mansions* (1711?; no extant copy except portions retained in the diary); *Proposals Touching the Accomplishment of Prophesies* (1713); *A Small Vial of Tears* (1717); *Early Piety* (1718; 4th ed., 1741); *Upon the Drying Up That Ancient River, the Merry-mak* (1721); *A Memorial Relating to the Kennebec Indians* (1721); *In Remembrance of Mr. Samuel Hirst* (1727); *The Diary of Samuel Sewall, 1673-1729* (1878-1882); *Letter-Book of Samuel Sewall*, 2 vols., CMHS, 50, 52 (1886, 1888).

Biography: Born at Bishop Stoke, Hampshire, Eng., on Mar. 28, 1652, Sewall immigrated to Mass. nine years later and at age 15 entered Harvard College. Like Michael Wigglesworth (q.v.) two decades earlier, Sewall began his diary shortly after becoming a tutor and fellow of the college. His marriage to Hannah Hull in 1675/6 greatly enhanced Sewall's fortune, and he followed his father-in-law John Hull (q.v.) into a career as a successful merchant. He also served the colony as overseer of the printing press, magistrate of the General Court, and captain of artillery, resigning the latter position in protest against marching under the cross of St. George. In 1692 Sewall was appointed as a justice for a Special Court of Oyer and Terminer to try those accused of witchcraft in Salem; twenty-one people were executed. Four years later, believing that personal tragedies were a divine judgment against his role in the trials, he publicly acknowledged his blame. Sewall went on to become a judge and later chief justice of the Superior Court, serving until 1728; he died in Boston Jan. 1, 1729/30.

Critical Appraisal: Samuel Sewall's importance in American literature depends primarily on his diary, which has been widely praised and even compared to that of Samuel Pepys. However, Sewall's style is undistinguished, and he rarely sustained a focus on subject or theme. Most entries are relatively brief, and content may shift abruptly from sentence to sentence. There are some exceptions, such as the often anthologized entries covering Sewall's courtship period following the death of his first wife in 1717.

For the real value of the diary, and it is substantial, one must not look for a smoothly written narrative, but rather for a portrait that must be pieced from entries spanning well over a half a century. It is the cumulative effect of these fragments that allows the reader to perceive the gradual transition of New Eng. from a colony whose laws, social organization, and activities focused on the religious mission of the Puritans to a large, well-established, and complex society with a multitude of secular concerns and a well-developed regional character. Sewall's prominent position in Boston society and his active and educated interest in his world made him an excellent observer. Sewall's own character developed along with that of New Eng., and although he never deserted the deep religious sentiment that early in his life had led him to consider a career in the ministry, the diary shows him gradually adapting to the secular life he chose.

Although it records behavior that must have come through intense introspection, the diary has little of the soul searching that marks Puritan spiritual journals. Sewall tried to record what he believed was fact and objective experience. Such experience seems to have been entered with little selection. There is no pronounced emphasis on events of major historical, social, or even personal importance. These occurrences were recorded, but even events of great moment get little more attention than comments on weather, deaths, or commercial transactions. Indeed, the diary makes relatively little mention of the Salem witchcraft trials that proved so personally as well as historically important. On the pages of the diary, Sewall meets, deals, and dines with many of the most prominent people of New Eng. They and their actions are presented to the reader not as special or unusual, but rather as the ordinary characters of a world that Sewall preserved in his diary.

Sewall also wrote poetry, and some of his verses were preserved on the pages of his diary and commonplace book. Others were published as broadsides during Sewall's lifetime. Individual poems and lines show wit and skill with language; but, at best, Sewall can only be considered a minor poet. More important than Sewall's poetry is his *The Selling of Joseph*, the first antislavery tract published in New Eng. Sewall relied on biblical evidence, especially comparisons influenced by Puritan typology. Considering the injustice committed when Joseph's brothers sold him into slavery, Sewall denied anyone's right to convert a free man to property or to assert a "proportion between twenty pieces of silver and *liberty*." Sewall was eloquent in arguing that as blacks were "the sons and daughters of the first Adam, the brethren and sisters of the last Adam and the offspring of God, they ought to be treated with a respect agreeable." In tracing the inherent right of all men to freedom to their descent from the biblical Adam, Sewall was also alluding to a contemporary slave named Adam.

A large part of this effectively argued work was devoted to contradicting arguments that would continue to be used in the defense of slavery until emancipation: the biblical precedent for and origin of slavery in the practice of Abraham and the curse of Cham, enslavement as the lawful consequence of war, and benefits to those enslaved by exposure to Christianity. Sewall maintained that slavery not only corrupted the slaveholder, but also the culture in which it existed. If, as he had argued in his *Phaenomena Quaedam Apocalyptica*, New Eng. was to be the site for the New Jerusalem of biblical prophesies, slavery was an obstacle to the realization of the divine plan.

The *Phaenomena* is notable not only for its argument of the kind of theological speculation common in early New Eng., but also for its renewal of the earlier Puritan assertion of a special divinely ordained role for New Eng. By extension such arguments have contributed to the development of the belief in America's special mission in the world. In rhythmically invoking the beauty, power, and fruitfulness of nature in America to suggest the spiritual development of the people who would dwell there, Sewall prefigured similar sentiments from the American Transcendentalists over a century later. His writings not only provide the reader with important insights and information about the time in which they were written, but also help to reveal the early development of some of the most central themes of American literature and society.

Suggested Readings: DAB; FCNEV; LHUS; Sibley-Shipton (II, 345-364); T_1. *See also* N[athan]. H. Chamberlain, *Samuel Sewall and the World He Lived In* (1897); Richard Mott Gummere, "Byrd and Sewall, Two Colonial Classicists," PCSM, 42 (1953), 156-173; Steven E. Kagle, *American Diary Literature* (1979), pp. 147-153; Cotton Mather, *Late Memorable Providences Relating to Witchcrafts and Possessions* (1691); Perry Miller, *The New England Mind: From Colony to Province* (1953); Josephine K. Piercy, *Studies in Literary Types in Seventeenth-Century America, 1607-1710* (1939), pp. 78-82, 342-347; T. B. Strandness, *Samuel Sewall, A Puritan Portrait* (1967); Ola Elizabeth Winslow, *Samuel Sewall of Boston* (1964). Recent editions of Sewall's writings include Sidney Kaplan, ed., *The Selling of Joseph* (1969) and M. Halsey Thomas, ed., *The Diary* (1973).

Steven E. Kagle
Illinois State University

JOHN SHAW (1778-1809)

Works: John Elihu Hall, ed., *Poems by the Late Doctor John Shaw* (1810).
Biography: Born at Annapolis, Md., May 4, 1778, John Shaw graduated from St. John's College in Oct. 1796 with his close friend Francis Scott Key. Shaw remained to earn an M.A. and then studied medicine under Dr. John Thomas Shaaff until 1798, when he left for Algiers as surgeon on the *Sophia*. He traveled widely in the Near East and Mediterranean, serving as William Eaton's secretary at Tunis for a few months, visiting London briefly on a diplomatic mission, and finally returning to Annapolis for a year in the summer of 1800. In

1801 he left America again to continue his medical studies at Edinburgh. He left Scot. in 1803 with Thomas Douglas, earl of Selkirk, for St. John's Island in Can., traveling as well in northern N.Y. and as far west as Detroit before returning to Annapolis in early 1805. There for the next two years, he practiced medicine with Dr. Shaaff. In Feb. 1807 he married Jane Selby and moved for financial reasons to Baltimore, where in 1808 he was chosen professor of chemistry in the College of Medicine of Maryland, forerunner of the University of Maryland, whose charter he had helped to gain. In the same year, he contracted tuberculosis; in Nov. he sailed from Baltimore to Charleston, S.C., for his health, later taking a ship to the Bahamas for the same reason. He died en route on Jan. 10, 1809.

Critical Appraisal: Although anthologized as a poet in the nineteenth century, John Shaw's scientific and literary skills also combine effectively in his detailed journal and letters, excerpted at length in John Hall's "Biographical Sketch." His poetic strengths here appear in his anecdotal travel descriptions, which he tempered with frequent humor and the naturalist's accurate observation. His prose also reveals the healthy skepticism (as he demythologized Scylla and Charybdis, for example), intense patriotism, and melancholy moralism that characterize his poems. His familiarity with Classical and modern languages, including several American Indian tongues, gained at college and through his travels, also colors his verse, both his specific, often free translations from Greek, Latin, Italian, Portuguese, and Arabic and his English compositions, which are frequently Latinate and academic in style and subject.

The body of Shaw's poetry is uneven and often forced and sentimental. "The Voice of Freedom: An Ode" is a youthful effort in which a passionate speaker extols in rigid rhyme and meter the "Freedom nature gave to all" that "All an equal share should have." Still, even his early verse is redeemed by moments of sharp observation, especially of nature, as when in "Spring," a college exercise, he noted the flight of swallows: "In mazy circles, now upon the stream / They skim and lightly brush the curling wave." Generally, however, his poems are emotional and competent, but dull.

Shaw's persistent melancholy and conventional erudition on subjects such as love, flowers, the muse, death, the seasons, forests, birds, and crickets do not finally promise more than Shaw achieved in his short life; his "Farewel to Edinburgh" (c. 1803) is typical: "Sorrow distils the big tear from my eye." Yet his less egocentric and more original verse suggests his entertaining and individual personality. His "songs" ("The Sailor's Departure," "A Sleighing Song," and his translation of four "Moorish" songs, for example) reveal a direct simplicity through concrete images. His few poems about native American material (especially "The Captive" and a late, untitled composition) are strong, original efforts in which he chronicled the white man's invasion of the Indian's wilderness; the last, an ode to Indian courage and pride, is forceful as Shaw addressed a young brave and emphasized "the tension of virtue that nerved your breast." Shaw was also capable of raw humor, and the characteristic "President Whiskey," in which he developed a debate over the choice of a congressional drink through "patriot Von Stagger" and his friends, is perhaps, as John Ruhräh noted, "the gem of the collection."

Suggested Readings: DAB. *See also* Eugene Fauntleroy Cordell, *Historical Sketch of the University of Maryland School of Medicine* (1891); E. A. and G.L. Duyckinck, *Cyclopaedia of American Literature* (1875), I, 684; John Elihu Hall, "Biographical Sketch" in *Poems of the Late Doctor John Shaw* (1810), pp. 1-103; Howard A. Kelly and Walter A. Burrage, eds., *American Medical Biographies* (1920), p. 1041; John Ruhräh, "John Shaw: A Medical Poet of Maryland," AMH, 3 (1921), 252-262.

Caroline Zilboorg
Lake Erie College

JEREMIAH SHEPARD (1648-1720)

Works: *An Ephemeris of the Celestial Motions* (1672); *Early Offerings Best Accepted* (1712); *A Sort of Believers Never Saved...The Substance of Two Sermons* (1712); *God's Conduct of His Church Through the Wilderness* (1715). "To the Reverend Mr. William Hubbard" (possible attribution; 1677).

Biography: Jeremiah Shepard was the youngest son of Thomas Shepard (q.v.) and was born in Cambridge on Aug. 11, 1648, just a year before his father's death. His stepfather Jonathan Mitchel (q.v.) was his father's successor in the Cambridge pulpit, and his older half-brothers Thomas Shepard (q.v.) and Samuel Shepard became well-known Mass. clergymen. In spite of this background, Jeremiah did not move smoothly into the ministry, and his early adult years were filled with controversy. Graduating from Harvard in 1669, trained for the ministry, he was not ordained until 1680—in fact, until then he neither joined a church nor made a public profession of faith. He preached irregularly until 1673, when he was called to Rowley (where Samuel Shepard had preached until his death in 1668). Soon a faction in the congregation opposed him, and when the question of his permanent settlement came up three years later, his opponents argued that he was disqualified by his lack of church membership. A town meeting voted to withhold the salary of fifty pounds voted earlier; Shepard went to court and eventually accepted a compromise settlement of twenty pounds. He moved to Chebacco parish (now Essex), where the issue of his being a nonmember and nonprofessor again arose and ended his tenure.

Shepard then moved to Lynn, was ordained in Oct. 1680, and continued successfully in the Lynn pulpit for over forty years until the end of his life. Nothing in his later career or surviving writings provides an explanation for those troubled early years, unless it is his temperament, described by some as impetuous and impatient. His customary manner was solemn, and his view of human nature melancholy; he was not fond of music in church and favored long sermons. Consistent with his orthodox Puritan theology was his intolerance of opposition whether religious or secular: he struggled vigorously against the "spiritual plague" of Quakerism, viewed the Indians as "savage tawnies" and "cursed devil worshipers" whom the Lord did well to sweep away by smallpox, and played a passionate role in the dispute with Governor Edmund Andros. He apparently enjoyed great respect and popularity in Lynn and in 1689 was elected representative to the General Court, perhaps the only New Eng. clergyman in this period so honored.

During the 1692 witchcraft scare, seven members of Shepard's congregation were imprisoned, and he himself was "cried out against" as a wizard, a charge that found no credence. Indeed, its unlikelihood, especially to Judge Samuel Sewall (q.v.), whose family was connected to Shepard's by marriage and whose diary contains a dozen references to Shepard, may have helped dispel the general hysteria. In 1700 Shepard was conspicuous among the ministers opposing the liberal views of Solomon Stoddard (q.v.). In 1715 he was invited to deliver the annual election sermon. Shepard married Mary Wainwright, the daughter of an Ipswich merchant, and the couple had nine children, four of whom survived them. He died Jun. 2, 1720.

Critical Appraisal: Jeremiah Shepard's surviving published work consists of several sermons and a brief lunar almanac for 1672; he may also have written the poem signed "J. S." in William Hubbard's (q.v.) *Indian Wars*. Attribution by John Mangan, John Sibley, and others, of these seventeen heroic couplets of standard prefatory praise to Shepard is based primarily on the known association of Shepard and Hubbard. They have also been attributed to John Sherman of Watertown.

Shepard's sermons are in the Puritan mainstream, with the traditional doctrine, themes, and spirit. His most engaging is his longest work, *Early Offerings Best Accepted* (1712), addressed to young people and urging early piety. Familiar Calvinist doctrine is emphasized in *A Sort of Believers Never Saved* (1712), in which Shepard is at pains to describe kinds of the faithful who are doomed. Faith based only on delight in hearing the word, without a solid foundation in humiliation, is not "saving faith," nor is "a bare historical faith," when the mind assents "without any work upon the Heart." This sermon, in style and content, resembles closely those of his famous father and shares some of their eloquence.

In 1715 Shepard delivered his most important sermon, *God's Conduct of His Church*, a good example of an early eighteenth-century New Eng. election sermon. He analyzed the condition of God's chosen people and drew the inevitable analogy with "Israel of Old," employing the familiar image of the protective wall or "hedge of Government" set about the people. He found God's purpose from the creation of the world to the tending of his people in "this American Desert, this vast howling Wilderness," to be making "himself an Everlasting Name." Shepard stressed the blessings of a stable civil order, free from a despotic or arbitrary government, as well as those of the true religion and material prosperity. He exhorted New Eng. not to provoke God to a withdrawal of these favors by ingratitude and sin. Notably, however, this sermon carries little of the jeremiad tone. The warning section is brief, the catalog of sins sketchy; no fierce denunciation of declension or concrete political criticism is to be found.

Suggested Readings: CCNE; FCNEV; Sibley-Shipton (II, 267-276). *See also* Alonzo Lewis and James R. Newhall, *History of Lynn* (1865), pp. 283-296, 314-318; John L. Mangan, *Life of Reverend Jeremiah Shepard* (1905); James R. Newhall, *Centennial Memorial of Lynn* (1876), pp. 45-46; George L. Shepard, *A Genealogical History of William Shepard* (1886), pp. 34-42.

Doris Grieser Marquit
University of Minnesota

THOMAS SHEPARD (1605-1649)

Works: *The Sincere Convert* (1641); *New Englands Lamentation for Old Englands Present Errours* (1645); *The Sound Believer* (1645); *Certain Select Cases Resolved* (1648); *The Clear Sun Shine of the Gospel Breaking Forth upon the Indians of New England* (1648); *Theses Sabbaticae* (1649); *A Short Catechism* (1654); *First Principles of the Oracles of God* (1655); *Parable of the Ten Virgins* (1660); *Church Membership of Children* (1663); *Wine for Gospel Wantons* (1668); *Three Valuable Pieces* (including *Select Cases, First Principles,* and *A Private Diary* [1747]; only selections were published, the diary not being published in full until Michael McGiffert, ed., *Journal* in *God's Plot,* 1972); *Autobiography* (1832).

Biography: Thomas Shepard was born on the day of the Gunpowder Plot, Nov. 5, 1605, in Towcester, Eng. His childhood was particularly unsettled, being orphaned by the age of 10, and having been moved from one relative to another since the age of 3. At 15 he was admitted pensioner at Emmanuel College, Cambridge, receiving the B.A. in 1623/24 and the M.A. in 1627. In the same year, he was ordained deacon and then priest. Three years later, he was silenced by Archbishop William Laud. He became tutor and chaplain to the family of Sir Richard Darley, at whose estate he met and married Margaret Tauteville. After an abortive first attempt, he sailed for the New World in 1635, reaching Boston on Oct. 3. Shepard was soon chosen pastor of the church at Newtown, subsequently known as Cambridge, from where he became active in the major religious issues of the day, playing a central role in the forging of New Eng. Congregationalism. His interest in education and the general esteem in which he was held were largely responsible for the locating of Harvard in Cambridge. After the death of his first wife, he married Joanna Hooker in 1637; in 1647, having been widowed a second time, he took Margaret Boradel as his third wife. Shepard died on Aug. 25, 1649.

Critical Appraisal: It is no surprise that Thomas Shepard's writings were among the most widely read of any seventeenth-century Puritan divine, for his tone is generally calm and persuasive, while his language is animated and vital.

Many of his works employ the strategy of question and answer, which sometimes most notably conveys a sense of Shepard's authority, and at other times, it enlivens a work with the human interest of distinctive personalities. The rationalistic side of the man reveals itself in the clearly catechetical works, such as *The First Principles of the Oracles of God* and *A Short Catechism*, but also in the sermons and treatises, which include lengthy passages of "objections" and their "answers." Shepard's sense of the importance of direct question can be seen in his account of the conversion of the Indians, *The Clear Sun Shine of the Gospel Breaking Forth upon the Indians of New England*, which reports, often in quotation marks, specific questions asked by Indians. In "The Soul's Invitation unto Jesus Christ," objections are consistently offered in the voice of a woman; thus even in the most formal, apparently most logical of rhetorical strategies, Shepard achieved human warmth and drama.

Although sometimes criticized as legalistic, Shepard was nevertheless revered as an especially penetrating preacher. In his *Wonder-Working Providence*, Edward Johnson (q.v.) referred to Shepard as a "soul-ravishing Minister," and Cotton Mather (q.v.), who titled his biography of Shepard in *Magnalia* "Pastor Evangelicus," wrote that Shepard was "as great a Converter of Souls, as has ordinarily been known in our Days." This man, apparently small and consistently weak, drove home his sermons not in the thundering voice of hell-fire, but through the peculiar, quiet penetration of a language informed with imagery from daily life, resonant with the cadences of common speech, and energized by a string of rhetorical devices ranging from balance and parallelism to the witty aphorism that remains in the hearer's head long after the sermon is over: for example, urging the insufficiency of Bible reading, Shepard warned, "Jesus Christ is not got with a wet finger."

The Sincere Convert, one of Shepard's best-known sermons, is remarkable for its vivid imagery: sinful men are "filthy toads"; man is a "snake," a "dog"; sins are "like plague-sores [which] run on thee." Analogies move from simple similes ("many have fallen from the glorious Gospell to Popery, as fast as leaves fall in *Autumn*") to more complex forms of argumentation ("If we have been long in hewing a block, and we can make no meet vessell of it, put it to no good use for our selves, we cast it into the fire: God heweth thee by *Sermons, sickness, losses,* and *crosses, sudden death, mercies,* and *miseries,* yet nothing makes thee better; what should God doe with thee, but cast thee hence?"). Although the sermon is perhaps not representative of Shepard's work because of its insistence on the terrors of judgment, in its employment of imagery from the near and common, it exemplifies the rich imagination and vivacity of image that characterize Shepard's style throughout the canon. Testifying to the impact of his ocean-crossing and seaboard living, Shepard is especially fond of maritime imagery, but imagery of the home and its domestic situations, the relationships between husband and wife and between parents and children, becomes more frequent as Shepard turns from sermons of fear to sermons emphasizing Christ's love for man.

Although the Shepard canon warrants sustained study for its shifts in image clusters and modulation of tone (sometimes calm, sometimes rendered excited through dialog, exclamation, and quick question), a major theme running throughout the canon and unifying it is the concern with hypocrisy. In *The Parable of the Ten Virgins*, for example, Shepard clearly acknowledged that the church has hypocrites as well as true saints, and although it may be difficult to distinguish them on the basis of externals (they are all virgins, after all), for Shepard there was a wide gap separating the "sincere Christian" and the "most refined hypocrite." Even the titles of his major works evidence Shepard's interest in finding true faith: *The Sincere Convert, The Sound Believer, Wine for Gospel Wantons*. Both the meditations of his *Journal* and the *Autobiography* testify to the haunting personal insecurity that plagued even this most devout of Puritans and caused him to lean toward an experiential form of religion.

The *Autobiography* is a consummate work of literary art, carefully structured to move from the personal and local to the public and communal unit as it narrates the journey from birth to death and gradually transforms the individual to an almost generic figure. Thus biography moves into history, and Shepard reveals his genuine love for New Eng. As he incorporates his particular cultural moment and eternal vision, they fuse into a unique signature that identifies a literary talent and a compelling mind that continues to influence Americans long after Jonathan Edwards (q.v.) and the writers of the American Renaissance.

Suggested Readings: CCNE; DAB; DNB; FCNEV; LHUS; Sprague (I, 59-68); T_1. *See also* John A. Albro, *The Life of Thomas Shepard* (1847); Michael McGiffert, Introduction, *God's Plot* (1972), pp. 3-32; Cotton Mather, *Magnalia Christi Americana* (1702), III, 84-93; Samuel Eliot Morison, *Builders of the Bay Colony* (1930), pp. 105-134; Kenneth B. Murdock, *Literature and Theology in Colonial New England* (1949), pp. 111-116; Daniel B. Shea, Jr, *Spiritual Autobiography in Early America* (1968).

Paula K. White
Upsala College

THOMAS SHEPARD (1635-1677)

Works: *An Almanack for...1656* (1656); *Eye-Salve* (1673).

Biography: Thomas Shepard was born to Thomas Shepard (q.v.) and Margaret (Touteville) Shepard in London on Apr. 5, 1635. Perhaps no other child of the period has so complete a record of the dangers threatening him before and after his birth, for these problems are recorded in the introductory material of his father's *Autobiography*. In 1653 Shepard was graduated from Harvard College and in 1654 chosen fellow of the college; his interest in the college continued virtually until his death. In 1656 he married the daughter of William Tyng. Having been ordained teacher of the church in Charlestown, Mass., on Apr. 13, 1659, he was instrumental in maintaining a conservative stand against the Anabaptists, and his election sermon delivered in Boston in 1672, *Eye-Salve*, documents his concern that toleration could weaken the church. He died on Dec. 22, 1677, having contracted smallpox from a sick parishioner who had requested a visitation.

Critical Appraisal: Thomas Shepard's *Eye-Salve* was delivered in Boston as the Election Day sermon, May 15, 1672. As such, its very existence testifies to the prominence of the preacher not only in Charlestown but throughout the Massachusetts Bay colony. In structure and subject matter, the sermon follows the pattern that had become established by 1672, the full title itself bearing witness to the conventional themes of apostasy, respect for the past, and exhortation for the future, which characterize the sermons given on Election Days. In contrast to the more individualistic slant of most sermons, Election Day sermons looked to the community as a whole and sought to assess its civic mission.

In *Eye-Salve* Shepard interpreted for church and commonwealth the meaning of the present moment in divine history. His biblical text, Jeremiah 2:31, is one of prophetic expostulation to a backslidden people. By rehearsing the usual figural applications of Israel's wilderness testing and recalling the necessity of the Josian reforms as narrated in II Kings, Shepard comforted, warned, and threatened his listeners with a thoroughly developed Deuteronomic reading of the New Eng. experience. The nation has two choices: it may continue to obey God and so be blessed or it may disobey and bring itself to disaster and ruin. As a chosen nation, the commonwealth has already experienced divine election; now its epigonic leaders, both ministry and magistracy, must bring this Israel *redivivus* to its promised glory. God has established, provided for, directed, delivered, protected, and prospered the nation. In turn, the nation must perceive its future with special clarity and build the city, the New Jerusalem, the foundations of which have already been laid.

The sermon thus looks alternately back with awe upon the achievement of the fathers and ahead with anxiety to a future burdened with the possibility of failure. In remembering the first generation of leaders, Shepard recalled the Lord's covenant with his New Eng. Christians and at times shared his own personal memories of the household of faith, especially its concord: "when I was a Child [I] have observed in my Fathers house: if there hapned to be some misunderstanding at any time, it was reasoned out placidly, and still Ministerial communion was maintained; and these things are known unto hundreds yet living that do remember the Ministers meetings." The collective achievement of men like John Cotton (q.v.), Thomas Hooker (q.v.), John Norton (q.v.), and his own father is celebrated with gratitude: "O call to remembrance those times, you of the old Generation; how notably did the Lord, in the way of *Council of Churches*, by that *famous Synod then met at Cambridge* [in 1637], free this wilderness from being *a land of darkness* by seasonably dispelling that hellish damp, and mist of errours and heresy!" Throughout the sermon, Shepard narrated the communal history of his people with all of the evocative grandeur the Lord's gracious covenant requires. More importantly, however, the sermon voices a fundamental fear for a loss of vision. As it attempts to preserve the integrity and energy of the heroic past, its warning and exhortations betray a pervasive uncertainty. Shepard feared that the wilderness planting might soon become a desert again. Above all else, he urged that laws of one generation should not be rewritten by the next. The whole of God's enterprise is at stake, and failure is a real possibility. Thus although *Eye-Salve* is divided conventionally into three parts (specific textual explication, general doctrinal clarification, and application), almost three-quarters of its text is devoted to "uses." The sermon remembers much, but it exhorts much more. Urging a social program for family, school, and nation, Shepard sought to institutionalize the experience of the fathers. It is absolutely requisite, he believed, that ministry and magistracy work together for the suppression of dissent lest a spirit of toleration eviscerate the New Eng. way. As New Eng. Christians experience the loss of their primal dream, Shepard, a latter-day Jeremiah, warned them of apostasy and called for their return to the original errand in the wilderness.

He did so in a style that is rapid and energetic, sparked by word play, emphatic repetition, and strong images. Shepard spoke in the authoritative tone of the plain style, where life's complexities are reduced to binary opposites: for example, one lives in either a garden or a wilderness; one is enveloped in either light or darkness; one remembers the terms of the covenant or one ignores them. Such Ramistic thinking leads to the hyperbolic rhetoric that punctuates the sermon, as in the following example: "And are there any that think to mend themselves by going back to *Leek and Onions*? yea to that very *vomit of the Dragon*, to lick up that vomit which he hath formerly cast out of his mouth, whereby to cause this poor Woman in this Wilderness also...to be carried away therewith even as by a flood?"

The image patterns are of course primarily biblical, but also full of the bold earthiness of rigorous seventeenth-century life (nautical and agricultural images, for example). Yet imagery is not pervasive in the sermon. Indeed, the informing symbol, eye-salve, is not overtly developed, but hidden in metaphors of sight and illumination. The Puritan audience, however, would have been well trained in the ramifications of sight imagery, attuned to the immediate moral implications of light and darkness. Being able to see the apostasy around them argued a moral condition that, if acted upon immediately, could prevent an abortion of the Puritan mission. The sermon itself was to be the salve for bad sight.

The central symbol, eye-salve, was especially sensitive to Shepard, and that Shepard employed it here signals the tremendous personal significance the sermon held for him. In the section of the *Autobiography* devoted to the son, Thomas Shepard told of the disease that afflicted the eyes of this younger Thomas Shepard and threatened him with blindness. Shepard wrote that it was by an eye-salve, "the oil of white pasec, [that] the Lord restored [his] child to his sight suddenly and strangely." By entitling his most prestigious sermon "Eye-Salve," Shepard praised God, thanked him for saving his eyes and his life, and acknowledged his obligation "to do the Lord's work," as his father had written many years before.

Eye-Salve is an impressive example of the election-sermon genre and a good piece to study as a gauge of the times. A comparison with the extant skeleton of his father's Election Day sermon of 1638 reveals that in the thirty-four years separating the two sermons, Puritans had become more aware of their place in history as situated between a glorious past and an uncertain future, more obsessed with the immediacy and urgency of reformation, and more constrained to a sense of form in the genre of the sermon itself. A sermon that more easily invites comparison is Samuel Danforth's (q.v.) Election Day sermon of 1670, *A Brief Recognition of New England's Errand into the Wilderness*. The wilderness theme is invoked in both Danforth's and Shepard's sermons to mark the extent of God's favor to New Eng. Yet interestingly, even though the wilderness would not seem so crucial to Shepard as to Danforth, Shepard's explication is the more detailed and the more rigorous. It indicates the greater intensity in Shepard, both in method and in attitude. Shepard explicated his text word for word, not, as did Danforth, question by question. Shepard's tone is generally more strident, more urgent than Danforth's. In keeping with this tone, Shepard offered more specific recommendations to arrest the backsliding and reestablish New Eng. as a chosen nation working out its God-given potential. Shepard's sermon, in a few short pages, combines the personal and communal respect for the past and vision for the future that characterizes Puritan writing, and it shows the energy and intellectual vivacity of one of the best minds of the period. It is a sermon worthy of one of the leading families of early New Eng.

Suggested Readings: CCNE; FCNEV; Sibley-Shipton (I, 327-335). *See also* Cotton Mather, *Magnalia Christi Americana* (1702), Book IV, pp. 189-191; Urian Oakes, "An Elegy upon the Death of Mr. Thomas Shepard" in *The Puritans*, ed. Perry Miller and Thomas H. Johnson (1963), pp. 641-650; A. W. Plumstead, "An Introductory Essay," *The Wall and the Garden* (1968), pp. 3-37; Thomas Shepard, *God's Plot* (1972), pp. 33-37.

H. Andrew Harnack
Eastern Kentucky University
Paula K. White
Upsala College

HENRY SHERBURNE (1741-1825)

Works: *The Oriental Philanthropist, or True Republican* (1800).

Biography: Although *The Oriental Philanthropist* is not mentioned in James McLachlan's *Princetonians 1748-1768*, it is probably the work of the Henry Sherburne who graduated from the College of New Jersey (now Princeton University) in 1759. Sherburne was born in Portsmouth, N.H., in Sep. 1741, the son of a merchant, judge, selectman, and member of the Provincial Council and the Albany Congress. While the family was Anglican, Henry's father was a friend of various revivalists and religious dissenters. One of thirteen children, he entered college on May 20, 1756. His main distinction as a student seems to have been his propensity for borrowing and falling into debt. When he graduated, he still owed the school forty pounds that, according to available records, was never repaid.

Returning to Portsmouth, Sherburne seems to have entered his father's business. Taking the patriots' side in the Revolution, he signed the N.H. association against the importation of British goods in 1776, and a year later joined in a call to expel all Loyalists from the state. In 1780 he was a prominent member of a Portsmouth "Committee for Supplying Soldier Familys."

Little is known of Sherburne's business activities, but apparently he continued to fall into debt until eventually his business failed. Although he petitioned the N.H. legislature for relief in 1790, he probably remained in debt until he died in 1825. Published in 1800, *The Oriental Philanthropist* is Sherburne's only known work, possibly written during the leisure afforded him by his failure in business, and no doubt with the hope that he would gain some profit by it.

Critical Appraisal: *The Oriental Philanthropist* is prefaced with a typical eighteenth-century apology for the use of the fable or fictitious tale, which "is agreeable to convey the most salutary truths that they may be effectively impressed upon the minds of those readers who are apt to be disgusted with dry treaties of morality." Sherburne continued, "let it still be permitted to lend its benevolent aid for our entertainment and instruction, till the expected aera [sic] fully arrive when genuine truth shall shine forth with claims superceding the necessity of the fascinating blandishments of fictitious tales."

Although in a sense *The Oriental Philanthropist* is a typical Oriental fairy tale, it is in many respects more utopian. The hero, the Chinese Prince Nytan, is banished by wicked usurpers and is eventually rescued from prison by Ravenzar, a genie, and taken to the Island of Ravenzar. Its inhabitants spend much time in discussing issues such as love, benevolent rule, and the banishment of slavery and tyranny. Serving as an ambassador to other lands, Nytan attempts to convince them that they should establish a benevolent government like that of the Island of Ravenzar. The moralizing of the novel is clearly set within the Christian context, as is apparent in Sherburne's poetic headings for the novel's books:

> What a rich sample of those happy times,
> Bards erst did sing, in sweetly flowing strains!
> Here I've a foretaste of the glory-bliss,
> Which Deity descends to pour on all his works!
> The proud shall cease the world to rule; No slave
> Shall bend low cringing at a tyrant's feet;
> No hostile beast, no murderous savage roam;
> Blest harmony prevail, and earth eternal bloom! (Book XII)

Not only is the message of the story Christian, but it is also suggests that America is the place where such a utopian society is possible. This is evident when Sherburne opens his novel with an address to the "Happy American States so richly adorned with sons and daughters of refined genius and exalted virtue" and closes with a lengthy passage in which he expressed the hope that Columbia's "defensive walls that inclose it around, remain solid and impregnable to every inimical assault!"

Although the story of *The Philanthropist* is interesting, many portions of the book become tedious as the characters carry on lengthy discourses about government, racial prejudice, slavery, and other issues. The book is highly moralistic and the fairy-tale approach serves as a thin mask for its didactic purpose. Nevertheless, Sherburne's novel should interest the student of issues such as utopian literature in America, slavery, and attitudes toward institutions such as government, marriage, and economics.

Suggested Readings: P. *See also* Herbert Ross Brown, *The Sentimental Novel in America, 1789-1860* (1940), pp. 146-147, 149-150; Henri Petter, *The Early American Novel* (1971), pp. 151-152.

Robert L. Mc Carron
Bryan College

SAMUEL SHERWOOD (1730-1783)

Works: *A Sermon, Containing Scriptural Instructions to Civil Rulers* (1774); *The Church's Flight into the Wilderness* (1776).

Biography: Born in Green's Farms (now Westport), Conn., in 1730, Samuel Sherwood was the second son of Capt. and Deacon Samuel Sherwood. His mother, Jane, was the sister of the Rev. Aaron Burr (q.v.). The young Sherwood graduated from Yale in 1749 and went to Newark as a tutor in the College of New Jersey (now Princeton University), of which his uncle was then president; there he completed his theological studies, was licensed to preach in 1751 by the Fairfield West Association, and served as a supply minister in various pulpits. On the Fourth of July 1757, he was called to settle in the small, newly organized town of Norfield (now Weston), Conn. He was to serve as minister there until his death in 1783 at the age of 54. He was survived by his wife, Rachel Hyde, whom he had married in 1754. Of their several children, one, Samuel Burr Sherwood, was to become a member of Congress.

Critical Appraisal: Samuel Sherwood's sermon on *The Church's Flight into the Wilderness* was delivered in Jan. 1776. In this address, Sherwood employed biblical exegesis to encourage the citizens of Norfield to support the Revolution against G.B. Sherwood's argument is based upon a section of the Bible that was especially important for Protestants in colonial America, the Book of Revelation. Reflecting the popular belief that the New World settlement enjoyed a special place in the providential plan of God, Sherwood explicated his text to reveal the struggle between Eng. and the American colonies prefigured:

he equated the conflict spoken of in verse seventeen with "the present war that is carrying on with such. . .fury against us." He concluded his address on a note of hope and encouragement, insisting that New Eng. enjoys a special favor in the eyes of God, that "God Almighty. . .is on our side." He pointed to the recent destruction of a large number of English ships and men as proof of God's judgment upon Eng.'s "wicked undertaking." Throughout his sermon, Sherwood was at pains to identify the British monarchy and its "tyrannical designs" upon the innocent and unoffending colonies with "papal conspiracy," apparently tapping the large reservoirs of anti-Catholic prejudice that had been instilled for generations in the New World Protestants. Thus his sermon can be seen as a reflection of both an American habit of mind and American conventions of pulpit rhetoric.

Suggested Readings: CCNE; Dexter (II, 219-221). *See also* Stephen J. Stein, "An Apocalyptic Rationale for the American Revolution," EAL, 9 (1975), 211-225; Ezra Stiles, *The Literary Diary of Ezra Stiles*, ed. Franklin B. Dexter (1901), III, 73; Ernest Lee Tuveson, *Redeemer Nation: The Idea of America's Millennial Role* (1968), Ch. 2.

Robert Colbert
Louisiana State University in Shreveport

JOSEPH SHIPPEN (1732-1810)

Works: "Winter" (1758); "The Glooms of Ligonier" (1760); "Military Letters. . .1756-1758," PMHB, 36 (1912), 367-378, 385-463.

Biography: Joseph Shippen was born in Philadelphia, Pa., in 1732, the eldest surviving son of Edward and Sarah Shippen. He graduated from Nassau Hall (Princeton) in 1753 and soon entered the Provincial Army, in which he served during the successful campaign to capture Fort Duquesne, and thereafter rose to the rank of colonel. During a 1760 business venture to engage in the sugar trade, Shippen accompanied John Allen and the painter Benjamin West on a voyage to It. Upon his return to Philadelphia in 1761, he was appointed secretary to the province. Four years later, he joined the American Philosophical Society, evidence of his interest in science. (Shippen likewise attended a gathering in 1769 at the observatory of David Rittenhouse to view Venus.) In 1768 he married Jane Galloway, who had earlier posed for a portrait by West. Because of failing health, Shippen and his family retired in 1773 to a country home in Lancaster County, where he was appointed judge for the county in 1789. He died in 1810.

Critical Appraisal: Most of the critical attention accorded Joseph Shippen has focused on the problems of attribution. Of the eight poems ascribed to Shippen, only two ("The Glooms of Ligonier" and "Lines Written in an Assembly") are definitely said to be his. Rufus Griswold and Moses Coit Tyler attributed "Upon Seeing the Portrait of Miss————[Jane Galloway] by Mr. West" to

Shippen, but George Everett Hastings in his 1926 biography of Francis Hopkinson (q.v.) assigned the poem to Hopkinson, and Theodore Hornberger suggested the possible authorship of William Hicks. Later scholars, such as Frank Mott, E. P. Richardson, and J. A. Leo Lemay followed Griswold and Tyler in ascribing the poem to Shippen.

A second problem of authorship concerns the series of five poems published in the *American Magazine* of 1758, all signed by "Annandius." Although Lemay questioned Shippen's authorship of two—"Wrote upon the Back of a Title Page of a Comedy" and "An Answer to an Enigma"—he did list Shippen as the probable author of "On the Glorious Victory. . . in Silesia," "Winter," and "Ode on the late Victory Obtained by the King of Prussia." Internal evidence suggests the likelihood of Shippen's authorship of all eight and similarly casts doubts on his claims as a major poet. The poems reveal a consistent regard for the sentiments of chivalry and the values of military life, as well as a taste for Classical allusions, flowery diction, and weak versification.

Shippen's two poems explicitly directed to Philadelphia's ladies of society, "Lines Written in an Assembly Hall" and "Upon Seeing a Portrait," show little originality or poetic gift: "In Sally Coxe's form and face / True index of her mind. / The most exact of human race / No one defect can find" ("Lines Written"). Shippen also seemed fond of "poetic" diction such as "languishingly sweet" and "nectareous sweets" ("Upon Seeing a Potrait"). In "The Glooms of Ligonier," he began with a description of "climes deform'd with frost severe" in order to contrast these with the charms of a lady "whose modest charms improve / The lightning of your eyes". . ."Of these possest, at fate we'll smile, / Defy the surly year, / Honour and love shall reconcile, / The Glooms of Ligonier."

Shippen also used the battlefield to praise the virtues of manly warfare, particularly as embodied in King Frederick of Prussia. "On the Heroic Victory Obtained by the Heroick King of Prussia Over the Imperial Army Near Newmark in Silesia, the 5th December 1757" compares Frederick to Hannibal, Caesar, Scipio, and Alexander and invokes the poetic muse of heroic verse:

> Such is th' event of human things,
> The fates of emp'rors and of kings,
> Death in the rear disasters brings
>   Dreadful to see!
> Such as great Pope or Homer sings,
>   Strains too high for me.

In the "Ode on the Late Victory Obtained by the King of Prussia," Shippen added traditional similes and Miltonic diction:

> As when a Lion rears his head,
> The forest wide is fill'd with dread,
>   Each creature seeks his den;
> As when Leviathan the great
> Displays himself in finny state,
>   He terrifies the main.

In his longest poem, "Winter," Shippen similarly began with stock images: "Fair autumn! now her pride is fled / And hoary winter shews his head. / The trees stand sad and leafles round / Fierce Eurus blows and storms abound." He went on to describe the effects of winter on the lives of sailors, merchants ("His ships detain'd, his purpose cross'd / And his dear hopes of gain are lost"), farmers ("the happy rustic clown"), the miller, country folk, and city gentlemen (in which section Shippen again lauded "great FRED'RICK'S noble feats"). He ended with a philosophic and traditional view of the cycles of the year: "Thus all is change we see on earth / 'T was so decreed since nature's birth."

Shippen was not a good poet. His rhyme and verse schemes are often clumsy, and his diction and images are seldom imaginative. He was, however, an important and respected figure in mideighteenth-century Pa., and his poems reflect many of the values of that society.

Suggested Readings: P; T$_1$. *See also* Thomas Balch, *Letters and Papers Relating Chiefly to the Provincial History of Pennsylvania with Some Notices of the Writers* (1855), pp. lxvii-lxxix; Theodore Hornberger, "Mr. Hicks of Philadelphia," PMHB, 53 (1929), 343-351; E. P. Richardson, "West's Voyage to Italy, 1760, and William Allen," PMHB, 102 (1978), 3-26.

Timothy K. Conley
Bradley University

WILLIAM SHIRLEY (1694-1771)

Works: *Journal of the Siege of Louisbourg* (1746); *A Letter from William Shirley* (1746); *Memoirs of the . . . War Between the English and French in North America* (1758); Charles H. Lincoln, ed., *Correspondence of William Shirley. . .1731-1760*, 2 vols. (1912).

Biography: Although several among his contemporaries accused him of being a social climber and a seeker after place, William Shirley became one of the most popular of colonial American governors. This colorful and dynamic man was born on Dec. 2, 1694, at Preston in Sussex, Eng., and received an A.B. at Pembroke College, Cambridge, in 1715. Before being called to the bar in 1720, he married Frances Barker, whose invaluable aid eventually would help him to achieve the governorship of Massachusetts Bay. Shirley practiced law for eleven years, but apparently in or about 1731 a financial crisis caused him to immigrate to America.

From 1731 until 1741, Shirley often distinguished himself in his Boston legal practice as a faithful supporter of imperial policies, contrary to the then governor, Jonathan Belcher. In 1736, with controversy growing over the alleged misuse of the king's woods in New Eng., Shirley's chance to apprise the mother country of his loyalty and Belcher's sympathies with the colonists arose. He stated his grievances in a letter that his wife, Frances, carried to Eng., where she lobbied steadily for some sixteen months before obtaining an appropriate hearing. After gaining appointments for her husband as collector of customs and as naval officer at Boston, she asked in 1739 that he be appointed governor. Although this request was denied, she persisted and was joined in Eng. by Shirley's friend Samuel Waldo, one of the wealthiest landowners of Mass. Through his influence, Frances's continued efforts, and Belcher's diminishing popularity, Shirley was finally commissioned governor on May 25, 1741.

Apparently Shirley's governorship was comparatively happy; he soon straightened out the currency problem left him by Belcher's mismanagement and, foreseeing the inevitability of new French hostilities, greatly strengthened the colony's defenses. As Thomas Hutchinson (q.v.) remarked, however, in his *History of...Massachusetts-Bay*, "the great event in this administration was the siege and reduction of Louisburgh." Shirley's role in this 1745 victory at Cape Breton, Nova Scotia, was decisive; according to his writings, he was the mastermind behind the operation.

Having traveled to Paris in 1749 to settle negotiations for peace, Shirley was appointed commander-in-chief of the Continental British forces shortly after his return to Boston in 1753. His campaigns during the Seven Years' War were not so spectacular as that of Louisbourg; indeed in 1756 Shirley was commanded to return to Eng. to answer for his conduct of the war. Shirley defended himself well, and his private secretary, William Alexander, drew up a tract, *The Conduct of Major Gen. Shirley* (1758), in which he argued convincingly that Shirley should "stand vindicated from all Imputations of having been any ways accessary to any of the Misfortunes, which have befallen his *Majesty's* Service in the Course of the present War." Although the charges were dropped for lack of evidence, Shirley had lost favor and was forced to accept the governorship of the Bahamas in 1761. In 1769, having retired from active political life, he returned to his home at Roxbury, Mass., where he died in Mar. 1771. As may be expected, Shirley did not observe the pre-Revolutionary unrest sympathetically. Samuel Eliot Morison has related the aging former governer's quip, when asked how he felt about the more vocal of the young "troublemakers": "Mr. Cushing I knew, and Mr. Hancock I knew; but where the devil this brace of Adamses came from, I know not."

Critical Appraisal: To be sure, William Shirley's contribution to colonial politics far out-distances his achievement in early American literature. His sizeable canon does, however, merit more attention than it has received. Shirley's *Journal of the Siege of Louisburgh* is a day-by-day account of this "great event," so vividly related that it resembles a film scenario. Shirley's flare for imaginative yet closely detailed description often shows to good advantage: "The transporting the cannon was with almost incredible Labour and Fatigue, for all the Roads over which they were drawn, saving here and there small Patches of rocky Hills, was a deep Morass, in which, while the cannon was upon the Wheels, they several Times sunk, so as to bury not only the Carriages, but the whole Body of the Cannon likewise."

The *Memoirs*, like Alexander's *Conduct of Major Gen. Shirley*, was written to garner favor at a time when Shirley's reputation was at its lowest point. These eighty pages detail the rationale the general employed in planning his strategy for the taking of Louisbourg. Avoiding the issue of his role in the Seven Years' War and concentrating instead on his immensely successful, earlier campaign, Shirley obviously hoped to shift attention from his alleged later shortcomings. A careful student of diplomacy, he soon showed that he grasped fully the strategic importance of keeping Nova Scotia English and not French. Nova Scotia gives the possessor "The Navigation of the Gulf of St. Lawrence" and hence easy access to the New Eng. colonies. Always assuming a third-person point of view to suggest a more convincing disinterestedness and credibility, "the Massachusetts Governor" or "Mr. Shirley" then gave a brief account of the history of the English-French controversy over these rights of navigation, as well as the dispute over fishing rights in the Newfoundland-Nova Scotia areas. Shirley then told how he anticipated before anyone else the probable renewed French aggression in the region, reconnoitered the French forces, and determined that they could be overcome by a colonial force. The details of the events leading up to and including the battle are a rehashing of his earlier pamphlets, the *Journal* and *A Letter from William Shirley*. But here Shirley calculatedly emphasized his role in shaping events rather than simply recording them.

Of more interest to students of literature are Shirley's letters. They display a self-conscious style that indicates that he probably intended them to be published (or at least to be publishable). He lived in an era that celebrated the epistolary style. His open "Letter to. . . Duke of Newcastle" published for the colonists as *A Letter from William Shirley* in 1746, exemplifies his cultivation of that epistolary style. Shirley's tone was formal and correct. His purpose was to give "a full Account of the Proceedings of the New England Forces raised under my Commission for the Reduction of Cape-Breton, during the late Siege of this Place, to the Time of its Surrender." At several points throughout the tract, the governor attempted to be painstakingly accurate, probably as a result of the period's rage for verisimilitude. At one point, he thus described the English ships as having moved "the Distance 5913 Feet from. . . an incessant Fire from the Enemy's Cannon and Mortars." Nor did he neglect to praise his men for their fortitude in the face of battle fatigue: "they went on cheerfully without being discouraged, or murmuring."

His *Correspondence* also includes responses and other missives to Shirley, so that the two-volume collection, covering the years 1731-1760, constitutes a veritable record of his administration as governor of Massachusetts Bay. Here as in the open "Letter," his tone was always correct and formal, and since most of these letters served as tools of government, Shirley's expertise in legal training assisted his most immediate purpose. Yet the governor's style sometimes reveals more than just a concern for the necessary. For example, at the outbreak of the Seven Years' War, Shirley sent a communiqué to the earl of Holderness (Jan. 7, 1754) requesting instructions for the presentation of a united front to the enemy. But rather than indicating that past experience had proved this unlikely, he wrote this inflated passage: "yet, I say, My Lord, there seems just reason to apprehend from past experience, that the want of such a settlement, and a method to enforce its taking effect, will be an obstacle to the carrying into execution any general plan for cementing an Union among His Majesty's subjects upon this continent, for the defence of His Majesty's territories committed to their trust." One must note the implicit ambiquity of the phrase "the defence of His Majesty's territories committed to their trust," for as early as 1754, what Shirley called the "king's trust" was already beginning to be thought of as the trust of those colonists who actually held and worked the land—hence a probable root of Shirley's incapacity to carry out royal commands more ably. But suffice it to say that Shirley here projected an inkling of intent to publish. For those interested in colonial American history just before the stir for independence, Shirley's works provide fascinating reading.

  Suggested Readings: DAB; DNB; T$_2$. *See also* William Alexander, *The Conduct of Major Gen. Shirley* (1758); Francis D. Haines, Jr., "Governor Shirley's Use of a Joint Legislative Committee in Colonial Massachusetts," RS, 23 (1955), 62-72; Thomas Hutchison, *The History of. . .Massachusetts-Bay* (1768), II, 304-333; III, 1-42, 48, 63, 67, 211, 225; Thomas H. Johnson, *The Oxford Companion to American History* (1966), pp. 722-723; Samuel Eliot Morison, *The Oxford History of the American People* (1965), pp. 158, 161-162, 174, 180, 202; John W. Raimo, *Biographical Directory of American Colonial and Revolutionary Governors: 1607-1789* (1980), pp. 142-143; Daniel L. Salay, "The William Johnson-William Shirley Dispute: Origins, Course, and Consequences" (M.A. thesis, Vanderbilt Univ., 1972); John A. Schutz, *William Shirley: King's Governor of Massachusetts* (1961); George A. Wood, *William Shirley: Governor of Massachusetts, 1741-1756* (1920).

John C. Shields
Illinois State University

WILLIAM SHURTLEFF (1689-1747)

  Works: *Distressing Dangers* (1727); *The Labour That Attends the Gospel-Ministry* (1727); *Gospel Ministers* (1739); *The Faith and Prayer* (1740); *The Obligations upon All Christians* (1741); *A Letter to Those of His Brethren Who Refuse to Admit. . .Whitefield* (1745).

  Biography: Born Apr. 4, 1689, William Shurtleff was the third child of Capt. William Shurtleff and Mrs. Suzannah Shurtleff of Plymouth, Mass. Although Plymouth's Church had admonished Capt. Shurtleff for his sin, pride, and hardness of heart, he had returned to respectability by the time of William's birth. Shurtleff earned his first degree at Harvard in 1707 and his second in 1710. In the years between degrees and immediately following, he served as a schoolmaster at Beverly and for a short time as the chaplain at Castle William in Boston Harbor. But in 1712 he obtained a permanent parish at the New Castle First Congregational Church in N.H. His marriage to Mary Atkinson, a woman of "whimsical ways," managed to test his "uncommon patience and meekness" with severe trials. A controversy over his salary caused his dismissal from New Castle in 1732, and he was immediately called to the Portsmouth Second Congregational Church, where he served until his death on May 9, 1747.

Critical Appraisal: In structuring his early sermons, William Shurtleff was addicted to the use of metaphor and simile. They were not always successful, for as he said himself, "on carrying on the simile, I shall not be solicitous to do it in every particular." The analogies are strained, and it would have been difficult to make the symbols consistently equal. In *Distressing Dangers*, his sermon on shipwrecked seamen, Shurtleff made the dangers faced upon the seas a metaphor for the dangers faced in life. His 1727 sermon on Gospel ministry points out that running a race requires "speed, strength, laborious exercise and persevering diligence," as do the duties and difficulties faced by ministers. At the ordination of the Rev. Gookin in 1739, Shurtleff preached a sermon in which ministers became likened to stars "on account of the use for which they are designated—to shine or shed forth light upon a dark and benighted world." Initially, these metaphors seem appropriate, but they are not developed consistently.

Shurtleff's published works also include *The Faith and Prayer*, a sermon preached before two young women condemned to die for the killing of their infant children, and a sermon delineating the obligations placed upon Christians to work for the salvation of their fellow men. But he is best remembered for his letter in defense of George Whitefield (q.v.). Shurtleff was impelled to invite Whitefield to his pulpit, because he thought that his congregation needed to be revitalized by Whitefield's evangelical fervor. Shurtleff saw his congregation as worldly and "rich and curiously dressed." Whitefield was an instrument to change those worldly attitudes. Shurtleff defended the disorders created by Whitefield on two grounds: one, that a change for the better inevitably involved disorder and disruption; and two, that the clergy who opposed Whitefield had the greater responsibility for creating the disorders.

As Perry Miller points out, only diehards like Shurtleff stood by Whitefield after he had been discredited. Moreover, as Edwin Scott Gaustad suggested, although Shurtleff may have had a brief and important reputation established because of his part in the Great Awakening, he was soon forgotten by laity and clergy alike. Yet he has also been characterized as a blunt and honest preacher, and his sermons were more memorable than those of many of his contemporaries.

Suggested Readings: CCNE; Sibley-Shipton (V, 396-403). *See also* Edwin Scott Gaustad, *The Great Awakening in New England* (1957), pp. 47, 102-103, 114; Alan Heimert and Perry Miller, *The Great Awakening* (1967), pp. 354-363; Perry Miller, *Jonathan Edwards* (1949).

George Craig
Edinboro State College

JOHN SMALLEY (1734-1820)

Works: *The Sinner's Inability to Comply with the Gospel* (1769); *Eternal Salvation on No Account a Matter of Just Debt* (1785); *The Law in All Respects Satisfied by Our Saviour* (1786); *On the Evils of a Weak Government* (1800); *Sermons on a Number of Connected Subjects* (1803); *Sermons on Various Subjects* (1814).

Biography: John Smalley was born on Jun. 4, 1734, in Lebanon, Conn. In spite of financial difficulties, he was able to leave the mechanical trade to which he had been apprenticed and attend Yale. His studies were sponsored by his pastor, Eleazar Wheelock (q.v.), and Ezra Stiles (q.v.). Smalley received a bachelor's degree from Yale in 1756 and soon after began to study theology under Dr. Joseph Bellamy (q.v.).

In 1758 Smalley was ordained and installed as the pastor of a newly founded Congregationalist Church in New Britain, Conn. He remained affiliated with that church for over fifty years, preaching his last sermon there in 1813. While serving at New Britain, Smalley tutored students of theology in his home. Later, he became a contributing editor of *The Connecticut Evangelical Magazine and Religious Intelligencer*.

Smalley was honored several times during his career as a Congregationalist minister. In 1787 he was invited to address the Yale graduates on the morning after their Commencement. The College of New Jersey conferred the degree of doctor of divinity on him in 1800. Although he had planned to retire at the age of 70, his congregation requested that he continue with the help of a younger colleague, the Rev. Newton Skinner. His last years were devoted to study. Smalley died on Jun. 1, 1820.

Critical Appraisal: In his sermons, John Smalley was not afraid to take controversial stands. At a time when the colonies were rebelling against authority, Smalley called for the recognition of higher powers and obedience to authority. Although he was not a Tory, Smalley had little sympathy for the Revolution. In 1774 he was required to defend his political position in the *Connecticut Courant*; the following week he was rebutted by the Committee of the Sons of Liberty in Farmington. When the new country was established, he stood firmly on the side of the Federalists, even though the majority of his parishioners were Democrats.

Although little concerning current events enters into his published sermons, the issues of authority and law are major themes throughout Smalley's work. In his last individually published sermon, *On the Evils of a Weak Government*, Smalley argued that too much liberty causes far more suffering and injustice than despotism does. He attributed the evils he saw in his society to widespread insubordination and lack of proper respect. He compared these evils to those described in the third chapter of Isaiah, where God removes his grace from Jerusalem and Judah, because they have defied his authority.

Ultimately, it is God's authority and law that Smalley wants his audience to recognize and obey. In his earlier sermons, he argued that God's law, as interpreted by the Calvinists, is just and reasonable. This stand was a reaction against the Universalists and Arminians, who argued that if God's law is just, he cannot punish sinners. Smalley's first sermon, *The Sinner's Inability to Comply with the Gospel*, began with an acknowledgement of the difficulties raised by these opposing theologies. He granted that it seems unreasonable and unjust to condemn men to eternal suffering, but he discounted certain theological arguments explaining the nature of grace. He disagreed with the premise that all men are given the capability to achieve grace if only they will exercise it. Nor did he accept the premise that the saved achieve their status by making themselves worthy of God's grace. Grace is God's doing, not man's, Smalley stated, drawing proof from Scripture: "No Man can come to me, except the Father which hath sent me draw him" (John 6:44). Smalley acknowledged that no one, by himself, can overcome sin, but he distinguished between two kinds of failures—moral and natural. *Moral inability* is simply a lack of will or heart; the morally unable might have the capacity to overcome their sins, but they are not inclined to do so. *Natural inability*, on the other hand, is a lack of physical power. The naturally unable are inclined to overcome sin but cannot accomplish it on their own. They should not be condemned, for we do not criticize an amputee for not being able to work with his hands. The naturally unable, however, do overcome sin, because their inclination leads them to a belief in Christ, who gives them divine grace. Through this grace, the believers become humble, obedient, and sinless. The morally unable remain rebellious to God's authority and, therefore, deserve the eternal punishment to which they are doomed.

Smalley's other sermons elaborate on the need for submission to God's authority. In *The Law in All Respects Satisfied by Christ*, he argued that the great pain Christ suffered on the cross demonstrates how fully man's sins must be punished. The only way to avoid that kind of punishment is to submit to God's authority. In *The Perfection of Divine Law*, a Commencement address delivered at Yale, Smalley stated that the prospect of eternal punishment is a useful tool in conversion.

By all accounts, Smalley was more respected for the rigor of his logical arguments than for his skill in delivering sermons from the pulpit. He is never described as a popular preacher, but his congregation in New Britain remained loyal to him for over fifty years in spite of political controversies. His sermons are marked by an appeal to reason rather than to emotion. His discussions of eternal punishment are not filled with terrifying images of the tortures of hell; instead, they are logical arguments defending the justness and reason of God's law.

Suggested Readings: CCNE; Dexter (II, 430-434); Sprague (I, 559-565). *See also* Stephen E. Berk, *Calvinism versus Democracy* (1974), pp. 3-17, 62-66.

Daniel C. Garver
University of Houston

ANNA YOUNG SMITH (1756-1780)

Works: *An Ode of Gratitude*; *Occasional Verses on the Anniversary of the Death of...Dr. Thomas Graeme*; *On Reading Swifts's Works* (all w. 1774; pub. 1790); "Ode to Sensibility" (1774); "A Song" (1774); "An Elegy to the Memory of American Volunteers" (1775).

Biography: Anna Young Smith was born in 1756 and raised by her aunt Elizabeth Graeme Fergusson (q.v.), who encouraged her literary efforts and influenced them. Smith favored independence and several of her poems celebrate it. Despite her father's opposition, she married Dr. William Smith in 1775. Having lived near Philadelphia throughout her life, she died from complications of childbirth in 1780.

Critical Appraisal: Anna Young Smith's poetry varied from themes typical of eighteenth-century women poets (gratitude to her aunt Elizabeth Fergusson, love for her grandfather Dr. Thomas Graeme and her husband, Dr. William Smith) to political verses celebrating the fallen minutemen of Lexington and Concord and quasi-feminist lines criticizing Dean Swift's satirical treatment even of his Stella.

For the most part, Smith's poetry demonstrates efforts expected of a daughter of a well-to-do Pa. family. Of greater moment than most of her verses was her criticism of Dean Swift, but even there her point was not to assert the rights of women but rather to criticize his cynicism. More appropriate to the greater role women were assuming in political discourse were her verses on Lexington and Concord. If women could not, and most at this time did not, demand the franchise, they could fashionably demonstrate patriotism like Smith or involve themselves in a host of spinning bees like many other women who showed their independence of Br. by making homespun.

Suggested Readings: Pattie Cowell, *Women Poets in Pre-Revolutionary America, 1650-1775* (1981).

Arthur Worrall
Colorado State University

ELIHU HUBBARD SMITH (1771-1798)

Works: *American Poems* (ed.; 1793); *Ten Letters on the Fever Which Prevailed in New York in 1795*, in Noah Webster, ed., *A Collection of Papers on...Bilious Fevers* (1796); *Edwin and Angelina, or, The Banditti* (1797); *The Medical Repository* (ed., with Edward Miller and Samuel L. Mitchill; 1797-1798); biographical essays on Joel Barlow, Timothy Dwight, John Trumbull, Lemuel Hopkins, and David Humphreys, and a review of *The Anarchiad, Monthly Magazine and British Register*, 6 (July through December, 1798); *A Discourse,*

Delivered April 11, 1798 (1798); *Diary* (w. 1795-1798; pub. 1973); miscellaneous articles, essays, poems, and prefaces.

Biography: Born on Sept. 4, 1771, Elihu Hubbard Smith was the only son of Dr. Reuben Smith and Abigail (Hubbard) Smith of Litchfield, Conn. A brilliant and precocious boy, he entered Yale at the age of 11 and graduated four years later. The college was over-crowded, and President Ezra Stiles's (q.v.) attempts to enforce higher academic standards led to student riots during Smith's senior year. His main accomplishments at Yale seem to have been to acquire a number of friends that he retained to the end of his life, a similarly long-lasting loss of faith that later led an acquaintance to label him "a terrible Freethinker," and academic deficiencies that caused his father to enroll the young college graduate in a preparatory school. Thus Smith entered Timothy Dwight's (q.v.) Greenfield Hill Academy, where he completed his basic education and began to write poetry, emulating his teacher. Smith then returned to Litchfield, where he studied medicine desultorily for three years. In 1790 he left to complete his medical education at the College of Philadelphia, studying under Benjamin Rush (q.v.). He remained in Philadelphia for some months after completing his studies, writing poetry and befriending Joseph Bringhurst, Jr., Charles Brockden Brown (q.v.), and John Fenno (q.v.).

Although Smith practiced medicine, he never received a medical degree and was never able to make a living as a physician. Between 1791 and 1793, he attempted to maintain a practice at Wethersfield, Conn. Although he had few patients, he led an active life, becoming associated with the Connecticut Wits, a loosely constituted school of writers that had originally included Timothy Dwight (Smith's teacher at Greenfield Hill) as well as Joel Barlow (q.v.), Lemuel Hopkins (q.v.), David Humphreys (q.v.), and John Trumbull (q.v.). Smith contributed to *The Echo* (1791-1795), a production of Hopkins and a younger group of Wits that included Richard Alsop (q.v.), Mason Fitch Cogswell (q.v.), and Theodore Dwight (q.v.). This period of intense literary activity ended with Smith's editing of *American Poems*, the first true anthology of poetry produced in America.

Shortly after *American Poems* was published in Litchfield, Smith left for New York City, where he took over a thriving medical practice—which promptly diminished. In New York Smith helped found the *Medical Repository*, associated with Noah Webster (q.v.) in the Manumission Society, and played a leading role in the Friendly Club, a discussion group of talented young N.Y. Federalists. He was an intimate friend of William Dunlap (q.v.) and saw his opera *Edwin and Angelina* produced by Dunlap and John Hodgkinson (q.v.). Smith continued to write and took on several editorial tasks, seeing Brockden Brown's *Alcuin* through the press and contributing a preface. Similarly, he prepared a verse preface for the first American edition of Erasmus Darwin's *The Botanic Garden*.

Elihu Hubbard Smith never married. His extraordinary life came to an early end when he contracted yellow fever during the epidemic of 1798. He died on Sept. 19, soon after his twenty-seventh birthday.

Critical Appraisal: In Oct. 1795, having learned from John Hodgkinson that the music for *Edwin and Angelina* had been completed, Smith wrote in his diary that success for his three-act verse opera "would be a new proof of the crudeness of the public taste." The remark was a token of Smith's undoubted critical abilities, not of his modesty. Although he published poetry throughout his life, Smith's poetic talent was slight. He is, however, an important figure in American literary history because he knew most of the important writers of his day, and because he left a thorough record of his intellectual, literary, and social life in his diary. First published in 1973, the diary amounts to more than 350,000 words and constitutes an indispensable historical source as well as an autobiographical document of inherent interest. In addition to recording his daily activities, Smith copied much of his correspondence into the diary, including letters to Brockden Brown, Joseph Dennie (q.v.), Theodore Dwight, and Benjamin Rush. The diary is prefaced by an autobiographical recollection of Smith's childhood and preparation for college.

James E. Cronin, the editor of Smith's diary, notes that it was intended to form the basis for a projected autobiography. If this autobiographical intention seems presumptuous in a man still in his twenties, it was nevertheless justified: the diary is Smith's most important work, and his life was of more significance than his literary accomplishments. *Edwin and Angelina*, for example, marked the first American appearance of the romantic outlaw theme, but Smith's plot and verse were derivative. He wrote a considerable amount of poetry in addition to this verse opera, including some of the earliest American sonnets, which appeared within a poetical correspondence with Bringhurst and a third writer carried on in Fenno's *Gazette of the United States*. Yet Smith never developed a poetic voice of his own, and as much of his poetry was published anonymously in newspapers and periodicals, it is impossible even to identify all the poems that he may have written.

Although Smith lacked creative talent, he was a gifted critic and editor. His friends Brockden Brown and William Dunlap both benefited from Smith's editorial revisions of their work and his pleasure in discussing "the disputes between *ands & ors*; & commas, semicolons, &c." But the great editorial work of Smith's life was *American Poems*. This anthology is a notable document in the rise of American literary nationalism, although much of the poetry it prints is derivative and imitative of English verse. In making his selections, Smith emphasized the work of his fellow Connecticut Wits, but he included poems by other poets, such as Philip Freneau (q.v.), William Livingston (q.v.), Sarah Wentworth Morton (q.v.), and Robert Treat Paine (q.v.). Smith planned further volumes of the anthology, but he died before he could bring these plans to fruition. His biographical articles on the major Connecticut Wits are also arguments for American literary nationalism. Published in the *Monthly Magazine and British Register* and reprinted after Smith's death in Dennie's *Farmer's Museum*, these essays are among the first serious discussions of American authors to appear in the British press. Smith advertised them to the editor of the *Monthly Magazine* as attempts to educate English readers and as signs of "the progress of fine arts in a new world"; Dennie, writing for an American readership, lamented that "for such modes of writing There Was No Curiosity in America." Smith was careful not to claim too much for his subjects. Given his personal relationship with Timothy Dwight, in particular, Smith's remarks suggest considerable objectivity and critical acumen.

Smith's remaining publications reflect his humanitarian and medical interests. His 1798 *Discourse* was delivered before New York City's Society for Promoting the Manumission of Slaves, for which Smith served as secretary and school trustee. His best medical writing appeared in *Ten Letters on the Fever*, but his collaboration in founding *The Medical Repository* is of particular significance because the *Repository* was the first American medical journal. Smith wrote for the journal and helped to edit the first six issues.

For the duration of his brief adult life, Elihu Hubbard Smith was in a position to observe an astonishing number of themes in American literary and intellectual history converging within the circle of his friends and acquaintances. Charles Brockden Brown, William Dunlap, Timothy Dwight, Benjamin Rush, and Noah Webster were central figures in Smith's life, and his diary and correspondence may supply fresh insights into the particularity of their world. Smith was an intelligent—and enthusiastic—observer of that world; his life and writings deserve to be better known.

Suggested Readings: DAB; Dexter (IV, 508-511); LHUS. *See also* Marcia Edgerton Bailey, *A Lesser Hartford Wit, Dr. Elihu Hubbard Smith* (1928); William K. Bottorff, "Introduction," *American Poems, Selected and Original* (1966); James E. Cronin, "Elihu Hubbard Smith and the New York Friendly Club," PMLA, 64 (1949), 471-479; idem, "Elihu Hubbard Smith and the New York Theatre (1793-1798)," NYH, 31 (1950), 136-148; idem, "Introduction," *The Diary of Elihu Hubbard Smith* (1973); idem, "Three Notes on Alexander Hamilton by Elihu Hubbard Smith," N&Q, 198 (1953), 210-211; Benjamin Franklin V, "The Published Commentary on the Minor Connecticut Wits," RALS, 8 (1978), 157-167.

Douglas R. Wilmes
The Pennsylvania State University

EUNICE SMITH (1757-1823)

Works: *Some Arguments Against Worldly-Mindedness* (also reprinted as *A Dialogue*; 1791); *Practical Language Interpreted* (1792); *Some of the Exercises of a Believing Soul* (1792); *Some Motives to Engage* (1798).

Biography: Eunice Smith was born in 1757 in a frontier community in western Mass. later named Ashfield. She was the daughter of Chileab Smith, an early settler and the founder of the Baptist Church in that community. The family were associated with the Warren (R.I.) Baptist Association. Chileab apparently controlled the Ashfield Baptist church's business affairs and occasionally traveled for the association. Eunice's brother Ebenezer was minister of the church until a falling out between father and son led to the establishment of separate churches in 1789. This separation lasted until 1796, five years after Eunice (who sided with her father) saw her first tract published. The Warren Association helped publish her tracts much as it had supported the family earlier in a struggle with Mass. to escape church taxes. All of Eunice Smith's published works were apparently written before her marriage to Benjamin Randall in 1792, although *Some Motives to Engage* was not published until 1798. She died in 1823 at the age of 66.

Critical Appraisal: Eunice Smith's tracts were part of a genre of writings by women for women that grew up after the American Revolution. Generally, they served as hortatory pieces to encourage good behavior free of corrupting worldly cares. Of greatest popularity was *Worldly-Mindedness*, first published in 1791 and reprinted nine times with only a few changes in the ensuing decade. The encouragement was to leave worldly cares and depend on Christ, an appropriate concern for Baptists like Eunice Smith living in the subsistence economy of western Mass. That Smith's audience was not limited to women is suggested by her next publication—*Practical Language Interpreted* (1792). Although *Worldly-Mindedness* presented a dialog between Mary and Martha, *Practical Language* offered a dialog between a believer and an unbeliever. Presumably appropriate for both sexes, this piece was reprinted four times. Here, as in *Worldly-Mindedness*, the reader is urged to abandon the carnal cares of this world while preparing for salvation in the next. Smith's other, less popular pamphlets—*Some Exercises of a Believing Soul* (1792) and *Some Motives to Engage* (1798)—were not reprinted.

Suggested Readings: Nancy Cott, *The Bonds of Womanhood: Woman's Sphere in New England, 1780-1835* (1977); Frederick G. Howes and Thomas Shepard, *History of the Town of Ashfield, Franklin County, Massachusetts from Its Settlement in 1742 to 1910* (c. 1910); William G. McLoughlin, *New England Dissent: The Baptists and the Separation of Church and State* (1971); Mary Beth Norton, *Liberty's Daughters: The Revolutionary Experience of American Women, 1750-1800* (1980).

Arthur Worrall
Colorado State University

CAPTAIN JOHN SMITH (1580-1631)

Works: *A True Relation of Virginia* (1608); *A Map of Virginia* [part] (1612); *A Description of New England* (1616); *New Englands Trials* (1620, 1622); *The Generall Historie of Virginia* (1624); *An Accidence* (1626); *A Sea Grammar* (1627); *The True Travels* (1630); *Advertisements for the Unexperienced Planters* (1631).

Biography: Born at Willoughby, Alford, Lincolnshire, Eng., in 1580, Smith was the son of a farmer. After service as a soldier with English troops in the Neth. while still in his teens, he joined the army of the Holy Roman Empire in battle against the Turks in Hung. There he was made a captain of horse-troops and then later was promoted to major and given the title of English gentleman. In time he was captured and enslaved. Sent to what is now southern Russia, he escaped and made his way back to the empire and ultimately to Eng. In 1606 he departed from Eng. again, this time for Va., where he was a colonist for two and a half years, during the last year officiating effectively as president of the governing Council. His return to Eng. was necessitated by his having been badly burned. In 1614 he explored the New Eng. coast. Later efforts to return to America as "Admiral of New England" proving unsuccessful, he turned to hack writing, propaganda, and historical compilation. He substituted the pen for the sword and then died at the age of 51.

Critical Appraisal: For many years Capt. John Smith was best known as an egotistical liar, and although modern biography has demonstrated his fundamental reliability, his reputation still suffers. He has several claims to significance. First, he prevented the collapse and failure of the Va. colony. Second, he wrote a number of works, some of historical importance only, some of continuing interest. He should be recognized as the first American writer; that is, he wrote the first work, a pamphlet composed in what is now the U.S. in the English language. It is little more than a letter on the Jamestown colony's first year. Much better is his first-hand description of the setting of the first permanent English colony in America, titled "A Description of the Countries, the Commodities, People, Government, and Religion," which was published in both *A Map of Virginia* and as Book Two of *The Generall Historie*. This was written in Eng., after Smith returned home. One who had traveled extensively, Smith brought a sharp eye to his observations, and his descriptions, especially of the Indians, have great historical significance. With remarkable objectivity and caution, Smith sought to describe what America offered to the European who was willing to work.

Much less objective is Smith's *Description of New England*, partly because he had seen little more than the area's coastline in an exploratory voyage that lasted five months. He offered a kind of summary catalog of the flora and fauna here, but most of this pamphlet is devoted to Smith's plans for a fishing colony. He continued his recommendations of New Eng. as a site for colonization in two editions of *New Englands Trials*.

Smith's most famous and substantial work is his *Generall Historie of Virginia, New England, and the Summer Isles*, in six books, published as a handsome folio with engraved title page, four engraved maps, a portrait of Pocahontas, and commentary poems, including one by John Donne. The originality of the work is distinctly limited. Consulting published accounts, Smith first compiled a record of pre-Jamestown exploration by the English in America and then reprinted his earlier description of Va. Book Three, on the Jamestown settlement, offered

Smith a chance to be an original writer of history. Although once again serving chiefly as an editor, this time he added much to the document before him, an account of the "Proceedings" of the Jamestown colony written by his friends and admirers and published in *A Map* of 1612. Most memorably, he recounted how the Indian princess Pocahontas saved his life when he was captured by her tribe. (No similar account appears in Smith's *True Relation* of 1608.) Presumably, the reason for the addition is that English readers were now much interested in the native Americans, who had killed some 400 English colonists in Mar. 1622. Book Four provides a jumbled record of the Va. colony after Smith's departure, with the former leader emphasizing the virtue of his own policies, notably toward the Indians. Book Five finds Smith strictly the editor and compiler, for he had never been to the Bermudas—the Summer Isles. For Book Six, he updated his own *Description of New England* and *Trials*. An addendum to the *Historie* appeared in 1630 in Smith's *True Travels*, which tells—again with much borrowing—the story of Smith's European adventures. This addendum or updating provides accounts of English explorations in Guiana and the W. Ind.

Smith's best book is his last, for now he was showing really literary skill. The *Advertisements*, a forty-eight-page quarto pamphlet, combines propaganda, advice, and autobiographical ramblings. Looking back philosophically at his own life and looking forward optimistically to America's future greatness, Smith offered himself with remarkable vividness to the reader first as a soldier but also as a self-made man, an individualist, a dreamer. He constantly turned his reader's attention from the author to reality, to Smith's own time and place, which he rendered with vivid concreteness. How did America appear to Englishmen of the early seventeenth century? In this work and elsewhere, Capt. John Smith provided excellent answers, and in the telling we meet a heroic figure.

Suggested Readings: DAB; DNB; LHUS; T_1. The best biography is Philip L. Barbour's *The Three Worlds of Captain John Smith* (1964). An overview of Smith as writer is provided by Everett Emerson in *Captain John Smith* (1971). *See also* Lewis Leary, "The Adventures of Captain John Smith as Heroic Legend" in *Essays in Early Virginia Literature*, ed. J. A. Leo Lemay (1977). A new edition of Smith's works is to appear under the editorship of the late Mr. Barbour.

Everett Emerson
University of Massachusetts, Amherst

JOHN SMITH (1722-1771)

Works: *The Doctrine of Christianity as Held by the People Called Quakers, Vindicated* (1748); "Atticus" essays, 70 numbers in *Pennsylvania Chronicle* (Jan. 1767-Aug. 1770); ms. diary, 11 vols. (in Pennsylvania Historical Society, edited in part by Albert C. Myers as *Hannah Logan's Courtship*; 1904).

Biography: The son of a wealthy and influential Quaker family, John Smith spent his minority in Burlington, N.J., where his prosperous merchant father was a member of the provincial Assembly. In 1743 Smith moved to Philadelphia, where he engaged in commerce, particularly the West Indian trade, and rapidly found his fortune and a secure place in the Quaker establishment (in 1748 he married the daughter of James Logan [q.v.], William Penn's [q.v.] former secretary and easily the most distinguished man in the colony). Smith moved easily in society and civic affairs, served as a member of the Pa. Assembly, and held memberships in the Library Company of Philadelphia and the American Philosophical Society. Retiring from active commerce in 1756, he returned to Burlington for the life of a provincial gentleman. During this period, he received a royal appointment to the N.J. Council, served as justice of the peace, and was one of the founders of the Library Company of Burlington. He died in Burlington in 1771.

Critical Appraisal: Smith's first venture into print, the *Doctrine of Christianity as Held by the People Called Quakers, Vindicated*, a defense of Quaker pacificism, was occasioned by a Gilbert Tennent (q.v.) sermon justifying war. Twenty years later, Smith began his series of "Atticus" essays in the *Pennsylvania Chronicle* (where they were joined by John Dickinson's [q.v.] "Letters from a Farmer in Pennsylvania"). Frankly modeled after the essays of Addison, Steele, and Johnson, Smith's essays took as their province all manner of subjects, from conversation and county fairs to "Kissing & Beards." "I shall take the privilege," he announced in the third number, "of treating on any subjects that may excite innocent mirth, or lead to, and promote just and proper reflections on conversation, or more important conduct in life." At times heavily moralistic, the Atticus essays nevertheless enjoy a modicum of grace and learned ease, and occasionally a light touch. They are also excellent examples of the developed sensibility and aesthetic attitude of eighteenth-century Quaker society in Pa. Smith's formal education was apparently restricted, but he was a learned man withal and an avid reader. "To read for delight and profit is a most rational way of employing a part of our time," Smith observed in his Oct. 24, 1768, essay, "and is what in this happy age and country, people of all classes, that can read at all, may do, in a greater or lesser variety." Nor was his taste in books—and the taste he recommended to his audience—narrowly sectarian: "There ought to be in every family some good books to be always at hand, not merely systematic treatises, to support the particular tenets of any sect or party...but such as are designed to enlarge the understanding and mend the heart." Smith's extensive diary is a revealing document, both for the light it sheds on public events as well as his private and spiritual life. In the former respect, it is unusual among Quaker journals and is thus a valuable reflection of life in colonial Philadelphia.

Suggested Readings: R. Morris Smith, *The Burlington Smiths* (1877); Frederick B. Tolles, "A Literary Quaker: John Smith of Burlington and Philadelphia," PMHB, 65 (1941), 300-333.

Donald P. Wharton
Castleton State College

JOHN SMITH (1752-1809)

Works: *A Dialogue Between an Englishman and an Indian* (w. 1779; pub. 1942); *A Little Teatable Chitchat, Alamode; Or, An Ancient Discovery Reduced to Modern Practice:—Being a Dialogue, and a Dish of Tea* (w. 1781; pub. 1942); *The Duty, Advantages, and Pleasure of Public Worship* (1795); *A Sermon, Preached in Randolph, June 3, 1801, at the Ordination of the Rev. Tilton Eastman* (1801); *A Chaldee Grammar* (1802); *The New Hampshire State Latin Grammar* (1802); *A Hebrew Grammar* (1803); *Cicero de Oratore* (1804); *A Grammar of the Greek Language* (1805).

Biography: John Smith was born in Rowley, Mass., on Dec. 21, 1752. A precocious reader of Classical literature in his youth, Smith studied at Dummer Academy, entered Dartmouth College as a member of the junior class, and took a degree in 1773. After graduation he remained at Dartmouth as a tutor for four years. By 1778 his low salary had stimulated Smith, always a timid man, to complain to President Eleazar Wheelock (q.v.) who arranged his promotion to professor of English, Latin, Greek, Hebrew, and Chaldee at a salary of 100 pounds annually, one-half in money and the other in foodstuff. He held this position until his death.

As a teacher, Smith appears to have been conscientious and extremely industrious but also dull. Students admired him as a linguist who contributed markedly to the pedagogy of his time, but otherwise regarded him as ineffectual. If his wit failed him in the classroom, his capacity for work was consistently illustrated. Economic circumstances forced him to open a bookstore in his home. Throughout his career at Dartmouth College, he functioned as librarian, trustee, and college pastor. In 1803 Brown University conferred upon him the degree of doctor of divinity. He was married and had at least two children; he died in Hanover, N.H., Apr. 30, 1809.

Critical Appraisal: At the time of his death, John Smith was eulogized by President Wheelock for his scholarly achievements, which were, he said, "attested by multitudes, scattered in the civilized world." With all respect to President Wheelock's assessment, Smith has been scarcely remembered—and, ironically, even then not for his linguistic scholarship but for two works composed, undoubtedly, as a consequence of his obligation to correct all student exercises at Dartmouth that were spoken on the stage. Although generally regarded as a ponderous and exceedingly formal man of undistinguished appearance but high purpose, he clearly enjoyed a sense of humor and perhaps other theatrical attitudes never recorded.

His two creative works—*A Dialogue Between an Englishman and an Indian* and *A Little Teatable Chitchat, Alamode*—were not published during the author's lifetime and were undoubtedly written as a less-than-serious exercise, yet with a point of view reflecting Smith's convictions. Neither can be regarded as drama, although the second might be called a skit, because five characters are involved. Both, however, were presented on the stage, and both represent the kind of staged reading or presentation then popular on college campuses. Since the early years of the eighteenth century, the students at the few colleges in the colonies had entertained themselves by performing plays—sometimes not to the pleasure of their professors, as demonstrated at Yale in 1756 when both the spectators at a play and the actors were fined for their offensive behavior. Spoken dialogs and odes, frequently of a patriotic or blatantly Loyalist nature, became popular during the dozen years preceding the Revolution. Dartmouth started this practice in 1774. Smith's contributions to this form of theatre are distinctive in revealing an authentic character, in contrast to the rhetorical presentations involving mythological figures with Greek and Roman names. Smith also made pointed comments on contemporary social problems.

A Dialogue Between an Englishman and an Indian reflects something of the history of Dartmouth College, which had its origins in "Moor's Indian Charity School" in Lebanon, Conn. The major force in establishing this school was Eleazar Wheelock, a pastor in that town who devoted much of his life to teaching the Indians the "polite arts of civilized life," which included Greek, Latin, and English oratory as well as the fundamentals of reading and writing. His most famous student—whose rhetorical ability would appear to be represented in this dialog—was Samson Occom (q.v.), a direct descendent of the great Uncas and a preacher of some note in both America and Eng. before his pathetic fall from Wheelock's grace during the score of years preceding his death in 1792. Wheelock's work with the Indians was the foundation upon which Dartmouth College was created. When Governor Wentworth of N.H., at Wheelock's specific request, chartered the new college in 1769, Eleazar Wheelock became its first president and moved his Indian Charity School to Hanover, N.H. John Smith's worshipful attitude toward Wheelock was common knowledge, and his dialog reveals a profound admiration for the Indians of America and a major focus of Wheelock's teaching.

John Smith's dialog between an Englishman and an Indian is dated Mar. 2, 1779, about a month before Wheelock died. Perhaps there is some relationship between the two events. In his letter to Dr. Phillips, to whom he sent both dialogs in 1782, Smith noted that "a real Aboriginal defended the part of the Indian," who in the dialog is identified as Joseph Yannhoohtough from Onaida. Unfortunately, the records at Dartmouth College for Indians attending school are not complete. Daniel Simmons, class of 1777, was the first Indian to graduate; Peter Pohquonnoppeet was in the class of 1780; Lewis Vincent graduated in 1781. Presumably because of his excellent character and unusual talents, Peter was commonly called Sir Peter and after graduation helped govern his tribe of Stockbridge Indians. He might well have played the part of Joseph in the dialog who defended the Indians against the harsh attacks of the Englishman in a forceful and intelligent manner that clearly established him as the more civilized of the two. Identifying himself as a student of Wheelock, Joseph effectively argues "that you are mistaken in your opinion that the American Indians surpass all other people, in cruelty," and he refers to Maj. Robert Rogers (q.v.), British soldier and author of an Indian play called *Ponteach*, to illustrate the white man's cruel conduct. At last, Joseph's superior intelligence and Christian ideology force the Englishman to admit that he "may have been too much prejudiced against the Indians," and the curtain falls upon this didactic and propagandistic dialog.

A Little Teatable Chitchat, composed in Jun. 1781, presents a light-hearted comment upon the times. Showing his knowledge of English drama in naming the characters, Smith presented Mr. and Mrs. Sharp, Miss Toast, and her Uncle Pendulum and Mrs. Twaddle. The skit begins topically as Sharp reveals himself as a poor man who took advantage of the currency depreciation in 1775 to pay his debts and then become a war-time profiteer. His shameless self-interest as a member of the Assembly brings him great joy as he creates laws for his own advantage and manipulates the payment of paper money debts in silver and gold. Sharp also notes that he is proposing a bill to abolish Christianity—which appeals to "all our gentlemen of importance." The few remaining lines in the skit are taken up with Miss Twaddle's gossip and an interest in gluttony that matches the group's fascination with greed.

In the history of education in America, John Smith deserves his moment as a tireless language teacher who contributed early textbooks to the disciplines that consumed his energies. But he also deserves particular comment in histories of American dramatic literature for his dialogs. Distinguished for their content and tone rather than form, they illustrate two of the kinds of dialogs or skits—Christian didacticism and satirical social humor—that eased the curriculum demands upon late eighteenth-century college students.

Suggested Readings: CCNE. *See also* John Farmer, "Sketches of the Graduates of Dartmouth College from the Foundations of That Institution in 1769," CNHamHS, 3 (1832), 106-107; Ralph N. Hill, ed., *The College on the Hill: A Dartmouth Chronicle* (1964); Walter J. Meserve, *An Emerging Entertainment: The Drama of the American People to 1828* (1977), pp. 42-45, 90-91; Richard Moody, ed., *Dramas from the American Theatre, 1762-1909* (1966), pp. 1-10; Leon Burr Richardson, *History of Dartmouth College* (1932); Harold Rugg, "The Dartmouth Plays, 1779-1782," TA, 1 (1942), 55-68.

Walter J. Meserve
Indiana University

JOSIAH SMITH (1704-1781)

Works: *A Discourse Delivered at Boston* (1726); *A Sermon Preached in Boston* (1726); *Humane Impositions* (1729); *The Divine Right of Private Judgment* (1730); *The Duty of Parents* (1730); *The Greatest Sufferers* (1730); *No New Thing to Be Slandered* (1730); *Solomon's Caution Against the Cup* (1730); *The Young Man Warn'd* (1730); *The Character and Duty of Minister and People* (1736); *A Sermon Deliver'd at Charles-Town* (1739); *The Character, Preaching,*

&c. of the Reverend Dr. George Whitefield (1740); A Christmas Sermon (1740); The Burning of Sodom (1741); The Doctrine and Glory of the Saint's Resurrection (1742); Jesus Persecuted in His Disciples (1745); A Zeal of God Encouraged (1745); Sermons on Several Important Subjects (1757); A Funeral Discourse (1766); The Church of Ephesus Arraign'd (1768); Success a Great Proof of St. Paul's Fidelity (1770); Death the End of All Men (1771); The Broken Heart Relieved (1773); St. Paul's Victory and Triumph (1774).

Biography: The foremost religious writer of colonial S.C., Josiah Smith was born in Charleston on Dec. 25, 1704, grandson of Landgrave Thomas Smith and son of Dr. George Smith. Sent to Boston for his education, Smith began a useful and enduring friendship with two eminent Boston ministers, Benjamin Colman (q.v.) and William Cooper (q.v.). Smith graduated from Harvard College in 1725 and one year later was ordained a Congregationalist minister by Colman, Cotton Mather (q.v.), and others. He then served as pastor in Bermuda and in 1727 returned to S.C. as pastor at Cainhoy. He continued to publish sermons in Boston and in 1728 was awarded an M.A. from Harvard. During these years, Smith entered the conflict within the Congregationalist-Independent Church in Charleston, supporting the Rev. Nathan Bassett against the Scotch Presbyterians of the Rev. Hugh Fisher. In several sermons, Smith upheld the right of liberty of conscience against enforced subscription. In 1734 he was called to Charleston as Bassett's colleague and six years later became sole pastor of the influential church, the first native Carolinian to hold that position. In the next decade, Smith emerged as a leader of the southern evangelicals, as evidenced by his enthusiastic support of the controversial revivalist George Whitefield (q.v.). Smith opened his pulpit to Whitefield, collected money for his Ga. orphanage, published the most influential defense of the fiery evangelist, and undertook an extensive editorial campaign in the South Carolina Gazette. Smith's activism was curtailed by a paralytic stroke in 1749. His speech impeded, he turned again to print, publishing sermons in Boston and Charleston during the next two decades. During the 1770s, Smith supported the patriot cause. As a result, Smith and his family were exiled as paroled prisoners of war when Charleston fell to the British. Smith moved to Philadelphia in 1781 and died in Oct. of the same year. He was buried at Arch Street Church alongside Samuel Finley (q.v.) and Gilbert Tennent (q.v.), both colleagues in the evangelical and patriotic movements.

Critical Appraisal: Josiah Smith was a prolific writer whose work spanned nearly fifty years and exerted an intercolonial influence. His work was characterized by a distinctive union of northern and southern influences. As a native Carolinian educated in Boston, he absorbed the stern Calvinism of New Eng. and encouraged its spread through the colonies. Through his sermons and his personal influence, he helped to assure the endurance of Puritan orthodoxy in the Deep South. Because he enjoyed the accessibility of Boston printers and the favor of Boston ministers, Smith was able to make the religious conflicts of Charleston matters of colonial importance. In most of his publications, he espoused a Calvinism that was tempered by toleration, restraint, and a respect for individual liberty. Drawing upon these diverse sources, Smith's work illustrates the complexity of the Great Awakening, its intercolonialism and regional variations, and its considerable impact on the political and religious ideas of the South.

Smith's pervasive Calvinism appears in his recurrent emphasis upon the doctrines of original sin, Free Grace, and the necessity of rebirth. Like his Boston contemporaries, he stressed the importance of piety, the value of education, and the role of minister as moral censor. Smith's most distinctive trait, however, was his consistent support of liberty of conscience. In the contradiction between predestination and liberty, Smith faced the basic dilemma of Puritanism. Like Jonathan Edwards (q.v.), he sought to reconcile faith and reason by affirming the value of both. This position underlies Smith's support of religious dissent, his defense of Whitefield's Calvinism against the Arminianism of the Wesleyan side of the Awakening, and his defense of the private religious experience. His writings also succeeded, whereas much of his contemporaries' work did not, in combining enthusiasm and restraint. His style is usually clear, forceful, and unadorned. Although thoroughly evangelical, Smith seldom, even in controversial polemics, degenerated into vindictiveness or abuse.

Smith's support of liberty is apparent in his resistance to enforced doctrinal unity within the Independent Church of Charleston, where Smith argued for the value of conscience and reason to decide doctrinal questions for the individual. Expressing these views, his *Humane Dispositions* (1729) led to rebuttals from Hugh Fisher and to charges of Arminian heresy. In *The Divine Right of Private Judgment* (1730), Smith answered the objections of Fisher, and in *No New Thing to Be Slandered* (1730), he defended his orthodoxy and reaffirmed his persistent defense of private conscience, faith, and reason. Delivered in Charleston and published in Boston, these works illustrate Smith's skill as a polemicist and a defender of liberty.

Other sermons of this period reveal the traditional evangelical emphasis upon personal piety. In works such as *The Duty of Parents* (1730) and *The Young Man Warn'd* (1730), Smith upheld the minister's authority to demand moral conformity from his congregation. A more direct attack upon impiety is his *Solomon's Caution* (1730), a vigorous defense of sobriety and seriousness and a condemnation of drunkenness. *The Greatest Sufferers* (1730) is an interesting example of the orthodox view of natural disasters, in this case an attempt to use a New Eng. earthquake as a warning to the more sinful people in Charleston.

Smith's support of both individual liberty and Calvinism is best seen in his enthusiastic response to George Whitefield. In 1740 Whitefield found in Charleston an alienated Anglican establishment, an openly secular way of life, growing rationalism, and Josiah Smith—his strongest defender. In print, Smith used Peter Timothy's *Gazette* to defend Whitefield against Commissary Alexander Garden (q.v.) and to defend the principles of the Awakening against attacks. In 1743 Smith wrote an account of Whitefield's orphanage that was published in Boston and Philadelphia. The best known, however, of all of Smith's writings was his 1740 *A Character*, hailed as a convincing defense of Whitefield and the entire revivalistic movement. Published in Boston, Glasgow, and later in Charleston, the sermon helped to create a favorable reception for the ideas of Whitefield and the Awakening.

   A Character is a determined exposition of the major doctrines, manner of preaching, and personal character of George Whitefield. More importantly, the work presents a concise analysis of evangelical attitudes and establishes Smith as one of the leading apologists of the Awakening. The section on doctrine begins with original sin. This belief is "fundamental" to Christianity and refers to an "inherent corruption" in nature and man. It underlies the next doctrine, justification by faith alone. As the foundation of the Reformation, this Paulist doctrine is central to the ministry of Whitefield. Works are "the necessary Fruits and Evidences of true Faith," but they are effects, not causes, of justification. The exaltation of "Free Grace" is thus not Antinomian; it is essential and orthodox. Smith next defined regeneration, or "Spiritual Birth," again made necessary by the taint of original sin. Emphasizing the experiential theology of the Awakening, Smith declared that true religion is "inward" and "of the Heart." The final tenet is the belief in "inward Feelings of the Spirit." Smith refuted the charges of egotism against Whitefield by affirming the eminence of feeling in religion. His enthusiasm approached a near-Romantic celebration of the primacy of the affections, the "sacred Raptures" whereby the individual is aware of the Spirit of God.

   Regarding Whitefield's manner of preaching, Smith acknowledged him a "Master" of exhortation. In the most aroused language of the sermon, Smith praised the evangelist's power over men's passions, his often unrehearsed eloquence, and his evident sincerity. As to Whitefield's character, Smith commended his tolerance, sobriety, and charity, the "good Fruits" of his righteousness. In an unusual confession, Smith declared, "he has taken my Heart." He concluded by lamenting the decline of religion into mere formality and envisioned a new "Reformation," led by the evangelicals.

   In the remainder of Smith's writings, he was consistently evangelical, stressing the importance of grace, piety, and moral perseverence. His most extensive work is the 1757 *Sermons on Several Important Subjects*, containing twenty-four sermons on traditional Puritan topics such as grace, death, and judgment. The more ardent exhortations of some of Smith's later jeremiads reveal the stylistic presence of Whitefield, who remained influential until his death in 1770. Less than a month after Whitefield's death, Smith presented his final vindication of the evangelist, *Success a Great Proof*. Toward the end of his life, Smith began to publish almost exclusively in his native Charleston. These works, many of them funeral sermons, indicate an increasing awareness of death and the possibility of immortality for the saints. In general, Smith's work combines the learned Calvinism of New Eng. with the independence and toleration of his native South. Through his writings, Smith provided an impetus for the spread of the Great Awakening throughout the colonies and a theological background for political independence. He deserves recognition, with Edwards, Gilbert Tennent (q.v.), William Tennent II (q.v.), and Samuel Davies (q.v.), as a leader of the evangelical movement in eighteenth-century America.

Suggested Readings: CCV; Sibley-Shipton (VII, 569-585); Sprague (I, 351-352). *See also* Richard Beale Davis, *Intellectual Life in the Colonial South* (1978), II, 697, 763-767; George Howe, *History of the Presbyterian Church in South Carolina* (1870), I, 185, 206, 229-232, 243-248; Andrew T. Nelson, " 'Enthusiasm' in Carolina," SAQ, 44 (1945), 402-405; David Ramsay, *History of the Independent or Congregational Church in Charleston, South Carolina* (1815), pp. 14-16; idem, *History of South Carolina* (1809), II, 273-274.

Tony J. Owens
Daniel International Corporation
Greenville, South Carolina

MICHAEL SMITH (1698-c. 1771)

Works: *Sermon, Preached in Christ-Church, in Newbern, in North-Carolina* (1756); "On the Reduction of Guadaloupe" (1760); *Twelve Sermons, Preached upon Several Occasions* (1770); *Christianity Unmasqued* (1771).

Biography: Michael Smith was born in County Meath, Ire., in 1698, the son of the Rev. Robert Smith. The circumstances of his early education are obscure. On the missionary roll of the Society for the Propagation of the Gospel in Foreign Parts, he is listed as having earned an M.A. at Trinity College, Dublin, but on the title pages of his publications, he appears simply as "Michael Smith, A.B." He was ordained a priest in the Anglican Church in 1747 and served as curate at Hertfordshire until 1752, when in Dec. he arrived in S.C. with his wife, eight children, and two servants. Early in his career as pastor to Prince Frederick's Parish and Prince George's Parish, his wife and three of his children died. By 1754 rumors began to spread about Smith's disreputable conduct, in particular his living with a woman whom he had not married according to law, borrowing of money, and neglect of parish duties. On May 2, 1756, the church officers of Prince Frederick's Parish wrote a letter to the SPG relating and elaborating on these atrocities.

On his many travels between 1753 and 1756, Smith acquired for himself a favorable reputation in regions northward, and in 1756 he left S.C. and began to minister to St. James Parish in Wilmington, N.C. He was an active preacher throughout the coastal region, in Cape Fear and in New Hanover and Brunswick Counties. Although he had a difficult time competing with Anabaptists and other "enthusiastical sects" in N.C., he reported some success in a 1758 letter to the SPG secretary. But in 1759 the SPG, acting on the complaints from his S.C. parishioners, relieved Smith of his duties. Two letters (1759 and 1760) defending his character and ability, one from the church wardens of St. James Parish and the other from a prominent N.C. politician, appear in the letter book of the SPG. Each notes the difficulties under which he worked—the number of places he had to travel, his small salary, his large family, and the popular prejudice against Anglican missionaries. Smith went to Eng. to defend himself, but the SPG refused to grant him a hearing. He was not restored to his mission, and by 1762 he had been made a chaplain on a British warship. Subsequently, he returned to Eng., found a patron in the earl of Hillsborough, published two books, and became vicar of South Mimms in Hertfordshire. Nothing is known of his death.

Critical Appraisal: Although Michael Smith spent only about ten years in America, all of his works either were composed in the colonies or reflect in some way his American experience. His published sermons are among the few surviving examples of Anglican preaching in colonial N.C., and although they are not as impressive as the literary accomplishments of his Anglican brethren in Va. and Md., they are nevertheless excellent examples of the plain-style eighteenth-century discourse extolling common sense and common decency. His *Sermon, Preached in Christ-Church, in Newbern, in North-Carolina...Before the Ancient and Honourable Society of Free and Accepted Masons* (1756) is a standard exercise on the theme of brotherly love. Based on the text "Faithful are the Wounds of a Friend; but the Kisses of an Enemy are deceitful" (Proverbs 27:6), the sermon is built on a formulaic comparison of solitary man and social man and a distinction between true brotherly love and false friendship. It is a celebration of the human social state and of God's goodness in providing companions, and it is a moral treatise gently warning against the abuse of the sacred gift of friendship and encouraging the spirit of fraternal societies like the Masons. The reasonableness of God's ways to man and the common duty to love one another are also the main themes in most of the *Twelve Sermons, Preached upon Several Occasions* (1770), which were originally composed for an American audience but were not collected and published until Smith's return to Eng. The plain style and unemotional approach to his subjects were most likely calculated as an antidote to the preaching of the "enthusiastical sects" and dissenters who predominated in colonial N.C. Smith's subjects included "Virtue and Religion the Only Ground of Peace and Friendship Amongst Men"; "National Calamities, Not Always the Effects of Divine Vengeance"; "The Peculiar Guilt and Infamy of Knowing and Not Practicing Our Duty"; and "Prejudice and Prepossession Removed by Virtue Only." "I have not introduced any nice notions and systems of religion," Smith wrote in his dedication to the earl of Hillsborough, "not only because they are unsuitable to the temper and genius of the Colonies; and I think do more hurt than good to the cause of God; but, because...many of them are above my comprehension." Instead he offered "Plain Christianity and sound Morality."

Smith was perhaps a more distinguished poet than preacher, although this is not readily obvious in his only poem published in America, "On the Reduction of Guadaloupe," which appeared in the *South Carolina Gazette* (Apr. 26-May 3, 1760). Its 165 lines in heroic couplets adequately demonstrate Smith's technical competence, and the apt biblical and Classical allusions show that he was a man of learning, but the patriotic glorification of William Pitt and the British military seems disproportionate to the event he celebrated. A much more significant work is *Christianity Unmasqued; Or, Unavoidable Ignorance Preferable to Corrupt Christianity. A Poem. In Twenty-one Cantos* (1771). The dedicatory preface to the earl of Hillsborough has historical value, because it contains Smith's views on the Anglican mission in America, and the poem itself is an important contribution to the Anglo-American literature of the eighteenth century. As a poetic essayist, Smith displayed a remarkable wit and versatility. He deftly altered his rhetoric and style to suit his varying subject matter. For his satire of "corrupt" forms of Christianity, he used octosyllabic "Hudibrastic" couplets, but he shifted to heroic couplets for his depiction of true Christianity in the last canto. The poem's narrative forms are similarly altered. Smith's satire of Catholicism, attacking the Catholic reliance on miracle and superstition and the gullible sanctification of an all-too-human and fallible clergy, employs the exemplum. This form is the core structure of the saint's life, a popular Catholic literary form. Smith provided an interesting negative exemplum, the bawdy story of a priest who, in the guise of an exorcist, demands and wins a young woman's favors as a penance for sins—"She lost her honour with her sense." To combat the railing of dissenters, Smith raised his own pitch and railed against their emotionalism, hypocrisy, and self-righteousness, but he gained distance and kept himself aloof from the attack by presenting it in a speech by a created character, a Deist libertine named Antigersis. Then to dispose of Antigersis, who as a Deist worships reason, Smith used a rational method of discourse, the dialog. The author's mouthpiece is a decent young Englishman, Pistiferos. Through calm reason and compassion, he eventually convinces Antigersis that Christianity is the most healthful and rational course for modern humanity. In the speeches of Pistiferos, in the summation of principles in the last canto, and in the discursive links between episodes, Smith expounded his beloved doctrines, common sense and common decency. If religion is corrupted, then unavoidable ignorance such as that of American Indians is preferable. Sectarianism must be destroyed and the unity of early Christianity restored by reliance on the Church of England, that most sensible of God's instruments. Christianity should not be a means by which inquisitors gain power over their victims, but a means of strengthening the love and respect on which the well-being of society rests. Few expositions of these principles are more lively and readable than *Christianity Unmasqued*.

Suggested Readings: CCV. *See also* Hennig Cohen, *The South Carolina Gazette, 1732-1775* (1953), p. 190; Richard Beale Davis, *Intellectual Life in the Colonial South, 1585-1763* (1978), pp. 604, 677, 754-755, 1491; David T. Morgan, "Scandal in Carolina: The Story of a Capricious Missionary," NCHR, 47 (1970), 233-243; C. F. Pascoe, *Two Hundred Years of the S.P.G.* (1901), II, 850; William L. Saunders, ed., *North Carolina Colonial Records* (1887), V, 665, 696, 961-962; VI, 58-60, 312-313, 709-710.

M. Jimmie Killingsworth
New Mexico Institute of Mining and Technology

SAMUEL STANHOPE SMITH (1751-1819)

Works: *Funeral Sermon on. . .Richard Stockton* (1781); *An Essay on the Causes of Variety of Complexion and Figure in the Human Species*, including "Strictures on Lord Kaim's 'Discourse on the Original Diversity of Mankind'" (1787; much enlarged 2nd. ed., 1810); *Three Discourses* [on slander, small faults, and shame of religion] (1791); *A Discourse on. . .Fasting* (1795); *The Divine Goodness to the United States* (1795); *A Discourse Delivered on the 22nd of February, 1797. . .at the Funeral of the Rev. Gilbert Tennent Snowden* (1797); *Sermons* (1799; rev., 1801); *An Oration on the Death of General George Washington* (1800); *A Discourse on. . .Baptism* (1808); *Lectures on the Evidences of the Christian Religion* (1809); *The Resurrection of the Body* (1809); *On the Love of Praise. A Sermon* (1810); *Lectures. . .on Moral and Political Philosophy*, 2 vols. (1812); *A Comprehensive View of. . .Natural and Revealed Religion* (1815; rev. 2nd ed., 1818); *Essays on the Church of God* (1815); *Oratoria Inauguralis* (1817); part of the "Continuation to the Treaty of Ghent" (pub. in David Ramsay, *History of the United States*, 1818); *Sermons of Samuel Stanhope Smith. . .To Which Is Prefixed a Brief Memoir of His Life and Writings*, 2 vols. (1821).

Biography: The eldest son of Robert Smith, a Scots-Irish Presbyterian minister, Samuel Stanhope Smith was born in Pequea, Pa., on Mar. 16, 1751, a date now well established. Smith obtained a superlative grounding in Latin and Greek at his father's academy in Pequea, which enabled him to enter the junior class of the College of New Jersey (now Princeton) at 16. He graduated in 1769, having been much influenced by the new president of the college, John Witherspoon (q.v.), of whose "common sense" philosophy Smith continued to be a moderate practitioner. Following brief positions as tutor at both the Pequea Academy and Princeton, Smith journeyed to the western counties of Va. on missionary work for the Presbyterian Church. There he became widely celebrated for his pulpit eloquence and was, resultantly, asked to teach and administrate at the Academy of Hampden-Sidney, all the while suffering from tuberculosis, which persisted throughout his life. Having married Witherspoon's eldest daughter while performing his missionary duties in Va., Smith was asked back to Princeton in 1779 as professor of moral philosophy.

Smith's long and distinguished career at Princeton was the capstone of his life. While Witherspoon was engaged in wide-ranging patriotic activities, Smith practically alone was responsible for administering the campus, which he largely had to rebuild after the Revolutionary War and twice thereafter following devastating fires. In 1795 Smith was appointed seventh president of the university and began instituting liberal changes in the curriculum. He brought John Maclean to the faculty from Scot. as the first undergraduate teacher of chemistry and natural science in the U.S. But Smith's liberal outlook in education was strenuously opposed by the Presbyterian trustees of the university, who after a long series of skirmishes finally forced his resignation in 1812. Thereafter, Smith remained near the campus, preparing his lectures and sermons for publication, collaborating with friends to finish David Ramsay's (q.v.) *History of the United States* and continuing to influence the undergraduates by his presence. He died on Aug. 21, 1819, survived by five of his nine children, and was buried near his presidential predecessors.

Critical Appraisal: Although Samuel Stanhope Smith produced an extensive and varied body of sermons and moral writing pursuant to his careers as minister and educator, he is remembered by modern readers primarily as the author of *An Essay on the Causes of Variety of Complexion and Figure in the Human Species*, which brought him a wide reputation in America and moderate fame as well in G.B. and on the Continent. Delivered before the American Philosophical Society in 1787 and substantially expanded in 1810, the *Essay* contains many arguments that appear briefly in the *Moral and Political Lectures* (1812). It seeks to demonstrate the unity of mankind as set forth in the Bible but, importantly, without recourse to that work as a source of authority. Accordingly, the *Essay* is the first significant document in America to be based on John Witherspoon's philosophy of "common sense," a rational approach to subjects both material and spiritual. It is also an early effort to attempt to prove a Lamarkian theory of evolutionary change: the differences in mankind may all be accounted for, said Smith, by the slow but incessant changes wrought by climate and society. Smith was a lifelong friend of science and did much to narrow the gap between the natural sciences and the more traditional curricula taught in American schools. It is, in fact, for his liberal attitude toward education that Smith is often most admired today, and the *Essay* is the clearest literary evidence of his efforts to unite science and religion, just as his bringing Maclean to Princeton is the best practical evidence.

If Smith took a liberal stance toward science in the *Essay*, his *Lectures . . . on Moral and Political Philosophy* (1812) reflects similarly broad-minded viewpoints. His discussion of marriage in the *Lectures* is highly tolerant, and he suggested that in certain circumstances of society, as in Old Testament Judea, polygamy might be the best approach to marriage. In the *Lectures*, he also took an enlightened view toward slavery and offered a rational plan for the eventual— for he was a "gradualist"—liberation of all American slaves. This series of lectures, as Samuel Holt Monk pointed out, is an effort to deal with the "whole duty of man" and can still be read with pleasure by those interested in late eighteenth-century views on beauty, natural theology, duty to God, man, and self (and a wide range of other moral issues), taxation and commerce, law, modes of government, and revolution.

Having lived through the Revolutionary War and having rebuilt Princeton from the literal ashes of that conflict, Smith took a keen interest in his country and was intensely patriotic in a few of his writings. In *The Divine Goodness to the United States* (1795), he preached a spirit of patriotism much akin to that of other famous patriots of the day, and his *Oration on the Death of General George Washington* remains important on two counts: it is a fervent eulogy for that great commander, and it reveals the esteem in which Smith was held by his own countrymen. To be asked to read the funeral sermon of Washington was no mean compliment in 1800.

Smith's religious writings reveal an ornate but lucid style that makes his work some of the best traditional pulpit literature to come down to us. Although never so liberal as the moral lectures and the *Essay* of 1787, the three volumes of sermons—together with *Lectures on the Evidence of the Christian Religion* (1809), *A Comprehensive View of the Leading and Most Important Principles of Natural and Revealed Religion* (1815), *Essays on the Church of God* (1815), and Smith's shorter published sermons and discourses—offer religious sentiments that are not yet out of date.

Samuel Stanhope Smith has been rightly called an "enlightened conservative" and a "friend of rational liberty"; his best writing, especially the *Essay* of 1787, also marks him as a member, and not the least important one, of a slowly gathering literary fraternity whose rolls included Thoreau and Emerson and whose hallmark was humanism.

Suggested Readings: DAB; P; Sprague (III, 335-345); T$_2$. *See also* David F. Bowers, "The Smith-Blair Correspondence, 1786-1791," PULC, 4 (1943), 123-134; Gladys Bryson, "Philosophy and the Modern Social Sciences: The Comparable Interests of the Old Moral Philosophy and the Modern Social Sciences," SF, 2 (1932), 19-27; William H. Hudnutt, III, "Samuel Stanhope Smith: Enlightened Conservative," JHI, 17 (1956), 540-552; Winthrop D. Jordan, ed., Introduction, *An Essay on the Causes of Variety of Complexion and Figure in the Human Species* (1965), pp. vii-liii; John Maclean, *History of the College of New Jersey* (1877), pp. 5-146; Leroy Bradbury Miles, "Adventures in Persuasion: John Witherspoon, Samuel Stanhope Smith, and Ashbel Green" (Ph.D. diss., Harvard Univ., 1967); Samuel Holt Monk, "Samuel Stanhope Smith: Friend of Rational Liberty" in *The Lives of Eighteen from Princeton*, ed. Willard Thorp (1946), pp. 86-110.

Stephen J. Stedman
Tennessee State University

WILLIAM SMITH (1727-1803)

Works: *Some Thoughts on Education* (1752); *A General Idea of the College of Mirania* (1753); *Ode on the New-Year* (c. 1753); *A Poem on Visiting the Academy of Philadelphia* (1753); *Personal Affliction* (1754); *Some Account of the North-American Indians* (1754); *A Brief History of the Rise and Progress of the Charitable Scheme* (1755); *A Brief State of the Province of Pennsylvania* (1755); *Eine Kurtze Nachricht, von der Christlichen und Liebreichen Anstalt* (1755); Prefatory letter, in Thomas Barton, *A Sermon, Preached at Carlisle* (1755); *A Sermon, Preached in Christ-Church, Philadelphia, Before the Provincial Grand Master* (1755); *A Brief View of the Conduct of Pennsylvania* (1756); *A Letter from a Gentleman in London, to His Friend in Pennsylvania* (1756); *The*

Reverend Mr. Smith Vindicated (1756); *The American Magazine and Monthly Chronicle* (editor; Oct., 1757-Oct., 1758); *A Charge, Delivered May 17, 1757* (1757); *The Christian Soldier's Duty* (1757); "The Hermit" essay series, *The American Magazine and Monthly Chronicle* (1757-1758); *Discourses on Public Occasions in America* (1759; 1762); *A Discourse Concerning the Conversion of the Heathen* (1760); *An Exercise, Consisting of a Dialogue and Ode* (1761); *The Great Duty of Public Worship* (1761); *Additional Discourses and Essays* (1762); *A Humble Representation. . .in Behalf of the Lately Erected Colleges of New York and Philadelphia* (1762); *The Last Summons* (1762); *An Answer to Mr. Franklin's Remarks* (1764); *An Historical Account of the Expedition Against the Ohio Indians* (1765); *Some Account of the Charitable Corporation* (1769); *An Oration, Delivered, January 22, 1773* (1773); *An Examination of the Connecticut Claim* (1774); *An Exercise, Containing a Dialogue and Two Odes* (1775); *A Sermon on the Present Situation* (1775); *An Oration in Memory of General Montgomery* (1776); *A Sermon Preached at Christ-Church* (1779); *An Account of Washington College* (1784); *A Sermon Preached in Christ-Church, Philadelphia, on Friday, October 7th, 1785* (1785); *An Address to the General Assembly* (1788); *A Masonic Oration* (1788); *Two Sermons, Delivered in Christ-Church, Philadelphia, Before the General Convention* (1789); *A Sermon, on Temporal and Spiritual Salvation* (1790); *Select Sermons* (1791); *Eulogium on Benjamin Franklin* (1792); *An Historical Account of the Rise. . .of the Canal Navigation in Pennsylvania* (1795); *A Funeral Address. . .Major-General Mifflin* (1800); *The Works of William Smith*, 2 vols. (1803); numerous newspaper essays, letters, and poems.

Biography: Born in Aberdeen, Scot., on Sept. 7, 1727, William Smith was educated at the Univ. of Aberdeen, where he received the A.M. in 1747. Moving to London, he pursued his educational and religious interests as an agent for the Society for the Education of Parochial Schoolmasters and the Society for the Propagation of the Gospel. In 1751, Smith was offered a position as tutor to the sons of a N.Y. resident. He accompanied the boys to America and continued to serve as their tutor until Aug., 1753.

An ambitious and talented man, Smith could not forbear entrance into any controversy touching on his manifold interests. Thus the struggle to determine whether King's College should be Anglican or nonsectarian soon engaged his attention, as did proposals to define the educational philosophy of the new college. Shortly after his arrival in N.Y., Smith enlisted on the Anglican side in the press wars over the college, joining writers such as Samuel Johnson (q.v.), Samuel Seabury (q.v.), and James Wetmore (q.v.) in their struggle against the anti-Anglican forces, notably the young, Yale-educated "Triumvirate" of Presbyterian lawyers, William Livingston (q.v.), John Morin Scott, and William Smith (1728-1793) (q.v.). This episode had enormous significance in Smith's life, as it established him as a noted educational writer and brought him to the attention of Benjamin Franklin (q.v.). Favorably impressed by Smith's *A General Idea of the College of Mirania*, Franklin invited the young educator to inspect the Academy and Charitable School at Philadelphia. Thereafter, Smith was appointed a professor of logic, rhetoric, and natural and moral philosophy and traveled to Eng. to be ordained as an Anglican priest, which would qualify him to serve as the academy's provost. After his return to Philadelphia in May, 1754, Smith and Francis Alison (q.v.), rector of the academy, prepared a new charter for the school, and in 1755 Philadelphia's academy became a college.

As Smith's experiences in N.Y. had revealed, colonial education and politics were inextricably connected. But if the provost of Philadelphia's only college necessarily had a political role to play, Smith made a virtue of necessity and soon became a major irritant in the complex world of Pennsylvanian politics, serving as a controversialist for the proprietary interests against the Quakers and the Germans, who favored passivity in the face of the French attacks. This course led to a bitter paper war with Franklin and his adherents, who favored compromise rather than the polarization that Smith's eloquent voice and pen encouraged. In time Smith's activities became so partisan that even the proprietor, Thomas Penn, became offended. On several occasions Smith's differences with the assembly led to his arrest, and he was forced to teach his classes in jail. Traveling to Eng., Smith obtained a legal victory over the assembly and was awarded the degree of doctor of divinity by Oxford and the Univ. of Aberdeen. In 1763, he received the same degree from the Univ. of Dublin, and in 1768 he was elected to the American Philosophical Society.

Smith opposed the Stamp Act and in 1775 preached a celebrated patriotic discourse, *A Sermon on the Present Situation*. But his attachment to Eng. and the proprietary interests prevented him from whole-heartedly supporting the Revolution. By 1779, Smith had made too many enemies in Pa., and his college's charter was voided by the assembly. Smith moved to Md., where he founded the Kent School (which in 1782 became Washington College), with Smith serving as its president. Active in religious affairs during this period, Smith was a founder of the Protestant Episcopal Church. When the charter of the College of Philadelphia was restored in 1789, Smith again became provost, serving until the formation of the Univ. of Pennsylvania in 1791. In 1758 Smith married Rebecca Moore, the daughter of a codefendant in Smith's legal battles with the Pa. assembly during the 1750s. He died on May 14, 1803, at the Philadelphia home of a daughter-in-law.

Critical Appraisal: By vocation a writer on educational, political, and religious topics, William Smith nevertheless harbored a love of literature and the fine arts that established an important place for him in American cultural history—although he was not above employing his literary pursuits for personal advantage. He was himself a competent poet, publishing in *Some Thoughts on Education* a long poem, "Copy of Verses, Addressed to the Gentlemen of the House of Representatives," which William D. Andrews has analyzed as an early treatment of the rising glory of America theme afterward made famous by Philip Freneau (q.v.), Hugh Henry Brackenridge (q.v.), and Joel Barlow (q.v.). But Smith's activities as a promoter of artists, musicians, and writers in the halls of his college and the drawing rooms of Philadelphia are probably more significant than his own literary efforts, although these have received insufficient attention. Smith encouraged the artist Benjamin West and was instrumental in securing funds for West's European studies. His circle also included the musician James Bremner and a number of promising writers: Jacob Duché (q.v.), Nathaniel Evans (q.v.), Elizabeth Graeme Fergusson (q.v.), Thomas Godfrey (q.v.), and Francis Hopkinson (q.v.). After the early deaths of Evans and Godfrey, Smith arranged for the publication of their poems. In 1757 Smith persuaded William Bradford the third (q.v.) to publish *The American Magazine and Monthly Chronicle*, which Smith edited for thirteen months until its demise in Oct., 1758. *The American* published poetry by John Beveridge (q.v.), Samuel Davies (q.v.), Thomas Godfrey, Francis Hopkinson, Joseph Shippen (q.v.), James Sterling (q.v.), and others. In addition, the magazine offered historical and political essays; a "Philosophical Miscellany" department that included scientific writings by John Winthrop (q.v.) of Harvard; and "Monthly Essays," which presented serial essays by "The Antigallican," "The Planter," "The Prattler," and "The Hermit." The eight essays in the "Hermit" series were written by Smith; they concerned religious topics and employed sermonic forms with romantic overtones that are particularly evident in the first essay. The originality and high literary quality of *The American* are notable in the history of colonial magazines, but its publication was clearly as much a political as a literary event, for its pages were replete with attacks on the French and efforts to rally support for the war then raging on Pa.'s frontier. The Quakers and others of Smith's political enemies were criticized at length, and the magazine's early death when Smith left for Eng. must have been applauded by opponents of his politics even as it was mourned by lovers of literature.

Politically, Smith early broke with his benefactor Franklin because he was incapable of sustained compromised or moderation. The driving force of his passion was his desire to safeguard in Pa. the vision of religion and culture that he brilliantly transmitted in the pulpit and the classroom. He saw all that he valued at risk to the external threats of the French and Indians and the internal threats of the quietism of the Quakers, the alien culture of Pa.'s large German population, and the enthusiasm of Presbyterians such as Gilbert Tennent (q.v.). The ends for which he fought were so personally compelling that he could scarcely control the means he employed to gain them. Writing a prefatory letter to his friend Thomas Barton's (q.v.) sermon on Gen. Edward Braddock's defeat, Smith could barely restrain his horror at the danger Pa. faced: *"Murderers stealing thro' Midnight Darkness and polluting the Bed of Rest with savage Death!"* Assaulted by such terrors, his natural reaction was to push back:

> methinks I should consider myself as one who had advanced to the very Frontiers of *Messiah's Kingdom*, and among the first who had unfolded his everlasting Banner in the remotest Parts of the *West*. Recede I would not, nor give back a single Inch to the gloomy Reign of *Heathenism* and *Error*.

The oneness of the external and internal threats in Smith's mind runs through his polemical writing. In his anonymous 1755 *Brief State of the Province of Pennsylvania*, which Franklin at first refused to believe was written by Smith, his bitterness toward the Quakers and the Germans nearly equaled his hatred of the French, as he proposed policies that would disenfranchise his enemies and remove them entirely from the political arena. Franklin, who sought to occupy the middle ground in these political battles, suffered for his very moderation. Eventually, Smith would go so far as to denigrate Franklin's scientific achievements—a far cry from Smith's sentiments in his *Poem on Visiting the Academy of Philadelphia*: "My Pennsylvania's Ornament and Pride, / Her Hope, her Soul, her Father, and her Guide; / When gentle *Hamilton* shall grace our Skies, / and with him *Allen, Peters, Franklin* rise." Smith goaded Franklin to uncharacteristic bitterness in their press wars, in part perhaps because Smith was an effective, and therefore wounding, writer and in part because the two men were, as Ralph Ketcham suggests, "by nature temperamentally incompatible." That one of Smith's last publications was a *Eulogium on Benjamin Franklin* is one of the more affecting ironies of Smith's tumultuous career.

As Smith was one of Pa.'s most ardent supporters of British policy during the French and Indian War, he welcomed Col. Henry Bouquet's invitation to chronicle Bouquet's 1763 victory over the Indians at Bushy Run, near Fort Pitt. This action and Bouquet's subsequent expedition into Ohio were parts of the British attempt to stabilize the western frontier against the Indians following the Treaty of Paris, which ended the French and Indian and Seven Years' Wars. "Published from authentic Documents, by a Lover of his Country," *An Historical Account* was one of Smith's most popular publications, although its author was heavily dependent upon his informant and sources. Smith produced a valuable historical account of Bouquet's victory and pacification of the Ohio Indians, but it was clearly history with a moral, concluding with Smith's rendition of the submissive speech of a Shawnee chief and the optimistic view that "we now have the pleasure once more to behold the temple of *Janus* shut, in this western world!" The narrative is followed by an essay of "Reflections on the War with the *Savages* of *North-America*" and by appendixes detailing the geography and native inhabitants of the western territories. Much of the "Reflections" is a military manual for Indian fighters, but anthropological comments on the Indians illuminate Smith's assumptions about the threat they posed. Inspired by a "love of liberty" organic to "the state of nature," the Indians' behavior was not informed by standards of morality or reason. They saw "strategems and cruelty" as equally appropriate to the hunting of beasts or men; they were at one with their natural and uncivilized world: "Like beasts of prey, they are patient, deceitful, and rendered by habit almost insensible to the common feelings of humanity."

Smith's thought and writings were split by polarities. He had an uncommon fear of savagery, perhaps because there was a hint of it in his own innate lack of moderation. As an Anglican priest, a patron of young poets, a teacher, and a writer on education and a projector of educational schemes, he was compelled to counter the challenges to his own view of civilization offered by the ultimate barbarity of the frontier and the lesser evils of alien cultures and religions within Pa. society. In Smith's view of the conflict of civilization and barbarity, education may have been more compelling than religion. Although he was not an original educational theorist, he was a great educator, perhaps more comfortably able to reconcile means and ends in the classroom than on the battlefields of political and religious strife. In *Some Thoughts on Education*, he lobbied for King's College and argued that it should be located in the heart of New York City, that its students might "know Men and the World." In his most important book of education, *A General Idea of the College of Mirania*, he advanced a view of the ideal American college, a utopia suffused with pragmatism, illustrating a shrewd attention to the American condition, where the English language would be far more useful than Greek or Latin, and young men would rise on the strength of the rhetorical skills they would learn by writing and declaiming in the college halls.

Smith's view of education was modern rather than medieval, though much indebted in its details to English sources such as Robert Dodsley's *The Preceptor* and Smith's early experiences at the Univ. of Aberdeen. Conveniently, it was also a view of education in keeping with Franklin's beliefs. Smith's educational genius was practical, and it extended beyond the curriculum he oversaw at the College of Philadelphia. In N.Y., he offered a plan for an elaborate system of preparatory schools that would supply the classrooms of King's College with qualified students. In Pa., he seized upon Michael Schlatter's (q.v.) plan to establish charity schools for German children. That Smith saw this as an opportunity to crack German cohesiveness with the educational tools of the English language and the Anglican religion was characteristic of his fear of pluralism and his use of the countervailing force of education to defeat it.

Smith was also an effective fund-raiser and propagandist, raising large sums to support the German schools and found a press and newspaper, the *Philadelphia Zeitlang*, to counter German publicists such as Christopher Sauer (q.v.). Like Samuel Davies, Gilbert Tennent, and Nathaniel Whitaker (q.v.), he traveled to Eng. to raise money for his college, publishing there *A Humble Representation . . . in Behalf of the Lately Erected Colleges of New York and Philadelphia*. The efficiency of his personal arguments and his pen is shown by his success, with James Jay, in raising 16,000 pounds for King's College and the College of Philadelphia. He later published *An Account of Washington College* and obtained more than 10,000 pounds for that institution.

Smith was a celebrated speaker and master of pulpit oratory, although the texts of his many sermons, even those such as *A Sermon on the Present Situation* that dealt with the dramatic issues of the Revolution, may "seem now to be little else than well-dressed and orderly platoons of windy words," as Moses Coit Tyler remarked. Ironically, although the Revolution inspired his eloquence, it could not inspire his allegiance, and Smith found himself for once confronting a polarity of forces in which he could enlist on neither side. Thus he delivered his *Oration in Memory of General Montgomery* with all his considerable rhetorical art, but with unaccustomed hints at compromise when he considered the larger issue of independence. Congress rejected a motion to thank him for his efforts. A talented man who suffered for his immoderate nature and personal failings, Provost William Smith deserves more attention than he has received. Occasionally his own worst enemy, he was also—like William Smith of N.Y.—a victim of history, a writer who might be better known but for his inability to applaud the coming of the Revolution.

   Suggested Readings: DAB; DARB; LHUS; Sprague (V, 158-163); T_1; T_2. *See also* William D. Andrews, "William Smith and the Rising Glory of America," EAL, 8 (1973), 33-43; Albert Frank Gegenheimer, *William Smith: Educator and Churchman* (1943); Peter C. Hoffer, "Law and Liberty: In the Matter of William Smith of Philadelphia, 1758," WMQ, 38 (1981), 681-701; Theodore Hornberger, "A Note on the Probable Source of Provost Smith's Famous Curriculum for the College of Philadelphia," PMHB, 58 (1934), 370-377; Ralph L. Ketcham, "Benjamin Franklin and William Smith: New Light on an Old Philadelphia Quarrel," PMHB, 88 (1964), 142-163; Bruce Richard Lively, "William Smith, The College and Academy of Philadelphia and Pennsylvania Politics 1753-1758," HMagPEC, 38 (1969), 237-258; Frank Luther Mott, *A History of American Magazines 1741-1850* (1930), pp. 25, 80-82; Lyon N. Richardson, *A History of Early American Magazines 1741-1789* (1931), pp. 99-123; Kenneth Silverman, ed., *Colonial American Poetry* (1968), pp. 380-386; Idem, *A Cultural History of the American Revolution* (1976), passim; Horace Wemyss Smith, *Life and Correspondence of the Rev. William Smith, D.D.*, 2 vols (1879; 1972); Charles J. Stillé, *A Memoir of the Rev. William Smith, D.D.* (1869).

Douglas R. Wilmes
The Pennsylvania State University

WILLIAM SMITH (1728-1793)

   Works: *Some Critical Observations upon a Late Poem, Entitled, The Breeches* (1750); *The Art of Pleading in Imitation of Part of Horace's Art of Poetry* (with William Livingston; 1751); *An Answer to a Bill in the Chancery of New-Jersey* (with William Livingston; 1752); *Laws of New York from the Year 1691 to 1751, Inclusive* (ed., with William Livingston; 1752); *The Craftsman: A Sermon from the Independent Whig* (ed., with William Livingston; 1752); *The Occasional Reverberator* (ed.; Sept. 7, 1753-Oct. 5, 1753); *The Preface to the Independent Reflector* (with William Livingston; 1754); *The Querist: or, a Letter to a Member of the General Assembly* (with William Livingston; 1754); *The History of the Province of New-York* (1757; 1972); *A Review of the Military Operations in North-America* (with William Livingston; 1757); *Laws of New-York from the 11th Nov. 1752, to 22d May 1762* (ed., with William Livingston; 1762); *Information to Emigrants* (1773); *The Candid Retrospect or the American War Exam-*

ined by Whig Principles (1780); *Continuation of the History of the Province of New-York* (1829; 1972); "Observations on the Loss of the American Colonies" (w. 1785; pub. 1942); William H. W. Sabine, ed., *Historical Memoirs from 16 March 1763 to 9 July 1776 of William Smith* (1956; 1958); L. F. S. Upton, ed., *The Diary and Selected Papers of Chief Justice William Smith, 1784-1793* (1963, 1965); "Thoughts upon the Dispute between Great Britain and her Colonies" (w. 1765; pub. 1965); Mss. diary, 1753-1783, N.Y. Public Library; numerous periodical essays and letters.

Biography: Born in New York City on Jun. 25, 1728, William Smith was the eldest son of William Smith, Sr. (1697-1769), and Mary (Het) Smith. Smith's father was a leading N.Y. lawyer, jurist, and politician; similarities in the careers of father and son have caused occasional confusion. In 1735, the elder Smith joined with James Alexander to defend John Peter Zenger (q.v.) against charges of seditious libel. Later, William Smith, Sr., served as a member of the Provincial Council, helped found the College of New Jersey, and fought against Anglican control of King's college.

Like his father, William Smith, Jr., attended Yale, graduating in 1745. After studying law in his father's office, Smith joined William Livingston (q.v.) in establishing an extremely successful law practice. Smith was self-consciously precocious, but his early accomplishments befitted his self-image. He and Livingston produced the first digest of N.Y.'s laws when Smith was only twenty-three, and Smith published his major work, *The History of the Province of New-York*, when he was twenty-nine. In the interim, Smith, Livingston, and John Morin Scott—all young Presbyterian lawyers and Yale graduates—had become known as the "New York Triumvirate." Political supporters of the Livingston faction against the DeLanceys, the Triumvirate published the *Independent Reflector* (1752-1753) and carried on a series of press wars in the pages of the *Reflector* and other N.Y. newspapers. Attacks on the established clergy and pleas for religious toleration brought responses from Samuel Johnson (q.v.), Samuel Seabury (q.v.), and James Wetmore (q.v.). Similarly, the Triumvirate opposed the Anglicans' efforts to charter King's College as an Anglican institution, an issue with implications for the development of the newly founded Presbyterian College of New Jersey and the continuing struggle of the Anglicans, led by Johnson, Seabury, and Thomas Bradbury Chandler (q.v.), to establish an American bishopric.

Smith became a key player in N.Y. politics during the years leading up to the Revolutionary War. He narrowly missed becoming chief justice in 1763, replaced his father on the council in 1767, continued to support the Livingstons as they gradually lost power to the DeLanceys, and made innumerable political friends and enemies. Smith delighted in the art of politics; his service as an advisor to Gov. Robert Monckton put him close to the executive seat of power in the 1760s, while his place on the council and his role as a powerful lawyer allowed him to intrigue against Lt. Gov. Cadwallader Colden (q.v.), Sir William Johnson, and other leading figures in the complex world of N.Y. politics. The

Stamp Act crisis of 1765 found Smith in uncomfortable alliance with the Sons of Liberty, but the escalating radicalism of the late 1760s and early 1770s conflicted with Smith's beliefs, for while he perceived that the British imperial system must change, he believed that it should change through the mechanisms of established political and legal forms.

When the Revolutionary War began, Smith attempted to remain neutral: "I think both Sides wrong," he wrote Gov. George Clinton (q.v.). But his refusal to swear allegiance to the state of N.Y. and his subsequent banishment from Livingston Manor to British-occupied New York City signaled his ultimate decision to join the Loyalists. He was appointed chief justice in 1780, but the continuance of military government in N.Y. prevented him from serving. In 1783, he left for Eng. with the defeated British army. Three years later, he was appointed chief justice of Canada and sailed for Quebec, where he lived until his death on Dec. 3, 1793. Smith married Janet Livingston in 1752; many of their eleven children died young, but a son, William Smith (1769-1847), lived to become a prominent Canadian historian and jurist.

Critical Appraisal: William Smith was a prolific, even compulsive writer. He kept a diary for most of his adult life, contributed essays and letters to N.Y. newspapers, carried on a busy law practice and an extensive personal correspondence, and wrote or co-authored some longer works of lasting significance. As most of Smith's periodical writings were anonymous, and many of his works were joint productions of members of the Triumvirate, a completely accurate bibliography cannot be produced.

Smith's most significant publication, *The History of the Province of New-York*, emerged from his earlier efforts to produce a digest of N.Y.'s laws. The original volume (1757) carried the history up to 1732; a later *Continuation*, not published in Smith's lifetime, drew heavily upon his personal experience and early diaries to chronicle the province's history to 1762. Like Thomas Hutchinson's (q.v.) *History of the Province of Massachusetts-Bay*, Smith's *History* reveals its author's political biases, while managing to rise above simple partisanship. Royal governors—with the exception of the Earl of Bellomont, an ally of the Livingstons—the Anglicans, and Cadwallader Colden are sacrificed at the altar of Smith's whig politics. But his character studies of the royal governors and an appendix analyzing the economic, political, and social conditions of the province make the *History* a document of enduring interest.

Smith saw historical research and interpretation both as an end in itself and as a political instrument, but the political dimension of his thought was not simply narrow and tactical. His intellect was capable of probing beyond the cluttered stage of provincial N.Y. politics, dominated by shifting allegiances and great families such as the Livingstons and the DeLanceys, to the larger field of British and American constitutional and national relationships. In this larger field, Smith believed that knowledge could be the facilitator of beneficial constitutional change, as opposed to chaotic extra-constitutional disruption. History, in Smith's view, should not be confined to the study, and historical ignorance would exact a price.

Writing his "Thoughts upon the Dispute between Great Britain and her Colonies" in 1765, Smith attacked Eng.'s colonial tax policies as "palpable Blundering," caused by "want of Knowledge concerning the Nature and State of our Trade." Similarly, he pointed out that an unwillingness to "bend" the constitution to accommodate historical change in the relationships between the mother country and her colonies seemed to arise from a fatal fixation on the present political structures of the colonies. Historically, he argued,

> the Colonies became separate, and with respect to each other independant Societies, by *Accident*; neither the Crown nor the Nation, had any Design in Splitting the Dominions into so many different, petty Governments. Thro' *Necessity* each acquired *Legislative* Powers, in a Mode somewhat similar to the grand Pattern in the Parent Country.

To understand history was to be freed from its seeming imperatives, and Smith's historicism and his constitutionalism come together in his proposals to avoid historical disaster by redefinition of the political framework of the American colonies in "Thoughts upon the Dispute," and elsewhere in his voluminous writings. Writing after the American victory, he similarly analyzed the weaknesses and potentialities for disaster in the Articles of Confederation in "Observations on the Loss of the American Colonies," again demonstrating the congruence of history to politics as he traced the multiple sources of dissatisfaction unleashed by the war and its aftermath. Throughout his writings, Smith revealed a sense of historical relevance that found its best expression in his *History*.

Attribution to Smith of the anonymous *A Review of the Military Operations in North-America* remains controversial. L. F. S. Upton, Smith's biographer, attributes the work to Smith. Milton M. Klein, however, argues for William Livingston as the author, while Michael Kammen, editor of Smith's *History*, refers to *A Review* as a collaborative effort of Smith and Livingston. Whether its authorship is assigned to Smith or Livingston, the *Review* expresses points of view held by both men and remains a valuable account of military campaigns during the French and Indian War and the political machinations of the colonial leaders. The *Review* was concerned with military developments following the defeat of Gen. Edward Braddock in July, 1755. Braddock had assigned Gov. William Shirley (q.v.) of Mass. to command an attack on Fort Niagara, while William Johnson had been directed to attack the French at Crown Point. Following Braddock's death, Shirley was given overall command of the colonial forces, and the two expeditions had proceeded. Shirley's force failed to gain its objective, but Johnson had defeated the French at Lake George in Sept., 1755. These events rapidly became fuel for political fires, as Shirley was a friend of Smith and Livingston and a political opponent of Lt. Gov. James DeLancey. Capitalizing on Johnson's brilliant victory, DeLancey and Thomas Pownall, with the assistance of Lewis Evans (q.v.), began a campaign to discredit Shirley. Early in 1756, Shirley was replaced by Lord Loudon as military commander and recalled from his post as governor of Mass., to be replaced by Thomas Pownall. William

Johnson was knighted. The *Review* thus represents an attempt to restore Shirley's reputation by attacking DeLancey and Johnson, despite the latter's undoubted military successes. In addition, the *Review* called for unification of the English colonies against the French, as had been suggested in the Albany Plan of 1754, which DeLancey opposed and the Livingstons and Smiths, father and son, supported.

If the authorship of the *Review* is clouded, equally difficult problems surround attempts to separate the newspaper writings of Smith, Livingston, and Scott. Their major production was the *Independent Reflector*, printed by James Parker (q.v.), to which Smith contributed ten essays. In 1753 Smith also edited the *Occasional Reverberator*; its four issues contain essays for and against the Triumvirate's position, and Smith may have written for both sides as he attempted to maintain the pressure on his Anglican opponents. Smith also published articles and letters in other N.Y. newspapers, including the *Journal*, the *Gazette*, and Hugh Gaine's (q.v.) *Mercury*, for which Smith wrote ten essays in the weekly "Watch Tower" column. Much of this journalistic outpouring concerned the King's College controversy, as did *The Querist*, co-authored by Smith and Livingston.

William Smith's writings reveal his deep concern for history, the law, constitutional reform, and politics. The Revolutionary War was a personal tragedy for him; afterwards he was distrusted by both sides. It was also an intellectual tragedy because it destroyed the historical continuity he had traced in his *History* and the political context in which he had fought so many youthful press wars. His legal writings retain only historical interest, while his constitutional proposals never received serious political consideration and had no effect on the course of colonial history. He was among the best writers of colonial history, yet he was also one of the most prominent victims of the historic events of 1776.

Suggested Readings: DAB; Dexter (II, 55-60); LHUS; T₁. *See also* Robert M. Calhoon, "William Smith, Jr.'s Alternative to the American Revolution," WMQ, 22 (1965), 105-118 (prints "Thoughts upon the Dispute"); Dorothy R. Dillon, *The New York Triumvirate: A Study of the Legal and Political Careers of William Livingston, John Morin Scott, and William Smith, Jr.* (1949); David C. Humphrey, *From King's College to Columbia, 1746-1800* (1976), passim; Michael Kammen, "Introduction," *The History of the Province of New-York*, 2 vols. (1972); Milton M. Klein, ed., *The Independent Reflector* (1963); idem, "William Livingston's *A Review of the Military Operations in North-America*," in *The Colonial Legacy: Some Eighteenth-Century Commentators*, ed. Lawrence H. Leder (1971); Hilda Neatby, "Chief Justice William Smith: An Eighteenth-Century Whig Imperialist," CanHR, 28 (1947), 44-67; Lorenzo Sabine, *Biographical Sketches of Loyalists of the American Revolution* (1864), II, 312-313; L. F. S. Upton, *The Loyal Whig: William Smith of New York & Quebec* (1969; includes bibliography of Smith's periodical essays and letters); Roger A. Wines, "William Smith: The Historian of New York," NYH, 57 (1959), 3-18; Oscar Zeichner, "William Smith's 'Observations on America,'" NYH, 40 (1942), 328-340.

Douglas R. Wilmes
The Pennsylvania State University

WILLIAM LOUGHTON SMITH (1758-1812)

Works: *To the Citizens of Charleston District* (1788); *The Politicks and Views of a Certain Party, Displayed* (1792); *An Address from William Smith of South Carolina, to His Constituents* (1794); *The Speeches of Mr. Smith, of South-Carolina, Delivered in the House of Representatives of the United States, in January, 1794, on the Subject of Certain Commercial Regulations, Proposed by Mr. Madison, in the Committee of the Whole, on the Report of the Secretary of State* (1794); *A Candid Examination of the Objections to the Treaty of Amity, Commerce, and Navigation, Between the United States and Great Britain, as Stated in the Report of the Committee, Appointed by the Citizens of the United States in Charleston, South Carolina* (1795); *The Speech of Mr. Smith, of South Carolina, in the House of Representatives of the United States, on the Subject of the Reduction of the Public Debt* (1795); *A Comparative View of the Constitutions of Several States with Each Other, and with That of the United States* (1796); *An Oration, Delivered in St. Philip's Church, Before the Inhabitants of Charleston, South-Carolina, on the Fourth of July, 1796, in Commemoration of American Independence* (1796); *The Pretensions of Thomas Jefferson to the Presidency Examined; and the Charges Against John Adams Refuted* (1796); *The Numbers of Phocion, Which Were Originally Published in the Charleston Courier, in 1806, on the Subject of Neutral Rights* (1806).

Biography: William Loughton Smith was born in 1758 to one of the wealthiest families in S.C. Both of his parents died before Smith reached adulthood. At the age of 12, he began his education in Eng. and Switz., returning to Charleston in 1783. An attorney by profession, Smith was elected to the First Congress of the U.S. and served as a member of that body until 1797. In that year, he resigned his office to become U.S. minister to Port. He was relieved from this post in 1801 and returned to Charleston two years later. After being defeated in a run for Congress in 1804, Smith resumed the practice of law. He died in Charleston in 1812.

Critical Appraisal: Political writings expounding elements of the position of the Federalist party comprise most of William Loughton Smith's literary production. Smith, whose political ideology was so similar to Alexander Hamilton's (q.v.) that their authorship was on occasion confused by the public, was at his best attacking the Republican opposition. His *The Politicks and Views of a Certain Party, Displayed* was written in response to Republican charges that he had personally profited from the federal assumption of state debts. This extremely partisan work analyzed the emergence of the Republican opposition, dating its origins to the return of Thomas Jefferson (q.v.) from Fr. Jefferson, according to Smith, was a second-rate individual in comparison with Hamilton. Smith argued that Jefferson hid behind a partisan press attacking Hamilton and attempting to convince the American people that as long as the Federalists controlled the government, they would be unhappy.

Smith established himself as a leading Federalist in the South three years later by his defense of the Jay Treaty in his pamphlet *A Candid Examination of the Objections to the Treaty of Amity, Commerce, and Navigation*. In this tract, the author presented sound, well-reasoned arguments of how the treaty did in fact benefit America. Smith's most imaginative work, however, remained his biting attacks on the Republicans—particularly Thomas Jefferson. The pamphlet *The Pretensions of Thomas Jefferson to the Presidency Examined* was an examination of whether Jefferson would make a good president. Originally published as a series of articles in the *Gazette of the United States* under the signature of "Phocion" and later reprinted in the *South-Carolina State Gazette*, this work was one of the most savage attacks leveled at Jefferson up to that time. Smith's tract examined the Republican's qualifications for president in a satirical manner, utilizing the arguments by a Virginian essayist that Jefferson would be a good president because he was a philosopher. Smith discounted Jefferson's abilities as a moral philosopher because of his support of the French Revolution and then argued that if he was a natural philosopher, his vocation did little to make him qualified to be president. Smith's works are important in understanding the political views of the Federalists in the last decade of the eighteenth century. His political writings touch every major issue before the U.S. Congress from 1792 to the turn of the century.

Suggested Readings: DAB. *See also* George C. Rogers, Jr., *Evolution of a Federalist, William Loughton Smith of Charleston, 1758-1812* (1962); Ulrich D. Philips, "The South Carolina Federalists II," AHR, 14 (1908), 713-743; John H. Wolfe, *Jeffersonian Democracy in South Carolina* (1940).

George D. Terry
University of South Carolina

ANTHONY SOMERBY (1610-1686)

Works: *The Holy Bible in Verse* (c. 1640; excerpts published in Harold S. Jantz, FCNEV, pp. 132-144, 1944; rep. 1962).

Biography: Born in Lincolnshire, Eng., in 1610, Anthony Somerby was a merchant in Bristol until he immigrated, for reasons unknown, to Newbury, Mass., in 1639. Although no record of his education has yet come to light, he was undoubtedly an educated and well-respected man, for he served as schoolmaster at Newbury for a short time and as town clerk for most of his life. Little is known about his private life, but we may safely assume, from a reading of his verse, that he was devoutly religious. *The Holy Bible in Verse* reveals one other salient fact about his life: in 1641 his wife gave birth to a son, Abiel. Somerby died in 1686, at the age of 76. The circumstances surrounding his death and the place of his burial are unknown.

Critical Appraisal: Written during the 1640s, Anthony Somerby's *The Holy Bible in Verse* is one of the longest poems written in seventeenth-century

New Eng. An unfinished synopsis of the Bible, the poem is composed of approximately 1,600 stanzas arranged alphabetically (from A to U) and written in relatively rough common measure. In the course of the poem, Somerby repeated his modified alphabet, with some inconsistencies, approximately eighty times. Although his use of the alphabet suggests a preoccupation with order, the poem is characterized by the surprising absence of other more essential methods of organization. As Harold Jantz has said of Somerby's alphabetical method, "One can only hope that he did not use it during his short period of school teaching, for the pupils would have been thoroughly confused by his bland disregard of chronology and by his 'method' of crowding three or four miscellaneous items into one stanza."

Although the poem's arbitrary organizational principle is a significant poetic liability, Somerby's reluctance to go beyond synopses of Bible stories limits his accomplishment even more seriously. Only rarely did Somerby pause from his cursory summaries to comment on God's word; instead, he merely glossed the Bible, telling his readers what they should examine in depth. He wrote, for example, "Know here the pedigree age and deth / of patriarchs related / from Adam to the dayes of noe," "observe here onans filthy fact," and "see here how Joseph gets the coyne. . . into king pharos hand." Hence although the poem is an obvious product of the religious concerns of the time, it nevertheless tells us little about Somerby's, or his age's, specific theological beliefs.

Despite its flaws, Somerby's *Bible in Verse* is a significant contribution to seventeenth-century American poetry because of its subject, length, and ambition. Even more importantly, perhaps, the poem is noteworthy for its extensive use of alliteration. As Jantz has said, the *Bible in Verse* is one of "the latest survivals by a century or more of this mainstay of old Germanic poetry." By combining the common measure of the present with the alliterative prosody of the past, Somerby created an original mode of poetic expression. More than most of his peers, he was concerned with extending and developing poetic tradition, thereby bringing the old into conjunction with the new. The following stanza is representative of Somerby's achievement: "Good david from his kingdom driven / was greatly greived in mind / for his great sin against the Lord / and could small comfort find."

Because *The Holy Bible in Verse* is an important work of early American poetry, it is regrettable that only brief excerpts from its Genesis and Book of Ruth sections have been published. The rest of the poem exists in manuscript form in the archives of the American Antiquarian Society. Only when the poem is published in its entirety will it receive the scholarly attention it merits.

Suggested Readings: FCNEV.

David Jauss
University of Arkansas at Little Rock

AUGUSTUS GOTTLIEB SPANGENBERG (1704-1792)

Works: *Darlegung Richtiger Antworten auf Mehr 300 Beschuldigungen Gegen den Ordinarium Fratrum* (1751); *Apologetische Schlusschrift* (1752);

Leben des Herrn Nichlaus Ludwig Grafen und Herrn Zinzendorf, 3 vols. (1772-1775); *Kurzgefasste Historische Nachright von der . . .Bruderunitat* (1774); *Reden an Kinder* (1782); *Das Wort von Krenz* (1791); *Vergebung der Sunde* (1792); *Idea Fidei Fratrum Oder Kurzer Begriff der Christlichen Lehr in den Evangelischen Brudergemeinen* (1799).

Biography: Augustus Gottlieb Spangenberg was born on Jul. 15, 1704, at Klettenberg (near Gottingen), Ger., where his father served as Lutheran pastor. Orphaned when he was but 10 years old, Spangenberg studied at the cloister school of Ilfeld. In 1722 he entered the University of Jena, where he became a live-in secretary to a noted pietistical leader, Johannes Franciscus Buddeus. Forsaking his original law curriculum for theology, Spangenberg was awarded an undergraduate degree in that field at Jena in 1726 and, while studying for the M.A. (which he received in 1729), was strongly attracted to Count Nicholas Ludwig Von Zinzendorf (q.v.), who had visited the university in 1728. In 1730 Spangenberg went to Herrnhut to assist in the county's religious experiment with the Brethren, refusing an offered lectureship at Copenhagen. In 1732, however, Spangenberg did accept a call to teach in the theological school and to assist in the orphans' institute of the University of Halle. Unfortunately, the moderate pietistic atmosphere of Halle was unsuited to Spangenberg's more leftist views. He was dismissed in 1733 for Separatist tendencies, and probably also for his close association with Von Zinzendorf, who was rapidly becoming anathema at Halle, and made his way back to Herrnhut, where he formally joined the Brethren. Quickly Spangenberg became Von Zinzendorf's right-hand man and a prime mover in Moravian mission work. In 1735 he brought Moravian colonists to Copenhagen and was responsible for Moravian settlements in Ga. in 1735. For a time, from 1736 to 1739, he labored among the Schwenkfelders in Pa., trying to gather these sometime tenants of Herrnhut into Von Zinzendorf's Church of God in the Spirit. When this failed, he returned to Europe, both to be wed (in 1740) and, in 1741, to found in London the Society for the Furtherance of the Gospel, a device to gain Anglican financial support for Moravian missions.

Consecrated a bishop in 1744, he sailed to America to assume control of the Moravian settlement at Bethlehem, Pa., founded three years earlier by Von Zinzendorf and David Nitschmann. Using Bethlehem as a center, Spangenberg had the Moravians labor mightily in the work of converting Indians. To solve the community's financial woes, he instituted a "common-economy," in reality a return to the primitive communism of the early church, where all worked for the community, which, in turn, provided for the needs of its members.

His influence temporarily waning, he was replaced at Bethlehem by Bishop John Nitschmann and returned to Europe in 1750. His exile, however, lasted but a year for, in 1751, he was back in America. Finding his "common-economy" at Bethlehem a shambles due to sloth, mismanagement, and human nature, he quickly abandoned the experiment and reverted to a capitalistic economy based on the family unit. In 1754 he undertook a large-scale settlement of Moravians in N.C. Finally, in 1762 his health was so undermined that he returned to Herrnhut, where he served as de facto head of the Moravian Church until his death on Sept. 28, 1792.

Critical Appraisal: Beyond doubt, the greatest work of Augustus Gottlieb Spangenberg is his *Idea Fidei Fratrum*, translated into English in 1784 as *Exposition of Christian Doctrine*. In this work, Spangenberg not only codified Moravian doctrines but did so in such a moderate way that he prevented the church from lapsing into sectarianism and kept it in the mainstream of the churchly denominations.

Because of Spangenberg's great interest in Indian missions, one of his more prominent works is "An Account of the Manner in Which the Protestant Church of the Unitas Fratrum or United Brethren Preach the Gospel and Carry on Their Missions Among the Heathen," translated from the German and published in London by H. Trapp in 1788.

In a forceful and plain style, with copious references to Scripture, Spangenberg argued that although God gave Jews a special revelation as his chosen people, he did not forget the heathen, for "He manifested himself to them by the works of creation." The Babylonian captivity itself was just one phase in God's unrelenting effort to spread his word to the heathen by having the Jews rub elbows, as it were, with them so they could learn of God and accept him if they had a mind to do so. Although Christ concentrated his mission on the Jews, he did go to Samaria, and more importantly, he sent Paul to labor among the heathen.

Moravian missioners, and this work is sort of a handbook for such, as well as an apologia for non-Moravians, should walk in Paul's steps eschewing the wisdom of the Greeks to preach in the foolishness of the people. By unpalatable wisdom, Spangenberg meant dogma and Revelation before Christ. Not only did it confuse the simple-minded heathen, but "the poor creatures commonly took the doctrine only into their heads; the heart experiencing little or nothing of it; It was therefore but too often the case that they became worse after their baptism than they had been before." Instead, Spangenberg insisted that they emphasize the Gospel of Christ, his suffering and death, this in accord with the blood and wounds theology Moravians then favored. This process would lead to conversion. Dogmatic knowledge would come later.

Baptism was granted once the heathen acknowledged their sinfulness, their intention to sin no more, and the power of Christ alone to save them. Infant baptism he allowed only for the children of the regenerate. The Lord's Supper was to be given only if the candidate passed a personal examination of the soul, and piety was to be fostered through conventicles.

In many ways, Spangenberg showed the adaptability that was the hallmark of Jesuit missioners before him. He insisted on translating hymns and Scripture into the native tongue and was tolerant of alien customs insofar as they were not sacrilegious. For instance, he urged his missioners not to denounce those laboring in hot climates for nudity while working. He took an equally pragmatic approach to the problem of polygamy. If a man had more than one wife before conversion, he could keep them, but he could not aspire to be a lay mission helper. If an Indian contracted a Christian marriage, then polygamy, and divorce, were forbidden to him forever. The vast success of the Moravian missions is a tribute to the effectiveness of Spangenberg's ideas.

Suggested Readings: CCMC; DAB; DARB. *See also* J. Taylor Hamilton, *A History of the Church Known as the Moravian Church* (1900); Edward Langton, *History of the Moravian Church* (1956); K. F. Ledderhose, *The Life of Augustus Spangenberg* (1855); Gerhard Reichel, *August Gottlieb Spangenberg* (1906); Levin Theodore Reichel, *The Early History of the Church of the United Brethren* (1888); Jeremiah Rissler, *Life of Spangenberg*, 4 vols. (1794).

Leonard R. Riforgiato
The Pennsylvania State University

HENRY SPELMAN (c. 1595-1623)

Works: *A Relation of Virginia, 1609* (w. c. 1611; pub. 1872).

Biography: Trader and interpreter for the Va. colony, Spelman first came to Va. from Eng. in 1609, "beinge in displeasuer of my frendes, and desirous to see other cuntryes." Only about 14 at the time, he was soon left by Capt. John Smith (q.v.) at an Indian village, presumably to serve as surety against English attack and to learn the language. Although William Symonds's assertion in Smith's *Generall Historie* that Pocahontas saved Spelman's life is dubious, he resided in several Indian villages for more than a year and was able to master the language. Ransomed by Capt. Argall late in 1610, he returned to Eng., where he composed *A Relation of Virginia*, probably during the next year. On his return to Va., he busied himself as an interpreter and trader, but lost his captain's rank in 1619 when the Assembly found him guilty of speaking maliciously of Governor Yeardley to the Indians. Described by a contemporary as "one that had in him more of the savage than of the Christian," Spelman seems to have had an ambiguous, marginal status that caused his fellow colonists to regard him with a mixture of respect and disquiet. Nevertheless, his language skills and understanding of Indian ways made him invaluable to the colony, until he was killed by Anacostan Indians along the Potomac in 1623. Spelman was also an important oral informant for Samuel Purchas's (q.v.) and William Strachey's (q.v.) accounts of Indian customs and myths.

Critical Appraisal: *A Relation of Virginia* is a brief, nearly illiterate account of Indian customs preceded by a summary of Henry Spelman's experiences during his first residence in Va. Because of his youth and inexperience, some of his claims are highly questionable, especially his assertions that he was sold by Smith to the Indians and that Smith conspired with Powhatan to kill Capt. West. The remainder of the narrative describes Indian religious practices, housing, marriage customs, the naming of children, medical treatments, justice, criminal executions, farming, eating, warfare, and games. The descriptions are fairly detailed and essentially neutral, neither criticizing nor praising Indian ways. The Indians, said Spelman at one point, "for ye most part . . . worship ye diuell, . . . yet neuer ye less in euery cuntry they haue a seuerall Image whom they call ther god." Spelman's description of the landscape is almost entirely couched in terms of its potential for hunting and agriculture, but his intent in most of the manuscript is less promotional than descriptive, for the benefit of those who are "desirus to heare ye fashions of that cuntrye." The narrative is notable as one of the first descriptions written by a long-term resident of Indian villages, and despite its laboring style, it serves as a useful ethnographic introduction, refreshing in its simplicity and dispassionate approach.

Suggested Readings: Edward Arber and A. G. Bradley, eds., *Travels and Works of Captain John Smith*, 2 vols. (1910), pp. ci-cxiv, passim; Alexander Brown, *The Genesis of the United States*, 2 vols. (1890), pp. 483-488 and 1020-1021; Richard Beale Davis, *Intellectual Life in the Colonial South, 1585-1763*, 3 vols. (1978), pp. 185, 223-224, passim; Richard L. Morton, *Colonial Virginia* (1960), I, 78-81. The manuscript of *A Relation* was first printed by J. F. Hunnewell in a small, private edition; a slightly different version under the title *A Relation of Virginea* is printed in Arber and Bradley.

David H. Stanley
The University of Utah

ALEXANDER SPOTSWOOD (1676-1740)

Works: *The Official Letters of Alexander Spotswood*, vol. I (1882); vol. II (1885).

Biography: Born on the African side of the Strait of Gibraltar, the son of a British garrison surgeon, Alexander Spotswood followed a family tradition into military service. As a young officer in Queen Anne's War, he won the confidence of the duke of Marlborough. Resigning his commission in 1709, he was named lieutenant governor of Va., an impressive post for a 33-year-old soldier of modest background. He served as governor of the colony from 1710 to 1722.

With 80,000 inhabitants, including 20,000 slaves, Va. was the foremost colony in the New World. It was, however, an uneasy province, where British policy contended with the ambitions of landed gentry and church officials. Young Spotswood, promptly asserting the royal prerogative, put Va. on the path to internal order and a new prosperity. He regulated the tobacco trade, curbed greedy land speculation, subdued pirates on the seaboard and Indian uprisings on the frontiers, and pushed settlement to and beyond the Blue Ridge mountains. In Williamsburg he directed architectural and town-planning developments befitting the capital of a favored colony.

When Queen Anne's death left the throne to a German prince, Spotswood's fortunes waned. George I chose to exploit the colony rather than develop it; his ministers annulled Spotswood's reform laws and diminished his authority. Spotswood was removed from office in 1722.

The later years of his life were devoted to Spotswood's own ambitions. In London, at age 48, he married advantageously, returning to Va. six years later with a wife and four children. In the Rappahannock wilderness, he cleared land, built a handsome "castle," and brought in German settlers to develop iron smelters and forest products. Now more a Virginian than an Englishman, he shared the colonial unrest that would eventually produce the American Revolution.

Critical Appraisal: The chief records of Spotswood's public career are his official letters, which made the long slow voyage from Va. to London. They bespeak his ambition, self-confidence, and strength of will, while revealing his attitudes toward colleagues and constituents. Many of the 185 letters were addressed to the lords commissioners of trade and the lords of the treasury. Less frequent correspondents were the lords of the admiralty, the bishop of London, and other officials in London. The letters embraced a broad range of concerns—economic, political, religious, and military—in the colony. Vexing problems were land use, regulation of tobacco commerce, and relations with the Indians. Underlying all was the contest between local colonial government and the royal authority.

On arrival in Va., Spotswood found that land speculators could entail large tracts and hold them tax free, without improvement, for future profit. His letters on quit rents clearly informed the Board of Trade (whose members had hazy concepts of Va.) of the extent and terrain of the colony and of the need for reform in land possession and land use. His modest proposal, that landholding should require a small measure of improvement and cultivation, was resisted by the House of Burgesses. But the governor prevailed.

Tobacco, Va.'s principal export, was subject to royal regulations that were generally ignored by the planters. Under a reform spelled out to the commissioners of trade, Spotswood had the tobacco harvest collected, inspected, and graded in government barns. The burning of inferior leaf enhanced the value of exported cargo and assured the queen of her just taxes.

On long journeys by horseback to the western wilds, Spotswood observed greed and corruption in the Indian trade. Curbing the traffic in rum and shoddy merchandise, he planned roads, bridges, and warehouses to serve the Indian commerce. He induced restless Sapony tribesmen to settle around Fort Christanna, deep in the forest, where a few soldiers helped them to police themselves, and a dedicated schoolmaster taught their children the rudiments of civilized learning. In correspondence with the bishop of London, he began a program of secondary education for selected Indian youth; brought to Williamsburg, they were given their own housing and curriculum at William and Mary College.

Spotswood's contribution to the developing town of Williamsburg appears in occasional letters. A gifted mathematician and amateur architect, he designed the Bruton Parish Church, the second building of the venerable college, the fortresslike magazine, and the stately governor's residence (derisively called "palace" by resentful burgesses) and its handsome gardens.

In asserting the royal prerogative, Spotswood increasingly provoked the Va. gentry. William Byrd of Westover (q.v.), who dubbed the governor "Arroganti," spent a long season in London lobbying against him, and the commissioners of trade received an unsigned bill of fifteen complaints from Va. Spotswood's longest and most fervent letter, posted Jan. 16, 1717, responded to the complaints, item by item, so that he remained securely in office. However, the underlying conflict of self-determination against royal authority remained, and contention smoldered like a fitful campfire. Conspicuously absent from Spotswood's letters is any account of his 1716 expedition to the Blue Ridge and the luring valley of the Shenandoah. More a personal adventure than an official mission and not officially recorded, the romantic episode carried Spotswood permanently into popular history and folklore.

On the matter of international rivalry for control of the American interior, Spotswood's foresight was important for the future, whether under dominion of the U.K. or of the as yet unborn U.S. In 1720 he wrote to the Board of Trade:

> there can be no doubt but that the French settlement on the Mississippi will (without timely precautions) greatly effect both the Trade and Safety of...his Majesty's Plantations. Tobacco, rice, and other commodities...will no doubt be produced in this new French Settlement, and they will become our rivals...in all foreign Markets.... By the communication which the French may maintain between Canada and the Mississippi...they have it in their power...to engross all the trade of the Indian Nations.

With the same logic, he pressed the importance of planting English settlements on the coast of Fla., and "of taking St. Augustine from the Spaniards." No other colonial leader saw so clearly the growing rivalry and the incalculable prize.

Through Spotswood's official letters gleam personal qualities of fervor, candor, and energy, along with a keen and broad intelligence. He wrote with a formality that carried his own tone of voice and mind. He could express warmth and esteem but also irony, scorn, and anger. He must have read much, although his letters seldom mention reading. Somehow this unschooled soldier had acquired poise and urbanity. In all he did and said, he had a confident style.

Suggested Readings: DAB; DNB. *See also* Leonidas Dodson, *Alexander Spotswood, Governor of Colonial Virginia, 1710-1722* (1939); Hugh Jones, *The Present State of Virginia* (1754; 1956); Ann Maury, *Memoirs of a Huguenot Family* (1853); H. R. McElwaine, ed., *Journals of the House of Burgesses, 1705-1712* (1912); idem, *Journals of the House of Burgesses, 1712-1726* (1912); Louis B. Wright and Marion Tinling, eds., *The London Diary, 1717-1721* (1958); idem, *The Secret Diary of William Byrd of Westover, 1709-1712* (1941).

Walter Havighurst
Oxford, Ohio

SAMUEL SPRING (1746-1819)

Works: *A Sermon Delivered at the North Congregational Church...on a Day of Public Thanksgiving* (1778); *A Sermon on Family Prayer* (1780); *A*

Sermon on the Importance of Sinners Coming Immediately to Christ (1780); *The Substance of a Discourse Delivered at Westford, October 4th, 1779* (1780); *Three Sermons to Little Children* (1783); *A Friendly Dialogue Between Philalethes [Samuel Spring] and Toletus [David Tappan] . . . upon the Nature of Duty* (1784); *The Nature and Importance of Rightly Dividing the Truth* (1784); *Christian Knowledge* (1785); *Moral Disquisitions and Strictures on the Reverend David Tappan's Letters to Philalethes* (1789); *The Exemplary Pastor* (1791); *A Sermon Preached at the Ordination of the Reverend Pearson Thurston* (1792); *A Discourse, Delivered at North Church in Newburyport* (1794); *A Sermon Preached at the Ordination of the Rev. Daniel Merril* (1794); *A Thanksgiving Sermon* (1798); *God the Author of Human Greatness . . . A Discourse on the Death of . . . Washington* (1800); *A Sermon Delivered Before the Massachusetts Missionary Society* (1802); *A Discourse Preached in Bradford . . . Before the Essex Middle Association* (1804); *The Sixth Commandment Friendly to Virtue, Honor and Politeness* (1804); *Truth Discriminated from Error* (1805); *Two Discourses on Christ's Selfexistence* (1805); *An Address to the Members of the Merrimack Humane Society* (1807); *A Discourse Delivered in Consequence of the Death of Deacon Thomas Thompson* (1808); *A Sermon at the Inauguration of the Rev. Edward D. Griffin . . . Professor of Pulpit Eloquence in the Theological Institution in Andover* (1809); *Two Sermons Addressed to the Second Congregational Society in Newburyport, Fast-day* (1809); *A Funeral Discourse Delivered at the Interment of the Rev. Nathaniel Noyes* (1810); *An Essay on the Discipline of Christ's House* (1816); *The United Agency of God and Man in Salvation* (1817); *A Charity Sermon Delivered at the Request of the Howard Benevolent Society* (1818); *A Sermon Preached at New Haven, Conn. Before the American Board of Commissioners for Foreign Missions* (1818); *The Youth's Assistant* (1818).

Biography: Samuel Spring was born at Northbridge (formerly Uxbridge), Mass., on Feb. 27, 1746. His father, a wealthy farmer and descendant of John Spring who settled in Watertown in 1634, intended that his son follow him in the generational line of prosperous New Eng. farmers. However, Samuel was more responsive to the noted piety of his mother, Sarah (Reed) Spring. Experiencing his conversion at the age of 18, he decided to prepare for the ministry. His mother's influence overcame his father's initial reluctance, and Samuel began studies under the Rev. Nathan Webb. In 1771 he graduated from the College of New Jersey (now Princeton University) and for the following three years studied theology under John Witherspoon (q.v.), as well as under Joseph Bellamy (q.v.), Samuel Hopkins (q.v.), and Stephen West. He then joined the Continental Army and was assigned as chaplain for Benedict Arnold's (q.v.) 1776 expedition to Can. In 1777 he was ordained pastor of the North (Central) Congregational Church in Newburyport, Mass., where he remained until his death in 1819. He was instrumental in the formation of the Massachusetts Missionary Society (1779) and was founding editor of its official organ, the *Massachusetts Missionary Magazine* (1803).

Spring is also known for his role in the establishment of the Massachusetts

General Association (1803), a union of the two Calvinist parties opposed to Unitarianism. Most notably, he was one of the founders of the Andover Theological Seminary (1808), which served as nursery and bastion for the nurture and preservation of orthodox Calvinism. Born at the close of the First Great Awakening, Spring was the most productive from the Revolution through the Second Great Awakening. He was an intimate and highly respected member of the "Hopkinsian" circle of Calvinist preachers, named for the Rev. Samuel Hopkins of Hadley, Mass., who was first Spring's mentor and, later, his father-in-law. Spring fathered eleven children, two of them ministers, and he published some twenty-five tracts and sermons.

Critical Appraisal: The strict (Hopkinsian) Calvinists' controversy with the Unitarians dominates the writings of Samuel Spring. *Two Discourses on Christ's Selfexistence*, for example, is a lucid critique of the Unitarian position on the humanity of Christ, the substitution of tabula rasa and "self-determination" for the doctrine of original sin, and the consequent rejection of "infinite atonement" that Calvinists believed to be established in the death and resurrection of the divine Christ. For all of his alarm over the rise in religious liberalism, Spring cultivated a dispassionate, empirical style of exegesis: "If the experiment were possible," he mused, "we would avail ourselves of the judgement of some enlightened, impartial man, relative to Christ's divinity, who has read the Bible carefully without any comment or human aid." Nevertheless, he was contented with the normal process of hermeneutics: "The Scripture is correct and decisive, and authorizes no diversity of religious theories." Spring perceived Unitarianism to be more than the growth of individual error: It was a divine judgment on "a declining people" who no longer kept the sabbath, catechized the children, or upheld "true" religion with the fervor of their ancestors. Thus Spring underscored the importance of "exemplary" pastors who were "under the guidance of disinterested benevolence" (a Hopkinsian term). Such pastors were "detached from the concerns of the world," preachers of "sorrow for sin," and of the "absolute eternity of hell torments."

Although he opposed the liberals' faith in perfectability and universal redemption, he was an advocate of "virtuous education" as a social corrective. In a sermon on *The Sixth Commandment*, preached against dueling, he suggested that crime resulted from "some material defects and mismanagement in the method of...education." Discoursing on the death of George Washington (q.v.) in a sermon titled *God the Author of Human Greatness*, he noted that "The agency of God is directly concerned in human greatness by amply furnishing the favoured sons of genius with an answerable education." Thus education was for Samuel Spring not the process of self-initiative and fulfillment, but an instrument and blessing of divine grace. All moral duty was unfolded in the vital center of God's "holy [disinterested] love." In reply to the moderate David Tappan (q.v.), Spring wrote his *Moral Disquisitions* to prove the doctrine of man's *total* depravity, arguing that motive could not be isolated from action, and that all good works were "selfish" and "carnal" if not performed under the influence of "holy love."

In short, pragmatism was not reconcilable with the workings of the Holy Spirit. Williston Walker has called Samuel Spring "the chief Hopkinsian in New England" next to Nathaniel Emmons (q.v.). Certainly, Spring's influence derived from a combination of effective preaching style and the ability to make Calvinist doctrine and piety relevant to current social and intellectual trends. For these reasons, he is a significant figure in the transition from Puritan to evangelical.

Suggested Readings: CCMC; DAB; P; Sprague (II, 85-89). *See also* Sarah L. Bailey, *Historical Sketches of Andover* (1880), pp. 560-561; Samuel Davies Alexander, *Princeton College During the Eighteenth Century* (1872), pp. 145-146; Williston Walker, *A History of the Congregational Churches in the United States* (1894), pp. 322-351; Leonard Woods, *The Usefulness of the Sacred Office; A Sermon Delivered, March 9, 1819, at the Funeral of the Rev. Samuel Spring, D.D.* (1819).

Barbara Ritter Dailey
Boston University

JOSEPH STANSBURY (1740-1809)

Works: *The Loyal Verses of Joseph Stansbury and Jonathan Odell* (w. 1771-1783; pub. 1857).

Biography: Born in London in 1740, Joseph Stansbury immigrated to America in Oct. 1767, settling in Philadelphia, Pa., where by the outbreak of the Revolutionary War, he had become a successful merchant. During the early years of the war, he published Loyalist verses in the Philadelphia *Evening Post* and, along with Jonathan Odell (q.v.), acted as an intermediary in the Benedict Arnold (q.v.) conspiracy. He was arrested in Nov. 1780 on suspicion of spying for the British and was banished to N.Y. in Dec. He lived there until after the war, publishing occasionally in *Rivington's Royal Gazette*. Stansbury attempted to resettle in Philadelphia following the war but met with public resentment. After a brief exile in Nova Scotia, a trip to Eng. to file legal claims, and another short stay in Philadelphia, he finally settled in N.Y., where he lived until his death in 1809.

Critical Appraisal: Perhaps better than any other Loyalist writer, Joseph Stansbury recorded in his verse the emotional cycles corresponding to the fortunes of the war and its aftermath. Although in 1771 he could still write, "We are Englishmen all," by Jun. 1776 in "A Welcome to Howe," he warned, "Brittania cries—forbear: Deluded Sons, nor urge the War." After the war actually broke out, Stansbury, like his friend and fellow poet Jonathan Odell, supported the Loyalist cause in verse, confidently anticipating British military successes in poems such as "The Lords of the Main" (1780) and "Song for a Venizon Dinner" (1781) and satirizing the Revolution and its leadership, as for example in these ironic lines from "Liberty" (1780): "Law and order prostrate lie; / *Commonwealth* is all the cry. / Tho' we slaves at present be / 'Tis all for glorious Liberty."

Although Stansbury ably wrote such partisan verse, his talents and temperament seem to have been better suited to occasional songs and personal verse. In returning to them near the end of the war, he effectively blended an enjoyment of the moment with the sadness of impending defeat. One of the best of his songs is "Let Us Be Happy as Long as We Can," which concludes: "Tonight let's enjoy this good wine and a Song / And relish the hour which we cannot prolong. / If Evil will come, we'll adhere to our Plan / And baffle Misfortune as long as we can." Shortly after the war, Stansbury wrote a short but eloquent poem, "The United States," calling for reunification of the two sides, "Blushing we were ever Foes." Postwar adjustment was not easy, however, as can be seen in "To Cordelia," written in Nova Scotia, describing the pain of exile, a common plight of Loyalists but one that was fortunately temporary for Stansbury. This final group of poems, expressing Stansbury's determination not only to bear up under adversity but also to be reconciled to the new regime and to reclaim his American identity, conveys a sincerity and charm that still retain their appeal.

Suggested Readings: DAB; T₂. *See also* Pastora S. Cafferty, "Loyalist Rhapsodies: The Poetry of Stansbury and Odell" (Ph.D. diss., George Washington Univ., 1971), contains texts of unpublished poems by Stansbury; Everett Emerson, ed., *American Literature, 1764-1789* (1977), pp. 59-71.

Charles Modlin
Virginia Polytechnic Institute and State University

DANIEL STANTON (1708-1770)

Works: *A Journal of the Life, Travels, and Gospel Labours of a Faithful Minister of Jesus Christ* (1772).

Biography: Daniel Stanton was born in 1708 in Philadelphia, Pa., the only child of Daniel Stanton, who was lost at sea shortly before his son's birth, and Abigail, who died when Daniel was still a child. Apprenticed to his uncle, Stanton lived, rather unhappily, in N.J. until his term of service was complete. He then embarked on a lifelong series of ministries for the Society of Friends, first in Bucks County, Pa.—where he met Sarah Lloyd, whom he wed in 1733—and later throughout N.Y. State and New Eng. After his wife's death in 1748, his journeys grew longer: to Barbados in 1748; through Ire., Eng., Wales, and Scot. (1749-1750); to N.Y. and New Eng. again (1753-1754); to Va., N.C., and S.C. (1760-1761); to Del. and Md. (1762); and additional trips throughout the Northeast (1763-1764, 1767, 1769). He died in Germantown near Philadelphia on Jun. 28, 1770.

Critical Appraisal: Obviously Daniel Stanton was not a literary figure, nor did he in any way pretend to be. His *Journal* is a prosaic account of his yearly travels and, more importantly, his yearly (and monthly) meetings with fellow Quakers. The *Journal* retains interest, however, both as a historical document and as an example of the personal literature so popular in colonial America.

The *Journal*'s historical interest lies not in its description of contemporary events (few of which Stanton noted) or contemporary scenes (the landscape seldom impinges upon the narrative). He faithfully recorded, however, Quaker meetings and the Friends in attendance throughout his travels. As such, the *Journal* finds a companion in John Smith's (q.v.) account of *Hannah Logan's Courtship: A True Narrative*, in which Stanton appears frequently.

The *Journal* also shares a place in American literary history as personal literature similar to the Quaker diaries of John Woolman (q.v.) and Thomas Chalkley (q.v.), and, in part, to Jonathan Edwards's (q.v.) *Personal Narrative* and Benjamin Franklin's (q.v.) *Autobiography*. The affinities between the religious experiences of Edwards and Stanton—two figures of decidedly different religious beliefs and intellectual powers—rest chiefly in their similarly emotional religious conversion scenes and subsequent dedication to a life of service. The parallels with Franklin's work are not as obvious, but they appear more intriguing.

Franklin and Stanton were born within two years of each other; both were apprenticed, unwillingly, to a near relation; and both recorded a rigorous program for self-discipline (as did Edwards, of course). Franklin's work is marked by the creation of a persona who early in life sets rational goals and succeeds in accomplishing them. Stanton quite early established his religious goals and, from the certain tone that characterizes his *Journal*, likewise succeeded.

According to the *Literary History of the United States*, in Stanton's work "the Quaker style showed signs of becoming stereotyped...colorless, drained of imaginative content." Stanton surely is not a literary stylist, but that "colorless" prose may be appropriate to a diary of such a confident Friend. External events seldom shake his equanimity: it is worth noting that only five events merit extended comment—a storm off the coast of Ire., a Cambridge meeting (which "much depressed my spirits"), the Indian treaties of 1756-1757, the death of his daughter (a "near trial"), and the death of a slave ("through the permission of Divine Providence his time was shortened"). If we can speak of a persona controlling the events recorded in the *Journal*, it is one who, as Stanton said in his conclusion, has a "fixed hope" of salvation.

Suggested Readings: LHUS. *See also* the testimony of the Philadelphia monthly meeting of the Friends, which serves as an introduction to the *Journal* and appears to be the only considerable discussion of Stanton's life and work.

Timothy K. Conley
Bradley University

GEORGE STARKEY (c. 1626-1665)

Works: *The Marrow of Alchemy* (as "Eirenaeus Philoponos Philalethes"; 1654-1655); *Natures Explication and Helmonts Vindication* (1657); *Pyrotechny Asserted and Illustrated* (1658); *Britains Triumph* (as "G.S."; 1660); *The Dignity* *of Kingship Asserted* (1660); prefatory poems, *Idea of the Law* (by John Heydon; 1660); *Royal and Other Innocent Blood* (1660); prefatory poems, *Theomagia* (by John Heydon; 1664); *A Smart Scourge for a Silly Sawcy Fool* (1664); *An Epistolar Discourse* (1665); *The Admirable Efficacy. . . of True Oyl* (1683); *George Starkey's Pill Vindicated* (n.d.).

Biography: Son of a Church of England minister serving the Southampton tribe, George Starkey (*Stirk, Stirke, Sterkey, Starkie*—his name appears in all forms) was born in the Bermudas in the late 1620s. For unrecorded reasons, he was sent not to Eng. but to Harvard for his education. Recommended in advance to Governor John Winthrop (q.v.), Starkey arrived in New Eng. late in 1639. Despite family plans that he would prepare for the ministry, he soon began chemical studies, probably under the guidance of the younger John Winthrop, Jr. (q.v.), to whose library and apparatus he was permitted access. Upon graduation in 1646 and after earning an M.A. the following year "in course," Starkey practiced medicine in the Boston vicinity at least through 1648. That year he made the acquaintance of Dr. Robert Child the Remonstrant. Through Child, Starkey gained admission to Eng.'s "Invisible College" of scientific experimenters (a group including Samuel Hartlib, Benjamin Worsley, Robert Boyle, John Dury, and Bassett Jones). Of this young physician "lately married to one Stoughton's daughter" in the colonies, Hartlib noted "a most incomparable universal Witt" and an ability to perform "a number of most strange and desperate cures." A gold-making venture with Worsley and others may have diverted Starkey's attention briefly after his arrival in London in 1650. But most of his energy was occupied in perfecting the formula for oil of Venus (copper), *ens veneris*, a curative Boyle sufficiently believed in to help finance the quest for this "Horizontal Gold" panacea. By 1653, scorned by these influential friends who detected a developing pattern of frenzied experimentation followed by periodic stays in London's jails and debtor's prisons, Starkey turned to writing defenses of his own iatrochemical theories, which frequently became attacks, often scurrilous, on the Galenist physicians for whom he held contempt. His *ad hominem* arguments, responded to in kind, may account for the unsupported rumor that a reprobate Starkey died in debtor's prison. More probable is John Allin's account that Starkey died in 1665 of the plague he was reported to have treated successfully, himself infected while performing an autopsy to verify his Paracelsian theories.

Critical Appraisal: George Starkey's major writings divide neatly into two groups: three political tracts celebrating the Restoration of the monarchy and an array of alchemical treatises. Both *Britains Triumph* and *Dignity of Kingship Asserted* include sharply satiric portraits of a John Milton irate at the collapse of his plan for a "Rump" Parliament. William Parker's efforts to identify this attacker place Starkey in the context of the many pamphleteers of flabby, vapid prose conspicuous at the time.

Modern concern with the alchemical tracts is noticeably lacking, excepting the continuing search for the creator of the Philalethes essays. These writings, revered in their own time and still esteemed within a history of ideas framework, have long been peripherally associated with Starkey, as well as Winthrop and Child. Earlier critics have charged Starkey with stealing *The Marrow of Alchemy* ("one of the most celebrated experimental treatises in the English language") from Philalethes. Current scholarship suggests Starkey and the Cosmopolite are one and the same.

The Marrow has been criticized for vague expression of ideas and imprecise language, yet praised for dexterous versification of "a by no means poetic theme." Following the logic of Starkey's rendition of the alchemical opus is difficult, because in this long treatise (556 six-line stanzas), he drew together history, tradition, empirical data, and esoteric images, often without signaling any shift from one level of meaning to another. The apparent structure of three books devoted to philosophic theory and four books to actual practice is misleading, for the subjects are indivisible. The sacredness of the art, moreover, precluded the poet from speaking plainly, and so he turned to eclectic, veiled language and a body of metaphoric identifications meant to be comprehended only by the enlightened. In so doing, Starkey demanded of the reader a prior knowledge of the rudiments of alchemy and familiarity with at least a small part of the vast body of alchemical literature that spans several continents and many centuries. The ambitiousness of Starkey's attempt is worth noting, for the scope and timing of *The Marrow*'s composition mark it as a watershed in the history of "scientific" thought.

Suggested Readings: DNB; Sibley-Shipton (I, 131-137). *See also* Robert C. Black, III, *The Younger John Winthrop* (1966), pp. 155-157, 234; John Ferguson, "The Marrow of Alchemy," ASJ, 3 (1915), 106-129; Harold Jantz, "America's First Cosmopolite," PMHS, 84 (1972), 3-25; William Riley Parker, Introduction, *The Dignity of Kingship Asserted* (facsimilie ed.; 1942); Arthur Edward Waite, ed., *Lives of Alchemistical Philosophers* (1888), pp. 27-30; Ronald Sterne Wilkinson, "George Starkey, Physician and Alchemist," *Ambix*, 11 (1963), 121-152; idem, "Some Bibliographical Problems Concerning George Starkey," *Ambix*, 10 (1973), 235-244.

Cheryl Z. Oreovicz
Purdue University

JACOB STEENDAM (1615-c. 1672)

Works: *The Goldfinch* (1649-1650); *The Complaint of New Netherlands to Her Mother* (1659); *The Praise of New Netherlands* (1661); *Spurring-Verses* (1662); *Moral Songs for Batavian Youth* (1671).

Biography: Jacob Steendam's origins are obscure, but he is believed to have been born in 1615 in Kniphausen, Hol., and later to have moved to Amsterdam. Steendam spent his life as a wanderer and was for fifteen years employed by the West India Company. In 1641 he was sent to the coast of Guinea in Africa and remained there until 1649. Upon returning to Amsterdam, he collected his first poems and published them under the title *The Goldfinch*.

In 1650, after leaving the West India Company, he traveled to New Neth. with the intention of settling permanently, and in 1652 purchased land on Long Island, N.Y., and houses on what are now Broadway and Pearl Street. Records also indicate that in 1653 and 1655, he contributed money for defending New Amsterdam against the Indians; in 1658 he sought redress from a business associate who overcharged him for commissions on goods sold for him; and in 1660 he sought permission to import slaves from and conduct trade with Africa.

In 1662 he returned to Hol., never to visit the property he still kept in America. Although he intended to venture back, his plans were abandoned when the English took possession of the colony in the name of the duke of York. In 1665 he embarked from Amsterdam for the E.Ind., and records indicate that he was appointed superintendent of the Orphan House at Batavia, Java, in 1671. There is no record of his life after this time, or of his death. We do know that his wife, Sara de Rosschou, succeeded him as superintendent at the Orphan House and that she died in 1673, when Steendam's daughter and son-in-law assumed the position. By all accounts, Steendam was an earnest, extremely pious man and member of the Dutch Reformed Church.

Critical Appraisal: Although he is regarded as the first poet in America, Jacob Steendam did not approach his verse as a vocation. As Henry C. Murphy remarked in his memoir, they were fugitive pieces, dashed off in spare moments from his active life. His poems are generally lyrical, usually revealing a strong didactic purpose. Steendam wrote exclusively in Dutch, apparently never learning English, and it was not until 1865 that Murphy translated and collected some of his poems and those of later poets of New Neth. Although scholars are aware of five publications, his *Complaint* and *Praise of New Netherlands* are of the greatest interest to American readers.

The Complaint is presented in the form of a child's plea to its mother for protection. Relying heavily on mythological imagery, Steendam fashioned an allegorical history of the Dutch colony in New Neth. The poem bemoans the neglect the colony has suffered and begs the mother country for protection from exploiters and hostile Indians. Although the metaphors are frequently mixed and awkward, the poem recounts the bounty of the area and foreshadows its eventual domination by opposing forces.

The 300-line poem, *The Praise of New Netherlands*, further develops this love of the new land in a lengthy paean extolling many of its more flattering and bountiful features. Steendam cataloged the pleasures and benefits of the climate, land, oceans, and animals, defining New Neth. as "a very Eden. . .the masterpiece of nature's hand; / Whatever does with breath of life expand, / Or comes from out the sea, or thrives on land, / On you conferring." The work ends with an invitation to those at home to emigrate "for [their] redemption."

Steendam's next piece, *Spurring-Verses*, recapitulates many of the observations made in *Praise* with the intention of encouraging others to join Peter

Cornelisen Plockhoy in settling in Del. Here the poet spoke with authority about his own experiences and about the likelihood that those joining Plockhoy would discover "the promised land of Jacob's seed." Much of the poem is couched in the imagery of The Old Testament and emphasizes the "treasures" the new land offers.

Steendam was a protégé of Jan Zoets, an Amsterdam innkeeper, satirist, and leader of a poet's club. Although largely solemn and pious, Steendam's poems reveal some of Zoets's comic influence in the pseudonym "noch vaster," which the poet always affixed to his works. Translated as "even firmer," this cognomen is a pun on Steendam's name, which means "stone dam."

Suggested Readings: DAB. *See also* William Loring Andrews, *Jacob Steendam: The First Poet in New Netherland* (contains three poems cited above; 1908); Mary L. D. Ferris, "A Note about Jacob Steendam," *De Halve Maen*, 90 (1976), 14; H. C. Murphy, *Jacob Steendam, Noch Vaster* (contains three poems; 1865); Ellis Lawrence Raesly, *Portrait of New Netherland* (1945); Henri and Barbara Van Der Zee, *A Sweet and Alien Land* (1978).

David W. Madden
University of California, Davis

RICHARD STEERE (1643-1721)

Works: *The History of the Babylonish Cabal; Or, The Intrigues, Progression, Opposition, Defeat, and Destruction of the Daniel Catchers; in a Poem* (1682); *A Message from Tory-Land to the Whig-Makers in Albian* (1682); *Romes Thunder-Bolt; Or, Antichrist Displaid* (1682); *A Monumental Memorial of Marine Mercy* (1684); "A Breviary of the Grounds of an Appeal" (1695); "To the Consideration of the Majestrates" (1695); "The Plea of Richard Steere" (1695); *The Daniel Catcher. The Life of the Prophet Daniel: In a Poem* (1713).

Biography: Born to an English clothworker in 1643, Richard Steere grew up in the village of Chertsey, Surrey, on the Thames some twenty miles above London. He was educated in a local singing school or "petty," later attended the Latin grammar school in Kingston-upon-Thames, and at age 13 was apprenticed to a cordwainer in London. In 1666 Steere was admitted to the Cordwainers Company, thereafter possessing the title "citizen of London," and was engaged in overseas commerce until 1682. Steere supported the earl of Shaftesbury and the Whigs with doggerel attacks on the Tories and—indirectly—on King Charles II. In 1683 Steere evaded Charles's suppression of the Whigs by taking ship to New Eng. He returned to London briefly the same year but removed permanently to the New World in 1684. In 1685 Steere settled in New London, Conn., where he found employment as a merchant and married the first of three successive wives—all widows. Ten years after his appearance in New London, Steere wrote and signed along with three others a petition to the governor protesting the imprisonment of John Rogers (q.v.) and his followers for their refusal to pay the minister's tax. Steere and the petitioners were arrested, indicted, and fined. Their subsequent appeal to the Court of Assistants was denied. In 1711 Steere moved across the Sound to Southold, Long Island, N.Y., where he died on Jun. 20, 1721.

Critical Appraisal: The range and quality of Richard Steere's verse are surprising among early American poets. His verse written while in Eng. was composed in the service of a political cause and is the work of a poet not yet the master of his craft. Nevertheless, *Romes Thunder-Bolt* is permeated with instances of acerbic wit, and in *A Message from Tory-Land*, Steere skillfully adapted the tune of a popular song to lyrics sharply satirizing his political foes. His contribution to American poetry is more durable. *A Monumental Memorial of Marine Mercy* is the finest example of the sea-deliverance tradition in the period. The dramatic voyage is contrived to enlarge the reader's understanding of human dependence on providence, and the narrative structure conveniently parallels the spiritual passage. The ocean crossing develops an intellectual progress from ignorance to truth, a move from moral indifference to spiritual insight. Steere's highly competent nativity poem is something of an anomaly in early American literature, being one of only half a dozen composed on that theme in seventeenth-century America. That he found the nativity congenial as a religious symbol is due largely to the Arminianism of his General Baptist persuasion, and for the poem's idea, he is indebted to Milton. "A Sea-Storm Nigh the Coast" draws on Steere's impressions gathered during storms at sea and along the Conn. shore. It may very well be his most fully realized poem. Meticulously controlled and metrically complex, "Sea-Storm Nigh the Coast" is one of the few fully rendered aesthetic contemplations of the era. "Earth's Felicities, Heaven's Allowances," a blank verse work at a time in American literature when few such were written, is an extended exposition of Steere's mature reflections, perhaps his best work. Taking as its province the nature of human happiness, the poem analyzes this phenomenon in the context of Christian doctrine. Steere's premise was that the quest for salvation and the proper enjoyment of earth's felicities are not mutually exclusive. The reverse of this conviction has often been thought— incorrectly—to dominate Puritan attitudes toward the world. But the analysis that develops from this premise is aesthetic as well as theological, for *felicity*, as Steere used the term, includes both beauty and happiness. Indeed, in the context of his poem, the two are inseparable.

Steere also wrote important prose. His 1695 protest against religious persecution in Conn. occupied an important cultural and historical position between the tolerationist tracts of Milton, Goodwin, Overton, and Roger Williams (q.v.) on the one hand and the libertarian principles of The Declaration of Independence and the Virginia Statute for Religious Freedom on the other. Men do not owe the free exercise of their civil or property rights to religious conformity, Steere argued, and in his perception property was itself a right, one deserving the protection of law against tyranny and distress. This brought him to declare "That

Liberty of Conscience is every mans natural birthright, Or that Conscience ought not to be forced in matters of Religion," and that "no man ought to be debarred of his property Civil Rights and priviledges, for the Sake of his Religious Opinions."

Suggested Readings: FCNEV; LHUS. *See also* Harrison T. Meserole, *Seventeenth-Century American Poetry* (1968), pp. 243-268; Donald P. Wharton, *In the Trough of the Sea: Selected American Sea-Deliverance Narratives, 1610-1766* (1979), pp. 131-141; idem, *Richard Steere, Colonial Merchant Poet* (prints 1695 prose; 1978).

Donald P. Wharton
Castleton State College

WILLIAM STEPHENS (1671-1753)

Works: *A Journal of the Proceedings in Georgia, Beginning October 20, 1737* (1742); *A State of the Province of Georgia* (1742); *The Journal of William Stephens, 1741-1745*, 2 vols. (1958-1959).

Biography: Born in Eng., the son of Sir William Stephens, lieutenant governor of the Isle of Wight, Stephens earned bachelor's and master's degrees at King's College, Cambridge, and served as MP for Newport for nearly thirty years. He became acquainted with James Edward Oglethorpe (q.v.) while in Parliament, and after a series of financial reverses and the loss of his estate and parliamentary seat, he went to S.C. to survey a barony in 1736. He became reacquainted with Oglethorpe in Ga. and subsequently was appointed secretary for the affairs of the Trust within the province of Ga., primarily because of the trustees' growing sense that Oglethorpe's indifferent correspondence was not accurately representing conditions in the colony. As secretary, Stephens was primarily responsible for reporting to the trustees as what one commentator has called an "official spy," but he also gradually took responsibility for civil affairs, since Oglethorpe's attention was increasingly directed at the military threat posed by the Spanish colony in Fla. During a reorganization of the colony in 1741, Stephens was named president of Savannah County, the northern half of Ga.; two years later, at age 72, he became president of Ga. and was assigned to be in charge of civil affairs, a post he retained until growing debility forced his resignation in 1750. He died at Bewlie, his estate on the Savannah River.

Critical Appraisal: Although William Stephens's journals for 1745-1750 are lost, the remainder are now published and provide a remarkably complete account of Ga. affairs over a crucial eight-year period. Despite their journal format, they were written in the expectation that full copies would be forwarded to the trustees and thus constitute a public, day-by-day commentary on colonial affairs rather than a private diary. At least seventy copies of the 1737-1741 journal were printed for the information of the trustees, who used portions to counterattacks made on the Ga. enterprise by "malcontents" such as Patrick Tailfer (q.v.) and Thomas Stephens, William's disinherited son. Because Stephens represented the trustees and depended on them for continued employment, his journals reflect an acute awareness of the trustees' principled opposition to rum, slavery, and any system of land inheritance other than tail-male. In criticizing the malcontents, consistently encouraging the silk, fruit, and wine industries—all of which failed—and blaming the colonists rather than administrative and policy errors for the colony's troubles, Stephens probably misled the trustees by reflecting their own views too narrowly and consistently.

Stephens was not a literary man, but the journals nevertheless provide the best description of the ordinary affairs of the colony in its early years. They demonstrate, too, the dilemma of the colonial civil servant, at once individual colonist on the frontier and manager of the colony's affairs, his opinions divided between the wishes of the trustees and his own observations. The entry from March 6-7, 1745, for example, describes a visit from S.C. planters to Savannah and their professed eagerness to "obtain Lands, when they saw once a door open to let in Negroes, under such limitations and Restrictions as the Trust Saw fit, to carry on Improvements. To which I could say little. . . but. . . very probably that affair might admit of farther Consideration, &c."

Stephens's only writing besides the journals is *A State of the Province of Georgia*, closely related to Oglethorpe's "State of Georgia" and perhaps the result of collaborative effort. It is a document intended for signature by Ga. colonists to assure the trustees of the colony's well-being in the face of petitions and letters of complaint from some colonists. The tract begins with a description of landscape and climate, avoiding the grossly inflated claims of some promotional tracts, but nevertheless optimistic for the eventual success of orange, silk, and wine production. The document admits the substantial desertion rate from the colony, but attributes it to the personal failings of the runaways; it suggests importing British servants and making other minor policy changes that might improve the colony. The document attracted only twenty-five signatures, probably because of its misrepresentation of actual conditions. Its circulation seems to have encouraged a reply by Patrick Tailfer and others, the well-known *A True and Historical Narrative of the Colony of Georgia*, and helped set off a pamphlet war between supporters of the colony and discontented colonists and former colonists.

Suggested Readings: DNB. *See also* Natalie F. Bocock, "William Stephens," GHQ, 17 (1933), 243-258; Leslie F. Church, *Oglethorpe: A Study of Philanthropy in England and Georgia* (1932), pp. 288-291, 310-313; E. Merton Coulter, Introduction, *The Journal of William Stephens, 1741-43* (1958); Trevor R. Reese, Introduction, *The Clamorous Malcontents* (1973); J. C. Ross, "Charles Ackers and William Stephens' Journal," GHQ, 52 (1968), 434-437; Albert B. Saye, *New Viewpoints in Georgia History* (1943), pp. 84-87; Phinizy Spalding, *Oglethorpe in America* (1977), pp. 37-41; Clarence L. Ver Steeg, Introduction, *A True and Historical Narrative of the Colony of Georgia* (1960). Stephens's journals for Oct. 1737 to Oct. 1741 have been reprinted in *The Colonial Records of Georgia*, vol. 4, and supplement (1904-1916, 1970). The 1741-1745 journals have been edited by E. Merton Coulter in 2 vols. (1958-1959). *A State of the Province* is in *The Clamorous Malcontents*.

David H. Stanley
The University of Utah

JAMES STERLING (1701-1763)

Works: *The Rival Generals: A Tragedy* (1722); *The Parricide: A Tragedy* (w. c. 1726; pub. 1736); *The Loves of Hero and Leander from the Greek of Musaeus* (1728); *A Poem on the Art of Printing* (1728); *Poetical Works* (1734); *An Ode on the Times, Address'd to the Hope of Britain* (1738); "The Sixteenth Ode of Horace's Second Book, Imitated and Inscribed to . . . Samuel Ogle, Esq.," *Maryland Gazette* (Mar. 31, 1747), p. 1; *An Epistle to the Hon. Arthur Dobbs* (1752); *A Sermon, Preached Before His Excellency the Governor of Maryland . . . December 13, 1754* (1755); "A Poem. On the Inventions of Letters and the Art of Printing" (Philadelphia) *American Magazine or Monthly Chronicle*, 1 (Mar. 1758), 281-290; "A Pastoral to His Excellency George Thomas," *American Magazine or Monthly Chronicle*, 1 (May 1758), 390-397; "The 22d Ode of the First Book of Horace Imitated; and Inscribed," *American Magazine or Monthly Chronicle*, 1 (Oct. 1758), 642-643; "Verses Occasioned by the Success of the British Arms in the Year 1759," *Maryland Gazette* (Jan. 3, 1760).

Biography: Born in Downrass, King's County, Ire., in 1701, James Sterling was educated in Dublin and graduated from King's College in 1720. Sometime around the date of his graduation, he wrote a tragedy—possibly the first by a native Irishman—titled *The Rival Generals* and followed it several years later with another, *The Parricide*. After the death of the first of his three wives, an actress of some note, he took an M.A. and had entered the Anglican clergy by the time his *Poetical Works* appeared in Dublin in 1734. Thwarted in his desire to immigrate to Boston as an assistant rector (the Bostonians regarded his theatrical past as scandalous), Rev. Sterling arrived in Anne Arundel County, Md., in 1737 to assume a post in All Hallows Parish. By the end of 1740, he had moved permanently to St. Paul's in Kent County on the Eastern Shore, where he was anything but satisfied to live the life of an unworldly parson. During an English sojourn in 1751-1752, he managed to have himself appointed collector of customs for the head of Chesapeake Bay, and he won himself the reputation of a scoundrel among some by his dubious attempts to secure a monopoly on the Labrador trade. Until his death on Nov. 10, 1763, Sterling remained actively interested in literary pursuits, colonial commerce, and efforts to limit French power in North America. The latter concern provided the subject for his most famous sermon, preached before Md.'s governor and legislature in 1754.

Critical Appraisal: James Sterling's qualities as a poet—his defects and virtues alike—are largely those of neo-Classical poetry in general. His stock in trade was the lofty theme treated in heroic couplets, a meter in which he wrote with obvious facility and sometimes monotonously unvaried rhythm. In an age of public literature, Sterling was a supremely public versifier (although most of his periodical pieces appeared unsigned) and "perhaps the most prolific Southern poet" of his time.

Sterling's work is typically encomiastic; yet his praise of governors, generals, and other prominent figures nearly always remained subordinate to his broader themes. For example, "The Sixteenth Ode of Horace's Second Book, Imitated" is ostensibly in praise of Governor Samuel Ogle, but most of the poem is devoted to the philosophical principle that contentment eludes man, because "He cannot leave his restless Soul behind." Similarly, although "On the Inventions of Letters" sets out to celebrate the moral example of the printer-novelist Samuel Richardson, it is in essence a concise history of the diffusion of knowledge through the written word. The most ambitious of Sterling's American poems is the *Epistle to Dobbs*. Epic in tone and perspective but seriously lacking in unity, the more than 1,500 lines of this verse-letter to the seeker of the Northwest Passage drift grandly from idealized descriptions of Md. to castigations of Spanish colonial policy to Miltonic images of an archangel in the northern sky. In the range and density of its allusions and the consistency of its stylized Augustan diction, however, the *Epistle to Dobbs* remains a remarkable tour de force.

Sterling spent less than half of his life in the New World, and his poems and sermons attest that he remained an enthusiastic subject of the crown. Still, he seems to have been sincerely eager for the forging of a distinctly American literary culture, and he gave this hope—together with American scenes and creatures—a conspicuous place in his work. The second part of the long pastoral that he addressed to former Pa. Governor George Thomas takes the form of an elegy for Alexander Pope (with whom Sterling claimed "intimacy" during his younger days); but the opening section is a visionary prayer inviting the muses to forsake Parnassus and fly to the young land where "fertile fields, and fishy streams abound: / Nothing is wanting but *Poetic* ground." In a bizarre mingling of Classical mythology and contemporary realism, Sterling presented the Indians shouting "loud YOHAWS" as they prepared to receive the foreign goddesses who would lift them out of ignorance. In several respects, the Md. cleric was clearly a precursor of the Connecticut Wits and of Joel Barlow (q.v.) in particular. "Verses Occasioned by the Success of the British Arms" paints scenes of rural peace and plenty (including an elevated description of the "Maize in extended Rows") strikingly like those later glorified in "The Hasty Pudding." Despite his neo-Classic stamp, Sterling has also been called "more sentimental than any previous American poet," partly on the basis of this poem's expression of sadness at the steady disappearance of the forests. Yet he was capable too of exercising his modest gift for comedy on the circumstances of colonial life, as when he represented himself as the "christian hero" unexpectedly meeting a buffalo in Governor Ogle's garden.

Writing conventional poetry in genteel anonymity for short-lived periodicals, Sterling pursued a life of letters that exemplifies much about the literary situation in the South of the mideighteenth century. The fugitive pieces he left behind him, however, broached a number of topics that were to trouble and inspire American authors in the succeeding centuries.

Suggested Readings: CCMDG; DAB; DNB; LHUS. *See also* J. A. Leo Lemay, *Men of Letters in Colonial Maryland* (1972), pp. 257-312 (see pp. 372-380 for a checklist of Sterling's publications); Kenneth Silverman, *Colonial American Poetry* (includes four poems known to be by, or attributed to, Sterling; 1968), pp. 257-269, 328-333, 339-346; Lawrence C. Wroth, "James Sterling: Poet, Priest, and Prophet of Empire," PAAS, 41 (1931), 25-76.

W. H. Ward
Appalachian State University

EZRA STILES (1727-1795)

Works: *Oratio Funebris...Pro Jonathan Law* (1751); Franklin Dexter, ed., *The Itineraries and Miscellanies of Ezra Stiles* (w. 1755-1794; pub. 1916); *A Discourse on the Christian Union* (1761); Franklin Dexter, ed., *The Literary Diary of Ezra Stiles* (w. 1769-1795; pub. 1901); *A Discourse on Saving Knowlege* (1770); *To the Candid Public* (1774); *To the Public* (1776); *Oratio Inauguralis* (1778); *A Sermon at the Death of Dr. Daggett* (1780); *An Oration Delivered at...Charleston* (1782); *The United States Elevated to Glory and Honor* (1783); *An Account of the Settlement of Bristol, Rhode Island* (1785); *A Funeral Sermon...for Mr. Chauncey Whittelsey* (1787); *A Sermon...at the Ordination of Henry Channing* (1787); *A History of Three of the Judges of Charles I* (1794); *An Ecclesiastical History of New England* (1795); Isabel Calder, ed., *The Letters and Papers of Ezra Stiles* (1933).

Biography: Ezra Stiles was born in Conn. in 1727. He graduated from Yale in 1746 and received an M.A. in 1749. Declining to enter the ministry because of religious doubts, he turned to law, being admitted to the bar in 1753. Two years later, his doubts resolved, he became a minister of the Second Congregational Church in Newport, R.I. During his two decades in Newport, Stiles, in addition to attending to his pastoral duties, served as librarian of the Redwood Library; performed experiments in chemistry, astronomy, and electricity (Benjamin Franklin [q.v.] was an early friend); studied Oriental languages; and helped found Rhode Island College (Brown Univ.).

With the advent of the Revolution, which he strongly supported, Stiles left Newport for brief clerical assignments in Bristol, Dighton, and Portsmouth, N.H. Then in 1778 he assumed the presidency of Yale, a post he characterized as a "Crown of Thorns." Beyond his executive function, Stiles taught Hebrew, ecclesiastical history, theology, philosophy, and a variety of other subjects. He was likewise active as a preacher and as first president of the Connecticut Society for the Abolition of Slavery. His administration was notable for its tolerance (he went so far as to allow his students to attend dancing classes) and its success in helping the college weather the difficulties, especially financial ones, attendant on the Revolution. Through his efforts in 1792, the college charter was changed to allow several state officials to serve as ex officio corporation members, with the result that state funds crucial to Yale's survival were granted. In 1795, at the age of 67, Stiles died, leaving to Yale some forty-five volumes of his manuscripts.

Critical Appraisal: Stiles's wide-ranging intellect and probing curiosity are reflected in the remarkable variety of topics in which he became knowledgeable. Beyond the ecclesiastical and legal scholarship one might expect from a man of his education and position, Stiles's writings show him performing (sometimes dilettantishly, but more often impressively) as a historian, philosopher, scientist, philologist, and protosociologist. The broad scope and frequent depth of his knowledge earned him a deserved reputation as one of the most learned men in America, although the same qualities, in conjunction with his passionate antiquarianism, led some of his contemporaries to satirize him as "Doctor Magpie."

A notable aspect of Stiles's eclecticism is the spirit of toleration and respect he showed for viewpoints and traditions different from his own. Thus while in Newport he was conspicuous for the close ties he maintained with the city's Roman Catholic and Jewish congregations. It is characteristic of Stiles that through his friendships at the synagogue, he in time became proficient at Hebrew and Jewish theology. His concern for securing and preserving the civil liberties of Americans of all religious faiths was a leading factor in his early and fervent advocacy of the movement for independence. To his liberality of mind may be added his intellectual honesty, as evidenced by his scrupulous refusal to take holy orders until a long period of private investigation and reflection had resolved his doubts concerning the validity of Revelation.

Although he wrote voluminously, Stiles's publications during his lifetime were limited to a relative handful of sermons, addresses, and historical essays. They, for all of their excellence, have been largely eclipsed by his less formal and more personal writings. It was in his diaries and correspondence that Stiles made his major literary contribution. Aside from their enormous factual and documentary value (Stiles was a meticulous recorder of statistics and sketcher of maps), such materials engagingly display to best advantage their author's lively intelligence and the diversity of his interests. In his correspondence, for example, Stiles carried on a multilingual exchange with scientists, statesmen, and theologians around the world.

Stiles's greatest work is his *Literary Diary*, compiled posthumously from the more extensive diaries he maintained from 1769 onwards. In it he recorded his experiences, reading, and reflections on public events. The diary is a treasure house of information and shrewd observation regarding his private and professional activities, but it likewise contains his invaluable accounts of the particulars of (and participants in) the American Revolution. In such matters, Stiles's breadth of curiosity and his love of the factual have served posterity especially well, since his diary is the sole source for much important and fascinating detail concerning the period. But one of the primary attractions of the diary is the self-portrait it entails. Although Stiles eschewed the intimate or confessional vein, his appealing personality—energetic, frank, inquisitive, and generous—comes through very vividly.

Suggested Readings: CCNE; DAB; DARB; Dexter (II, 92-97); Sprague (I, 470-479); T₂. *See also* Abiel Holmes, *The Life of Ezra Stiles* (1798); G. A. Kohut, *Ezra*

Stiles and the Jews (1902); Edmund Morgan, "Ezra Stiles: The Education of a Yale Man, 1742-1746," HLQ, 17 (1954), 251-268; idem, *The Gentle Puritan: A Life of Ezra Stiles* (1962); H. R. Stiles, *The Stiles Family in America* (1895); A. P. Stokes, *Memorials of Eminent Yale Men* (1914); T. D. Woolsey, *An Historical Discourse* (1850).

Richard I. Cook

Kent State University

ISAAC STILES (1697-1760)

Works: *A Prospect of the City of Jerusalem, in Its Spiritual Building, Beauty and Glory* (1742); *A Looking-glass for Changlings. A Seasonable Caveat Against Meddling with Them That Are Given to Change* (1743); *The Character and Duty of Soldiers* (1755); *A Sermon...at the Ordination of...Ezra Stiles* (1755).

Biography: Isaac Stiles was born at Windsor, Conn., on Jul. 30, 1697. The eldest son of John and Ruth (Bancroft) Stiles, Isaac was a third generation New Englander whose paternal grandfather and great-grandfather were among the original settlers of Windsor in 1635. Although raised to be a weaver, Stiles and his parents decided that he should be prepared for college. He studied for a while under his pastor, the Rev. Timothy Edwards, father of Jonathan Edwards (q.v.), and eventually, he entered Yale College from which he obtained an A.B. in 1722. After graduation he taught school at Westfield, Mass., his mother's native town, and he continued his study of theology under the Rev. Edward Taylor (q.v.). Stiles preached at Westfield in 1722 and 1723 and for a while was under consideration as a potential colleague for the then-aged Taylor. That appointment never materialized, and after coming in second to Jonathan Edwards when the church at Bolton, Conn., was looking for a pastor in 1723, Stiles moved back to Conn., where he began to preach to the church in the north parish of New Haven (now called North Haven) in Jan. 1724. The pulpit of the church, which had been vacant since the withdrawal of the Rev. James Wetmore (q.v.) more than a year before, was offered to Stiles, and he accepted, being ordained over the church on Nov. 11, 1724. For the next thirty-five years, he faithfully served the needs of his North Haven congregation. During the Great Awakening, he was an outspoken member of the Old Light camp and was called to speak for that persuasion at the Conn. election in 1742 . The final ascendency of the New Lights in Conn. political and religious affairs during the period after 1745 and continued harassment by members of that faction are said to have contributed to Stiles's death on May 14, 1760. Married twice—first in 1725 to Keziah, the youngest daughter of Edward Taylor, by whom he had Ezra Stiles (q.v.), who would serve as president of Yale College from 1777 to 1795, and then in 1728 to Esther Hooker, by whom he had five sons and five daughters—Stiles was survived by Esther, Ezra, two other sons, and two daughters.

Critical Appraisal: During his life, attitudes toward Isaac Stiles were mixed because of his Old Light bias and his staunch political conservatism. After his death, however, opponents and supporters alike agreed that he was a preacher of uncommon talent. According to one account published after his death, "[Stiles] was an excellent preacher; nature, it seems, had formed him for this, and his greatest talent lay here," and according to another account, he was "a zealous, engaging preacher." Final acknowledgement appears on his tombstone on which is inscribed praise for his "natural gift of eloquence." Although only four of his sermons were printed during his life, their high quality and the fact that one was an invited election sermon suggest that Stiles likely deserved the grand testimony noticed above.

The occasions for Stiles's published sermons indicate that he was comfortable before any audience. For instance, *A Looking-glass for Changlings* was preached at a meeting of Conn. freemen in 1743, and *The Character and Duty of Soldiers* was preached to a company of New Haven soldiers about to depart for battle against the French in 1755. Of the sermons, *A Prospect of the City of Jerusalem*, which was preached at the Conn. election on May 13, 1742, is the most competent literarily and provides sufficient evidence of Stiles's "natural gift of eloquence." Preached at a high point of the Awakening in Conn., the sermon is very much in the mainstream of Conn. and Mass. election sermons of the late seventeenth and early eighteenth centuries. In it Stiles traced the terms and conditions under which New Eng. was established as the "New Jerusalem" and the ways in which that original intention, supported by a covenant between God and his latest chosen people, had become frustrated by the appearance of secularism and doctrinal divisiveness throughout the land. Stiles argued that New Eng.'s salvation depended upon the ability of civil and ecclesiastic leaders—today's Moses and Aaron figures—to bring about a reform of evil and a return to New Eng.'s original purpose. To support his view, he drew on the errand motif so popular among earlier election preachers, and with a flair for the Classical, he cited Tertullian to prove that the interests of religion, which were in decline, are equal to those of the state. Thus, he concluded, it behooved civil leaders to join with the clergy to preserve and, as necessary, legislate the old moral vision of New Eng. Only through such cooperation could Conn.'s leaders hope to correct the "many growing Evils and prevailing Sins, for which the Land Mourns, and which have a very awful tendency to Undermine our Foundations, to Sap our Walls, to Bury us in...Desolation, and lay our Jerusalem utterly Waste."

An interesting aspect of *A Prospect of the City of Jerusalem* is Stiles's defense of the Old Light position. In the sermon, Stiles pointed to the New Light movement as one of the primary "Evils" that have compromised New Eng.'s religious strength. He criticized the New Lights for their blindness to truth and to the clear lessons of Scripture, as clear, he said, as the "Rays of the Sun": "The pale Moon beams, the glimmering Twilight, the feeble, inconstant, unsteady Resemblance or faint Appearance of Light in a variable Glow-worm, does not more dazzle their Eyes, and is thought to afford more Light than the direct Rays of the Sun shining in its meridian Lustre and Brightness." Aware that the New Lights were gaining in popularity and power, Stiles consoled his fellow Old Lights thus: Be it so, that we are treated... *as the Off-scouring of all things*, made *the Song of the Drunkard*, or stigmatiz'd as *Carnal, Pharisees, Hypocrites*, [and] *Dumb Dogs*.... Tis enough *that the Disciple be as his Master*.... The world hated Christ before it hated his Ministers.

A Prospect of the City of Jerusalem and other sermons by Stiles reveal the preacher's lively and inventive mind, one certainly equal to the training Stiles enjoyed at the hands of the elder Edwards and Taylor. For that reason, they merit further study along with the manuscripts of Stiles's sermons kept by the Massachusetts Historical Society.

Suggested Readings: CCNE; Dexter (I, 264-267). *See also* Alan Heimert and Perry Miller, eds., *The Great Awakening* (1967), pp. 305-322.

Ronald A. Bosco
State University of New York at Albany

WILLIAM STITH (1707-1755)

Works: *A Sermon Preached Before the General Assembly* (1745-1746); *The History of the First Discovery and Settlement of Virginia* (1747); *The Sinfulness and Pernicious Nature of Gaming* (1752); *The Nature and Extent of Christs's Redemption* (1753).

Biography: William Stith—clergyman, teacher, historian, antiquarian, college president—was born in 1707 into one of the most powerful families in Va. As the grandson of William and Mary (Isham) Randolph of Turkey Island ("the Adam and Eve of Virginia"), the nephew of Sir John Randolph (king's attorney), and the cousin of men such as Richard Bland (q.v.) and Peyton Randolph, the intelligent young Stith had many opportunities available to him. After receiving a secondary education at the grammar school of the College of William and Mary and his bachelor's and master's degrees from Queen's College, Oxford, he was elected master of the grammar school at William and Mary. He tired of teaching boys after five years and became rector of the affluent Henrico Parish, where he stayed for sixteen years. During this period, he was also chaplain to the Va. House of Burgesses. In 1752 the death of Stith's brother-in-law William Dawson (q.v.) left vacant the traditionally conjoined offices of president of William and Mary, Anglican commissary, and councilor. Governor Robert Dinwiddie violently opposed Stith as a candidate for the offices because of Stith's involvement in the opposition to Dinwiddie's fee of one pistole for signing land patents. Stith was credited with coining a toast much used during the heated dispute—"Liberty and Property and No Pistole." Dinwiddie successfully blocked Stith's appointment as commissary and councilor; in a bitter contest before the Board of Visitors, however, Stith won election to the presidency of the college, a position he occupied until his untimely death in 1755.

Critical Appraisal: A major southern colonial historian, William Stith was one of the ablest men of his generation in Va. As an antiquarian and historian, he made a significant contribution to the tradition of modern historical scholarship; as a pulpiteer, he left three printed sermons that demand respect as both theology and literature. Stith's writing style has been criticized by many later critics, including his cousin Thomas Jefferson (q.v.); however, it is an effective, sophisticated plain style, the controlled plain style of a learned writer. The author's extensive learning is revealed in the steady flow of casual references to a host of Classical and modern sources.

Stith's *The History of the First Discovery and Settlement of Virginia* appeared in at least two Williamsburg issues in 1747 and in London and Williamsburg issues in 1753. His uncle Sir John Randolph had planned to write a history of Va., a project Stith discussed with both Randolph and his friend William Byrd II of Westover (q.v.). After Randolph's death in 1737, Stith took up the project and had at his disposal the books and manuscripts of his uncle's library as well as the library of Byrd, one of the greatest of southern colonial book collections, which also included certain significant manuscripts. In addition, Stith had access to the partially preserved official records in Williamsburg. The author's plan was to write a comprehensive history of the colony from its beginning through his own day; however, he managed only to fill a rather large volume with the period ending in 1624 and the dissolution of the Virginia Company.

Stith's was the first history of Va. that attempted simply to tell the story of Va. based upon a detailed, factual reporting of the primary sources. The author's impressive work as an antiquarian placed in his hands well over 50 percent of all of the manuscripts extant today for the story of Va.'s earliest history; however, the documents provided a disproportionate and somewhat one-sided coverage of events. Although he used many printed and manuscript sources, his main printed source was Capt. John Smith's (q.v.) *Generall Historie*, and his chief manuscript source was the copy of the Virginia Company's Court Records for 1619-1624 found in Byrd's library. About one-third of Stith's *History* is devoted to the 1607-1609 period during which Smith was active in the colony, and about one-half concerns the 1619-1624 period covered by the Virginia Company records. Smith's *Historie* tells his side of his battles with his opponents, and the Virginia Company records relate the Sir Edwin Sandys-earl of Southampton administration's side of its struggle with King James I.

Not only did Stith produce a landmark work in his attempt to write history for its own purposes based upon primary sources, but he made a significant contribution to modern historical methodology. He used his primary sources exclusively, synthesizing them into a single narrative. When he had several sources, he drew his own conclusions and occasionally showed a sophisticated use of evidence by drawing conclusions from several sources not positively stated in any single source. In the section covering 1619-1624, where he had an abundance of sources,

Stith exhibited an increasing awareness of the need for specific evidence to support his conclusions. Indeed, he included so many details that his *History* is marked by an undue prolixity. Stith also revealed a perceptive critical attitude toward his sources, whether he was making judgments between disparate accounts or noting obvious error or bias in a single source. In no case, however, did he guess beyond his evidence.

Stith belongs to an established tradition of southern colonial historians in his secular New World patriotism and his Whiggish interpretation of his colony's early history. Like his contemporary and subsequent American Whig historians, Stith read the principles and concerns of his own time into the events of history. He saw history in terms of men, not in terms of God's providence as did New Eng. historians or in terms of great social or economic forces as have modern historians. A contemporary in Whig principles of men such as Richard Bland and Thomas Jefferson, Stith saw history as a record of politically good men resisting politically evil men and interpreted the good in terms of his own day. For example, the Virginia Company represented the liberty of the people resisting crown prerogative just as Stith and his friends were to do in the Pistole Fee dispute. As he wrote to the bishop of London in 1753, "I must have been quite blind, not to have seen the illegality of laying taxes upon the people without law." Building upon John Smith's foundations, Stith employed an eighteenth-century American Whig frame of reference to develop a Va. mythology that historians after the Revolutionary War disseminated to the American populace: the heroic John Smith, champion of the people; "darling" Pocahontas; gracious Sir Edwin Sandys, who ensured the liberty of colonials by establishing the House of Burgesses; and the villain King James I, who destroyed the Virginia Company.

The three extant sermons, delivered before the General Assembly at the official request of the Burgesses, show Stith to be an able preacher. *A Sermon Preached Before the General Assembly* (1745/1746) is a perceptive, effectively reasoned Whig political sermon that uses the Bible and Roman history to prove that Christian doctrine does not support tyranny. His second sermon before the Assembly, *The Sinfulness and Pernicious Nature of Gaming* (1752), is a specific pastoral sermon denouncing a major evil of his day. *The Nature and Extent of Christ's Redemption* (1753), Stith's third sermon, embroiled its author in controversy by presenting an extreme expression of Christianity as commonsense reason. Although Stith was accused of Deism, he never really went beyond Arminian Christianity or Lockean Christianity. Many fellow Anglicans considered Stith liberal, and the Presbyterians thought him to be virtually heretical. In the sermon, Stith alluded to a pamphlet by the New Light Presbyterian minister Samuel Davies (q.v.) titled *The Impartial Trial, Impartially Tried, and Convicted of Partiality* (1748). Davies penned an answer to Stith's sermon in Jul. 1755 titled *Charity and Truth United* but did not publish it, partially because Stith died in Sept. before Davies was ready to take his piece to the press.

Suggested Readings: CCV; DAB; LHUS; T₁. *See also* Richard Beale Davis, *Intellectual Life in the Colonial South, 1585-1763*, 3 vols. (1978); Darrett B. Rutman,

Introduction, *The History of the First Discovery and Settlement of Virginia* (a Johnson Reprint Corporation facsimile of Joseph Sabin's 1865 reprint of the 1747 edition; 1969); William Stith, *The History of the First Discovery and Settlement of Virginia* (the Reprint Company's facsimile of the 1747 edition, 1965; with Morgan P. Robinson's bibliographical notes and index originally published in 1912 in the *Bulletin of the Virginia State Library*, 5, no. 1); Thad W. Tate, "William Stith and the Virginia Tradition," *The Colonial Legacy, Volumes III and IV*, ed. Lawrence H. Leder (1973), pp. 121-145; Toshiko Tsuruta, "William Stith, Historian of Colonial Virginia" (Ph.D. diss., Univ. of Washington, 1957), for the most complete biographical discussion; Alden T. Vaughan, "The Evolution of Virginia History: Early Historians of the First Colony," in *Perspectives on Early American History: Essays in Honor of Richard B. Morris*, ed. A. T. Vaughan and George A. Billias (1973), pp. 9-39.

Homer D. Kemp
Tennessee Technological University

ANNIS BOUDINOT STOCKTON (1736-1801)

Works: "Epistle to Mr. S[tockton]" (1758); "By a Lady in America to Her Husband in England" (1775); "An Elegy Sacred to the Memory of Richard Stockton" (1781); "An Extempore Ode in a Sleepless Night" (1781); "Addresses to General Washington in the Year 1777 After the Battles of Trenton and Princeton" (1787); and many other poems.

Biography: Annis Boudinot Stockton was born in Darby, Pa., in 1736. She married Richard Stockton, a N.J. lawyer, in approximately 1755 and moved to his home near Princeton, an estate named "Morven" by Annis. When Stockton died in 1781, she remained at Morven until, with her children grown and her eldest son married, she moved in with her youngest daughter, Abigail Field.

The Stocktons were committed to the American cause in the War for Independence, actively supporting independence efforts from the family estate. Probably because the Stocktons had so openly and vigorously supported independence, their home was ransacked by British forces late in 1776. Indeed, Annis had hidden papers of the American Whig Society and other Revolutionary groups just before British forces took the area around Princeton.

Critical Appraisal: Like most women poets of the colonial period, Annis Stockton has remained unknown until recently. Her work was partially revealed by L. H. Butterfield in 1941, and in 1981 Pattie Cowell printed Stockton's extant poems, which reflect the interests expected of a woman until the War for Independence led her, like many other women, to turn to political themes. Thus her early poems like the "Epistle to Mr. S[tockton]" indicate a woman given to conventional poetry. Yet clearly, Annis Stockton's themes were not restricted to romance even before the outbreak of fighting in 1775, although equally clearly, wartime events sharpened her political poems. She had demonstrated her awareness of contemporary events with a piece for Col. Peter Schuyler, taken prisoner by the French, after his return from captivity in 1758. But her poem on the death of Dr. Joseph Warren (q.v.) at the Battle of Bunker Hill demonstrates a sharpening of political awareness not noted earlier. After her poems on her husband's death in 1781, she wrote little, and that, like much of her earlier work, was imitative of earlier poets, notably Pope.

Suggested Readings: Pattie Cowell, *Women Poets in a Pre-Revolutionary America, 1650-1775: An Anthology* (1981); L. H. Butterfield, "Morven: A Colonial Outpost of Sensibility. With Some Hitherto Unpublished Poems by Annis Boudinot Stockton," PULC, 6 (1944), 1-16.

Arthur J. Worrall
Colorado State University

SOLOMON STODDARD (1643-1729)

Works: "Nine Arguments Against Examinations Concerning a Work of Grace" (w. 1679; pub. 1976); *The Safety of Appearing at the Day of Judgment in the Righteousness of Christ* (1687); "The Sermon on Paul's Epistle to the Galatians" (w. 1690; pub. 1975); *The Tryal of Assurance* (1698); *The Doctrine of the Instituted Churches* (1700); *The Necessity of Acknowledgment* (1701); *God's Frown in the Death of Usefull Men* (1703); *The Way for a People to Live Long in the Land* (1703); *The Danger of Speedy Degeneracy* (1705); *The Falseness of the Hopes of Many Professors* (1708); *The Inexcusableness of Neglecting the Worship of God* (1708); *An Appeal to the Learned* (1709); *Those Taught by God the Father* (1712); *The Efficacy of the Fear of Hell* (1713); *A Guide to Christ* (1714); *Three Sermons Lately Preach'd at Boston* (1717); *The Duty of Gospel-Ministers* (1718); *The Presence of Christ with the Ministers* [with] *an Examination of the Power of the Fraternity* (1718); *The Way to Know Sincerity* [with] *a Treatise Concerning Conversion* (1719); *An Answer to Some Cases of Conscience* (1722); *Question Whether God Is Not Angry* (1723); *The Defects of Preachers Reproved* (1724).

Biography: Solomon Stoddard was born in Boston in 1643, son of the prominent merchant Anthony Stoddard and Mary Downing, niece of Governor John Winthrop (q.v.). He graduated from Harvard College in 1662, was named librarian of the college, and then spent two years in the Barbados for his health. In 1669 he accepted a call as minister to the frontier settlement of Northampton, Mass., where Eleazer Mather (q.v.), son of Richard Mather (q.v.) and brother to Increase Mather (q.v.), recently had died. Stoddard married Mather's widow, Esther, by whom he would have twelve children, and entered upon a ministry he would hold until his death.

In Northampton Stoddard quickly gained a reputation for his liberal theological views, later termed "Stoddardism." Upon his arrival, he instituted the principles of the Half-Way Covenant, which his predecessor had strongly resisted.

More significantly, in 1677 he stopped recording distinctions between full and half-way members in the church record book, allowing all members to come to the sacrament of the Lord's Supper. By 1690 he had openly declared the Lord's Supper a "converting ordinance," open to all who professed an interest in Christ and who were not scandalous in their outward behavior. As early as 1677, Increase Mather and others attacked these innovations, and at the Reforming Synod of 1679, Mather challenged Stoddard to debate the principles for admission to full communion, an encounter from which Stoddard emerged victorious. In 1700 he further shocked the conservative clergy by his advocacy of the "Instituted Church," a catholic, sacramental institution that offered men the promises of the Gospel through ordinances such as baptism, prayer, preaching, censure, and the Lord's Supper and to which all people belonged by virtue of their presence within a certain geographical area.

Through the next decade, he and the Mathers engaged in a long and sometimes acrimonious pamphlet war over these innovations. But by 1710, as Stoddard realized he was not gaining support for his novel ecclesiastical reforms, he shifted his interest to a presbyterial system of church government similar to that which Conn. had instituted with the Saybrook Platform of 1708. Furthermore, he was instrumental in the establishment of the Hampshire Association of ministers, a countywide organization through which he spread his ideas of the minister's evangelical duties. During the course of his career, Stoddard had witnessed several "harvests" of souls in his parish, and in these last years, he shared his experiences in these revivals with younger ministers in the valley who were members of this ministerial association and who helped Stoddard prepare the ground for the Great Awakening of the 1740s. Among these younger men was Stoddard's grandson, Jonathan Edwards (q.v.), whom he chose to be his assistant in 1727, and at Stoddard's death in 1729, Edwards assumed the mantle of his grandfather's esteemed position in the valley.

Critical Appraisal: Between 1670 and 1730, Solomon Stoddard was one of the most influential ministers in New Eng., second only to the Mathers in importance. He challenged the Mathers' pious pronouncements about the supposedly sacrosanct nature of the New Eng. Way, and the success of his evangelical labors legitimated his plan to breathe new life into the churches at a time when they were widely perceived as degenerate. Stoddard made experience, and not allegiance to tradition, the measure of his theology, and in his many books and pamphlets, he criticized what he considered an ill-advised and thoughtless worship of tradition. Although his ecclesiastical innovations at first drew few supporters, his defense of them, offered in powerfully persuasive and commonsensical prose, preoccupied the intellectual leaders of the colony throughout the early eighteenth century.

Because of his involvement in ecclesiastical reform, many of Stoddard's works were more polemical than explicitly theological. In his first publication, *The Safety of Appearing at the Day of Judgment in the Righteousness of Christ* (1687), his only doctrinal treatise, he argued strongly that church members should participate in the Lord's Supper even if they were not sure of a work of saving grace upon their souls. His next important publication, *The Doctrine of the Instituted Churches* (London, 1700), consolidated the fruits of his thinking about the organization of the church and illustrated how his ecclesiastical position differed significantly from both the Conn. Presbyterians and the liberal Brattle Street Church group, with whom he often was identified by the Mathers as contributing to the pollution of the churches. This brief work, in which he rejected the notion of a gathered or "covenanted" church as it had been defined by the Massachusetts Bay Puritans, was a carefully reasoned argument for proper ecclesiastical organization, but the pamphlets of the next decade, particularly *The Inexcusableness of Neglecting the Worship of God* (1708) and *An Appeal to the Learned* (1709), while displaying his skill as a polemicist, show him increasingly drawn into rhetorical combat to defend his views. To many readers, however, these works, in which he attacked the Mathers and their supporters for their position on church membership and the efficacy of the sacraments, remain his most accessible and interesting publications.

After 1710 Stoddard's writings became more openly evangelical. *A Guide to Christ* (1714) was offered as a manual of instructions for young ministers who were learning to deal with the intricacies of the process of conversion in their parishioners and stands between Thomas Shepard's (q.v.) *The Sound Believer* (1645) and Jonathan Edwards's *Treatise Concerning Religious Affections* (1746) as one of the most acute psychological analyses of the conversion experience. In other works like *A Treatise Concerning Conversion* (1719) and *The Defects of Preachers Reproved* (1724), he continued this evangelical emphasis, leading the younger ministers of the Connecticut Valley into that path which would culminate in the revivals of 1735 and 1740. Always open to ideas that would make his theology more applicable to the situation of his parishioners and that of New Eng. as a whole, Stoddard exerted a significant influence on the gradual liberalization of Puritanism in America. Although not as polished or forceful a writer as his grandson, for his day Stoddard occupied a comparable position as a strong believer in the mystery and joy of the spiritual life who gave his entire career to furthering man's understanding of how he could best approach his God.

Suggested Readings: CCNE; DAB; DARB; FCNEV; Sibley-Shipton (II, 111-122); Sprague (I, 172-174); T₁. *See also* Ralph J. Coffman, *Solomon Stoddard* (1978); E. Brooks Holifield, *The Covenant Sealed: The Development of Puritan Sacramental Theology in Old and New England* (1974), pp. 168-224; idem, "The Intellectual Sources of Stoddardeanism," NEQ, 45 (1972), 373-392; Karl Keller, "The Loose, Large Principles of Solomon Stoddard," EAL, 16 (1981), 27-41; Paul R. Lucas, " 'An Appeal to the Learned': The Mind of Solomon Stoddard," WMQ, 30 (1973), 257-292; idem, *Valley of Discord: Church and Society Along the Connecticut River, 1636-1725* (1976), pp. 143-188; Perry Miller, "Solomon Stoddard, 1643-1729," HTR, 34 (1941), 277-320; Thomas A. Schafer, "Solomon Stoddard and the Theology of the Revival" in *A Miscellany of American Christianity: Essays in Honor of H. Shelton Smith*, ed. Stuart C. Henry (1963), pp. 328-361; Robert Lee Stuart, " 'Mr. Stoddard's Way': Church and Sacraments in Northampton," AQ, 24 (1972), 243-253; James P. Walsh, "Solomon Stoddard's Open Communion: A Reexamination," NEQ, 43 (1970), 97-114.

Philip F. Gura
University of Colorado, Boulder

SAMUEL STONE (1602-1663)

Works: *A Congregational Church Is a Catholike Visible Church* (1652); *A Short Catechism Drawn Out of the Word of God* (1684). Other works listed in Donald Wing's *Short-Title Catalogue* (3 vols., 1945-1951) are by a different Samuel Stone.

Biography: Samuel Stone, the son of John Stone, freeholder, was born in Hertford, Eng., in 1602. He matriculated pensioner at Emmanuel College, Cambridge, in 1620, where he received a B.A. in 1623 and an M.A. in 1627. He took holy orders at Peterborough and studied divinity further with Richard Blackerby in Ashen, Essex. In 1627 he became curate at Stisted, Essex; he remained there until 1630, when he was suspended for nonconformity. Upon the recommendation of Thomas Shepard (q.v.), Stone then secured a lectureship at Torcester, Northamptonshire. He migrated to New Eng. in 1633 as Thomas Hooker's (q.v.) colleague and assistant; Hooker and Stone were ordained pastor and teacher, respectively, of the Newtown church on Oct. 11, 1633. They left for Conn. in 1636 with most of their congregation; their new settlement, Hartford, was presumably named in honor of Stone's birthplace.

Hartford's frontier location brought Stone into various contacts with the native American population: he served as a chaplain in the 1637 Pequot War, trained the Pequot John Minor in his own home as a missionary-interpreter, and with his later nemesis, elder William Goodwin, attempted (unsuccessfully) to negotiate a compromise over Conn.'s differences with the sachem Sowheag. After his first wife (whose name is unknown) died in 1640, "having smoaked out her days in the darkness of melancholy," he married Mrs. Elizabeth Allen in 1641.

Hooker's death in 1647 left Stone to serve the Hartford church alone. Attempts to secure him an associate led to a bitter personal quarrel between Stone and ruling elder Goodwin and eventually to the notorious "Hartford Church controversy" (1653-1659). During this period, Stone attempted to assert his authority over the congregation, resigned his office, was reinstated but then refused to celebrate the sacrament, and finally watched a large minority of his congregation secede and form a new church at Hadley, Mass. In 1660 John Whiting (q.v.) assumed the position as Stone's associate, and Whiting continued to lead the church after Stone's death on Jul. 20, 1663. Stone left an estate valued at 563 pounds, including 127 pounds worth of books.

Stone's opponents accused him of "Presbyterianism." He was in fact an early supporter of what became the Half-Way Covenant, spoke publicly against requiring prospective church members to make a "relation" of their experience of grace, and accurately expressed his notion of ministerial authority in his famous characterization of Congregational polity as "a speaking aristocracy in the face of a silent democracy." But he defended Congregationalism in print, taught divinity in his home to future Congregational ministers (including John Cotton, Jr. [q.v.]), and represented his church at the Synods of 1637, 1643, 1646-1648, and 1657.

Critical Appraisal: Stone's most important works were never published. The manuscript of his confutation of the English Antinomians Tobias Crisp and John Saltmarsh, although sent to Eng. for publication, had already disappeared by Cotton Mather's (q.v.) day. His monumental "Body of Divinity," which his divinity students were apparently required to copy out in longhand, was also sent to Eng. but failed to find a publisher; a manuscript copy in Samuel Willard's (q.v.) handwriting survives in the Massachusetts Historical Society. That society also possesses a manuscript of Stone's brief discourse "Against ye binding persons to make a Relation of ye time and manner of there conversion in order to there Admission into ye Church."

Apart from his undistinguished *Short Catechism*—used in the Hartford church but first published twenty years after his death—Stone published only *A Congregational Church Is a Catholike Visible Church*. Much of his reputation as an arid, pedantic writer has arisen from judgments of this work, but critics have failed to place it in its proper context: the controversial literature of Stone's day. While composing his comprehensive *Survey of the Summe of Church Discipline*, Thomas Hooker had come upon a copy of *The Essence and Unitie of the Church Catholike Visible, and the Prioritie Thereof in Regard of Particular Churches* (1645) by the English Presbyterian Samuel Hudson. Hudson denied "a particular explicit holy covenant to be the *forme* of a particular church" and argued that Christians are members primarily of the universal "Church Catholike" and only secondarily of particular churches, each of which partook "of part of the matter and part of the form" of the whole.

Hooker devoted Chapter 15 of Part I of the *Survey* to refuting Hudson's position. The Church Catholic was not an "integral whole," as Hudson had argued, made up of the particular churches as members, but rather, a *genus* or general that existed and was preserved in each particular church as *species*. Hudson responded in *A Vindication of the Essence and Unitie of the Church Catholike Visible* (1650), advancing a number of arguments to demonstrate that the Church Catholic could not be a *genus*. Stone then came to the defense of his deceased colleague.

As Samuel Mather (q.v.) saw in the dedicatory epistle to Stone's work, the discussion turned entirely on a "seemingly slight logical question": was the visible Church Catholic a genus or an integral whole? If particular churches were simply fractions of the whole, as Hudson argued, they could not claim to exercise functions reserved to the whole, such as ordaining elders or excommunicating errant members. The basic premise of Congregational polity would be negated. On the other hand, argued Hooker and Stone, if each particular church as *species* contained the whole essence, properties, and operations of the visible Church Catholic as *genus*, then it would follow that "every individual church hath the entire nature of a church in it," and the Congregational Way would rest on firm ground.

Samuel Mather call Stone's book "a patterne for all discourses of this nature in clearness, and succinctness, and close pursuing of the point in hand without distasteful reflections and diversions from things to men." Modern readers might wish for an occasional diversion to lighten Stone's relentless pursuit of what is now an ancient argument, but they, too, will respect Stone's thoroughness, command of Ramist and Aristotelian logic—the first half of the work is a careful explication of the logical terms at issue—and fairness to his opponent.

Suggested Readings: CCNE; DAB; DNB; FCNEV; Sprague (I, 37-38); T_1. *See also* Paul Lucas, *Valley of Discord* (1976), pp. 35-50; "Papers Relating to the Controversy in the Church in Hartford, 1656-59," CHSC, 2 (1870), 51-125; George Leon Walker, *History of the First Church in Hartford* (Stone's will; 1884), pp. 146-181, 445-449. Outlines of a number of Stone's Hartford sermons appear in Douglas Shepard, "The Wolcott Shorthand Notebook, Transcribed" (Ph.D. diss., State Univ. of Ia. 1957).

Baird Tipson
Central Michigan University

ISAAC STORY (1774-1803)

Works: *Liberty. A Poem, Delivered on the Fourth of July* (1795); *All the World's a Stage* (1796); *Consolatory Odes, Dedicated with Christian Piety to Those Unfortunate Beings Who Labor Under the Malignant Influence of the Democratic Mania* (1799); *An Eulogy on...Washington* (1800); *An Oration of the Anniversary of the Independence of the United States of America* (1801); *A Parnassian Shop, Opened in the Pindaric Stile* (1801).

Biography: Little is known about the brief life of Isaac Story. He was born Aug. 7, 1774, in Marblehead, Mass., the second son of Rev. Isaac and Rebecca (Bradstreet) Story and the cousin of the distinguished jurist Joseph Story. He graduated from Harvard in 1793 and then studied law. Story settled in Castine, Maine, in 1797 but moved back to central Mass. in 1799, residing first in Sterling and later in Rutland. He died on Jul. 19, 1803, unmarried and not yet 30, while visiting his relatives in Marblehead.

Critical Appraisal: Isaac Story's brief literary career was much like that of other minor lawyer-poets of his day such as Royall Tyler (q.v.). His works are accurately characterized in the short obituary that appeared in the *Salem Register* for Jul. 25, 1803: "Wit and humor were provinces in which he sought peculiar favor; though he not unfrequently mingled in his poetic effusions the gravity of sententiousness with the lighter graces." Story wrote seriously moral personal essays, light verse, and political and patriotic verse and prose for newspapers. In 1795 he published a Jul. 4 oration, *Liberty*, a juvenile production in competent heroic couplets. Printed under the pseudonym "The Stranger," the poem begins with a dedication in which Story admitted that he "aspires not to the elegance of refinement." The next year under the same pseudonym, Story published *All the World's a Stage* in which he abandoned the couplet in favor of blank verse, a medium he handled with considerably more grace. The work is a series of "characters," mildly satirical character sketches of the kind that were highly popular during the eighteenth century.

Both of these early works were printed by William Barrett of Newburyport, who was also the printer and publisher of the *Political Gazette* in which Story published a series of essays "from the desk of Beri Headin." Strongly reminiscent of Joseph Dennie's (q.v.) "Lay Preacher" essays, these works are serious in tone and highly conventional in content. A second series of essays by Story, much like the first but signed by "The Traveler," appeared in the Boston *Columbian Centinel*. Apparently, while he was in Castine, Maine, Story also wrote some things for Daniel Waters's *Castine Gazette*, but just which poems or essays in that newspaper may be his has not been established.

Story's best-known work is a collected volume of poems that appeared in Boston in 1801, *A Parnassian Shop, Opened in the Pindaric Stile: By Peter Quince, Esq.* Most of these poems are "odes" written in imitation of those by Peter Pinda (that is, John Walcot, 1738-1819), and all of them had appeared over Story's pseudonym first in Barrett's *Political Gazette* and, after that paper ceased publications in 1797, in Joseph Dennie's *Farmer's Weekly Museum.* The poems are fairly short and varied. The first stanza of the "Ode to Poverty" is typical of the lighter verse:

> Come, Poverty, with placid hue,
> With ragged garments, worn-out shoe;
> Come, hear the jovial Peter!
> Thy squalid looks and haggard mien,
> Protub'rant bones and eyes scarce seen,
> Now swell his solemn metre.

The poems contain a number of echoes of Milton's *L'Allegro.* Somewhat more somber is "Peter's Adieu to the City," in which the reader finds the conventional praise of nature and pastoral withdrawal from hectic city life: "Our wants are both simple and few, / Where virtue and modesty reign; / But the phantoms of bliss we pursue, / And the counsels of wisdom disdain." As these lines demonstrate, Story was a competent and sometimes clever poet, but his literary reputation is limited by three circumstances: his career was too brief for him to develop a mature or distinctive voice; many of his poems are topical and therefore lack modern interest; those poems that are not topical are highly conventional in both subject and treatment.

Suggested Readings: DAB. *See also* Perley Derby and F. A. Gardner, *Elisha Story of Boston* (1915); H. M. Ellis, *Joseph Dennie and His Circle, University of Texas Bulletin, Studies in English,* no. 4 (1915).

Carl R. Kropf
Georgia State University

THOMAS STORY (c. 1670-1742)

Works: *A Journal of the Life of Thomas Story* (1747); *Two Discourses Delivered in the Public Assemblies of the People Called Quakers* (w. 1737; pub. 1769); *The Means, Nature, Properties and Effects of True Faith Considered* (w. 1738; pub. 1793).

Biography: Born in the parish of Kirklinton, Eng., and educated at Carlisle grammar school, Thomas Story read law in Cumberland. Although a good churchman, he began to have scruples about baptism and other religious rites and in 1689 experienced a conversion to Quakerism. Giving up the parts of his legal work that he thought would interfere with his religious duties, he began to preach in 1693. After settling in London, Story met William Penn (q.v.), who helped him find legal employment among the Quakers. In 1678 Story sailed to Pa. He was chosen first recorder of Philadelphia in 1701, member of the Council of State, keeper of the great seal, master of the rolls, land commissioner, and treasurer of the Pennsylvania Land Company. In 1706 he was elected mayor of Philadelphia and fined for declining. A dedicated missionary of the Society of Friends, Story traveled to N.J., N.Y., Mass., R.I., and Va.; he visited Jamaica and Barbados. In 1714 he returned to London and preached in Hol., Ire., Scot., and Wales. Several attacks of paralysis gradually deprived Story of speech, and he eventually became unable to leave his home in Carlisle, where he died in 1742.

Critical Appraisal: Journals recording daily life and personal feelings were not uncommon in the eighteenth century. One of the most readable of those journals is that of Thomas Story. Published in 1747, Story's most well-known work contains the account of his conversion to Quakerism and the history of his life, travels, labors, sufferings, debates, discourses, and remarkable occurrences and observations. In his will, Story directed that the journal be published and stated that he kept the journal to preserve a faithful account of his own conduct, to contemplate and adore the divine goodness and mercies of God, and to instruct others. That the journal is meant to be a spiritual autobiography is evident from his selection of details. He made no mention of his marriage or the years he was engaged in affairs in Pa. (1705-1709) or of 1720-1727, when he was involved with several lawsuits. The *Journal* instead is informed by his religious concerns— his conversion in a dream, temptations, preaching, and debates. The introspective account of his life is punctuated by songs of praise, prayers, and voluminous quotations from the Bible. Full of rich detail, the large volume relates entire conversations with officials in the colonies; offers anecdotes about religious figures; records conferences and disputes with dukes, priests, and archbishops; and includes texts of letters, documents, and sermons.

Although the Quakers technically did not preach formal sermons, their testimonies were frequently very close to preaching. Story's testimonies in particular were often comparable to written sermons; his editors considered his discourses superior to many published sermons. In his *Journal*, Story gave long excerpts and complete transcriptions of his debates and testimonies. Other of his testimonies were taken in shorthand, transcribed, and then approved by Story for publication. Before he allowed them to be printed, however, he added scriptural references to support the doctrines he had presented.

Story's missionary zeal is evident in his constant willingness to accept the challenge of any Quaker opponent. The debates were long and lively, the testimonies moving and powerful. Story's favorite subjects included water baptism, the Inner Light, and the unpardonable sin. Whether he was preaching about those subjects or the means of faith, the necessity of knowing one's self, or the insufficiency of natural knowledge, the message he presented was clear and vivid. The doctrines and the theology were presented in a logical, organized manner and in plain language agreeable to the simplicity of the Gospel. The language was passionate as he exhorted his people to forsake sin; it was graceful as he discussed God as a soul-melting presence.

Story's *Journal* provides modern readers with much of the religious history of the times, including descriptions of the services of religions other than Quakerism. The interviews and conversations he recorded, moreover, shed light on contemporary religious doctrines. Many Quaker journals provide little specific information, but the extensive detail, long excerpts, and transcriptions of testimonies and debates provide an important record of the condition and growth of Quakerism in the eighteenth century. A movement hated and feared at first was aided by men like Story, who could hold his own in debates and whose missionary enthusiasm was not offensive to officials. By the end of the century, Quakers were tolerated, respected, and were even becoming influential in the colonies. It is through the dedication of men like Story that the religious mind and actions of a particular people at a particular time can be discovered.

Suggested Readings: DNB. *See also* Richard Beale Davis, *Intellectual History of the Colonial South* (1978); Rufus M. Jones, *The Quakers in the American Colonies* (1911); *Quaker Biographies: A Series of Sketches*, vol. 3 (1912).

Meta R. Braymer
Virginia Commonwealth University

WILLIAM STOUGHTON (1631-1701)

Works: *New Englands True Interest; Not to Lie* (1670); *A Narrative of the Proceedings of Sir Edmund Androsse and His Accomplices, Who Acted by an Illegal and Arbitrary Commission from the Late King James* (with others; 1691).

Biography: Israel Stoughton came to New Eng. in 1630. There he helped found Dorchester, Mass., and became a prominent landowner; and there his second son, William, was born in 1631. Guided by his father's hope that he would dedicate himself to studying the holy Scriptures, William soon became a serious and successful student. Having completed preparatory schools, he entered Harvard College, from which he graduated in 1650. Following one additional year of study at Harvard, he decided to continue his studies in Eng. In 1653 he received an M.A. from New College, Oxford, where he was named a fellow. Later he served as a curate in Sussex. But at the Restoration, he lost both his fellowship and his church, and in 1662 he returned to Mass.

Having quickly established himself as an able, pious man and a powerful preacher, Stoughton seemed destined to follow the path charted for him by his father. But after he had refused several chances to be ordained as minister of the church in Dorchester and one to follow Jonathan Mitchel (q.v.) at the prestigious church in Cambridge, Stoughton finally made a decisive move toward politics and law. From 1671 to 1674, he served as selectman of Dorchester; from 1674 to 1676 and again from 1680 to 1686, he served as commissioner of the United Colonies. In addition, he undertook several important diplomatic missions to Eng. During the late 1680s and early 1690s, he survived a series of shifts and reversals and in 1692 was named both lieutenant governor of Mass. and chief justice of the special tribunal charged with conducting the witchcraft trials of Salem. Throughout the trials, Stoughton remained ardent in his desire to procure convictions. In the process, he enhanced his power in New Eng. and secured a large place in the darkest episode of New Eng.'s early history. On Jul. 7, 1701, when he died, he remained one of the colony's most prominent leaders and least repentant judges. Having never married and having no direct descendants, Stoughton bequeathed most of his considerable estate to Harvard College. Together with earlier bequests, his will made him the largest single benefactor of Harvard during its first century.

Critical Appraisal: Although Stoughton clearly possessed the ability to make a large place for himself in America's early literature, he spent most of his time and energy on public affairs. Only two of his works survive—one that belongs to his later career as a public figure and one that belongs to his early career as a preacher.

A Narrative of the Proceedings of Sir Edmund Androsse (1691) played an important role in New Eng.'s effort to justify its opposition to Andros. Although it is considered to be chiefly the work of Stoughton, its first named author, it bears all of the marks of an official statement and is signed by four other men. Together these "gentlemen of great integrity" proposed "to vindicate their majesties loyal subjects in New-England" by giving "a true representation of things." Finally, however, the *Narrative* reflects both the awkwardness of committee writing and the caution of public statements: it is disappointingly awkward and disappointingly dull.

Delivered as an election sermon on Apr. 29, 1668, *New Englands True Interest* (1670) is both earlier and better. In it Stoughton recalled New Eng.'s original errand in an effort to recover her sense of purpose and rekindle her sense of hope. In the process, he engaged all of the major themes of the Puritan jeremiad, several of them through unforgettable images. "*O New England,*" he wrote, "thy

God did expect better things of thee and thy Children," whereupon he began to catalog sins that ranged from bickering and backbiting through surliness and arrogance to worldliness, fornication, and drunkenness. "Not these things," he continued, "but better things, *O New England*, hath thy God expected from thee." The first-generation New Englanders Stoughton depicted as heroes and giants: "God sifted a whole Nation that he might send choice Grain over into this Wilderness." But in depicting the second and third generations, he posed hard questions: "But we who rise up to tread out the footsteps of them that are gone before us, alas! what are we?" Still, although he saw danger ("It is a sad name to be styled *Children that are corrupters*"), he found hope: "The times are come. . . wherein faithfulness to God. . . will be the most glorious Crown that can be worn upon Earth. . . .*Let no man take this Crown from you.*" In exploring both the danger he saw and the hope he retained, Stoughton set forth the basic tension that defines the Puritan jeremiad.

Suggested Readings: CCNE; DAB; Sibley-Shipton (I, 194-208); T_1. *See also* Perry Miller and Thomas H. Johnson, eds., *The Puritans: A Sourcebook of their Writings* (1963), I, 243-246.

David Minter
Emory University

WILLIAM STRACHEY (1572-1621)

Works: *A True Reportory of the Wreck and Redemption of Sir Thomas Gates, Knight* (1609); *For the Colony in Virginea Britannia: Lawes Divine, Morall and Martiall* (1612); *Historie of Travell into Virginia Britannia* (1612).

Biography: William Strachey was born in 1572 into an English family of "minor gentry." His education, background, and abilities brought him into the company of the leading literary figures of London. As a young man, he wrote some well-received verses and was a member of Blackfriars Theatre and probably also of Gray's Inn. Needing to establish himself, especially after several unsuccessful ventures in Turkey and Constantinople, he turned to Va. in 1609 as did so many gentleman-adventurers of his day. It was this Va. voyage that was to bring him his measure of fame, particularly for *A True Reportory*, his letter about the shipwreck off Bermuda that is generally believed to have been a source of Shakespeare's *The Tempest*. He further proved his capabilities as a writer as well as a man of action throughout his residency in the New World, a period during which he served as first secretary and recorder of the Va. colony. In 1611 he was recalled to Eng. by the Virginia Company for reasons unknown, but that he was still in good standing seems likely, since he remained a shareholder of the company until his death ten years later. Strachey's last years were luckless, and he died unknown except for his debts.

Critical Appraisal: William Strachey's writings give evidence of his competence in both prose and poetry and show that he was adept in the writing styles favored in the seventeenth century. If he is best known for one letter of 1609, *A True Reportory of the Wreck and Redemption of Sir Thomas Gates, Knight*, it is a just renown for it is his best piece of writing. Voyage narratives were eagerly read, and Strachey offered his readers a choice combination of level-headed reality and stirring excitement. There are early pedestrian portions, but they make more convincing the later electrifying descriptions of the shipwreck terrors. So graphically did he render their despair and desolation that the radiant rhetoric of the "redemption" still carries a moving grace. It is reasonable indeed to accept that the manuscript circulated among Strachey's literary friends, reached Shakespeare, and served as the probable source for *The Tempest*.

His two other prose works offer further proof of his cognizance of the era's literary tastes. His history and the treatise on laws are never less than competent, although they do not have the writing flair of *A True Reportory*. *Lawes Divine, Morall and Maritiall* is a sturdy compilation. Historically valued as the first such collection of common laws in America, its literary interest lies primarily in showing an ability to fit style to subject. Like his famous letter, it is clearly the work of an educated and literate man with a sonnet as its preface and many literary allusions sprinkled throughout, but for the most part, Strachey in *Lawes* kept to language earnest and judicious.

His third prose work, *Historie of Travell into Virginia Britannia*, seems to encapsulate the "might-have-been" aspects of William Strachey's influence. Compared with his contemporary John Smith (q.v.), Strachey proved himself the more skilled writer, with better organization and smoother phrasing. He was more observant than Smith of the Indians, their language, and their beliefs. But Smith captured the imagination of his age with his bold self-portrayals as the hero of his every adventure. Strachey's *Historie*, written after his return to Eng., was strongest when he offered his own observations, but almost as if he gave way to Smith's greater repute, he turned more and more to compilations of various accounts rather than relying on his own findings. As a result, there is a lessened impact to his *Historie*.

With his various verses seldom seen and his *Historie* overshadowed, William Strachey's literary fame rests on his voyage letter-narrative, the stylistically controlled and often dramatic *A True Reportory*.

Suggested Readings: DAB; DNB; T₁. *See also* S. G. Culliford, *William Strachey, 1572-1621* (1965); Richard Beale Davis, *Intellectual Life in the Colonial South, 1585-1763*, vol. I (1978); Howard Mumford Jones, *The Literature of Virginia in the Seventeenth Century*, 2nd. ed. (1968). For William Strachey's prose works, see David H. Flaherty, ed., *Lawes Divine, Morall and Martiall* (1969); Louis B. Wright and Virginia Freund, eds., *Historie of Travell into Virginia Britannia* (1953); Louis B. Wright, ed., *A True Reportory* in *A Voyage to Virginia in 1609* (1964).

Leota Harris Hirsch
Rosary College

NICHOLAS STREET (1730-1806)

Works: *The American States* (1777).

Biography: Born in Wallingford, Conn., in 1730, Nicholas Street was the fourth son of a well-established family of that town. After graduating from Yale College in 1751, he was called to the pastorate of the Congregational Society in East Haven, Conn., in 1755. He remained pastor of this congregation of 100 members until his death in 1806, at the age of 76. In his respected, if unspectacular, ministry, he adhered to relatively traditional theology and preaching methods, even through the Revolutionary period, as his one published sermon demonstrates. Although not widely renowned, he was warmly admired and respected in and around his community, as an obituary notice in the *Connecticut Journal* indicates: "Uniting sound discretion with a meek and benevolent spirit, his public and private instructions were always seasonable.... He was gentle towards all, as a father cherishes his children."

Critical Appraisal: Although Nicholas Street claims only a modest literary position, his sermon *The American States* clearly demonstrates how a relatively traditional Congregationalist explained, interpreted, and supported the colonial quest for independence from Br. Although the tone of this sermon is clearly patriotic, Street emphasized the sins of the colonies more than the sins of Br. Despite its concern with current events and its reference to Thomas Paine (q.v.), the sermon in its form and theology resembles New Eng. sermons of an earlier day. Still, it was probably the timeliness of its subject, along with its rhetorical effectiveness, that led Street's hearers to have this sermon published in 1777.

Street built this sermon upon an analogy between the American colonists and the Israelites after their escape from Egypt. Both groups had escaped oppression only to find themselves in a wilderness of "trouble and difficulty," and members of both groups turned against their leaders when their respective escapes did not immediately produce prosperity and freedom. Street contended that God brought both groups to their difficulties to show them their own sinfulness and humbled them into repentance. Within this basic analogy, Street isolated a number of charges against the colonists. He sharply attacked Tories who "look upon it as a greater crime to oppose the king in his most arbitrary measures, than to violate the law of the realm and of their God," those who futilely try to remain neutral, and those extremists who ignore laws for the sake of liberty. His primary attacks, however, were directed against the moderate colonists who supported independence:

> We are apt to think our cause is so righteous with regard to Great-Britain, that I fear we are ready to forget our unrighteousness towards God; and while we are endeavoring to get rid of the unreasonable commands of an earthly sovereign, I fear we forget to obey the most reasonable commands of the rightful Sovereign of the Universe.

More specifically, he found among the colonists a lack of faith in God and colonial leaders and a lack of a sacrificial public spirit as well as selfishness, greed, deceit, oppression, treachery, falsehood, profaneness, and a failure to keep the Sabbath. Against all of these vices, Street contended, the colonists must return to God with humility and repentance, and then God may be entreated to extricate them from their political and military problems. His final emphasis was that colonial righteousness must precede colonial independence.

Although his emphasis was clearly on colonial unrighteousness, Street minced no words in his occasional attacks on Br. and its leadership. Comparing George III to the Egyptian pharoah, he noted "the unreasonable vileness and cruelty of the British tyrant and his ministry" who "oppress, enslave and destroy these American states, who have been some of his most peaceable and profitable subjects." George III, he continued, who "should have been our father and protector, has become the bloody murderer of his best subjects!....I now boldly assert him to be a cruel tyrant, who seeks to govern us without law, without reason, or the sacred dictates of revelation." Street unequivocally concluded that he never again wanted to be connected with the British government.

The effectiveness of this sermon comes largely from Street's mastery of traditional New Eng. homiletics. Its carefully organized structure; its repetition of main points; its catalogs of supporting biblical cases; its construction of the central analogy between the colonists and the Israelites; its skillful, yet traditional, use of imagery (for example, water imagery: "some people have no notion of trusting in God; they rise and fall just like a ship at anchor with ebbing and flowing tide"); its concise, aphoristic syntax ("for to govern without law is tyranny; for law is the guardian of liberty"); its powers of analysis that can see both sides of issues and can explore one issue in numerous directions; and its ultimate emphasis on the unrighteousness of its audience combine to produce a sermon that shows Street to be a late representative of New Eng. Calvinism. Although his rhetoric seems more traditional than imaginative, his skillful application of the traditional theology and rhetoric to contemporary social and political events makes one wish that other sermons of his had been published.

Suggested Readings: CCNE; Dexter (II, 271-273). *See also* Alan Heimert, *Religion and the American Mind* (1966), pp. 495, 561.

John S. Hardt
Ferrum College

NATHAN STRONG (1748-1816)

Works: *The Reasons and Design of Public Punishments* (1777); *A Sermon, Preached March 18, 1778* (1778); *The Agency and Providence of God* (1780); *A Sermon, Delivered in Presence of His Excellency* (1790); *A Sermon, Delivered at the Ordination of. . .Ichabod Lord Skinner* (1794); *The Doctrine of Eternal*

Misery Reconcileable with the Infinite Benevolence of God (1796); *A Sermon, Preached at the Annual Thanksgiving* (1797); *A Sermon, Preached in Hartford June 10th, 1797* (1797); *Political Instruction from the Prophecies* (1798); *A Sermon, Preached at the Installation of. . .David Huntington* (1798); *A Sermon Preached on the State Fast* (1798); *Sermons, on Various Subjects, Doctrinal, Experimental and Practical,* 2 vols, (1798, 1800); *A Discourse [on] . . .the Death of Gen. George Washington* (1799); *The Hartford Selection of Hymns* (1799); *A Sermon, Delivered at the Funeral of Mrs. Sarah Williams* (1800); *A Thanksgiving Sermon* (1800).

Biography: Born in Coventry, Conn., in 1748, Nathan Strong was the son of a Congregational pastor by the same name. The younger Strong went to Yale, where he served as tutor a few years after graduating in 1769 with highest honors. One of his classmates was Timothy Dwight (q.v.), later to become another leader with Strong in the Second Great Awakening. At first inclined to study law, Strong soon shifted his energies toward the ministry. He began his career upon ordination to the pastorship of First Church, Hartford in 1774, at a critical juncture in the life of the congregation and of the emerging nation.

With the outbreak of war, Strong offered his services as chaplain in the Revolutionary army. He also wrote articles to defend the cause of independence and, later, to reconcile public sentiment to adopting the federal Constitution. But his early record as a minister was marred by an ill-fated engagement in the distillery business, which landed him in disrepute and bankruptcy by 1794.

Surprisingly, the episode did no permanent harm to Strong's career. In fact the ministry in Hartford began to attract new renown in that same year of 1794 with a revival driven, it seems, by Strong's personal crisis of self-renewal. Under Strong's leadership and consistent with the general revival sweeping New Eng., still more fruitful seasons of awakening came in 1798, 1800, 1808, 1813, and 1815. Partly to lend guidance to the revivals, Strong published his two large volumes of *Sermons on Various Subjects* (1798, 1800). He also contributed his extensive treatise on *The Doctrine of Eternal Misery*. In 1799 he published *The Hartford Selection of Hymns*, compiled chiefly by him, and he became the main founder and sustainer of the *Connecticut Evangelical Magazine* and the Connecticut Missionary Society. Strong died in Hartford in 1816.

Critical Appraisal: In one of his ordination sermons, Nathan Strong instructed the ordinand to "avoid not plain preaching, because it is growing unfashionable." For the most part, Strong's large and varied legacy of writings shows the author's willingness to follow his own advice. As a New Divinity man, Strong made himself receptive to the emotional tides of the Second Awakening; and before that he had set himself behind the cause of national independence. But in the end, Strong's prose is best characterized as a moderating, conservative force: conservative theologically, in its promotion of the Edwardsean-Hopkinsian school of orthodox Calvinism; politically, in its defense of American civil pieties; and stylistically, in the chastened logic of its typically unflorid and unfigured rhetoric.

Strong revealed his conservative political and social temper in a plentiful array of thanksgiving, fast day, execution, and election sermons. That Divine Providence favored preservation of the American "temple of civilized religious freedom" against the corrupting revolutionaries of Europe, especially the "infidels of France," is a persistent theme in these addresses. Civil and religious obedience, the church and the civil state, become nearly coextensive. Strong held up his myth of the forefathers as "brave and hardy—virtuous and wise" in opposition to the millennial signs of apostasy and declension he discerned in an era of political ferment. His discourse on George Washington (q.v.) elevated this hero to the providential status of a new Moses, come to "rescue from bondage the modern and western Israel of the Lord." Fearing his fellow citizens might be seduced into sullying their godly inheritance, Strong exhorted them in his 1800 thanksgiving sermon to eschew all "new gods," "new institutions," and "new opinions" in morality and religion. "Change is dangerous," he warned, "lest it be for the worse."

Theologically, the rising popularity of Universalist doctrine was in Strong's mind decidedly a change for the worse. To defend the orthodox belief that some sinners will be punished interminably after death, he produced his seemingly interminable treatise (408 pages) *The Doctrine of Eternal Misery*. Written most directly in response to a posthumous publication by Joseph Huntington of Coventry, the treatise also addressed the more general challenge presented by "those gentlemen who have endeavored to criticize misery out of the universe." Strong marshaled the full range of usable arguments from Scripture, tradition, and logic to establish that a benevolent God may admit the "partial evil" of selective damnation to achieve the highest good of the scheme as a whole. For Strong genuine "benevolence" should not be reduced to benign feeling toward individuals, but should consist rather in "a friendliness of the heart to the general good, to which all private, separate and individual interests are subordinated." Some of Strong's arguments seem weak or well worn, and often his phrasings merely echo formulations set forth earlier by Jonathan Edwards (q.v.) (both elder and younger), Samuel Hopkins (q.v.), and others. Still, *The Doctrine* is probably Strong's most impressive work. There are moments when the author's speculative vigor manages to raise the treatise above narrow polemics toward a more sublime genre of theodicy. But along with his higher theologizing, Stong voiced the predictably practical worry: "the tendency of this [Universalist] doctrine will be to promote vice, and make men careless concerning their own salvation."

That terror has its sanctified uses in the evangelical scheme is likewise a governing motif in Strong's two volumes of *Sermons on Various Subjects* associated with the revival. A rhetoric of fear may serve not only to awaken sinners to their insecurity, but to excite them toward apprehending that "new taste" that marks the gracious presence of God. Even as Strong insisted unequivocally on the Calvinist doctrines of total depravity and divine sovereignty, he observed that "There cannot be religion without feeling, deep feeling." Hence he defended the latest appearance of "experimental religion" as something quite distinct from both "formalism" and "enthusiasm." A good deal of this, of course, hearkens back to the elder Jonathan Edwards, and although Strong made his case lucidly enough, he did not isolate the signs of genuine faith with anything like the compelling detail Edwards had provided in a work like the *Treatise Concerning Religious Affections*.

Suggested Readings: CCNE; Dexter (III, 357-363); Sprague (II, 34-41). *See also* Stephen E. Berk, *Calvinism versus Democracy: Timothy Dwight and the Origins of American Evangelical Orthodoxy* (1974), pp. 65, 164; Joseph Haroutounian, *Piety versus Moralism: The Passing of the New England Theology*, 3rd ed. (1970), pp. 131-156; J. Hammond Trumbull, *The Memorial History of Hartford County Conn., 1633-1884* (1886), I, 286.

John J. Gatta, Jr.
University of Connecticut

THOMAS SYMMES (1678-1725)

Works: *A Monitor for Delaying Sinners* (1719); *Good Soldiers* (1720); *The Reasonableness of Regular Singing* (1720); *A Discourse Concerning Prejudice in Matters of Religion* (1722); *An Ordination Sermon Preached at Malden. . . When the Reverend Mr. Joseph Emerson Was Ordained* (1722); *Utile Dulce* (1723); *The People's Interest* (1724); *Lovewell Lamented* (1725).

Biography: The career of Thomas Symmes, minister at Boxford and Bradford, Mass., typified the experience of many of the third generation of New Eng. clergymen. Symmes's career choice was foreordained, since both his father and grandfather were ministers, so he entered Harvard College. After graduating, he accepted a pulpit at Boxford, but not without considerable discussion about salary and the matter of a separate pew for his new wife, Elizabeth. This haggling about proper maintenance and respect for his calling was a portent, for in 1708 a church council granted him a release from Boxford, because the congregation could not pay the salary he demanded. He immediately took over his father's Bradford church, but there too his insistence on clerical prerogatives caused trouble. He quarreled with his parishioners over the correct form of hymn singing, berated them for falling asleep during sermons, and even had the meeting-house door locked to prevent the unappreciative from slipping out before services had ended. These problems reflected the growing restiveness of New Englanders with the pastoral style of Symmes's generation of ministers. In their concern for proper respect and salaries, ministers like Thomas Symmes revealed a rigidity and self-interest that alienated their parishioners and ironically paved the way for the charismatic itinerant preachers of the Great Awakening. This alienation was especially evident in Symmes's career, for despite his almost obsessive demands for a better salary, he died in 1725 as he had lived—in poverty.

Critical Appraisal: Like his career, the writings of Thomas Symmes reflect the troubles faced by New Eng. ministers during the first half of the eighteenth century. Symmes was neither a renowned scholar nor a brilliant pulpit orator. Only four of his sermons were published, and all exhibit the standard theology and homiletics of his generation of Harvard-trained ministers. More important are his tracts on the proper form of hymn singing and *The People's Interest*, a stinging indictment of New Englanders' parsimony toward their pastors. These writings are good examples of the strident rhetoric and professional arrogance that exacerbated relations between pew and pulpit in the years before the Great Awakening.

Symmes was among the ministers converted to the practice of singing by note after reading a 1715 pamphlet written by John Tufts, a young Harvard graduate. Tufts had argued that this form of singing was a far better way to praise God than the old way, in which a congregation repeated each verse of a hymn after a deacon had chanted it. Each member of the congregation chose his or her own pitch, tone, and tempo in this response, and Increase Mather's (q.v.) characterization of it as an "Odd Noise" was probably too charitable. Many parishioners, however, resisted the changes in traditional singing that Tufts recommended. These laymen thought that such reforms smacked of papist ceremony and decreased the power of deacons as well. In *The Reasonableness of Regular Singing*, Symmes became the first minister to answer these criticisms. There he provided scriptural precedents for singing by note, pointed out that New Eng.'s founders had sung in this manner, and argued that its melodiousness and arithmetical rationality were more pleasing to God than the cacophony of the old way. These arguments were not immediately successful; Symmes was unable for a number of years to convince even his own church to adopt his reforms. Yet he persisted, repeating his case in *A Discourse Concerning Prejudice in Matters of Religion* and in *Utile Dulce*, a stylized debate on singing between a minister and a recalcitrant parishioner, in which the former easily prevailed. Symmes eventually won over his Bradford congregation, but the final victory of the new way of singing was achieved only after years of acrimonious disputes between clergy and laiety.

Published in 1724, *The People's Interest* represents a new genre of New Eng. pastoral writing that began to appear around 1710. This genre outlined the holy and honorable nature of ministers' work, emphasized their material needs, and excoriated parishioners for paying their pastors neither adequate salaries nor proper respect. Symmes began *The People's Interest* with a preface to Mass. Lieutenant Governor William Dummer and clearly hoped, in vain as it turned out, that this account of starving ministers would result in financial assistance from the government. The arguments presented in this pamphlet were not scriptural, but rather references to earlier works on the same subject by Increase Mather (q.v.) and Cotton Mather (q.v.) and some secular writers; it also included a comparison of the standards of living of ministers, lawyers, and physicians. Like most pamphlets and sermons of this genre, *The People's Interest* was a secular document, written for secular purposes. Like these other writings, it was singularly unsuccessful in accomplishing its purposes.

Since most of Symmes's writings were persuasive pieces meant for a general audience, his prose is more accessible than much of the ministerial literature of colonial America. *Utile Dulce* and *Lovewell Lamented*, a sermon on the defeat of a Mass. militia company by the Indians, are especially good examples of this clarity. Symmes was a convincing causist, but the tone of arrogance that prevails throughout his work clearly lessened the impact of his pleas. He could never forget that he was a member of New Eng.'s only learned profession and was better educated than his parishioners. In the patronizing tone of *The People's Interest* and *Utile Dulce* lies a major reason why New Englanders were not moved by his arguments.

Suggested Readings: CCNE; Sibley-Shipton (IV, 411-417). *See also* James W. Schmotter, "The Irony of Clerical Professionalism: New England's Congregational Ministers and the Great Awakening," AQ, 31 (1979), 148-168; Ola E. Winslow, *Meetinghouse Hill, 1630-1783* (1952), pp. 150-170; J. William T. Youngs, Jr., *God's Messengers: Religious Leadership in Colonial New England, 1700-1750* (1976).

James W. Schmotter
Cornell University

T

PATRICK TAILFER (fl. 1734-1741)

Works: *A True and Historical Narrative of the Colony of Georgia in America, from the First Settlement Thereof Until This Present Period* (with Hugh Anderson, Da. Douglas, and others; 1741).

Biography: Little is known of the life of Patrick Tailfer, and nothing is known of the years before his arrival in the colony of Ga. on Aug. 1, 1734, although he was said to be a physician from Edinburgh, Scot. In Ga. he settled on a small plantation near the larger holdings of John and Robert Williams, the brothers of his wife, Mary. Finding himself ill suited to plantation life, Tailfer moved to Savannah to practice medicine.

In Savannah, too, discontent soon overtook Tailfer. Joining other disgruntled colonists, he began sponsoring clubs and meetings that opposed several policies—including prohibitions against selling rum and trafficking in black slaves—that were dear to the heart of Gen. James Edward Oglethorpe (q.v.), the founder of the colony. Tailfer and his fellow dissidents also opposed the presence and influence of Charles and John Wesley, whom Oglethorpe had brought over to direct the spiritual life of Ga.

Although Oglethorpe and his trustees were quick to call Tailfer and his associates clamorous malcontents, they were slow to take action against them. By 1741, however, with conditions in Ga. worsening and discontent spreading, Tailfer was forced into exile in S.C., where he joined Hugh Anderson, David Douglas, and other "Landholders of Georgia" in writing *A True and Historical Narrative of the Colony of Georgia*. This book shows that Tailfer was a witty, urbane man, and it has given him a place in American literature. Of his life after 1741 as of his life before 1734, we know nothing.

Critical Appraisal: Patrick Tailfer presented *A True and Historical Narrative* as a straightforward account of Ga.'s early history, "Containing the most authentick Facts, Matters and Transactions" of the colony. But from his six-page dedication, "To his Excellency James Oglethorpe, Esq.," to his last paragraph, describing the sad fate of Ga. and her "poor Inhabitants," Tailfer informed his account of the planning, settlement, and difficulties of Ga. with irony and satire.

Throughout he addressed both Oglethorpe ("your Excellence") and the trustees ("Honourable Gentlemen") with feigned reverence, and he consistently presented himself and his associates with mock deference, "Most devoted Servants." But his laudatory dedication is a burlesque, and his wit, although occasionally detached and elegant, is often caustic and even vicious. The primary manifestation of Oglethorpe's status as a visionary philanthropist, whose proper concern is with the "perpetual welfare" of his subjects, is his total disregard for "transitory advantages" such as food, shelter, and clothing. Having reduced all Georgians to "more than primitive poverty," the better to teach them the "valuable virtue of humility," he destroyed their ambition and robbed them of hope. Consequently, we not only come to see Ga. as immersed in suffering; we also come to see Oglethorpe and the trustees as the tyrannical architects of disaster. Oglethorpe in particular emerges, not as a visionary leader, but as a selfish, greedy despot enamored of foolish schemes, and his deputy, Thomas Causton, emerges as a brutal, sadistic creature whom Oglethorpe deliberately used to commit deeds too vile for his own hand. Although Tailfer enumerated various causes of the ruin and desolation of the colony—stressing its policies governing land, rum, and slaves—he traced the root causes to Oglethorpe and his cohorts. They turned Ga. into "a Desart," an "Object of Pity to Friends, and of Insult, Contempt and Ridicule to Enemies," scattering her "poor Inhabitants...over the Face of the Earth."

Suggested Readings: LHUS; T_1. *See also* David L. Minter, *The Interpreted Design as a Structural Principle in American Prose* (1969), pp. 41-42, 50-51; Clarence L. Ver Steeg, Introduction, *A True and Historical Narrative* (1960); Robert M. Willingham, Jr., "Patrick Tailfer" in *Southern Writers: A Biographical Dictionary*, ed. Robert Bain et al. (1969), pp. 443-444.

David Minter
Emory University

DAVID TAPPAN (1752-1803)

Works: *The Duty of Private Christians to Pray for Their Ministers* (1778); *The Character and Best Exercises of Unregenerate Sinners* (1782); *A Discourse Delivered at the Third Parish in Newbury* (1783); *The Question Answered, "Watchman, What of the Night?"* (1783); *The Character and Death of the Servant of God* (1784); *Two Friendly Letters from Toletus to Philalethes* (1785); *A Sermon, Delivered at the Ordination of the Rev. Timothy Dickinson* (1789); *The Connexion Between Faith in God* (1792); *A Sermon Preached Before His Excellency John Hancock* (1792); *A Minister's Solemn Farewell to His People* (1793); *A Sermon, Delivered to the First Congregation in Cambridge* (1793); *Copy of an Address Delivered to the Students of Phillips Academy* (1794); *A Discourse, Delivered in the Chapel of Harvard College, June 17, 1794* (1794); *A*

Discourse Delivered in the Chapel of Harvard College, September 16, 1794 (1794); *A Sermon Delivered at the Ordination of the Rev. John Thornton Kirkland* (1794); *A Sermon, Delivered at the Third Parish in Newbury* (1794); *Christian Thankfulness Explained and Enforced* (1795); *A Discourse Delivered in the Chapel of Harvard College, November 17, 1795* (1795); *A Discourse Delivered to the Students of Harvard College, September 6, 1796* (1796); *A Sermon, Delivered Before the Annual Convention of the Congregational Ministers* (1797); *A Discourse Delivered in the Chapel of Harvard College, June 19, 1798* (1798); *A Discourse, Delivered to the Religious Society in Brattle-Street* (1798); *The Beauty and Benefits of the Christian Church* (1800); *A Sermon Delivered at Kennebunk* (1800); *A Discourse, Delivered in the South Meeting-House in Andover* (1802); *A Sermon, Delivered at Wiscasset* (1802); *A Funeral Discourse* (1803); *A Sermon Delivered April 18, 1803* (1803); *Lectures on Jewish Antiquities* (1807); *Sermons on Important Subjects* (1807).

Biography: One of the most prolific authors of the eighteenth century, David Tappan was born in Manchester, Mass., on Apr. 21, 1752. His father Benjamin was a Harvard graduate and Congregationalist minister, and the son followed in his father's path. Tappan was admitted to Harvard College at the age of 14 and received a B.A. in 1771. In Apr. 1774 he was ordained a Congregationalist minister and became pastor in Newbury, Mass., where he served for the next eighteen years. Tappan married Hannah Sawyer in 1780; they had ten children but five died in infancy. In Dec. 1792 he was appointed Hollis professor of divinity at Harvard and served in that capacity until his death. At Harvard he directed much of his energy to combating perceived Deistic influences on the theology students. Tappan was a moderate Calvinist acceptable to both wings of Mass. Congregationalism, the more orthodox Calvinists who followed Jedidiah Morse (q.v.) and the Unitarians. His death on Aug. 27, 1803, set off a power struggle between these factions for control of Harvard. Tappan's funeral sermon was preached by Abiel Holmes (q.v.).

Critical Appraisal: His fellow minister Daniel Dana observed that David Tappan's "prime and prominent excellence was that of a preacher," and certainly most of his published works were sermons. Tappan was noted for his plain style of preaching, theological moderation, and staunch Federalism.

Several consistent themes run throughout Tappan's writings: concern for public virtue; the need for calm, orderly religious life; and respect for authority. In his 1792 election sermon, for instance, he vigorously asserted "the necessity of religion to public order and happiness" and spoke of the need for political leaders to be "public religious instructors." He reminded the general population that "virtue enlightened and invigorated by political and Christian knowledge, is eminently the soul of a republic." Like many of his fellow clergy, he perceived his time as one of assaults on Christianity by "the spirit of infidelity and libertinism, which reigns in the world," and in his 1797 address to the Congregationalist ministers of his state defended clerics as necessary components of society.

Like most Protestant clergymen, Tappan at first supported the French Revolution, because he saw it as the means to the destruction of Roman Catholicism and the hastening of the millennium. In his 1789 fast sermon, however, he abjured his earlier support and—along with Jedidiah Morse and Timothy Dwight (q.v.) —swallowed the story of the "Bavarian Illuminati." Tappan's reputation suffered somewhat from the subsequent exposure of this fictitious conspiracy.

Four years after his death, Tappan's most ambitious work, *Lectures on Jewish Antiquities*, was published by his friends. Consisting of lectures given at Harvard in 1802 and 1803, the book analyzed Hebrew government, worship, ministers, prophets, rituals, and law. His *Sermons on Important Subjects* (1807) consisted of previously unpublished manuscript sermons; even more than his political sermons of the 1790s, they show Tappan as a minister dedicated to promoting personal holiness and commitment among his congregation.

Suggested Readings: Sibley-Shipton (XVII, 638-645); Sprague (II, 97-103). *See also* Henry F. May, *The Enlightenment in America* (1976), pp. 194-195, 264-268. Prefixed to *Sermons on Important Subjects* is a sketch of Tappan's life by Abiel Holmes and a copy of the sermon Holmes preached on the occasion of Tappan's funeral.

John F. Berens
Northern Michigan University

EDWARD TAYLOR (c. 1642-1729)

Works: Stanzas 5 and 7 of "Upon Wedlock and Death of Children" (pub. in Cotton Mather, *Right Thoughts in Sad Hours*; 1689); *The Poetical Works of Edward Taylor* (1939, 1943); *The Poems of Edward Taylor* (1960); *Edward Taylor's Christographia* (1962); *A Transcript of Edward Taylor's Metrical History of Christianity* (1962); *The Diary of Edward Taylor* (1964); *Edward Taylor's Treatise Concerning the Lord's Supper* (1965); *Edward Taylor vs. Solomon Stoddard: The Nature of the Lord's Supper* (1981); *Edward Taylor's "Church Records" and Related Sermons* (1981); *Edward Taylor's Minor Poetry* (1981); *Edward Taylor's Harmony of the Gospels* (1982).

Biography: Born in Sketchley, Leicestershire, Eng., about 1642, Edward Taylor received a nonconformist education that was completed, after he immigrated to Massachusetts Bay in 1668, at Harvard College. Shortly following his graduation from Harvard in 1671, he accepted a call to Westfield, a Mass. frontier town. Although subsequently denied immediate participation in the intellectual activity of the coastal towns, an activity with which he privately identified, Taylor spent the remainder of his life in unquestioned dedicated service, as minister and physician, to orthodox Congregationalism and his parish. On Nov. 5, 1674, he married Elizabeth Fitch of Norwich, and three years after the death of his first wife in 1689, he married Ruth Wyllys of Hartford. Taylor possessed a remarkable library of nearly 200 works, and he also copied extensive passages from borrowed books. He corresponded with Increase Mather (q.v.), Samuel

Sewall (q.v.), and Solomon Stoddard (q.v.), but very few of his letters survive. Several of his sermons and a substantial number of his poems are extant, although save for two stanzas, they were not published in his lifetime. Aside from the fact that he resided in a frontier town, it remains uncertain why his poetry did not appear in print during his life, and it is even more surprising that his reply to Stoddard, eight sermons written about 1694, and his Christological treatise, fourteen sermons written between 1701 and 1703—both of which appear to have been prepared for the press—were not published before the twentieth century. In 1725 Taylor, very ill, accepted assistance from Nehemiah Bull; three years later, Taylor died and was buried in Westfield.

Critical Appraisal: Although as a minister Edward Taylor wrote sermons, many especially noteworthy for their documentation of his ideas about Christ and the Lord's Supper, his literary reputation as the most outstanding literary artist of Puritan New Eng. emanates from the *Preparatory Meditations*, poetry he wrote in apparent conjunction with certain of his sermons. These devotional poems in the meditative tradition of the sixteenth and seventeenth centuries were written in preparation for his participation in the Lord's Supper, although evidence suggests that he revised and recast several of them at later times. These poems may reflect the traits of seventeenth-century English "metaphysical" poetry—the work of, say, George Herbert, whose poetry Taylor occasionally echoed—but in fact they evince genuinely idiosyncratic features such as a deliberately executed decorum of imperfection, an adherence to an exclusionist typological system, and a management of persona that conveys the essential ambivalence of Puritan culture as well as, in the process, permitting the poet to assert self and arrest that assertion, to be simultaneously within and outside his poem. *Preparatory Meditations* has disturbed some critics, and the earliest scholarship pertaining to it tends to emphasize its congruence with Anglican sources and its alleged Roman Catholic dimensions. In spite of the fact that this latter belief and the supportive notion that Taylor enjoined his heirs never to publish his work have properly declined in recent scholarship, critics still tend to approach the sacramental features of Taylor's poetry as if they stand apart from the mainstream of Puritan orthodoxy, an attitude that is nonetheless slowly fading away before a more clarified perception of Puritan sacramentality (for example, E. Brooks Holifield's *The Covenant Sealed* [1974]) and of the pluralism of Puritan culture generally. Current interest in the *Preparatory Meditations* still emphasizes theme, theology, intellectual heritage, and aesthetic theory—each indeed a valid concern—but several critics have most recently confronted the notion that these poems imagistically develop in a baroque and free-associative manner by demonstrating in select examples an intricate artistic integrity, a developmental consistency of imagery, and a logical pattern of transition, albeit they may evince an idiosyncratic and private variety.

Taylor's ostensibly more public *Gods Determinations Touching His Elect*, a long sequence of doctrinal verse in diverse manner, is less aesthetically rich than the *Preparatory Meditations*. Possible influences upon it such as morality plays,

Theocritan song contests, Ignatian meditative practices, and homiletic tradition have been remarked by scholars. Less discussed but, perhaps, more significant is the exhibition in *Gods Determinations* of Taylor's capacity for the dramatic, his relish for paradox, and his ability to organize a work through several modes of unity.

Taylor's minor work includes a brief diary, an incomplete commentary on the Gospels, a long narrative poem on the history of Christianity, and miscellaneous poems, various church records, many extracts from or transcriptions of works by others, and a few extant letters. Taylor's stature as the greatest New Eng. Puritan literary artist is secure, and in the offing is the recognition that in broader terms, he ranks among the greatest of American writers.

Suggested Readings: CCNE; DAB (Sup. I); FCNEV; LHUS; Sibley-Shipton (II, 397-412, 534-536); Sprague (I, 177-181). *See also* Robert Daly, *God's Altar: The World and the Flesh in Puritan Poetry* (1978); Norman S. Grabo, *Edward Taylor* (1961); Karl Keller, *The Example of Edward Taylor* (1975); William J. Scheick, *The Will and the Word: The Poetry of Edward Taylor* (1974); William J. Scheick and JoElla Doggett, *Seventeenth-Century American Poetry: A Reference Guide* (1977); Donald E. Stanford, *Edward Taylor* (1965).

William J. Scheick
The University of Texas at Austin

JACOB TAYLOR (d. 1746)

Works: *Tenebrae in; Or, The Eclip[ses]* (1698); Almanacs (1700-1746); *Pennsylvania* (1728).

Biography: Jacob Taylor's name first appears as the author of *Tenebrae in; Or, The Eclip[ses]*, published in N.Y. in 1698. In 1700 came the first of his yearly almanacs, printed by Reinier Jansen, in whose shop Taylor apparently worked. Upon Jansen's death four years later, Taylor assumed control of the press, issuing his own almanacs and several publications for the Friends' meetings. Taylor showed little interest in printing, however, and after 1712 he yielded all such concerns to Andrew Bradford (q.v.). In 1706 Taylor became surveyor general of Pa., a post he held until 1733. (In 1725 he added the title of surveyor general of Philadelphia.) We know little else of his life in these years, save that in 1708 he took charge of the Friends' school and that in 1702, as James Logan (q.v.) recorded, he was stricken with smallpox. Apparently, he benefited in part from the illness: Joshua Fisher stated that in addition to his many other duties, Taylor was a "successful practitioner of physic." Until his death in 1746, however, Taylor was chiefly occupied with astrological and mathematical calculations for his almanacs.

Critical Appraisal: Printer, schoolmaster, physician, poet, almanac maker, mathematician, astronomer, surveyor, satirist—Jacob Taylor is indeed a difficult figure to evaluate. His many interests rivaled those of Benjamin Franklin (q.v.), but unfortunately, his talent did not.

Taylor's chief claim for our attention rests on his almanacs, begun in 1700 and issued continuously (with the exception of 1701 and 1707) until his death in 1746. Although principally collections of monthly astrological calculations, like most almanacs, they also collected a potpourri of anecdotes, reflections, and literature. The almanac of 1705, for example, includes a table of the kings of Eng., several poems by Taylor, monthly calendars and weather predictions, and a schedule of the year's eclipses. In the almanac for 1741, Taylor reprinted selections from *Paradise Lost*; 1743's edition added a narrative of "The Indian Prophecy" based on the appearance of the comet of 1680. Fisher pointed out that "before the publication of Franklin's well known production, his [Taylor's] almanac was the best and most popular of several issued in Philadelphia," surpassing those of Taylor's principal rival, Daniel Leeds (q.v.). Taylor, however, too often neglected the fine points of composition: as Henry Phillips suggested, "The orthography is extremely unsettled [even for the early eighteenth century] and the grammar equally uncertain."

Included in most of these almanacs are specimens of Taylor's own poetry—poetry that won the praise of several of his contemporaries. Joseph Breintnall (q.v.) wrote a poem extolling "Thy lasting sense and spirit," and the anonymous author of "The Wits and Poets of Pennsylvania" echoed these words: "With Years oppresst, and compass'd round with Woes, / A Muse with Fire fraught yet T—y—r shoes, / His fancy's bold, harmonious are his Lays, / And were he more correct, He'd reach the Bays." A hundred years later, Joshua Fisher offered more reserved praise: "some of the pieces have considerable merit. . .[but his poems] were never remarkable for their vigour or sublimity."

Chief among these poems, in addition to the brief verses in his almanacs, were Taylor's "Story of Whackum," a satire of rural physicians; the "Testimony in Favour of Poor Richard's Almanac"; and his several satires directed at Samuel Keimer (q.v.), who incurred Taylor's wrath both for his self-righteous pose and his plan to institute a religious school for "male negroes to read the Holy Scripture": "A school for thee! a most commodious place / To nod and wink, and print with such a grace." Subtlety was not Taylor's forté, and if we can judge from this extract from his almanac for 1705, neither was versification: "To them that shall presume that Risque to run, / To let us know how we're imposed on, / Detraction, envy, slander shall accrue / From that ill-natured, vaunting, lying Artles Crue." The verse is, as Henry Phillips suggested, "a piece of terrible poetry, most shockingly printed."

Taylor's longest poem, *Pennsylvania*, belongs in the tradition of descriptive verse first established in Pa. by John Holme (q.v.) and Richard Frame (q.v.) and continued, somewhat more skillfully than by Taylor, by Thomas Makin (q.v.). Taylor focused on the natural bounty of the area and explicitly linked the province with the biblical Promised Land: "Like Palestine a land of good repute, / For wheat and barley, honey, milk, and fruit." He relied heavily on a catalog of crops and trees, and unfortunately, he often selected most unfelicitous diction: "The ground producing ev'ry sort of grain, / Pomarious profit, and the hortensian gain." As his "wild unbounded fancy roves," Taylor alights on the products of Pa.'s arbors: "As for the nuts, they may with acorns join, / A noble mast for saginating swine." Taylor was not suited for such a poetic task; he clearly was at his best when he seized upon a topic for his satiric pen.

But Taylor was not a gifted poet, and although we should be familiar with his verse, we should look primarily to his almanacs for his literary and historical significance. He supplied Philadelphia with an important source of amusement and instruction, and Franklin's final praise of Taylor's works ("the most compleat Ephemeris and most accurate Calculations that have hitherto appear'd in America") supplies a fitting close: "He was an ingenious Mathematician as well as an expert and skillful Astronomer; and moreover, no mean Philosopher, but what is more than all, He was a PIOUS and Honest Man. *Requiescat in pace.*"

Suggested Readings: T_1. *See also* Joshua Fisher, "Some Account of the Early Poets and Poetry of Pennsylvania," MHSP, 2, pt. ii (1830), 65-67; Henry Phillips, Jr., "Certain Almanacs Published in Philadelphia between 1705 and 1744," PAPS, 19 (1881), 291-297; Marion Barber Stowell, *Early American Almanacs: The Colonial Weekday Bible* (1977), pp. 156-158; John William Wallace, "Early Printing in Philadelphia," PMHB, 4 (1880), 432-445.

Timothy K. Conley
Bradley University

JOHN TAYLOR OF CAROLINE (1753-1824)

Works: *An Examination of the Late Proceedings in Congress, Respecting the Official Conduct of the Secretary of the Treasury* (1793); *A Definition of Parties; Or, The Political Effects of the Paper System Considered* (1794); *An Inquiry into the Principles and Tendency of Certain Public Measures* (1794); *An Argument Respecting the Constitutionality of the Carriage Tax* (1795); *A Defense of the Administration of Thomas Jefferson* (1805); *Arator: Being a Series of Agricultural Essays, Practical and Political* (1813); *Construction Construed, and Constitutions Vindicated* (1820); *Tyranny Unmasked* (1822); *New Views of the Constitution of the United States* (1823).

Biography: Born on Dec. 19, 1753, at Mill Farm, Caroline County, Va., John Taylor of Caroline was the son of James and Ann (Pollard) Taylor. After the deaths of both of his parents, he was cared for by his uncle Edmund Pendleton, who placed him in Donald Robertson's Classical school in King and Queen County, where he became a classmate of James Madison (q.v.).

In 1770 Taylor entered the College of William and Mary. Reading for the law under Edmund Pendleton, Taylor was licensed to practice in Va. in 1774. His study of law accounts, in part at least, for his deep interest in American politics, particularly during the formative years of the new nation.

Taylor's marriage in 1783 to Lucy Penn greatly improved his fortunes, which had suffered from deflation following the Revolution. His wife's handsome dowry, combined with Taylor's genius for husbandry and his successful experiments in crop rotation, made him one of the most successful farmers in his region. "Hazlewood," his home on the banks of the Rappahannock in Caroline County, was, indeed, a model of agrarian efficiency.

As Roy Nichols has suggested, Taylor came from an Enlightenment background, having reached his majority in 1774. Because of his agrarian interest, study of law, and Enlightenment disposition, he served with distinction at both the state and federal levels: in the Va. House of Delegates, 1779-1785 and 1796-1800, and in the U.S. Senate, 1792-1794, 1803, and 1822. He died at "Hazlewood" on Aug. 21, 1824.

Critical Appraisal: John Taylor's political and economic arguments are rooted in Enlightenment Classicism and are strongly influenced by the teachings of the French Physiocrats. In the Jeffersonian, agrarian tradition, he came to see the farmer as a child of God and held that in recognition of man's proclivity to both good and evil, the only justification for government was the keeping of public order. Both *A Definition of Parties* (1794) and *An Inquiry into the Principles of Certain Public Measures* (1794) were highly critical of Alexander Hamilton's (q.v.) policies on funding and banking. *A Defense of the Administration of Thomas Jefferson* (1805) attests, on the other hand, to Taylor's ardent support of the president, despite Thomas Jefferson's (q.v.) purchase of the Louisiana Territory, which the Va. economist had difficulty accepting.

Published first as essays in the newspaper *The Spirit of Seventy-Six* beginning on Dec. 25, 1810 (see Robert Shallope for proper dating), *The Arator*, Taylor's most widely read work, advocated crop rotation, proper drainage, and the use of lime and manures long before such methods became accepted farm practices or before any real concern over soil depletion had been voiced in the South. The author, like Jefferson before him, praised the character developed in those who till the earth. M. E. Bradford placed the collection in the tradition of *De Agri Cultura* of Cato the Censor (220 *B.C.*) and Vergil's *Georgics*.

An Inquiry into the Principles and Policy of the Government of the United States (1814), his most important work, is a rebuttal to John Adams's (q.v.) *A Defense of the Constitution of Government of the United States of America* (1787-1788). Taylor argued that the rise of American capitalism is at the expense of farmers and laborers and that the method of that exploitation is "inflated public paper, bank stock, and a protective tariff" (Hubbell, p. 221). Long before the evolution of secession, Taylor saw contemporary American economic policy as favoring business interests and exploiting agrarian support of the Union. The work, to Charles Beard, is "among the two or three really historic contributions to political science" in American history. *Construction Construed* (1820), the author's attack on Chief Justice John Marshall and the Supreme Court, is motivated by similar political reservations concerning union as opposed to confederation.

To an agrarian of the twentieth century like Andrew Lytle, Taylor's emphasis on confederation and his mistrust of union anticipate nineteenth-century secessionists like John C. Calhoun. Vernon Parrington, on the other hand, judged him the "most penetrating critic of Hamiltonian finance and the most original economist of his generation." Taylor's real achievement, however, seems to have been his effort to warn against the "fusion of political and economic power within a centralized government," a fusion he saw as threatening to the freedoms of an American republic.

Suggested Readings: DAB. *See also* Keith M. Bailor, "John Taylor of Caroline: Continuity, Change, and Discontinuity in Virginia's Sentiments toward Slavery, 1790-1820," VMHB, 75 (1967), 290-304; Charles A. Beard, *Economic Origins of Jeffersonian Democracy* (1915); M. E. Bradford, Introduction, *Arator*, Liberty Classic Edition (1977), pp. 11-43; Avery O. Craven, "The Agricultural Reformers of the Antebellum South," AHR, 32 (1928), 302-314; William E. Dodd, "John Taylor of Caroline, Prophet of Secession," BrHP, 2 (1908), 214-252; idem, "John Taylor of Caroline and the Preservation of an Old Social Order," VMHB, 46 (1938), 285-298; Maurice Duke, "John Taylor of Caroline, 1753-1824: Notes Towards a Bibliography," EAL, 6 (1971), 69-72; William D. Grampp, "John Taylor: Economist of Southern Agrarianism," SEJ, 11 (1945), 255-268; Jay B. Hubbell, *The South in American Literature, 1607-1900* (1954), pp. 219-223; Andrew N. Lytle, "John Taylor and the Political Economy of Agriculture," AmR, 3 (1934), 84-99, 630-643; Eugene Tenbroeck Mudge, *The Social Philosophy of John Taylor of Caroline* (1939); Roy F. Nichols, Introduction, *An Inquiry into the Principles of the Government of the United States* (1950), pp. 7-29; Vernon Louis Parrington, *Main Currents in American Thought* (1927), pp. 14-19; Robert E. Shallope, "The Arator Essays and the 'Fallacy of the Prevalent Proof,'" VMHB, 84 (1976), 283-286; Henry H. Simms, *Life of John Taylor* (1932); B. F. Wright, "The Philosopher of Jeffersonian Democracy," PSR, 22 (1928), 870-892.

George C. Longest
Virginia Commonwealth University

GILBERT TENNENT (1703-1764)

Works: *The Danger of Forgetting God* (1735); *The Espousals* (1735); "An Expostulatory Address to Saints and Sinners" (pub. in John Tennent, *The Nature of Regeneration*; 1735); *The Necessity of Receiving the Truth in Love* (1735); *The Necessity of Religious Violence* (1735); *A Solemn Warning* (1735); *The Divinity of the Sacred Scriptures* (1739); *The Duty of Self Examination* (1739); *The Legal Bow Bent* (1739); *The Preciousness of Christ* (1739); *The Solemn Scene* (1739); *Three Letters to the Reverend George Whitefield* (1739); *The Unsearchable Riches* (1739); *The Danger of an Unconverted Ministry* (1740); *Die Gefahr* (1740); *A Discourse Upon Christ's Kingly-Office* (1741); "A Letter to Mr. Whitefield" (w. 1741; pub. in *Historical Collections Relating to Remarkable Periods of the Success of the Gospel*, ed. John Gillies [1754], II, 130-132); *Remarks upon a*

Protestation (1741); *The Righteousness of the Scribes* (1741); *A Sermon upon Justification* (1741); "Extract of a Letter. . .to the Rev. Mr. Dickinson" (pub. in *The Boston Evening-Post*, Jul. 26, 1742); *Two Sermons Preached at New-Brunswick* (1742); *The Examiner, Examined* (1743); *The Necessity of Holding Fast* (1743); *Some Account of the Principles of the Moravians* (1743); "A Letter. . .Relating Chiefly to the Late Glorious Revival of Religion" (pub. in the *Christian History for the Year 1744*, ed. Thomas Prince, Jr.); *Love to Christ* (1744); *The Necessity of Studying* (1744); *The Necessity of Thankfulness* (1744); *Twenty-Three Sermons* (1744); *All Things Come Alike to All* (1745); *The Danger of Spiritual Pride* (1745); *Discourses, on Several Subjects* (1745); *A Funeral Sermon Occasion'd by the Death of. . .John Rowland* (1745); *The Necessity of Keeping the Soul* (1745); *The Necessity of Praising God* (1745); *A Sermon Preach'd in Greenwich* (1746); *Brotherly Love* (1748); *The Late Association for Defense, Encourag'd* (1748); *The Late Association for Defense Farther Encourag'd* (1748); *A Sermon Preach'd at Philadelphia, January 7, 1747-8* (1748); *Irenicum Ecclesiasticum* (1749); *A Sermon Preach'd at Burlington. . .November 23, 1749* (1749); *A Sermon Preach'd at Philadelphia, July 20, 1748* (1749); *Several Discourses upon Important Subjects* (1749); *The Substance and Scope of Both Testaments* (1749); *The Terrors of the Lord* (1749); *Two Sermons Preach'd at Burlington. . . April 27,1749* (1749); *The Divine Government* (1752); *The Good Mans Character* (1756); *The Happiness of Rewarding* (1756); *Sermons on Important Subjects* (1758); Preface, *Self Disclaimed* (by David Bostwick; 1759); *A Persuasive, to the Right Use of the Passions* (1760); *A Sermon on I Chronicles xxix, 28* (1761); *The Blessedness of Peace-Makers* (1765).

Biography: Born in County Armagh, Ire., on Feb. 5, 1703, Gilbert Tennent was the eldest son of William and Catharine (Kennedy) Tennent. Although William Tennent (1673-1745) was to play an important role in the development of the Presbyterian church in America, in Ulster he subscribed to the established Church of Ireland, graduating from the Univ. of Edinburgh in 1695 and being ordained a priest in 1706. However, he seems to have had non-conformist sympathies that undoubtedly played a part in his decision to join the thousands of other Scotch-Irish who immigrated to America in the early eighteenth century. The Tennents arrived at Philadelphia in or about 1718, when Gilbert was in his early teens. After gaining admission to the Presbyterian ministry, the elder Tennent served at several churches before settling at Neshaminy, Pa., where in 1735 he established his "Log College." William Tennent trained many ministers in the years before and after he founded his Neshaminy academy, including his sons William Tennent II (q.v.), John, and Charles, and a number of preachers later prominent in the Great Awakening, such as Samuel Blair (q.v.), Samuel Finley (q.v.), and John Rowland. But his most famous student was his oldest son Gilbert, who, like his three brothers, had decided on a career in the Presbyterian ministry.

In Gilbert's case, the decision to enter the ministry had been difficult. His conversion experience had been intense and troubled by doubt; for a year, he studied medicine. But in 1725 he accepted the honorary A.M. degree offered to him by Yale and became a candidate for the ministry, applying to the Philadelphia Presbytery for licensure. In the spring of 1725 he passed the presbytery's examination, and in Dec. he began to preach at Newcastle, Del. However, he soon left the Newcastle congregation and was admonished by the synod for this abrupt departure. But Tennent's call to the New Brunswick, N.J., church in the fall of 1726 led to happier results; after a severe illness and early failures to inspire his congregation, he quickly established himself as a popular preacher. Tennent remained at New Brunswick until 1743, when he accepted a call from a newly formed Presbyterian church in Philadelphia.

Tennent's sixteen years at New Brunswick were clearly the most fruitful—and controversial—of his life. He was an aggressive, rough, passionate man whose emotions required the control of commitment to a cause, and this he found in the evangelical preaching for which he became famous, first in N.J. and then throughout the colonies. Encouraged by the example of Theodore Frelinghuysen (q.v.), the Dutch Reformed minister of New Brunswick, Tennent began in the 1720s to preach a powerful message of a new birth to be experienced through a conversion attended by emotional upheaval. His theology was Calvinist and his persuasions founded upon a dramatic dualism of terror and joy: the security of faith alone was insufficient and must lead to the horror of "conviction" of the sinner's insufficiency for salvation. Only then might the joy of "assurance" that one was a Christian replace the terror of the perception of utter sinfulness. In talented and confident hands, this message could have enormous effect on the listener. By the early 1730s, the Tennent brothers had led several revivals in N.J., and by 1739, when George Whitefield (q.v.) arrived in Philadelphia, the surviving Tennents and the graduates of the Log College had begun the Great Awakening in the middle colonies.

The profoundly disturbing implications of the Tennent family's emphasis on an emotional experience of conviction and assurance soon began to create disquiet within the Synod of Philadelphia, with the Log College men and a group led by Jonathan Dickinson (q.v.) forming about half the synod's membership in opposition to the antirevivalist faction. A struggle for power broke out and grew in intensity during the late 1730s. The fitness of the Log College graduates to preach was no longer considered on the basis of their individual merits. In 1740, Tennent preached his Nottingham sermon, *The Danger of an Unconverted Ministry*, attacking the spiritual qualifications of ministers who could not welcome the revivals then growing in intensity and scope. In 1741 the synod suffered a schism that would continue until 1758. The antirevival faction, led by John Thomson (q.v.), remained in control of the synod, while the Tennents and their supporters withdrew, later to form the New Side Synod of New York. The Old Side, meanwhile, suffered a gradual decline in numbers and influence.

Samuel Davies (q.v.) and Jonathan Edwards (q.v.) played leading roles in the history of the Great Awakening, but it was Gilbert Tennent and George Whitefield who were the chief instruments in effecting the spread of the Awakening.

To Whitefield, Tennent was "a Son of Thunder," a preacher whose elemental, polarizing force could not be ignored: "Hypocrites must either soon be converted or enraged at his Preaching." After their first meeting in Nov., 1739, Whitefield departed for the north to begin his great evangelistic tour of 1739-1740. A year later, he again passed through New Brunswick, accompanied by Daniel Rogers of Harvard. Rogers and Whitefield urged Tennent to undertake a tour of New Eng.; Tennent accepted and arrived in Boston approximately a month later. For the next three months, he traveled through Mass. and Conn., enjoying great success. Reporting the results of his efforts to Whitefield, Tennent noted that in the college town of Cambridge "the shaking among the dry bones was general, and several of the students have received consolation." At Plymouth, the Rev. Nathaniel Leonard recorded that Tennent "Preached Eight Sermons to great Acceptance which by the Blessing of God greatly awakened this People." And in Boston, the anonymous author of a celebratory broadside poem crudely yet effectively defended Tennent against his many detractors: "What mad besotted Disperado can / Take Prejudice against this holy Man?" Nevertheless, many sober Old Side ministers in New Eng. must have been relieved when Tennent returned to N.J. in the early spring of 1741. The schism in the Philadelphia synod occurred soon after his return, and Tennent was busy seeing to the affairs of the New Brunswick Presbytery, defending his role in the schism, and harrying the Moravians.

Tennent's life after he left New Brunswick for Philadelphia in 1743 had an anticlimactic tone. Tennent became, like the Awakening, less intense. He became less controversial; be began to read his sermons from a fully prepared text, and the fire glowed less intensely in his spoken words. Although he occasionally returned to the attack, severely criticizing the Quakers' failure to support defense efforts in 1748, he grew closer in spirit to his gentler brother William.

In later life, Tennent increasingly appeared in constructive roles, even, as Benjamin Franklin (q.v.) observed in his *Autobiography*, as a "Projector." The new Philadelphia congregation lacked a meeting place, and Tennent approached Franklin for assistance in raising money. Franklin refused and instead offered shrewd advice so that Tennent "obtain'd a much larger Sum than he expected." Similarly, Tennent and Samuel Davies raised a larger than expected sum for the College of New Jersey during a fund-raising trip to Eng. in 1753-1754. Like his brother William, Tennent became a trustee of the new college. In these later endeavors to promote the cause of the College of New Jersey, as in his attempts to undo the effects of the schism of 1741, Tennent was haunted by his past. William Smith (q.v.) of the rival College of Philadelphia and other enemies of New Side ambitions saw to it that Tennent's Nottingham sermon was well known in Eng. when Davies and Tennent arrived. Similarly, Tennent's conciliatory efforts within the Presbyterian church had to overcome a vast reservoir of animosity; this he attempted to confront in *Irenicum Ecclesiasticum, or a Humble Impartial Essay upon the Peace of Jerusalem* and in other publications.

Tennent lived to see the Presbyterians reunited by the merger of the N.Y. and

Philadelphia synods in 1758; he even served as moderator after the consolidation. He died in Philadelphia on Jul. 23, 1764, survived by his third wife and three children. The funeral sermon was preached by Samuel Finley, then president of the College of New Jersey, and published as *The Successful Minister of Christ Distinguished in Glory*.

Critical Appraisal: Of the many thousands of early American sermons that have been printed or otherwise preserved, very few have had a lasting individual significance. John Winthrop's (q.v.) *A Model of Christian Charity* and Jonathan Edwards's *Sinners in the Hands of an Angry God* have frequently appeared in anthologies of American literature, yet for the most part colonial sermons are read by experts and assimilated for the concerns and ideas they collectively reveal. But on Mar. 8, 1740, Gilbert Tennent preached at Nottingham, Pa., one of those rare sermons in which occasion and rhetoric combined dramatically to mark a significant point in the history of American culture. Although *The Danger of an Unconverted Ministry* has long been recognized as a key document of the Great Awakening, its implications extend beyond the 1740s to illuminate a classic American dilemma: how can the tension of individual freedom and structures of authority remain creative? How are centrifugal and centripetal forces to be balanced? In his most famous sermon, Tennent momentarily destroyed this balance of forces, and it was only by a fortunate combination of actions and circumstances that chaos was prevented. Tennent's intention was to attack the antirevivalists by striking through an open gate that was indefensible, and thus undefended. He accused many of his fellow ministers of being unregenerate, unqualified in spiritual substance although they were qualified in form by virtue of their ordination. It was a spiritual *ad hominem* attack.

In destroying a structure of formal authority embodied in the church organization, Tennent believed he was tactically justified. He was losing a war within the church so he turned to the laity. But his own anger drove him to portray a conflict not only of principle and church practice, but of something more: "an ungodly Ministry is a great Curse and Judgment: These Caterpillars labour to devour every green Thing." His polemic had an elemental force; he decried a crime against fruitfulness and growth, against life. Allegorically, his opponents were as "the Pharisee-Teachers in Christ's Time," hypocrites, enemies of "vital Religion," and enemies of the people: "for they feared the People. They must keep the People in their Interests: Ay, that was the main Chance . . . and therefore such sly cautious Methods must be pursued as might consist herewith. They wanted to root vital Religion out of the World; but they found it beyond their Thumb." Tennent urged a vision of polarity, outlining a spiritual and social conflict of unendurable tension: "a cruel Oppression of tender Consciences, a compelling of Men to Sin." Individuals necessarily had to seek new authorities in such a conflict, and Tennent confidently expected that he and his followers possessed the spiritual substance and force to attract them amid the chaos. His evidence was the ongoing success of the revivals and his contempt for the empty formalities of a clericalism that he believed had become an end in itself. For these reasons at

Nottingham he was willing to unleash a whirlwind. *The Danger* was the single most important text produced by the Great Awakening in the Middle Colonies. In addition, it suggests the precariousness of an essential American balance of social forces in times when communal stress is confronted by passionate spokesmen for change.

Tennent seems rapidly to have realized that he had gone too far at Nottingham. His 1742 "Extract of a Letter" to Jonathan Dickinson spoke of having "mismanag'd" the events leading up to the schism and admitted "the *excessive heat of Temper* which has sometimes appear'd in my Conduct." The activities of extreme New Lights such as James Davenport in New Eng. had given Tennent a glimpse of the actualities of chaos. In the Nottingham sermon, he had named no names, but others had been less particular in applying the principles Tennent had espoused. He could not support those actions or their effects: "The Practice of *openly exposing Ministers* who are supposed to be unconverted in publick Discourse, by particular Application of such Times and Places, serves only to provoke them . . . and to declare our own Arrogance." More extensive—and less self-critical—defenses of Tennent's actions may be found in *Remarks upon a Protestation*, which presented the New Side view of the schism, and *The Examiner, Examined, or Gilbert Tennent, Harmonious*, which responded to John Hancock's (q.v.) *The Examiner, or Gilbert Against Tennent*. Tennent's activities in New Eng. during the winter of 1741-1742, his abundant publications, and his attacks on the Moravians in *The Necessity of Holding Fast* had provided Hancock with material that could be used to show contradictions in Tennent's positions and actions. In response, Tennent restated the theme of the Nottingham sermon in more moderate language and defended his actions in words that were alternately harsh and designedly ingenuous: "It is strange to think how the most generous and noble Actions, thro' the Force of some Craft and Artifice, assisted with Prejudice and Falsehood, may be represented in the darkest Dress, as if they were Vices of the most sordid kind." In the years immediately following the Nottingham sermon, Tennent's polemical writings characteristically reveal him fighting a rear-guard action from a position of strength. He had become both famous and infamous.

But Tennent was preeminently a great revivalist, a preacher who strove to move his audiences to conviction and assurance. Although the published sermons of George Whitefield notoriously fail to suggest the power of his spoken words, Tennent's sermons retain considerable force in their printed form. In sermons such as *The Necessity of Religious Violence, The Righteousness of the Scribes*, and *A Solemn Warning to the Secure World*, Tennent carried on the work of the revival, contrasting the terrors of damnation with the joy of assurance and conversion, sarcastically attacking the secure sinner, and balancing his audience's hesitations on the points of uncomfortable questions. Damnation, he observed in *The Danger of Forgetting God*, "may strike Terror into the Consciences of all those *that forget God*: But who are those?" His questions allowed no compromise, no relaxation of tension: "Are you repenting and obeying the Gospel or not? Or, only carrying a dead hypocritical Form?" As Finley observed in *The Successful Minister*, "with admirable Dexterity he detected the bold Presumer, discovered the vanity of his Confidence, and exposed the formal Hypocrite to his own View."

Tennent published relatively few funeral and ordination sermons, although he did author a number of occasional sermons on military and patriotic events. *A Funeral Sermon Occasion'd by the Death of. . .John Rowland* commemorated the death of a leading revivalist and Log College graduate, while *Love to Christ* was preached at the ordination of Charles Beatty (q.v.), another graduate of the Log College. In *All Things Come Alike to All*, a funeral sermon occasioned by the death of a member of Tennent's congregation who had been struck by lightning, his improvement was enlivened by an account of his own recent narrow escape from the same fate: "the Flash of the Lightning was so violent as to tear my shoes to Pieces, twist one of my Buckles, and melt a little of two Corners of the other."

He was a popular interpreter of public issues; he attacked Quaker pacifism in *The Late Association for Defense, Encourag'd* and *Farther Encourag'd*, celebrated the colonial victory at Louisbourg in 1745 (*The Necessity of Praising God*) and a British naval victory in the Mediterranean (*The Necessity of Thankfulness*), and supported the colonial forces during the French and Indian War (*The Happiness of Rewarding the Enemies of Our Religion and Liberty*). In *A Sermon on I Chronicles*, he memorialized the death of George II and the coronation of his successor, "our young Solomon, our British *Josias*."

Tennent's last publication, *The Blessedness of Peace-Makers*, appeared in 1765, the year after his death. It printed two sermons that he had delivered to the united Synod of Philadelphia and New York City in May, 1759. In the first of these sermons, Tennent proclaimed the virtue of striving to attain social tranquility: "Such as duly consider the value of peace to society, must needs have a high esteem of it, which naturally tends to excite proportional desire and labour." In the second, he surveyed the history of religious persecution and defended the cause of religious liberty. He defended, in short, the virtue of a stable and enlightened structure of social authority, whether within or without the confines of his church. It was a very different theme than the message he had preached at Nottingham at the height of the Great Awakening, nineteen years before.

Suggested Readings: DAB; DARB; Sprague (III, 35-41); T₂. *See also* Archibald Alexander, *Biographical Sketches of the Founder and Principal Alumni of the Log College* (1851); Edwin Scott Gaustad, *The Great Awakening in New England* (1957); Alan Heimert, *Religion and the American Mind* (1966); Alan Heimert and Perry Miller, eds., *The Great Awakening* (1967; repts. *The Danger of an Unconverted Ministry* and excerpts from other writings by Tennent); David S. Lovejoy, ed., *Religious Enthusiasm and the Great Awakening* (1969; repts. "Extract of a Letter"); William G. McLoughlin, *Revivals, Awakenings, and Reform* (1978); Charles H. Maxson, *The Great Awakening in the Middle Colonies* (1920); Leonard J. Trinterud, *The Forming of an American Tradition: A Re-examination of Colonial Presbyterianism* (1949).

Douglas R. Wilmes
The Pennsylvania State University

JOHN TENNENT (c. 1700-1748)

Works: *Every Man His Own Doctor* (1734); *Essay on the Pleurisy* (1736); *Detection of a Conspiracy* (1743).

Biography: John Tennent was born in Eng. around 1700. Little is known of his early life until his arrival in Va. in 1725. He settled in Spotsylvania County and is known to have acquired land there and in Fredericksburg and Prince William Counties in addition to practicing medicine. He married Dorothy Paul sometime around 1730.

By the mid-1730s Tennent was living in Williamsburg, where, in 1734, William Parks (q.v.) published his *Every Man His Own Doctor*—"a Plain and Easy Means for Persons to cure themselves" through medicinal plants grown in America— followed by *Essay on the Pleurisy* two years later. The latter book advocated the use of the seneca snakeroot plant (*polygala seneca*) in treating pleurisy and related diseases and became the center of some controversy. In the summer of 1737, Tennent went to London with a letter of introduction from William Byrd of Westover (q.v.) to Sir Hans Sloane (president of the Royal Society) in an ill-fated attempt to garner English medical support for his discovery. Although his snakeroot treatment showed success in experiments performed in both Eng. and Fr., support from the medical community at large was not forthcoming, and he returned to Va., where attacks on and defenses of his discovery had been published in several issues of the *Virginia Gazette*. In 1738 he petitioned the House of Burgesses for a monetary reward for what he thought was a discovery beneficial to the common good of both the colony and the world. It was at first denied, but Tennent persisted, produced witnesses on his behalf, and was granted 100 pounds. The Burgesses snubbed him, however, by dividing the money among his waiting and anxious creditors, who had materialized at the news of his good fortune. Then, "not enjoying Health in America, and meeting with Ingratitude in the Colony," Tennent left for Eng., where he spent the rest of his life.

Tennent appears to have fallen into a decline in Eng. He married a wealthy widow of Huntingdon but was accused of bigamy a year later and put on trial in Old Bailey. Although Tennent was acquitted of the charge, his wife and her sorely needed (by Tennent) fortune left him. Faced with charges of quackery by his peers, Tennent spent a great deal of time in pursuit of medical charlatans and in vindication of his own research. He published *Detection of a Conspiracy. . .The Singular Case of John Tennent, M.D.* in 1743. Tennent died, virtually ignored by his colleagues, on Oct. 27, 1748. In 1760 his son John petitioned the Va. Assembly for aid in obtaining a medical education in recompense and recognition for his father's work. He was unsuccessful in this regard, but later served as a surgeon in the Continental Army.

Critical Appraisal: Although many of Tennent's medical treatments sound quaint, if not barbaric, to us today, they must have worked on occasion, because many a life's salvation was obtained through or ascribed to use of his home remedies. Tennent was a pioneer in self-medication, and it was this that set his peers in the medical world against him. They were not against the use of botanical remedies, and their usual course of treatment was no more refined than the bleedings and purges he described. But *Every Man His Own Doctor* is subtitled "The Poor Planter's Physician," and although it admits that many harbor "such an unreasonable aversion to Physick," it allows that the fees and practices of many doctors have made them loathsome to their patients, especially the poor. Tennent, therefore, exhorted the poor planters to seek health through plants that "grow at their own Doors."

Every Man His Own Doctor is, perhaps, the first work to discuss the use of native American plants to treat disease, and Tennent described medical care for those diseases most common among the Va. colonists. It appears to have been highly regarded among lay people, if not among medical men, and was published in several editions, including a few by Benjamin Franklin (q.v.), who even published a 1749 German edition (*Ein Jeder sein eigener Doctor*) for immigrants.

Every Man makes for interesting reading today, if only for the bizarre and somewhat rigorous medical advice it contains. Tennent addressed himself to all manner of fevers, dropsies, agues, and complaints, including cancer, colic, consumption, epilepsy, gout, nosebleed, palsy, piles, pox, quinsy, rupture, vapors, and yaws. Tennent's standby "Physicks" (until snakeroot, which he did not mention here and, presumably, had not yet discovered) are bleeding the patient and purging him well with ipecac, both as an emetic and as an enema.

Each particular complaint requires embellishments to these basics. Palsy (or stroke) victims are advised to take plunges into cold water, to take snuff up the nose, and to roll a ball of rosemary leaves between the palms. Dr. Tennent's seven-month sure cure for epileptics (especially effective if administered to children) involves (in addition to bleeding): burning feathers, leather, or hooves under the nose and taking ipecac during the four days preceding and following the full moon and powdered mistletoe and snuff on all other days. For those afflicted with worms, a tobacco leaf soaked in vinegar and applied to the stomach is guaranteed to "make the Worms much sicker than it doth the Patient," and a rupture may be relieved by a truss, provided cow dung is liberally applied to it.

A "decoction" of comfrey leaves applied externally is recommended for those suffering the "excessive bleeding piles," provided they "fall not into violent Passions either of Love or Anger." Taken internally, it is helpful to women for relief of "Flooding...of their Courses," but only if they rest, especially their tongues. The unlucky woman prone to the vapors is advised to:

> Plunge, three Mornings every Week, into cold Water, over Head and Ears; or if you have no Convenience for that, it will have the same effect, if you suffer yourself to be whip'd with smart little Rods. It can't be imagin'd how this will brace the Nerves, and rouze the sluggish Spirits (as some grave Gentlemen find, when they try it for a merrier Purpose).

The vapor-prone lady is well-advised to avoid beef, which "inclines People, too much, to hang themselves," and men who wish to avoid the pox are told to "eat seldom of fresh Pork...live not too near a swamp, or ever venture upon strange Women, especially upon Ethiopians."

Tennent's *Essay on Pleurisy* is confined to his discovery of treating this most epidemic of diseases in Va. with an old Indian remedy of seneca snakeroot. He discussed at length the disease, determining it to be characterized as a "viscidity" of the blood, aggravated by climate and diet. Through some extrapolation and a primitive sort of biophysics, he concluded that the state of the blood of a pleurisy sufferer is not unlike that of a snakebite victim, and that conditions with similar symptoms might be cured by similar means. Hence in addition to bleeding and blistering, Tennent recommended snakeroot.

Tennent claimed that he could produce evidence that his treatment had worked and that he had a cure rate of over 90 percent while doctors using other methods lost two-thirds of their patients. Problems arose when it was found that snakeroot was a name given to several plants, although according to Tennent, only the *polygala seneca* was effective. In the end, however, Tennent's greatest failures were his ostracism by established medicine, which seems to have reacted in large part to his unorthodox views of medical practice, namely self-medication, and the fact, as Tennent himself admitted, that he made enemies easily: "I had spoke my Mind some times too freely and allowed my Tongue a little unreasonable license." His works record one man's good although single-minded intention to aid the colonists of the New World, often far from available medical help, to cure themselves with what they had at hand.

Suggested Readings: DAB. *See also* Wyndham B. Blanton, *Medicine in Virginia in the Eighteenth Century* (1931), pp. 119-129; Richard M. Jellison, "Dr. John Tennent and the Universal Specific," BHM, 37 (1963), 336-346; H. A. Kelly, *American Medical Biography* (1920).

Randal A. Owen
St. Mary's Dominican College

WILLIAM TENNENT II (1705-1777)

Works: *Exhortations to Walk in Christ* (1739); "An Account of the Revival at Freehold" (pub. in the *Christian History for the Year 1744*, ed. Thomas Prince, Jr., pp. 298-310); *A Sermon upon Matthew v. 23, 24* (1769).

Biography: William Tennent II was born in County Armagh, Ire., on Jun. 3, 1705, the second son of William and Catharine (Kennedy) Tennent. Educated at the Univ. of Edinburgh, the elder William Tennent (1673-1745) was a Presbyterian minister who immigrated to Philadelphia in or about 1718, later settling at Neshaminy, Pa. Working in his home and in the "Log College" he constructed late in 1735, he educated most of the young ministers who would assure the success of the Great Awakening in the Middle Colonies. Among these students were his four sons: Gilbert Tennent (q.v.), William Tennent II, John, and Charles. Gilbert having received a call to the Presbyterian church at New Brunswick, N.J., William moved to N.J. to continue his theological studies under his older brother. Meanwhile, John had become minister of the church at Freehold, N.J., where he led a successful revival. John, however, died in the spring of 1732, and on Oct. 25, 1733, William Tennent II was ordained by the Presbytery of Philadelphia as pastor of the Freehold church where his late brother had enjoyed such success. There he would serve until his death on Mar. 8, 1777.

Freehold had been the scene of much contention prior to William Tennent's arrival. The community was split between Dutch Reformed and Presbyterian congregations; from 1707 to 1729, the two churches had been served by Joseph Morgan (q.v.), whose abilities were insufficient to restrain unrest among the Dutch, who desired a preacher who could speak their language, and the Presbyterians, who harbored a faction desirous of a less formalistic and more spiritually satisfying brand of preaching. These tensions led to visits by Theodore Frelinghuysen (q.v.) and Gilbert Tennent; ultimately, they led to Morgan's replacement by John Tennent, and after his early death, by William Tennent. William was just the man to achieve success in such a highly charged situation; he combined natural abilities as a peace-maker with a reputation for piety and spiritual intensity. Although he supported the Great Awakening and served as an itinerant minister, making trips to the south and west with Samuel Blair (q.v.) and John Rowland, his deepest concerns were pastoral. William was content to minister to the needs of his own congregation. Thus his fame in later life was partially a reflection of the accomplishments of his father and older brother, but this is not to suggest that William's interests were narrow: he inherited his father's educational concerns, instructing students in his own home and serving as a trustee of the College of New Jersey (now Princeton University). In his old age, he joined his son William Tennent III (q.v.) in ardently supporting the revolutionary cause.

William Tennent's contributions to the reputation acquired by the Tennent family during the Great Awakening seem inseparable from his peculiar character. Gilbert supplied the fire and the leadership, while William reified the Tennents' emphasis on emotional experience of religion. Like Gilbert and John, William seems to have undergone an extraordinarily intense conversion experience, and his biography suggests his unusual ability to recall and relive this intensity in later life. His character displayed a combination of eccentricity and patently authentic spiritual sensitivity, for he was in many ways unworldly and clearly incapable of dissembling. His eccentricity and his religious emotion combined to produce a number of variously extraordinary and improbable legends and anecdotes. In the most famous of these incidents, Tennent became ill while studying for the Presbytery's examination for licensure. He continued his studies, but the intense strain caused him to faint while conversing in Latin with Gilbert. He could not be revived, and Gilbert became convinced that his brother had died.

The body was prepared for burial, but a doctor intervened, and William was finally resuscitated three days later. Thereafter he suffered from amnesia and could neither read nor remember any of his studies, although his memory and intellectual attainments were later restored.

Tennent indicated that he believed he had entered heaven and that he retained a vivid memory of the experience. In a similarly mystifying incident, he was reputed to have lost several toes by traumatic amputation one night as he slept; this he imputed to satanic malice. On another occasion, members of his congregation discovered him overcome with religious emotion, lying on the ground unable to return to the church to preach the afternoon sermon. Yet another legend recorded his acquittal on a charge of perjury because of the seemingly miraculous arrival of witnesses who could testify for him. His marriage to Catherine (Van Brugh) Noble was contracted with eccentric suddenness, and his love of horses and horsemanship was similarly productive of anecdote. Tennent's secular eccentricity and mystical experiences created an image of otherworldliness that his undoubtedly powerful abilities in the pulpit enabled him to project into his listeners' own experiences. By joining his unusual personality and mysticism with communicative talent, William Tennent contributed to the aura of enthusiasm in pursuit of religious renewal that the Tennent family acquired in the 1730s and 1740s.

Critical Appraisal: Among William Tennent's publications are two texts relevant to the history of the Awakening. *An Exhortation to Walk in Christ* was preached in New Brunswick on Aug. 8, 1737, and published in *Sermons on Sacramental Occasions by Divers Ministers*, a collection that also included works by Gilbert Tennent. This collection was part of a barrage of publications issued by the elder William Tennent's former students during 1739. When considered in conjunction with the arrival of George Whitefield (q.v.) on Nov. 2, 1739, and his subsequent travels through the colonies, these books and pamphlets signaled that the Awakening had broken out of its formerly local boundaries within New Eng. and the Middle Colonies and assumed inter-colonial dimensions. Tennent's sermon thus played a small part in what Leonard J. Trinterud has identified as "a critical hour" in the fortunes of the Log College group, a moment when the colonial revivalists were able to capitalize upon the momentum supplied by the young English evangelist to spread their message throughout the colonies.

In Oct., 1744, William Tennent supplied "An Account of the Revival at Freehold" to Thomas Prince, Jr., for publication in his *Christian History*. This letter constitutes an important source for the study of the course of the Awakening in N.J., and it may be read as a narrative representative of the progress of the revival in many other communities. Tennent's opening paragraphs described the history of the congregation and his younger brother's unwilling decision to accept its call, as he believed "that they were a people whom God had given up." References to the spiritual malaise and anti-clericalism that prepared the ground for the great revivals led into Tennent's account of the progressively unfolding drama of the revival: the "miserable, helpless, and almost hopeless condition" of the congregation; the storm of emotion as the revival gathered force, "both minister and people wet with their tears, as with a bedewing rain"; the spiritual agonies of conviction, when the awakened "looked upon themselves to be mere monsters of nature, and that none were worse, if any so bad"; and the shifting gains and losses of confidence over time, as the climactic intensity of the revival ebbed and flowed through the congregation. In light of his own experiences, Tennent was particularly careful to defend the Freehold revival against charges of enthusiasm, stating that he had seen no evidence of the unnatural "impulses of their own minds" in his congregation and specifically disclaiming existence of visions, revelations, and trances.

A Sermon upon Matthew shows Tennent in his role as peacemaker within the Presbyterian church. The schism of 1741 had been the most dramatic institutional effect of the differences between the Old Side and the New Side during the Great Awakening, and William's father and brother had done much to bring on the schism. But the differences between the two factions had been papered over in the Plan of Union of 1758, and Gilbert Tennent had died in 1764. In 1769, when William Tennent's last published sermon appeared, the New Side was firmly in control. Ironically, the brother of the man who had so severely attacked religious formalism and hypocrisy could now agree to sit quietly beside a hypocrite:

> Shall we omit positive Duties, because there will always be Sinners in the Church? Upon this Plan all social Duties of Religion must cease. Sure I may confess. . . in Company with an Hypocrite, and yet not be an Hypocrite. I may sit down with an impious Man, and yet not patronize his Iniquity.

William Tennent lacked the force and aggressive passion of his more famous older brother, but he dealt more constructively with the inevitable day when the stressful intensity of the Awakening had passed, and congregations once again had to deal with the quieter tensions of normalcy.

Suggested Readings: CCMC; DAB; Sprague (III, 52-62). *See also* Archibald Alexander, *Biographical Sketches of the Founder and Principal Alumni of the Log College* (1851; repts. Tennent's *Christian History* letter); Elias Boudinot, *Memoirs of the Life of the Rev. William Tennent* (1807); J. M. Bumsted and John E. Van de Wetering, *What Must I Do To Be Saved? The Great Awakening in Colonial America* (1976), pp. 63-67; "Catharine Tennent," PMHB, 7 (1883), 113-115; Ned Landsman, "Revivalism and Nativism in the Middle Colonies: The Great Awakening and the Scots Community in East New Jersey," AQ, 34 (1982), 149-164; Leonard J. Trinterud, *The Forming of an American Tradition: A Re-examination of Colonial Presbyterianism* (1949), passim.

Douglas R. Wilmes
The Pennsylvania State University

WILLIAM TENNENT III (1740-1777)

Works: *God's Sovereignty* (1765); *An Address, Occasioned by the Late Invasion of the Liberties of the American Colonies* (1774); *Mr. Tennent's Speech,* *on the Dissenting Petition* (1777); "Fragments of a Journal...Describing his Journey, in 1775, to Upper South Carolina," in R. W. Gibbs, *Documentary History of the American Revolution...in South Carolina* (1855-1857) I, 225-239; Newton B. Jones, ed., "Writings of the Reverend William Tennent, 1740-1777," SCHM, 61 (1960), 129-145, 189-208.

Biography: Born in Freehold, N.J. in 1740, William Tennent III was the son of William Tennent II (q.v.) and Catherine (Van Brugh) Tennent. His father and his uncle Gilbert Tennent (q.v.) were famous Presbyterian ministers and leaders of the Great Awakening; his grandfather William Tennent (1673-1745) had established the Log College and trained a generation of New Side Presbyterian ministers. William Tennent II was a trustee of the College of New Jersey and a friend of Pres. Aaron Burr (q.v.). In Dec. 1754 he took his sons William and John to Newark to begin their studies. The boys lived for a month with Pres. Burr and his wife Esther Burr (q.v.), the daughter of Jonathan Edwards (q.v.), completing their preparation for collegiate studies at the local grammar school. In 1756, the college was moved to Princeton, and in 1758 William and John Tennent graduated from the College of New Jersey. John then pursued medical studies in Br., but William had decided to become a minister. He received the A.M. from the College of New Jersey in 1761, and the same degree from Harvard two years later. On Jul. 29, 1761, he was licensed by the Presbytery of New Brunswick. Ordained the following year, he served as a supply preacher in New York City, where he met Susanne Vergereau. After overcoming the opposition of her wealthy family, the couple were married in 1764.

Tennent's ministerial career was notably successful. On Nov. 13, 1764, the First Congregational Church of Norwalk, Conn., issued a call, inviting Tennent to serve as junior pastor to Moses Dickinson (q.v.). However, Tennent did not wish to renounce his membership in the Presbytery of New Brunswick and the Synod of New York and Philadelphia, and he requested that he maintain these affiliations while simultaneously joining the Consociation of the Western District of Fairfield County, Conn. Negotiations between the interested parties led to a compromise that assured the Conn. parish that it would not be placed under the authority of the Presbytery, and Tennent became assistant pastor at Norwalk in Nov. 1765. As Tennent was an able and popular preacher, he soon acquired an enviable reputation. Ebenezer Pemberton (q.v.) of Boston failed in an attempt to name Tennent as his successor, but in Nov. 1771, the Independent Church of Charleston, S.C., issued a call to Tennent, offering him "a more lucrative and honorable" position, as Ezra Stiles (q.v.) remarked as he disapprovingly recorded the young minister's decision to sail south. On Apr. 12, 1772, Tennent was installed as minister of the Charleston church.

Tennent's activities in S.C. led to even greater successes. An exponent of religious toleration, he did not attempt to impose Presbyterianism upon his own church, and he maintained friendly relations with all denominations except the Episcopalians. His popularity and Whig beliefs soon led to political responsibilities; he was elected to the first and second provincial congresses and the S.C.

Assembly. A member of the Committee of Correspondence, Tennent joined William Henry Drayton (q.v.), Oliver Hart (q.v.), and two other prominent Whigs on a dangerous journey into the colony's back country to combat Loyalist sentiment as the Revolution approached. Tennent's record of this trip was published as "Fragments of a Journal." When his father died in 1777, Tennent traveled to N.J. to settle the estate and bring his mother to S.C. He died on Aug. 11, 1777, at the High Hills of Santee, while returning from this mission. Tennent was survived by his wife and five children.

   Critical Appraisal: The high quality of William Tennent's published writings supports his reputation as an excellent preacher and orator. The life was not driven from his prose as he prepared it for publication, as was often the case with other celebrated exponents of pulpit oratory. Unfortunately, he published only two sermons and a speech given to the S.C. Assembly. These texts, his 1775 "Journal," and manuscript materials edited by Newton B. Jones and published in 1960 constitute Tennent's literary works. *God's Sovereignty, No Objection to the Sinner's Striving*, was a sermon preached on Jan. 20, 1765, during Tennent's tenure as a supply preacher in N.Y.'s English Presbyterian Church. *God's Sovereignty* was very much in the Tennent family tradition, revealing its author's clear, strong sense of audience. It urged that audience forward through dramatic contrasts, forcing them to choose between the difficult way of striving toward a saving conversion and the easy way of damnation: "go on ye profane! laugh at heaven, despise the terrors of God—blaspheme the awful name—exceed hell itself, and cause the damn'd to shudder at superior crimes!" The issues and the rhetoric of the Awakening were echoed in Tennent's concern for the spiritual substance of ritual: "*Praying* is the matter of a duty—*with faith*, is the form of it. *Hearing* is the matter of a duty—*with love*, is the form." Finally, there were more specific echoes of Gilbert Tennent's methods in his nephew's rebuttals, which ridiculed his opponents' positions by exaggeration and then disposed of all opposition with the final twist of a sarcastic question: "Is it giving more glory to his grace to say, that it is readier to alight on a great transgressor than a small one? that the more guilty, the more fit objects for his mercy? does this give a lovely idea of the nature of the best of beings?"

   Tennent's evangelical powers were clearly formidable, and the political tremors of the coming revolution led him to employ those abilities to support the patriot cause. Indeed, the problematic connection between the Awakening and the Revolution is illuminated by Tennent's two published sermons, for while the attitudes and rhetoric of *God's Sovereignty* mark that sermon as a text that might well have been preached during the Awakening, *An Address, Occasioned by the Late Invasion of the Liberties of the American Colonies by the British Parliament* reveals many of the same rhetorical devices employed in the political context. The audience's options were dramatically absolute: "We are threatened with Slavery. War, Pestilence and Earthquakes, those ordinary Ministers of God's Vengeance, are transient, partial or local Evils. Slavery is a general and perpetual Evil." Preached on the text of Lamentations 3:22, Tennent's jeremiad melded the revivalist's thrust toward an emotional experience of religion with the need now to reform not only for the sake of the individual's soul, but for the sake of the emergent nation. Also persistent in this process was Tennent's willingness to goad his audience with sarcasm:

> How little do we find even the *Form* of Religion among us! I do not mean here that there are few who go to Church, or have their Children baptised, or call themselves Christians. There was a Time indeed when these Things were considered as true Badges of the Christian Profession, but in our wiser Age the very Ideas of these things are changed.

Tennent's pitiless survey of this "wiser Age" cataloged the profanity, drunkenness, and even "the *secret* Vices of our Nation. . . covered only by the Curtain of Night," calling finally for "a general Reformation" to accompany the efforts of the "mere Politician" who must calculate his nation's purely military capacities.

In the last years of his life, Tennent had become both a "Christian Patriot" and a military-minded "mere Politician," conducting unsuccessful experiments to manufacture gunpowder and establishing himself as a voice to be reckoned with in the provincial congresses and assembly. On Jan. 11, 1777, he delivered a *Speech, on the Dissenting Petition* explaining his views on the place to be accorded religion under the new state constitution then being debated in the S.C. Assembly. He opposed infringements of religious liberty inherent in a plan, which he supposed was mandated by the language of the proposed constitution, to assess taxes for the support of religion on a territorial, parish-by-parish basis. This he saw as a device that would force the minority in each parish to support an established religion in violation of individual conscience. In fact, the proposed language did not have the intent that Tennent imputed to it, and the issue was resolved to his satisfaction, but his *Speech* was on broader grounds an eloquent plea for religious liberty in the new nation. It reveals, moreover, the same energy, sure sense of audience, and occasionally sarcastic aggressiveness that marked Tennent's sermons: "Should not the Constitution take care of the religious as well as the civil Liberties of the People? Or do you think the former of less importance than the latter?"

William Tennent III's reputation might have been greater but for his early death and his failure to publish more of his work. But he was a worthy member of one of early America's most extraordinary families, and his sermons and speech in defense of religious liberty retain uncommon interest.

Suggested Readings: CCNE; CCV; P; Sibley-Shipton (XIV, 338-345); Sprague (III, 242-245). *See also* Hugh Alison, *The Faithful Servant of Christ Honoured* (1777); William M. Dabney and Marion Dargan, *William Henry Drayton and the American Revolution* (1962), pp. 93-106; Oliver Hart, *The Character of a Truly Great Man Delineated* (1777); William G. McLoughlin, "The Role of Religion in the Revolution," in *Essays on the American Revolution*, ed. Stephen G. Kurtz and James H. Hutson (1973), pp. 216-217.

Douglas R. Wilmes
The Pennsylvania State University

LUCY TERRY (1730-1821)

Works: "Bars Fight" (w. 1746; pub. 1855).

Biography: While still a child, Lucy Terry was taken from her native Africa as a slave and brought to New Eng. At the age of 5, she was sold to Ebenezer Wells. Therefore, she was living in Deerfield, Mass., at the time of an Indian raid there in Aug. 1746, which she witnessed and then described in twenty-eight lines of couplets. Baptized before 1746, she was later admitted to the church, and in 1756 married a free Negro, Abijah (or Obijah) Prince, who purchased her freedom. The couple became landowners and also were charter members of the town of Sunderland, Vt. They had six children. When the oldest was of college age, she tried, unsuccessfully for three hours, to persuade the trustees of Williams College to change their segregation policy and admit him. He later served in the Revolution, probably with the Green Mountain Boys under their near neighbor Ethan Allen (q.v.). When another neighbor tried to claim some of the Princes' land, she argued the case all the way to the U.S. Supreme Court, where she won. Her home was a rendezvous for young people who enjoyed the many stories that earned her a wide reputation as a raconteur, including the reciting of "Bars Fight."

Critical Appraisal: The term *poet* hardly fits Lucy Terry, but she has the distinction of apparently being the first black American to write verse, although the one surviving example of her work was not published until over 100 years after its composition. Although "Bars Fight" (*bars* here apparently means "meadow") has been called doggerel because of awkward syntax, sometimes strained rhyme, bouncing meter, and fragmentary content, it also has been called vivid and dramatic. In addition, it has been called the best account of the bloody massacre it records, sometimes with macabre details ("Simeon Amsden they found dead, / Not many rods off from his head"). Its form owes a clear debt to the oral heroic tradition; however, it records few heroes, focusing mostly on those who lost in one way or another. It does not celebrate a victory but is more a lament of a local tragedy by a relatively uneducated, 16-year-old servant slave girl recording for posterity her memories of a gruesome occasion, in the tradition of ancient poetic historians. In this context and as perhaps the earliest belletristic effort by a black American, the poem is worthy of attention in spite of its aesthetic deficiencies, for it is the earliest known poem by a black American.

Suggested Readings: Angelo Constanzo, "Three Black Poets in Eighteenth Century America," *SSC* [Shippenburg State College] *Review* (1973), pp. 89-101; Pattie Cowell, *Women Poets in Pre-Revolutionary America, 1650-1775* (1981); Lorenzo J. Greene, *The Negro in Colonial New England* (1968), pp. 242-243, 314-415; Sidney Kaplan, *The Black Presence in the Era of the American Revolution, 1770-1800* (1973), pp. 209-211; Bernard Katz, "A Second Version of Lucy Terry's Early Ballad," NHB, 29 (1966), 183-184; William L. Katz, *Eyewitness: The Negro in American History* (1967), pp. 24, 37; Eugene B. Redmond, *Drumvoices: The Mission of Afro-American Poetry* (1976), pp. 50-51; William H. Robinson, ed., *Early Black American Poets* (1969), pp.

3-4; Theressa G. Rush et al., *Black American Writers Past and Present* (1975), II, 691-693; George Sheldon, *A History of Deerfield, Massachusetts* (1895), I, 545-549; idem, "Slavery in Old Deerfield," NEM, 8 (1893), 49-60; Roger Whitlow, *Black American Literature: A Critical History* (1974), pp. 15-16; Martha R. Wright, "Bijah's Luce of Guilford," NHB, 27 (1965), 152-153, 159. The poem also can be found in various anthologies of writing by black Americans.

Julian Mason
The University of North Carolina at Charlotte

JAMES THACHER (1754-1844)

Works: *Military Journal, 1775-1783* (1823); *American New Dispensatory* (1810-1821); *Observations on Hydrophobia* (1812); *American Modern Practice* (1818-1826); *American Orchardist* (1822); *American Medical Biography* (1828); *Management of Bees* (1829); *Essay on Demonology* (1831); *History of Plymouth* (1832).

Biography: Born in Mass., James Thacher was twenty-one when he joined the Continental Army, shortly after the beginning of the Revolution, as a surgeon's mate. Although he had completed a five-year apprenticeship, he had no formal higher education. However, his later career as both a physician and a writer indicates that his skill and individual effort compensated for the lack of academic preparation. Thacher served in various units and seemed fortuitously to have been near the scene of major events of the war from its beginning until its end. He was near the American successes in the siege of Boston and the Battle of Saratoga, and he was involved in setbacks at Ticonderoga and in the Penobscot Campaign. Thacher watched the suffering of George Washington's (q.v.) troops at Morristown in 1779, the execution of Maj. John André in 1780, and the surrender of Gen. Cornwallis in 1781. All of these events were recorded in his diary. After leaving the army, Thacher practiced and taught medicine in Plymouth, Mass.; in his mid-50s, he turned the writing skill evident in his diary to works intended for publication. His scientific writings ranged from medicine and pharmacology to arbor culture and beekeeping. His historical works include the first biography of American medicine and a book on witchcraft at Salem. His position as a fellow of the American Academy of Arts and Sciences, his honorary membership in the New York Historical Society, and his honorary M.D. from Harvard are indications of how far his personal skills allowed him to surmount early disadvantages.

Critical Appraisal: James Thacher's most enduring work is his *Military Journal*. Considered in the context of other diaries of the Revolution, the Thacher diary has epic qualities. The most obvious of them is its scope. Few other diaries of the war are so extensive, and in them the quality of the writing and the artistic unity of the account are much weaker. Thacher's presence at so many of the crucial incidents of war placed him in an advantageous position, but even when he relied on second-hand accounts, he so skillfully wove them into the fabric of the record that readers will scarcely notice any change. Thacher's diary presents a vital portrait of the war. His accounts are detailed and include effective sections of dialog. Thacher supplements material from his experiences with background information about the geography and history of the region and even provides moments of comic relief. His style is extremely elevated, but given the significance of the events, such excesses may be excused. Thacher repeatedly shows his readers that he considered the Revolution to be dramatic when viewed closely and monumental when taken as a whole. All of these elements make the diary an important personal document. The skills at characterization that Thacher demonstrated in his diary are also apparent in his *American Medical Biography*. However, although that work is still useful for researchers, it and Thacher's other books are rarely considered today. Thacher's reputation still rests primarily on his diary.

   Suggested Readings: DAB; T_2. *See also* Steven E. Kagle, *American Diary Literature* (1979), pp. 121-127.

Steven E. Kagle
Illinois State University

OXENBRIDGE THACHER (1719-1765)

   Works: *Considerations on the Election of Counselors* (1761); *Considerations on Lowering the Value of Gold Coins* (1762); *Sentiments of a British American* (1764).

   Biography: Oxenbridge Thacher, Boston lawyer and pre-Revolutionary pamphleteer, was born in Boston on Dec. 29, 1719. While an undergraduate at Harvard, Thacher gave indication of his free-spiritedness when he was fined for the use of forbidden liquors. Thacher entered the ministry, but his small voice and poor state of health eventually caused him to give it up for a practice in law. In Jul. 1741 he married Sarah Doggett, whose mother his father had wed a year earlier. During the early years of his law practice, he made the acquaintance of Josiah Quincy, Jr. (q.v.), John Lowell, and John Adams (q.v.). Adams later observed of Thacher, "there was not a citizen of Boston more universally beloved for his learning, ingenuity, every domestic and social virtue, and conscientious conduct in every relation of life." America's second president also claimed that only the voice of James Otis (q.v.) surpassed Thacher's in influence among those of the early Revolutionary movement.

   The two early pamphlets, *Considerations on the Election of Counselors* and *Considerations on Lowering the Value of Gold Coins,* display an unmistakable passion for the cause of liberty. But it is in his last pamphlet, *Sentiments of a British American,* that Thacher most effectively sounded the voice of freedom, troubled by what appeared to be unreasonable restrictions. Thacher was destined, however, never to enjoy the fruits of the Revolution, for in 1765 he died from the deleterious effects of smallpox inoculation. A contemporary eulogized him in these affectionate lines: "A Patriot's Flame, with pious Zeal sustain'd, / His Country's Rights with jealous Care maintain'd." Seven children survived him, including his famous son, Peter Thacher (q.v.), who unlike his father achieved fame "as a model of the pulpit orator."

Critical Appraisal: Best known to students of early American literature as the author of carefully reasoned but severely critical pamphlets directed at pre-Revolutionary British injustices, Oxenbridge Thacher doubtless influenced later, more inflammatory pamphleteers. Thacher's criticism of British colonial policy toward America becomes progressively more harsh in his three pamphlets. The earliest, *Considerations on the Election of Counselors*, is an admonishment to the electorate to select representatives who are willing, and even eager, to preserve the balance of power between elected officials and the judiciary. Thacher's rhetoric at one point predicts the U.S. Constitution's establishment of a balance of power: "The essence of liberty in any state is preserved by the due adjustment of the several powers of the community. Where this is lost or one branch of power swallows up other branches, it becomes a tyranny."

Thacher's second pamphlet, *Considerations on Lowering the Value of Gold Coins*, argues for a standardization of the currency in silver rather than the inflationary gold. But perhaps of greater interest to students of the Revolution is Thacher's inclusion of an argument for freedom of the press. Thacher closed his article with a defense of his use of the press as a vehicle for criticism against government policy. Appropriately, the daring lawyer selected as his final statement the famous opening lines of *Areopagitica*, Milton's groundbreaking essay arguing for freedom of the press.

Sentiments of a British American is, from the outset, an open objection to economic restrictions imposed by the "mother state." As Thacher declared, his objective was to oppose an act passed by Parliament that levied "certain duties in the British Colonies and plantations in America." Much of Thacher's language closely resembled that of later pamphleteers such as Thomas Paine (q.v.), as well as that of the Declaration of Independence. Some of Thacher's principal objections were that the colonists were not heard from when Parliament levied these economic restrictions, that the great distance from the "mother state" demanded the colonies be granted more power of government at home (obviously an inchoate plea for independence), that the colonies were becoming progressively alienated from the "mother state," that the exchange of trade between the colonies and the "mother state" was decidedly structured in the economic favor of Br., and finally that the colonies would not indefinitely endure such injustices. Thacher extended his muted threat by remarking that if Eng. persisted in its abuses, the colonies "must then adopt Jack Straw's Verses; 'When Adam delved, and Eve span, / Who was then the Gentleman?'" It is clear from his conclusion that

Thacher preferred to remain British but that it was becoming increasingly difficult to do so.

Moses Coit Tyler has observed of this tract that it represents "the very essence of the best American thought in its earliest stage of dissent from the new and firmer policy of the empire." All three of Thacher's pamphlets are evidence that the issue of freedom was vital at least a decade before the Declaration of Independence. Thacher's sound, reasoned approach directed future pamphleteers toward the construction of arguments designed to convince not by emotionalism but by solid logic and by the appeal of equality for all men.

Suggested Readings: Sibley-Shipton (X, 322-328); T$_2$. *See also* John Adams, *Works* (1850-1856), II, 47n, 67, 74-75, 124n, 472n; X, 247, 285-287; Bernard Bailyn, ed., *Pamphlets of the American Revolution*, vol. I (reprints *The Sentiments of a British American*; 1965).

John C. Shields
Illinois State University

PETER THACHER (1688-1744)

Works: *The Fear of God Restraining Men* (1720); "Attestations," "Revival of Religion at Middleborough," and "Revival of Religion at Middleborough Continued" (all pub. in Thomas Prince, Jr., ed., *Christian History*, I, 171-173, 412-416; II, 87-99; 1744-1745).

Biography: Acknowledged as one of the saints of the Great Awakening, Peter Thacher was born on Oct. 6, 1688, in Milton, Mass., where his father Peter Thacher was minister. After receiving a B.A. from Harvard in 1706, he headed the grammar school at Dorchester and occasionally preached at Malden and Middleborough. Asked to be the pastor of the First Church of Middleborough late in 1707, he was not ordained until some internal church problems had been settled and he had received an M.A. from Harvard in 1709. During his sophomore year, Thacher met Thomas Prince (q.v.), whose sister Mary he wed on Jan. 24, 1711, and whose *Christian History* he backed. An enterprising businessman, Thacher was a partner in the Land Bank of 1749 and helped establish the Plymouth iron works.

Although successful in business, Thacher was primarily noted for his "great Seriousness and Solemnity" as well as for his orthodox Puritanism, which he gleaned from a large collection of works by Puritan divines, a library that Thomas Prince said was the largest such collection he had seen in New Eng. Since philosophically he was a seventeenth-century Puritan living in the eighteenth century, it is not surprising that Thacher wholeheartedly supported the Great Awakening immediately after hearing Gilbert Tennent (q.v.) preach during his visit to Middleborough in 1741. Thacher was a tireless supporter of the revival. Although he became ill, he continued preaching—during one week, eight times. Already in poor health, Thacher was unable to survive an attack of dysentery and died on Apr. 22, 1744.

Critical Appraisal: Peter Thacher's extant works reveal that he was the "free, bold and faithful Reprover to all Sorts" whom his brother-in-law Thomas Prince described in *The Christian History*. Much respected by orthodox Puritans, Thacher earned the praise of men such as Samuel Sewall (q.v.) and Gilbert Tennent.

The Fear of God Restraining Men (1720), Thacher's only extant sermon, was delivered in 1718, during a period of spiritual decline and increasing materialism. After declaring that "it hath been, and still ought to be" a minister's duty "to shew the Generation they live in, their sin and danger," Thacher firmly and clearly enumerated the evils associated with materialism. Those individuals who do not evidence a "fear of God" when dealing with others are guilty of typical Puritan sins such as sloth and extravagance. Thacher also mentioned a frequent complaint of the New Eng. clergy: lack of financial support from the laity. According to Thacher, these individuals are barbarians; "when a people withhold from their Pastors. . . a plentiful and honourable Maintenance, for them and their Families, they act barbarously." As is common in this type of sermon, Thacher exhorted his listeners to relinquish their materialism; furthermore, and perhaps significantly, he called for governmental intervention so that "these Grievances. . . will [not] become Publick Sins." In general, this sermon lucidly reveals Thacher's orthodoxy.

More significant historically are Thacher's brief but dramatic accounts of the Great Awakening. Apparently, his congregation did not follow his advice of 1720 until after the respective visits of Gilbert Tennent and Josiah Crocker to Middleborough in 1741. Before their arrivals, Thacher pictured the spiritual laxity of his congregation as a "Time of fatal Deadness." But in Nov. 1741, he joyfully exclaimed, "our Frolicks are turned into Prayers and Praises!"

His brief accounts provide useful historical details. For instance, the hysteria that accompanied many conversions apparently did not occur in Middleborough, for Thacher noted that "we have *not known Visions,* nor *Trances,* nor *Revelations.* But *brotherly exhorting* with more Modesty and Affection than hath been represented. . .*free* from *censurable Enthusiasm.*" These often vivid accounts, embellished with brief confessions, effectively portray the success of the Great Awakening in Middleborough. So successful was the revival that by the time of his death in 1744, Peter Thacher had added 174 members to his church.

Suggested Readings: CCNE; Sibley-Shipton (V, 317-322). *See also* Alice M. Baldwin, *The New England Clergy and the American Revolution* (1928), p. 63n55; Edwin Scott Gaustad, *The Great Awakening in New England* (1957), pp. 52-53, 76; C. C. Goen, *Revivalism and Separatism in New England* (1962), p. 218.

Susan A. Leazer
Illinois State University

PETER THACHER (1752-1802)

Works: *An Oration Delivered at Watertown* (1776); *The Rest Which Remaineth* (1778); *Observations upon the Present State of the Clergy* (1783); *That the Punishment of the Finally Impenitent* (1783); *A Reply to the Strictures of Mr. J. S.* (1784); *A Sermon, Preached at Charlestown* (1788); *A Sermon, Preached October, 1788* (1788); *A Sermon, Preached at Exeter* (1790); *A Sermon, Preached to the Society in Brattle Street* (1791); *A Sermon, Preached Before the Ancient and Honorable Artillery Company* (1793); *A Sermon, Preached to the Society in Brattle Street* (1793); *The Nature and Effects of Christian Sympathy* (1794); *A Sermon, Preached at Lynn* (1794); *A Sermon, Preached in Boston* (1795); *A Sermon, Preached at Charlestown* (1796); *A Sermon, Preached to the Society in Brattle-Street* (1796); *A Sermon, Preached at Dorchester* (1797); *Brief Account of the Society for Propagating the Gospel...in North-America* (1798); *A Sermon, Delivered at the First Church* (1798); *A Sermon Preached to the Society in Brattle-Street* (1798); *A Sermon Preached June 12, 1799* (1799); *A Sermon, Occasioned by the Death of...Washington* (1800); *A Sermon Preached to the Church and Society in Brattle-Street* (1800).

Biography: Patriot and clergyman, Peter Thacher was born on Mar. 21, 1752, in Milton, Mass. The eldest son of Oxenbridge Thacher (q.v.), he graduated from Harvard with highest honors in 1769. Thacher began his ministry at Malden in 1769; shortly after his installation, he married the widowed Elizabeth Pool. Late in 1784 Thacher left the Malden congregation to become minister at the Brattle Street Church, Boston, on Jan. 12, 1785, where he remained until his retirement in 1802. Thacher was awarded the doctor of divinity degree from the University of Edinburgh in 1791.

In addition to being an active as well as a much respected clergyman, Thacher participated fully in many aspects of colonial life. During the Revolutionary War, he championed the cause of freedom and received "beating orders" that granted him recruiting powers to defend the Mass. shore. He was also appointed chaplain of the General Court. In 1780 Thacher was a delegate to the Mass. Constitutional Convention. Furthermore, he found time to support organizations such as the Society for the Propagation of the Gospel among the Indians, the American Academy of Arts and Sciences, and the Boston Town Library. In 1791 he helped organize the Massachusetts Historical Society. Active until pulmonary tuberculosis forced him to leave Boston, Thacher died in Savannah, Ga., on Dec. 16, 1802, six weeks after his arrival.

Critical Appraisal: A consistently polished and dynamic orator, Peter Thacher deserves George Whitefield's (q.v.) compliment that he was "the young Elijah." His lengthy canon is diverse: an oration delivered to commemorate the Boston Massacre; a pamphlet denouncing the treatment of the New Eng. clergy; a pamphlet outlining the purpose and structure of the Society for Propagating the

Gospel; ordinations preached throughout Mass.; and funeral sermons including those for James Bowdoin (q.v), John Hancock, and Increase Sumner, all former governors of Mass. It is regrettable that this consistently fine and diverse canon has escaped critical notice.

Thacher was said to be most effective when he wrote "with studied brevity...clearness [and] warmth." Any type of tyranny especially aroused his "warmth" or anger, an appropriate reaction for the eldest son of Oxenbridge Thacher, a pre-Revolutionary patriot. For example, his *Observations upon the Present State of the Clergy* is a diatribe concerning the lack of lay support for the clergy. Although this situation outraged Thacher, he carefully noted that he had not been victimized by his congregation. In this well-organized pamphlet, he discussed common problems that faced the New Eng. clergy: elderly pastors being summarily dismissed and ministers not receiving adequate salaries. According to Thacher, such congregations had usurped their powers. He proclaimed that conditions must change, for "every man...is entitled to equal justice. No one man ought to have it in his power to tyrannize over, to injure nor defraud any body of men."

Thacher's *An Oration Delivered at Watertown* (1776) to commemorate the Boston Massacre deserves much more attention than it has received, especially since it is a prime example of a philippic; in fact, it has been suggested that Thacher may have been the only Boston orator who understood how to produce this Classical form. This rapidly moving and dramatic oration covers three points: the crimes perpetrated by George III, the contrasts between Eng. and New Eng., and a call for divinely sanctioned war. Although Thacher usually relied on concrete nouns, verbs, and adjectives rather than on figures of speech to make his points, in this philippic he combined both techniques to develop the contrasts between Eng. and New Eng. and to lead into his call for independence. He pictured the English as beasts, acquiescing to the tyranny of George III and his supporters: a corrupt legislature, "cringing, base-souled Priests," and a licentious standing army. On the other hand, the colonists inhabited a rich country full of resources to fight a war and would not permit their rights to be infringed. To emphasize the contrast between the two countries, Thacher used effective leonine imagery. The once formidable "British lion...hath now lost his teeth," whereas America is a land whose people responded to the outrageous Boston Massacre "like a lion, awaking from his slumber" ready to spring into action.

Like many New Eng. ministers, Thacher indicated that freedom had been banished from both Eng. and the Continent. Before exclaiming that God should permit America's independence, he personified freedom who "invites us to accept her blessings" and who "wishes to find an asylum in the wilds of America." So stirring was his *Oration Delivered at Watertown* that Thacher was asked to repeat it in Boston.

Suggested Readings: CCNE; DAB; Sibley-Shipton (XVII, 237-247); Sprague (I, 719-723). *See also Appleton's Cyclopaedia of American Biography* (1897), VI, 69-70;

Alice M. Baldwin, *The New England Clergy and the American Revolution* (1928), passim; Alan Heimert, *Religion and the American Mind* (1966), pp. 474, 512.

Susan A. Leazer
Illinois State University

THOMAS THACHER (1620-1678)

Works: *A Fast of Gods Chusing* (1678); *A Brief Rule* (1678); "To the Reader" (pub. in Nathaniel Morton, *New Englands Memoriall*; with John Higginson, 1669).

Biography: Thomas Thacher was born in 1620 in Milton Clevedon, Somersetshire, Eng. He was educated at the grammar school in Salisbury by his father Peter Thacher, who became rector there in 1622, but he never attended the university, because he was unable to subscribe to the religious vows required for matriculation. He arrived at Boston in 1635 on the *James* with his uncle Anthony Thacher and cousin Joseph Avery. He then entered the family of Charles Chauncy (q.v.) and began a course of study that included theology, logic, mechanics, and medicine as well as extensive work in Hebrew, Arabic, and Syriac. He achieved some local fame as a scholar in most of these areas, earning Cotton Mather's (q.v.) unrestrained praise for a one-page lexicon of Hebrew and his beautiful transcriptions of Syriac and other oriental characters. In 1643 he married Elizabeth, daughter of Ralph Partridge, the minister of Duxbury, and eight months later, he obtained his first ministerial position when he succeeded Samuel Newman as pastor of the church at Weymouth. He left Weymouth in 1664 after his wife died, possibly because he had been dismissed from his post. He soon married Margret Webb Scheafe, daughter of a wealthy Boston merchant, and moved there in 1669 to practice medicine and preach occasionally until he was installed as pastor of the Third (Old South) Church that same year. In Boston, as at Weymouth, the fervent eloquence of Thacher's prayers and his fond attention to the children under his care increased his congregation rapidly. This success earned him a reputation as one of the most popular preachers in the colony that he enjoyed until his death in 1678.

Critical Appraisal: Despite his fame among the colonists as a scholar and a man of powerful and efficacious prayer, Thomas Thacher is remembered today solely as the author of the first medical tract published in Mass., *A Brief Rule to Guide the Common-People of New-England How to Order Themselves and Theirs in the Small Pocks, or Measels*. Smallpox had struck the colonies repeatedly since the first recorded epidemic in 1633, although the disease had not been widespread in New Eng. until the second wave of immigration. In 1666 forty people died of smallpox in Boston alone, and in 1677 a ship arrived at Nantasket that infected most of the northern colonies, killing at least 700 by the middle of the year. Thacher's son Peter was visiting Eng. at that time, and he probably sent Thacher the works that became the basis for *A Brief Rule*, Thomas Sydenham's *Methodus Curandi Febres* (1666) and *Observationes Medicae* (1676). Although Thacher also relied on a Greek or Latin edition of a text by the Arab Rhazes, *A Treatise on the Smallpox and Measles*, most of *A Brief Rule* follows Sydenham closely, especially in his description of the disease as the blood's endeavor to renew itself and his warning not to try to impede or hurry the course of the disease.

Thacher modestly presented himself as "no Physitian, yet a well wisher to the sick" and clearly did not consider this broadside as a token of his literary or scholarly ability. But through its periodic reprintings, *A Brief Rule* became one of the best-known texts in New Eng. It was reprinted as a pamphlet during smallpox epidemics in 1702 and 1721 or 1722 and even today is still respected as the most sensible and useful response to the disease possible in the seventeenth century.

Thacher's other writings are unremarkable. In addition to his fast sermon and the preface to Nathaniel Morton's (q.v.) *New-Englands Memoriall*, which is memorable only for its connection with that important work, he authored or coauthored prefaces to works by Thomas Shepard (q.v.), Samuel Arnold (q.v.), and John Wilson (q.v.). More interesting are the letters published in the *Collections of the Massachusetts Historical Society* and the *New England Historical and Genealogical Register*. There Thacher emerged as a reasonable and thoughtful participant in the crises of the colony, and in a letter defending a woman accused of witchcraft before the most powerful men in New Eng., Thacher demonstrated the compassion and argumentative skill that earned him the respect of his contemporaries.

Suggested Readings: CCNE; Sprague (I, 126-129). *See also* William Bradford, *History of Plymouth Plantation* (1856; rep., 1912), II, 304n; Daniel J. Boorstin, *The Americans: The Colonial Experience* (1958), pp. 214-215; CMHS, 5th ser., 1 (1871), 355-357; Cotton Mather, *Magnalia Christi Americana* (1702; rep., 1855), III, pt. ii, ch. 4, 488-497; NEHGR, 8 (1854), 177-178; Harrison T. Meserole, *Seventeenth-Century American Poetry* (1968), pp. 405-408; Benjamin B. Wisner, *History of the Old South Church, Boston* (1830).

Michael P. Clark
The University of Michigan

GABRIEL THOMAS (1661-1714)

Works: *An Historical and Geographical Account of Pensilvania and of West-New-Jersey* (1698).

Biography: Gabriel Thomas was born in Monmouthshire, Wales, in Mar. 1661, the son of Quaker parents. In 1681 Thomas joined the first group of William Penn's (q.v.) colonists and crossed the Atlantic to settle in Philadelphia. In 1697 Thomas returned to London, where he saw his book through the press, remaining there until 1702. Ironically, Thomas who had dedicated his *Account* to Penn, had a falling out with the proprietor after it was published. Claiming a share of the colony's prosperity for the promotional efforts of his book, Thomas sought to secure the proprietary post of collector of quitrents for New Castle County. Penn's failure to meet this request prompted an acrimonious exchange between the two, including Thomas's complaint to the British Board of Trade accusing Penn of "unjust dealings," and Penn's characterization of Thomas as "beggarly" and "base." In later years, Thomas resided in Sussex County in the present state of Del. and again in Philadelphia after 1712. He died in 1714.

Critical Appraisal: Gabriel Thomas's one published work, *Historical and Geographical Account of Pensilvania*, is one of the multitudinous promotional tracts of early America, albeit one of the better ones and certainly the best of those written about the colony of Pa. Frankly written to encourage immigration to Penn's settlement on the Delaware, Thomas's *Account* paints an extremely rosy picture of conditions and opportunities in the new colony. A portion of the work consists of catalogs of flora and fauna, and another enumerates the particular occupations most needed by the province. Altogether it is an entertaining mixture of natural history, geography, history, and promotion. Thomas was evidently a man of limited learning but of ample wit, and his breathless style contains moments of charm and amusement. Obvious promotions such as "Poor People both Men and Women, will get near three times more Wages for their Labour in this Country, than they can earn either in England or Wales" are leavened by the author's own humorous prejudices, for example, "Of Lawyers and Physicians I shall say nothing, because this Countrey is very Peaceable and Healty; long may it so continue and never have occasion for the Tongue of the one, nor the Pen of the other, both equally destructive to Mens Estates and Lives; besides forsooth, they, Hang-Man like, have a License to Murder and make Mischief." All in all, Thomas's rhetoric, appropriately plain for a Quaker, is nonetheless characterized by an unaffected and infectuous enthusiasm for his subject, a manner quite engaging even if we may doubt that in Pa. "Jealousie among Men is here very rare, and Barrenness among Women hardly to be heard of, nor are old Maids to be met with; for all commonly Marry before they are Twenty Years of Age, and seldom any young Married Woman but hath a child in her Belly, or one upon her Lap."

Suggested Readings: LHUS; T$_1$. *See also* M. Katherine Jackson, *Outlines of the Literary History of Pennsylvania* (1907; 1966); Albert C. Myers, *Narratives of Early Pennsylvania, West New Jersey and Delaware, 1630-1707* (1912; 1966).

Donald P. Wharton
Castleton State College

ISAIAH THOMAS (1749-1831)

Works: [Boston] *Massachusetts Spy* (Jul. 17, 1770-Apr. 6, 1775): triweekly, established by Z. Fowle and I. Thomas; Jul. 17, 1770, prospectus; Aug. 7, 1770, vol. 1, no. 2, 1st true issue; Oct. 11, 1770, last issue with Fowle and Thomas imprint; Oct. 30, 1770, 1st issue with single Thomas imprint; Nov. 5, 1770, *Spy* became semiweekly; Feb. 1, 1771, vol. 1, no. 65, last issue in quarto; newspaper suspended, resumed with Mar. 7, 1771, issue in folio as a weekly with new volume numbering system; Oct. 8, 1772, title became *The Massachusetts Spy, or Thomas's Boston Journal*; Apr. 6, 1775, vol. 5, no. 218, ceased publication in Boston; resumed in Worcester on May 3, 1775, as *The Massachusetts Spy, or American Oracle of Liberty*; no issues published on Feb. 23, Mar. 8-Apr. 5, or Apr. 19, 1776; May 31, 1776-Jun. 25, 1778, publication leased and appeared under various titles; Jun. 25, 1778, Thomas resumed publication as *Thomas's Massachusetts Spy, or American Oracle of Liberty*; May 24, 1781, title became *Thomas's Massachusetts Spy, or The Worcester Gazette*; Mar. 30, 1786, vol. 16, no. 782, newspaper replaced by *The Worcester Magazine*, which first appeared in Apr. 1786, in octavo, and continued through Mar. 1788, vol. 4, no. 26; Apr. 3, 1788, newspaper reappeared as *Thomas's Massachusetts Spy: Or, The Worcester Gazette*, vol. 17, no. 783; Jan. 5, 1792, Leonard Worcester joined as partner; Mar. 6, 1799, printed under arrangement with Isaiah Thomas, Jr.; Jun. 10, 1801, Isaiah Thomas, Jr., became proprietor.

[Newburyport] *The Essex Journal and Merrimack Packet: Or, The Massachusetts and New-Hampshire General Advertiser* (Dec. 4, 1773-Aug. 17, 1774): weekly, established by I. Thomas and Henry Walter Tinges; 2nd number appeared on Dec. 29, 1773, and thereafter publication was regular; Aug. 17, 1774, Thomas withdrew from firm.

[Walpole] *The New Hampshire Journal: Or, The Farmer's Weekly Museum* (Apr. 11, 1793-Apr. 5, 1796); Thomas resumed proprietorship on Feb. 20, 1798, and admitted Alexander Thomas to firm with issue of May 29, 1798: weekly, established by I. Thomas and David Carlisle, Jr.; Apr. 11, 1794, title became *The New Hampshire and Vermont Journal: Or, The Farmer's Weekly Museum*; Apr. 5, 1796, Thomas left firm, with Joseph Dennie rising as editor. Alexander Thomas later conducted the firm with aid of Dennie.

[Boston] *The Royal American Magazine, or Universal Repository of Instruction and Amusement* (Jan. 1774-Mar. 1775): monthly, established by I. Thomas, who edited the magazine through Jun. 1774; resumed with Joseph Greenleaf, Jul. 1774-Mar. 1775.

[Boston] *The Massachusetts Magazine: Or, Monthly Museum of Knowledge and Rational Entertainment* (Jan. 1789-Dec. 1796): monthly, suspended Jan.-Mar. 1795; established by Isaiah Thomas and Company, Jan.-Aug. 1789; Isaiah Thomas and Ebenezer T. Andrews, Sept. 1789-1793; others followed.

The History of Printing in America, with a Biography of Printers and an Account of Newspapers (2 vols. in octavo, 1810; 2nd ed. based on his notes for a corrected edition, 1874).

Biography: Born in Boston, Mass., on Jan. 19, 1749, Isaiah Thomas was the youngest son of Moses and Fidelity (Grant) Thomas. His adventurous father sailed to Cuba as a soldier of fortune and later to the Mediterranean before settling in N.C., where he died in 1752. Left virtually destitute as the result of Isaiah's paternal grandfather's will, Fidelity Thomas possessed sufficient business acumen to set up her own shop and support her five children. On Jun. 4, 1756, she apprenticed Isaiah to Boston printer Zechariah Fowle. Thomas's earliest experience with a composing stick concerned the ribald ballad "The Law-[y]er's Pedigree, Tune, Our Polly is a Sad Slut." Although Fowle was a careless craftsman, Thomas managed to learn the rudiments of setting type from Samuel Draper and another local printer, Gamaliel Rogers. Following a "sharp disagreement" with Fowle in 1765, Thomas plotted secretly to sail for Eng., via Halifax, Nova Scotia.

On Sept. 24, 1765, he arrived in Halifax and secured employment with the government printer, Anthony Henry, who also published the *Halifax Gazette or Weekly Advertiser*. Henry's indolence prompted Thomas to emerge as the newspaper's true voice. Thomas soon ran amiss of the Stamp Act, publishing a "seditious" newspaper without the authorization provided by the infamous stamps—suspiciously missing from the paper stock. Both he and his publisher were summoned several times before the governor and Council, but narrowly avoided such confrontations despite threats of prosecution. With Henry's government printing contracts in jeopardy, Thomas chose to ease the situation by removing to Portsmouth, N.H. His Halifax sojourn had lasted six months.

In Portsmouth, he labored with Z. Fowle's older brother, Daniel, on the *New Hampshire Gazette* for thirteen days. He then spent several weeks with the Portsmouth *Mercury and Weekly Advertiser*, before returning to Fowle's shop in Boston. Further disagreements with Fowle led Thomas to abandon Boston again—this time for a trip to N.C. There he attempted to negotiate for a press, without success. An opportunity with the *South Carolina and American General Gazette* emerged, and Thomas was persuaded to join the staunch Royalist publisher Robert Wells in Charleston. During his two-year stay, he met and married Mary Dill (1769), whom he later divorced for alleged adultery (1777).

By spring 1770 Thomas had returned to Boston where, in partnership with Fowle, he issued the first number of the thrice-weekly *Massachusetts Spy* on Jul. 17, 1770. By late Oct. 1770, Thomas had bought out his partner's interest and had secured a loan to purchase Fowle's equipment. Although Thomas proposed an expanded biweekly version of the *Spy*, he changed his mind; within three months, Thomas had opted for a weekly publication projected on a grander scale than any previous Boston newspaper. On Mar. 7, 1771, the revised *Massachusetts Spy* appeared from its new office on Union Street, proclaiming its editorial neutrality to fewer than 200 subscribers. Initially, Thomas's columns were open to Whigs and Royalists alike, but the rapid polarization of political views soon thwarted this arrangement.

Within two years, Thomas's "sedition foundry" had forged the largest circulation in Boston. Loyalist efforts to buy, cajole, or suppress the *Spy* failed. Thomas was refused access even to mundane government news, including Custom House accounts of the arrivals and clearances within Boston harbor. Through his columns, anonymous Sons of Liberty cast scathing diatribes against the tyrannical rule of Governor Thomas Hutchinson (q.v.), which depicted him as a petty usurper. Thomas refused to appear before the governor and his Council to explain his editorial policies, questioning the legality of such a demand. Efforts to entangle Thomas in a libel action came to naught. The shrewd editor countered that far more "disloyal" statements had appeared in the English press without reprisals. On Oct. 10, 1772, Thomas charged in the *Spy* that efforts to prosecute him were malicious. He noted, "we may next have padlocks on our lips and fetters on our legs, or FIGHT OUR WAY TO CONSTITUTIONAL FREE-DOM." Loyalists throughout the colonies burned Thomas in effigy or had copies of his newspaper burned by the hangman. Thomas had seized the most radical of editorial positions, demanding—as his grandson Benjamin F. Thomas later wrote—not only the rights of Englishmen but the rights of man. Isaiah Thomas sought to extend his influence beyond his provincial 2,500 subscribers through patriotic devices, such as the segmented snake representing each of the colonies.

Hostilities forced him to flee Boston on Apr.18, 1775, two days after he secretly had shipped his presses and types to Worcester, Mass., "in the dead of night." Thomas accepted the uncertainties of publishing during a revolution and knew the risks. Failure was a familiar bedfellow. The *Royal American Magazine; Or, Universal Repository of Instruction and Amusement*, which Thomas had first issued on Feb. 6, 1774, had passed into the hands of Joseph Greenleaf and now lay fallow. Even the appearance of Governor Hutchinson's *History of the Colony of Massachusetts-Bay* within its columns failed to rescue it from oblivion. A similar newspaper venture with Henry Walter Tinges in 1773 to establish *The Essex Journal, and Merrimack Packet; Or, The Massachusetts and New Hampshire General Advertiser* at Newburyport found Thomas selling his share to Ezra Hunt after about one year.

On May 3, 1775, the *Massachusetts Spy, or American Oracle of Liberty* emerged from Worcester. The Committee of Safety recognized Thomas's contribution to the cause, voting to provide him with "sixty reams of printing crown paper and eight reams of printing demy paper." The years 1775 and 1776 proved difficult for Thomas, as rags, subscribers, hard money, and government support became scarce. On Nov. 17, 1775, the *Spy* announced Thomas's appointment by the Continental Congress as local postmaster—a commission ultimately renewed until 1802.

In 1776 Thomas leased the *Spy* and part of his equipment to William Stearns and Daniel Bigelow, Jr., while he explored the feasibility of establishing a newspaper in Salem, Mass. Three writs of attachment upon his remaining press and types compelled him to sell the articles to pay unspecified debts. With the Salem venture scuttled, Thomas again decided to lease the *Spy*—this time to Antony Haswell in 1777. That same year, Thomas charged his wife "with having been guilty of the Crime of Adultery with one Major Thompson." The marriage was dissolved formally on May 27, 1777.

During the spring of 1778, Thomas returned to Worcester, retrieved his beloved *Spy*, and resumed his newspaper career. With the issue of Jun. 25, 1778, the paper became *Thomas's Massachusetts Spy*. Following the peace of 1783, Thomas prospered. He had remarried on May 26, 1779—this time to his "half-cousin" Mary Fowle—and had found stability in both personal and professional affairs. From Mar. 1786 until Mar. 1788, the *Spy* was suspended and replaced by the *Worcester Magazine* in octavo. The threat of stamp duties and the imposition of a duty on all newspaper advertisements published in Mass. led Thomas to the format change. With the adoption of the Constitution (which Thomas favored and actively supported), Thomas embarked upon more diversified publishing schemes. He built a large paper mill at Quinsigamond in 1793, established a bindery, and controlled at least sixteen presses. His bookstores spread from Mass. to Md. Issued under the imprint of Thomas and a former apprentice, Ebenezer T. Andrews, was the *Massachusetts Magazine* (1789-1793). In Apr. 1793 David Carlisle joined forces with Thomas as manager of the *New Hampshire Journal* at Walpole. Thomas remained affiliated with the newspaper for at least three years, as Joseph Dennie (q.v.) struggled to transform it into the literary and political spokesman for the Federalist cause—known chiefly as *The Farmer's Weekly Museum*. During the 1790s, Thomas became the proprietor of one of the largest printing concerns on either side of the Atlantic, issuing numerous Bibles, juvenile works, almanacs, dictionaries, musical songbooks, novels, school texts, and Classical works. In 1802 he turned over his business to his son Isaiah Thomas, Jr., and began organizing his massive collection of newspapers and books to support two projects: the publication of the *History of Printing in America, with a Biography of Printers, and an Account of Newspapers* (1810, two volumes in octavo) and the organization of the American Antiquarian Society (Nov. 19, 1812). Within months of the death of his second wife in 1818, Thomas married her cousin Rebecca Armstrong on Aug. 10, 1819. Isaiah Thomas spent his final years engrossed in projects as diverse as the Worcester to Boston Turnpike and the collection of works for the American Antiquarian Society. He died on Apr. 4, 1831.

    Critical Appraisal:

      To Print or not to Print—that is the question,
      Whether 'tis better in a trunk to bury
      The quirks and crotchets of outrageous fancy,
      Or send a well wrote Essay to the press
      (No matter which, whether on timid *cowardice* or *courage*)
      And by imprinting, end them. To print, no doubt,
      No more; and by one act to say we end.

    This, then, exemplified the *Massachusetts Spy* of Isaiah Thomas: brazen, bitter, besieged. Thomas had established his *Spy* as a nonpartisan organ, "Open to all Parties, but influenced by None." He soon discovered, however, that the rhetoric of independence carried the burden of action. He had begun his newspaper with the intention of writing for the masses—the mechanics. He explained,

Common sense in common language is necessary to influence one class of citizens as much as learning and elegance of composition to produce an effect upon another: the cause of America was just, and it was only necessary to state this cause in a clear and impressive manner to unite the American people in its support.

Yet the anonymous contributors drawn to his "sedition factory" were hardly the common, disenfranchised masses. James Otis (q.v.), Joseph Warren (q.v.), Paul Revere, Joseph Greenleaf, and John Hancock proved to be the influential names behind the literary masks. Whig principles and the burning pens of firebrands were the order of the day.

In 1770 three major newspapers held ground in Boston: the Boston *News Letter* (a formidable opponent with substantial government support), the Boston *Evening Post* (the organ of John and Thomas Fleet), and the strident Boston *Gazette and Country Journal* (whose printers were the influential Benjamin Edes and John Gill). Against them, Thomas introduced his *Massachusetts Spy*, cluttering its columns with proceedings of town meetings, charges of treason on the part of government toadies, and reports of the activities of the Sons of Liberty and the Committees of Correspondence. Thomas quickly outdistanced another competitor, the Boston *Chronicle*, whose fiery printers John Mein and John Fleming set out to depict controversial issues with editorial balance. Their castigation of both patriots and public officials made them *personae non gratae* in both camps. Mein enraged the mechanics and retired from the fray; Thomas rushed headlong into incendiary journalism and established a circulation of 3,500 subscribers before fleeing the city.

Thomas's previous quarrels with civil authorities eased his transition from simple printer to patriot. As the *Spy* grew in influence in Boston, the young publisher became bolder in his assessment of the prerogatives of liberty:

The Free Use of the Press to defend the *Glorious Cause of Liberty*, and to point out to the world, those base and wicked arts of designing men, who fain would set nations together by the ears, and involve whole kingdoms in Slavery! to help as much as possible in maintaining and supporting that LIBERTY for which our Fathers suffered in transferring it to us.

Thomas's editorial voice flowed harmoniously with those of "Monitor," "Massachusettensis," "The Centinel," and "Mucius Scaevola." "Scaevola"—probably Joseph Greenleaf—relished baiting the "usurper" Governor Hutchinson. Greenleaf wrote,

A ruler, independent of the people, is a monster in government;...A Massachusetts Governor, the King by compact, with his people may *nominate* and *appoint* but not pay: For his support he must stipulate with the people, and until he does, he is no legal Governor.

"Monitor" viewed the government with indignant alarm at best; "Scaevola" deemed it the instrument of a usurper. But it was "Monitor" who in the early

1770s enlarged his series of essays to charge the existence of treason within the Hutchinson administration. The *Massachusetts Spy*, then, served as a conduit of controversy, whether in Boston or later in Worcester. Thomas successfully "clarified" the issues and laid the literary breastworks for at least the semblance of unified colonial defense against the British. He chose symbols ("Join or Die") and emotional occurrences (Boston "massacre") to polarize further public opinion. In addition, he supplemented the political tirades within the columns of his *Spy* with the publication of *Thomas' New England Almanack*, which appeared in Boston in 1775. By 1790 his almanac contained more than mere weather predictions: the text of the Tariff of 1789 and the proposed Amendments to the Constitution were among the offerings. The *Massachusetts Spy* served the populace as both a political barometer and a daily diary of dissent.

Isaiah Thomas's three sallies into magazine journalism were no less uneventful. On Jun. 24, 1773, Thomas issued the prospectus for *The Royal American Magazine* on the front page of his *Massachusetts Spy*. In it Thomas denigrated newspapers as not "fit to convey to posterity the labours of the learned." In language suggestive of that used by both Thomas and Dennie twenty years later in *The Farmer's Weekly Museum*, Thomas announced his subscription to the major magazines and reviews of G.B. as well as the appropriate periodicals of the American colonies. Literature, Thomas explained, was "the great fountain head from whence springs all that is requisite to accomplish rational beings."

Yet the "disordered state of public affairs" and the untoward wreck of the ship carrying his precious types from Eng. unsettled Thomas and his venture. The first issue was dated Jan. 1774. For more than a year and a half, no magazine had been published in the colonies, with the last general magazine defunct for more than four years. Thomas's contents were predictable: selections culled from the English press; a variety of articles touching upon science, religion, and the arts; and commentaries upon current events. "Sedition" ran rampant. The Boston Massacre was memorialized by John Hancock; "liberty" was the favorite literary mistress ("Liberty in General," "The Character of an American Patriot"). The passage of the Boston Port Bill evoked this response in *The Royal American Magazine*: "How matters will end, God only knows, but it is thought that, by the blessing of heaven, if the colonies unite and stand firm, that they will preserve their liberties and cast off the iron yoke of bondage." Thomas used the closure of the Boston harbor and mechanical difficulties within his shop as reasons for withdrawing from the magazine. In addition, he admitted that his contributors— "those good Gentlemen"—had favored the magazine "with but few original Pieces."

Joseph Greenleaf, the accused "Mucius Scaevola," assumed publication in Aug. 1774 and attempted—ironically—to use the serialization of Hutchinson's *History of the Colony of Massachusetts-Bay* as an inducement for subscribers. He even offered to omit the Hutchinson work for those readers desiring to pay less for the magazine. Less strident than Thomas, Greenleaf nevertheless failed to sustain the magazine beyond the third number of the second volume.

As noted by historian Lyon N. Richardson, despite mechanical and financial problems (and a paucity of much original material), Thomas did succeed in bringing the short story to the attention of American readers. "The Thunder Storm" (Jan. 1774), "Justice and Generosity" (Feb.-Mar. 1774), and "The Fortune Hunter" clearly piqued interest in the genre. "Sex, sorrow, and sentimentality" were brought forth in a profusion unknown previously in the colonies, according to Richardson. In addition, perhaps as many as sixteen of the twenty-two important engravings found in *The Royal American Magazine* were executed by Paul Revere. In Apr. 1774 Thomas inserted in his magazine the first American engraving of the words and music of a song ("The Hill-Tops"). Despite these achievements, he waited until Apr. 1786—twelve years—before attempting another magazine.

Thomas issued *The Worcester Magazine* in an effort to circumvent a legislative act taxing advertisements in newspapers such as his *Massachusetts Spy*. The change was easily accomplished, since the periodical types available to eighteenth-century printers of both magazines and newspapers were virtually indistinguishable. The only major accommodation was the switch from a four-page folio to a sixteen-page octavo format. Essentially, *The Worcester Magazine* was a made-over weekly newspaper concerned with the federal Constitution, civil order, and currency. Shays' Rebellion, troubles in R.I., and proceedings of the Mass. General Court set the tone. Of particular importance, as emphasized by Frank Luther Mott, was the magazine's commitment to running diverse arguments concerning the proposed federal Constitution. Perhaps the most important literary contribution was that of "The Worcester Speculator," often attributed to Pliny Merrick of Brookfield. This series, reprinted by the *American Museum*, was sometimes favorably compared with essays in the *Spectator*. However, the essays of "Tom Taciturn" (Edward Bangs of Worcester?) evinced more rhetorical flourish than substance, although one essay favored the abolition of the legal system in deference to a judiciary run by local pastors. Thomas generally shied away from religious debate in all of his publications, generally offering "orthodoxy" rather than more heretical views. The poetry department, "Pegasus of Apollo," carried the previously published work of wordsmiths such as Timothy Dwight (q.v.), David Humphreys (q.v.), and Jonathan Swift. With the lifting of the tax on advertisements, Thomas suspended *The Worcester Magazine* and resumed his *Massachusetts Spy* in Apr. 1788.

Before the advent of the *Port Folio* in 1801, Thomas's *Massachusetts Magazine* was in the vanguard of American efforts to emulate European Enlightenment. Sounding surprisingly like his contributor Joseph Dennie, Thomas promised his readers a periodical that would "improve the taste, the language and the manners of the age." Within its eight volumes, Thomas included poetry, music, "morality," natural science, and an admixture of marriages and mortality. Essay serials proved the mainstay, with luminaries such as Joseph Dennie ("Socialis"), Judith Sargent Murray (q.v.) ("Constantia"), and William Bigelow ("Charles Chatterbox") providing the intellectual kindling for heated discussion. Thomas continued publishing short stories as well as original American dramatic scripts. He had published drama before, particularly Mercy Otis Warren's (q.v.) controversial attack upon Governor Hutchinson ("The Adulateur"), which had appeared in the Mar. 1772 issue of the *Massachusetts Spy*. In Oct.-Nov. 1789, Thomas introduced William Dunlap's (q.v.) "The Father," produced in N.Y. but unavailable in Boston, which did not permit theatre. The *Massachusetts Magazine* remains a rich source of original lyric and didactic poetry, including the work of Sarah Wentworth Morton (q.v.). As "Philenia," Morton exchanged literary "familiarities" with Joseph Dennie ("Meander"). Despite Dennie's cooperation with Thomas on the *Massachusetts Magazine* and, later, *The Farmer's Museum*, it remains unclear why Thomas's later praise for "The Lay Preacher's" author was so tempered. In *The History of Printing in America*, Thomas wrote simply, "Mr. Dennie was reckoned among the first scholars in the belles-lettres, which our country has produced."

By 1791 Thomas and Ebenezer T. Andrews were forced to admit what Thomas had discovered in earlier magazine ventures: original American prose and poetry did not appear spontaneously for publication. They wrote, "A copious selection, both Foreign and Domestick, has therefore supplied those vacant pages, that long waited for the effusions of American Genius—and languished, but in vain—for the genial embrace of Columbian Science." Again, Thomas turned to music, filling out portions of the magazine with forty-five pieces (much of it American vintage) by Sept. 1792. When he and Andrews disposed of the publication in 1793, financial rather than literary considerations seemed responsible. Thomas, in his last decade before "retirement," broadened his publishing base as well as his ultimate impact upon the issuance of religious, musical, and juvenile literature.

During his career, Isaiah Thomas published roughly 900 titles, including several of singular importance: a folio edition of the Bible (1791), complete with fifty copper plates engraved by Samuel Hill, John Norman, Joseph Seymour; *Laus Deo! The Worcester Collection of Sacred Harmony* (1786), the first American musical edition prepared from type; first American editions of William Blackstone's *Commentaries*, Daniel Defoe's *Travels of Robinson Crusoe* (as a book, already serialized in several colonial newspapers), and John Bunyan's *Pilgrim's Progress; Mother Goose's Melody*, and *Little Goody Two-Shoes*; the first edition of William Hill Brown's (q.v.) *The Power of Sympathy*; and more than 100 children's books. Thomas's *The History of Printing in America* (2 vols., 1810), although at best a flawed and at worst a jaundiced rendering, continues to serve as a departure point for scholars interested in the genesis of modern American printing. Thomas's initial collection of some 3,000 volumes formed the basis upon which the American Antiquarian Society began assembling its own massive holdings. Perhaps the explorer Brissot de Warville summed up Thomas's contribution most succinctly when he observed in 1788, "He is the Didot of the United States."

Suggested Readings: DAB; LHUS; T$_2$. *See also* Frederick E. Bauer, Jr., "The American Antiquarian Society and Children's Literature," *Phaedrus*, 3 (1976), 5-8; Joseph T. Buckingham, *Specimens of Newspaper Literature; with Personal Memoirs, Anecdotes and Reminiscences* (1850); Philip Davidson, *Propaganda and the American Revolution* (1941); Everett Emerson, ed., *American Literature, 1764-1789: The Revolutionary Years* (1977); Worthington C. Ford, "The Isaiah Thomas Collection of Ballads," PAAS, 33, pt.1 (1923), 34-112; Benjamin T. Hall, ed., "The Diary of Isaiah Thomas, 1805-1828," TAAS, 9, 10 (1909); Karl Kroeger, "Isaiah Thomas as a Music Publisher," PAAS, 86, pt. 2 (1976), 321-341; Levi Lincoln, *Reminiscences of the Original Associates of the Worcester Fire Society* (1862); Annie Russell Marble, *From 'Prentice to Patron: The Life Story of Isaiah Thomas* (1935); Marcus A. McCorison, "To the Suburbs, Eighteenth Century Style," NEG, 6, no. 3 (1965), 25-33; Frank Luther Mott, *American Journalism: A History of Newspapers in the United States Through 250 Years, 1690 to 1940* (1947); idem, *A History of American Magazines, 1741-1850* (1966); C. L. Nichols, "Extracts from the Diaries and Accounts of Isaiah Thomas from the Year 1782 to 1804 and His Diary for 1808," PAAS, 26, pt. 1 (1916), 58-79; idem, *Isaiah Thomas: Printer, Writer and Collector* (1912, 1971); John R. Osterholm, "The Literary Career of Isaiah Thomas, 1749-1831," DAI, 39 (1978), University of Massachusetts, 2277-A; Lyon N. Richardson, *A History of Early American Magazines, 1741-1789* (1931); Arthur M. Schlesinger, *Prelude to Independence: The Newspaper War on Britain, 1764-1776* (1958); C. K. Shipton, "Bibliotheca Americana," PBSA, 62 (1968), 351-359; idem, *Isaiah Thomas: Printer, Patriot and Philanthropist, 1749-1831* (1948); Madeleine B. Stern, "Saint-Pierre in America: Joseph Nancrede and Isaiah Thomas," PBSA, 68 (1974), 312-325; G. Thomas Tanselle, "Attribution of Authorship in 'The Spirit of the Farmers' Museum,'" PBSA, 59 (1965), 170-176; Benjamin F. Thomas, "Memoir of Isaiah Thomas," TAAS, 5 (1874), xvii-lxxxvii; James d'Alté Welch, *A Bibliography of American Children's Books Printed Prior to 1821* (1972); Edwin Wolf II, "Some Books of Early New England Provenance in the 1823 Library of Alleghany College," PAAS, 73 (1963), 13-44; Lawrence C. Wroth, *The Colonial Printer* (1931, 1964).

For Isaiah Thomas manuscript materials, see Isaiah Thomas Papers, 28 volumes and seven boxes, including letters, diaries, accounts, and the manuscript of Thomas's *History of Printing in America* in American Antiquarian Society, Worcester, Mass.; Mathew Carey (1760-1839) Papers (1787-1795), three reels of microfilm in American Philosophical Society Library, Philadelphia, Pa., made from originals owned by the American Antiquarian Society, Worcester, Mass., and the Historical Society of Pennsylvania, Philadelphia, Pa.; Jacob Merritt Howard (1805-1871) Papers (1702-1870), in Burton Historical Collection, Detroit Public Library, Detroit, Mich.

William F. Vartorella
Mary Baldwin College

JOHN THOMAS (1743-1815)

Works: "Washington" (pub. in *From the Genius of America*; 1783); "Written Under a Young Lady's Picture at Tulip Hill" and other poems (pub. in *A Lady in Maryland, Extracts in Prose and Verse*; 1808).

Biography: John Thomas, the youngest son of Philip and Anne (Chew) Thomas, was born on Aug. 26, 1743. The Thomases were descendants of one of

Anne Arundel County, Md.'s first Quaker families, and John resided for most of his life at the family seat, "Lebanon," situated on the West River. While serving as a captain in the local militia during the early stages of the Revolution, Thomas married Sarah Murray in 1777. In later years, he distinguished himself as a member of Md.'s General Assembly and as president of the state Senate and became one of the first visitors and governors of St. John's College, Annapolis. John Thomas died at "Lebanon" on Feb. 13, 1815, and was buried in The Old Quaker Burial Ground adjoining a nearby plantation, "Tulip Hill."

Critical Appraisal: Obviously not a prolific writer, John Thomas appears, in all senses of the word, an "occasional" writer. Two occasions—one public and one personal—serve as the foci for two of his extant poems. The public occasion is the return of George Washington (q.v.)—hero and statesman— to Mt. Vernon and the peace of country life in 1783. A mixture of panegyric, encomium, and pindaric ode, "Washington" is relatively unenergetic. The images are standard neo-Classical fare, and the message of getting down to peaceful concerns and the epithets are stock.

Thomas does, however, seem to have been more at home with the familiar ode, the form he espoused in his earlier poem "Written Under a Young Lady's Picture at Tulip Hill" (1762). The poem expresses ardent admiration for Jane Galloway, "Jenny" in the picture, who resided at Tulip Hill. Penned in couplets, the poem invokes the Classical "Damon" beholding the picture and pondering whether the artistic rendering or the subject in the flesh (art or nature) be the fairest. The conclusion, of course, is that art "must yield" to nature, that Jenny's form cannot be duplicated.

Suggested Readings: J. Reaney Kelly, "Tulip Hill, Its History and Its People," MdHM, 60 (1965), 349-403; *A Lady in Maryland, Extracts in Prose and Verse* (1808), II, 166, 167; Edward M. Noble and Edward T. Tubbs, eds., *Maryland in Prose and Poetry* (1909), pp. 113, 245; Lawrence Buckley Thomas, D.D., *The Thomas Book* (1906), p. 52.

A. Franklin Parks
Frostburg State College

ROBERT BAILEY THOMAS (1766-1846)

Works: *The Farmer's Almanack* for 1793-1831; *Old Farmer's Almanac* for 1832-1847. Published today in Dublin, N.H., by Yankee, Inc., the original Robert B. Thomas almanacs were printed in Boston, usually by Belknap and Hall and later by Manning and Loring, generally the year before the date mentioned in the title.

Biography: Almanac-maker Robert B. Thomas, son of William and Azubah (Goodale) Thomas, was born in Grafton, Mass. His grandfather William Thomas had studied at Christ's College, Cambridge. He came to America from Wales about 1718, settled in Marblehead about 1720, married Lydia Eager, and had six children. The eldest was Robert's father, who had little formal education but made good use of his father's library and became a schoolmaster. Robert grew up on his father's farm in Sterling in the North Parish of Shrewsbury, now West Boylston. Although William Thomas offered his son a college education, Robert preferred to study as his father had before him, reading the books in the family library. His father also instructed him at home. One of the library textbooks was James Ferguson's *Astronomy Explained* (1756), which both fascinated and frustrated him: he wanted to calculate his own almanac but lacked the skill. Following in his father's footsteps, he became a schoolmaster in 1786; he met Hannah Beaman in 1792 and married her in 1803. Robert soon gave up teaching to learn bookbinding and to become a bookseller. In 1792 he and his younger brother Aaron formed a partnership in the bookbinding business. During the summer of 1792, he used the profit from his first bookbinding venture to study under Osgood Carleton, an almanac-maker and "Teacher of Mathematicks." Thomas was then able to calculate his first *Farmer's Almanack* (for 1793), thus realizing his earlier ambition. He continued the series for fifty-six years, until his death at age 80 in West Boylston on May 19, 1846. He was survived by his widow and two nephews, to whom he entrusted his almanac business, having no children of his own. He was reputed to be honest, hardworking, forthright, practical, generous, and highly respected by all who knew him.

Critical Appraisal: Robert B. Thomas's *Farmer's Almanack* (later *Old Farmer's Almanac*) is significant not only for his length of association with this single publication (fifty-six years) but for its value to the social and intellectual historian and for Thomas's genial and folksy literary style. He began his almanac at a critical time in American history, shortly after the Constitution was adopted, when nationalism and optimism were newly part of the American scene. His almanacs, which circulated from Boston, Salem, N.Y., and Philadelphia, therefore reflect the development of the country itself. George Kittredge has compared Thomas and Benjamin Franklin (q.v.) as almanac makers, and Thomas comes out well. From the beginning, Thomas solicited correspondence from his readers, especially on agricultural matters. Readers also submitted puzzles and poems, and Thomas often commented on them in the pages of his almanac. He had a secure hold on his readers: since he did not take astrology seriously, Thomas consistently omitted the Man of Signs, an almost heretical departure from conventional almanac format. He respected his readers and was too gentlemanly to offend them, as shown by his avuncular, amusing, and frank printed correspondence with them. In 1837 when his readers demanded a likeness of the author, Thomas obliged with a "Pickwickian" woodcut of himself, in keeping with the tone of the almanac. The 1833, 1837, and 1839 editions all carried his brief autobiography.

In addition to the usual almanac fare (prefaces, advice, weather, proverbs, road conditions), Thomas began to expand his literary talents by inserting character sketches such as "Old Hunks" in 1808, "Old Betty Blab" in 1817, "Margaret and the Mare" in 1816, "The Cattle Show" in 1824, and "The Baker" in 1837.

His jovial, homely good humor is evident throughout. His style is unpretentious, unself-conscious, sometimes whimsical, and always in good taste even when satirical. The sketches were sometimes anecdotal, the individuals so lifelike that many readers thought they recognized their friends and neighbors. The author was a perceptive and shrewd observer who indeed could have used prototypes to make his "genre" portraits. He used dialog simply and naturally, frequently employing hyperbole to make his point. His glimpses of typical customs such as huskings are revealing; his satirical allusions to lawyers and quacks are typical of contemporary attitudes; and his anecdotes, unlike those used generally as filler, are often as didactic as his little essays. His advice on economy is in the vein of Franklin, as is the wit in his proverbs. He also occasionally commented on the books that he advertised for sale.

Although his prefaces and his character sketches were his most outstanding literary contributions, he also tried poetry. Unlike many other almanac-makers, he would permit no bawdy material in his almanacs and was so much embarrassed in 1796 when his printer inserted some "highly disgusting" material that he apologized in the following issue. His prose was sometimes stately (for example, his 1842 preface, "Fifty Years Ago"), but it was more often sprightly— and even cutting at times, as in his famous feud with Isaiah Thomas (q.v.), which ran in both of their almanac prefaces. Robert B. Thomas had soon become the leader in the almanac field, forcing his rival Isaiah Thomas in 1798 to add "Isaiah" to the title of his "Thomas" almanac so that he would not be confused with Robert B. The competition between the two Thomases naturally resulted in superior almanacs for the Mass. region. Robert B. Thomas's almanac is the second most widely known in America (Franklin's *Poor Richard*, of course, being the first), largely because the *Old Farmer's Almanac* still carries his name on the title page. Since his death, these words have appeared: "Established in 1793, by Robert B. Thomas." The prefaces today usually conclude with a quotation from Thomas and a facsimile of his signature.

Suggested Readings: DAB. *See also* James H. Fitts, "The Thomas Almanacs," EIHC, 12 (1874), 243-270; George Lyman Kittredge, *The Old Farmer and His Almanack* (1924); Henry Morton Robinson, "The Almanac," *The Bookman*, 75 (1932), 218-224; Marion Barber Stowell, "American Almanacs and Feuds," EAL, 4 (1975), 276-285; idem, *Early American Almanacs* (1977), pp. 95-101.

Marion Barber Stowell
Milledgeville, Georgia

CHARLES THOMSON (1729-1824)

Works: *An Enquiry into the Causes of the Alienation of the Delaware and Shawanese Indians from the British Interests* (1759); *The Holy Bible* (translation of the Septuagint; 1808).

Biography: Charles Thomson was born in Northern Ire. in 1729, the youngest son of widower John Thomson, a prosperous linen tradesman. Charles and three of his brothers arrived at New Castle, Del., in 1739, their father having died on the voyage to America. Thomson attended Francis Alison's (q.v.) academy at New London, Pa., until he was able to organize his own school and, in 1750, move to Philadelphia, where he met Benjamin Franklin (q.v.) and subsequently became a tutor at the Academy of Philadelphia. In 1755 Thomson was named master of the Friends' School. This connection with the Quakers enabled him to become a member of the commission negotiating with the Delaware Indians, his work culminating in the publication of the *Enquiry into the Causes of the Alienation of the Delaware*. In this same period, Thomson was active in Philadelphia's literary and scientific societies and was instrumental in the organization of the American Philosophical Society. In 1760, one year after his first marriage, Thomson resigned his post at the Friends' School and established himself as a dry-goods merchant. Five years later, he became one of the most vocal and determined opponents of the Stamp Act and, later, the Townshend Acts and the East India Company tea monopoly. By 1774 Thomson had corresponded with Samuel Adams (q.v.) and John Hancock and had organized the Pa. Revolutionary party; in Sept. he was elected secretary of the Continental Congress (a position he held for fifteen years) and assumed a major role in the drafting of the Declaration of Independence and the Articles of Confederation, the conduct of the war, the enactment of the Northwest Ordinance of 1787, the design of the Great Seal, and the framing of the Constitution. After his retirement in 1789, Thomson devoted himself to a translation of the Septuagint. Although he retained some interest in national politics, Thomson held no other office before his death in 1824.

Critical Appraisal: Certain difficulties present themselves to anyone attempting a literary evaluation of Charles Thomson's work. First, he was an active political figure whose values were not primarily aesthetic. We do have much material available among Thomson's essays, papers, and letters, but few of them would interest the literary critic. Second, Thomson's work is often obscured by his life: his historical roles as negotiator, radical organizer of the Revolution in Pa., and secretary to the Continental Congress dominate any evaluation we make of his works, and no one judgment or title seems to include all of his activity. The Indians knew him as the "Man of Truth"; to John Adams (q.v.), he was the "Sam Adams of Philadelphia"; biblical scholars of the nineteenth century were familiar with him as the first translator of the Septuagint. Although these epithets may establish too strict boundaries, they do provide one useful classification of his works.

Thomson's first extended writing was the *Enquiry into the Causes of the Alienation of the Delaware*. *Literary History of the United States* tells us that Thomson's attempt "to vindicate the Quaker policy of seeking the friendship and respect of the Indians" was the product of "sober and painstaking scholarship," and so it was. Thomson began with the Conestoga Treaty of 1722 and continued through treaties, Council minutes, Assembly records, deeds, memoirs, letters, journals, and his own memory of peace conferences through 1757. His purpose, as he stated in the introduction, was to examine why so many Indians had "become our most bitter enemies." He found that this enmity was primarily the result of the English (not Quaker) policy of manipulation and exploitation by traders, settlers, and politicians. Thomson carefully and at some length distinguished the actions of these Englishmen from those of the French, who "use all the means in their power to draw as many into their Alliances as possible."

This method of contrast forms perhaps the dominant feature of Thomson's style: he presented villains (Gen. Braddock, Sir William Johnson) and heroes (Chief Teedyuscung, the Quakers), effective policy and disastrous injustice. The Indians themselves were "capable of being our most useful friends, or most dangerous Enemies." Thomson made this balanced antithesis—between friends and enemies, English and French—a keynote to his essay, and thus he constructed a clear, comprehensive, and persuasive argument.

In the decade following the *Enquiry*, Thomson's prose served the cause of the Revolution, and again he proved the master of convincing argument. In "A Letter from a Merchant in Philadelphia," sent to and published in London by Franklin (and included in volume two of *The Papers of Benjamin Franklin*, edited by Leonard Labaree), Thomson's periodic sentences and carefully wrought parallel structures convey the weight of cumulative grievances borne by the colonists. In a letter to William Drayton, Thomson admirably defended John Dickinson (q.v.) and his attempts at conciliation with Br. (a move Thomson opposed):

> But this petition, which was drawn up in the most submissive and unexceptional terms, meeting with same fate as others [i.e., rejection by the King], obviated objections that would have been raised, and had a powerful effect in suppressing opposition, preserving unanimity, and bringing the province in a united body into contest.

Thomson's final work, an English translation of the Septuagint, occupied most of his final years and provides another example of his attention to details and clear prose style. C. A. Muses, editor of a revised and enlarged version of Thomson's translation, said that "Thomson's work of translation and scholarship was sound and honest as were his official activities," and this type of evaluation dominates critical reception of the work. According to William Orme's *Bibliotheca Biblica* (1824), the translation is "creditable to America and the learned author"; Hartwell Horne in the *Manual of Biblical Bibliography* (1839) called it "very respectfully executed." Albert Edmunds (1891) stated that "the simple, untraditional translation...might well be regarded as the Quaker Testament." Although perhaps not imaginative, Thomson's scrupulous translation stands as an appropriate final testament to his life.

Indeed, Thomson's entire canon seems more a testimonial to his character and energy than a lasting achievement in belles lettres. His prose is careful, persuasive, and clear, if not memorable. Yet typically, he was not intent on aesthetic effect but on action, and in this he seems to have succeeded.

Suggested Readings: DAB; LHUS; T$_2$. *See also* Kenneth R. Bowling, "Good-by 'Charles': The Lee-Adams Interest and the Political Demise of Charles Thomson, Secretary of Congress, 1774-1789," PMHB, 100 (1976), 314-335; "Early Days of the Revolution in Philadelphia," PMHB, 2 (1878), 411-423 (letter to William Drayton); Albert Edmunds, "Charles Thomson's New Testament," **PMHB**, 15 (1891), 327-335; Lewis R. Harley, *The Life of Charles Thomson* (1900); J. Edwin Hendricks, *Charles Thomson and the Making of a New Nation, 1729-1824* (1979); Fred S. Rolater, "Charles Thomson, 'Prime Minister' of the United States," PMHB, 101 (1977), 322-348; James J. Zimmerman, "Charles Thomson: 'The Sam Adams of Philadelphia,'" MVHR, 40 (1958), 464-480.

Timothy K. Conley
Bradley University

JOHN THOMSON (c. 1690-1753)

Works: *An Overture Presented to the Reverend Synod of Dissenting Ministers, Sitting in Philadelphia* (1729); *The Poor Orphans Legacy* (1734); *An Essay upon the Faith of Assurance* (1740); *The Doctrine of Convictions Set in a Clear Light* (1741); *The Government of the Church of Christ* (1741); *An Explication of the Shorter Catechism* (1749).

Biography: John Thomson (spelled *Thompson* in most records of colonial Va.) was probably born in Scot., about 1690, since he entered the University of Glasgow in 1706. His studies at Glasgow continued until 1710 or 1711, when he was awarded an M.A. A Scots-Irishman, Thomson was licensed to preach by the General Synod of Ulster in 1713. He came to America with his wife and daughter in 1715 and began to preach regularly at Lewes, Del. Late in 1716 he received a call from this congregation and was ordained and installed as pastor in Apr. of the next year. A long train of financial troubles then began for Thomson. He resigned as pastor at Lewes in 1729, because his parishioners were remiss in paying his salary. In 1730 he accepted a call from Middle Octorora, but again financial support was lacking, and by 1732 he had accepted a new position at Chestnut Level, Pa. He was in such financial trouble by the following year that the congregations of the Donegal Presbytery took collections for his relief. About this time his wife died and left him with a large family, which then included ten children. He later remarried and fathered another child.

Thomson's difficulties with his congregations may have been caused or exacerbated by his frequent travels, many of which were occasioned by his duties in the church government. He was a moderator and powerful member of the Presbytery and the Philadelphia Synod, in which he performed both secretarial and judicial services. He was also by nature a pioneer very interested in the fate of the Presbyterian Church in the backwoods regions of the South. As early as 1738, he visited Va. and in 1739 asked permission to go there to help establish Presbyterianism in remote areas. But this request was refused until 1744, when he was released from his duties at Chestnut Level. Thomson had family and friends at Buffalo in Amelia (now Prince Edward) County, Va., where he settled in 1744 and remained until 1750 directing missions throughout western Va. He founded a school for young men that may have been the forerunner of Hampton-Sidney College. About 1751 Thomson extended his missionary efforts to N.C., and it is likely he was the first minister of any denomination to preach in the region of Rowan County. He settled near his son-in-law in what is now Iredell County, N.C., and established thereabouts a preaching circuit consisting of many stations over an area of 314 square miles. He died in 1753 and was buried under the floor of his cabin in N.C.

Critical Appraisal: John Thomson's writings fall into two categories, one mainly concerned with Christian education, the other with Presbyterian doctrine. His writings on Christian education exerted a strong influence on the ministry of the early Presbyterian Church in America, but Thomson is most vividly remembered as the great representative of Old Light Presbyterianism in the Philadelphia Synod during the Great Awakening. His pamphlets on the dangers that the New Lights' doctrine and practice posed for the church are not only compelling, but are also relatively calm and sensible. Thomson was one of the few, if not the only, Old Light minister whose criticism of Great Awakening revivalism amounted to more than fierce satire and personal abuse. The New Lights were thus forced to acknowledge him, and when the animosities of the early 1740s ended, Thomson emerged with the respect of both sides.

Thomson's Old Light church politics are most clearly set forth in his tract *The Government of the Church of Christ* (1741). A background against which to understand this significant work is Thomson's *Overture* of 1729, which advocates the adoption of the Westminster Confession and Catechisms on the grounds that uniformity of doctrine protects the church from the errors of ministers who, although well intentioned, are "corrupt in Doctrinals." In Thomson's definition, the church is not merely the sum of individual opinion, but it is a unified body in agreement about doctrine. When the disagreements began in the late 1730s, Thomson became the spokesman for those in the Philadelphia Synod who opposed the Great Awakening, and his *Government of the Church of Christ* has become known as the clearest statement of the antirevivalist position. In the preface, he attacked George Whitefield (q.v.) and referred to him as a "downright Deceiver, or under a dreadful Delusion." In the text, he challenged the "protesting Brethren," especially Samuel Blair (q.v.) and the Tennents, on two particular points—their attack on their fellow clergymen (most notably Gilbert Tennent's [q.v.] infamous Nottingham sermon on unconverted ministers, which was so intemperate that Tennent was later forced to admit it was a mistake) and their refusal to acknowledge the authority of the Presbyterian Church government. The protesting ministers wanted to define the Presbyteries and the Synod as mere advisory boards, whose decisions on matters such as rules governing the movement of itinerant preachers among established parishes were not binding for dissenting ministers. But Thomson insisted that the church government must be granted full authority if it were to be effective at all.

During the revival, Thomson was the spokesman for the Synod on doctrinal as well as political matters. His anonymous *Essay on the Faith of Assurance*, printed by Benjamin Franklin (q.v.) in 1740, is an exposition of the doctrine that although it is a Christian's duty to "make sure Work of his Calling and Conversion," this business should be neither sorrowful nor necessarily attended by revelations or miraculous occurrences, for "an infallible and certain knowledge of our being in a State of Grace . . . is . . . attainable by the true Believer, in this life, in the diligent Use of ordinary Means . . . without immediate Revelation or infallible Inspiration." The *Essay* thus treats a problem central to the Great Awakening, the author's purpose being to give the traditional Calvinist view of assurance, so that the audience might avoid any perversion of the doctrine encountered in the revival. Although Thomson never stated this purpose directly, his intention was clear in the section of the *Essay* dealing with common mistakes about assurance. The fullest and most powerful treatment of these errors appears not in this work, however, but in his 1741 tract *The Doctrine of Convictions*, in which Thomson dropped the pretense of anonymity and oblique references to the revivalists and in his own voice spoke directly to those preachers who in his opinion were guilty of promulgating doctrinal errors. The tract was apparently occasioned by the fact that Thomson was named in Gilbert Tennent's sermon on unconverted ministers. Thomson's preface is given over entirely to dealing with Tennent's sermon and with the problem of "some Ministers taking upon them to judge and condemn their Brethren, as carnal unconverted Men, who cannot nor are desirous to do good to the Souls of others." In the tract proper, after arguing that even "true and Faithful Ministers" are liable to error in interpreting the Scriptures, Thomson gave a full account of the revivalists' errors concerning "the Main and Fundamental Doctrine of Regeneration." Among them are the mistaken notions that before true conversion occurs, "there must be an awakening Conviction of Sin and Misery raised in the Soul"; that the sense of assurance is as clear to the truly converted as any physical sense such as seeing or hearing; that conversion must be accompanied by great inner turmoil or by great emotion, inward or outward; and that although a minister may be called and ordained, even he is not yet converted unless he has received an "inward call." Thomson argued that faith in God is the usual cause of conversion and that remorse for the repentance from sins usually follows rather than precedes conversion. The grace that affects a new convert "is supposed not to be awful and terrible, but sweet, soft and encouraging, like a spiritual Song of Love." If fear, terror, or strong emotion is the prime motivation for a person's conversion, it is likely that he is only reacting to a moment's impulse or under the strong influence of a powerful, emotional sermon. The "work of self-Examination," Thomson noted, is "not only a necessary Work, but also of great difficulty, and wherein Persons are in no small Danger of Mistaking and going Astray." If a person is often unsure of the nature of his own convictions, certainly he cannot claim authority to judge others. The one revivalist tenet that raised Thomson's ire above all was the claim that one converted person could recognize another merely from a short conversation with him. The use of this erroneous doctrine to condemn ministers already examined by the church government and found to be sound in doctrine was, according to Thomson, the work of judgmental hypocrisy. The reason and power of *The Doctrine of Convictions* was so great that by 1749, when the heat of the revival had abated, even Gilbert Tennent could quote from Thomson's book and on the basis of it defend Old Light ministers and argue for repairing the divisions caused by the revival.

Before and after the Great Awakening, Thomson's concern over doctrine led him to write books of instruction aimed primarily at an audience of initiates to Christianity. The anonymous *Poor Orphans Legacy* (printed by Franklin in 1734) is directed to children and was supposedly inspired by the death of Thomson's first wife and by his anxiety over the condition his children would have been left in had he also died. His last book, the influential and popular *Explication of the Shorter Catechism*, again demonstrates his concern for the "new arising Generation" and for the "Weak and Ignorant of more advanced Years." It also shows Thomson's steadfast allegiance to the official doctrines of the Presbyterian Church and his fear that these doctrines were being ignored by those entrusted with the instruction of new converts. In an appendix to the *Explication*, Thomson compared the thirty-nine articles of the Church of England with Presbyterian doctrine and found only a few points of difference. This essay shows that although he was conservative, he was not aggressively combative or radically sectarian. His role in the Great Awakening was thus probably the result of his desire to protect a sound body of doctrine, on which foundation a unified church could be built even in the uncertain setting of the American frontier.

Suggested Readings: CCMC; CCMDG; CCV; Sprague (III, 22). *See also* Richard Beale Davis, *Intellectual Life in the Colonial South, 1585-1763* (1978), pp. 602, 686, 758-759, 784; Wesley M. Gewehr, *The Great Awakening in Virginia, 1740-1790* (1930), pp. 43-45, 62-67; Alan Heimert, *Religion and the American Mind* (1966), pp. 39, 176, 202, 217; Alan Heimert and Perry Miller, eds., *The Great Awakening: Documents Illustrating the Crisis and Its Consequences* (1967), pp. 110-126, 169; John G. Herndon, "The Reverend John Thomson," JPHS, 20 (1942), 116-158; 21 (1943), 34-59; George William Pilcher, *Samuel Davies: Apostle of Dissent in Colonial Virginia* (1971), pp. 32-33; Richard Webster, *A History of the Presbyterian Church in America, from Its Origin Until the Year 1760* (1857), pp. 355-357.

M. Jimmie Killingsworth
New Mexico Institute of Mining and Technology

THOMAS TILLAM (d. after 1668)

Works: "Uppon the First Sight of New-England June 29, 1638" (1638); *The Two Witnesses* (1651); "A Hymn Celebrating the Lord's Sabbath...at Colchester"

(1657); *The Seventh-Day Sabbath* (1757); "The Seventh Angel Sounding" (attributed author, signed T. T.; 1667); "More Verses Concerning the Same Subject" (attributed author, signed T. T.; 1667).

Biography: Little biographical information exists on Thomas Tillam. He was born in Eng., arrived in Mass. in 1638, and then returned to Europe. His religious affiliations were with the Seventh Day Baptist Church, Millenarianism, and Utopianism. While in Eng., he was a pastor in Hexham, Northumberland, and Chichester, Essex. Between 1661 and 1667, Tillam helped establish his followers within a communal monastic society in Heidelberg, Ger. Two religious poems ("Seventh Angel" and "More Verses") attributed to Tillam appear in Samuel Hutchinson's *A Declaration of a Future Glorious Estate* (1667), but the exact connection between the two men is unclear.

Critical Appraisal: Although both poems by "T. T." (attributed to Thomas Tillam) are based on Revelation 20, they are formally different. "The Seventh Angel Sounding" lists fifteen changes that occur on the Day of Doom. Basically iambic pentameter, the lines split into half, and each pair of lines rhymes in the middle and at the end, which forms an interesting and unusual pattern: "The Saints deceased———Royal Jesus brings: / The rest released,———Mount on Angels Wings." The apocalyptic diction of this poem continues in "More Verses Concerning the Same Subject"; however, the latter is arranged in eight quatrains. Although the two poems are not exceptional in style or content, they convey a sense of wonderment that also pervades Tillam's best and only signed poem, "Uppon the First Sight of New-England."

Tillam composed this poem in 1638, one of the great years of immigration to America. But whereas documents like William Bradford's (q.v.) *History of Plymouth Plantation* include the literal as well as the typological, Tillam's lyric attempts "to obliterate the sea experience in a feeling of Holy wonder." The poet's spiritual optimism is evident in his opening lines, "Hayle holy-land wherin our holy lord / Hath planted his most true and holy word / Hayle happye people who have dispossest / Your selves of friends, and meanes, to find some rest," where he chose the cognates "hail" and "holy" five times to emphasize the Pilgrims' religious enterprise. Tillam used enjambement throughout the verses, probably to heighten his hopes for the settlement's continuity and success in overcoming "Sathans wylye baites." Critics have rightly drawn attention to this beautiful twenty-two-line lyric and called it "unmistakably inspired," of "brief lyric intensity," and a "noble expression."

Suggested Readings: FCNEV. *See also* Harrison T. Meserole, ed., *Seventeenth-Century American Poetry* (prints "Upon the First Sight"; 1972), pp. 397-398; William J. Scheick and JoElla Doggett, *Seventeenth-Century American Poetry: A Reference Guide* (1977), p. 158; Roger B. Stein, "Seascape and the American Imagination: The Puritan Seventeenth Century," EAL, 7 (1972), 17-37.

Kathryn Zabelle Derounian
University of Arkansas at Little Rock

HENRY TIMBERLAKE (1730-1765)

Works: *The Memoirs of Lieut. Henry Timberlake* (1765).

Biography: Henry Timberlake was born in Hanover County, Va., in 1730. At his father's death, Timberlake was left with a small estate and apparently engaged in commerce. In 1756 he entered the military service but saw no action in campaigns during 1756, 1758, and 1759. He was an ensign in the regiment of Col. William Byrd III, who marched against the Cherokees in 1761. After peace was made on Nov. 19, Timberlake volunteered to accompany the Cherokees to their country as a demonstration of the crown's good faith. After living with the Cherokees for three months, he accompanied the Cherokee chief Outacity and two other Indians to Eng., where they remained in his charge for several months, exhausting his personal funds. A commission as lieutenant allowed him to return to Va., where he began to recover financially, but he became impoverished once more when, in 1764, he accompanied another group of Cherokees to Eng. Ironically, on both excursions, Timberlake was accused of having made money by "showing" the Indians. To vindicate himself and recover financially, he wrote his *Memoirs* and was in Eng. seeing to its publication when he died on Sept. 30, 1765.

Critical Appraisal: Timberlake's *Memoirs* is a fast-moving narrative told in a straightforward style. His comments on his early life are unfortunately brief. A dislike for anything that might "relish of romance" and the purpose of self-justification for which he wrote made him enter directly into an exposition of the circumstances that had led to accusations against him. In following Timberlake's narrative, the reader gains vivid insights into the dangers of traveling on the eighteenth-century frontier, the life style, manners, and customs of the Cherokees, and Outacity's 1762 sojourn to Eng.

Timberlake's work contradicts established generalizations concerning the stereotyping of Indians in eighteenth-century writing. He tended to view the Cherokees as individuals sometimes driven, for instance, by petty jealousies or rivalries, and he complained of intrusions upon the privacy of the Cherokees in Eng. by the rabble and royalty alike, while chronicling their meetings with persons such as King George, Oliver Goldsmith, and Sir Joshua Reynolds.

The work was translated into German and was reprinted in the first volume of Johann Tobias Köhler's *Sammlung Neuer Reisebeschreibungen* (1767), and it was translated into French by J.B.L.J. Billecocq and published as *Voyages du Lieutenant Henri Timberlake* (1797). His observations of matters such as Cherokee habits, practices, and government are accurate and remain a valuable source for ethnologists. Literary artists have also found the narrative useful. Robert Southey, for example, used it extensively in his epic poem *Madoc* (1805), and American novelist Mary Noailles Murfree drew on it in her works dealing with the Cherokees, particularly *The Story of Old Fort Loudon* (1899).

Suggested Readings: DAB (XIV, 111-112). *See also* Samuel Cole Williams, ed., Introduction and annotations, *Lieut. Henry Timberlake's Memoirs, 1756-1765* (Rep., 1971).

Daniel F. Littlefield, Jr.
Little Rock, Arkansas

JONATHAN TODD (1713-1791)

Works: *The Young People Warned. Or, The Voice of God to the Young People in the Late. . .Judgment of the Throat-Distemper* (1741); *Be Followers* (1743); *The Soldier Waxing Strong* (1747); *A Defence of the Doings of the Reverend Consociation and Association of New Haven County* (1748); *Civil Rulers the Ministers of God, for Good to Men* (1749); *Public Mourning at the Death of Godly, and Useful Men. Two Sermons. . .[on the] Death of the Rev. Nathanael Chauncey* (1756); *A Faithful Narrative, of the Proceedings of the First Society and Church in Wallingford* (1759); *A Reply to the Rev. Mr. Eell's Serious Remarks, upon the Faithful Narrative* (1760); *Judgment and Mercy: Or, Aaron Dead and Lamented, and Eleazaer in His Office. Two Sermons. . .[on the Late] Rev. Mr. Thomas Ruggles* (1770); *The Good Man Useful in Life; Rewarded at Death. Two Sermons. . .[on the Late] Worshipful Capt. Timothy Hill* (1781); *The Peaceful and Happy End of an Useful Life. A Sermon. . .at the Interment of the Rev. Wm. Seaward* (1782); *The Vanity of Expectations from the World, and the Wisdom of Setting Our Hope in God. A Sermon. . .at the Funeral of Mrs. Amanda Redfield* (1783).

Biography: The son of Jonathan and Sarah (Morrison) Todd, Jonathan Todd was born in that part of New Haven now called North Haven, Conn., on Mar. 9, 1713. Little is recorded about either his formative years or his college preparation. A graduate of Yale College (class of 1732) from which he obtained both A.B. and A.M. degrees, Todd studied theology for a time after graduation under the Rev. Daniel Chapman of Fairfield, Conn., and he was subsequently invited in May 1733 to preach as a candidate for the then vacant pulpit in East Guilford (now Madison), Conn. On Aug. 27 he was given a call to settle there. He accepted on Sept. 17 and was ordained over the church on Oct. 24, 1733. For the next fifty-seven years, Todd served the needs of his East Guilford flock, outliving all in his parish who were heads-of-household at the time of his ordination and holding the position of minister longer than any person then alive in Conn. Although during the Great Awakening he was a spokesman for the Old Light camp, in the controversy surrounding the installation of the Rev. James Dana (q.v.) at Wallingford in 1758, he was one of Dana's chief supporters. On that occasion, he published *A Faithful Narrative* (1759) in support of Dana and the proceedings, and in *A Reply* (1760) he answered the charge of irregularity in the Dana proceedings and charges against the independence of churches in local affairs all brought by Edward Eells, son of Nathaniel Eells (q.v.). According to one account published after his death, these activities aroused doubt among Todd's fellow ministers about "whether, properly speaking, [Todd] was a Calvinist." These doubts notwithstanding, Todd continued to hold a privileged position in Conn. for the rest of his life. When Todd died on Feb. 24, 1791, Ezra Stiles (q.v.) praised him as "one of the most learned and pious divines New England ever produced; a great reader, of most vigorous mental powers, strong and penetrating acumen, mild and placid, calm and benevolent." Todd married Elizabeth Couch of Fairfield in 1735; she died in 1783. Although they had no children, Todd was nonetheless concerned about the integrity of his reputation and estate after his death as this statement from his will suggests: "I have long been convinced in my own mind that the enslaving of the Africans . . . is unjust; and it is one of the sins of the land, and I would endeavor to free my estate from the cry of such a sin against it." Accordingly, upon his death, Todd freed and generously endowed all of his slaves.

Critical Appraisal: Jonathan Todd's literary reputation, as the subjects of most of his published work indicate, derives largely from his reputation as a preacher. One midnineteenth-century account credits Todd thus: "As a preacher, he held a highly respectable standing among his brethren." The number of times Todd was called upon to preach at the funerals of fellow ministers testifies to the probable accuracy of this appraisal. In the five printed sermons on deceased ministers as well as in three additional printed funeral sermons, Todd preached to the occasion out of predictable texts, instructing survivors on how by following the affecting example of God's saints they too might live and die well. Whether discussing the life of a minister, military man, or townswoman, Todd invariably told survivors to make their lives useful and fruitful and to be mindful always of God's work and the needs of their fellow man. In a fashion that anticipates the humanitarian bent of religion in the late eighteenth century, Todd argued that only through such a life can one find genuine happiness in this world.

Of Todd's four sermons in print in addition to his funeral sermons, two deserve special attention: *The Young People Warned*, a fast-and-humiliation sermon preached during an epidemic among East Guilford's children in Aug. 1740, and *Civil Rulers the Ministers of God, for Good to Men*, an election sermon preached before the Conn. General Assembly on May 11, 1749. In *The Young People Warned*, Todd assumed the Jeremiah persona popular among late seventeenth- and early eighteenth-century New Eng. preachers and warned the audience that despite the effort of the Awakening, indeed, perhaps because of its apparent failure by 1740 to revive the cause of religion in New Eng., God was displeased to the point of anger with His people. In the sermon, Todd joined forces with ministers like Benjamin Colman (q.v.), Thomas Foxcroft (q.v.), Thomas Prince (q.v.), and John Webb (q.v.), who after the 1720s decided to make a direct appeal to New Eng.'s rising generations in a last effort to stay New Eng.'s backsliding. That God would yet speak to his people through events and that the event in question here was so obviously negative combined in Todd's view to represent hope for New Eng. and a spur to immediate reform.

Civil Rulers the Ministers of God, for Good to Men is noteworthy as an unusually spirited defense of the political and religious bias suggested by its title. In the sermon, Todd argued that the political interests of Conn. are identical to the colony's religious interests, and he asserted that just as a healthy political environment is crucial to the cause of religion, the prosperity of religion is a necessary condition for political prosperity: "Religion *is profitable unto all Things*.... 'Tis profitable to obtain the *Blessing of GOD*, and to promote those *social Vertues* that are the Glory & Strength of a Society." Todd reminded the rulers before him that "All *wise* Governments... have th[ough]t, that it belong'd to them, to take Care of the Cause of Religion," thereby challenging them to do likewise. In this effort, the rulers must be strong, for after reviewing Conn.'s current political and social realities, Todd told the officials that they must now protect the interest of religion by enforcing the sanctity of the Sabbath, raising public payments in support of the clergy, and controlling the rate of inflation in the colony. Echoing the political conviction of New Eng.'s founders, Todd concluded the sermon by stating that upon a "stable [religious] Foundation," a stable society would grow.

Read in conjunction with his printed funeral sermons or by themselves, *The Young People Warned* and *Civil Rulers the Ministers of God* substantiate claims about Todd's lively and inventive mind. Todd's talent as a preacher for days of election or humiliation is equal to any in Conn. during the eighteenth century, and although his political beliefs generally define him as a follower of the old New Eng. Way, his praise of humanitarianism in the funeral sermons shows that he was sensitive to the subtle shifts in religious attitudes during the late eighteenth century.

Suggested Readings: CCNE; Dexter (I, 465-468); Sprague (I, 383-384).

Ronald A. Bosco
State University of New York at Albany

BENJAMIN TOMPSON (1642-1714)

Works: "Gulielmi Tompsoni Braintreensis" (w. 1666); "Remarks on the Bright, and Dark Side of Mr. William Tompson" (1666-1702); "The Grammarians Funeral" (1667-1708); "A FUNERAL TRIBUTE to John Winthrope" (1676); *New Englands Crisis* (1676); *New-Englands Tears* (1676); "UPON the NATIVES" (1677); "John Leverett" (w. 1678-1679); "Mr. Peter Hubbard" (w. 1678); "EDMUND DAVIE" (w. 1682); "HUMPHERY Davie" (w. 1682); "To Lord Bellamont" (w. 1699); "Celeberrimi COTTONI MATHERI, Celebratio" (1702); "Upon the Very Reverend SAMUEL WHITING" (1702); "Fitz-John Winthrop" (w. 1708);

"A Neighbour's TEARS...Mrs. Rebekah Sewall" (1710); "The Translation of Mr. JAMES ALLEN" (1710); "...His Last Lines" (w. 1713).

Biography: Benjamin Tompson, one of America's first native-born poets, was born on Jul. 14, 1642, to William and Abigail Tompson in Braintree, Mass. William Tompson was one of the most zealous of the Puritan patriarchs of the seventeenth century, ministering to the Indians in northern New Eng. and to the Anglicans in Va. and Md. Benjamin, who was raised by the Blanchards of Charlestown, graduated from Harvard College in 1662 and thereafter practiced medicine, taught school, and wrote poetry. He taught in the grammar schools of Boston, Roxbury, Charlestown, and Braintree. His most famous pupil, Cotton Mather (q.v.), admired his Classical learning, mathematical skills, and poetry, including three (perhaps four) of Tompson's poems in the *Magnalia Christi Americana*. Although we possess only the outline of Tompson's life, we do know that he was twice married, often involved in legal disputes with his neighbors, closely associated with influential families like the Winthrops, Sewalls, Mathers, and Davies, and that he exercised his wit and humor on several public occasions. For example, he once dressed as the Simple Cobbler of Aggawam and greeted the new governor, Lord Bellamont, with a pastoral, poetic skit. His gravestone in Roxbury, Mass., lauds him as the "Renouned Poet of New England." He died on Apr. 13, 1714, at the age of 72.

Critical Appraisal: Benjamin Tompson is one of seventeenth-century New Eng.'s more important poets. About thirty separate poems, a fraction of what he probably wrote, survive in early printed and manuscript forms in various libraries and historical societies in the Boston area. Tompson wrote the first volume of American poetry to be reprinted in Eng.; he published prefatory poems in William Hubbard's (q.v.) and Mather's histories; he was the leading actor in a pastoral "play" performed in Boston in 1699; he incorporated the Anglo-Indian language into his work for satirical purposes; and his elegies may be considered as quintessential examples of that popular and important early American genre. Many of his poems are witty, personal and poignant, learned and ornamental, or vivid, graphic, and realistic portraits of life in colonial America.

A reader of Tompson's poetry must realize that we possess only two poems in the poet's own hand. The other, relatively few poems that have survived were transcribed and preserved by members of his family and important colonial families like the Winthrops or the Sewalls, or were deposited in local historical societies by benefactors or antiquarians. Scholars have been unable to locate Benjamin Tompson's journal, diary, commonplace book, or any other personal record of his literary career. But with over 2,000 lines of extant poetry, we can confidently conclude that Tompson was a conscious and dedicated artist whose favorite forms were the elegy and the occasional poem.

Today, his fame rests chiefly on *New Englands Crisis* (1676), a mock-heroic poem on the Narragansett (and Algonkian) Indian war called King Philip's War. The first two parts of *New Englands Crisis* reappeared in London in 1676 as *Sad* and Deplorable NEWES FROM NEW ENGLAND. Later that same year, this apparently pirated text was superseded by another London edition, *New-Englands Tears*, which contained authorial revisions and additions to *New Englands Crisis*. The English and American editions, written in the midst of the war, clearly demonstrate that Tompson rapidly composed and revised, that as a colonial journalist he was reporting to the world New Eng.'s tragic encounter with the forces of evil in the American wilderness. The jeremiadlike theme and the satirical tone, coupled with a graphic realism on the one hand and a mythic perspective on the other, make *New Englands Crisis* one of the most interesting poetic achievements in seventeenth-century Massachusetts Bay. The poet, as an omniscient bard, sang the praises of God's Puritan warriors; mocked the false courage, pretentiousness, and brutishness of the Indian "savages"; and bewailed the sacking and burning of Medfield, Marlbury, Providence, Rehoboth, Chelmsford, and settlements on the outskirts of Boston. In over 600 lines of heroic couplets, Tompson employed traditional colonial American themes to characterize this particular disaster: he saw the war as the result of Puritan greed, generational confusion in the Holy Commonwealth, a supernaturally designed conspiracy to chastise or test, and perhaps to ruin, a backsliding community. Tompson boldly modulated the tone of this "epic" so that he could survey the causes, motives, and responsibility for this tragic contest, but in refusing to predict the outcome of the war, he created and sustained a state of dramatic suspension and immediacy, thereby investing the poem with the power of an eyewitness report from the battlefront.

Particular sections of *New Englands Crisis* have been singled out by scholars as worthy of extended commentary. The mock-epic "set-speech" delivered by the "pagan" commander, King Philip (whose Wampanoag Indian name was Metacomet), has justly been considered an outstanding instance of Tompson's satirical talent and as a representative example of Puritan bigotry and militarism. This short address (lines 111-134) perfectly exemplifies Tompson's double-edged satirical method: through the "greazy *Lout*" Philip, who harangues his serpentlike slaves in American Indian Pidgin English, the poet criticized the Puritans for proselytizing the Indians, stealing their land, meddling with squaws, falling into drunkenness, pursuing materialism—all through the voice of the supposed "savage." In another section, but still using the same method, Tompson chided his masculine Boston neighbors for allowing their tender wives and daughters to begin the work of fortifying, or sandbagging, Boston Neck against a potential invasion by the enemy. Employing a series of extended domestic metaphors for the construction of the bulwark, Tompson laughed at the "Amazonian Dames" who deserted their spinning wheels and kitchens to show the stronger but negligent males how to defend their town. This poem, "On a FORTIFICATION at Boston Begun by Women," is often included in anthologies and critical studies of American humor.

Benjamin Tompson is also recognized today, as he was in his own day, for his skills as an elegiac poet. Generally, his elegies are classified as Baroque, having a complex interweaving of the metaphysical conceit, elaborate and ornate image patterns, exotic diction, and a startling mixture of allusion and reference in the larger context of subtle and shifting philosophical argumentation. Others have seen in his elegies a combination of plainness, characteristic of Puritan writing in general, and genuine feeling and passion, a search for certainty and meaning in this world, and an American mythologizing temperament.

Most remarkable among the elegies are those on his zealot father, William Tompson, and those on important and influential colonial figures. He wrote elegies for John Winthrop, Jr. (q.v.), and Fitz-John Winthrop, the governor and the fellow of the Royal Society, respectively; on ministers James Allen, Samuel Whiting (q.v.), and Peter Hubbard; and most probably the elegy on John Wilson (q.v.) printed in Mather's *Magnalia Christi Americana*. His most unusual tribute is a long, but mainly light-hearted, elegy on Ezekiel Cheever (q.v.), Puritan New Eng.'s most respected and eminent schoolmaster. Two poems addressed to Humphrey Davie on the death in Eng. of his son Edmund, the brilliant Harvard graduate and medical student, contain remarkable examples of the traditional anagram, here "AD Deum Veni," the epistolary form, and the dream-vision soliloquy. In his elegy on Governor John Leverett, Tompson demonstrated his use of almanac material, meteorological and astronomical information, and contemporary military and political strategy. Throughout other elegies, Tompson showed a wide familiarity with Latin and Greek authors, the writings of the church fathers, earlier colonial history, alchemy, anatomy, and geography, as well as the orthodox theological positions held and reinforced throughout the century by the great clerical patriarchs of "the city upon a hill." Many of his private elegies upon family members, although obviously less learned, allusive, and formal, are carefully constructed character sketches of idealized mothers, fathers, brothers, granddaughters, deacons, and pastors—all good, simple, and humble Christians.

A few of Tompson's poems are noticeably innovative in methodology or content, although one could not call them radically different from the standard fare of the time. "Celeberrimi COTTONI MATHERI, Celebratio" boldly satirizes his former pupil but does so in a most genial and cordial manner, neatly mixing a formal Latin tribute with more homely English puns. The address "To Lord Bellamont" transfers the Classical pastoral poem to an American landscape while it proposes that this Garden of Eden is also a place of mirth and pageantry. Tompson's last lines of 1713 present a most unusual view of the Puritan, once the biting satirist and confident announcer of America's special nature, now wracked by infirmity both physical and spiritual.

Suggested Readings: DAB; FCNEV; Sibley-Shipton (II, 103-111); T$_1$. *See also* Neil T. Eckstein, "The Pastoral and the Primitive in Benjamin Tompson's 'Address to Lord Bellamont,'" EAL, 8 (1973), 111-116; Edwin S. Fussell, "Benjamin Tompson, Public Poet," NEQ, 26 (1953), 494-511; Howard Judson Hall, ed., *Benjamin Tompson...His Poems* (1924); Kenneth B. Murdock, ed., *Handkerchiefs from Paul* (1927); Peter White, ed., *Benjamin Tompson, Colonial Bard: A Critical Edition* (1980).

Peter White
The University of New Mexico

EDWARD TOMPSON (1666-1705)

Works: *An Elegiack Tribute to the Reverend and Worthy Seaborn Cotton* (1686).

Biography: Edward Tompson was born in 1666, probably in Mass. He may have been one of the sons of the poet Benjamin Tompson (q.v.) of Braintree. After graduating from Harvard College in 1684, he taught school in Newbury for several years. Then in 1696 he was ordained minister of Marshfield, where he remained until his death in 1705. Two of his sons graduated from Harvard College and became ministers. Tompson's one known published work is an elegy commemorating the 1686 death of Seaborn Cotton, John Cotton's (q.v.) first-born son.

Critical Appraisal: Tompson's elegy appeared in two posthumous editions: one in 1712 and another in 1715. The later editions were published under the revised title *Heaven the Best Country*. In the early eighteenth century, at a time when the Plymouth Separatists and the Massachusetts Bay colonists were in the third or fourth generation and theocracy was on the wane, the alteration in the title, emphasizing elegiac contemplation instead of hagiographical praise, is no surprise. Yet the contents of the subsequent editions remain unchanged.

Although the structure of Tompson's elegy follows the Classic triadic division of lament, praise, and consolation, the narrative voice and the style diverge enough from the norm to merit special attention. Following tradition, Tompson began by identifying himself with the "wailing *Mourners* drove," justifying his grief, and protesting his inadequacy to eulogize. "A *Diapason* of each *Muses* Moan," he wrote, "Is a due Tribute. Yet Griefs passions spent / Are eas'd when broach't, cur'd when they have vent." Immediately, a certain reasoned practicality is sensed and reflected in the use of asyndeton. Like the lines quoted above, the whole elegy is stylistically packed tightly and characterized by a predominance of medial caesuras. Sentences end and colons appear in the middle of stanzaic lines to give a jolting, halting effect, perhaps mirroring the disruptive and disharmonious death of a second-generation son and noted elder. Later in the consolation, the narrator speculates on "What to the COTTONS Stock *N-England* owes."

Having set the mood and tone in the introduction, Tompson subtly wove the idea of the "*heav'n-born* soul" sent to earth in the body into the fabric of his elegy. He cleverly alluded to the circumstances of Seaborn's birth (on the ship en route to America) as "Heav'n sent by *Sea* his *heav'n-born* soul to *shore*" and then bluntly confessed, "I need to *imitate*, but not *praise* / I ever hated flatt'ring of the dead." Well into the praise section, and after enumerating Seaborn's qualities in a curt, anecdotal manner heavy with either asyndeton or medial caesuras such as "*Ears* to the *deaf. Strength* to the *feeble Knee* / A *Mouth* to *dumb. A Churches eye* was hee," the narrator exclaims: "Never had Body such a Soul within" and "What earth does hide, in *heaven* will be *prais'd*." Throughout, Tompson intensified his praise of Seaborn through internal rhyme ("souls *start, smart, feel* to heal") and repetition of the same verb in different tenses ("it may, *must, shall* be se'd"). Then again he would hint at the theme of the soul's preexistence in a style prosaic and unembellished: "Scarce second to an Angel was his Tongue. / I wonder how he tarried here so long." The theme is not original nor is the dichotomy of soul and body, but the force of words cascading in quick succession, "O what a *brood* / His sed'lous *care, love, labour, bred, fed, rais'd!*" and the monosyllabic and frequently rhyming or nearly rhyming words thrown together are reminiscent of Edward Taylor's (q.v.) style in *Preparatory Meditations*, although not as startling or as well wrought. Not unlike Urian Oakes's (q.v.) "An Elegy upon the Death of the Reverend Mr. Thomas Shepard," the lament is full of ominous forebodings and rhetorical prognostications about the future of New Eng. now that a Cotton has departed: "That Worthies leave us to our Overthrow, / These are bad Symptoms of a *future* Blow." Seaborn was a "Guid midst sinful sullen times, / Which are uneven, and won't stand in Rhymes." (The many medial caesuras reflect an unevenness, but Tompson's elegy never deviates significantly from the regular rhyme scheme *ab, ab.*)

Finally, Tompson reassured his audience that although our *"Pillars, Posts, Propps* [are] cut down," there may be some good coming from "COTTONS Stock." The consolation for the most part follows the fertility metaphor derived from the pun on Seaborn's last name. "Tho' earth has Coffin'd up most of the studs, / [Blest] be the Heavens wee have yet some buds" successfully counters the earlier lament "Well may the *earth* grow *wast* when *heav'n* grows" through Seaborn's death. The parallel opposites of body-soul and earth-heaven painfully noticeable with Seaborn's departure from both earth and body are resolved in the consolatory observation: "Heavens waters make them *shoot* / [And] shew the world they come of COTTONS *Root*." Tompson assuaged the fear of ensuing chaos that might have been New Eng.'s *"future* Blow" through the extended fertility metaphor and pun dominating the last section, and at the same time, he effected a harmonious working together of heaven and earth to perpetuate God's chosen people in this Promised Land called New Eng.

Suggested Readings: CCNE; FCNEV; Sibley-Shipton (III, 306-310). *See also Farmer's Register of First Settlers of New-England* (1829), p. 289.

L. A. Norman
University of Cincinnati

SAMUEL TORREY (1632-1707)

Works: *An Exhortation unto Reformation, Amplified, by a Discourse Concerning the Parts and Progress of That Work* (1674); *A Plea for the Life of Dying Religion* (1683); *Man's Extremity, Gods Opportunity* (1695); "Upon the Death of Mr William Tompson" (w. c. 1666; pub. in Kenneth B. Murdock, *Handker-

chiefs from Paul: Being Pious and Consolatory Verses of Puritan Massachusetts, 1927).

Biography: Samuel Torrey was born at Combe St. Nicholas in Eng. in 1632. The son of Capt. William and Jane (Haviland) Torrey, he was brought to New Eng. by his father, who settled in Weymouth, Mass., in 1640. Little is recorded about his formative years or his college preparation. In Nov. 1653 he entered Harvard College, where he remained until 1656, when, in protest against a recent ruling of the Harvard Corporation mandating that students spend four years in preparation for the A.B., he left without taking a degree. Between 1656 and 1666, Torrey preached in the vicinity of Hull. Early in 1666 he was invited to settle as minister of the church of Weymouth, which had been under the care of Thomas Thacher (q.v.). Torrey was ordained over the church on Feb. 14, 1666, thereby formally beginning a distinguished career of service to both church and commonwealth. About this time, he composed his one preserved piece of verse, a memorial to William Tompson, his friend and pastor of the church in nearby Braintree, who died on Mar. 10, 1666. Known throughout the colony as a preacher of uncommon talent and persuasiveness, Torrey was invited to give the Artillery Election Sermon for 1669 and the Mass. election sermons for 1674, 1683, and 1695. The latter honor is testimony to Torrey's pulpit gifts and sterling orthodoxy, for before 1695 only Richard Mather (q.v.) and the eldest John Norton (q.v.) had been asked to appear at the election desk on three occasions. Despite his earlier difficulty with the Harvard Corporation, in 1682 Torrey was unanimously elected president of the college, following the death of President Urian Oakes (q.v.). Although he declined that particular tribute, the extent of his associations and the diversity of his service as recollected by Thomas Prince (q.v.) in the 1750s demonstrate that Torrey continued to play a significant role in the colony's intellectual, political, and religious affairs: "There was . . . a singular Esteem and Intimacy between [Torrey] and Lieut. Governor [William] Stoughton [q.v.], the Honourable Chief Justice Samuel Sewall, Esq [q.v.], the Rev. Mr. Joshua Moodey [q.v.], the Rev. Mr. Vice President [Samuel] Willard [q.v.]." The list goes on, with the level of Torrey's involvement in the affairs of Mass. used to indicate the great loss suffered by all with Torrey's death on Apr. 27, 1707. Married twice, first in 1657 to Mary Rawson, daughter of Edward Rawson, secretary of the colony of Mass., and then in 1695 to Mary Symmes of Charlestown, Torrey, who had no children, was survived by his second wife.

Critical Appraisal: Fifty years after Samuel Torrey's death, Thomas Prince wrote of the preacher: "His. . . Sermons were very scriptural, experimental, pathetical, sensibly flowing from a warm and pious Heart, and with wondrous Freedom and Variety. When he treated on awful Subjects, it was with most awakening Solemnity: but otherwise He usually express'd Himself with the most tender and moving Affection." On the evidence of Torrey's printed work, which with the exception of the single piece of verse consists exclusively of his three election sermons, Prince's estimate requires both qualification and a filtering out of sentiment. Although, in the final analysis, Torrey may have occasionally "express'd Himself with...tender and moving Affection," usually "He treated on awful Subjects," invariably with "awakening Solemnity." Along with Increase Mather (q.v.), William Stoughton, Michael Wigglesworth (q.v.), Samuel Willard, and other principal preachers of the 1670s and 1680s, Torrey was one of the architects of the "orthodox" plan to correct New Eng.'s decline from the piety and ideals of the founders, to rid New Eng. of its increasing sinfulness and backsliding, and to relieve New Eng. of the negative effects of its controversy with God. Speaking as late seventeenth-century Jeremiah figures, Torrey and his colleagues preached the necessity of both New Eng.'s humiliation before God and New Eng.'s reform.

It is likely that Torrey had a hand in formally defining the "sins of the Land" and remedies for the same during the 1679 "Reforming Synod" of New Eng. ministers. The results of that Synod, said to have been collected and written by Increase Mather, appeared in 1679 under the title *The Necessity of Reformation*. Yet as is true of the sermons of many preachers during this period, in *An Exhortation unto Reformation* (1674), Torrey rehearsed the list of New Eng.'s sins that would become a veritable litany of sins by 1679. In his two election sermons published after the Synod, Torrey repeated himself and the findings of his colleagues as he urged his contemporaries to consider how, among other things, their pride, their unnatural affection for this world, and their sensuality threatened to wreck New Eng. as a cooperative venture between God and his newest chosen people.

A Plea for the Life of Dying Religion, the election sermon preached on May 16, 1683, is Torrey's fullest statement on these matters. There he acknowledged that the original purpose for New Eng.'s settlement, namely, the establishment of a "plantation Religious," had been frustrated by "Declension": "nothing [is] more deadly to Religion than declension of Christians, which strikes at the very *heart and life* of it." In this sermon, as in his others, Torrey recited the "errand" myth to remind his audience of its privileged calling, and in typical jeremiad fashion, he pointed accusingly at New Eng.'s backsliding at the same time as he held out the hope that New Eng.'s troubled time was but part of a process whereby God was testing and strengthening his people. He stated,

> We have been Originally a People *seperated and set apart* unto and for
> *Religion*; we have seen as much of the beauty and glory of it, experienced
> as much of the light, life, power, grace and blessing of it, injoyed as much
> tranquility, prosperity, and felicity, in the profession and practice of it,
> as...can be.

"[Although] (we being deeply and generally declined) God may cause us to pass under purging and refining dispensations," Torrey told his audience, "believe and pray" that "God will keep Religion alive with us," lest "it be totally extinguished in these ends of the Earth."

Like most members of his generation, Torrey was confident that religion and God's plan as conceived by the founders could and would be revived in New

Eng. Later generations of New Eng. clergymen would have to deal with the reality that, at least in Puritan terms, such confidence was misplaced. But that fact does not diminish the significance of Torrey's sermons as gifted expressions of ideas and issues central to the Puritan cause in late seventeenth-century New Eng.

Suggested Readings: CCNE; FCNEV; Sibley-Shipton (I, 564-567). *See also* Kenneth B. Murdock, Editor's Introduction, *Handkerchiefs from Paul* (1927); Thomas Prince, Preface, *A Brief Discourse Concerning Futurities*, by William Torrey (1757).

Ronald A. Bosco
State University of New York at Albany

HARRY TOULMIN (1766-1823)

Works: *A Description of Kentucky* (1792); *Thoughts on Emigration...and a Short Account of the State of Kentucky* (1792); *A Short View of the Life of...John Mort* (1793); *The Western Country in 1793: Reports on Kentucky and Virginia* (w. 1793-1794; pub. 1948); *A Collection of All of the Permanent and Public Acts of the General Assembly of Kentucky* (1802); *A Summary of the Criminal Law of Kentucky* (1802); *An Oration* (1802); *Review of the Criminal Law of the Commonwealth of Kentucky*, 3 vols. (with James Blair; 1804-1806); *The American Attorney's Pocket Book* (1806); *The Magistrates' Assistant* (1807); *The Statutes of the Mississippi Territory* (1807); *A Digest of the Territorial Laws of Alabama* (1823).

Biography: Harry Toulmin was born in Eng. on Apr. 7, 1766. His father was a minister and his mother a bookseller. Largely self-educated, Toulmin became a minister and aroused some opposition with his Unitarian doctrines. Fascinated by accounts of the U.S., particularly the western country, Toulmin emigrated in 1793 with Joseph Priestley. His mission was to examine American prospects for members of his congregation, to whom he sent several reports. When Toulmin reached Ky., he had letters of introduction from Thomas Jefferson (q.v.) and James Madison (q.v.), and in 1794 he was elected president of Transylvania Seminary. From 1796 to 1804, he was Ky.'s secretary of state, which apparently interested him in compiling state laws. Appointed superior court judge in the Mississippi Territory, he played an active role in that region's political affairs. In 1819 he was a prominent member of the convention that drafted a state constitution for Ala., where he died on Mar. 11, 1823.

Critical Appraisal: Although there is some doubt about his participation, Harry Toulmin was the probable editor and compiler of *Thoughts on Emigration* and *A Description of Kentucky* in 1792, the year before he left Eng. Attributing excerpts to his sources, he added some comments of his own. The works are useful in describing the contemporary arguments for and against emigration and in showing what knowledge Englishmen then had of the U.S. in general and the

Ky. area in particular. But the first-hand accounts edited from his journals, reports, and letters by Marion Tinling and Godfrey Davies as *The Western Country in 1793: Reports on Kentucky and Virginia,* are more interesting than Toulmin's own edited works. He was a careful observer who sought additional information from knowledgeable inhabitants, and his account is one of the best sources available on Ky. and Va. in the 1790s. Well educated and well read, Toulmin wrote in a plain, straightforward style that reads much better than most nineteenth-century prose.

During his Ky. years, Toulmin recognized the need for compiled acts of the state legislature, and his work in that area was invaluable to the legal profession in Ky. and, later, in the territories of Miss. and Ala. He also recognized that poorly trained attorneys and magistrates needed help, and he wrote two handbooks, *The American Attorney's Pocket Book* and *The Magistrates' Assistant,* which must have been consulted frequently by grateful lawyers.

Suggested Readings: DAB. *See also* Thomas D. Clark, ed., *A Description of Kentucky* (1945); Willard Rouse Jillson, *A Transylvania Trilogy* (1932); N. H. Sonne, *Liberal Kentucky* (1939); Marion Tinling and Godfrey Davies, eds., *The Western Country in 1793* (1948).

Lowell H. Harrison
Western Kentucky University

JONATHAN TOWNSEND (1697-1762)

Works: "To the Reader" (with others; pub. in Daniel Baker, *Two Sermons*; 1728); *An Exhortation* (1729); *Comfort for the Afflicted* (1738); *God's Terrible Doings* (1746); *Ministers, and Other Christians* (1758).

Biography: Son of a prosperous tenant farmer, Jonathan Townsend was born on Dec. 30, 1697, probably in Boston, Mass., where his birth was recorded. He graduated with the Harvard class of 1715 and later earned an M.A. After preaching at Lynn and Nantucket in 1717-1719, Townsend was invited to become the first minister of the Congregational Church in Needham, Mass. On May 26, 1720, he married Mary Sugars, daughter of Capt. Gregory Sugars, whose fleet was sent against Can. during King William's War (1690). Although not active in any military campaigns, Townsend participated in many good causes: speaking on behalf of the unpopular Scotch-Irish, helping Thomas Prince (q.v.) publish his *Chronological History,* supporting the missionary efforts of Joshua Cotton in R.I., and engaging in missionary work in Mass.

For over twenty-five years, Townsend apparently had a harmonious relationship with his parishioners; however, in 1746 some of them seceded to form a New Light Church, because they objected to his style of preaching. This secession aggravated Townsend's already shaky financial position. Finally, at a town meeting in 1754, Townsend threatened to resign if his past wages, often based on depreciated paper money, were not repaid. Although the meeting supported Townsend's request, its decision was challenged. The matter was still being litigated in 1758, when Townsend delivered a sermon at the annual ministerial convention in Boston and used the occasion to remind the laity to support ministers. He died after a long illness on Sept. 30, 1762.

Critical Appraisal: Known for his "dignified and orthodox preaching," Jonathan Townsend generally reflected traditional Puritan beliefs in his sermons. As he stated in his preface to *An Exhortation*, a collection of two sermons, "The reader will find nothing curious in the Subsequent Discourses but only plain practical truths deliver'd mostly in the Scripture-Language which gives...life, beauty, and solemnity to the Diction." His first three sermons are lucid explanations of the Puritan cosmology. Each sermon focuses upon a contemporary event: the storm of Sept. 16, 1727; the drowning of two youths; the death by lightning of a young man. Furthermore, in each discourse, Townsend proclaimed that the respective event reveals God's displeasure with his people and admonished them to change their ways, since Townsend's God is not one "to be jested with" or to "be mocked" (1746).

More significant historically is his final sermon, *Ministers, and Other Christians*, which can be compared with Peter Thacher's (q.v.) *Observations upon the Present State of the Clergy* (1783). Both works discuss the often difficult lives of the New Eng. clergy and the duty of congregations to support them. Townsend's sermon, delivered before the annual ministerial convention in Boston, apparently was inspired by the problems he had with the Needham congregation concerning his salary. Unlike Thacher's impassioned attack, Townsend's sermon is tactful (perhaps surprisingly so considering the difficulties he was facing). Composing a balanced discourse, Townsend outlined six ways, respectively, that the clergy and "private Christians" can work together and among themselves to propagate the Gospel. His remarks to his fellow ministers offer further evidence that the Congregational pastors were certainly not a unified group, for he reminded them that they must advise, encourage, and support each other, especially if they are innocent victims of gossip. When addressing the "private Christians," he mentioned certain problems that must be solved before they can participate fully in the clergy's "great work": lay interference in ecclesiastical affairs and failure to attend religious services. Townsend's final remark to the laity may refer implicitly to his financial straits; he stated that "private Christians" can advance the work of the clergy by contributing money and especially books, since "Ministers ordinarily are not able to do much in this way at their own charge." In general, this well-organized and developed sermon illuminates the significant problems facing the Congregational clergy in the eighteenth century.

Suggested Readings: CCNE; Sibley-Shipton (VI, 150-153).

Susan A. Leazer
Illinois State University

NICHOLAS TROTT (1663-1740)

Works: *Clavis Linguae Sanctae* (1719); *The Tryals of Major Stede Bonnet* (1719); *The Laws of the British Plantations* (1721); *The Laws of the Province of South Carolina* (1736); "Eight Charges" (Ms., n.d.).

Biography: Nicholas Trott was born in London, Eng., in 1663 into a family of colonial promoters and officials. His grandfather Perient was husband of the Somers Island Company in Bermuda, and his uncle Nicholas, a notorious pirate harborer with whom he is occasionally confused, was a governor of the Bahamas. His father, Nicholas Trott, was a London merchant. Educated at Merchant Taylor's School and the Inner Temple, Trott became attorney general of Bermuda and in 1699 went to Charleston, S.C., as attorney general. Trott was appointed chief justice of the colony in 1703 and vice admiralty judge in 1716, but the overthrow of proprietary government in 1719 put an end to his judicial career. He was twice married, first to Jane Willis of Bermuda and after her death to Sarah Rhett. A devout High-Church Anglican, he was an early and faithful member of the Society for the Propagation of the Gospel. He was honored with a doctor of civil law degree from Oxford in 1720 and a doctor of laws from the University of Aberdeen in 1726. Trott spent the remainder of his life in Charleston, working on a Hebrew lexicon of which no trace remains, until his death there in 1740.

Critical Appraisal: Trott has been accurately called "the ablest known essayist of the period before 1764 in South Carolina." His essays, in the form of grand jury charges, were expositions of jurisprudence for the instruction and inspiration of grand jurors and ultimately legal-philosophic essays. They are principally found in a collection, "Eight Charges," that also includes a sentencing speech. The subject matter of the charges is conventional, even formulaic, but his treatment of it is not. His separate charges examine the nature and origin of law, its necessity and usefulness, the happiness of living under law, the obligation to obey civil laws, the nature and obligation of oaths, the grand juror's oath, the excellency and reasonableness of the laws of Eng., and an exhortation to enforce these laws against offenders. The most interesting feature of the "Eight Charges" is an elaborate charge on colonial witchcraft law, including a vindication of belief in witches that Dr. Thomas Cooper (q.v.), a legal scholar and friend of Thomas Jefferson (q.v.), called "undoubtedly the most learned and elaborate defense of the existence of witchcraft as a crime, that I have had an opportunity of perusing."

Trott's most widely known literary effort is his account of *The Tryals of Major Stede Bonnet* (1719), including Trott's moving speech sentencing Bonnet to be hanged, which was incorporated verbatim by Daniel Defoe into his immensely popular *A General History of the Robberies and Murders of the Most Notorious Pyrates* (1724).

Although his other writings, two collections of colonial laws and his lexicon of the Psalms, are practical works of scant literary merit, they reflect Trott's erudition and scholarship. His "Charges" demonstrates "his literary gift of lucid, learned, and lively prose," entitling him to be numbered among the first rank of colonial writers with men like Increase Mather (q.v.), whom he quoted, and Judge Samuel Sewall (q.v.).

Suggested Readings: DAB. *See also* Randall Bridwell, "Mr. Nicholas Trott and the South Carolina Vice Admiralty Court: An Essay on Precedural Reform and Colonial Politics," SCLR, 28 (1976), 181-217; Richard Beale Davis, *Intellectual Life in the Colonial South, 1585-1763* (1978), pp. 586-587, 661-662, 1455-1456, 1605, 1622-1623; L. Lynn Hogue, "An Edition of 'Eight Charges Delivered, at So Many General Sessions, & Goal Deliveries: Held at Charles Town. . .1703. . .1707 by Nicholas Trott, Esq; Chief Justice of the Province of South Carolina'" (Ph.D. diss., Univ. of Tenn., 1972); idem, "Nicholas Trott: Man of Law and Letters," SCHM, 76 (1975), 25-34; idem, "The Sources of Trott's Grand Jury Charges" in *South Carolina Legal History*, ed. Herbert A. Johnson (1980), pp. 23-37.

L. Lynn Hogue
Georgia State University at Atlanta

BENJAMIN TRUMBULL (1735-1820)

Works: *A Letter to an Honourable Gentleman of the Council Board* (1766); *A Discourse, Delivered at the Anniversary Meeting* (1773); *A Plea, in Vindication of the Connecticut Title to the Contested Lands Lying West of New York*, 2 eds. (1774); *Illustrations on the Counsel of God* (1783); *God Is to Be Praised for the Glory*, 2 eds. (1784); *An Appeal to the Public with Respect to the Unlawfulness of Divorces* (1788; rep. and abridged, 1789); *A Sermon, Delivered at the Ordination of Thomas Holt* (1790); *Illustrations on the Nature* (1791); *A Sermon, Delivered at the Installation of Alexander Gillet* (1793); *A Sermon, Delivered at the Ordination of Lemuel Tyler* (1793); *A Sermon, Delivered at the Ordination of Reuben Moss* (1793); *A Sermon, Delivered at the Ordination of Aaron Woodward* (1794); *Charge for the Ordination of Bezaleel Pinneo* (1796); *Proposals for Publishing by Subscription a Complete History of Connecticut* (1796); *A Complete History of Connecticut from 1630 to 1713* (1797); *Address of the General Association* (1798); *Twelve Discourses on the Divine Origin of the Holy Scriptures* (1799); *Funeral Discourse on the Death of General George Washington* (1800); *A Century Sermon or Sketches of the History of the Eighteenth Century Interspersed and Closed with Serious Remarks* (1801); *The Dignity of Man* (1801); *An Address on Prayer and Family Religion* (1804); *An Appeal to the Public on the Unlawfulness of Marrying a Wife's Sister* (two parts; 1810); *A General History of the United States, 1492-1792* (only vol. I to 1765 completed; 1810); *A Treatise on Covenanting with God* (1810); *A Sermon, on the Death of Rev. Noah Williston* (1812); *A Complete History of Connecticut to the Year*

1764 (1818; rep., 1898); "A Compendium of the Indian Wars in New England" (unpublished ms. of 1767 edited by Frederick Berg Hartranft; 1924).

Biography: Benjamin Trumbull was born on Dec. 19, 1735, in Hebron, Conn., a state to which he devoted much of his preaching and historical writings. He graduated from Yale University in 1759 and took his theological studies with Rev. Eleazar Wheelock (q.v.). On May 21, 1760, he was licensed to preach, and in Dec. of that year, he began as pastor of the Congregational Church of North Haven. Also in Dec. he married Martha Tillotson Phelps, with whom he had seven children. As a result of his contributions to the Congregational Church, where he preached throughout his life, Yale awarded Trumbull the degree of doctor of divinity in 1796.

Many of Trumbull's critics believe that his success as a preacher resulted from his popularity as patriot and historian. He interrupted his preachings at North Haven to serve as chaplain for Gen. Wooster's regiment in the Revolutionary War; he also captained a company of sixty volunteers. After the war, while still preaching, he began *A History of Connecticut* at the request of his family and spent twenty years compiling it. Upon completing *A History of Connecticut*, he began a general history of the U.S. but died on Feb. 2, 1820, after finishing only one of the projected three volumes.

Critical Appraisal: Benjamin Trumbull's contribution to American letters rests primarily with his two major histories: *A History of Connecticut* and *A General History of the United States*. Both of these books present accurate historical accounts, colored by the Puritan belief in the manifestation of God's work in history. Trumbull's knowledge and respect of history also emerge in his other writings: political tracts, letters, and sermons.

A History of Connecticut and *A General History*, written from the annals of Conn. and the other colonies, are representative pieces from the beginning and end of Trumbull's career as an historian. Trumbull undertook the writing of *A History of Connecticut* in 1777 at the request of his father's first cousin, Governor Jonathan Trumbull, and twenty years later, he completed the *History* up to 1713; in 1818 he again published the *History*, updating it to 1764. Trumbull's love of state and devotion to religious principles lend a romantic quality to a book that is an otherwise accurate historical account of the state of Conn. The *History's* purpose, Trumbull wrote in the introduction, is to instruct the readers of the present about the past; he achieved this through biographies of prominent religious and political personages and lesser known colonial founders and accounts of important discoveries, struggles, and political developments. Underlying the historical account is the growth of the American character as one consistently in search of self-improvement and righteously upholding religious and civil liberties.

A General History is an accurate historical account that exhibits little of the nostalgia that makes *A History of Connecticut* a period piece that captures the growth of the American character. *A General History* begins with the discovery of America in 1492 and a geographic description of the land; it progresses through colonization and some of the conflicts with Br. Although Trumbull completed only one of the projected three volumes before his death, *A General History*, like *A History of Connecticut*, served as a valuable source of historical information through the nineteenth century.

The remainder of Trumbull's writing includes sermons, theological treatises, political statements in letters and pamphlets, and an unpublished history of the Indian Wars, excerpts of which were published in 1924. The sermons and theological treatises were written in the Puritan tradition, that is, emphasizing the importance of leading a conservative, religious life; the political statements are laden with religious and historical commentary. The most influential of these lesser works was *Plea in Vindication*, a political pamphlet; there Trumbull sustained the claim of Conn. to the Susquehanna purchase. Through the pamphlet, Trumbull succeeded in persuading Congress of the validity of the state's claim.

Trumbull's political statements are persuasive and indicative of his devotion to his state. His religious statements reflect a man well learned in the Puritan philosophy of life. But his histories, particularly *A History of Connecticut*, remain his main contribution to American letters; the book is an accurate, industrious account of a state to which his ancestors and descendants dedicated much of their lives; it is also a chronicle of the growth of the American character.

Suggested Readings: CCNE; DAB; Dexter (II, 621-627); Sprague (I, 584-590); T$_2$. *See also* CS, 2 (Mar. 1820), 113-119; H. P. Johnston, *Yale and Her Honor Role in the American Revolution* (1888), pp. 222-223; J. H. Lea, *Contributions to a Trumbull Genealogy* (1895); PMHS, 17 (1880), 138-139; S. B. Thorpe, *North Haven Annals* (1892), pp. 184-222, 244-248; Benjamin Trumbull, Introduction, *A Complete History of Connecticut to the Year 1764* (1898).

Donna Casella Kern
Michigan State University

JOHN TRUMBULL (1750-1831)

Works: "The Meddler," *Boston Chronicle*, 10 numbers (Sept. 7, 1769-Jan. 22, 1770); "The Correspondent," *Connecticut Journal*, nos. 1-8 (Feb. 23-Jul. 6, 1770); nos. 9-38 (Feb. 12-Sept. 3, 1773); *An Essay on the Use and Advantages of the Fine Arts* (1770); *An Elegy, on the Death of Mr. Buckingham St. John* (1771); *The Progress of Dulness* (1772, 1773); *M'Fingal* (1775, 1782); *The Poetical Works of John Trumbull* (1820).

Biography: John Trumbull was born in 1750 at Westbury, Conn., the son of a Congregational minister. He entered Yale College in 1763 and spent eight of the next ten years there. Toward the end of this time, he began to write Hudibrastic poetry and Addisonian essays. Rather than follow his father into the ministry, he moved to Boston in 1773 and studied law under John Adams (q.v.), an association that helped precipitate his most famous poem, *M'Fingal*. Settling down at

Hartford in 1781, he practiced law and became a strong Federalist, a fact apparent in his collaboration with other Connecticut Wits on *The Anarchiad* (1786-1787).Abandoning letters, between 1789 and 1819, he held public office as state's attorney for the county of Hartford, twice as a member of the state legislature, and as judge of the Superior Court of Conn. and the Supreme Court of Errors. The appearance of his *Poetical Works* in 1820 reminded the world that before he became a successful lawyer and jurist, John Trumbull had been a man of letters. He spent the last six years of his life in Detroit, dying there in 1831.

Critical Appraisal: Always a religious and political moderate, in the field of letters John Trumbull pushed beyond the limits of his formal education, which was heavily Classical and theological, to become a burlesque poet and, what is not so well known, a periodical essayist. He launched his literary career in both genres while still at New Haven, recalling in after years that when he attended Yale College in the 1760s, "English poetry and the belles-lettres were called folly, nonsense and an idle waste of time." "Epithalamion Stephani et Hannae" (1769) was a sometimes bawdy travesty occasioned by the wedding of the Yale tutor Stephen Mix Mitchell to Hannah Grant. More ambitious and certainly far better known was the long Hudibrastic poem of a few years later, *The Progress of Dulness*. Beginning as a staunch critic of college and church, Trumbull wrote the first part, "The Rare Adventures of Tom Brainless," to point out "those general errors, that hinder the advantages of education, and the growth of piety." Attacked for having written "a satire upon Yale College and the ten commandments," he shifted the emphasis in the second and third parts of the poem, exposing two conventional eighteenth-century types, the fop (Dick Hairbrain) and the coquette (Harriet Simper). *The Progress of Dulness*, although scarcely the equal of *The Rape of the Lock*, stands forth as one of the most skillful social satires of the century.

Concurrent with these early poetic efforts, Trumbull ventured into the essay serial for the only time in his career. Among the literary exercises he engaged in to stimulate an interest in belles-lettres while a graduate student and a tutor at Yale were *The Meddler* and *The Correspondent*. At a time when most American writers were participating in the Revolutionary debate, Trumbull avoided politics as steadily as Addison's Spectator. *The Meddler*, although frequently clumsy and amateurish in execution, depicts the ever-popular coquette and fop, castigates false wit, and satirizes trifling projectors in a manner reminiscent of Swift. *The Correspondent*, a more ambitious serial, moves beyond well-worn topics such as dunces and medical quacks to others less expected, notably an attack in the eighth number on slavery at a time when almost the only antislavery advocates in America were Quakers.

The work that won Trumbull the position of leader of the Connecticut Wits and secured him a permanent if secondary place in American literary history is *M'Fingal*. Undertaken in 1775 as a satirical attack on Thomas Gage, military governor of Mass., this poem when finally completed seven years later became, in Alexander Cowie's words, "the most popular American poem of its length before Longfellow's *Evangeline*." Squire M'Fingal, a New Eng. Tory double-dyed, is twice bested by the Whigs, first in extended debate with Honorius in a town meeting and then in armed combat before the Liberty Pole. Like his literary ancestor Hudibras, M'Fingal is quarrelsome, boastful, stubborn, one who would bully his opponent into submission in meeting or on the field of battle but never quite succeeds in doing either. *M'Fingal* towers above all other Hudibrastic poems written in America in largeness of design, artistic control, and invention.

Trumbull the lawyer and jurist regarded his literary career as an avocation, and perhaps it was just as well. Although he possessed ability as a burlesque poet and periodical essayist, these genres make fewer demands on the writer than, say, the epic or fiction or drama. He came closer to mastery in poetry than in prose. The Meddler and the Correspondent are thin disguises assumed by a young man who was unable, or perhaps unwilling, to put sufficient dramatic distance between himself and the reader. In *The Progress of Dulness* and *M'Fingal*, however, Trumbull achieved greater success than other American writers in the Hudibrastic tradition such as Ebenezer Cooke (q.v.), Philip Freneau (q.v.), Jacob Bailey (q.v.), and Hugh Henry Brackenridge (q.v.), displaying skill in the use of epic and romantic conventions, ingenious rhyming, sharp characterization, comic narrative, and an inexhaustible variety of low-burlesque comparisons.

Suggested Readings: DAB; LHUS; T_2. See also Edwin T. Bowden, ed., *The Satiric Poems of John Trumbull* (1962); Alexander Cowie, *John Trumbull: Connecticut Wit* (1936); Victor E. Gimmestad, *John Trumbull* (1974); Bruce Granger, *American Essay Serials from Franklin to Irving* (1978), pp. 97-115; idem, "John Trumbull and Religion," AL, 23 (1951), 57-79; Leon Howard, *The Connecticut Wits* (1943), pp. 37-78.

Bruce Granger
The University of Oklahoma

NATHANIEL TUCKER (1750-1807)

Works: *The Bermudian* (1775); *The Anchoret* (1776); *Columbinus* (1974).

Biography: Born in Bermuda of a family long prominent in island affairs, Nathaniel Tucker came to Charleston in 1771 to prepare himself for a career in medicine under the tutelage of his older brother, Thomas Tudor Tucker, who had settled in S.C. as a physician after study in Edinburgh. Nathaniel Tucker had been apparently working for some time on a poem about his native island, called *The Bermudian*. He hoped that its publication and sale would provide money for his own medical training abroad. With that in mind, he sent copies of the manuscript to his brother St. George Tucker (q.v.), then a student at the College of William and Mary in Williamsburg, Va., and another copy to friends in Edinburgh. The poem appeared in both places in 1775, with no spectacular financial or critical success. Undaunted, Nathaniel went abroad for study, first at Edinburgh and then at Leiden, publishing meanwhile in 1776 in the former city a second, equally unsuccessful long poem called *The Anchoret*. On receiving his medical degree in 1777, he lived briefly in London, where, attracted by the theater, he apparently tried his hand at playwriting. Among his manuscript remains is a drama, *The Queen of Jewry*, said to have been, then or later, "refused by the managers of both playhouses" there. Settling in 1779 as a physician at Malden in Yorkshire, he felt himself an alien, he said, in a strange land. He envied his brothers who could actively participate in the struggle of the American colonies for independence. He wanted to contribute his own patriotic share. So he set to work on an epic poem that he planned to call *America Delivered* and sent copies of what he wrote to St. George in Va. and to relatives in Bermuda. Persuaded by their criticism that it was too imitative of Milton, he set it aside and wrote a masque called *Columbinus*, an allegory of the triumph of the colonies over tyranny. In 1784 he sent the manuscript to his brother in Va., expressing hope that it would be accepted by the Congress of the new U.S. as an official dramatic poem, to be performed annually on every Fourth of July. It was not, nor was it printed until 1974 and then as a curious relic of good intentions. In 1786 Tucker moved to Hull, where he spent the rest of his life in desultory practice of medicine, fathered seven children, and translated volumes of Swedenborg on *Divine Wisdom* (1788), *Divine Providence* (1790), and *The Apocalypse Revealed* (1791). After his death on Dec. 3, 1807, a new edition of *The Bermudian* was issued for the benefit of his grieving and impoverished widow.

Critical Appraisal: Nathaniel Tucker—"Poor Natty," his brothers called him—followed a literary path paved with good intentions. He wanted almost more than anything "to turn author," he said, "and live in a garret," but time and talent both ran out. He published occasionally in periodicals in America and in Eng., but much of his literary work lies in manuscript in the Tucker-Coleman Collection at the College of William and Mary at Williamsburg, largely unnoticed. In idea and expression, he can be thought of as a weathercock turning successively with each breeze of influence that disturbed the times in which he wrote. In the 1770s he followed paths laid out by Goldsmith and Gray, in regularized couplet and in the spirit of humane rationalism derived from Pope. In the 1780s he found Milton and Shakespeare better models for the expression of expanding freedoms promised by that Revolutionary decade. By the 1790s he was drawn to the Transcendental revelations of Swedenborg and translated them into editions read by William Blake, Samuel Taylor Coleridge, and other forward-looking people. But Tucker's gaze was most often on scenes left behind. His *The Bermudian* is a homesick pastoral, important principally because unique. *Columbinus*, certainly among the first written long poems to celebrate American independence, is a curious blend of nostalgia and deft adaption of scenes and rhythms derived from better poems. Only by desire an American, Nathaniel Tucker is, at best, an honorary inhabitant of whatever Pantheon is erected for her early writers.

Suggested Readings: LHUS. *See also* Lewis Leary, *The Literary Life of Nathaniel Tucker* (1951).

Lewis Leary
The University of North Carolina at Chapel Hill

ST. GEORGE TUCKER (1752-1827)

Works: *The Knight and the Friars: An Historical Tale* (1786); *Reflections on the Policy and Necessity of Encouraging the Commerce...of the United States* (1786); *Liberty: A Poem on the Independence of America* (1788); *Cautionary Hints to Congress Respecting the Sale of the Western Lands* (1795); *A Letter to the Reverend Jedediah Morse* (1795); *Dissertation on Slavery: With a Proposal for the Gradual Abolition of It, in the State of Virginia* (1796); *Probationary Odes of Jonathan Pindar, Esq.* (1796); *Remarks on the Treaty of Amity, Navigation and Commerce* (1796); *A Letter to a Member of Congress* (1799); *A Letter to a Member of the General Assembly of Virginia, on the Subject of the Late Conspiracy of Slaves; with a Proposal for Their Colonization* (1801); *Blackstone's Commentaries: With Notes of Reference, to the Constitution and Laws, of the Federal Government of the United States; and of the Commonwealth of Virginia*, 5 vols. (1803); William S. Prince, ed., *Poems of St. George Tucker of Williamsburg, Va., 1752-1827* (1977).

Biography: St. George Tucker was born Jun. 29, 1752, in Port Royal, Bermuda, and lived there with his parents, Henry and Anne Butterfield Tucker, until his late teens, when he immigrated to Va. There he attended William and Mary College, from which he graduated in 1772. Two years later, he was admitted to the bar and began practicing law in Williamsburg. During the Revolutionary War, he served with the Va. militia, fighting with conspicuous bravery at the battle of Guilford Court House and later at Yorktown, where he was wounded. Having attained the rank of colonel by the end of the war, he then returned to Va. In 1778 he married Frances Bland Randolph, widow of John Randolph. In 1791, three years after the death of his first wife, he married another prominent Virginian, Lelia Skipworth Carter.

Tucker's age was a political age, particularly in Va., where he spent most of his adult life. Like his age, Tucker focused his attention on law, politics, and public affairs. He served as a judge on the General Court of Va., as a professor of law at William and Mary, as a judge on the Va. Court of Appeals, and by appointment of President James Madison (q.v.), as a judge on the federal District Court of Va. In 1825 he retired from public life to a quiet life in Nelson County, Va., where he died on Nov. 10, 1827.

Critical Appraisal: Although the political context in which St. George Tucker lived valued pamphlets and condoned satire, it put limited stock in poetry and drama. Asked by a younger man whether being known as a writer might not damage his reputation as a lawyer, Tucker replied that indeed it might. Although there is no evidence to suggest that Tucker's reputation suffered from his publication of *Liberty, Probationary Odes*, or the "occasional" poems he contributed to periodicals, there is clear evidence that his published writings, like his life, concerned politics, law, and public affairs and clear evidence, too, that during his lifetime, his reputation owed far more to his public letters, essays, and tracts than to his poetry. His redaction of *Blackstone's Commentaries* became one of the most important and influential legal works of his time; his *Dissertation on Slavery*, which advocated gradual emancipation through the freeing of all children born to slave mothers, was widely read and discussed, as were other of his letters and proposals.

In addition, however, Tucker published minor poetry of considerable charm. His *Probationary Odes*, first published in the *National Gazette* and often mistakenly attributed to the more famous Philip Freneau (q.v.), won him readers, if not acclaim. "Liberty, a Poem on the Independence of America" (1788) was also popular. The more Romantic "Days of My Youth, Ye Have Glided Away" not only attracted readers but kept them; several times anthologized, this simple lyric did more than any other single work to keep Tucker's reputation as a minor poet alive. Tucker left unpublished, however, a surprisingly large number of poems, plays, and essays, and they have begun to stimulate new interest in him. Although full-scale appraisal of his achievement must await further publication of his works, it is clear, primarily as a result of William S. Prince's *The Poems of St. George Tucker of Williamsburg, Va., 1752-1827* (1977), that Tucker's writings are more varied and accomplished than had long been assumed.

Suggested Readings: DAB; LHUS; T₂. *See also* Lewis Leary, "St. George Tucker" in *Southern Writers: A Bibliographical Dictionary*, ed. Robert Bain et al. (1979), pp. 465-466.

David Minter
Emory University

HENRY TUFTS (1748-1831)

Works: *A Narrative of the Life, Adventures, Travels and Sufferings of Henry Tufts* (1807).

Biography: Henry Tufts was born in New Market, N.H., on Jun. 24, 1748, into what has been described as a New Eng. Brahmin family. His grandfather was a highly respected Boston clergyman. His father was a tailor remembered for leading a "blameless life." His mother, however, was described as "an old witch woman." Tufts did not attribute what he confessed to be his "depraved disposition" to his mother and described his early years as being perfectly innocent. But after one unfortunate incident involving currency belonging to a neighbor, he acquired the reputation of a thief and rascal. Unable and somewhat unwilling to escape such a designation in his rural society, he accepted his predestination and practiced his vocation with much zeal. His career lasted forty years and covered the territory from Maine to Va. Always individualistic and opportunistic, and invariably riding a stolen horse, he wandered from town to town (or was chased) looking for ways to turn a fast dollar, often choosing to pose as either a doctor, preacher, or fortune-teller. He variously accepted the roles of a devout family man, lecher, soldier, deserter, jailbreaker, counterfeiter, and smuggler. After nearly being executed in 1795, he retired to Maine, where, with the help of a ghostwriter, he set down his life story. He died at the age of 83 in 1831, a respected member of his town.

Critical Appraisal: Although Henry Tufts had little redeeming value in his own life, his value today is manifest. In spite of the fact that the printer's shop mysteriously burned down a year or so after publication, in spite of the fact that persons by the name of Tufts purchased copies of the book and destroyed them, and in spite of the fact that certain writers of genteel New Eng. history attacked the "detestable" book without bothering to read it, the book has survived, although barely. As a result, we now have a remarkable and entertaining picture of the colonial underworld during the late eighteenth century, including the Revolutionary period.

Tufts's narrative is important for both historical and literary reasons. This account of his unscrupulous (although not vicious) wanderings and experiences during the nation's formative years gives us great insight into the daily lives of those who lived on farms and in small towns. Their concerns over small items such as a hammer, basket of apples, or shirt reminds us that our culture was not always so material. The narrative also contains much information concerning colonial justice, since Tufts was often apprehended and usually whipped or jailed. We are reminded that sin and crime were often confused in early New Eng., and that justice was unevenly administered. More importantly, however, Tufts's narrative provides much information concerning the critical difficulties that George Washington (q.v.) and his generals faced during the Revolution. Tufts is not the patriot soldier who took up arms to defend his family and country, filled with democratic ideology. He enlisted because soldiering, he thought, is more honorable than thieving, although he quickly learned the two are not contradictory. He served his country, not with his musket, but with his skill as a thief, stealing livestock and produce from angry farmers to help feed his regiment. Moreover, Tufts served three consecutive two-month enlistments, but when Washington finally succeeded in convincing Congress to pass longer enlistments, he deserted at the first opportunity. He was in every sense a "summer soldier and sunshine patriot." Much of the later narrative is filled with descriptions of Tufts hiding from bands of armed men scouring the countryside for deserters, attesting to the acute manpower shortage.

From a literary standpoint, the narrative again has much to offer. Although by no means a great work of literature, the book is part of a line of development in American fiction often overlooked—American picaresque literature. Both "autobiographical" and episodic, the book is concerned with Tufts's low-life exploits as a rogue. He was launched somewhat prematurely into the world without either profession or estate and had to survive only through his own cleverness. This cleverness is seen throughout the narrative. On one occasion, he used the leg and cloven foot of an ox to impersonate the Devil in order to pass a sentry post. At another time, he used a black robe to impersonate the newly fashionable New Light preachers. Arrayed in such a fashion, he traveled to various frontier towns, where his sermons became popular. Technically, the narrative is too episodic, and consequently structurally weak, to be good fiction. Yet many of the parts of a novel are present, especially action, dialog, and characterization. Ostensibly written as a warning to youth, the book is far too enjoyable (and often comic) to warn anyone. Tufts is not even particularly contrite in the end. Although he has vowed never to steal again, his vow does not stop him from stealing away with a neighbor's daughter at the age of 52. The style is lively. Tufts, through his anonymous ghostwriter, was fond of recounting and embellishing his experiences as a scoundrel.

Suggested Readings: Thomas Wentworth Higginson, "A New England Vagabond," *Harper's New Monthly Magazine*, 76 (1888), 605-611; Edmond Pearson, ed., *The Autobiography of a Criminal* (1930).

Daniel E. Williams
Abteilung für Amerikanistik
Universität Tübingen

JOHN TULLEY (1638-c. 1702)

Works: *An Almanack* for 1687-1701 (1687-1701); *Tulley's Farewel 1702. An Almanack* for 1702 (1702).

Biography: The almanac maker John Tulley (spelled both *Tulley* and *Tully*) was the son of John Tulley and Sarah Fenner of Horley parish in Surrey, about twenty miles from London. After her husband's death, the widow Sarah left Eng. in 1646 or 1647 for Mass. with her young son and a daughter, Sarah (three years younger than John), and her two brothers, Arthur and William Fenner. Already a wealthy woman, Sarah (Fenner) Tulley later married the prominent Robert Say of Saybrook, Conn.

In 1671 John Tulley married Mary Beamont, daughter of a Scots immigrant and the sister of a former deputy governor of Mass., Thomas Danforth. The Tulleys bought a house and lot in Potapaugh from John's stepfather and lived there until 1701. John and Mary had eight children: John, Sarah, William, Lydia, Mary, Deborah, Lucy, and Hepsibah. Tulley sold his agricultural property and taught arithmetic, navigation, and astronomy. He also served as town clerk. From 1681 to 1702, he published an annual almanac, the last one titled *Tulley's Farewel* and printed after his death. (*Vital Records* unaccountably lists Tulley's death as 1711.)

Critical Appraisal: John Tulley's contributions to the American almanac were chiefly in format and tone. He was responsible for several "firsts." He was the first to use Jan. as the first month of the year, rather than Mar., although British almanac makers had followed this practice for years. He was also the first to affront the orthodox clergy with the insertion of "pagan" holidays: Valentine's Day, New Year's Day, Shrove Sunday, and Easter. It was he who introduced weather forecasts, and in 1691 he included the first of many tables that dealt with interest and currency conversions.

He lightened the seriousness of the existing almanacs with lively and bawdy material. Although he was sometimes facetious in his astrological prognostications, some of his readers may not have noticed. Occasionally, however, his satire was flagrant: for example, for May 1688, he wrote: *"Mars* in a Trine aspect with *Jupiter*, denotes, that a Dung Cart full of nail pareings will be better to Dung Land than a Bushel of live Buggs or *Musquitoes."* An irresistible example of his levity (Jul. 1688): "Now wanton Lads and Lasses do make Hay, / Which unto lewd temptation makes great way, / With tumbling on the cocks, which acted duly, / Doth cause much mischief in this month of July." Tulley appeared irrepressible, but he was actually a careful man who knew exactly how far he could go, particularly since his almanacs were printed in Boston under the noses of Increase Mather (q.v.) and Cotton Mather (q.v.). He apologized in his 1686 edition for his printer's having included something the year before that might have been "displeasing to God, whatever it were to man." Yet his five pages in 1695 on "The Cruelty of the Papists" would probably have helped to appease the Puritan clergy, had they been upset. Tulley was also careful to obtain the signature of the official censor: "Imprimatur Edw. Randolph, secr." appeared on his title page for 1688, the first almanac to include the censor's name. The early almanacs are generally fun to read; Tulley's works are particularly delightful.

Suggested Readings: Gilman Gates, *Saybrook at the Mouth of the Connecticut* (1935), pp. 157-158, 167-169; "Letters of John Tulley," PMHS, 3rd. Ser., 30 (1916), 74-77; "The Tulley Family of Saybrook, Ct.," NEHGR, 3 (1849), 157-160; Marion Barber Stowell, *Early American Almanacs* (1977), pp. 14, 17, 28, 58-61, 64; Arthur Tourtellot, *The Charles* (1941), pp. 105-107; *Vital Records of Saybrook, 1647-1834* (1952), pp. 11, 18, 35.

Marion Barber Stowell
Milledgeville, Georgia

EBENEZER TURELL (1702-1778)

Works: *Memoirs of the Life and Death of Jane Colman Turell* (pub. with two sermons by Benjamin Colman and titled *Reliquiae Turellae*; 1735); *Ministers Should Carefully Avoid Giving Offense in Any Thing* (1740); *Mr. Turell's Dialogue Between a Minister and His Neighbor About the Times* (1742); *Mr. Turell's Directions to His People with Relation to the Present Times* (includes a verse paraphrase of Isaiah 44; 1742); *Mr. Turell's Brief and Plain Exhortation* (1748); *The Life and Character of the Reverend Benjamin Colman* (1749). For a transcript of Turell's manuscript pamphlet titled "Detection of Witchcraft," see CMHS, 2nd ser., 10 (1823), 6-22.

Biography: Ebenezer Turell was born in Boston, Mass., on Feb. 5, 1702, the youngest of five children of Samuel and Lydia Stoddard Turell, and at the age of 3 days, he was baptized in the Mather church. He attended Harvard, where he became the scribe of a literary club that produced a journal modishly titled the "Telltale." The original, in Turell's hand, can still be read in the Harvard Library Archives, and his exhortation to some of his correspondents reveals how universal are the problems of an editor: "My advice then is, dress and express your ideas in the most concise and clear language that you may speak much in a few words and not be tax'd as monsters in nature having two tongues and but one ear." He was graduated in 1721, received an M.A. in 1724, and continued his studies for about a year with Benjamin Colman (q.v.), pastor of the Brattle Street Church in Boston. On Nov. 25, 1724, he was ordained pastor of the church in Medford, Mass., where he was to spend his entire pastorate. An appreciative parishioner, Thomas Seccombe, kept an account of Mr. Turell's services in four notebooks that he titled "An Account of All the Texts Preached in Our New Meeting House on Sabbath Days, Fast Days, and Thanksgiving Days, and Also All the Baptisms." Although this manuscript may have been lost, some use of it was made in Charles Brooks's *History of Medford* (1855) to show Turell to be a preacher of some insight and courage. He got along well with his congregation, which continued to support him in good style even during the years of the Awakening when many churches were using the inflation of the time as a means of starving their pastors out.

On Aug. 11, 1726, Turell married Jane Colman (Turell) (q.v.), and before her death in 1735, she gave birth to four children, only one of whom survived his mother and that only for a brief time. On Oct. 23, 1735, he married Lucy Davenport, a lady of charm and social polish who evidently enjoyed fulfilling her role as mistress of the parsonage. After her death on May 17, 1759, Turell was married once again, this time to Jane Pepperrell, the widow of both Benjamin Clark and William Tyler. Her presence graced the parsonage until her death in 1765, after which Turell resigned himself to living alone. He preached his last sermon on Apr. 17, 1774, on the text: "If a man die, shall he live again?" Turell's own death did not take place until four years later on Dec. 5, 1778.

Critical Appraisal: Ebenezer Turell's ordination sermon, *Ministers Should Carefully Avoid Giving Offense in Any Thing*, is far from being the spineless message that its title implies. The sermon acknowledges that there are congregations that will take offense at anything the pastor might do and warns the minister against sacrificing his own calling and integrity to bastardize his message and his ministry. A slight uneasiness at the early ripples of the Awakening is evident in his injunction to use the midnight oil, for preaching is more dependent on scriptural exegesis and theological understanding than it is on mere inspiration; but at the same time he warned against the rising countermovement of rationalism, then rampant in Eng. In his calls, the pastor should avoid "unsavory Wordiness and trifling" matters, and in his public prayers, he is warned against "rambling impertinences and needless Tautologies." The pastor should certainly not try to avoid offense by neglecting the duty of discipline, in which honest indictment of real sin is a necessity, but at the same time, he should take care to avoid the pit of clerical tyranny.

Mr. Turell's Brief and Plain Exhortation to Repentance and Reformation is a brief jeremiad on the occasion of the burning of the courthouse with all of its records, which Turell interpreted as a divine call to a sharp reduction in immorality and private selfishness as well as a call for a strong increase in a godly public spirit designed to unite the community. *Mr. Turell's Directions* is a brief but interesting exhortation to his people warning them against the excesses of the Great Awakening. Although still praising the work of George Whitefield (q.v.) and Gilbert Tennent (q.v.) and claiming to be a friend of the renewed interest in religion, Turell warned against thirteen dire practices that he considered to be aberrations of the movement. *Mr. Turell's Dialogue* further examines these thirteen principles in the form of an eighteen-page conversation between a minister and his neighbor in which the visitor conveniently asks the minister questions regarding his stand on most of the principles. Again, it shows Turell to be exceedingly wary about the effects of the Awakening, although he still affirmed the movement to be of God, at least when it was duly mediated through his established ministers.

A pamphlet recounting an alleged case of witchcraft was left among Turell's manuscripts and later published by the Massachusetts Historical Society. This shows Turell in the curious but prevalent position of believing in the possibility of witches but finding no credibility in any current manifestations of witchcraft. "'Tis a pity the world has been so credulous, and furnished these sceptics with matters to make sport of," he wrote. "At the same time, it is a thing horrid to think of, that we should be imposed upon by false relations, and our understanding daily affronted by lies." He closed the work with a paean of advice including the injunction: "Truth is the food of an immortal soul. Feed not any longer on the fabulous husks of falsehood. Never use any of the devil's playthings. The horseshoe is a vain thing, and has no natural tendency to keep off witches or evil spirits. Be warned against all such trading with the devil."

But deservedly, the best known of Turell's works are his two biographical studies, *The Life and Character of Benjamin Colman* and the *Memoirs of the Life and Death of Jane Colman Turell*. These biographies are in no way excuses to produce propaganda of any kind; he wrote simply from a thorough appreciation of the lives he presented and from a deep sense of the value of human life in general. In each case, he included in his biography huge quantities of his subjects' own writings as well as some letters written to them. We know some of the poetry of both Benjamin Colman and Jane Turell only because their biographer has included them, although in both cases, he also mentioned works that were omitted, works, now lost, that we wish he had included instead of some of the correspondence he considered to be prestigious. In his life of Colman, he gave us some insight into his goal as a biographer: "I hope I have been preserved in a good measure from that error which many biographers and eulogists insensibly slide into in Narratives of this kind, *scil.*, Making their subject to excell in every Thing by drawing a perfect Character. . .without showing *the Man*, scil. those particular excelling qualities which distinguish him from others." Although Turell can hardly be objective, since one of his subjects was a beloved mentor who later became his father-in-law, and the other was his own wife, he did endeavor to give a complete picture. He was particularly successful in analyzing Jane Turell's strengths as a budding intellectual poet at the same time that he did nothing to conceal the tension she felt in conforming to her role as his wife and enduring her "religious melancholy," which bordered on the neurotic.

Suggested Readings: CCNE; Sibley-Shipton (VI, 574-582); T_1. *See also* Perry Miller and Thomas H. Johnson, eds., *The Puritans* (1963), pp. 464-465, 536-544.

Howard C. Adams
Frostburg State College

JANE COLMAN TURELL (1708-1735)

Works: All of Turell's known works—a selection of poems, letters, and extracts from her diary—are published in Ebenezer Turell, ed., *Memoirs of the Life and Death of the Pious and Ingenious Mrs. Jane Turell* (1735), including two funeral sermons by Benjamin Colman titled *Reliquiae Turellae* (1735).

Biography: Jane Colman was born to the Rev. Benjamin Colman (q.v.) and his wife, Jane, on Feb. 25, 1708, in Mass. She was an intellectually precocious child, and from an early age, her father sought to develop her writing style by playfully carrying on a written correspondence in both prose and verse even while they were living in the same household. She was evidently a shy girl, and at the age of 10, her father wrote to her in Brookline, where she was visiting, to be less "shame-fac'd" and to "look People in the Face speak freely and behave decently," although in the same letter, he gave the somewhat contradictory advice to be "very humble and modest, womanly and discreet." She early took her writing seriously and at 17 expressed a wish that she might write as well as her father, in response to which he gave her strong encouragement, nonetheless adding that her work ought to be kept within proper feminine bounds. That she wanted to publish poetry is suggested in his strong urging to relegate her poetry to a spare hour or two, rather than letting it be a prime force in her life. Before she was 18, she had read every book in her father's huge library. Jane had an unfortunate propensity to religious melancholy and only became a communicate member of the church under the strong and repeated encouragement of her father and her clergyman husband, the Rev. Ebenezer Turell (q.v.), whom she married on Aug. 11, 1726. The tension between poetry and propriety, so early engendered in her life, continued, and she sent a poem for her father's perusal with the self-conscious apology: "I find my Inclinations to *Poetry* still continue, tho' I hope I do not follow them to the omitting more necessary Things. It is my Study and Endeavour to be a *Blessing*." She gave birth to four children, only one of whom outlived her and that by only a year. Her overdeveloped conscience continued to oppress her, and she professed amazement that "one so Young as I, scarce Twenty Years Old,...should have heap'd up so much Sin and Guilt." This was still a concern when she died after a continued illness on Mar. 26, 1735.

Critical Appraisal: All that we have of Jane Colman Turell's poetry is what her husband and father chose to include in her memoirs, but this is enough to show that in many ways, she was an accomplished poet. She wrote almost entirely in the couplet form, and among the poems written when she was about 17 are some highly successful psalm paraphrases in which she managed to use the form to fuse her own concerns with those of the psalmist. Particularly effective are versions of the 137th Psalm and a portion from the fifth chapter of the Song of Solomon. Some passages in the Psalm paraphrases show that Turell was a self-conscious artist, and this is even more apparent in an early poem, addressed to her muse, in which she hoped to take her place among strong, established female poets: Sappho, Orinda (Katherine Philips), and Philomela (Elizabeth Rowe). "Go lead the way, my Muse," she wrote, "nor must we stop, / 'Till we have gain'd *Parnassus* shady Top." Overtones of an early Puritan feminist are heard in a poem inspired by Philomela in which she praised the "*Female* Pen" that can strike at a man's world with all of the force of the ancient prophetess Hulda. "A *Woman's* Pen strikes the curs'd *Serpents* Head, / And lays the Monster gasping, if not dead."

Among her later poems, written after her marriage, there is a charming imitation of Horace, inviting her father to forsake the crowded and sophisticated environs of Boston to spend a day in the idyllic pastoral surroundings of her Medford home. At this time also, she wrote poems of praise to both Edmund Waller and Richard Blackmore; the latter, although perhaps not totally successful as a poem, displays a highly accomplished use of the couplet, with a Pope-like use of balance and zeugma. The most moving and personal of Jane Turell's poems was written in the late months of her third pregnancy: "Again in Travail Pains my Nerves are wreck'd, / My Eye-balls start, my Heart strings almost crack'd." Movingly, she remembered the first child, born dead, and the second, which she was allowed to hold for just ten days, and finally prays "That when the Hour arrives with painful Throws, / Which shall my Burden to the World disclose, / I may Deliverance have, and joy to see / A living Child, to Dedicate to Thee."

Suggested Readings: DAB. *See also* Clayton Harding Chapman, "Benjamin Colman and His Daughters," NEQ, 32 (1953), 169-192; Pattie Cowell, "Jane Colman Turell: 'Inclinations to Poetry,'" SCN, 36 (1978), 93-94; idem, *Women Poets in Pre-Revolutionary America, 1650-1775* (1981).

Howard C. Adams
Frostburg State College

ROYALL TYLER (1757-1826)

Works: *The Contrast* (1790); *The Origin of Evil* (1793); *The Algerine Captive* (1797); *Moral Tales for the Instruction of Youth* (1800); *An Oration. . .[on] the Death of General George Washington* (1800); *The Yankey in London* (1809); *The Chestnut Tree* (1931); *Four Plays* (1941); *The Verse of Royall Tyler* (1967); *The Prose of Royall Tyler* (1972).

Biography: Born in Boston on Jul. 18, 1757, of a prominent and well-to-do family, Royall Tyler entered Harvard at the age of 15, receiving a degree in Jul. 1776. After graduation, he studied law, served briefly in the colonial militia, was admitted to the bar in 1780, and began his legal career in Falmouth (now Portland), Maine. After two years, he returned to the Boston area, a young lawyer endowed with a comfortable patrimony and a reputation of being also a somewhat rakish young man about town. His courtship of Abigail Adams was cut short when her father, John Adams (q.v.), who seems not to have approved of young Tyler, insisted that she and her mother join him in Europe, where he was negotiating the treaty of peace. In 1786 Tyler joined Gen. Benjamin Lincoln in helping put down Shays's Rebellion and early in the next year set out for N.Y. on a mission somehow connected with that insurrection. Five weeks after his arrival, he had written a comedy, *The Contrast*, and had seen it produced, on Apr. 6, 1787, at the John Street Theatre, the first play by a citizen of the U.S. to appear on the professional stage. Other plays followed, acted but not preserved: *May Day in Town* later in 1787, *The Farmhouse, or Female Duellists* and *The Doctor in Spite of Himself* in 1795, and *The Georgia Spec* in 1797. Four further plays, three of them on biblical subjects, were printed from manuscript in 1941, probably all deriving from a later period. But Tyler's first large reputation was as a poet. In 1791 he moved his practice to Guilford, Vt., and from there, with Joseph Dennie (q.v.) as a nearby collaborator, submitted verse and prose to various periodicals, as "From the Shop of Messrs. Colon and Spondee," with Dennie as "Colon" producing much of the prose and Tyler as "Spondee," most of the verse. Their popularity was immediate, their wit and sly wisdom admired. When in 1797 Tyler's novel *The Algerine Captive* appeared in two volumes in Boston, it was advertised as by the "Rabelais of America." A picaresque tale, partly about its author's early life in Boston and partly about imaginary adventures in the Mediterranean, it brought heady success, reprinted with praise in London three years later. In 1801 Tyler moved to Brattleboro, from where he was elected a judge of the Supreme Court of Vt., six years later becoming its chief justice. But legal activities did not quiet his pen, as he continued to contribute brisk snippets in verse and prose to periodicals such as *Polyanthus* in Boston and Joseph Dennie's *Port Folio* in Philadelphia. From 1811 to 1814, he was professor of jurisprudence at the University of Vermont, of which he was also elected a trustee. His later years were pinched with poverty and illness, but with continued writing also. When he died on Aug. 16, 1826, he left the manuscript of a collection of tales for children, several poems, and an autobiographical narrative, "The Bay Boy," not published until 1972.

Critical Appraisal: Tyler was a deft and witty person, quick with rhyme and with an ear for rhythm, and with enough imagination to write in prose of lands that he had never seen, in Europe and North Africa. His range was large. As dramatist, essayist, novelist, and poet, he caught the temper of his time and reproduced it adequately well. But little that he wrote stands the test of time, except a few brief lyrics of rhythmic inconsequentialities. As a young man, he effectively ridiculed the simpering pretentions of rhyming contemporaries who imitated the sentimental manner of Della Crusca. But writing was for Tyler at best his second occupation; law was his first and was the more respectable. His pose was that of a cultivated man of leisure to whom writing was an avocation, done for his own amusement or that of his friends. But a suspicion lurks that Tyler wanted more than that of literature. As he grew older, he became more serious, so that his posthumously published "The Bay Boy" can be seen as an effort to present himself and his experiences in growing up in a new country in an instructive and perhaps lasting form. His handicap throughout much of his life had been that he wrote, as perhaps every writer must, what he thought people would read. In a censorious time, he lightly censored his contemporaries with wit that overrode rancor and with lightness of touch not unlike that of his older contemporary in Philadelphia, Francis Hopkinson (q.v.), or his younger contemporary, Oliver Wendell Holmes, who was growing toward wit in his father's parsonage in Cambridge. As some of his later writings seem to indicate, Tyler would have liked finally to be remembered as a serious writer, but his trials seem mainly to have been in imitation of other writers who were serious—as in his later attempts at drama based on fables by Cervantes and Moliere and biblical story. In all, Tyler's invention, although quick, was perhaps too often like the invention of someone else, his verse indistinguishable from other sprightly verse, and his *The Contrast* so like antecedent comedies that it has become a playground for scholars who discover it deriving from one or more earlier transatlantic plays. He had perhaps a more jovial wit than many of his native contemporaries, and a better control of rhythm than they, but he left no telling mark that guarantees the several anonymous pieces suspected to be his as surely his. But what has been identified does guarantee him a small but secure place as a talented workman who cannot be overlooked.

Suggested Readings: DAB; LHUS. *See also* Marius B. Péladeau, ed., *The Prose of Royal Tyler* (1972); idem, *The Verse of Royal Tyler* (1968); G. Thomas Tanselle, *Royall Tyler* (1967); Mary Palmer Tyler, *Grandmother Tyler's Book* (1925).

Lewis Leary
The University of North Carolina at Chapel Hill

U

JOHN UNDERHILL (c. 1597-1672)

Works: *News from America, or A New and Experimentall Discoverie of New England* (1638).

Biography: John Underhill was born sometime around 1597 in Kenilworth, Warwickshire, Eng., into a family whose members had served the earls of Leicester as retainers and stewards. Underhill embarked on a military career and during the 1620s served in the Neth. in the guard of the prince of Orange.

In 1630 he arrived in Massachusetts Bay to oversee military affairs and was chosen as both a deputy and selectman in Boston. His military career blossomed during the Pequot War of 1636-1637, when he served as a captain in the Mass. forces. But it quickly withered, for in 1638 Underhill publicly supported the Antinomians and consequently was disfranchised, dismissed from military service, and disarmed. In rapid succession, he moved to Eng., returned to Mass., and immigrated to the Piscataqua settlement in N.H., where he was elected governor. Dissension forced him to move first to Mass. and then to Stamford, Conn., where he served as deputy to the New Haven General Court in 1643. But soon he was called to put down an Indian uprising in New Neth. He remained there and filled various offices until he charged Director Peter Stuyvesant with plotting the destruction of the English in 1653. He eventually settled in English-controlled Long Island and held local offices until after the English conquest of New Neth., when he occupied provincial offices in N.Y. until his retirement in 1667. From 1661 until his death, he resided in Oyster Bay.

Critical Appraisal: Although written in Eng. during Underhill's self-imposed exile from Mass., *News from America* was a spirited defense of the New Eng. Way. Ostensibly a justification of the author's military role in the Pequot War, it was a promotional tract describing the virtue of the land, rationalizing the hardships faced by the colonists, and answering criticisms of Mass. heard in Eng.

In Underhill's view, "the old serpent stirred up [the Pequot Indians of eastern Conn.] against the church of Christ." The murder of two traders by the Indians called for revenge, which was achieved by the destruction of the Indians' fort at

Mystic and the massacre of its 400 inhabitants. Underhill referred those who questioned this carnage to Scripture and King "David's War." Puritans suffered in the war as well, and Underhill tried to explain the purpose of adversity by presenting a rudimentary captivity narrative about a Puritan girl. Captured by the Pequots, she maintained her virtue and came to appreciate God's purposes and mercy through the experience. She symbolized the English who through suffering in the wilderness acquired a deeper knowledge of Christ. "Know that Christ can not be had without a cross," Underhill wrote; consequently prospective immigrants should not hesitate to embark for New Eng. Material rewards also awaited the settlers, for Underhill described the farming, fishing, and commercial opportunities of various localities in New Eng. He encouraged women to migrate as well by relating an anecdote of his wife's influence on him to dispel the rumor that New Eng. men kept wives in "servile subjection."

Recent scholarship has attributed the Pequot War to Puritan land hunger rather than justice, but *News* remains an eloquent defense of the Puritans. Underhill's use of biblical metaphor and references to the Old Testament clearly identified the children of New Eng. as the successors of God's children of Israel.

Suggested Readings: DAB; DNB; T₁. *See also* Louis Effingham De Forest and Anne Lawrence De Forest, *Captain John Underhill, Gentleman, Soldier of Fortune* (1934); Francis Jennings, *The Invasion of America: Indians, Colonialism, and the Cant of Conquest* (1975), pp. 202-227; Henry C. Shelley, *John Underhill of New England and New Netherland* (1952). *News from America* was reprinted in CMHS, 3rd ser., 6 (1837), 3-28.

Robert Brunkow
Santa Barbara, California

V

ROGER VIETS (1738-1811)

Works: *A Serious Address and Farewell* (1787); *A Sermon Preached at St. Andrews Church* (1787); *Annapolis Royal* (1788); *A Sermon on the Duty of Attending* (1789); *A Sermon Preached to the...Society...of Masons* (1793); *A Sermon Preached at Sissabo* (1799); *A Sermon, Preached Before the...Masons* (1800); *A Sermon Preached in St. Peter's Church* (1800).

Biography: Roger Viets was born at Simsbury, Conn., on Mar. 9, 1738, and received his early schooling there. He entered Yale College and prepared himself for the Church of England priesthood, graduating in 1758. After a few years as a lay reader, he sailed to Eng. and was ordained to London in Apr. 1763. Upon his return to America, he served as parish priest at Simsbury and the surrounding area until Dec. 1785.

During the American Revolution, Viets's sympathies for the crown and his role as representative of the Established Church made his position in the community increasingly untenable. In 1777 he was jailed on suspicion of having aided British fugitives. The undermining of his social and moral authority in the community, together with the withdrawal of British financial support for the American churches, led him to seek a new post in Nova Scotia after the Peace of 1784. He was assigned to Digby, Nova Scotia, a new town established by Loyalist refugees, and arrived there in the early summer of 1786. He served as rector of Digby until his death on Aug. 15, 1811. While living in Digby, he was an important leader in the secular and religious life of that community.

Critical Appraisal: Roger Viets's published sermons fall into two categories: those that deal specifically with theological subjects and those that amount to speeches delivered on special occasions. His theological sermons argue very orthodox positions with a skillful blend of logic and rhetorical exhortation. Although not particularly interesting intellectually, they have moments of effective persuasive rhetoric. In his "occasional" sermons, Viets drew even more heavily on his rhetorical skills. The most interesting of them, *A Serious Address and Farewell* (1787), was his valedictory to his Simsbury congregation, delivered when he returned to gather his family and belongings after his initial visit to

Nova Scotia. The sermon is partly an *apologia* justifying his removal to Nova Scotia, partly a subtle condemnation of the social and political circumstances that precipitated his removal, and partly an implicit assertion of the superiority of the topography and social environment of his new home. Consciously or unconsciously, his intention seems to have been to persuade his auditors (and readers) that life in Loyalist Nova Scotia embodied all of the central ideals of the prevailing eighteenth-century conservative vision of human social contentment: he presented a stable community of amiable, reasonable men living in harmony with benevolent nature and in accordance with the accepted principles of moral propriety, under the guiding spirit of their religious faith. It was a social vision marked by a fundamental belief that the principles of order, cohesion, and unanimity lay at the heart of human affairs. By implication, the lives of his Conn. readers are projected as being inherently inferior, and probably irretrievably so as a result of the antithetical sociopolitical ideals spawned by the Revolution. The social vision presented by Viets is implicitly incompatible with a democratic society (and a revolutionary one at that) that gave priority to the principles of individual responsibility and self-realization.

This vision of a contented, ordered society becomes explicit and central in Viets's poem *Annapolis Royal* (1788), written not to spite Conn. Yankees but to encourage and inspire Nova Scotian Loyalists as they struggled to rebuild their lives in a new land. The poem begins as a simple topographical poem, but moves on to describe the social environment of the emerging community. In both cases, the poet's emphasis falls on harmoniousness, depicting a contented people in a pastoral landscape. In the final part of the poem, focus shifts to the spiritual quality of life at Annapolis, completing the picture of harmony, a harmony encompassing and reaffirming the integral, ordered relationship between the natural, human, and divine aspects of reality.

The ultimate significance of the picture that emerges lies not so much in the poet's describing what might be or should be, as in his implicit assertion (given the scope of his vision) that life in Loyalist Nova Scotia was part of the mainstream of eighteenth-century human experience. The poem suggests that although they were refugees recently cast onto a new, undeveloped terrain, the Loyalists were not isolated from civilization as they understood it. Civilization lay in the vision of reality that they shared with all reasonable men and that they realized in their communal life in this new land. They were part of the universal order of things and had to see themselves in this context to appreciate the true value of their lives. *Annapolis Royal* was Viets's way of asserting that all was essentially right with the world, that all had not been lost in the Revolution.

Suggested Readings: CCNE; Dexter (II, 557-560). *See also* J. Fingard, *The Anglican Design in Loyalist Nova Scotia* (1972); T. Vincent, Introduction, *Annapolis Royal, A Poem, 1788* (1979).

Thomas B. Vincent
Royal Military College of Canada

PHILIP VINCENT (b. 1600)

Works: *The Lamentations of Germany* (1638); *A True Relation of the Late Battle Fought in New-England Between the English and Salvages, with the Present State of Things There* (1638).

Biography: Philip Vincent was born in 1600 in Frisby, Yorkshire, Eng., one of three sons of John Vincent, a gentleman. He attended Peterhouse College, Cambridge, where he received an M.A. He was ordained and presented to the Rectory of Stoke d'Abernon in Surrey in 1625, a living he resigned in 1629. After the death of his wife in 1630, he began a period of wandering in the New World and Europe, sailing for Guiana probably in 1632. His work *The Lamentations of Germany* describes travels in southern Ger. between 1633 and 1635, and he was apparently in New Eng. at the time of the Pequot War (1637). Nothing is known of the remainder of his life.

Critical Appraisal: Philip Vincent's *A True Relation* is a brief history of the significant war fought between early settlers and the Pequot tribe of Conn. in 1637, a conflict that virtually exterminated the formidable tribe and revealed the New Eng. colonists' success in dividing and conquering their Indian neighbors. Although Vincent's work is evidently not an eye-witness account, its use of detail suggests that his sources were participants.

Vincent's attitude toward the Indians is more Virginian than Puritan in its tolerance. "Their correspondency of disposition with us," he wrote, "argueth all to be of the same constitution and the sons of Adam. . . . Only art and grace have given us that perfection which yet they want, but many perhaps be as capable thereof as we." At the same time, Vincent justified the harsh treatment of the Pequots, because such "barbarians, ever treacherous, abuse the goodness of those that condescend to their rudeness and imperfections."

Although Vincent was a clergyman, *A True Relation* notably lacks the sense of God's providential design that informs other contemporary narratives of the war; instead he was intent upon demonstrating a sensible human policy at work on the colonial side. Parallels with the history of Va. are pursued to illustrate the superiority of the New Englanders, whom Vincent commended for dealing with the Pequots in such a manner as to avoid future trouble and ensure the developing prosperity of the colony.

Whereas the more celebrated accounts of the war were written for a colonial audience by military commanders—John Mason (q.v.), John Underhill (q.v.), and Lion Gardiner (q.v.)—Vincent's *True Relation* is valuable for providing an outsider's view for an English audience. A traveler passing through New Eng., Vincent managed to combine immediacy and distance: his narrative relates the particulars of the Pequot War to the larger perspective of colonial history and makes frequent reference to general paradigms of human experience. In spite of his eagerness to praise the colonial side for its heroism and sound strategy,

Vincent's manner is restrained: he described the actions of both sides matter-of-factly and without embellishment.

Suggested Readings: DNB. *See also* Howard Bradstreet, *The Story of the War with the Pequots Re-Told* (1933); Charles Orr, ed., *History of the Pequot War* (1897; 1980), for Vincent's *True Relation* from the text of CMHS, 3rd ser., 6 (1836), with Joseph Hunter's "Biographical Notice of Philip Vincent"; Alden T. Vaughan, "Pequots and Puritans: The Causes of the War of 1637," WMQ, 21 (1964), 256-269.

Louise K. Barnett
Rutgers University

NICHOLAS LUDWIG COUNT VON ZINZENDORF (1700-1760)

Works: *Bedenken und Besondere Sendschreiben in Allerhand Practischen Materien* (1734); *Kleine Schrifften* (1740); *Sixteen Discourses on the Redemption of Man* (1740); *Hymns Composed for the Use of the Brethren* (1749); *Theological Ideas and Sentences* (1751).

Biography: Nicholas Ludwig Count Von Zinzendorf was born at Dresden on May 26, 1700, of a noble German family. His father, a high Saxon court official who died when Nicholas was in his infancy, wanted his son to follow a career in the Saxon civil service. Accordingly, his family sent him to the University of Halle in 1706 to study under the noted pietistic scholar Dr. August Hermann Francke. Unfortunately, the young count's interests took a decidedly theological turn, much to his family's irritation. As a result, he was transferred to Wittenberg to study law from 1716 to 1719, although he managed to spend his spare time in prayer, meditation, and theological reading. In 1721 Von Zinzendorf became a counselor in Dresden and, the following year, married Countess Erdmute Dorothea. Seemingly, he had settled into the comfortable life of the German ruling class, but his heart was not in it. He purchased a small estate at Bertholdsdorf (later named Herrnhut) and attempted to model it after the famous Halle institute. Von Zinzendorf gathered around himself a little group of like-minded pietists whom he organized into an *ecclesiola*—a sort of religious order—modeled after the Pietistic conventicles. Legally, his group had to remain a part of Lutheranism, the state church in that part of Ger. In fact, it had deviated doctrinally from the state church.

In 1722 the remnants of the Moravian Church, or the Unitas Fratrum, fled Bohemian persecution to find sanctuary in Herrnhut. Von Zinzendorf was fascinated by these descendants of the old Slavonic reformer John Huss. Soon he began steps to reconstitute the church at Herrnhut. He resigned his court position in 1728 to devote full time to this scheme. Unfortunately, these activities led to a government investigation and an official order in 1732 to sell his estates and leave Saxony. Von Zinzendorf, reprieved by a change in ministry, instead received Lutheran orders in Tübingen in 1734 and dispatched Moravian missionaries to the W. Ind. and Greenland to seek asylum. America appeared to be the most likely refuge, so the count sent one of his followers, August Gottlieb Spangenberg (q.v.), first to Ga., then to Pa., to see if he could make any headway among German settlers there.

In 1737 Von Zinzendorf was himself consecrated a Moravian bishop. Four years later, he went to Pa. to foster his new ecumenical scheme. He wanted to reunite all Christians into an Invisible Church of Christ, using the Moravians as a nucleus around which the other sects could coalesce. Each sect would retain its denominational and doctrinal distinctiveness as a tropus within the whole church. The true church would be a loose association of tropi. In Jan. 1742 the count summoned a meeting of German sectarians at Philadelphia to put the scheme into effect. When the stubbornly independent sectarians resisted amalgamation, Von Zinzendorf abandoned the idea and instead concentrated on infiltrating the Lutheran congregations by placing Moravian pastors at vacant congregations. This scheme too was thwarted by the arrival of Henry Melchior Muhlenberg (q.v.), who expelled the Moravians and united the German Lutheran congregations into a doctrinally pure consistory.

Frustrated, the count left America in 1743. American Moravians, abandoning the tropus scheme, petitioned for and were granted by Eng. in 1749 recognition as a legal church. Von Zinzendorf worked in Eng. until 1755 and then spent the remaining years of his life, until his death in 1760, visiting Moravian congregations around the world.

Critical Appraisal: Von Zinzendorf's writings are mystical and heavily christocentric, so christocentric, in fact, that his trinitarianism is highly suspect. He seems to have held that God the Father is not our father until after Christ's mediation and reconciliation.

With more orthodox theologians, Von Zinzendorf believed that human nature was corrupted by the Fall, but unlike them, he reduced all sin to one—disbelief in the Lord Jesus. The process of justification for him was merely the positing of an act of faith in the divinity of the suffering God-man who freely chose to die for our sins. Faith is man's sole duty and obligation. Christ himself, Von Zinzendorf believed, would initiate justification and impart saving grace. Man need give only passive acceptance. Von Zinzendorf did not require a conscious struggle with the sinful self before conversion is had. The process is completed in a flash of inspiration, a twinkling of God's eye.

For Von Zinzendorf there is no set pattern in attaining sanctification. God deals with each soul in a unique way. Since Christ died for all men, all men can be saved. There is no such thing as a predestined body of the elect. Whence comes this knowledge of Christ that leads to faith? Not from the law, since the law merely tempts man to pursue evil by emphasizing that which is forbidden. Not from education, since education merely impresses ideas in the head, not on the heart. This knowledge, instead, comes from an immediate illumination by Christ. Once Christ enters the soul, sin is cleansed away. Indeed, Von Zinzendorf appears to have held that the justified are incapable of sinning any more. Even a man who has lived all of his life in the basest sin, yet received Christ on his deathbed, is saved. Moreover, since we do not know when and to whom Christ will present himself, we have no right to condemn the natural man for his failure to know God.

In Zinzendorfian theology, sanctification is accompanied by a divine certitude of redemption. Like the faithful steward, one need only say "I believe" and rest assured in the certain knowledge of eternal reward. Christ has chosen me; he will not give me up. There is no place in Von Zinzendorf's theology for good works, for salvation cannot be earned. Likewise, any business or recreation is permissible provided it not be itself evil, that is a denial of faith. Holiness becomes man's nature, not the object of so-called moral activity. Yet man should be grateful for this salvation earned by Christ's redemptive death. One of the aspects of Von Zinzendorf's theology that most repelled more orthodox churches was his maudlin and mawkish expressions of devotion to Christ's blood and wounds to the point of describing true Christians as maggot worms crawling in the wounds of Christ.

To a great degree, however, Von Zinzendorf's theology lay within the mainstream of left-wing Pietism. His greatest ecclesiastical contributions were his theories on the possibility of ecumenical unity.

Suggested Readings: CCMC; DAB; DARB. *See also* J. Taylor Hamilton, *A True History of the Church Known as the Moravian Church* (1900); Edward Langton, *History of the Moravian Church* (1956); A. J. Lewis, *Zinzendorf: The Ecumenical Pioneer* (1962); Augustus Gottlieb Spangenberg, *Leben des Herrn Nichlaus Ludwig Grafen und Herrn Zinzendorf und Pottendorf*, 3 vols. (1772-1775); John R. Weinlick, *Count Zinzendorf* (1956).

Leonard R. Riforgiato
The Pennsylvania State University

BENJAMIN WADSWORTH (1670-1737)

Works: *Wadsworth's Journal* (w. 1694; pub. 1850); *Rulers Feeding & Guiding Their People* (1716); *The Well-Ordered Family*, 2nd ed. (1719); "A Sermon Setting Forth the Nature of Early Piety" (pub. in *A Course of Sermons on Early Piety*; 1721); *Benjamin Wadsworth's Book...Relating to College Affairs* (w. 1727-1737; pub. 1935). See also *The Short-Title Evans* (1969), II, 955-956, for additional works by Wadsworth.

Biography: Benjamin Wadsworth, pastor of the First Church in Boston and eighth president of Harvard College, was born in Milton, Mass., on Feb. 28, 1670. He attended the college of which he was destined to be president, taking the B.A. in 1690 and the M.A. in 1692. Both in the affairs of church and college, he was a moderate and as such named a fellow of Harvard College in 1697 (a member of its governing corporation) and acted on and off in this capacity for the next twenty-eight years. When the corporation chose one of their own members to the highest post the college offered, they recognized Wadsworth's dedication to the vital and necessary task of educating the rising generation to piety and productivity in a still harsh and primitive country. In this post, he served the college well. He was meticulous and methodical, searching the records for college property to recover funds lost through the neglect of previous officers. He supervised improvements in the curriculum, and under him Thomas Hollis founded the Hollis professorship of mathematics and natural philosophy with an endowment of 1,200 pounds and telescopes to go with the grant. Hollis's munificence marked the heightened interest in science that characterized the eighteenth century.

Wadsworth died in office on Mar. 16, 1737. He had served as Harvard's president for ten years and had published in his lifetime some forty-seven sermons. Married in 1696 to Ruth Bordman, he died without issue.

Critical Appraisal: When, in 1727, Benjamin Wadsworth came to the presidency of Harvard, the college founded "in this Wilderness," he was already the experienced and adept pastor of the First Church in Boston. He had further served the pressing and practical needs of his colony, accompanying the commissioners of Mass., empowered, in 1694, to negotiate with the Five Nations, at Albany. A decade before the redoubtable Mrs. Sarah Kemble Knight (q.v.), who, traveling alone, kept a journal of her trip from Boston to N.Y., he recorded his daily difficulties and observations on the nearly month-long excursion south. The manuscript has been published under the title *Wadsworth's Journal*. A dedicated recorder of his professional experiences, he also kept a detailed account of his years at Harvard, titled *Benjamin Wadsworth's Book. . .Relating to College Affairs.*

With a keen and ironic eye, Wadsworth viewed the hardships and pleasures of wilderness travel. The company was good and the commissioners lightened their mishaps and discomforts with witty conversation. The second day out, Aug. 7, one Mr. Durte of Hartford "did accidentally fall into our company, and after the same manner. . .accidentally, he and his horse both together fell into a brook; but both rose again without damage." The same day, the company dined in the woods without mishap. "Pleasant descants" were made upon the dining room. It was noted that the room "was large, high curiously hung with green. . .[and] accommodated with the pleasancy of a murmuring rivulet."

In addition to a clever tongue, Wadsworth had an eye for factual detail. The *Journal* records the demographic and topographic peculiarities of the towns through which the company passed and sometimes found shelter for the night. He was particularly curious to record the state of their religious institutions. Thus Waterbury was approached by "a very bad road," consisted of twenty-five families, "tho very compact," and had as its minister Mr. Peck and a new meeting house, "tho unfinished."

Finally, Wadsworth recorded that under the "smiles of Providence," the commissioners returned safely home on the thirty-first of the same month in which they journeyed forth.

As a devoted alumnus of Harvard College, Wadsworth promoted its fame and fortunes within the colonies as a necessary and exemplary means by which his coreligionists might know and do God's will. Thus educated to "Search Scriptures," they might "avert the Evil Tokens, at which they who dwell in the Wilderness may be afraid." To live the life of pious Christians under such inhospitable circumstances, children as well as adults must be able to read the Bible and to read with persistent and intelligent dedication. Ten years before he became president of Harvard, he delivered a sermon, *Rulers Feeding & Guiding Their People*, before the Great and General Court of the Bay Colony. The "Colledge" he noted was founded "in this Wilderness to Educate and qualify Persons. . .for special & eminent. . .Services both in Church and State." Despite "our cold Climate, severe Winters, and hard Labour for a livelihood; yet I reckon our Colledge has been a greater blessing. . .than all the Gold and Silver Mines of the Spanish West Indies."

With the goal of preserving this community of saints, Wadsworth did all he could "to countenance and incourage" Harvard's survival and growth. The record of his difficulties and successes he kept in his *Book*. On an almost daily basis, he noted expenditures, receipts, commencements, and problems of curriculum, housing, food, and discipline. In so small a fellowship of scholars—the class of 1721 had only thirty-seven members—he acted as college preacher, overseer of accounts and repairs, dispenser of monies, and disciplinarian to rebellious undergraduates. He had frequent and direct personal contact with candidates seeking the B.A. and M.A. degrees. Typically, he interceded in a quarrel between freshmen and sophomores. On complaint from several of the former that they were "greatly abus'd" by their seniors "who struck & beat them," Wadsworth himself sent for two of the accused and, one by one, "discours'd 'em, and refer'd their affair to be consider'd by myself" with the "Fellows [members of the governing corporation of Harvard]." In due course, the offenders were publicly chastised and fined.

Despite the modest beginnings of the college struggling to survive in a hard environment with few endowments and small income, it prospered under Wadsworth's tutelage. When Wadsworth died in 1737 while still in office, Joseph Sewall (q.v.), pastor of the Church of Christ in Boston, praised his "unwearied" diligence in "attending" college business and attributed Wadsworth's illness to "too intense Labour and close Application" in furthering the "Welfare" of Harvard.

Suggested Readings: CCNE; Sibley-Shipton (IV, 1-6); Sprague (I, 220-223). *See also* Nathaniel Appleton, *Reviving Thoughts in a Dying Hour* (1737), which refers to Wadsworth's presidency and accomplishments at Harvard; Samuel Eliot Morison, *Three Centuries of Harvard* (1936), pp. 72, 77-82, 114, and very briefly mentioned in his *Harvard College in the Seventeenth Century*, 2 vols. (1936); Joseph Sewall, *When the Godly Cease* (a funeral sermon; 1737). *Wadsworth's Journal* has been printed in CMHS, ser. 4, 1 (1852), 102-110. *Benjamin Wadsworth's Book...Relating to College Affairs* has been printed in PCSM, 31 (1935), 443-507.

Betty Kushen
West Orange, New Jersey

TIMOTHY WALKER (1705-1782)

Works: *The Way to Try All Pretended Apostles* (1743); *Diaries of Rev. Timothy Walker* (w. 1746-1780; pub. 1889); *Those Who Have the Form of Godliness* (1772).

Biography: Timothy Walker, a founder of Concord, N.H., was a prominent religious and political figure in the northern wilderness of eighteenth-century New Eng. Born on Jul. 27, 1705, in Woburn, Mass., Walker was the son of Samuel Walker and Judith Howard. He received an A.B. from Harvard in 1725 and an M.A. in 1728. After a brief apprenticeship with John Barnard (q.v.) of Andover, Walker was ordained as the first pastor of the plantation of Penacook (later Concord) on Nov. 18, 1730.

During the following fifty-two years, Walker's ministry was marked by wise counsel and able leadership. In its first meeting held within a newly built block-house, Walker's church adopted the Half-Way Covenant, adding a shade of liberalism to the congregation's reputation. Although Walker sided with the Old Lights during the Great Awakening, he perpetuated his liberal attitude, especially during his later years, and was sometimes accused of Arminianism. A moderate Calvinist, he sided with his friend Charles Chauncy (q.v.) to oppose those preachers who attempted to impose severe Calvinism upon Congregationalism. Walker's ministry was characterized by a desire for unity and a willingness to overlook differences of opinion.

Walker was regarded as the political leader of the community. In 1737 the plantation was incorporated as the town of Rumford, but this incorporation was invalidated by the settlement of a boundary dispute between Mass. and N.H. Walker's parish became a N.H. rather than a Mass. settlement, and a dispute arose with a group of rich Portsmouth landowners concerning ownership of the land. On three occasions between 1753 and 1762, the Mass. government commissioned Walker to travel to Eng., where he appealed the case to the king on behalf of his community. The final ruling was in Walker's favor, but the N.H. courts were uncooperative. Eventually, the settlers had to pay the proprietors to obtain sole ownership of their land. As a concession to Walker and his friends, Mass. granted them the town of Rumford, Me. This grant greatly increased the bounds of Walker's unofficial parish, which stretched over 100 miles from Penacook to Rumford and required four days of riding to reach the most remote frontiers. Walker's influence began to fade during the early days of the American Revolution. He died on Sept. 1, 1782, after over half of a century of service to his community.

Critical Appraisal: The published sermons of Timothy Walker evidence varying reactions to the Great Awakening. Although Walker did not approve of itinerant Calvinists, neither did he oppose them with the same intensity as Charles Chauncy. Walker probably did not attend the sermons of these traveling preachers, and as late as 1772, he was defending his right to abstain from attendance and was encouraging his congregation to do likewise. Walker's parish was located over thirty miles from the nearest town in which George Whitefield (q.v.), Gilbert Tennent (q.v.), or James Davenport visited; yet inevitably, the spiritual fever reached his community. At the height of the Awakening, Walker delivered his sermon *The Way to Try All Pretended Apostles*.

In *The Way to Try* Walker preached against the potential harm inherent in listening to false teachers. With particular emphasis upon the refutation of his opponents' arguments, Walker refuted the Calvinistic doctrine of unconditional election that was being adamantly promoted by the itinerants, quoting Thomas Hooker (q.v.) and other prominent ministers to support his arguments. As an admonition to Gilbert Tennent and others, he encouraged his flock to bring to his parsonage any "extraordinary Messenger" so he might talk to such an individual personally. Walker accused the itinerants of gathering large crowds of the unlearned and confusing them with "the surprising Effects of Error and Enthusiasm." The sermon concluded with a plea to all of the members of the congregation to refrain from attending lectures given by itinerant preachers.

Within this sermon, Walker introduced an important idea to the Great Awakening. Many of the itinerant preachers were not ordained, yet claimed to be enthused with God's spirit. Walker maintained that ministers could be chosen only by the laying on of hands of the orthodox authorities or by the direct operation of Christ. Walker contended that those chosen directly by Christ would give evidence of their selection by performing miracles. Since none of the itinerants were able to demonstrate this kind of power, they were left without a defense against Walker's charge. Although the concept had been used by Catholics against Protestant ministers in the sixteenth century, Walker may be the first to apply the principle during his era.

Those Who Have the Form of Godliness was published thirty years later and dealt with the same subject. During the late 1760's, the Baptist minister Hezekiah Smith journeyed through the land proselytizing. Walker blamed him for "the bleeding state of Haverhill, and about twenty parishes round." Walker's attitude toward itinerants had remained constant throughout the years, as suggested by two allusions to his earlier sermon *The Way to Try*: "as I then thought, and still think, supported by weighty and sufficient reasons." But Walker was willing to compromise on the doctrinal point of infant baptism to preserve spiritual unity in his congregation. He admitted "reviewing that controversy over and over again"; yet he still remained dedicated to scriptural grounds for infant baptism. Although the majority of Congregationalists shared his belief, he nevertheless stated that he would not withdraw his ministry from any who refused to baptize their children. Such an admission by a prominent minister was not common in eighteenth-century New Eng.

Although Walker's sermons employed the standard form of delivery, he differed from his colleagues in his style. The average New Eng. sermon lasted one hour and was delivered with a calm, dispassionate tone. Walker's sermons seldom exceeded thirty minutes. His orations were characterized by dignity, precision, and brevity. Although his use of imagery was sparing, Walker was able to create a meaningful metaphoric image. In *The Way to Try*, Walker described the rejection of sound religion as the rejection of good food: "the Old Divinity, which has stood the Test of above seventeen hundred Years, is become stale and unsavory, to many wanton Palates." In the introduction to *Those Who Have the Form of Godliness*, Walker painted a vivid picture of the biblical concept of journeying on the narrow path toward heaven. Walker praised "the man who is wise enough to steer a safe and middle course" between "the rock of self-righteousness" and "the fatal quicksand of libertinism." Concepts of pride and license are vivid in Walker's metaphor.

Walker kept a line-a-day diary from 1746 to 1780 published in 1889 by his great-grandson Joseph Burbeen Walker. The diary is a collection of weather reports, religious records, and catastrophic occurrences. Instances of scalping

and gunfire are interspersed among the records of infant deaths, frequent marriages, and the purchasing of slaves as Walker mixed the morbid with the
mundane. The death of a child is mentioned in the same line with the killing of
four hogs. Although the notes are brief, the diary provides an interesting account
of life in a New Eng. frontier village. Walker's papers are located in the New
Hampshire Historical Society collections.

Suggested Readings: CCNE; DAB; Sibley-Shipton (VII, 603-614). *See also*
Edwin Scott Gaustad, *The Great Awakening in New England* (1957); Phyllis M. Jones and
Nicholas R. Jones, eds., *Salvation in New England: Selections from the Sermons of the
First Preachers* (1977).

Paul Thornton
University of Houston

BENJAMIN WALLER (1716-1786)

Works: "On the Aforegoing Essays [by Charles Hansford]" (w. 1750; pub.
1961); three untitled lyrics (w. 1750, 1765; pub. 1961); "Myrtilla to Damon"
(1759); "A Biographical Sketch of the Poet [Charles Hansford]" (w. 1765; pub.
1961).

Biography: Benjamin Waller, son of Col. John and Dorothy King Waller,
was born Oct. 1, 1716, at "Endfield," the family home in King William County,
Va. Although Col. Waller called himself "Gentleman" and served his colony in
several significant capacities, he seems to have been only modestly successful.
According to Littleton Waller Tazewell, Benjamin Waller's grandson and later a
governor of Va., the colonel "was a plain planter" who "possessed a competent
fortune," but "was not wealthy, and had a numerous family." Because of these
circumstances, perhaps, he allowed Benjamin to move to Williamsburg when he
was approximately 10 years old to become the protégé of John Carter, the
colony's wealthy and influential secretary of state, who, according to Tazewell,
saw in young Waller "a boy of uncommon parts, which would not probably be
fully developed in his situation, for the want of proper education."

From this time until Carter's death in 1743, Waller seems to have profited
from his favor. Apparently through his sponsorship, Waller attended the College
of William and Mary, achieving a distinguished record and completing the
prescribed curriculum when he was 17 or 18. Then he gained valuable political
experience by serving as a clerk in Carter's office. Later, probably early in 1737,
under Carter's guidance, he began to study law in one of the finest libraries in
eighteenth-century Va.—that of the deceased Sir John Randolph, permission to
use that excellent facility having been granted by the widow, Lady Susan Randolph. In 1738 Waller passed the Va. bar and immediately began to practice in
and around Williamsburg.

Waller's subsequent rise to success as lawyer, businessman, and public official resulted in part from his training and native ability—or as Tazewell put the matter, his "industry, punctuality, integrity, and skill." But in the months immediately following admission to the bar, the continued patronage of Secretary Carter and a timely friendship with Governor William Gooch were significant factors. In May 1738, for example, the governor appointed him king's attorney for Gloucester County and in early Dec. 1739, king's attorney for James City County. A few weeks later, Carter appointed him clerk of James City County, and the governor made him clerk of the General Court. Then in Aug. 1740 the governor arranged for him to become clerk-assistant of the House of Burgesses. Four years later—in 1744—he was elected to that body as representative for James City County, a position he held until 1761. In the meantime, he had become increasingly involved with his private legal practice and an assortment of business ventures, chief among which seems to have been his work as agent for numerous British merchants. In fact, from the early 1740s until the eve of the Revolution, a significant—and lucrative—portion of his legal and business activity seems to have involved collecting bills for these merchants.

In the early 1760s in Va., as elsewhere in the colonies, political and economic differences with G.B. were becoming pronounced. Since Waller continued to hold appointments from the crown, such as king's attorney for the Court of Admiralty, he was reluctant openly to oppose the measures of the crown's major representatives, but he was also unwilling to oppose the contrary measures of dissident Virginians—probably because he often was in sympathy with their views. Consequently, he began to decline both appointive and elective positions and lived for some time as a private citizen. With the reorganization of the Va. government during and after the Revolution, however, he once again offered his services. From Dec. 1778 until May 1779, he served as a member of the Council. He resigned this post to become presiding judge of the three-member Court of Admiralty and also a judge of the first state Court of Appeals. Even after Richmond replaced Williamsburg as the seat of Va.'s government, sessions of these two bodies continued to be held in Williamsburg merely for Waller's convenience. Even so, declining health prompted his resignation from both courts in Jan. 1786. He died at his home May 31, 1786, one of the most highly regarded legal figures in Va.

Critical Appraisal: According to Littleton Waller Tazewell, Benjamin Waller was a "studious" man who "found time to read a great deal" despite "his numerous public engagements." In addition, Tazewell continued, "He was an excellent scholar; and kept alive his scholastic learning until his death." Some of this "scholastic learning" he shared with others by guiding them in the study of law, his most famous student being George Wythe, who later taught Thomas Jefferson (q.v.) and at William and Mary held the first law professorship in the U.S. Waller was also the patron of untried writers like the blacksmith-poet Charles Hansford (q.v.), whose extant verses he was responsible for preserving. But of major interest here of course is the writing produced by Waller himself. Unfortunately, much of it is unidentifiable, and some that might be identifiable has been lost. For example, the Archives of the Colonial Williamsburg Foundation contain a collection of satiric letters and verses written by Henry Wood of Goochland between 1745 and 1755 that are addressed to Waller. Some refer to poems that Waller had written and sent to Wood, but copies of none of them have been discovered. Then Waller may have been author of some or all of the "Dinwiddianae" papers, a group of poems and prose pieces dated between 1754 and 1757 that express strong opposition to the policies of Lieutenant Governor Robert Dinwiddie, but Waller is only one of several possible candidates for their authorship.

Fortunately, a handful of poems almost certainly written by Waller have been identified and preserved. None displays literary genius, but all are skillfully written lyrics that reflect taste and talent beyond those of a mere versifier. Three of these lyrics are brief untitled tributes to Charles Hansford discovered in a manuscript version of his poems along with two epistolary prose statements bearing Waller's signature. One of the latter is a brief biographical account of Hansford and a statement revealing how his poems came into Waller's possession; the other is a generous letter to Hansford commending him for his work. Written in heroic couplets, the Waller poems are unrestrained in their response both to Hansford and to his verses. One, citing Hansford's deafness and advanced age, implicitly compares him with Vergil, Pope, Homer, and Milton, who all endured physical frailties but triumphed over them through their poetry— as, Waller said, did Hansford: "The loss is gain, the sorrow turn'd to joy, / When nobly thus we our last stake employ." Another lyric is especially interesting, because it is adapted from a piece by Edmund Waller, the Restoration poet, from whom Benjamin Waller claimed to have been descended. Again Waller cited Hansford's deafness and age, but here his chief aim was to laud numerous reflections of religious zeal sprinkled throughout the Hansford collection. These lines are representative: "The soul, with nobler resolutions deck'd, / The body stooping, does herself erect. / No mortal parts are requisite to raise / Her that, unbodied, can her Maker praise." The third lyric, couched as an elegy, is nonetheless essentially a political statement. It attributes to the late poet pro-American sentiments that surely were Waller's in 1766, when he composed the poem. Were Hansford alive to witness "this fatal day / When liberty, Heaven's best and brightest ray," has been "torn" from his country, Waller said, he would surely "plead her cause" and "vindicate her from oppressive laws!" No doubt among these "oppressive laws" was the recently enacted Stamp Act, which seems to have intensified the growing disenchantment of Waller and many other colonials with British domination during the 1760s.

The only other significant extant work that with reasonable certainty can be placed in the Waller canon is a song, "Myrtilla to Damon," appearing in the *Gentleman's Magazine* for May 1759. A manuscript version of this lyric may be found in colonial Williamsburg's collection of Waller Family Papers—the same collection containing the previously mentioned pieces by Henry Wood. In quatrains of alternating iambic tetrameter and iambic trimeter lines, "Myrtilla to

Damon" is a pastoral piece in which Myrtilla laments Damon's faithlessness to her as he "whistles o'er the plain" and "sings the merriest strain" to other "nymphs" to whom he "Vows ever to be true." Despite such fickleness, Myrtilla says, Damon continues to hold "my chain." She closes with this caution to her fellow "nymphs": "Trust me the tale who best can prove, / By sad experience wise, / Each may by turns obtain his love, / But none can keep the prize." This song, like the earlier tributes to Charles Hansford, has a felicity of diction and sprightliness of meter pleasing both to the ear and eye. As a result, one is all the more disappointed that so few examples of the work of an obviously gifted poet are currently available and can only hope that others may be unearthed in the future.

Suggested Readings: Randolph B. Campbell, "The Case of the 'Three Friends,'" VMHB, 74 (1966), 190-209; Richard Beale Davis, ed., *The Colonial Virginia Satirist*, TAPS, 57 (1967), 5-42; idem, *Intellectual Life in the Colonial South, 1585-1763* (1978), I, 347; II, 545-546, 551; III, 1159, 1213, 1247, 1377-1378, 1421, 1424, 1472, 1477, 1485-1486, 1607; Hugh Blair Grigsby, *Discourse on the Life and Character of the Hon. Littleton Waller Tazewell* (1860), pp. 9-11, 100; Rev. Horace Edwin Hayden, *Virginia Genealogies* (1966), pp. 382-383; Lynda Rees Heaton, ed., "'This Excellent Man': Littleton Waller Tazewell's Sketch of Benjamin Waller," VMHB, 89 (1981), 143-152; Andrew Lewis Riffe, "The Wallers of Endfield, King William County, Virginia," VMHB, 59 (1951), 337-352, 458-493; James A. Servies and Carl R. Dolmetsch, eds., *The Poems of Charles Hansford* (1961), pp. xvii-xix, xxxv-xlii, 69-70, 73-74, 94-95.

William H. Castles, Jr.
University of South Carolina

THOMAS WALLEY (1618-1679)

Works: *Balm in Gilead to Heal Sions Wounds* (1669).

Biography: Thomas Walley, born in Eng. in 1618, was a Puritan clergyman who fled to New Eng. after the Restoration, when many Puritans were driven from their pulpits. A graduate of Pembroke College, Oxford, and rector of St. Mary's Church, Whitechapel, Walley sailed to Boston with his wife and five children in the summer of 1662. Later that year, he was "settled" as pastor of the church at Barnstable on Cape Cod, where he remained until his death at age 61 on Mar. 24, 1678/9. Walley attained a reputation for extraordinary piety. Roger Williams (q.v.) referred to him as "that heavenly Mr. Walley," and John Cotton (q.v.) marveled that at his death "many young ones...flocked to his bed-side" to hear his last words.

Critical Appraisal: Thomas Walley's contribution to American literature consists of a single election sermon, but it is a notable example of the Puritan plain style as well as a clear reflection of the closeness of church and state in early New Eng. The complete title best describes the subject matter: *Balm in*

Gilead to Heal Sions Wounds, or A Treatise Wherein There Is a Clear Discovery of the Most Prevailing Sicknesses of New-England, Both in the Civill and Ecclesiastical State; As Also Sutable Remedies for the Care of Them, Collected Out of That Spirituall Directory, the Word of God. In strong, simple prose, Walley lamented that *"Faith* is dead, and *Love* is cold, and *Zeal* is gone" and reminded the magistrates of New Eng. that "God hath called you to be *Healers* to a poor sick country." Most of the sermon is an extended metaphor of sin as illness, with the conclusion that "If there be Sickness in the Church, there will be little health in the Common-wealth." A 2nd edition of *Balm in Gilead* was published in 1670, but with no alterations in the text. [For a description of the typographical differences between the two editions, see Massachusetts Historical Society *Proceedings,* 29 (1894-95), 274-275.]

Suggested Readings: CCNE. *See also* Frederick Freeman, *The History of Cape Cod: The Annals of Barnstable County,* 2nd ed. (1965), pp. 249, 290-293; CMHS, 38 (1868), 195, 242-243; Cotton Mather, *Magnalia Christi Americana,* 2nd American ed. (1855), I, 599-601; Amos Otis, *Genealogical Notes of Barnstable Families,* 2nd ed. (1979), I, 257; II, 46, 61, 106-109, 242; *PMHS,* 29 (1894-1895), 274-275.

Virginia Bernhard
University of St. Thomas

NEHEMIAH WALTER (1663-1750)

Works: "An Elegiack Verse, on the Death of...Mr. Elijah Corlet" (1687); *The Charitable Samarian* (translator; by Ezechiel Carre; 1689); *The Answer of Several Ministers* (1695); *Unfruitful Hearers Detected and Warned* (1696); *Letter, About the Present State of Christianity Among the Christians and Indians of New England* (with Increase Mather; 1705); *The Body of Death Anatomized* (1707); *A Discourse Concerning the Wonderfulness of Christ* (1713); *A Plain Discourse on Vain Thoughts* (1721); *Faithfulness in the Ministry* (1723); *Practical Discourses on the Holiness of Heaven* (1726); *The Sentiments and Resolutions of an Association of Ministers...Concerning the Reverend Mr. George Whitefield* (1745); *Discourses on the Whole LVth Chapter of Isaiah* (1755); *Thirsty Souls Invited by Christ* (1825).

Biography: Nehemiah Walter was born to an English family in Younghall, Ire., in 1663. About 1680 he and his father, threatened by popery, immigrated to Boston, where the young man's knowledge of Latin allowed him to enter Harvard College. He proved a fine scholar and received the B.A. in 1684 and the M.A. in 1687. When a Boston merchant offered him a trip to Port Royal, Nova Scotia, Walter gladly welcomed the opportunity to travel, found a home with a French family, and easily became fluent in French. Throughout his life, Walter read French theological disputes, and on occasion he preached in French to the Huguenot congregation of Boston.

After returning from Nova Scotia, Walter continued his studies at Harvard College, concentrating on Greek, Latin, Hebrew, and church history. He was recognized as a scholar and taught in the grammar school of Elijah Corlet, on whom he later wrote an elegy. Walter wanted to pursue his studies further and had planned to leave New Eng. in 1688, when he was invited to preach at John Eliot's (q.v.) church in Roxbury. He received a unanimous call to the ministry as colleague to Eliot, and the two worked together until Eliot's death in 1690.

Walter's learning, orthodoxy, and good humor made him popular with his congregation and the noted men of his day. In 1691 Walter married Sarah Mather, the daughter of Increase Mather (q.v.). The couple had nine children. Walter was known for his moving and eloquent extempore sermons on Scripture and his valuable and kindly counsel. Walter died on Sept. 17, 1750. Cotton Mather (q.v.) preached the funeral sermon, and Samuel Sewall (q.v.), Walter's lifelong friend, was among the bearers.

Critical Appraisal: Nehemiah Walter's sermons address the primary tenets of Puritan beliefs such as original sin, the centrality and glory of Christ, or the role of the minister as shepherd. He did not display his unusual knowledge of the Classics, the church's fathers, or Protestant disputes but concerned himself with forthright typological openings of biblical texts.

Walter's "An Elegiack Verse, on the Death...of Mr. Elijah Corlet" is a rhetorical tribute to Corlet's scholarship in Latin and Greek. Walter used Classical and biblical figures in his attempts to describe Corlet's skill as a grammarian and rhetorician. The length of the elegy and its numerous images gratified the Puritan taste for amplification and allusion. The poem is notable as an early example of blank verse and for Walter's assertion that "jingling Rhythme" is not appropriate for elegies.

Suggested Readings: CCNE; FCNEV; Sibley-Shipton (III, 294-301); Sprague (I, 217-220). *See also* Robert D. Arner, "Nehemiah Walter: Milton's Earliest American Disciple?" EAL, 8 (1973), 62-65; William Kellaway, *The New England Company, 1649-1776* (1961); David Levin, *Cotton Mather* (1978), pp. 159, 192-193; Cotton Mather, *Magnalia Christi Americana* (1702), I. i.vii, I. iii. xxxi, II. iv.i; idem, *Selected Letters of Cotton Mather*, ed. Kenneth Silverman (1971), p. 346; Harrison T. Meserole, *Seventeenth-Century American Poetry* (1968), pp. 464-466; Thomas Prince and Thomas Foxcroft, Preface, *Discourses on the Whole, LVth Chapter of Isaiah*, by Nehemiah Walter (1755), pp. i-xxvi; Samuel Sewall, *The Diary of Samuel Sewall*, ed. M. Halsey Thomas (1973); Kenneth Silverman, *Colonial American Poetry* (1968), pp. 121-132; Frederick L. Weis, "The New England Company of 1649 and Its Missionary Enterprises," PCSM, 38 (1959), 134-218.

Cheryl Rivers
Manhattanville College

THOMAS WALTER (1696-1725)

Works: *A Choice Dialogue Between John Faustus, a Conjurer, and Jack Tory His Friend* (1720); *The Grounds and Rules of Musick Explained, or An*

Introduction to the Art of Singing by Note (1721); *The Little-Compton Scourge* (1721); *The Sweet Psalmist of Israel* (1722); *The Scriptures the Only Rule of Faith* (1723); *An Essay upon That Paradox, Infallibility* (1724).

Biography: Thomas Walter was born in Roxbury, Mass., Dec. 7, 1696, the son of the Rev. Nehemiah Walter (q.v.) and Sarah Mather. Through his mother, he was the grandson of Increase Mather (q.v.) and Maria Cotton and a great-grandson of John Cotton (q.v.). As a boy, he was distinguished for retentive memory and quick perception. C. K. Dillaway, in his *History of the Grammar School in Roxbury*, wrote that "there was no subject but what Walter was intimately acquainted with." When he entered Harvard College, his uncle Cotton Mather (q.v.) wrote in his diary: "I have a Nephew now a Student at Cambridge....I would send for him, talk with him, and bestow agreeable Books of Piety upon him." Apparently his frequent conversations with his uncle admirably supplemented his formal learning, for he was graduated from Harvard in 1713 at the age of 17 with the A.M. degree and a reputation for brilliance and conviviality.

Walter was ordained on Oct. 29, 1718, as his father's assistant pastor at Roxbury, on which occasion his grandfather Increase Mather preached the ordination sermon. The congregation had met earlier in Mar. and had chosen him unanimously; furthermore, the townspeople had voted to pay him 500 pounds. It was an eventful year for him; on Christmas Day 1718 he married Rebecca Belcher, daughter of the Rev. Joseph Belcher of Dedham. One daughter, Rebecca, was born in 1722.

He was evidently a popular preacher who did not hesitate to enter into controversial theological arguments. His disputation with John Checkley (q.v.) resulted in his *Choice Dialogue Between John Faustus...and Jack Tory*. Other writings of his pastorate include *An Essay upon...Infallibility, The Scriptures the Only Rule of Faith* and *The Sweet Psalmist of Israel*. Rev. Nathaniel Chauncy (q.v.), in a letter written in 1768, said that he often had occasion to admire Walter's "superlative excellence of...material and acquired accomplishments. His genius was universal. . . . There was no subject but he was acquainted with...he could readily and without any pains write or speak just what he would."

One personal incident, recorded in Cotton Mather's diary, is interesting for its sensationalism; indeed, it nearly cost Thomas Walter his life. Cotton Mather had become intensely interested in inoculation procedures for smallpox and had enlisted the influence of his nephew Thomas to inoculate the people of Boston. The Mather crusade for inoculation was unfortunately terrifying and alienated many Bostonians who believed that inoculation actually spread the disease. At three o'clock in the morning of Nov. 14, 1721, someone threw a "granado" into the room where Thomas Walter lay; he would certainly have been killed had the explosive not spilled out instead of detonating as planned. The assailant evidently thought the room was occupied by Mather (whose room it customarily was), for a note attached to the grenade read: "Cotton Mather, you dog, damn you; I'll inoculate you with this, with a pox to you."

Later entries in Mather's diary give details of Walter's advancing consumption and his death Jan. 10, 1725, from pneumonia. He was buried in Roxbury Cemetery in the same tomb where his father would be laid a few years later. The funeral sermon was preached by Cotton Mather, whose text was printed as *Christodulus: A Good Reward of a Good Servant*.

Critical Appraisal: Thomas Walter is recognized by music historians as an important reformer in the development of American church music; that is, a reformer and organizer in the forward move of congregational psalm singing to accuracy of note and tonal beauty. Singing in American churches of the eighteenth century was declining into an unmelodious mishmash of individual song-by-ear. Not only did each church have its own way of singing a tune, but each person in the congregation interpolated his own fancies. People for the most part could not read music; there was no standard by which to keep everyone singing the same note, or the same rhythm, together. The result was a hideously cacophonous and individually embellished attempt at melody singing.

The reform that plainly was called for was spearheaded by three young Harvard graduates—Thomas Symmes (q.v.), John Tufts (1689-1750), and Thomas Walter. They were supported by other clergymen such as Cotton Mather and Nathaniel Chauncy, who preached and wrote in favor of "Regular Singing or Singing by Note." They advocated singing schools where citizens could be taught the rudiments of music. Although there was some bitter hostility among diehards who did not want the old way changed, the singing school became an established tradition by 1760.

Walter's book, *The Grounds and Rules of Musick Explained*, was his effort to correct what he called in his preface "an horrid medley of confused and disorderly sound," in the churches of New Eng. It was the first practical American music-instruction book; as first published, it was oblong and had sixteen pages of engraved music, using diamond-shaped notes. The music was printed only on one side of the page, and the G-clef (or "clift," as he called it) has a very peculiar form. This was the first music book with bar lines to be printed in the North American colonies; also it was the earliest known example of engraving on copper to be published in Boston. It was printed on the press of James Franklin (q.v.), at a time when his younger brother Benjamin Franklin (q.v.), then only 15, was learning the printer's trade as his apprentice.

Walter's book opens with a Preface containing a long and earnest argument in favor of singing by note. Instructions then follow on the elements of music and the major and minor modes, which he called the "sharp key" and the "flat key." He spoke of "the Length or Shortness of the Notes" in his discussion of time. There is a page headed "Rules for Tuning the Voice," containing a number of short, well-chosen exercises in scales, broken chords, and skips, illustrating the various intervals. George Hood said that "the tunes are composed in three parts only, and are made up of half and whole-notes. . . . The harmony is full, rich, and correct; and the whole style, purely choral." The twenty-four melodies include all thirteen tunes found in the *Bay Psalm Book* of 1698. Apparently John Playford's *Whole Book of Psalms...Composed in Three Parts* (1677) was the principal source for Walter's settings.

Although Thomas Walter's text is variously described by scholars as "confusing," "vague," "turgid," and "lacking in conciseness," it was enormously influential and appeared in six subsequent editions until 1765. Irving Lowens said that the only significant American tune books published by 1764 were those of John Tufts, James Lyon, and Thomas Walter. Before the advent of William Billings (q.v.) in 1770, the primary lasting influence on the style of church music in New Eng. was that of Thomas Walter.

Suggested Readings: CCNE; DAB; Sibley-Shipton (VI, 18-24); Sprague (I, 219-220). *See also* C. F. Adams, Jr., "Some Notices of the Walter Family," NEHGR (1854); *Boston News-Letter*, Nov. 20, 1721; Gilbert Chase, *America's Music* (1966); Ralph T. Daniel, *The Anthem in New England Before 1800* (1966); Francis Samuel Drake, *The Town of Roxbury* (1878); L. C. Elson, *History of American Music* (1925); W. A. Fisher, *Notes on Music in Old Boston* (1918); idem, *One Hundred Years of Music Publishing in the U.S.* (1933); Henry W. Foote, *Three Centuries of American Hymnody* (1940); George Hood, *A History of Music in New England* (1846); John Tasker Howard, *Our American Music* (1931); M. B. Jones, "Bibliographical Notes on Thomas Walter's *Grounds and Rules of Musick Explained*," PAAS, 42 (1933), 235-246; Irving Lowens, *Music and Musicians in Early America* (1964); Hamilton C. MacDougall, *Early New England Psalmody* (1969); Thomas Marrocco and Harold Gleason, *Music in America: An Anthology* (1964); Cotton Mather, *Diary*, CMHS, 7th ser., 7-8 (1911-1912); Frank J. Metcalf, *American Psalmody* (1917); idem, *American Writers and Compilers of Sacred Music* (1925); idem, "Thomas Walter, the Second Native Compiler," CHer (Sept. 1913); E. H. Pierce, "The Rise and Fall of the 'Fugue-Tune' in America," MusQ (Apr. 1910); *A Report of the Record Commissioners, Containing the Roxbury Church Records* (1881); Oscar G. T. Sonneck, *Francis Hopkinson and James Lyon* (1905); Robert Stevenson, *Protestant Church Music in America* (1966); Elwyn A. Wienandt and Robert H. Young, *The Anthem in England and America* (1970).

Elena I. Zimmerman
Forest Park, Georgia

NATHANIEL WARD (c. 1578-1652)

Works: *A Religious Retreat Sounded to a Religious Army* (1647); *A Sermon Preached Before the Honourable House of Commons* (1647); *The Simple Cobler of Aggawam in America* (1647).

Biography: A descendant of minor gentry and yeoman farmers, Nathaniel Ward was born, probably in 1578, in Haverhill, Suffolk, Eng. In 1596 he was admitted to Emmanuel College, Cambridge, from which he received the M.A. in 1603. He entered Lincoln's Inn in 1607 and was admitted to the bar in 1615. On a continental tour about 1616, he met David Pareus who persuaded him to take up the ministry. He served as chaplain to the English merchants in Elbing, Prus., returning to Eng. in 1622, where be became rector of Stondon-Massey on Feb. 10, 1625/26. He was one of forty-nine clergymen who in 1629 addressed a petition to Archbishop Laud on behalf of Thomas Hooker (q.v.). He was twice charged with refusing to follow the prescribed Anglican ceremonies, and in 1631 Laud ordered him to stop preaching. He was suspended on Sept. 27, 1632, excommunicated on Oct. 30, and deprived of his benefice on Dec. 16. After the death of his wife, he immigrated to the Massachusetts Bay colony in 1634 with his daughter Susan (21) and his son James (10), to be joined later by his son John. At 56 or 57, he was one of the oldest—if not the oldest—of the emigrant ministers. He was elected minister of Aggawam (later Ipswich, Mass.) and for a time involved himself deeply in the spiritual affairs of his parish, which included in its congregation Simon and Anne Bradstreet (q.v.). On Feb. 20, 1637/38, he was replaced by Nathaniel Rogers, giving ill health as his reason for seeking his release. He turned to politics and was a member of the committee that drafted the 1641 *Body of Liberties*. For this service, he was granted 600 acres at what is now Haverhill, Mass. Ill health apparently prevented him from settling this land with his family and instead he went to Boston, where he wrote *The Simple Cobler* in 1645-1646 after having, on Dec. 10, 1641, deeded the Haverhill land to Harvard College. He returned to Eng. in 1647 and became pastor at Shenfield. *The Simple Cobler* brought him temporary popularity in Parliament. In 1647 he preached their Jun. Fast Day sermon in which, in addition to repeating the exhortations of the book, he called for the disbanding of much of the army and the enforcing of religious discipline upon the rest. Because Parliament was afraid of the army, the sermon was published by anonymous "friends" of the author. In Aug. of the same year, nothing daunted, he published *A Religious Retreat*, this time addressed to the army itself, in which he repeated his demands. During the following years, he may have authored other pamphlets in the same vein. In 1647 as well he contributed an introductory epistle "To the Reader" in *The Day-Breaking, If Not the Sun-Rising of the Gospell with the Indians in New-England* and in 1650 an introductory poem ("Mercury Show'd Apollo, Bartas' Book") to Anne Bradstreet's *Tenth Muse Lately Sprung Up in America*. In 1652 he died without having achieved religious or political influence.

Critical Appraisal: Frequently cited as the first American satire or the first humorous book written in America, *The Simple Cobler of Aggawam* was published in London on Jan. 29, 1647, and went through four editions that year. Ward arrived back in Eng. in time to make extensive revisions in the 3rd and 4th editions. (A 5th edition was published sixty-six years later.) Obviously something of an overnight sensation in its own time, the book can prove bewildering to the modern reader who may be unversed in its firmly Renaissance techniques and in the topical nature of its concerns.

For his satiric and homiletic purposes, Ward created a persona, one Theodore (Greek for *Nathaniel*) de la Guard (French for *Ward*), a "simple cobbler" under whose name the book was published and who addresses from New Eng. the

Parliament that had in 1645 executed Ward's old enemy, Archbishop Laud. The persona, in and out of which Ward slips at will, is a stock character of Renaissance comedy and satire and can be traced to the "mechanic preacher" of the Martin Marprelate tracts, the *Cobler of Canterbury* (1608), and, more significantly, to Democritus, Jr., the "laughing philosopher" who is the persona of Robert Burton's *Anatomy of Melancholy* (1621).

The persona's message is essentially conservative: he calls upon Parliament to cease its toleration of the numerous religious sects springing up in Eng. —Independents, Separatists, Anabaptists, and so on—providing a list of seventeen such "Religious Men but pernicious Heretiques" and arguing the diabolic origins of sects and schisms: "If the devill might have his free option, I beleeve he would ask nothing else, but liberty to enfranchize all false Religions." He urges the *via media* between separation and Rome and urges Charles I to compromise with Parliament so that an end may be put to the continuing political disorder in Eng. He exhorts Parliament to take firm control of religion, to compromise on political differences, to put an end to the Civil War *or* to wage it more vigorously for Parliament's own victory.

Besides the exaggerated language—including vernacular usages, analogies, antitheses, parallelisms, puns in more than one language, allusions, epigrams, and quotations in foreign languages and from philosophy, poetry, drama, and pornography—the modern reader's ability to follow Ward's argument may also be hampered by the persona's tendency to digress. We may seem to be left with only the persona as the central structural element (and even he appears and disappears at apparent random). Consequently, it is essential to remember that Ward is working in the Burton tradition in which apparent madness in sense or structure provides an index to the madness of the system under satiric attack. Even without the tradition, we have Ward's reminder that "I speak it seriously, according to my meaning."

For example, in the midst of bewailing "Errors in Religion" (the subject of the book), Ward digressed to condemn current women's fashions: his heart was broken "to see so many goodly English-women imprisoned in French Cages, peering out of their hood-holes for some men of mercy to help them with a little wit, and no body relieves them." It becomes clear from his argument, however, that madness in fashion follows from madness in religion, and that madness is the object of the satire, and that it can be dealt with only madly, for as he pointed out in one of the doggerel verses scattered throughout his text, *"He that instructs a foole, may act th'unwise."* Thus it is perfectly fitting that the cobbler be allowed to develop outrageous metaphors, as when he speaks of these fashionable women's "long-wasted, but short-skirted patience."

One admits therefore that Ward's social thought had no influence in America or Eng. and that the very literary genre he chose indicates a certain pessimism from the beginning. Nevertheless, the robust, cantankerous, sententious, eccentric, sheer high spirits of the work, qualities that we find nowhere else in New

Eng. at the time, make *The Simple Cobler* a *vade mecum* for any serious student
of early American literature.

Suggested Readings: CCNE; DAB; DNB; FCNEV; LHUS; Sprague (I, 39-40);
T_1. *See also* Robert D. Arner, *"The Simple Cobler of Aggawam*: Nathaniel Ward and the
Rhetoric of Satire," EAL, 5 (1971), 3-16; Jean Béranger, *Nathaniel Ward* (1969); Wil-
liam J. Scheick, "The Widower Narrator in Nathaniel Ward's *The Simple Cobler of
Aggawam*," NEQ, 47 (1974), 87-96; P. M. Zall, ed., *The Simple Cobler of Aggawam in
America* (1969), pp. ix-xviii.

John J. Teunissen
University of Manitoba

JOSEPH WARREN (1741-1775)

Works: *An Oration, Delivered March 5th, 1772* (1772); *An Oration; Delivered March Sixth, 1775* (1775).

Biography: A fourth-generation American, Joseph Warren was born in
Roxbury, Mass., in 1741. The son of a substantial farmer, he graduated from
Harvard College in 1759. After serving an apprenticeship to a leading Boston
physician, Warren embarked upon a medical career distinguished by concern in
practice and innovation in teaching. His popularity as a practitioner was doubtless enhanced by personal charm and sincerity, warmth and sensitivity, dignity
and confidence. Such leadership qualities drew Warren into the thick of political
broils that centered locally upon the control by conservatives over policymaking
and officeholding in Mass. and imperially upon the nature and extent of parliamentary powers of taxation and legislation over the American colonies.

From the time of the Stamp Act until his death, Warren held to a consistently
radical posture in advocating American rights, often much in advance of other
future Boston revolutionaries excepting Samuel Adams (q.v.). Mingling intimately with both the well-to-do and the humble, he influenced political decision
making by serving as the chief informal director of the mechanics caucus of the
North End of Boston and as the grand master of St. Andrews Masonic lodge.
Although little concerned with economic, political, or military personal ambition, his major role in shaping Boston policies was formally recognized in 1774
when the town elected him as a representative to the Provincial Congress, from
whence he came to head the Committee of Safety of Massachusetts, was elected
president of the Third Provincial Congress, and was appointed a major general
by that Congress in Jun. 1775. While fulfilling his duties at the battle of Bunker
Hill, dressed in fine apparel, he was killed by a bullet to the skull as he slowly
walked away during the retreat—"always a gentleman from sole to crown."

Critical Appraisal: Like so many of his contemporaries, Joseph Warren
cloaked most of his writing under a thin veil of pseudonymous authorship.

Although not as active a pamphlet polemicist as other Boston patriots, he did contribute numerous and significant pieces to the newspaper press. Despite a restrained and kindly nature, Warren at times became so emotionally embroiled in an issue that his press attacks upon the actions and motives of a protagonist bordered upon malicious, scurrilous, even libelous, character assassination. More restrained but especially effective were lengthier pamphlets or broadsides that he either authored or drafted himself or in collaboration with others, such as *A Short Narrative of the Horrid Massacre in Boston*, an inflammatory account of the Boston Massacre composed in conjunction with James Bowdoin (q.v.) and Samuel Pemberton; the Solemn League and Covenant, calling for a boycott of British goods following the tea incident; the Suffolk Resolves, a polished rendition of the response of Suffolk County delegates to the Intolerable Acts; and the *Narrative of the Excursion and Ravages of the King's Troops*, an emotional description of the Lexington engagement whereby Warren charged Br. with war guilt for supposedly firing the first shot.

However clouded the authorship or sentiments of such compositions might be, Warren's two published Boston Massacre orations give explicit evidence of the force of his varied writings in forwarding the American cause. Of the early massacre commemorations, those of Warren are easily the most affecting. He avoided the pedestrian style of James Lovell (1771), the unimaginative didacticism of Benjamin Church (q.v.) (1773), and the stilted phraseology of John Hancock (1774). Instead, Warren addressed his hearers in direct and succinct language with an easy and flowing style that proved both intelligible to the mind and pleasing to the ear. In these orations, he passed by logical progression from prefatory summations of natural law political theory, through filiopietistic historical interpretations of founding settler motives and rights, to critical evaluations of recent events judged inimical to the legitimate constitutional relationship of Br. and her colonies. But before calling for resistance against these invasions of American rights, Warren skillfully aroused the emotions of his hearers by impassioned descriptions of British atrocities during the massacre. Only then would he conclude with a thinly veiled plea for active opposition to oppression.

For his time, Warren was advanced not only in style but in content, as when, for example, in his 1772 oration he declared that any "state must be flourishing and happy" where there existed a "noble attachment to a constitution, founded on free and benevolent principles." He went on—perhaps unwittingly—to invert the traditional New Eng. philosophy of history however. Instead of portraying moral and religious corruption as the result of loss of dedication to constitutional principles—a secularized rendition of the jeremiad emphasizing political, rather than moral and religious, roots for decline. This 1772 oration is the more moving and powerful of the two. That of 1775, presented at a time when the outbreak of open hostilities threatened, paradoxically appears both more controlled and more discursive, neither as moving nor direct as the 1772 oration. Nonetheless, the aim of both pieces, to strike—in typical New Eng. fashion—that delicate balance between intellectual conviction and emotional arousal, is worthily accomplished.

Suggested Readings: DAB; Sibley-Shipton (XIV, 510-527); T$_2$. *See also* John Cary, *Joseph Warren: Physician, Politician, Patriot* (1961).

John G. Buchanan
California State University, Long Beach

MERCY OTIS WARREN (1728-1814)

Works: *The Adulateur* (1772, 1773); *The Defeat* (1773); *The Group* (1775); *The Blockheads; Or, The Affrighted Officers* (1776); *The Motley Assembly* (1779); *Sans Souci* (1785); *Observations on the New Constitution* (1788); *Poems Dramatic and Miscellaneous* (1790); *History of the Rise, Progress and Termination of the American Revolution* (1805); *The Retreat* (possible or attributed author; n.d.).

Biography: Born in Barnstable, Mass., in 1728, Mercy Otis Warren played a significant role in the Mass. political and literary scene during the Revolutionary War. Her involvement stemmed from the liberal political interests of her father, James Otis; brother, the younger James Otis (q.v.); and husband, James Warren, a gentleman farmer, merchant, and, later, Revolutionary War general. Marriage in 1754 brought her to Plymouth, where, except for a short residence in Milton, she raised five sons and with her husband carried on an extensive correspondence and friendship with many important American and European political and literary personages, including John Adams (q.v.) and Abigail Adams (q.v.), George Washington (q.v.) and Martha Washington, Thomas Jefferson (q.v.), James Bowdoin (q.v.), Dr. John Winthrop (q.v.) and Hannah Winthrop, Lady Montague, Catherine Macaulay, and Marquis de Lafayette. In her personal associations, she was known to be "affable without familiarity," "gracious to equals," but "condescending to inferiors," elegant, dignified, and logical.

In addition to influencing Revolutionary policies from her Plymouth home, Mercy Warren expressed her strong political and social views through satiric propaganda plays and verse and wrote one of the important contemporary histories of the American Revolution. Although she had no formal education, having received only some tutoring from Rev. Jonathan Russell, the Barnstable clergyman, she became widely read; she held Addison, Pope, and Dryden as her literary ideals and read Raynal, Gibbon, Hume, and Moliere, among other notables. John Adams viewed her as "an imcomparable Satyrist" whose "poetical pen...has no equal that I know of in this country." In addition, her first-hand knowledge of the leading Revolutionary figures contributed to an intimate characterization of those personalities in her *History*. Until her death in 1814, she was sought out as an authority on the Revolutionary era.

Critical Appraisal: In her plays, largely patterned on neo-Classical techniques, Mercy Warren contributed to the satiric political propaganda that accompanied the American Revolution. More importantly, in *The Adulateur, The Group,* and *The Blockheads*, she created an imaginative contribution to American literary and cultural history: the motif of America as a "Revolutionary Theater" in which a drama of significant scope and importance was being acted through the dramatization of real and imagined incidents as tragedies, farces, and comedies, and the representation of significant Revolutionary figures as "actors" on the American stage. In the manner of a Roman heroic drama, *The Adulateur* satirizes Governor Thomas Hutchinson's (q.v.) connivance and duplicity in his dealings with the Mass. patriots, the Tory actions identified as a "Tragedy as it is now acted in Upper Servia"; *The Group* farcically portrays the "scenes" played by the ruling Tory Council, appointed by Charles II, in removing the freedom of Mass. citizens; and *The Blockheads*, generally attributed to Warren and written in reaction to Gen. Burgoyne's *The Blockade of Boston* (1775), ridicules the abortive, comedic attempt of Gen. Howe to seize the fortifications in Boston and the consequential confusion among the Tory refugees who left with the British army. Although an antitheatrical milieu prevailed in New Eng., Warren justified her "theatrical amusements" as enforcing "lessons of morality" and as the "exhibition of great historical events" for the contemplation of reflecting and philosophical minds. Nevertheless, in the actions and words of the lambasted British and Tories, there was also an "entertaining" quality that Warren herself recognized.

Warren's dramatic pieces are generally written in a refined, academic style, although her blank verse is occasionally notable. Soliloquies and direct revelation of thoughts by characters to their accomplices predominate. With the exception of the dramatic conflicts and suspense in *The Ladies of Castille* and *The Sack of Rome*, published in her *Poems*, her plays have limited plot and character development, their primary purpose being to create strong political satire.

Warren's poetry, published in contemporary newspapers and collected in her *Poems*, is occasional verse, including poems written to and about family members, nature, public figures, and the effect that suspension of trade with Br. will have on a lady's toilet; the volume had wide circulation among political and other public notables.

Her three-volume *History*, written over a twenty-five-year period, is "Interspersed with Biographical, Political, and Moral Observations" that reveal her personal involvement. Although her historic narrative partly reflects an anti-Federalist bias and caused a temporary break in her friendship with John Adams, the factual accuracy, biographical portraits, and thorough explanation of the political causes of the Revolution won a far-ranging and long-lasting respect among her contemporaries and historians.

Suggested Readings: DAB; LHUS; NAW; T₂. *See also* Katherine Anthony, *First Lady of the Revolution: The Life of Mercy Otis Warren* (1958); Alice Brown, *Women of Colonial and Revolutionary Times: Mercy Otis Warren* (1896); Lester H. Cohen, "Explaining the Revolution: Ideology and Ethics in Mercy Otis Warren's Historical Theory," WMQ, 37 (1980), 200-218; Pattie Cowell, *Women Poets in Pre-Revolutionary America* (1981); W. C. Ford, ed., *Warren-Adams Letters*, 2 vols. (1917); Lawrence J. Friedman and Arthur H. Shaffer, "Mercy Otis Warren and the Politics of Historical Nationalism," NEQ, 48 (1975), 194-215; Edmund M. Hayes, "Mercy Otis Warren: *The Defeat*," NEQ,

49 (1976), 440-458; Maud M. Hutcheson, "Mercy Warren, 1728-1814," WMQ, 10 (1953), 378-402; Norman Philbrick, ed., *Trumpets Sounding: Propaganda Plays of the American Revolution* (1972); Kenneth Silverman, *A Cultural History of the American Revolution* (1976), pp. 212-213, 255-256, 295.

Dennis Gartner
Frostburg State College

GEORGE WASHINGTON (1732-1799)

Works: Worthington C. Ford, ed., *The Writings of George Washington*, 14 vols. (1889-1893); John C. Fitzpatrick, *The Writings of George Washington*, 39 vols. (1931-1944); *The Diaries of George Washington*, 6 vols. (1976-1979).

Biography: George Washington, the first president of the U.S., was born in Westmoreland County, Va., in 1732. His seven or eight years of formal schooling grounded him not only in mathematics and trigonometry, enabling him to take up surveying in his early career, but also introduced him to the world of letters. His reading included the leading works of fiction of his day (*Tom Jones, Humphrey Clinker*, and *Peregrine Pickle*), ethical works, the writings of Pope and Addison, and the Bible. After the death of his elder half-brother Lawrence, George became owner of Mount Vernon. He was appointed by Governor Dinwiddie to be district adjutant for the southern district of Va. and later transferred to the northern neck and Eastern Shore. In 1753 he accepted Dinwiddie's appointment to deliver an ultimatum to the French who were allegedly encroaching on English lands in the Ohio country. The report to Dinwiddie of Washington's harrowing exploits was printed as *The Journal of Major George Washington* (1754). After leading other military expeditions, Washington married Martha, widow of Daniel Parke Custis, in 1759 and settled down at Mount Vernon to the life of a gentleman-farmer until public service summoned him to renewed duties in the Va. House of Burgesses. From 1760 until 1774, he was a justice of Fairfax and held court in Alexandria.

Washington's close observations of the deteriorating relations with G.B. caused particularly by her taxation policies made him a logical choice for delegate to the First (1774) and Second (1775) Continental Congresses, and he was elected in 1775 to assume command of the continental armies. Following victory over the British, he resigned his commission to Congress, relinquishing "with satisfaction the appointment I accepted with diffidence." He then turned to restoring to self-support the financial base of Mount Vernon, which had fallen into a shambles while he was away. When the Federal Convention was summoned, he attended and served as its president. In time he would become the nation's president followed by an unopposed second term. As president he molded the contours of the new nation financially and militarily so that it might assume its proper rank among nations. He retired from the presidency in 1797 only to be summoned again to the country's aid to lead an army raised in expectation of war with Fr. by President John Adams (q.v.), although Washington never personally commanded it. He died in Dec. 1799 on the threshold of a new century he had already done much to shape.

Critical Appraisal: George Washington's writings consist of letters, diaries, military records, and financial documents, but his *Diaries* are perhaps his best known works. Not the effort of a literary diarist, the *Diaries* present instead a practical mirror of Washington's life. They stretch from the spring of 1748 when he set out in a surveying party engaged by Lord Fairfax, the account of which Washington preserved in a small notebook, until Dec. 1799 when he died. For Washington his *Diaries* were an accounting of "Where & How my Time is Spent," a utilitarian accounting in an age preoccupied with taking stock. Washington, who "strove, not always successfully, to restrict himself to a 'plain stile,'" bequeathed us ringing if not always memorable phrases such as the injunction in his 1796 Farewell Address ("'Tis our true policy to steer clear of permanent alliances, with any portion of the foreign world"), which is frequently misquoted by political orators who confuse it with Thomas Jefferson's (q.v.) phrase about "entangling alliances." His prodigious literary legacy is a wealth of writing reflecting America in her formative state.

Suggested Readings: DAB; LHUS; T$_1$; T$_2$. *See also* William A. Bryan, *George Washington in America, 1775-1865* (1952); James Thomas Flexner, *George Washington in the American Revolution, 1775-1783* (1968); idem, *George Washington: Anguish and Farewell, 1793-1799* (1972); idem, *George Washington: The Forge of Experience, 1732-1775* (1965); idem, *George Washington and the New Nation, 1783-1793* (1970); J. H. Penniman, *George Washington as Man of Letters* (1918).

L. Lynn Hogue
Georgia State University, Atlanta

GEORGE WEBB (b.c. 1708)

Works: *Bachelors Hall* (1731).

Biography: According to Benjamin Franklin's (q.v.) *Autobiography*, the principal source for biographical information, George Webb was born in Gloucester, Eng., in 1708 and educated at a local grammar school. Joseph Foster's *Alumni Oxoniensis* reports that Webb matriculated at Baliol College in 1724 at age 16 but left after a year to seek employment as an actor in London. Lack of success induced him to sign as an indentured servant bound for America. In Philadelphia, Webb served as an apprentice in Samuel Keimer's (q.v.) printing shop, although he was eventually able to join with Keimer as a partner. Despite revealing Franklin's plans for a weekly paper to Keimer, Webb became a member of Franklin's Junto in 1727. Four years later, Franklin also published Webb's twelve-page folio poem. The remainder of Webb's life remains largely a matter of conjecture. Douglas McMurtrie suggested that Webb may be the George Webb who established the first press in S.C. in 1731. Lawrence Wroth in *The Colonial Printer* (1964) acknowledged this possibility and linked Webb with the George Webb of Annapolis. Both also suggest the possibility that Webb died in S.C. in 1732 or perhaps returned to Eng. about the same time. Foster reported that Webb was in Eng. in 1734 serving as a barrister in the Middle Temple.

Critical Appraisal: Franklin's evaluation of George Webb remains the best known: "He was lively, witty, good-natured, and a pleasant companion; but idle, thoughtless, and imprudent to the last degree." Contemporary reaction to Webb's poetry seems to share at least part of these sentiments. *Bachelors Hall* occasioned complimentary verses by Jacob Taylor (q.v.) and Joseph Breintnall (q.v.) (both included in Franklin's edition of the poem) and the following praise from "The Wits and Poets of Pennsylvania": "For thro' the Piece Poetick Genius shines, / Where Thoughts sublime Meet in harmonious Lines; / Where hounding Pegasus with loosen'd Rein, / Proud of the Course, shows a well order'd Flame."

Later estimates range from warm praise to modest acknowledgment. Joshua Fisher (1830) called the poem "altogether a very creditable performance." In their *History of Philadelphia* (1884), J. Thomas Scharff and Thompson Westcott noted that the poem exhibits "a poetical gift of respectable degree," and Joseph Jackson thought that Webb's poem "was quite as good as the average poem of his time, and rather superior to the majority of poems that saw light in the Colonies before him." William P. Trent's *Cambridge History of American Literature* offers a sterner judgment: "Webb's heroic couplets are as conventional as could be desired, and, together with the verses written by other members of his circle, they recall the dominant hand of Pope."

Although Webb did (probably) compose poems for the *Gentleman's Magazine* and the *American Weekly Mercury*, he is remembered by Trent and others for *Bachelors Hall*. In this poem, Webb's subject is a Philadelphia gentlemen's club, noted in its day for the often boisterous antics of its members. (Franklin's Junto, or the Leather Apron Club, included the less affluent yet more enterprising young men; the Merchants' Every Night drew mainly the respectable and established gentlemen.) Webb's purpose was to acquit the club of those accusations of licentiousness:

> Fir'd with business of the noisy town,
> The weary Batchelors their cares disown;
> For this loved seat they all at once prepare,
> And long to breathe the sweets of country air;
> On nobler thoughts their active minds employ,
> And a select variety enjoy.

Certainly, such lines bear testimony to Pope's influence, if not dominance. Webb likewise employed the couplet, as of course did Pope, to provide his readers with memorable aphorism: "But condescending, genuine, apt, and fit, /

Good nature is the parent of true wit." The influence of Franklin's Junto and the
tenets of inquisitive and confident Deism are also evident:
>   Mysterious nature here unveil'd shall be,
>   And knotty points of deep philosophy;
>   Whatever wonders undiscover'd are,
>   Deep hid in earth, or floating high in air,
>   Though in the darkest womb of night involv'd,
>   Shall by the curious searcher here be solv'd.

Webb did not, however, strike memorable images or impress the reader with
original poetics; this probably was not his intention. His poetry serves a social
function: *Bachelors Hall* is a witty apology for the lives of clever young men.
Webb's own life would seem to retain more interest for the fictional biographer
than his poetry does for the literary critic.

Suggested Readings: T₁. *See also* Benjamin Franklin, *The Autobiography of
Benjamin Franklin*, ed. Leonard W. Labaree et al. (1964); Joseph Jackson, *Literary
Landmarks of Philadelphia* (1939), pp. 301-303; Douglas C. McMurtrie, "The First
Decade of Printing in the Royal Province of South Carolina," *Library*, 4th ser., 13
(1932-1933), 425-452.

Timothy K. Conley
Bradley University

JOHN WEBB (1687-1750)

Works: *The Young Mans Duty, Explained...to a Society of Young Men*
(1718); *The Peculiar Advantages of Early Piety* (pub. in Cotton Mather, *A
Course of Sermons on Early Piety*; 1721); *A Sermon...at the Thursday Lecture
in Boston* (1722); *Practical Discourses on Death, Judgment, Heaven & Hell. In
Twenty-Four Sermons* (1726); *A Seasonable Warning Against Bad Company-
Keeping* (1726); *The Duty of Ministers...Occasion'd by the...Death of the
Reverend Mr. William Waldron* (1727); *The Believer's Redemption* (1728); *Vows
Made unto God* (1728); *Some Plain and Necessary Directions to Obtain Eternal
Salvation. In Six Sermons* (1729); *A Brief Discourse at the Ordination of a
Deacon* (1731); *The Great Concern of New-England* (1731); *The Duty of a
Degenerate People* (1734); *The Greatness of Sin Improv'd...A Sermon...in the
Hearing of...Condemned Malefactors* (1734); *The Government of Christ...
Preached...the Anniversary for the Election* (1738); *The Duty of Sur-
vivers...Preach'd...After the Death of the Reverend Mr. Peter Thacher* (1739);
Christ's Suit to the Sinner...Preach'd in a Time of Great Awakening (1741).

Biography: John Webb, chaplain of Castle William, first minister of the
New North Church of Boston, early supporter of Zabdiel Boylston (q.v.) and his
inoculations against smallpox, overseer of Harvard College, and chaplain of the

Mass. House of Representatives, was born in Braintree, Mass., on Aug. 21, 1687. His parents were John and Bethiah (Adams) Webb, and in the town of Braintree, where the elder Webb was selectman, the Webbs were known as a family of property and distinction. Prepared for college at the Braintree Grammar School, Webb attended Harvard, obtaining an A.B. in 1708. From Oct. 1708 to Oct. 1709, he served as schoolmaster in the town of Reading, where, according to one posthumous account of Webb's early career, "He was especially careful to impress the Minds of those under his Charge with a Sense of Divine Things; often exhorting them to remember their Creator in the Days of their Youth." In fact, an interest in the religious education of young people would later become a special feature of Webb's ministry. After preparing for and taking the A.M. in 1711, Webb began to preach in the Boston area. He is known to have preached early in his career before Harvard's President John Leverett and in one of the parishes of Newbury. Late in 1713 he was appointed chaplain of Castle William, after failing in his bid for the Charlestown pulpit. In 1714, supported by Cotton Mather (q.v.) and Increase Mather (q.v.), Thomas Bridge, and several other local conservative preachers, Webb was selected pastor of the New North Church, which was formed by a group of "Substantial mechanicks," who were once part of the Mathers' congregation at the North Church. Webb's selection was a personal victory and a victory for the Boston conservative camp, for his competitor for the position was the bright, energetic, and liberal John Barnard (q.v.), who had the support of Benjamin Colman (q.v.) and his followers. Webb was ordained over the New North on Oct. 20, 1714, in a ceremony participated in by the Mathers, Bridge, and Ebenezer Pemberton (q.v.). In the years that followed, Webb kept close to the Mathers and their fellow conservatives. He supported them in their opposition to Governor Joseph Dudley (q.v.); Increase Mather prepared a preface for *The Young Mans Duty, Explained*, Webb's first printed sermon, and Webb preached one of the lecture sermons for Cotton Mather's "course" on early piety in 1721. In 1720 Peter Thacher (q.v.) was settled as Webb's colleague, and since Thacher was the older man, Webb accorded him the rank of senior pastor. The Thacher-Webb partnership, which lasted for eighteen years until Thacher's death, was a happy one and helped to free Webb from his dependence upon the Mathers. For instance, with Thacher's support, Webb ordained ruling elders for the New North, a move that shocked the Mather faction. As time passed, Webb's increased popularity and his election as chaplain of the House of Representatives further relieved him of dependence upon any party. He continued to be an essential conservative, and throughout the 1730s, his voice was raised often to support the revival of religion that became the Great Awakening. Webb was prominent among the preachers who welcomed George Whitefield (q.v.) to Boston, and he invited Whitefield to the New North, where the evangelist preached to an overflow audience of more than 6,000. Forced by poor health to relinquish part of his pastoral duties, Webb accepted Andrew Eliot (q.v.) as his colleague in 1742. Mourned by many as "a very pious holy man of God, and an Excellent and Faithful Minister of Jesus Christ," Webb died on Apr. 16, 1750. Married twice, first in 1715 to Frances Bromfield, who died during the 1721 smallpox epidemic, leaving no children, and then in 1727 to Elizabeth Jackson. Webb was survived by Elizabeth, a daughter Elizabeth born in 1730, and a son John born in 1732.

Critical Appraisal: In *A Burning and Shining Light*, the funeral sermon that Eliot preached for his colleague in 1750, John Webb is celebrated as, among other things, a conscientious preacher of uncommon talent. In his sermons, Eliot reported, "[Webb] laboured to be plain and close, that he might inform the Understanding, and awaken the Conscience at the same time.—He studied the Sense more than the Language, and had rather had his Hearers into right Sentiments and practice, than tickle their Ears with smooth and well turned Periods." Eliot's appraisal of Webb's talent is supported by a review of Webb's printed sermons. There we discover a great command of language and emotion as Webb spoke, for instance, at one time as a spiritual father pleading for the souls of his flock and at another time as a modern-day Jeremiah informing his flock of the horrors that await those who die outside of Christ and his church. That his talent was undoubtedly appreciated by his contemporaries is apparent from the fact that early in his career he was invited to preach the Artillery Election Sermon for 1719, and during the decades that followed, he was invited to preach repeatedly for members of the House. In 1731 he preached at the special session of the Mass. General Court, and in 1738 he preached the annual election sermon. Nor do these moments of triumph in the pulpit tell the whole story, for no typical Puritan occasion for a sermon is absent from among Webb's forty-four printed sermons, and several pieces—among them *The Young Mans Duty, Explained, A Seasonable Warning Against Bad Company-Keeping*, and *Some Plain and Necessary Directions*, which is a collection of sermons—went through multiple printings or editions, in all, a very respectable record for an early eighteenth-century conservative minister.

Although a case might be made for Webb's *The Duty of a Degenerate People* (1734) or his *The Government of Christ* (1738) as a particularly noteworthy sermon, no one Webb sermon is, in the final analysis, the best or most typical of his work. Indeed, it is more fair to Webb's gifted and complex mind and to his sermonic talent to collect evidence of his views and pulpit manners from various sources. For instance, Webb's lifelong interest in the religious education of New Eng.'s children has already been noticed, but the intensity of his interest in that cause is apparent only by noticing that two of his earliest printed sermons were exclusively for young audiences, and that throughout his career, he usually devoted a section of a sermon's applications to the particular edification of the young. At the same time, he constantly challenged New Eng.'s elders to take care of the young, as in 1722, when in *A Sermon...at the Thursday Lecture* he inquired whether enough was being done in schools "to restrain the exhorbitant Lusts, and form the Manners of Youth." In that same sermon, he reminded the tutors of Harvard College that "together with the advancement of good Literature...proper measures [should] be taken to promote vital Religion."

Of course, Webb had other interests that he was equally concerned to promote. As a conservative holding to the old New Eng. Way, Webb subscribed to the belief that New Eng. stood in the utmost peril in the 1720s and 1730s lest the "sins of the Land" be answered to with reform. Taking his form from the fast and humiliation exercises led by the Mathers and others of their party, Webb incorporated their litany of New Eng.'s sins and their repeated cries for reform into his own sermons. In *The Great Concern of New-England*, which he preached on Feb. 11, 1731, before the General Court, Webb begged his audience to pass and enforce laws to stem the "Flood of Irreligion and Prophaness... pernicious Lying, Slandering, and Backbiting [of] one another... filthy Lewdness and Uncleanness... [and] open and horrible contempt cast upon the sacred Name, and Day" that threatened New Eng.'s very existence. In *The Duty of a Degenerate People*, which he preached before his New North congregation on Jun. 18, 1734, Webb appealed to his people "that in this day of Declension... [they] beg earnestly of God... [to] *revive the Work of Grace in [their] Hearts*." "[You] must confess and bewail your late slothfulness and negligence in Duty," he told them; "own that the languishing state of your Graces are fallen into, is owing to this guilty cause; and then fly to the Blood of Jesus for a new, and a sealed Pardon." Little wonder then that Webb rejoiced at the early signs of the Awakening or that he played a large and willing role in bringing the spirit of revival to Boston. From Webb's hopeful point of view, the Awakening was to be New Eng.'s "saving Grace."

As a preacher of talent and worth, an inheritor of the pastoral dynasty left unattended at the death of the Mathers, and an insightful spokesman for the old New Eng. Way, John Webb deserves more credit and attention than scholars have thus far given him. In any future considerations of the politics and religion of New Eng. between 1720 and 1750, Webb's position in New Eng. affairs and the impact of his sermons upon the opinion of public officials and fellow clergymen merit examination and comment.

Suggested Readings: CCNE; Sibley-Shipton (V, 463-471). *See also* Andrew Eliot, *A Burning and Shining Light* (1750).

Ronald A. Bosco
State University of New York at Albany

NOAH WEBSTER (1758-1843)

Works: *A Grammatical Institute of the English Language, Comprising, an Easy, Concise, and Systematic Method of Education, Designed for the Use of English Schools in America. In Three Parts* (Pt. I, 1783; Pt. II, 1784; Pt. III, 1785); *An Examination into the Leading Principles of the Federal Constitution Proposed by the Late Convention Held at Philadelphia* (1787); *Dissertations on the English Language: With Notes, Historical and Critical. To Which Is Added,* *by Way of Appendix, an Essay on a Reformed Mode of Spelling, with Dr. Franklin's Arguments on That Subject* (1789); *The New England Primer, Amended and Improved* (1789); *A Collection of Essays and Fugitive Writings on Moral, Historical, Political and Literary Subjects* (1790); *The Little Reader's Assistant* (1790); *Effects of Slavery, on Morals and Industry* (1793); *The Revolution in France Considered in Respect to Its Progress and Effects. By an American* (1794); *A Brief History of Epidemic and Pestilential Diseases,* 2 vols. (1799); *A Compendious Dictionary of the English Language* (1806); *An American Dictionary of the English Language* (1828); *The Holy Bible, Containing the Old and New Testament, in the Common Version. With Amendments of the Language* (1833); *The Elementary Spelling Book; Being an Improved American Spelling Book* (1834).

[New York] *American Minerva* (1793-1796): daily, established Dec. 9, 1793, by George Bunce & Company (Webster as editor), with the subtitle *Patroness of Peace, Commerce, and the Liberal Arts;* title changed on Mar. 19, 1794, with the addition *And the New-York (Evening) Advertiser;* became *American Minerva, and the New-York (Evening) Advertiser* on Mar. 20, 1794; later, *American Minerva; an Evening Advertiser* on May 6, 1775; on May 2, 1796, the Bunce-Webster partnership was dissolved and the newspaper became the *Minerva, & Mercantile Evening Advertiser* under the guidance of Hopkins, Webb & Co. (Webster); succeeded by the *Commercial Advertiser* after Sept. 30, 1797.

[New York] *Herald* (1794-1797): semiweekly edition of the *American Minerva;* established Jun. 4, 1794, with subtitle *A Gazette for the Country;* succeeded by *The Spectator* after Sept. 30, 1797.

[New York] *Commercial Advertiser* (1797-1803): daily, begun on Oct. 2, 1797, as successor of *The Minerva;* the Webster-Hopkins partnership was terminated on Jul. 1, 1799, with Webster taking his nephew Ebenezer Belden as a partner; on Nov. 4, 1803, Webster retired and the paper was published under various titles and management until after 1820.

The American Magazine. Containing a Miscellaneous Collection of Original and Other Valuable Essays in Prose and Verse, and Calculated for Both Instruction and Amusement (Dec. 1787-Nov. 1788): monthly, with Noah Webster, editor, and the following publishers: Samuel Loudon, N.Y., Dec. 1787-Feb. 1788; S. and J. Loudon, N.Y., Mar.-Nov. 1788.

Biography: Noah Webster was born on Oct. 16, 1758, at West Hartford, Conn., the fourth of five children of Noah and Mercy Webster. He received his early education from his local pastor, the Rev. Nathan Perkins (q.v.), and a Hartford schoolmaster, a Mr. Wales. Despite the threat of a severe strain upon the family's finances, the Websters enrolled their youngest son in Yale College in Sept. 1774. Webster's experience in New Haven coincided with the anticlericalism of a vocal faction that demanded reforms in the Classical curriculum. Webster was caught up in the Enlightenment spirit, exploring natural philosophy and the achievements of the "immortal Newton." Yale's spirited debates concerning the morality of slavery may have presaged his later writings on the subject.

Despite interruptions caused by the Revolutionary War, in which Webster briefly served, he was graduated in 1778. Dissatisfied with farming, Webster turned to schoolteaching, clerical work, and, later, law to earn a meager living. In 1781 he sat successfully for the bar at Hartford, after failing the examination in Litchfield. A scarcity of clients forced him to abandon the profession and to return to teaching, this time at his own school in Sharon, Conn. There he engaged the Rev. John Peter Tetard as his mentor and pursued foreign languages. He returned briefly to New Haven, where he accepted an M.A. from Yale. A disastrous love affair with Rebecca Pardee may have thrust Webster into a self-imposed exile in Goshen, N.Y. While teaching in Goshen, Webster found time to evaluate school textbooks, focusing his attention upon the dissemination of American culture.

In 1783 Webster released the first part of his *A Grammatical Institute of the English Language*, titled *The American Spelling Book*. This "blue-backed speller" was destined to appear in no fewer than 400 editions, with estimated sales in excess of 100 million copies. It provided Webster's family with much of its financial support while he pursued scholarship. Parts II (the grammar) and III (a reader) set the tone of Webster's patriotic approach toward American education. The grammar was predicated upon Webster's assumption that "grammar is formed on language, and not language on grammar." This theme gained importance in Webster's later lexicological investigations. "Federal English," he explained, should take precedence over the affectations employed by the pretentious British. Webster emerged as a polemicist while in Goshen, advocating a return to the colonies' glorious past. Yet the present posed special problems, with the absence of a federal copyright exposing Webster's popular works to "piracy." He immediately began the agitation for a uniform copyright provision, petitioning state legislatures and stumping before any influential audience that would hear him. His efforts led to the adoption of a federal statute in 1790. Unfortunately, contracts he entered into with shrewd printers ultimately deprived him of much of the profits. However, his efforts as an early lobbyist did enflame his passion for political discourse, and Webster became a staunch Federalist, whose strong voice for the emerging ethic of honesty, perseverance, and frugality made sense amidst the clamor of faction.

His articles in the *Connecticut Courant* in 1783 had attracted attention from Federalist Loyalists; his *Sketches of American Policy* in 1785 captured the interest of even James Madison (q.v.) and George Washington (q.v.). By 1787 Webster's support for the adoption of the federal Constitution was well known. He combined his views on government with those concerning literary criticism and a plethora of other subjects in his short-lived *American Magazine* (1787-1788). Yet his optimism toward America's future was diminishing nearly as quickly as the colonial landscape he idealized. Concepts of authority and freedom were becoming polarized within his philosophy. "Too much liberty," he wrote, "is the worst tyranny." *Sketches of American Policy* (1785) was his intellectual watershed: he was beginning to cross over from Revolutionary ideology to the harmony of order, control, and sacrifice embodied in a central government. *An Examination into the Leading Principles of the Federal Constitution* (1787) was Webster's response to the Constitutional Convention and the product of intense conversations with delegates. In it he advocated the "tolerable equal distribution of landed property" as the "basis of natural freedom" and the underpinning of "real power."

With the failure of his *American Magazine*, Webster retreated to Hartford, where he remained until 1793. Within months of his return, he married Rebecca Greenleaf in Oct. 1789 and resumed his law practice. With the security of a devoted wife, Webster turned to his etymological research. *Dissertations on the English Language* (1789) opened the way for his assertion of the need for a "national language" as the ultimate embodiment of the new "national union." To Webster, language served as both a stabilizing and liberating force, creating a national unity of purpose and providing a common framework for exploring disparate issues such as the national economy or slavery.

In 1791 Webster helped establish an abolitionist society in Hartford and emerged as a proponent of the "free tenant" approach to emancipation. His book, *The Little Reader's Assistant* (1790), had been received as something more than a mere student's reader; it contained two slavery tales of wretched bondage, outrages against humanity, and stark barbarism. It was followed by his *Effects of Slavery, on Morals and Industry* (1793). Webster had not forgotten the Yale debates or the propagandistic fervor he once had accepted without question. Webster's utopia needed reform, if not simple reaffirmation.

On Dec. 9, 1793, Webster founded the *American Minerva* in New York City as an effort to quell insidious Jacobinism. His *The Revolution in France* (1794) marked his departure from his tenets espousing the rights of man to self-enhancement. The indiscriminate use of the guillotine made him shudder; his philosophical foundation crumbled under the strain and man, a sullen being, emerged as depraved. His *American Minerva* alienated his friends through its forceful columns, leading Webster further to withdraw into his work. *A Brief History of Epidemic and Pestilential Diseases* (two volumes, 1799) brought him praise from the medical community and established the book as a seminal work.

With the turn of the century, Webster withdrew from *American Minerva* (which had become the *Commercial Advertiser*) and retired to a study cluttered with dictionaries and linguistic aids. The resolution of ambiguity, both within the culture and its language, preoccupied Webster as he prepared his *Compendious Dictionary of the English Language* (1806), the precursor to his larger, more famous study.

Two years after the issuance of his *Compendious Dictionary of the English Language*, Webster discovered the emotional and philosophical panacea he had sought so long: the acceptance of an omnipotent God. The French Revolution had challenged, then shattered, his belief in man's innate goodness. Religion now filled the breach, and Webster, to the consternation of scholars, applied biblical Scripture and divine creation to all avenues of his etymological research.

Safe within his own linguistic Garden of Eden, he expelled his learned German colleagues. His new edition of *The New England Primer* (1801) became a throwback to the earlier examples that used the Calvinistic catechism. *The Panoplist* carried an account of his conversion; Webster began submitting essays to the *Religious Intelligencer*.

The Second Great Awakening had captured Noah Webster, mind, body, and soul. Part of Webster's perceived "duty" under the new order was the revision of the obsolete and vulgar expressions of Scripture. "The language of the Bible," he wrote, "has no inconsiderable influence in forming and preserving our national heritage." Antiquated phraseology, however, impaired man's understanding of the inspired document. "This may be a real misfortune," Webster explained, "for the use of words and phrases, when they have ceased to be a part of the living language, and appear odd or singular, impairs the purity of language. . . . It may require some effort to subdue this predilection; but it may be done, and for the sake of the rising generation, it is desirable." In his rendering of *The Holy Bible* (1833), Webster demonstrated his skills as a euphemist. In his "Introduction," he wrote,

> In no respect does the present version of the scriptures require amendments, more than in the use of many words and phrases which cannot now be uttered, especially in promiscuous company, without violence to decency. . . . Purity of mind is a christian virtue that ought to be carefully cherished; and purity of language is one of the guards which protect this virtue.

Words such as *teat, womb, stink, suck,* and *fornication* were excised and replaced with respectable substitutes.

Webster had experienced analogous scriptural problems in preparing his *An American Dictionary of the English Language* (two volumes, 1828). His solution to a multitude of etymological problems was biblical. Johnson's *Dictionary*, which he deplored yet borrowed from freely, and the *Bible* became his benchmarks for linguistic research. He ignored the evolving German linguistic school, dabbling instead in at least twenty languages and making a shambles of the inquiry. He deprecated the work of his colleagues, believing in the superiority of his endeavor. *An American Dictionary* sold reasonably well in Eng., despite its unconventional spellings. Yet the effort failed to prove entirely profitable, and the 1841 revision was not successful. Following Webster's death on May 28, 1843, Charles and George Merriam arranged with his estate for the transfer of the rights to the *American Dictionary*.

Critical Appraisal: On the eve of the Civil War, Jefferson Davis lauded Noah Webster for his former role in unifying a now increasingly sectional nation: "above all other people we are one, and above all books which have united us in the bond of common language, I place the good old Spelling-Book of Noah Webster." Davis was overly optimistic on both counts: the South seceded from the Union and Webster's "blue-backed speller" was denigrated in some quarters as responsible for the decay of American culture.

Yet perhaps Davis was not that far from the mark. Webster, especially during his formative period, used Revolutionary rhetoric similar to that cited by Davis. In his "Essay on a Reformed Mode of Spelling," Webster wrote,

Every engine should be employed to render the people of this country *national*; to call their attachments home to their own country; and to inspire them with the pride of national character. However they may boast of independence, and the freedom of their government, yet their *opinions* are not sufficiently independent; an astonishing respect for the arts and literature of their parent country, and a blind imitation of its manners, are still prevalent among the Americans.

Webster has been branded by numerous historians as a nationalist intensely committed to the Revolutionary idealism of the founding fathers. In fact, he was a man driven by philosophical extremes. Progress and innovation he deplored; yet he sought to enliven debate over the true etymology of thousands of words. He looked to the past for his utopian idea, while agitating for the abolition of slavery and the establishment of an educational system committed to the erosion of social class distinctions. Webster vacillated over the question of public virtue, finally embracing the conclusion that man was depraved. Although an advocate of an unfettered press, he opposed the bill of rights.

In his scholarly affairs, he was perceived as an egotistical tyrant, whose insensitivity to constructive criticism led to the discrediting of his work within his own lifetime. A Federalist once respected by Joseph Dennie (q.v.) and other anthologists, Webster later was ridiculed, satirized, and vilified as a fomenter of counter-Federalist rebellions. After 1794 Webster abandoned his agitation for the extension of man's freedom and sought limitations on the behavior of Americans. Language seemed the logical medium of social control.

"There is a manly pride in true independence which is equally remote from insolence and meanness," Webster wrote in his "Remarks on the Manners, Government and Debt of the United States." This pride, he believed, had to be tempered with an exacting preoccupation with the transmission of a truly American culture. Although most Federalists held tenuously for the preservation of the old order, Webster strove for separation. "America," he noted, "must be independent in literature as she is in politics." In the preface to his *Speller*, Webster pointed to the "folly, corruption and tyranny" of Europe and warned,

For America in her infancy to adopt the maxims of the Old World would be to stamp the wrinkles of decrepit old age upon the bloom of youth, and to plant the seeds of decay in a vigorous constitution. American glory begins to dawn at a favourable period.

This was the first step in what Henry Steele Commager identified as Webster's true accomplishment: the manumission of "generations of Americans from a sense of inferiority about their language, [giving them] a sense of dignity of their speech." Webster's reader (the third part of the *Institute*) included selections from the Declaration of Independence (despite his growing dislike for Thomas Jefferson [q.v.] and poetry from Philip Freneau (q.v.) and Joel Barlow (q.v.) (whom he would later oppose).

As a Federalist, Webster feared faction and francophobia. Federalists winced when Webster wrote, "The United States are in no danger of monarch or the aristocracy of hereditary estates and offices," but surely embraced his disclaimer, "But these states will always be exposed to *anarchy* and *faction*, because these evils approach under the delusive but specious guise of *patriotism*." Webster sought uniformity through a linguistic cultural standard. David Tyack has pointed to the indecisiveness of Webster in formulating a view of the role of "public information." In 1796 Webster maintained faction could be overcome through knowledge of public affairs. He later changed his mind: "But from what evidence can we infer that men who *know* what is right will do what is right? In what history of mankind, political or ecclesiastical, are the facts recorded which authorize the presumption, much less the belief, that correct action will proceed from correct knowledge?"

Webster, perhaps, was unfortunate enough to straddle two centuries whose views upon the nature and purpose of knowledge and language differed. As noted by Daniel H. Calhoun, oratorial persuasion in the nineteenth century was overshadowing literature, which many deemed "frivolous or immoral." Webster's work to simplify spelling and grammar was perceived as an expansion of the oratorial function to the detriment of literary pursuits. According to Calhoun, Webster "slipped from his real-usage standard to a moral propriety standard" in tune with the times. This gradual slippage proved more ameliorating than it was radical. Webster had abandoned much of his Revolutionary rhetoric after the appearance of his political pamphlets and his journalistic contributions.

Webster's journalistic career began roughly simultaneously with his efforts for the enactment of federal copyright legislation. In 1782 he submitted a series of articles calling for the revitalization of American culture to the N.Y. *Packet* —published by his cousin Bavil Webster. He also supplied the *Connecticut Courant*—which printed his speller—with occasional essays and some editorial assistance. Writing under the pseudonym "Honorius," Webster admitted that participatory journalism exposed him to "the derision of meanness, the snarling of petulance, and the attacks of malevolence." Furthermore, in another context, Webster denied that the "liberty of the press" fell "within the jurisdiction of federal government." Rather, "it is in the power of the state to reserve the liberty of the press, or any other fundamental privilege, and make it an immutable condition of the grant." Gary Coll has noted Webster's disquietude over the actions of the rabble during the mid-1780s, forcing the former Revolutionary to write in the *Connecticut Courant* that he favored a limited monarchy rather than the "passions and ignorance of a multitude." He despised the American rabble, but hated European snobbery more.

In his *American Magazine* (1787-1788), Webster deplored European traditions and sought to encourage American letters. Yet the paucity of original American submissions forced him to reprint numerous essays of foreign vintage. Edward W. Pitcher has demonstrated the dominance of reprinted fiction from English sources, demolishing the assumption that much of it was contributed by American authors. Although Coll seemingly differed in his assessment of the magazine's composition, it is clear that Webster was the dominant (more than 25 percent?) American contributor.

Webster spent much of his space extolling reforms in American education, while offering women greater literary attention than had occurred in previous ventures. Extracts from Capt. John Smith's (q.v.) *General History* and even Jefferson's *Notes on Virginia* graced the *American Magazine*'s columns. The poetry department emerged as an outlet for the work of Yale alumni. Barlow, John Trumbull (q.v.), and Timothy Dwight (q.v.) were Webster's poetic lights. Webster and Dwight joined forces to censure an impertinent English reviewer who dared to suggest Dwight's *The Conquest of Canaan* was thinly veiled allegory of the American Revolution.

Webster's choice of causes proved interesting: he opposed the use of the *Bible* in schools, dissuaded students from foreign travel, and condemned the employment of schoolmasters expected to teach a multitude of courses. He encouraged women, yet, as pointed out by Frank Luther Mott, had the audacity to suggest in "An Address to the Ladies" (1788): "To be *lovely* you must be content to be *women*; to be mild, social, and sentimental—to be acquainted with all that belongs to your department—and leave the masculine virtues, and the profound researches of study to the province of the other sex." Webster had promised his magazine would avoid "personal invective, ribaldry, and immoral writings," a promise he assiduously followed. He may have appeared gentle with women— he considered himself a ladies' man—but he proved tough with literary entrepreneurs eager to lift the fruits of his labors for their own gain. He stood ready to prosecute copyright infringements, despite the lack of appropriate law. In Feb. 1788 he became the first proprietor of an American magazine to assert that the contents were private property.

As emphasized by Lyon N. Richardson, Webster's crusading spirit did not reflect business acumen. His proposal for a shared magazine venture based upon an alliance of seaboard editors was tolerated by friends, although dismissed. "The Monarch," wrote one colleague to Jeremy Belknap (q.v.) concerning the scheme, "[is] a literary puppy. . . . He certainly does not want understanding, and yet there is a mixture of self-sufficiency, all-sufficiency, and. . .a degree of insufficiency about him, which is (to me) intolerable." Webster failed, despite his enlightening essays titled "Education" and "Government" (the latter over the pseudonym of "Giles Hickory"). Perhaps the low point in Webster's editorship was his devastating review of Timothy Dwight's *The Triumph of Infidelity*. Richardson has suggested Webster's review may have been precipitated in part because of Dwight's affiliation with Mathew Carey (q.v.) and *The American Museum*. Webster's critique cited Dwight's penchant for "borrow[ing] lines without giving credit" and his friend's appearance as a "theological dogmatist."

Dwight's friendship apparently had been devalued. Despite Webster's efforts to conduct a Federalist magazine, his publication proved as ephemeral as the poetry of his prolific contributor "Aspasio." Webster abandoned N.Y. and its first monthly magazine by Jan. 1789, touching base in Boston, where he attempted unsuccessfully to merge his defunct periodical with Isaiah Thomas's (q.v.) *Massachusetts Magazine*—then in preparation.

By 1790 Webster again was prepared to joust with his sharp pen, this time as the author of a series of twenty-eight essays titled "The Prompter." His mission was to say little, but for that little to prompt readers to action. His articles caught the attention of prominent Federalists seeking a strong voice to counter Republican attacks upon the Washington administration for the president's declaration of neutrality and his demand for the recall of Citizen Genêt. The New York *Journal* of Thomas Greenleaf had to be opposed, and Alexander Hamilton (q.v.), Rufus King, and John Jay (q.v.) were prepared to pay the price. Webster agreed to issue the daily *American Minerva* as a "chaste and impartial" Federalist organ. Webster informed his public that such newspapers "supercede the use of Magazines and Pamphlets" and "like schools, they should be considered the auxiliaries of government, and placed on a respectable footing; they should be heralds of truth; the protectors of peace and good order."

In fact, Webster's herald of truth drew freely from the vituperative prints of John Fenno (q.v.) and William "Peter Porcupine" Cobbett (q.v.). Webster started a series of essays whose placement was a precursor to the modern editorial and improved upon the example set by Thomas Greenleaf by establishing his own semiweekly edition (*Herald*) for "country readers."

Webster clearly saw himself as a bastion of Federalism, especially within the realm of foreign affairs. Writing as "Brutus" in 1793, Webster questioned the intentions of foreign powers; as "Curtius" in 1795, he drafted a defense of the Jay Treaty, which won him the admiration of even his most unregenerate Federalist critics. His twelve letters to the *Minerva* were buttressed by thirty-eight letters drafted by "Camillus" (Hamilton and King), the last thirteen of which appeared in Webster's newspaper. As emphasized by H. E. Scudder, Rufus King's praise for Webster knew no boundaries. His letter to Jay was explicit: "the essays of Curtius had contributed more than any other papers of the same kind to allay the discontent and opposition to the treaty," because they were addressed to the common mechanic. Jefferson attributed all of the *Minerva* letters to Hamilton and beseeched Madison on Sept. 21, 1795, to "take up your pen, and give a fundamental reply to Curtius & Camillus." This was the high-water mark of Webster's influence both as an editor (he preferred the title "compiler") and as a supporter of Hamilton. After the treaty defense, the Hamilton-Webster alliance grew tenuous. Both were besieged by the press.

Benjamin Franklin Bache's (q.v.) *Aurora* characterized Webster as the "jackall of the British faction" and continued, "If ever a man prostituted the little sense that he had, to serve the purposes of a monarchic and aristocratic junto, Noah Webster, Esq. must be the man." Webster equally was capable of gutter billingsgate, often choosing Philip Freneau and the *Time-Piece* as ready foils. Webster suggested Freneau was a "fit inhabitant for Botany Bay" (the English penal colony in Aust.) and, in another context, smeared the *Time-Piece* as "copiously bespattered with filth like the *National Gazette* formerly."

After mid-1797 Webster contributed only a smattering of items to the *Minerva*; fewer, following his departure from N.Y. in Apr. 1798. In 1800 Webster published a scathing *Letter to General Hamilton, Occasioned by His Letter to President Adams*, which depicted Hamilton as "the evil genius of America." His action further alienated fellow Federalists and brought down the wrath of numerous party editors. His disillusionment with the press led him to observe that year, "I. . . aver. . . no government can be durable and quiet under the licentiousness of the press that now disgraces our country." Webster sold his interest in the *Commercial Advertiser* (the old *Minerva*) in 1803.

With the turn of the century, Webster turned to other projects. Several years before the appearance of Isaiah Thomas's *The History of Printing in America* (two volumes, 1810), Webster contemplated writing a description of "the origin and progress of the public prints in the United States." As Allen Walker Read has demonstrated, Webster's survey was met with suspicion or, at best, disinterest. The response from John Carter of the Providence *Gazette* implied that the release of information regarding circulation could be used by an unscrupulous government to impose new stamp duties upon publishers. After abandoning this and a plan to write the definitive life of George Washington, Webster settled down to lexicographical pursuits.

His interest in education and, particularly, the role of the schools in accomplishing progressive social change had diminished since the 1770s and 1780s. Religion preoccupied Webster in the nineteenth century, and he confessed that "eminent abilities, accompanied with depravity of heart render the possessor tenfold more dangerous in a community." Webster's second volume of *Dissertations* and his *Compendious Dictionary of the English Language* (1806) were ridiculed by even those who had been early admirers. Joseph Dennie, who had attributed the "merits in the short essays of 'The Lay Preacher'" to Webster, later cut him to the quick over the issue of standards of speech. Samuel Johnson was the literary hero of Federalist writers who contributed to the *Monthly Anthology and Boston Review* and the *Port Folio*. John Gardner dubbed Webster's lexicographical efforts as "Noah's Ark"—a derisive phrase that stuck in the public prints. The *Anthology* carried a running debate over the merits of the *Compendious Dictionary*, which included replies by Webster. The Anthology Society's *Journal* for Aug. 29, 1809, noted brusquely, "The conversation of the evening was chiefly at the expense of Noah Webster, as long as the Secretary kept awake." The inclusion of such Americanisms as "anti-fogmatic," "hellniferous," and "to bottom" in Webster's listing provided critics with no end to character assassination.

Webster isolated himself in his study, laboring to finish his "Synopsis" (a reference work still in manuscript form) and his *American Dictionary of the*

English Language (1828). As Allen Walker Read has noted, the "Synopsis" research convinced Webster that his etymological theories were sound and that it was safe to proceed without further interruption by continental linguistic advances. Attempts by James Gates Percival to persuade Webster that a methodology dependent upon a mere "comparison of dictionaries and vocabularies" was fraught with the promise of linguistic disaster left Webster unmoved. The chinks in Webster's lexicographical armor were numerous. The studies of Jacob Grimm first were eased and then thrust upon him with little effect. Webster considered himself the premier lexicographer of the age, despite his excessive dependancy upon the work of Samuel Johnson and his want of extensive grounding in linguistics.

In his narrowly drawn but illuminating study of Webster's debt to Johnson's *Dictionary of the English Language* (1799), Joseph W. Reed, Jr., demonstrated in the case of entries under Webster's letter "L" (2,024 words) about one-third of the 4,505 definitions "were culled from Johnson or show unmistakable signs of Johnson's influence." Few true Americanisms appeared. In addition, Webster's penchant for scriptural authority led him to include a liberal saturation of biblical illustrations—at least for the "L's." Webster, the critic of Johnson's "want of discrimination," was indiscrete—if not indiscriminate—in borrowing from his English colleague. In spite of his untenable position, Webster had the audacity to write in 1839,

> The process of tracing words to their primary sense, and from that sense deducing the secondary significations and terms to express them is probably *new*. . . . In this branch of etymology, even the German scholars, the most accurate philologists in Europe, appear to be wholly deficient.

As demonstrated by Charlton Laird, the most original of Webster's research emerged as the least defensible to both contemporary and modern critics. Laird's striking case for Webster's relative ignorance of Anglo-Saxon assails Webster's rendering of the elements of grammar, constructions, and common words. At best, Webster was able, with difficulty, to "translate simple prose rather accurately," according to Laird. Harry Warfel's assertion that Webster "studied, as far as American libraries could supply him with books, Anglo-Saxon" goes wanting for evidence.

Webster's *American Dictionary of the English Language* (1828), with its 70,000 entries, had a far broader purpose than mere etymological investigation. Whether critics characterize it within the context of rising nationalism (John D. Hicks, Oscar Handlin, Charles Beard), patriotism (Merle Curti, Lawrence J. Friedman), or as a medium of social control (Richard M. Rollins), clearly Webster was obsessed with the equilibrium necessary between Revolutionary idealism and the stable fabric of society. On the surface, the title *American Dictionary* implies the nascent nationalism so often associated with the work. Yet as Richard M. Rollins strongly argued, Webster "did not advocate the development of a new language, or even a new dialect." In Webster's words, "It is desirable to perpetuate that sameness [the English body of language]." Fewer than 100 Americanisms have been isolated within Webster's entries, a fact that led H. L. Mencken to castigate him as an incompetent observer of the American scene. Webster's literal belief in biblical verities narrowed his etymological approach to ridiculous boundaries that permanently flawed his work. His need for order and his fear of insatiable Revolutionaries cast within a godless world led Webster to define political terms in the most restrictive modes imaginable. As Rollins so aptly stated, Webster's "faith in equality among men is conspicuous only by its absence."

When he published what he regarded as his greatest accomplishment—*The Holy Bible, Containing the Old and New Testaments, in the Common Version, with Amendments of the Language* (1833)—Webster apparently had come full circle from the robust, rough-and-tumble polemicist of the Enlightenment to the publicist of nineteenth-century piety. His previous attention to the purity of language (although some Federalists did not perceive his efforts in such a light) now led to euphemism. Words suddenly needed a *raison d'être* even within a scriptural context. "The language of the Bible," Webster wrote, "has no inconsiderable influence in forming and preserving our national language." Unfortunately, Webster failed to follow his own dictum: language—and the study of linguistics—was an evolving form with nuances constantly in flux. Perhaps it was Webster who lived a life predicated upon nuance, sometimes failing to perceive subtle changes within himself and his social milieu that posed long-term effects upon his achievements. Webster succeeded, perhaps, in giving new living definition to two critical words: *submission* and *duty*. In such living language, he became lost amidst the sacrifices each demanded of him.

Suggested Readings: DAB; Dexter (IV, 66-79); LHUS. *See also* Homer Babbidge, ed., *Noah Webster: On Being American, Selected Writings, 1783-1828* (1967); Clarence S. Brigham, *History and Bibliography of American Newspapers, 1690-1820, Volume I* (1947); Bonnie Bromberger, "Noah Webster's Notes on His Early Political Essays in the *Connecticut Courant*," BNYPL, 74 (1970), 338-342; Thomas Howard Brown, "A Study of the *American Magazine* and Its Contributions to the Literature of the Early National Period," DAI, 34 (1974), University of Georgia, 4188-A; Vincent P. Bynack, "Language and the Order of the World: Noah Webster and the Idea of an American Culture," DAI, 39 (1978), Yale University, 2375-A; Daniel H. Calhoun, "From Noah Webster to Chauncey Wright: The Intellectual as Prognostic," HER, 36 (1966), 427-446; Gary Coll, "Noah Webster, Journalist, 1783-1803" in *Newsletters to Newspapers: Eighteenth-Century Journalism*, ed. Donovan H. Bond and W. Reynolds McLeod (1977), pp. 303-318; Henry Steele Commager, "Noah Webster, 1758-1958: 'Schoolmaster to America,'" SatR, 41 (Oct. 18, 1958), 10-12, 66-67; Emily E. F. Ford, comp., *Notes on the Life of Noah Webster*, 2 vols. (1912); Charlton Laird, "Etymology, Anglo-Saxon, and Noah Webster," AS, 21 (1946), 3-15; Kemp Malone, "A Linguistic Patriot," AS, 1 (1925), 26-31; Dennis E. Minor, "The Evolution of Puritanism into the Mass Culture of Early Nineteenth-Century America," DAI, 24 (1974), Texas A&M University, 7714-A; John S. Morgan, *Noah Webster* (1975); Frank Luther Mott, *American Journalism: A History of Newspapers in the United States Through 250 Years, 1690 to 1940* (1947); idem, *A History of American Magazines, 1741-1850* (1966); Edward W. Pitcher, "Signatures and Sources for Fiction in Webster's *American Magazine* (Dec. 1787-Nov. 1788)," EAL, 13 (1978),

102-106; Allen W. Read, "Noah Webster as a Euphemist," DiaN, 6 (1934), 385-391; idem, "Noah Webster's Project in 1801 for a History of American Newspapers," JQ, 11 (1934), 258-275; idem, "The Spread of German Linguistic Learning in New England During the Lifetime of Noah Webster," AS, 41 (1966), 163-181; Joseph W. Reed, Jr., "Noah Webster's Debt to Samuel Johnson," AS, 37 (1962), 95-105; Lyon N. Richardson, *A History of Early American Magazines, 1741-1789* (1931); Richard M. Rollins, *The Long Journey of Noah Webster* (1980); idem, "Words as Social Control: Noah Webster and the Creation of the *American Dictionary*," AQ, 28 (1976), 415-430; Dennis P. Rusche, "An Empire of Reason: A Study of the Writings of Noah Webster," DAI, 36 (1976), University of Iowa, 5500-A; Ervin C. Shoemaker, *Noah Webster, Pioneer of Learning* (1936); H. E. Scudder, *Noah Webster* (1883); Emily E. F. Skeel, comp., and Edwin H. Carpenter, Jr., ed., *A Bibliography of the Writings of Noah Webster* (1958); Gerald F. Smith, "Noah Webster's Conservatism," AS, 25 (1950), 101-104; David Tyack, "Forming the National Character: Paradox in the Educational Thought of the Revolutionary Generation," HER, 36 (1966), 29-41; Harry R. Warfel, "The Centenary of Noah Webster's *Bible*," NEQ, 7 (1934), 578-582; idem, ed., *Letters of Noah Webster* (1953); idem, *Noah Webster: Schoolmaster to America* (1936); Ruth F. Warfel and Harry R. Warfel, eds., *Poems by Noah Webster* (1936); Theodore A. Zunder, "Noah Webster and *The Conquest of Canäan*," AL, 1 (1929), 200-202.

For manuscript collections, see the following repositories: Mathew Carey (1760-1839) Papers (1787-1795) in American Philosophical Society Library, Philadelphia, Pa.; Poulson Family Papers (1816-1864) in Dickinson College Library, Carlisle, Pa.; Noah Webster (1758-1843) Papers (1796-1863), about 150 items, in Connecticut Historical Society Collections, Hartford, Conn. (includes correspondence of Webster's children and materials relating to Webster's *Dictionary*); Noah Webster (1758-1843) Papers (1787-1843) in Jones Library, Amherst, Mass. (unpublished calendar of letters in the library); Noah Webster (1758-1843) Papers in New York Public Library, New York City, N.Y. (14 boxes); Noah Webster (1758-1843) Papers in Pierpont Morgan Library, New York City, N.Y. See the Library of Congress for collection of the Pennsylvania Abolitionist Society (5 reels of microfilm; 1748-), which includes correspondence of Webster. Original documents are held by the Historical Society of Pennsylvania.

William F. Vartorella
Mary Baldwin College

PELATIAH WEBSTER (1726-1795)

Works: *An Essay on Free Trade and Finance* (1779); *A Second Essay* (1779); *A Third Essay* (1780); *A Fourth Essay* (1780); *A Fifth Essay* (1780); *A Sixth Essay* (1783); *A Dissertation on the Political Union and Constitution of the Thirteen United States of North-America* (1783); *A Seventh Essay* (1785); *An Essay on Credit* (1786); *Reasons for Repealing the Act of the Legislature of Pennsylvania, of Sept. 13, 1785* (1786); *Remarks on the Address of Sixteen Members of the Assembly of Pennsylvania* (1787); *The Weaknesses of Brutus Exposed* (1787); *An Essay on the Seat of the Federal Government* (1789); *An*

Essay on the Culture of Silk (attributed author; 1790); *A Plea for the Poor Soldiers* (1790); *An Address to the Stock-Holders of the Bank of North-America* (1791); *Political Essays on the Nature and Operation of Money, Public Finances, and Other Subjects* (1791).

Biography: Pelatiah Webster was born in Lebanon, Conn. After graduating from Yale College (1746), he studied theology. In 1749 he was ordained as pastor of the Congregational Church in Greenwich, Conn.; seven years later, his parish dismissed him for unknown reasons. Shortly thereafter, Webster established himself as a merchant in Philadelphia. He prospered in his new occupation and became one of the city's leading mercantile supporters of the Revolution. The British imprisoned him briefly in 1777 and Gen. Howe confiscated some of his property in 1778, but with no lasting effect on his business. During and after the War of Independence, Webster published a pseudonymous and influential series of papers on public finance and politics, which he eventually collected under his own name in a volume of *Political Essays* (1791). He died in Philadelphia in 1795.

Critical Appraisal: One of the outstanding political economists of the early Republic, Webster as much as any individual was responsible for the growing influence in America of the theory of free trade. The sources of his thought were two-fold. Eric Foner has described his economic ideas as "pure Adam Smith," and there is little doubt that Webster, a well-read man, was influenced by the European intellectual climate that produced *The Wealth of Nations* (1776). But he never admitted to imitation: "I endeavoured, as far as I could, to make myself *my own original*." This evaluation has some weight, for he felt no compulsion to write until confronted with economic problems that were distinctly American and closely related to his own business concerns.

The Revolutionary War dislocated many parts of the American economy. Webster was primarily concerned with problems of currency and public finance. He early warned his countrymen against the dangers of too large a circulation of paper money. He explained the runaway inflation of the late 1770s, contrary to the widespread opinion that it was caused by the schemings of selfish middlemen, as the impersonal result of an excessive quantity of paper. He was a leader in the campaign of Philadelphia's merchants against the practice of price fixing by popular committees, arguing in his *Essays on Free Trade and Finance* that public restraints on commerce were unjust and self-defeating. In his opinion, the only basis for a sound economy was free trade, which would maintain prices at their "natural" level, and business morality, which would uphold confidence in public credit. Free trade, he wrote, "is absolutely necessary to the property of every community, and to the happiness of all individuals who compose it."

Webster's solution for the problem of inflation—taxes that would both enhance the value of the paper money and gradually withdraw it from circulation—led him to consider the problem of governmental organization. The Continental Congress under the Articles of Confederation did not have the authority to tax. In his *Dissertation on the Political Union* (1783), Webster argued that the central government must be given that and other powers. He advocated a number of the reforms that the Philadelphia Convention made in 1787, but the legend that he was the "architect" of the federal Constitution has been disproved by Edward S. Corwin. The ideas Webster advocated in his *Dissertation* had wide currency before the pamphlet was written; he failed to anticipate some of the key features of the new Constitution; and the Convention ignored many of his specific proposals.

Webster's essays on finance and politics were partisan documents. He allied himself with the Pa. Federalists, who opposed price regulation and called for the replacement of the Articles of Confederation with a stronger form of national government. In 1787 he wrote two pieces in favor of the proposed Constitution. Like most Federalists, Webster was a committed advocate for the new nation's merchants. Indeed, few went so far in praising their probity: "the merchants are not only *qualified to give the fullest and most important information* to our supreme legislature concerning the state of our trade...but are also the most likely to do it *fairly* and *truly*." But he was not a rigid partisan. In the early 1790s, when Alexander Hamilton (q.v.) called for the reorganization of the national debt, Webster found himself on the side of Hamilton's opponent James Madison (q.v.) and advocated, in *A Plea for the Poor Soldiers*, a discrimination between original holders of debt certificates and the mercantile speculators who had purchased them at a fraction of face value. In this instance, he disagreed not only with the Federalist administration, but with many of his commercial associates.

The cogency, vigor, and resourcefulness of argument in Webster's essays lifted them above most economic writings of the period. If he was not truly a detached analyst, as he often claimed to be, he was a prolific spokesman for both the American mercantile community and for a program of free trade that had much influence in the nineteenth century.

Suggested Readings: CCNE; DAB; Dexter (II, 97-102); T$_2$. *See also* Douglas M. Arnold, "Political Ideology and the Internal Revolution in Pennsylvania, 1776-1790" (Ph.D. diss., Princeton Univ., 1976), pp. 136-137, 198-199; Edward S. Corwin, *The Doctrine of Judicial Review* (1914), pp. 111-126; Joseph Dorfman, *The Economic Mind in American Civilization* (1946), I, 212-213, 219-222, 227-228, 244-245, 260-261, 263-265, 270, 293-295, 369; Eric Foner, *Tom Paine and Revolutionary America* (1976), pp. 170-171; E.A.J. Johnson, *The Foundations of American Economic Freedom: Government and Enterprise in the Age of Washington* (1973), pp. 28-29, 42, 57-58, 79n, 80-82, 97, 127, 136-137, 144n, 147n, 148n, 154, 158, 167-169, 171, 174, 176, 186-187, 189, 198, 199, 203, 300, 310.

Douglas M. Arnold
Yale University

MASON LOCKE WEEMS (1759-1825)

Works: *The Lover's Almanac* (c. 1798); *The Bachelor's Almanac* (c. 1799); *Hymen's Recruiting Serjeant* (1799); *The Philanthropist* (c. 1799); *The Virginia*

Almanac (1799); *The Virginia and North Carolina Almanac* (1799); *The Life of Washington* (1800), 5th ed. (1806), 6th ed. (1808); *Carey's Franklin Almanac* (1802, 1804); *The True Patriot* (1802); *Weem's Washington Almanack* (1803); *The Grand Republican Almanac* (1806); *God's Revenge Against Murder* (c. 1807); *God's Revenge Against Gambling* (c. 1810); *The Life of Francis Marion* (1810); *The Devil Done Over* (c. 1812); *The Drunkard's Looking Glass* (c. 1812); *God's Revenge Against Adultry* (1815); *The Life of Doctor Franklin* (1815); *Anecdotes of Gamblers* (1816); *Peter and John Hay* (c. 1816); *God's Revenge Against Duelling* (1820); *The Effects of Drunkeness* (1822); *The Life of William Penn* (1822); *The Bad Wife's Looking Glass* (1823).

Biography: Mason Locke Weems was born at Marshes Seat, Herring Bay, Anne Arundel County, Md., on Oct. 11, 1759. He was the youngest of twelve children of David and his second wife, Hester (Hill) Weems. (David had seven other children from an earlier marriage.) Mason attended Kent County School across the bay from Baltimore, and presumably, he went to sea as a young man aboard vessels owned by his older brothers. Some evidence suggests he studied medicine in Edinburgh and London, and he was reported to be a surgeon in the Revolutionary War serving in the Royal Navy. He returned to America when his father died but then was again in Eng. studying for the ministry at a later date. After the Revolutionary War, Weems's life was more well recorded. He wanted to be ordained in the Anglican Church, but in the post-Revolutionary period, his status was uncertain; as an American citizen, he could not well take the oath of allegiance to Eng., a requirement for his ordination. He wrote to John Adams (q.v.), then American minister to the Hague, and to Benjamin Franklin (q.v.) in Paris, for assistance; evidently, some accommodation was made, for Weems was ordained as priest by the archbishop of Canterbury on Sept. 12, 1784.

That same year, he became rector of All Hallows, at South River, Herring Creek, in his native county and remained there for five years. In 1791 he took a similar position at St. Margaret's, Westminster, Md., where he entered into his lifelong career as seller, promoter, and author of books and pamphlets. After 1793, although yet an Episcopalian minister, he held no permanent clerical posts, preferring to wander the countryside hawking literary wares.

His first literary efforts were simply reprinting others' writing, usually sermons or pamphlets warning of the dangers of evil habits; a typical example is *Onania* (c. 1792) describing the consequences of masturbation. He became acquainted somehow with Col. Jesse Ewell of Prince William County, Va., for in Jul. 1795 Weems married Ewell's daughter Frances. They lived in Dumfries, Va., until the death of Frances's father, whereupon they moved to the Ewell homestead, which became Weems's base of operations until his death. Weems became agent for the publisher Mathew Carey (q.v.) in 1794, and the business associates maintained a lively economic and letter exchange for thirty years. Weems sold Carey's books on commission and became the epitome of the itinerant bookmonger ever widening his travels in the quest for profit; he journeyed into Pa., N.Y., and N.J. and south into Ga. and the Carolinas.

Weems often added his own name to the title pages of the works he was selling; for example, in 1799 a pamphlet lauding George Washington (q.v.) was printed, which contained some small additions by Weems, although most of the text was taken from an earlier biography. In 1800 Weems's own edition of the life of Washington appeared and, after much editing and expansion, became one of the most popular histories ever printed, eventually going through eighty-two editions. Thereafter, Weems tried to duplicate his success, bringing out biographies of Francis "Swamp Fox" Marion, Benjamin Franklin, and William Penn (q.v.). Finding authorship rewarding, he also produced several pamphlets condemning vices such as gambling, drinking, pride, adultery, and duelling. Weems died on one of his promotional journeys in Beaufort, S.C., on May 23, 1825.

Critical Appraisal: Essentially a peddler of culture, Mason Locke Weems traveled throughout the new nation of America, producing for it anecdotal histories that have become mainstays of American folklore about its early leaders. Weems's chief claims to fame are the incidents he created to illustrate the virtues of George Washington; Weems is personally responsible for the image of the boy Washington confessing to his father that he had, indeed, chopped down the cherry tree and the tale of Washington's father planting cabbages in such a fashion that the sprouts spelled out George's name.

Weems's aim was to fill what he perceived as a need on the part of his buying public to have more readable histories of America's heroes. The official biography of Washington was entrusted to Chief Justice John Marshall, who produced a six-volume work. But these volumes were formal, impersonal, and only indirectly concerned with Washington himself, focusing instead on the general happenings of the Revolution. Marshall's biography, for example, redacted Washington's entire boyhood to only a few pages. Disappointed with Marshall's product and realizing an audience existed for an expensive biography of Washington, which Weems believed would be purchased as acts of patriotism and piety if that biography were less stiffly written, Weems revised his early pamphlet. To his 5th edition (1806), he added the lively anecdotes to become so popular, and to the 6th (1808), he added even more "personal" although fictitious material, resulting in a volume well over 200 pages. The added image of Washington on his knees at prayer during the Valley Forge campaign, inclusions of the dreams of Washington's mother told in vivid detail, and accounts of an Indian firing seventeen times at Washington to no avail were exactly what the public wanted.

The other biographies Weems produced are in the same vein; he began with the skeletal facts of a person's life and hung upon them anecdotes, associates' impressions, and laudatory gossip to create one-sided, unsullied characterizations. Weems's other works use the same feature of a biographical base upon which he built didactic exemplums; he usually recounted the life of some wretched person who had succumbed to a particular vice and suffered "God's revenge." Weems, although only tangentially a preacher in later life, was affectionately known as "Parson" and was one of the most beloved characters in early America. His immense popularity resulted from his genial combination of preaching, fiddling, and aggressive selling of America's heritage in book form as well as his willingness to travel the backroads to even the smallest villages; hardly a person living at his time had not heard of him by word of mouth. Perhaps a fitting measure of his contemporary stature was his reported presence on the road even years after his death—Weems had perpetuated himself into the folklore of America.

Weems is not a literary figure of high regard; much of the material attributed to him was culled from others or hastily written and rewritten to produce sometimes little-changed editions to make a quick profit. Weems's importance lies rather in the figures he made of his imagination to make a new nation proud of its founders. Although Weems's histories were debunked by later historians, they are sources for that mythic America that by now has become cultural fact by virtue of repetition. Whatever his detractors might say, Weems wrote the most successful historical books of his time.

Suggested Readings: DAB; LHUS. *See also* William A. Bryan, "The Genesis of Weems's 'Life of Washington,' " *Americana*, 36 (Apr. 1942), 147-165; idem, *George Washington in American Literature, 1775-1865* (1952); Marcus Cunliffe, Introduction, *The Life of Washington* (1962), pp. ix-lxii; William Gilmore Simms, "Weems, the Biographer and Historian" in *Views and Reviews, Second Series* (1845), pp. 123-141; Harold Kellock, *Parson Weems of the Cherry Tree* (1928); Mrs. Emily E. Ford Skeel, *Mason Locke Weems: His Works and Ways* (1929); Jerry Wallace, *A Parson at Large* (1927); Lawrence C. Wroth, *Parson Weems: A Biographical and Critical Study* (1911).

Dean G. Hall
Wayne State University

EDMUND WELD (1631-1668)

Works: *A Funeral Elegy by Way of Dialogue Between Death, Soul, Body, World, and Jesus Christ* (c. 1720).

Biography: Edmund Weld (also spelled *Welde*) was born on July 8, 1631, in Terling, in the county of Essex, Eng. His father was Thomas Welde (q.v.), a graduate of Trinity College, Cambridge, and the nonconformist minister of the parish in Terling where the younger Weld was born and baptized. It was Thomas Welde who, together with Richard Mather (q.v.) and John Eliot (q.v.), compiled the first edition of the famous *Whole Booke of Psalmes*, better known as the *Bay Psalm Book*. In March of 1632, Thomas Welde and his family boarded the *William and Francis* and sailed for the freer shores of North America, arriving in Mass. on June 5 and settling soon thereafter in Roxbury. After graduation from Harvard College in 1650, Edmund Weld left Mass. for Inniskean, Ire., where he began a career in the ministry. He died in Inniskean on March 2, 1668, at the age of 37.

Critical Appraisal: Edmund Weld published only one work: *A Funeral Elegy by Way of Dialogue Between Death, Soul, Body, World, and Jesus Christ*.

Printed as a broadside sometime in the 1720s, Weld's *Funeral Elegy* was popular enough among New Eng. audiences to merit reprinting at least eight more times during the eighteenth century. According to a note printed with early issues of the broadside, the author, aware that he was soon to die, wrote his *Dialogue* as a type of contemplation concerning his own mortality. After Weld's death, continues the note, the manuscript of the *Dialogue* "was sent hither in a Letter from his Wife" to his relations in America, where it was later published.

Written in nineteen stanzas of ten lines each, Weld's *Dialogue* begins with a statement by "Death" that all people are his followers: "My Name is DEATH, / I'll stop thy Breath; / From mine Arrests thou can'st not hide." After "Death's" speech, "Soul" replies that he is weary of life and ready for heaven: "Ah Death thou'rt dead, / Broke is thy head; / Thy Sting and Strength removed quite." "Body," however, is not yet ready to die, and he complains to his "dearest Mate," the "Soul," about "Soul's" eagerness to part with life: "But ah, poor I / Must rotting lye, / As one forgot among the Dead." "Soul" then reminds "Body" that at the Last Judgement they shall be "Made one again," but "World" interrupts, disgruntled that his "Guest unkind" is so willing to leave him. After "Soul" instructs "World" that his "flattering Smiles begin to smell," "Jesus Christ" joyously welcomes "Soul" to heaven as his "lovely Bride," and the poem concludes with "Soul's" thanking "the Lamb so freely slain" for the gift of everlasting life.

Although they often lacked the quality of great poetry, "Dialogues" like that by Weld were extremely popular among the audiences of seventeenth- and eighteenth-century New Eng. Deprived as they were of dramatic entertainment, our Puritan forefathers sometimes turned to poetic "dialogue" as a substitute for the stage. In this respect, Weld's *Dialogue* fulfilled a social and moral function not unlike that performed by the morality plays of the Middle Ages, whose types and figures the allegorical characters in the *Dialogue* resemble.

Suggested Readings: FCNEV; Sibley-Shipton (I, 220). *See also* Emory Elliott, "The Development of the Puritan Funeral Sermon and Elegy: 1660-1750," EAL, 15 (1980), 151-164; Robert Henson, "Form and Content of the Puritan Funeral Elegy," AL, 32 (1960), 11-27.

James A. Levernier
University of Arkansas at Little Rock

THOMAS WELDE (1595-1661)

Works: *The Whole Book of Psalmes* (1640); *New England's First Fruits* (1643); *An Answer to W. [illiam] R. [athband]* (1644); *A Short Story of the Rise, Reign, and Ruine of the Antinomians* (1644); *A Brief Narrative of the Practices of the Churches in New England* (1645); *A False Jew* (1653); *The Perfect Pharisee Under Monkish Holines . . . in the Generation . . . Called Quakers* (1653);

A Further Discovery of That Generation...Called Quakers (1654); *A Vindication of Mr. Weld* (1658).

Biography: Thomas Welde, Puritan divine, was born in Sudbury, Suffolk, Eng., on July 15, 1595. He graduated from Trinity College, Cambridge, with a B.A. in 1613 and an M.A. in 1618 and that same year was ordained a minister. He then served as vicar at Haverhill, Suffolk, and in 1624 was appointed vicar at Terling, Essex. Because of Welde's support of nonconformist Thomas Hooker (q.v.), Archbishop William Laud deposed Welde on Nov. 24, 1631, charging him with "contumacy."

Welde then immigrated to Boston, arriving on Jun. 5, 1632. In Jul. he was appointed the first pastor of the church in Roxbury. Welde became a member of the first Puritan Synod of New Eng. and in this capacity participated in the trials of the Antinomian leaders John Wheelwright (q.v.) and his sister-in-law, Anne Hutchinson, during 1637-1638. In 1638 Welde became an overseer of Harvard College and in Jul. of that year began working with John Eliot (q.v.) and Richard Mather (q.v.) on a metrical translation of the Psalme from the original Hebrew. Published in Cambridge in 1640 as *The Whole Booke of Psalmes*, this work is more widely referred to as the *Bay Psalm Book*. It was the first book printed in the British American colonies.

In 1641 Welde accompanied Hugh Peter (q.v.) to Eng. as an agent of the Mass. colony for the principal purpose of obtaining financial aid. He and Peter then joined Alexander, Lord Forbes on his 1642 expedition to Ire. and in 1643 became involved in a plot to sent Archbishop Laud to New Eng. to prevent the latter's execution. His preoccupation with English affairs and his failure to defeat Roger Williams's (q.v.) plan to acquire a patent to the Narragansett territory led to Welde's dismissal as a colonial agent on Oct. 1, 1645. He never returned to America but instead became rector first at Wanlip, Leicester, in 1646 and then at St. Mary's, Gateshead, Durham, until his retirement in 1657. He died in London on Mar. 23, 1661, and was survived by his third wife and four sons.

Critical Appraisal: Thomas Welde's most important literary contribution is clearly his work in preparing the *Bay Psalm Book*. This metrical translation of the Psalms was intended for use as a hymnal and would supersede the earlier psalters such as the Sternhold and Hopkins Psalter, the earl of Stirling's translation, and the Ainsworth Psalter, among others. At least two other clergymen, John Eliot and Richard Mather, joined Welde in preparing the *Bay Psalm Book*; in fact, Zoltán Haraszti has suggested that even more translators may have been involved with the project because of the evidence of differences in diction and versification. However, Welde, Eliot, and Mather are the only known contributors.

From the standpoint of poetic merit, the *Bay Psalm Book* has been widely viewed as a clumsy effort, at best. Moses Coit Tyler found its "sentences wrenched about end for end, clauses heaved up and abandoned in chaos, words disembowelled...and dissonant combinations of sound." As Richard Mather noted in his preface to the psalter, the verse was "not always so smooth and elegant as some may desire or expect"; however, he added, "Gods Altar needs not our polishings." Indeed, the *Bay Psalm Book* was intended to be a literal translation that could be metrically adapted to the musical settings of Thomas Ravenscroft and sung by the Bay colony's Puritan congregations. Consistent with their Puritan temperament, the authors were more concerned with making a functional rather than a literary psalter. The opening lines of Psalm 23 illustrate the problems of making a metrical translation while maintaining literal accuracy: "The Lord to mee a shepheard is, / want therefore shall not I, / Hee in the folds of tender-grasse, / doth cause mee downe to lie:" Yet, as Norman S. Grabo has convincingly demonstrated by comparing the Psalm translations of Welde's contemporaries in Eng. to those in the *Bay Psalm Book*, the Bay psalters "did as well as anyone could—[and] when that 'anyone' includes poets of the rank of Sidney, Herbert, and Milton—elevates their accomplishment considerably." In addition, since many of the major English poets, including Shakespeare, were not widely known in colonial America, the familiarity of rhymes and meter of the *Bay Psalm Book* came to represent, as Robert Douglas Mead noted, "the possibilities of poetry and thus defined the context in which, later in the century, the first poets of America began to find their voices."

Although Welde's other work is less notable and nothing else he wrote was published in America, three works did concern the colonies. In 1643 Welde and Hugh Peter wrote *New England's First Fruits* to augment their fund-raising efforts as colonial agents. This book's success is indicated by the fact that its authors were able to raise 2,000 pounds in money and goods. The following year, Welde edited the manuscript of Governor John Winthrop's (q.v.) account of the Antinomian controversy of 1637-1638 and added a preface and conclusion of his own. In 1645 Welde published *A Brief Narrative of the Practices of the Churches in New England*, his last work concerning the colonies.

Suggested Readings: CCNE; DAB; DNB; FCNEV; LHUS; Sprague (I, 24-25); T$_1$. *See also* Norman S. Grabo, "How Bad Is the *Bay Psalm Book*?" PMichA, 46 (1961), 605-615; Zoltán Haraszti, *The Enigma of the Bay Psalm Book* (1956); Robert Douglas Mead, *Colonial American Literature* (1976), pp. 55-56.

Francis J. Bosha
Aoyama Gakuin University
Tokyo, Japan

NOAH WELLES (1718-1776)

Works: "To the Ingenious Author of the Poem Entitled 'Philosophic Solitude,' etc." (pub. in William Livingston, *Philosophic Solitude*; 1747); *The Real Advantage Which Ministers and People May Enjoy Especially in the Colonies* (1762); *The Divine Right of Presbyterian Ordination Asserted* (1763); *Animadversions, Critical and Candid* (1763); *Patriotism Described and Recommended*

(1764); *A Vindication of the Validity and Divine Right of Presbyterian Ordination* (1767; 1796); *A Discourse Delivered at Fairfield. . .for the Funeral of Noah Hobart* (1774); *Debates at the Robin Hood Society* (1774).

Biography: Noah Welles was born on Sept. 25, 1718, to Noah and Sarah (Wyatt) Welles, a farm family in Colchester, Conn. A friend and classmate of William Livingston (q.v.), Welles attended Yale College, class of 1741, receiving A.B. and A.M. degrees. From 1741 to 1746, he studied theology while teaching both at Yale, as tutor, and at Hopkins Grammar School, Hartford. In the first of these postgraduate years, Welles was a Dean's Scholar; in 1774 he was awarded the degree of doctor of sacred theology by Princeton and Yale, where he became a fellow of the college, also in 1774. After interim service at the First Congregational Church, Stamford, Welles was ordained and installed as pastor on Dec. 31, 1746; the Rev. Noah Hobart (q.v.), whose funeral sermon Welles was to deliver in 1773 and publish in the next year, gave the ordination sermon. On Sept. 17, 1751, Welles married Abigail Woolsey (daughter of the Rev. Benjamin Woolsey), and the couple had thirteen children. Throughout his thirty-year ministry at Stamford, Welles was highly regarded as a spokesman for Presbyterianism and American independence. On these merits, he was considered for the Yale presidency in 1766. In 1776, while ministering to imprisoned British soldiers, he contracted a fever and died on Dec. 31.

Critical Appraisal: Combining spiritual faith with secular gifts, Noah Welles revealed a thirst for religious controversy in a series of works defending Presbyterianism against the false claims of the Church of England. In these works, he was alternately reasonable, lightly satiric, and vigorously argumentative. In *The Real Advantages*, Welles posed as an advocate for the Church of England, welcoming still another dissolute young gentleman into the clergy. Welles claimed that Anglicanism suits a merry, spendthrift opportunist, because the faith is free of doctrine, moral discipline, and theological study. He assured the new convert that wealth and preferment awaited him, as well as the assurance of absolution for his sins. In this epistolary satire, Welles articulated the differences in social behavior, theology, church government, and religious practices that distinguish the Church of England supporters from the Presbyterian and Congregationalist dissenters, thereby condemning in the mode of Swift's "A Modest Proposal" all aspects of the English church and its clergy. In *Animadversions*, also in letter form, Welles replied to John Beach's (q.v.) attempt in *A Friendly Expostulation* to rehabilitate Charles I. Cutting and contemptuous, Welles attacked both Beach and his arguments, finding the former crude and indecorous, the latter an offense to all dissenters. In *The Divine Right*, Welles printed the sermon he had delivered on Apr. 10, 1773, with enlargements on the objections to ministerial authority subsequently put forward by his episcopal opponents. Arguing that the Bible defines only one order of ministry and that Presbyterians fit those scriptural criteria, Welles attacked the Church of England hierarchy of priests, thereby affirming the correctness of Presbyterian ordination. In *A Vindication*, Welles again attacked the argument for a diocesan episcopacy.

Supporting and replacing as spokesman Dr. Charles Chauncy (q.v.) (who at the Dudleian Lecture had drawn written objections from Jeremiah Leaming), Welles repeated the arguments of *The Divine Right. A Vindication* is more caustic than his other tracts; the biting voice suggests the freedom Welles gains by dropping the form (and consequent decorum) of the sermon. It suggests as well the frustration of Welles's supporters as they continued to argue for their sect's method of ordination.

Hand in glove with the denunciation of the Church of England is Welles's political support of the divided colonies. In his election day sermon titled *Patriotism Described and Recommended*, Welles delivered an inspirational address that exalted the Christian patriot who valued liberty and learning. Briefly critical of his colony's penchant for litigation, Welles urged his listeners, in accordance with a royal proclamation, to reform in such a way that the state would harmoniously reflect the order and charity of its citizens. Although not satiric, this address nonetheless shows a lucidity and tough-mindedness throughout.

One of Welles's publications, the funeral sermon for Noah Hobart, reveals yet another voice. There, in the solemn and ponderous tones of the elegy, Welles praised the service of the deceased minister and urged the example of his faith. Both articulate and persuasive, Welles showed the multiple and varied gifts of the New Eng. preacher.

Suggested Readings: CCNE; DAB; Dexter (III, 693-694); Sprague (I, 461-462). *See also Appleton's Cyclopaedia of American Biography*, VI, 426.

Roslyn L. Knutson
University of Arkansas at Little Rock

HELENA WELLS (c. 1760-c. 1809)

Works: *The Step-Mother* (1798); *Letters on Subjects of Importance to the Happiness of Young Females* (1799); *Constantia Neville, or The West Indian* (1800); *Thoughts . . . on Establishing an Institution for the Education of Unportioned Respectable Females* (1809).

Biography: Although she was born in America, Helena Wells considered herself an Englishwoman. She was born about 1760, daughter of Robert and Mary Wells, in Charleston, S.C. Her father, a successful bookseller and newspaper publisher, supervised her education at home and stressed the importance of proper language usage. In 1774, as staunch Loyalists, the Wellses removed to Eng., where Helena Wells apparently spent the remainder of her life, although her works indicate considerable familiarity with the W. Ind.

In London Wells entered into partnership with another woman to open a boarding school for girls. When forced to retire for reasons of health, she turned to writing and produced three books in two years. In 1801 or 1802, she married a man named Whitford and soon bore four children, although she continued to suffer poor health. She lived in Yorkshire for at least part of this time. Recovering after prolonged illness incurred during the birth of her last son, she published in 1809 her last-known work. Nothing more is known of her life.

Critical Appraisal: The novels and prose writings of Helena Wells reflect strong opinions on controversial subjects. Her main themes are women's needs for education, especially about finances, and independence of thought. Her first novel, *The Step-Mother* (1798), portrays a proud and independent woman who defies social convention by withholding her respect from any but those few who merit it. When the heroine's husband dies, she dismisses her lawyer and handles her own finances as well as her house and property. The book reflects the author's preoccupation with practical handling of money matters, detailing the division of property under a will and the heroine's sound investment practices. The novel proceeds slowly, as the author seems to want to show in day-by-day detail how a woman of sense handles her life. Volume one unfolds in first-person narration, but volume two becomes hard to follow when the narrator includes several long letters without indicating to whom the letters are addressed. The structure further breaks down in this volume as a number of subplots arise and the narrator details in third person the life histories of various relations of a man to whom her daughter (herself not even a main character) is engaged. The novel ends with a description of the way each character now spends her or his days. The bad characters, of whom there are but few, die off and everyone else lives happily, we assume, ever after.

The book received a number of London reviews, generally unenthusiastic. Critics found it "natural" but dull. They appreciated that it did not threaten the morals of young readers, but they found the lives of two generations too much to condense into one work.

In *Constantia Neville* Wells expressed more directly her concern for women's education and thus actually fulfilled her avowed didactic purpose. Wells derided the popular notion that all young ladies must be "accomplished" in music, and she insisted that young women learn to speak well in mixed company. She preached Christianity by presenting lengthy arguments with a Deist and a Unitarian. As in *The Step-Mother*, she created a heroine who demonstrated her intelligence and a knowledge of bankruptcy laws and other financial affairs. In the end, Wells rewarded her heroine with a rich and loving husband, merited not merely through long-suffering virtue, as typified by so many novels of the time, but for having lived an unsentimental and sensible life.

Constantia Neville holds autobiographical interest for its revelation of Wells's Scottish sympathies and its demonstration of the author's close acquaintance with the laws and culture of Jamaica, which suggest she may have lived there. The novel also includes an attack on Mary Wollstonecraft.

Wells's third book, *Letters on Subjects of Importance to the Happiness of Young Females*, was addressed to Wells's pupils. Each letter dealt with one or more specific topics. On the popular subject of novel reading, Wells denounced novels only if read to the exclusion of other studies, and she recommended a steady diet of history and epic poetry. The final chapter dealt with English grammar and usage, the importance of which Wells had derived from her father, an occasional writer. Wells's list of commonly mispronounced words provides an interesting description of the language as pronounced in London at the turn of the nineteenth century.

Wells's final published work proposed a social improvement, the establishment of a school to be sponsored by the Episcopal Church much as convent schools were operated by Catholics. The first half of the book deplored the state of women's educational institutions staffed by uneducated teachers who often "murdered" the English language. Wells cited the seduction of a student by a governess's husband and her own interview for a job at a school where the governess did not rise from her bed until noon. Wells also condemned a public who held unrealistic expectations of private governesses or who failed to acknowledge their proper place in society. She believed governesses deserved prestige in society "in proportion to what is generally awarded to a tutor of sons."

In the second portion of the book, Wells laid out a plan for her school. Located in Yorkshire, this "Protestant Nunnery" should have a chapel as well as a spacious house, gardens, and orchard. Four teachers could instruct 100 pupils in English, French, writing, arithmetic, geography, astronomy, sewing, music, and dancing. Special care should be taken with the students' diet and health, and all inhabitants should contribute to daily chores and upkeep of house and grounds. The garden should provide food, and the "inmates" could sell their handiwork to meet expenses. Tuition should be charged according to one's ability to pay. This book thus posed a realistic solution to a problem that had troubled Wells since her first arrival in Eng., the education of well-bred but financially distressed women.

Helena Wells's life and works invite critical examination, although her books belong only peripherally to the canon of American letters.

Suggested Readings: DAB (see "William Charles Wells": X, 644-645). *See also* Elisha Bartlett, *A Brief Sketch of the Life, Character, and Writings of William Charles Wells* (1899); Henri Petter, *The Early American Novel* (1971); William Charles Wells, *Two Essays...with a Memoir of His Life, Written by Himself* (1818).

Patricia L. Parker
Salem State College

BENJAMIN WEST (1730-1813)

Works: *The New-England Almanack* (1763-1801, and perhaps later), sometimes with "or Lady's and Gentleman's Diary," and with "by Isaac Bickerstaff" added to the title (Providence, R.I.; 1782-1801); *Bickerstaff's Boston Almanack* (most years; 1768-1793), titled "Bickerstaff's Genuine Boston Almanack" (Boston; 1786, 1791-1793); *Bickerstaff's New-England Almanack* (Boston; 1777-1796);

Wheeler's North-American Calendar; Or, The Rhode Island Almanack (Providence, R.I., 1781-1788); *An Astronomical Diary* (by "Isaac Bickerstaff"; most years, Hartford, Conn., and Boston; 1785-1797); *Town and Country Almanack* (by "Isaac Bickerstaff"; Norwich, Conn.; 1795-1799); *An Account of the Observations of Venus upon the Sun* (1769); "An Account of the Observation made in Providence. . .on the Eclipse of the Sun" (1781); *Memoirs of the American Academy of Arts and Sciences* (1785), I, 156-158; "On the Extraction of [Mathematical] Roots," *Memoirs* (1785), I, 165-169.

Biography: Benjamin West suffers from both bibliographical and biographical ambiguity, for he shares a name with the nearly contemporaneous and much better known historical painter. West was born in Rehoboth, Mass., but was raised on his father's R.I. farm and reputedly was self-educated with books borrowed from friends. Although West's religious affiliation is unknown, his almanacs seem somewhat more frequently than others to include lists of Friends' meetings, perhaps indicating at least sympathy for the Quakers and for religious dissent in general. West was definitely no Tory in his politics. After publishing his first almanac in 1763 and becoming noted throughout Mass. and R.I. for the accuracy of his almanacs by 1767, West gained publishing success during the period leading to the Revolution. He furthered the American cause by producing clothes for Revolutionary soldiers in Providence and by promoting independence, often in subtle ways, in his almanacs of the 1770s and 1780s. West taught mathematics and astronomy at Rhode Island College (later Brown), 1786-1799; received honorary degrees from Brown, Harvard, and Dartmouth; and was a member of the American Academy of Arts and Sciences (but not of the American Philosophical Society, to which his more famous contemporary namesake belonged). He died Aug. 26, 1813, at Providence.

Critical Appraisal: Identifying the author of even a single eighteenth-century almanac is difficult; identifying the author of a corpus of almanacs is harder. All eighteenth-century almanacs borrowed from others, and almost all plagiarized others. Many were written under pseudonyms, even pirated ones like "Isaac Bickerstaff," which was smuggled to America out of Jonathan Swift. Many playfully acknowledged their uncertain origins, admitting a preference for good stolen over bad original verse, to which "Poor Richard" confessed; confusing the contributions of writer and printer, even when both were the same person; or predicting the death of a rival and confirming it by noting a decline in the quality of his almanacs, which were then proclaimed to be the work of an imposter, a deception practiced, but not originated, by Benjamin Franklin (q.v.). A definitive list of the almanacs for which Benjamin West was responsible will never be compiled. Surely, he had nothing to do with several almanacs bearing his name, and surely, he made all or parts of almanacs for which he will never be given credit.

Benjamin West-Isaac Bickerstaff exists today as a name assigned to many examples of an eighteenth-century literary form for which there was no necessary correspondence between a work and a person. The absence of reliable attributions is characteristic of most eighteenth-century almanacs, including those ascribed to more prominent figures such as Nathaniel Ames (q.v.), Daniel Leeds (q.v.), Titan Leeds (q.v.), or Franklin. The mark of one hand, in style, organization, or computation, cannot be found among these almanacs; beyond unattributed quotations from countless sources, many contain graffiti ("Moll, don't curse folks," "Ronald's drunk today") interpolated in calendars as fillers, probably by whoever happened to be setting the type. This realization suggests that the West-Bickerstaff almanacs are not a corruption but an epitome of eighteenth-century serial publication and thus an authentic and revealing document of popular culture.

The anonymous or polynomial character of West-Bickerstaff is paralleled by what may be a related lack of individuation of the observer in the accounts of Venus's passage across the sun in 1769 and the solar eclipse of 1781, both undeniably the work of Benjamin West alone. As individual sightings, the observations meant little. But when added to other observations that were supervised and gathered by international learned societies, West's observations constituted a small part of a collective attempt to know the truth. The modesty of West's role in this scientific, corporate attempt to approximate omniscience was consistent with the meticulous piety expressed in his introduction to the account of Venus, where he presumed to be helping to further providence. He carefully qualified the claim that his account would not only improve navigation but also help prove the symmetry of the universe with the implied caution that such demonstrations cannot convert atheists, but only confirm the faith of former atheists already reclaimed by God.

The West-Bickerstaff almanacs are representative of a relatively unstudied form of eighteenth-century literature worthy of examination for its own sake and for what it could imply about the eighteenth-century conception of authorship and, perhaps, the underlying conception of the self.

Suggested Readings: BDAS; DAB. *See also* James D. Hart, *The Popular Book, A History of America's Literary Taste* (1950); Marion Barber Stowell, *Early American Almanacs* (1977).

R. C. De Prospo
Washington College

THOMAS WEST, BARON de la WARR (1577-1618)

Works: *The Relation...of the Colonie Planted in Virginia*, 2 eds. (1611; rep., 1858).

Biography: Thomas West, third (or twelfth) Baron de la Warr, was born in Hampshire, Eng., attended Oxford without taking a degree, and began his travels early with a journey to It. in 1595. In 1596 he married Cecilia Shirley, daughter of Sir Thomas Shirley of Wison, his godfather. West's lengthy entry in the

Dictionary of National Biography lists services to the public as a member of Parliament, a diplomat in the Low Countries, a soldier with Essex in Ire., a member of both Elizabeth I's and James I's Privy Council, a leader of the Council of the Virginia Company, and the first lord governor and captain general of Va. West was knighted by Essex in Ire. in 1599 and on the death of his father in 1602 became Baron de la Warr. In 1601 he was briefly imprisoned on suspicion of involvement in Essex's rebellious plot against the queen and was freed when Essex declared that West "was unacquainted with the whole matter." After 1608 West devoted his life to the establishment of a permanent Protestant settlement in America. He died in 1618, on his return journey to Va., after having recuperated from a series of illnesses suffered earlier in America.

Although West has appeared to some as a mere figurehead, he was, in fact, one of the unsung heroes of early American history. He reached Jamestown in 1609, just as the colony was about to fall apart. Sir Thomas Gates had been sent to serve as governor of Va. and to enforce a new charter, but had not arrived. Political tensions and physical miseries had destroyed all vestiges of communal harmony. West immediately dispatched groups in search of food. He quickly set up a governing council and began to codify the colonial laws. At the same time, he took every opportunity to put heavy pressure on the authorities in Eng. to improve both the level of financial support for Va. and the quality of settlers they sent there. As a result of the Baron's commitment and obvious dignity under such circumstances, the gentlemen of the colony united in their support of him. Soon after, he fell ill, and in 1611 he returned to Eng., where he busied himself advertising the virtues of Va. and writing his *Relation* in its defense.

Baron de la Warr was sent to Va. primarily to play a symbolic role. He was to show the world that the British government regarded its colony as an integral part of the kingdom. In 1609 the Council for Va. published a document titled "A True and Sincere Declaration," designed to draw support for the colony from the middle and upper classes. The document argues that the presence of a *"Baron and Peere* of this Kingdome (whose Honour nor Fortune needs not any desperate medicine)" in Va. is enough to assure doubters of the colony's importance. As Alexander Brown remarked, the dignity of the enterprise is demonstrated by the fact that "one of so approved courage, temper, and experience, shall expose himself for the common-good to all these hazards and paines . . . and beare a great part upon his own charge." As it turned out, of course, the baron became more than a symbol. Edmund Hawes, in his *Chronicles* (1615), is but one contemporary who testified to his heroism: "The L. De La Ware used his best diligence and industry and therefore withall tooke such extraordinary paines that he fell into extreame sickness." Alexander Brown, after examining the evidence, declared that "if any one man can be called the founder of Virginia," de la Warr "is that man."

Critical Appraisal: Published on the authority of the Council for Va., de la Warr's *Relation* is an elegant defense of himself and the colony. Writing it was necessary because of suspicions aroused by his sudden return to Eng. Since many had sought to withdraw from the project, "making this my returne, the colour of their needlesse backwardnes and unjust protraction," the author was compelled to describe the series of illnesses that "successively and severally assailed me." Agues, gout, cramps, and, finally, scurvy combined to drive him home. But his return should not hamper Va.'s growth, he noted, because the colony was thriving. Forts had been built, and a ten-month supply of food was in storage; contracts for corn had been drawn with the Indians; the livestock was healthy; and now that Argall had discovered the Potomac River, and both Sir Thomas Gates and Sir Thomas Dale were en route to Va. with supplies, the colony's future was very bright indeed. "There is no want of anything, if the action can be upheld with constancy and resolution." De la Warr was resolved to return to the settlement, and although "a weake Instrument," he would lay all he was worth "upon the adventure of the Action, rather than so honourable a worke should faile."

Suggested Readings: DNB. *See also* Alexander Brown, *The Genesis of the United States*, 2 vols. (1890; rep., 1964); William Crashaw, *A Sermon Preached in London Before the Right Honourable Lord La Warre* (1610); Howard Mumford Jones, *O Strange New World: American Culture: The Formative Years* (1964), pp. 100-103; Captain John Smith, "A Map of Virginia" in *The Jamestown Voyages Under the First Charter: 1606-1609*, ed. Philip L. Barbour (1969), II, 462-464; William Strachey, *Historie of Travaile into Virginia Brittania* (w. 1613; pub. 1849); Lyon G. Tyler, *England in America: 1580-1652* (1904), pp. 61-78; Louis B. Wright, *Religion and Empire: The Alliance Between Piety and Commerce in English Expansion: 1558-1625* (1943), pp. 99-107.

James Stephens
Marquette University

JAMES WETMORE (1695-1760)

Works: *A Letter from a Minister of the Church of England* (1730); *Quakerism* (1731); *Eleutherius Enervatus* (1733); *A Letter Occasioned by Mr. Dickinson's Remarks* (1744); *A Vindication of the Professors* (1747).

Biography: The life of James Wetmore turned upon his participation in the Great Apostasy of 1722, which Carl Bridenbaugh termed "possibly the most dramatic event in the ecclesiastical history of the American colonies." Wetmore was born in Middletown, Conn., grandson of the town's first minister, and had received an orthodox Congregational education at Yale College (A.B., 1714). Three years after his graduation, he was called as minister to the first Congregational society of New Haven, where he settled and married. Wetmore then became one of five Yale men to join Samuel Johnson (q.v.) and Timothy Cutler in a discussion group on the "New Learning." In Sept. 1722 all seven men declared their conversion to the Church of England. Expressions of outrage from authorities in the college and throughout the colony caused four of the weaker apostates to reconsider their commitment. Wetmore was one of these temporizers. Eventually, however, he reaffirmed his conversion (the other three did not), and in London in Jul. of 1723 he was ordained in the Church of England. Wetmore then returned to America and under an appointment from the Society for the Propagation of the Gospel engaged himself largely in catechizing black slaves in New York City. In 1726 he accepted a call from the Anglican community in Rye, N.Y., and served there as rector until his death from smallpox in 1760.

Critical Appraisal: James Wetmore's publications consist entirely of polemical defenses of the theological and ecclesiastical principles of the Church of England, which he so dramatically embraced in 1722. Thus his most substantial production (116 pages), *Eleutherius Enervatus* (composed "in concert" with his mentor Samuel Johnson), comprises "an Answer to a Pamphlet" by Jonathan Dickinson. Earlier Dickinson had defended the legitimacy of Presbyterian ordination (in *The Scripture-Bishop*, 1732); Wetmore denied it. Dickinson also provided the stimulus for Wetmore's statement of the Anglican position regarding baptism and regeneration (*A Letter Occasioned by Mr. Dickinson's Remarks on Dr. Waterland's Discourse of Regeneration*). Wetmore also chose to join a standing dispute between the Anglicans and Rev. Noah Hobart (q.v.). Wetmore's *A Vindication of the Professors of the Church of England in Connecticut* proved to be more vigorous than judicious. In a curious postscript, he attempted to demonstrate that John Winthrop (q.v.) and other founders were in fact loyal Anglicans. Hobart scored effectively against Wetmore in his reply, *A Serious Address* (1748). John Beach (q.v.) now took up the standard for the Church of England with his *A Calm and Dispassionate Vindication* (1749), to which Wetmore contributed an appendix. Late in his life (1754-1755), Wetmore involved himself in yet another topic of controversy, a newspaper battle over the future religious orientation of King's College, New York City. The primary antagonist was the competent William Livingston (q.v.), and once again Wetmore's contribution to the argument was by no means decisive.

Wetmore's literary skills were thus totally devoted to polemical exercises, and judged by their efficiency, they were minimal. Nonetheless, one aspect of his art deserved consideration. In *Eleutherius Enervatus* and the earlier *Quakerism*, Wetmore employed a structure of dialog to present his apologetics. Thus *Quakerism* consists of three short debates. In the first, Tremulous, who is inclining toward Quakerism, encounters the secure Anglican Eusebius. In the second debate, these two are joined by the zealous Quaker Titius, whose appearance seems to suggest an impartiality on the part of the author Wetmore but of course serves only as a device to clarify his prejudice. In the final dialog, the reconfirmed Tremulous declares his intention to spurn the obvious heresy of Quakerism. The dramatic effects produced here by Wetmore are transparent, but they are not unattractive.

Suggested Readings: CCMC; CCNE; Dexter (I, 133-138). *See also* Carl Bridenbaugh, *Mitre and Sceptre* (1962); Joseph J. Ellis, *The New England Mind in Transition* (1973).

Kenneth Van Dover
Lincoln University

PHILLIS WHEATLEY (c. 1754-1784)

Works: *Poems on Various Subjects* (1773); "To His Excellency General Washington," *The Pennsylvania Magazine*, 2 (Apr. 1776), 193; *An Elegy, Sacred to the Memory of...Samuel Cooper* (1784); *Liberty and Peace, A Poem* (1784).

Biography: Phillis Wheatley was born in Africa, probably in the Gambia-Senegal region. In 1761, when she was about 7, she was kidnapped and brought to Boston, Mass., where she was purchased by John Wheatley, a wealthy tailor, as a servant for his wife, Susanna. Within sixteen months of arriving, with the help of the Wheatleys' daughter Mary, Phillis had learned to speak English and to read even difficult passages from the Bible. From 1767 on, her work was published in newspapers and magazines, as broadsides and pamphlets, and in a book. In 1773 she went to Eng., where she met members of an international missionary group connected with the Wheatleys. She returned to America in Sept. to be with Susanna Wheatley, then seriously ill. Later that year, or in Jan. 1774, she was freed. Thereafter her fortunes declined. The Wheatley family circle broke up, and in 1778 Phillis Wheatley married John Peters, a freeman who had difficulty in supporting her and the three children born to them, all of whom died in infancy. The poet spent the last months of her life working in a cheap boardinghouse. She died on Dec. 5, 1784.

Critical Appraisal: Phillis Wheatley's first appearance in print was "On Messrs. Hussey and Coffin" in the Newport, R.I., *Mercury*, Dec. 21, 1767, when she was about 13; but it was her "Elegiac Poem on the Death of...George Whitefield," a broadside of 1770, that brought her wide public attention. During the next three years, she published three other broadsides, all elegies. Besides such occasional poetry, she wrote on abstract topics favored in the period—recollection, virtue, imagination, morning, and evening. She also wrote on current topics: to the king on the repeal of the Stamp Act, to Commodore Hood on pardoning a deserter, "On the Death of Mr Snider Murder'd by Richardson," "America," "On the Arrival of the Ships of War, and Landing of the Troops," and "On the Affray in King-Street," that is, the Boston Massacre. With the exception of the poem on the king, the existence of these unpublished poems has only recently been discovered, and manuscripts of the last two have not yet come to light. The original proposal for her book called for publication in Boston, but it finally appeared from a London house in 1773 under the title *Poems on Various Subjects*. The fact of English publication may account for the dropping of the two lost poems.

Without these and other topical poems, Wheatley's writing reflects even more clearly the strong religious influence that came from her life with the Wheatley family. While displaying a variety of neo-Classical motifs, particularly the invocation, the poems retain a strongly Christian character. Elegies on the death of prominent Bostonians or their children occupy much of the book. Although the funeral elegy had been popular in New Eng. since its founding, Wheatley's versions are original in her choice of elements to be stressed and their structural arrangement. In almost every case, they depict the departed in heaven, sometimes on a throne, surrounded by heavenly choirs, leaning out momentarily toward the earthbound spouse or parent. The mourner is encouraged to look forward to an eventual reunion in heaven. The emphasis on heavenly music and the manner of transcending this world by flying or by crossing over water are suggestive of black spirituals.

The poems on abstract subjects offer the poet more scope. "Thoughts on the Works of Providence," for example, contains a good description of the world as a machine, but unlike the Deists and atheists, against whom Wheatley warned in other poems, she saw the world as proof of God's intimate care.

With few exceptions, her poems follow the close couplet form she learned from Pope, but her tone was always sincere and completely without irony. Her couplets are notable for their quality of harmonious sound. Although they are used more often for reflective or elegiac verse than for narrative, when the poet sometimes turned to narrative, she wrote skillfully. Her poems on Goliath and on Niobe are among her best.

Wheatley's religious expression often emphasized the Christian promise of eventual equality for all. Again and again, she referred to freedom; her poem to the earl of Dartmouth, for example, juxtaposes a desire for freedom for New Eng. next to an account of her parents' anguish when she was seized and taken from her homeland. But her feelings against slavery are more strongly presented in her letters, especially in that written to the Rev. Samson Occom (q.v.), Feb. 11, 1774.

Unbiased judgments on Wheatley as a poet writing in America in the late eighteenth century have been rare until the last few years. Both her life and her poetry have been used to demonstrate the beliefs of others. In her own time, she was a showpiece in the drawing rooms of Boston and the missionary circles of Eng., until the loss of the Wheatleys, the upheaval of war, and her husband's financial problems left her destitute. During the early nineteenth century, her work was reprinted by the abolitionists to demonstrate the ability of blacks as an argument for emancipation. In the twentieth century, she has been praised as an early black American author. On the other hand, she has been criticized for accepting her lot without anger and for failing to speak out more boldly against slavery, despite the frequent references to freedom in her poems and her letters.

A considerable number of new poems or drafts of those previously known, as well as letters and other material on her life and opinions, has come to light in recent years. They call for a continuing revaluation of her place in American literature.

Suggested Readings: DAB; NAW; T₂. *See also* Mukhtar Ali Isani, "The First Proposed Edition of *Poems on Various Subjects* and the Phillis Wheatley Canon," AL, 49 (1977), 97-103; Sidney Kaplan, *The Black Presence in the Era of the American Revolution, 1770-1880* (1973), pp. 150-170; Robert C. Kuncio, "Some Unpublished Poems of Phillis Wheatley," NEQ, 43 (1970), 287-297; Phil Lapsansky, "Deism—An Unpublished Poem by Phillis Wheatley," NEQ, 50 (1977), 517-520; Julian D. Mason, Jr., Introduction, *The Poems of Phillis Wheatley* (1966); R. Lynn Matson, "Phillis Wheatley—Soul Sister?" *Phylon*, 33 (1972), 222-230; [Margaretta Matilda Odell], "Memoir" in *Memoir and Poems of Phillis Wheatley* (1834); Dorothy B. Porter, "Historical and Bibliographical Data of Phillis Wheatley's Publications," JSR, 6, i (1974), 54-60; M. A. Richmond, *Bid the Vassal Soar* (1974), pp. 1-78; Gregory Rigsby, "Form and Content in Phillis Wheatley's Elegies," CLAJ, 19 (1975), 248-257; William H. Robinson, *Phillis Wheatley in the Black American Beginnings* (1975); idem, "Phillis Wheatley in London," CLAJ, 21 (1977), 187-201; Kenneth Silverman, "Four New Letters by Phillis Wheatley," EAL, 8 (1974), 257-271.

Ann Stanford
California State University, Northridge

THOMAS WHEELER (fl. 1640-1676)

Works: *A True Narrative of the Lord's Providences Towards Edward Hutchinson of Boston and Myself* (1675)—rept. 1676 as *A Thankefull Remembrance of Gods Mercy to Several Persons at Quabaug.*

Biography: Biographical information about Thomas Wheeler is sorely limited and not entirely reliable, chiefly because of the lack of records; the Wheeler name was common in New Eng. and this Thomas and his family are sometimes confused with persons with the same name. Even Wheeler's birth and death dates cannot be confirmed. He is believed, however, to have died on Dec. 10, 1676, in Concord, Mass., where he had settled with his family during the late 1630s or early 1640s, and to have been survived by his widow, Ruth Wheeler (the daughter of William Wood [q.v.]), and at least two children. According to a nineteenth-century source, whose reliability is by no means certain, "Capt. Thomas was admitted freeman in 1642, was sergeant of the foot company of Concord in 1662, was appointed, at its organization in 1669, captain of the horse company, made up of troopers from several adjoining towns," and "was in command of this company in July, 1675," at the fight at Brookfield, Mass., with the Indians.

Critical Appraisal: Thomas Wheeler's reputation, today nearly nonexistent in American letters, relies upon his one narrative about his experiences in King Philip's War. As the record of a soldier-participant, the narrative resembles many similar military accounts that, like captivity narratives, were a recognized genre in the seventeenth century. Unlike the more famous and inclusive narrations of William Hubbard (q.v.) and Thomas Church (q.v.), Wheeler's tale simply reports the facts as he knew them. Wheeler's narrative limits itself to the tactics and results of only one minor skirmish and siege and does not seek to overview military strategy either before or after the event. Both Hubbard and Church relied on Wheeler's narrative, with and without giving Wheeler credit, and both attested to the accuracy of the account.

Wheeler began by relating the fate of his party when sent to counsel with the Nipmuck Indians, continued through an ambushment wherein several men were killed or, like Wheeler himself and his son, were wounded, and spent the narrative's major portion on the siege of Brookfield. These events took place between Jul. 28 and Aug. 5, 1675, when Wheeler ended the narration except to add that Capt. Hutchinson died on Aug. 19 and he himself returned home Aug. 21. As the title indicates, Wheeler obtruded upon the narration his understanding of God's "providence" in the events, asserting his purpose was "to give... an account of the Lord's dealing with us." As a result, he credited God as the puppeteer: about the ambush, he believed that to find the cause one must "look higher than man the instrument," and later when rain foiled the Indians' attempts to fire the wooden structure wherein all of the survivors and Brookfield residents were holed up, Wheeler concluded that the rain was God's interference. Some of Wheeler's images are powerful; he mentioned, for example, the Indians' playing "football" with a man's head just beyond the range of the townspeople's guns. Although lively, the narrative is understated, letting the fact of the event, unembellished by much description or personal swaggering, convey the fear and horror he and the settlers must have felt. Wheeler gave the impression of a truly humble man retelling a horrible experience not for his own but for God's glory.

Suggested Readings: George Madison Bodge, "Soldiers in King Philip's War," NEHGR, 38 (1884), 34-46; idem, Soldiers in King Philip's War (1906); William Hubbard, History of the Indian Wars in New England (1777; rep., 1969); Douglas Edward Leach, Flintlock and Tomahawk: New England in King Philip's War (1958); Richard Slotkin, Regeneration Through Violence: The Mythology of the American Frontier, 1600-1800 (1973), pp. 87, 184. The entire Wheeler narrative is reprinted in CNHamHS, 2 (1827), 5-23, and in Richard Slotkin and James K. Folsom, eds., So Dreadfull a Judgment: Puritan Responses to King Philip's War, 1676-1677 (1978), pp. 234-257.

Dean G. Hall
Wayne State University

ELEAZAR WHEELOCK (1711-1779)

Works: "Diary" (w. 1741; pub. 1869); The Preaching of Christ (1761); A Plain and Faithful Narrative (1763); A Sermon Preached Before the Second

Society (w. 1763; pub. 1767); *A Continuation of the Narrative* (1765, 1769, 1771, 1772, 1773, 1774, 1775); *A Brief Narrative* (1767); *Liberty of Conscience* (1776).

Biography: Eleazar Wheelock was born at Windham, Conn., on Apr. 22, 1711. In 1733 he graduated from Yale, where he shared the first Dean Berkeley Award. He remained at Yale one year to study divinity, received a license to preach in 1734, and in 1735 became pastor of the Second Society at Lebanon, Conn., where he remained until 1770. He was attacked by some of his fellow Congregationalists as an enthusiast during the Great Awakening because of his extensive activities as an itinerant preacher. To supplement his salary, Wheelock tutored students for college. Samson Occom (q.v.), a Mohegan, became his student in 1743, and this experience led Wheelock to become interested in educating Indians for mission work among their own people. In 1754 he founded Moor's Indian Charity School at Lebanon, where he taught both whites and Indians, among them Joseph Brant. In 1765 Occom and Nathaniel Whitaker (q.v.) went to Eng., where they raised about 12,000 pounds for the school. Dissatisfaction with his congregation and a loss of favor among the Six Nations caused Wheelock to seek a new location for his school. On the basis of the English fund, he negotiated a land patent in N. H., where, at Hanover in 1770, he founded Dartmouth College. Wheelock served as president of the college and of the Indian Charity School, educating Canadian Indians and white students for mission work. He died at Dartmouth on Apr. 24, 1779.

Critical Appraisal: Eleazar Wheelock became widely known as an itinerant preacher during the Great Awakening, preaching 465 sermons during one year. Religious fervor struck his church shortly after it had struck Jonathan Edwards's (q.v.) church at Northampton. In his *Narrative of Surprising Conversions*, Edwards noted the work of the young preacher and later called on him to preach at Scantic and Northampton to rouse the congregations when fervor cooled. Wheelock's diary (published in 1869) of a trip to Boston in 1741 indicates that he was popular, large crowds gathering and even following him where he went. He aroused the ire of some fellow Congregationalists such as Charles Chauncy (q.v.), who in *Seasonable Thoughts* accused him of enthusiasm. Some of the criticism may have resulted from his kinship to his two "enthusiastic" brothers-in-law, James Davenport and Benjamin Pomeroy, and from his friendship with George Whitefield (q.v.). Nevertheless, he was accused of yelling and pounding the pulpit, among other things, and members of other congregations who attended his services were sometimes excluded from communion in their own churches. No sermons from this period were published, perhaps because he wrote few of them; he preached from notes or delivered his sermons extemporaneously. More a man of action than of thought, Wheelock was not a scholar. Although he participated extensively in the revivalist movement, he was moved by the spirit of the day and made no significant original contribution to the religious thought of the time. He left two typical ordination sermons, *The Preaching of Christ* (1761) and *A Sermon Preached Before the Second Society* (1763).

Wheelock's importance rests on his work with the Indians. He left a detailed account of his work at Moor's Indian Charity School and at Dartmouth in *A Plain and Faithful Narrative* (1763) and the six subsequent narratives of continuation. In the former, he reflected the idealism with which he undertook to absolve himself and his family of "the public guilt" that resulted from neglect of the charter-bound duty of the colonies to Christianize the natives. That could be done best, he believed, by training Indians as missionaries. In the process of narrating his succinct history of the school and describing its activities and methods of funding, Wheelock gave insights into the character of his students and revealed himself as a strict disciplinarian and an able administrator. The first three continuation narratives relate the hardships and privations of Wheelock's Indian missionaries in the field and their tendency to desert their stations and turn to drink. By 1770 he was convinced that Indians did not make the best missionaries. Caught in the developing rift between American Calvinism and the Church of England, he and his missionaries fell out of favor with Sir William Johnson, who maintained a powerful influence over the Six Nations. Upon losing the favor of those tribes, Wheelock moved his school to Hanover, where he established Dartmouth College and reestablished his charity school. The last three continuation narratives relate the early history of Dartmouth, Wheelock's efforts to recruit students among the Canadian Indians, and the work of his missionaries among them. Moor's Indian Charity School was a significant contribution to the Indian mission activity during the middle third of the century. The work of men such as John Sergeant (q.v.), Jonathan Edwards, David Brainerd (q.v.), John Brainerd, and Wheelock foreshadowed the widespread interest in Indian mission work that began in the early nineteenth century, and some of Wheelock's administrative practices and theories of Indian education anticipate, albeit crudely, some of the theories of Richard Henry Pratt regarding Indian boarding schools over a century later.

During the Revolutionary War, Dartmouth College was in an exposed area of the frontier. Wheelock's missionaries were instrumental in reducing the hostilities of the Six Nations and in establishing good relations with the Canadian Indians; James Dean, one of his missionaries, was appointed Indian agent by the Continental Congress. Like many clergymen, Wheelock used the pulpit to speak to the issues of the day. In *Liberty of Conscience* (1776), he defended himself against the charge of Toryism for failing to observe Thanksgiving on the date set by the N.H. Provincial Assembly. Such legislatures might proclaim holidays but could not enforce observance of them without violating one's "liberty of conscience." The enlightened mind was compelled to resist any encroachment of civil power upon the prerogatives of Christ, he said.

Although Wheelock's major works indicate that he was headstrong and sometimes filled with his own importance, he was a tireless worker and a good administrator. Spending little time in study, he devoted great energy to his educational projects. Although his lack of scholarship may have hampered his literary output, the significance of his educational activities as a contribution to American society cannot be denied.

Suggested Readings: CCNE; DAB; DARB; Dexter (I, 493-498); Sprague (I, 397-403). *See also* "Diary of Rev. Eleazar Wheelock," HM, 15 (1869), 237-242; Alan Heimert, *Religion and the American Mind* (1966), pp. 367-368; James Dow McCallum, *Eleazar Wheelock* (1939); idem, *The Letters of Eleazar Wheelock's Indians* (1932), p. 11-32; David McClure, *Memoirs of the Rev. Eleazar Wheelock* (1811); Baxter Perry Smith, *The History of Dartmouth College* (1878), pp. 6-75.

Daniel F. Littlefield, Jr.

Little Rock, Arkansas

JOHN WHEELWRIGHT (c. 1592-1679)

Works: *A Fast-Day Sermon* (w. 1637; pub. 1867); *Mercurius Americanus* (1645).

Biography: John Wheelwright, Jr., was born at Saleby in East Lincolnshire, Eng., about 1592. He spent seven years at Sidney Sussex College, Cambridge, earning an M.A. in 1618 and taking holy orders. After a brief service as deacon at Peterborough Cathedral, he became vicar at Bilsby, near his birthplace, in 1621. Upon the death of his first wife, Wheelwright married Mary Hutchinson, Anne Hutchinson's sister-in-law. Deprived of his Bilsby living in 1632, most likely for his Puritan sentiments, Wheelwright lived off his modest private income until 1636, when he immigrated to New Eng. Some members of the Boston church attempted to secure him a call there as teacher, but the attempt was thwarted by John Winthrop (q.v.). Wheelwright then accepted a petition to minister to the not-yet-gathered church at Mount Wollaston, ten miles to Boston's south. His *Fast-Day Sermon*, preached the afternoon of Jan. 19, 1637, appeared to align him with Anne Hutchinson and her Antinomian followers and further alienated Winthrop and his party; the sermon provoked charges of contempt and sedition upon him from the General Court of the Massachusetts Bay colony. Wheelwright was convicted, and in Nov. 1637 he was sentenced to be disenfranchised and banished from the colony. He duly removed to N.H. and the next year founded the colony at Exeter and became pastor of its church. There he remained until 1643, when he moved to Wells to serve that church. The following year, after Wheelwright had written two conciliatory letters to Winthrop and the General Court, the court rescinded his banishment. In 1645 appeared his only work to be published in his lifetime, a vindication of his role in the Antinomian controversy titled *Mercurius Americanus*. He moved once again in 1647, serving the church at Hampton as pastor. Wheelwright returned to Eng. in 1655 or early 1656, but after the Restoration, he once more accepted a call from a New Eng. church, this time at Salisbury, Mass. He ministered there from 1662 to 1679, when he died at age 87.

Critical Appraisal: Wheelwright's significance stems almost entirely from his part in the Antinomian controversy, which troubled Massachusetts Bay from 1636 to 1638. The manuscript of his 1637 *Fast-Day Sermon*, although unpublished until the nineteenth century, served as a powerful weapon in the hands of his seventeenth-century opponents; today it provides historians with a unique example of a sustained theological statement by a minister openly aligned with the Hutchinsonian party. In *Mercurius Americanus* a more subdued Wheelwright distanced himself from the excesses of the Hutchinsonians but resolutely rejected the "official" interpretation of the controversy published by Winthrop and his supporters.

Wheelwright chose as the text for his *Fast-Day Sermon* Jesus's words from Matthew 9:15: "but the days will come, when the bridegroom shall be taken from them, and then they shall fast." The General Court had declared a day of general fasting and humiliation in hopes of healing "the dissensions in our churches," and Wheelwright quickly traced the root cause of the colony's troubles to the absence of Christ. Too many church members know Christ only by the good works they perform, presumably as "fruits and effects" of his presence in them; "they labour under a covenant of works." Ideally, fasting should teach them the need "to looke upon the Lord with a direct eye of faith." But Wheelwright did not expect so swift a change; he termed the actions of the errant church members "Antichristian" and warned of a coming spiritual combat when true Christians would "prepare for batell and come out against the enimyes of the Lord . . . those under a covenant of works." The struggle would be fierce. "Those that run under a covenant of works are very strong" and in appearance "wondrous holy people," so Wheelwright anticipated "a combustion in the Church and comon wealth."

A remarkable series of apocalyptic images follows. Wheelwright likened the approaching struggle to the battle between the angelic hosts of Satan and the archangel Michael (Revelation 12:7-9); pointed to the coming "day of the Lord" when the opponents of God shall be burnt up root and branch (Malachi 4:1); and reminded his hearers that Antichrist must be consumed by the fire of the Gospel before the day of Christ may come (Revelation 18:8, 2 Thessalonians 2:3 ff.). Such imagery not only reinforces his earlier identification of his opponents as anti-Christian but also feeds hopes that the last days are approaching. He urged believers to "be willing to be killed like sheepe" if they hoped to overcome and finally to "looke for the Spirit of the Lord to come upon us, and then to do mighty things through the Lord."

The Wheelwright of *Mercurius Americanus* wrote in a far different manner. Gone were the martyr's confidence and the apocalyptic expectations. Wheelwright and his sympathizers were scattered; at best he could set the record straight and clear his own reputation. The tract's full title reveals its polemical purpose: *Mercurius Americanus, Mr. Welds His Antitype, or Massachusetts Great Apologie Examined, Being Observations upon a Paper Styled, A Short Story of the Rise, Reign, and Ruine of the Familists, Libertines, &c. Which Infected the Churches of New England, &c. Wherein Some Parties Therein*

Concerned Are Vindicated, and the Truth Generally Cleared. Wheelwright, who styled himself *philalethes* (lover of truth), would provide the antitype for which the Bay colony's *Short-Story* (attributed by Wheelwright to Thomas Welde [q.v.] but today recognized to be by John Winthrop) was but a deceptive shadow. Not only did Wheelwright find the *Short Story* pregnant with "a spirit of censure and malice," but he also tried at every opportunity to demonstrate his superiority to it in wit, rhetoric, logic, and erudition. Wordplays abound, as do lapses into technical Greek and Latin terminology.

Although the reader without prior knowledge of the theological issues at stake in the Antinomian controversy will find it hard to follow Wheelwright's argument closely, his conclusions are easily summarized. He began by putting as much ground as possible between himself and the more radical Hutchinsonians, including Anne. As one possessed by "many strange fancies and erroneous tenents," Anne Hutchinson is judged "guilty of most of these errors" charged against her in the *Short-Story*. Many of her followers have likewise been disposed "through melancholy fumes...to strange fancies in Divinity."

Wheelwright's own position, on the other hand, had become virtually that of the Bay elders who opposed him. He allowed good works and dispositions (sanctification) to serve as reliable signs of true faith; he accepted evidence from conditional promises (New Testament passages where Christ promises salvation *on condition* that a person perform some action); he argued that Christians themselves are the primary actors in gracious works; and he agreed that Christians are still bound to the law.

So orthodox is he, indeed, that some other explanation must obviously be sought for his banishment. He admitted that his *Fast-Day Sermon* was contentious and his preaching of it vehement, but he argued that he meant spiritual contention only. Since he was in fact guilty of neither contempt nor sedition, he blamed his conviction and banishment on Winthrop's melancholy temper, reinforced by envy of Sir Henry Vane and "by a sullen constellation then predominant." Winthrop needed some outlet for his frustration and found it in the unfortunate Wheelwright.

Suggested Readings: CCNE; DAB; Sprague (I, 83-87). *See also* Emory Battis, *Saints and Sectaries* (1962); David D. Hall, ed., *The Antinomian Controversy, 1636-1638: A Documentary History* (prints fast-day sermon; 1968); James F. Maclear, "New England and the Fifth Monarchy," WMQ, 32 (1975), 223-260; John Wheelwright, *Writings*, ed. Charles H. Bell (contains texts of both Wheelwright's works; 1876).

Baird Tipson
Central Michigan University

ALEXANDER WHITAKER (1585-1617)

Works: *Good Newes from Virginia* (1613).

Biography: Alexander Whitaker was born in 1585 at Cambridge, Eng., where his father was to become master of St. John's College in 1587. His mother was Susan Culverall Whitaker, daughter to the wealthy London merchant Nicholas Culverall. After four years at Eton, Whitaker entered Trinity College, Cambridge, receiving a B.A. in 1605 and an M.A. in 1608. Ordained within the Church of England in 1609, he served for two years in the north of Eng., most likely in Yorkshire. In Mar. 1611 he gave up his prosperous and comfortable living and sailed for Va. with a group of colonists headed by Sir Thomas Dale.

Whitaker became the first rector to serve at the new settlement of Henrico fifty miles upriver from Jamestown. He built Rock Hall, the parsonage house, on the south bank of the James River, from which he ministered to Henrico and to another settlement at Bermuda Hundred. With Sir Thomas Dale, he explored the James River seventy miles up from Henrico, to the site of the falls below Richmond. Also, Whitaker was apparently the minister responsible for the instruction and baptism of Pocahontas into Christianity. Whitaker drowned while crossing the James River near Henrico, Va., in the spring of 1617.

Critical Appraisal: Written in the form of a sermon, Alexander Whitaker's *Good Newes from Virginia* follows from the text of Ecclesiastes 11: 1: "Cast thy bread upon the waters; for after many days thou shalt find it." Addressed to the Virginia Company in London, the essay pleads for greater support for the Va. colonies. The sermon itself is preceded by a lengthy Epistle Dedicatorie addressed to Lord Ure and written by William Crashawe, who attempted to answer various slanderous charges regarding the success of the Va. colony. Crashawe held up Whitaker as an example of a person with a good living who had volunteered to serve in Va. The sermon is also preceded by a brief dedication written by Whitaker to Thomas Smith, his distant relation and treasurer of the English colony in Va.

As a promotion tract, *Good Newes* attests to the providential conditions at the Jamestown and Henrico settlements. Whitaker urged both increased investment and settlement as he denied rumors of unfavorable conditions such as disease, unfavorable climate, and hostile Indians. On the contrary, Whitaker found that "the finger of God hath been the onely true worker heere: that God first shewed us the place, God first called us hither, and here God by his speciall providence hath maintained us."

Following the moderate Puritan leanings of his famous father, William Whitaker, Alexander Whitaker stressed the serious duty of Christians to establish the Church of England in the New World and to convert the Indians to Christianity. The attitude toward the Indians was essentially ambivalent: they were viewed as highly competent, healthy, disciplined persons, equal in capacity to Europeans in every regard, but they followed the "witchcraft" of heathen priests.

The Christian duty of liberality in charitable giving also enforces on those in Eng. the duty to supply the needs of the struggling colony. Throughout Whitaker's short essay, one hears the voice of a youthful, impassioned idealist, one who is engaged in translating his Puritan religious training into worthy deeds. The essay is intelligent and highly coherent, written in the "plain style" of Cambridge Puritan William Perkins.

Although the greater part of the essay deals with the religious duty to support the new colony, Whitaker eagerly reassured his British audience that secular reward would also follow upon a liberal investment. For this reason, he ended his essay with a laudatory account of Va.'s geography, climate, mineral wealth, soil, game, fish, and forests.

Suggested Readings: CCV; DAB; LHUS; T_1. *See also* G. Brydon, *Virginia's Mother Church* (1951), pp. 24-27; Joan St. C. Crane, "Good Newes from Virginia," *Serif*, 2, iv (1965), 3-11; Richard Beale Davis, *Intellectual Life in the Colonial South, 1585-1763* (1978), pp. 708-713, passim; William H. Littleton, "Alexander Whitaker (1585-1617) 'The Apostle of Virginia,'" HMagPEC, 29 (1960), 325-348; Harry Culverwell Porter, "Alexander Whitaker: Cambridge Apostle to Virginia," WMQ, 14 (1957), 317-343.

Jeffrey J. Folks
Tennessee Wesleyan College

NATHANIEL WHITAKER (1730-1795)

Works: *The Trial of the Spirits* (1762); *A Sermon Preached. . .at the Ordination of the Rev. Mr. Charles-Jeffry Smith* (w. 1763; pub. 1767); *A Sermon Preached at the Ordination of. . .Isaac Foster* (1765); *A Brief Narrative of the Indian Charity-School* (1766, 1767, 1769); *Two Sermons in Which the Doctrine of Reconciliation Is Plainly and Briefly Stated* (1768; rev., 1770); *A Funeral Sermon, on. . .George Whitefield* (1770); *A Confutation of Two Tracts* (1774); *An Antidote Against Toryism* (1777); *The Reward of Toryism* (1783); *A Brief History of the Settlement of the Third Church* (1784); *The Mutual Care the Members of Christ's Body Owe to Each Other* (1785).

Biography: Born on Long Island in 1730 and reared in N.J., Nathaniel Whitaker graduated in 1752 from the College of New Jersey and in 1755 became minister of the Presbyterian Church at Woodbridge and in 1760 of the Chelsea Parish at Norwich, Conn. At Norwich he also engaged in trade and was a neighbor of Eleazar Wheelock (q.v.), founder of Moor's Indian Charity School at nearby Lebanon. In 1765 Whitaker accompanied Samson Occom (q.v.), an educated Mohegan preacher, to Eng. and Scot. where, during the next year and a half, they raised about 12,000 pounds for Wheelock's school. The money, placed in trust, became the financial base for the founding of Dartmouth College. After his return to America, Whitaker served as minister of the Third Church at Salem from 1769 to 1784 and of the Presbyterian Church at Skowhegan, Maine, from 1785 to 1790. An ardent Presbyterian, he often became embroiled in controversies with other New Eng. clergymen and with his own congregations. During the Revolutionary War, he was an outspoken supporter of the colonists' cause. Whitaker died at Hampton, Va., in Jan. 1795. Among his descendants was Daniel Kimball Whitaker (1801-1881), his grandson, founder and editor of the *Southern Literary Journal*, the *Southern Quarterly Review*, and the *New Orleans Monthly Review*.

Critical Appraisal: Whitaker's religious works reflect the controversies that surrounded him as a clergyman during the decades following the Great Awakening. Whitaker preached and wrote about the issues that arose in the breakdown of religious unity in New Eng.: the verbal attacks of clergy upon clergy, the necessity of church attendance, congregational factions, the multiplication of sects, and the nature of salvation. In his essays, he joined the debate on salvation, church structure, and dogma.

A supporter of the evangelical movement, a friend of George Whitefield (q.v.), and a zealous Presbyterian who believed that salvation resulted from an operation of the Holy Ghost in man's soul, Whitaker often found himself at odds with other clergymen and with some elements of his own congregations. His sermon *The Trial of the Spirits* attacked the extreme dogmatism of those who, without reason, opposed any religion that appeared to be "experimental." Apparently in response to difficulties with his own flock, *A Sermon Preached at the Ordination of the Reverend Isaac Foster* was a plea for church unity; he exhorted the congregation to attend Foster's public ministry and to support him without complaint. In 1768 Whitaker instigated a public debate on the nature of salvation when *Two Sermons* on reconciliation, which he had preached in Eng., were published. Whitaker revised and republished them in 1770 in response to William Hart's *Brief Remarks* (1769), published as an answer to Whitaker and Samuel Hopkins (q.v.). Whitaker asserted the absolute necessity of regeneration in salvation and man himself as the source of his ruin and misery; Hart, who answered Whitaker again in *A Letter* (1771), rejected depravity and asserted that man, because he was essentially righteous and intelligent, could work out his own salvation. The debate, although inconclusive, dramatically emphasized a major divisive doctrinal issue of the day.

Other works reflect the ecclesiastical debates of the period. In 1773 a faction of his congregation asked his removal, charging that he had craftily led them along the path to Presbyterianism while they wanted a congregational, or "true," church structure. In response, Whitaker published *A Confutation of Two Tracts* in which he attacked John Wise's (q.v.) argument, presented nearly sixty years earlier and recently reprinted, that the New Eng. churches were rightly constituted. Presbyterianism, unlike Congregationalism, allowed the congregation freedom and was not a domineering and magisterial form of government that robbed them of their just rights and privileges. Whitaker survived the controversy of 1773, but in 1784 a large segment of his congregation severed pastoral ties. In response, he published *A Brief History*, reviewing both controversies, defending his actions, and charging that the congregation's actions were "cruel oppression" that denied his "liberty of conscience." That summer, at the Presbytery of Salem, he preached *The Mutual Care*. Using his case as an example, he emphasized the responsibilities of all members of the church to one another. The Presbytery exonerated Whitaker and dissolved his pastoral relation with the Third Church.

Whitaker was also strongly committed to social and political issues. Long supportive of Wheelock's Indian mission work, he vigorously campaigned in behalf of the school throughout Eng. and Scot. In 1766 and 1767, he published *A Brief Narrative of the Indian Charity-School*. Based on Wheelock's own narrative, the work was basically propagandistic, aimed at raising funds. Also published in Eng. in 1767 was Wheelock's 1763 sermon on the ordination of Charles Jeffry Smith, who was going out as a missionary to the Indians. Attached to the sermon was one by Whitaker on the same occasion. As the Revolutionary War approached, Whitaker demonstrated a growing concern for the matter of civil and political freedom. When Whitefield died in 1770, Whitaker's *A Funeral Sermon* called the evangelist a friend to America's "religious and civil liberties." In 1771 Whitaker preached a sermon, which was not published, on the Boston Massacre. In *A Confutation of Two Tracts*, he clearly perceived the parallel between civil freedom and freedom of conscience, as he did in *A Brief History* and *The Mutual Care*. Whitaker took the issue of independence to the pulpit, directing his attention to the Loyalists. His discourse *An Antidote Against Toryism*, dedicated to George Washington (q.v.) with "the frankness, and openness of one determined to live and die free," asserted that the cause of liberty was the cause of God and truth. God approved of war against oppression, and it was lawful to wage war against oppressors even when they, like the Tories, were not in arms. Citing Locke in his definition of liberty, Whitaker argued that only those who opposed good government were rebels. In *The Reward of Toryism*, delivered shortly after the war's end, he urged his countrymen to purge the nation of Tories, who still represented a threat to society.

Whitaker's sermons have typical structures, but unlike those of many of his predecessors and contemporaries, they are not laden with scriptural passages. Instead, Whitaker often refers to published works, past and present, secular and religious. Emphasis, as in his other works, is on man's spiritual, social, and political responsibilities to his fellow man. The emotionally charged language of his discourses on Toryism demonstrates his imaginative propagandistic skills, calling Washington "a hero," his army "a band of heroes," and the Tories "those cowardly, selfish, half-way people," whom he compared, in an expanded metaphor that informs both discourses, to the people of Meroz, who refused to take arms to oppose Fabin, the oppressor of Israel. The personality of a determined, stubborn, sometimes petulant man pervades his work, giving his writing a mildly informal quality as he personalized many of the issues he took up. His literary expression of those issues brought into sharp focus some of the major religious, social, and political currents of his day and demonstrated the significant contribution of the clergy to the Revolutionary spirit of the age. Indeed, as Heimert said, his "career and eloquence" epitomized the "moral and intellectual history of the Revolutionary years."

Suggested Readings: CCMC; CCNE; DAB; P; T$_2$. *See also* Joseph B. Felt, *Annals of Salem* (1849), II, 550, 601-605; Joseph Haroutunian, *Piety Versus Moralism* (1932), pp. 1-80; Alan Heimert, *Religion and the American Mind* (1966), pp. 494-509.

Daniel F. Littlefield, Jr.
Little Rock, Arkansas

ANDREW WHITE, S.J. (1579-c. 1655)

Works: *Relatio Itineris in Marylandiam* (1634); catechism in Piscataway; letters; theological treatises.

Biography: Andrew White was born in London, Eng., in 1579. After studies at the English Catholic colleges at Douay and Seville, he was ordained a priest and went to Eng., where he was arrested and banished for life with forty-six other priests in 1606 after the Gunpowder Plot. In 1607 he entered the Jesuits at Louvain and again returned to Eng. He afterwards taught theology, Scripture, and Hebrew at the Jesuit colleges at Liège, Louvain, Valladolid, and Seville. He became a friend of George Calvert, a convert to Roman Catholicism and the First Lord Baltimore, who, after an unsuccessful colonization venture in Newfoundland, petitioned Charles II for a grant of land north of Va. In 1632 the king issued the charter for Md. to Cecil Calvert, the Second Lord Baltimore. Although the new colony was to have religious liberty and no established church, the Calverts had arranged for Jesuits to go to the colony as ordinary settlers. White was appointed the first superior of the Jesuits and, with Father John Altham (*alias* Gravenor) and Brother Thomas Gervase, joined the expedition, which sailed from the Isle of Wight on Nov. 23, 1633, and landed in Md. on Mar. 25, 1634. In addition to ministering to the Catholic settlers, White worked among the Indians of the Patuxent and Piscataway tribes. This brought him the opposition of Governor Leonard Calvert, who ordered him back to St. Mary's City. Nevertheless, White converted the Tayac or chief of the Piscataways in 1640 and composed a simple catechism in the Piscataway language. White's Md. career ended in 1645, when Richard Ingle and William Claiborne invaded Md. from Va. and overthrew the proprietary government. Three Jesuits fled into Va., where they died. White and Thomas Copley, then the superior of the mission, were carried back to Eng., where they were charged with treason for being Catholic priests and for having entered Eng. without permission. The court banished both Jesuits for life. Copley returned to Md., but White, after unsuccessfully petitioning his superiors to go back to the colony, secretly reentered Eng., where he served as a chaplain to a private family in Hampshire. He died on either Jan. 6, 1656, or Sept. 27, 1655.

Critical Appraisal: Andrew White's theological treatises were intended as lecture notes for his students at the English colleges on the Continent. Of primary interest for Md. history and literature, however, is his *Relatio Itineris*, which was his account as superior of the Jesuit mission to the general of the order in Rome. Written in Latin, it is more than a travel account, although it has many of the characteristics of that genre. He thus narrated in great detail the hazards of the voyage, described at length Barbados, where the settlers stopped to take on supplies, and finally gave the first account of the Md. settlement itself.

But his detailed description of the soil and vegetation of Md. was more than an advertisement for the colony; it was intended to provide information to the Jesuit general about the future possibilities of the mission. Only by reading between the lines in the light of other early Md. documents can one discern that White was also describing an experiment in religious liberty for Catholics and non-Catholics alike. The Protestant settlers had boarded the *Ark* and the *Dove* in Eng. after taking the oath of allegiance and supremacy to the king. White and the Catholic settlers joined the expedition at the Isle of Wight, where they would not be subjected to the oath. White suspected that the sailors then delayed setting sail in order to betray the Catholics, but their plot was thwarted when the *Dove* was forced to cut its anchor and head for open sea to avoid high winds and collision with another ship. White was careful to note that this occurred on the feast of St. Clement, who was martyred by being tied to an anchor and cast into the sea. He made no direct allusion to Cecil Calvert's instructions that the Catholic colonists keep their acts of worship as private as possible to avoid offense to the Protestants, but he did record that it was the Catholics who offered prayers for a safe voyage and who, upon reaching Md., gathered to celebrate Mass and erect a cross on St. Clement's Island.

In the manner typical of the more famous Jesuit *Relationes* from New Fr., White described the Indians he encountered with a view to informing future missionaries. He carefully recorded their manner of dress; the food they produced; their character, religious beliefs, and potentiality for accepting Christianity; and the type of huts they built, in one of which White and his companions had established a chapel.

Although not a literary masterpiece, White's *Relatio* is a lively, first-hand account of the settlement of Md. He added touches of humor, as when he described the loss of his laundry when the settlers first landed or the surprise of the Indians that there could be trees large enough from which could be hewn a "canoe" as large as the *Ark*. Primarily intended as White's report to his superior in Rome, the *Relatio* also served as the basis for Lord Baltimore's tracts promoting the colony. Whether White was directly responsible for any of these tracts is uncertain. Leo LeMay argued that White was the author of *Objections Answered* (1633), in which, among other reasons, the author stated that "conversion in matter of Religion, if it bee forced, should give little satisfaction to a wise State of the fidelity of such convertites, for those who for worldly respects will breake their faith with God doubtlesse wil doe it, upon a fit occasion, much sooner with men." It would be safer to conclude that the authorship cannot be definitely assigned to White but that the pamphlet reflected the mentality of White and the other Catholic adventurers who sought to establish a colony without establishing a state church. It was to provide for such a separation of church and state that the priests were to take up property like any other settlers, a provision that became a major argument for later Md. Jesuit writers, notably Peter Attwood (q.v.) and George Hunter (q.v.).

White's "catechism" in the Piscataway language, preserved in manuscript at Georgetown University, is better described as a list of prayers and commandments. Its primary importance is in providing the earliest written example of the

Piscataway language. There are, finally, several additional letters of White to his Jesuit superiors and one to Lord Baltimore. The latter describes in some detail the original "Conditions of Plantation" and explains the motive for the Jesuits accepting the use of land from the Indians for support of their missionary work, an action that provoked a serious dispute between the Jesuits and the proprietor. For that controversy, see Edward Knott (q.v.).

Suggested Readings: CCMDG; DAB; DARB; T₁. *See also Calvert Papers*, I, *Maryland Historical Society, Fund Publication*, no. 28 (1889); Thomas Hughes, S.J., *History of the Society of Jesus in North America, Documents*, I, pt. I (for the Latin of the *Relatio* and for *Objections Answered*; 1908); J. A. Leo LeMay, *Men of Letters in Colonial Maryland* (1972); *Relatio Itineris in Marylandiam, Maryland Historical Society, Fund Publication*, no. 7 (1874) and Supplement (1875).

Gerald P. Fogarty, S. J.
University of Virginia

ELIZABETH WHITE (d. 1669)

Works: *The Experiences of God's Gracious Dealing with Mrs. Elizabeth White* (w. 1660; pub. 1741).

Biography: Elizabeth White lived in New Eng. during the midseventeenth century. However, few biographical facts are available concerning her. Even in her own spiritual autobiography she revealed hardly any personal information except those facts relating to her autobiographical motive in detailing the steps of her conversion. For example, she noted 1657 as the year of her marriage only because it precipitated her initial concern for her salvation. Likewise, when she referred to her family, she never mentioned any of their names; in fact, she even refrained from stating her maiden name. It is known that White died during childbirth in 1669, twelve years after her marriage. This was the very manner of death she related as foretold to her in a dream-vision. Although her dream prophecised how she would die, it did not tell her when.

Critical Appraisal: Spiritual autobiographies were fairly popular among seventeenth-century Puritans. Written primarily as records of conversion, they offered a means of self-examination and confession. As such they provided the Puritan a way to determine his progression in God's grace and thereby to know whether or not he might be one of God's elect. Because they were personal, the genre afforded the writer a degree of freedom within the otherwise strictly defined church doctrine of predestination.

White's *Experiences* concentrates on approximately three years, from 1657, shortly before her marriage, to about 1660, probably the year she wrote her spiritual autobiography. Following the established pattern of this genre, she began by looking back at the profound ignorance and false pride that she felt characterized her youth. But it was her father's desire that she partake of the sacrament a month before her marriage that caused her to realize how truly deficient her spiritual life was. White then described the series of demonic temptations she experienced. She sought to overcome these temptations by seeking comfort in Scripture and a *Book of Instructions for Comforting Afflicted Consciouses*.

White's narrative demonstrates a danger many spiritual autobiographers faced in losing the genre's necessary sense of spontaneity, and thus becoming overly ambiguous and abstract. Since the spiritual autobiographer often did not recognize his conversion until some time after he had experienced it, he later had to write about that past experience as a present happening without admitting the advantage of having been able to review it retrospectively. White strove to overcome this difficulty by using various animal images to depict her despair and quoting the Bible passages she relied on for comfort. Nevertheless, at times her accounts resemble well-rehearsed, prepared texts.

When White's autobiography was published in 1741, it was presumably to serve the genre's secondary purpose of helping in the edification of others. The reasoning underlying such publications was that if God in his infinite mercy was willing to forgive and thereby select the writer, his mercy might be extended to the reader as well.

Even though White's *Experiences* is not of the highest literary merit when compared with better-known spiritual autobiographies, her work does offer a modern reader insight into how a New Eng. Puritan laywoman judged herself in accordance with the strict standards of her religion's doctrines.

Suggested Readings: Daniel B. Shea, Jr., *Spiritual Autobiography in Early America* (1968), pp. 183-187.

Mindy Janak and Maurice Duke
Virginia Commonwealth University

HENRY WHITE (c. 1642-1712)

Works: Religious poem and epistle (1698), manuscript in Quaker Collection, Guilford College, in *Eastern Quarter: Symonds Creek Monthly Meeting Records 1678, 1715-1768*, I, 185-189; pub. by Thomas E. Terrell, Jr., as "'Some Holsom Exhortations': Henry White's Seventeenth-Century Southern Religious Narrative in Verse," EAL, 18 (1983).

Biography: Born about 1642 in Isle of Wight County, Va., Henry White was the son of a cooper. In 1663 he bought land in the Albemarle region of N.C. and soon thereafter built a plantation along the west bank of Little River in the Perquimans precinct. Between 1672 and 1679, White became one of the early converts to Quakerism in the Carolinas and soon became a leader in that group. One of the handful of Quaker meetings in that area met in his home until 1707 when the first meetinghouse was built, partly under his leadership. He served as the meeting's recording clerk and probably as an elder and minister. White was not a large landholder, but he was active in colonial affairs, serving at various times in the precinct county courts and for awhile on the N.C. higher court. He died in 1712.

Critical Appraisal: Although Henry White was not known during his lifetime for his literary achievements, his importance today is that he is the earliest known person in colonial N.C. to have written poetry or a religious epistle. A single example of each survives in manuscript form at Guilford College in Greensboro, N.C. White's untitled poem, written in 1698, is a 302-line narrative describing the fall of man and his restoration through Christ. White relied heavily upon biblical narrative for the Garden of Eden story, drew occasionally from Psalms and Old Testament prophetic Scriptures, and related man's salvation through Christ. He also offered "some holsom exhortations for everyone to take notis of." White was apparently influenced by a variety of theological traditions, and distinct Quaker themes emerge only infrequently, as in references to the light. The religious dimension is particularly significant since there was then no precedent in the South for religious poetry, which continued to be less prominent in the South than in New Eng. throughout most of the eighteenth century. Only scattered samples emerge in the South in the years following White.

White's epistle was written in the same year as the poem and was directed to "friends everywhere," most likely in places such as N.J., Pa., Va., Md., and Eng. Approximately 400 words long, White's epistle is both sermonic in its call to obedience and faith and confessional in its profession of God's love and peace as experienced by White and his fellow Quakers. This, too, is one of the earliest statements of religious conviction in the South and certainly the earliest such from a habitant of N.C.

Suggested Readings: Mrs. Watson Winslow, *The History of Perquimans County* (1931); Luella M. Wright, *The Literary Life of the Early Friends, 1650-1725* (1932).

Thomas E. Terrell, Jr.
The University of Chicago

JOHN WHITE (1575-1648)

Works: *The Ten Vows* (n.d.); *General Observations for the Plantation of New England* (1629); *The Humble Request* (1630); *The Planters Plea* (1630); *The Troubles of Jerusalem* (1646); *A Way to the Tree of Life* (1647); *A Sermon* (1648); *David's Psalms* (1655); *A Commentary on Genesis* (1656).

Biography: John White was born during the Christmas season, 1575, in Stanton St. John, Oxfordshire, Eng., the son of John and Isabel White. He was educated at Winchester College and entered New College, Oxford, in 1593, receiving his master's degree in 1600. He remained there as a fellow until 1606, when he became rector of Trinity Church in Dorchester, a position White held for the next forty years. In the same year, he married Anne Burgess and subsequently sired four sons. During his ministry in Dorchester, White gained the reputation of a clear and careful sermonizer who interpreted the entire Bible one and a half times.

About 1623 White and a number of friends projected the new colony of Mass. as a refuge for persecuted nonconformist Puritans and thus helped found the Dorchester Company (1623) and the Massachusetts Bay Company (1629). The project met with numerous difficulties, and at one point, it appeared that the colonists would return to Eng. However, White, who himself never visited America, eventually managed to secure a patent and the necessary supplies for the colonists.

In 1635 White was charged with fiscal improprieties and brought before the Court of High Commission. Although the court's decision is unclear, White did live to see his greatest detractor, Archbishop Laud, impeached for high treason and in 1640 was appointed to a committee charged with reforming the church. In 1643 White received another appointment, this time as a member of the Puritan Assembly of the Divines, a body established by Parliament to offer advice on the best form of uniform church government to be adopted in the country. He resigned his position in 1646 and returned to Dorchester as a pastor, where he died two years later.

Critical Appraisal: Although John White earned the reputation of an energetic sermonizer and the body of his literary works attests to his religious zeal, American audiences are especially interested in *The Humble Request* and *The Planters Plea* for the light they shed on the early efforts of British colonization in Mass. The first of them is a brief letter of leave-taking that a company of twelve new officers of the Massachusetts Bay Company tendered to the king. Written by White some years before, *The Humble Request* attempts to explain the reasons for the emigration, implores the king's understanding and approval, and offers an interesting vision of the spirit in which the colonial settlements were undertaken. In beseeching the king's approval, the request notes that "your charitie may have met with some occasion of discouragement through the disaffection, or indiscretion, of some of us." It goes on to explain that these citizens are not leaving "as loathing that milk wherewith we were nourished" but rather "to relieve and rescue with our utmost and speediest power, such as are deare unto us, when wee conceive them to be running uncomfortable hazards."

The Planters Plea, published in the same year, offers a more extensive explanation of White's advocacy of colonization. He began by arguing that the Bible clearly reveals the divine inspiration for colonization, noting that "Colonies (and other conditions and states in humane society) have their warrant from Gods direction and command; who as soone as men were, set them their taske, to replanish the earth, and to subdue it, Gen. I. 28." Continuing with the argument that God granted this continent to Christians in order that they would bring the divine word to the inhabitants and thus convert them, White contended that the

New World's agricultural and spatial abundance is intended for an ever-increasing society such as his own and not simply for a few native savages. Consequently, this land is seen as offering not only limitless possibilities for homesteading but physically restorative conditions that "manie of our people that have found them selves alway weake and sickly at home, have become strong, and healthy there."

Arguing further that "the principall scope whereat the Colonie aimes...must be Religion," White denounced the practice of sending a society's worst citizens as its colonists, individuals obviously unfit for the sacred mission he envisioned. Finally, he maintained that through proper management, colonies can provide innumerable economic advantages for both the parent country and the colony itself. Throughout, White organized his treatise by offering first his own views, then paraphrasing the opposition's contentions, and eventually countering with more of his own contentions. Although he acknowledged that many colonists may emigrate with the hope of enjoying greater religious liberty, White continually insisted that the colonists' primary loyalties were to the word of God and to the authority of the crown.

Ultimately, each of these works, as well as White's other writings, reveals a serious, pious, and learned man who always sought to promote religious and individual freedom. Despite his numerous religious exegeses, White will be remembered best by American audiences for the crucial role he played in the founding of the Mass. colony.

Suggested Readings: DNB. *See also* Francis Dillon, *A Place for Habitation* (1973); Everett Emerson, ed., *Letters From New England* (1976); Henry F. Howe, *Massachusetts: There She Is—Behold Her* (1960); Lawrence Shaw Mayo, *Hutchinson's History of Massachusetts Bay* (1936); Samuel Eliot Morison, *Builders of the Colony* (1930); Frances Rose-Troup, *John White, the Founder of Massachusetts* (1930).

David W. Madden
University of California, Davis

GEORGE WHITEFIELD (1714-1770)

Works: *The Eternity of Hell Torments* (1738); *A Journal of a Voyage from London to Savannah in Georgia* (Journal I; 1738); *Thankfulness for Mercies Received a Necessary Duty* (1738); *A Continuation of the Reverend Mr. Whitefield's Journal, During the Time He Was Detained in England by the Embargo* (Journal IV; 1739); *A Continuation of the Reverend Mr. Whitefield's Journal, from His Arrival at London, to His Departure from Thence on His Way to Georgia* (Journal III; 1739); *A Continuation of the Reverend Mr. Whitefield's Journal, from His Arrival at Savannah, to His Return to London* (Journal II; 1739); *The Heinous Sin of Drunkenness* (1739); *A Continuation of the Reverend Mr. Whitefield's Journal, from His Embarking After the Embargo, to His Arrival at Savannah in Georgia* (Journal V; 1740); *A Short Account of God's Dealings* *with the Reverend Mr. George Whitefield* (1740); *A Continuation of the Reverend Mr. Whitefield's Journal, After His Arrival at Georgia* (Journal VI; 1741); *A Continuation of the Reverend Mr. Whitefield's Journal from Savannah, June 25. 1740. to His Arrival at Rhode-Island* (Journal VII, title varies; 1741); *Britain's Mercies, and Britain's Duty* (1746); *A Further Account of God's Dealings with the Rev. Mr. George Whitefield* (1746); *Eighteen Sermons Preached by the Late Rev. George Whitefield* (1771); *The Works of the Reverend George Whitefield*, 6 vols. (1771-1772); *Fifteen Sermons, Preached on Various Important Subjects*, 3rd ed. (contains a sermon on Whitefield by the Rev. Joseph [*sic* Josiah] Smith of South Carolina; 1772); *A Selection of Letters of the Late George Whitefield*, 3 vols. (1772); *Memoirs of Rev. George Whitefield: by John Gillies, D.D.* (1838, 1934); Roland Austin, "Bibliography of the Works of George Whitefield," PWHS, 10 (1916), 169-184, 211-223 (over 133 items); Earnest E. Eells, ed., "An Unpublished Journal of George Whitefield," CH, 7 (1938), 297-345; John W. Christie, ed., "Newly Discovered Letters of George Whitefield, 1745-46," JPHS, 32 (1954), 69-90, 159-186, 241-270.

Biography: This Methodist leader was born in the Bell Inn, Gloucester, Eng., on Dec. 16, 1714. After a self-proclaimed degenerate early life, Whitefield entered Pembroke College on Nov. 7, 1732, as a servitor and met Charles and John Wesley. Neither frequent fasts nor the "method" of the "Holy Club" of Oxford, however, brought him inner peace. His spiritual uncertainty was finally vanquished by a "new birth" in 1735, a conversion experience that launched his ministerial career. Ordained a deacon on Jun. 20, 1736, he rose to unprecedented popularity and was accepted into the priesthood on Jan. 14, 1739. Active in Eng., Scot., Ire., and Wales, Whitefield also made seven visits to America (1738, 1739-1741, 1744-1748, 1751-1752, 1754-1755, 1763-1765, 1769-1770) and founded an orphanage called Bethesda in Georgia (1740). He reawakened religious fervor from Ga. to Maine primarily through open-air sermons to huge crowds and often stimulated resentment in members of the organized church. Whitefield preached approximately 18,000 times in his career. He survived his wife, Elizabeth James, whom he wed on Nov. 14, 1741, by two years, dying in Newburyport, Mass., on Sept. 30, 1770.

Critical Appraisal: Termed both saint and demon, man of destiny and charlatan, humble servant of God and self-promoting egotist, George Whitefield was a man who generated extreme responses. In Augustan Eng. and the colonies, enthusiasm in religion was generally regarded by those in authority as suspect and in bad taste. Whitefield's effusive comments about his intimate relationship with God published in his first journal provided evidence of his sanctimonious affectation and hypocrisy to his detractors and proof of his godly zeal to his supporters. Upon his return to Eng. in 1738, most pulpits were closed to him, and of necessity he began the open-air preaching that was to bring him his greatest fame. Whitefield's confidence in his mission's inspired nature left no room for disagreement. He had no patience with the established clergy, many of whom he thought were "wolves in sheep's clothing" and "blind unregenerate, carnal, luke warm, and unskillful guides." Unconcerned with rank, he even attacked the very popular Archbishop Tillotson and the bishop of London. His unshakeable faith in predestination and in regeneration through a "new birth" in fact required this assault on good works as a means to salvation to prevent men from following a path that, in his estimate, led inexorably to hell. Such egotism made him an easy target for the wits of his day: Johnson thought him a "mixture of politicks and ostentation"; Fielding's narrator in *Tom Jones* paralleled him to the character of Thwackum and preferred Whitefield's brother, who was "absolutely untainted with the pernicious principles of Methodism"; Samuel Foote lampooned him as Dr. Squintum (referring to the preacher's crossed eyes) in his comedy *The Minor*; and Pope likened him to a braying ass in the *Dunciad*. Whitefield fared better with the poets Cowper and Blake, who depicted him, respectively, as a saint and a prophet.

The texts of Whitefield's letters, journals, and sermons ironically give insufficient reason for these strong reactions or for his profound effect on his listeners and his immense popularity. His work reveals no unusual theological expertise in its heavy reliance upon the Bible, the thirty-nine articles, and Whitefield's own conversion experience. His sermons instead document his inability to discern a conflict between two fundamental tenets of his ministry. Theoretically, he propounded a strict interpretation of predestination, as when he struck a pulpit in Maine and cried out, "Works carry a man to Heaven! It were not more presumptious than for a person to climb to the moon by a rope of sand!" Practically, however, he concluded many sermons with a plea for good works that tacitly acknowledged their efficacy. Speaking of Christ's sacrifice, he said: "Shall we spend our time in those things which are offensive to him? Shall we not rather do all we can to promote his glory, and act according to his commands? O my dear brethren, . . . let me beseech you to love, fear, honour and obey him, more than ever you have done yet." Such theological inconsistency was subsumed by the vitality and the sincerity of Whitefield's own belief just as organized religion was subsumed in the grand scope of his vision: "all the world is my parish, and I will preach wherever God gives me opportunity, but you will never find me disputing about the outward appendages of religion; don't tell me you are a Baptist, an Independant, Presbyterian, a Dissenter, tell me you are a Christian, that is all I want."

The key to Whitefield's success cannot be found in his writings; it is the man himself that makes his religion of the heart succeed. The spellbinding effect of his extemporaneous oratory, attested to by Benjamin Franklin (q.v.), Lord Chesterfield, and David Hume, is precisely what is missing from the printed page. David Garrick, the famous actor, envied the range and richness of Whitefield's voice, and Franklin computed that it could reach an audience of 30,000 people. Imagine these forces brought to bear on the following extract on Christ crucified and its effect upon a congregation eager to believe:

> There, There, by faith, O mourners in *Sion*, may you see your Saviour
> hanging with arms stretched out, and hear him, as it were, thus speaking to

your souls; "Behold how I have loved you! Behold my hands and my feet! Look, look into my wounded side, and see a heart flaming with love: love stronger than death. Come into my arms, O sinners, come wash your spotted souls in my heart's blood.

Although the statement that Whitefield gave "churchgoing America its first taste of theatre under the flag of salvation" was certainly exaggerated, the charismatic evangelist was inclined to the theatrical. These dramatic sermons were no doubt heightened by his tendency to view himself in a messianic role. To Whitefield, his birth in the Bell Inn portended his future imitation of "the Example of my dear Saviour, who was born in a Manger belonging to an Inn." He also acquainted drunkards with their fate on the last day with words that stressed his identification with the Son of God: "And I summon you, in the name of that God whom I serve, to meet me at the judgment-seat of Christ, that you may acquit both my Master and me."

These brief insights are not meant to question Whitefield's creed, methods, or sincerity, but to point out the need for further critical evaluation that moves beyond advocacy or disparagement. He is central to the understanding of eighteenth-century America. Both a prime mover in the Great Awakening and in part its creation, Whitefield's impact was and is hard to underestimate: millions heard his voice and thousands were "reborn"; early missionary and philanthropic efforts begun by Thomas Bray (q.v.) and others were given new vitality; and a catholicity of religious spirit was initiated. In addition, the success of his intinerant ministry in the colonies indirectly hastened the break with Eng. by increasing the number of dissenters and, by forming them into loosely affiliated, intercolonial, interdenominational "congregations," perceptibly encouraged American independence.

Suggested Readings: CCNE; DAB; DARB; DNB; LHUS; Sprague (V, 94-108); T₂. *See also* Joseph Belcher, *George Whitefield: A Biography* (1857); Albert D. Belden, *George Whitefield—The Awakener* (1930); James Downey, *The Eighteenth Century Pulpit* (1969), pp. 155-188; Thomas Gamble, *Bethesda* (1902); Wesley M. Gewehr, *The Great Awakening in Virginia, 1740-1790* (1930); Edwin N. Hardy, *George Whitefield: The Matchless Soul Winner* (1938); Stuart C. Henry, *George Whitefield, Wayfaring Witness* (1957); Albert M. Lyles, *Methodism Mocked* (1960); W. Fraser Mitchell, *English Pulpit Oratory from Andrews to Tillotson* (1932); John Pollock, *George Whitefield and the Great Awakening* (1972); Luke Tyerman, *The Life of the Rev. George Whitefield*, 2 vols. (1877); Joseph B. Wakeley, *The Prince of Pulpit Orators* (1871); George L. Walker, *Some Aspects of the Religious Life of New England* (1897); Ola E. Winslow, *Jonathan Edwards* (1941). A more complete early bibliography of works and articles relating to Whitefield is Francis A. Hyett and Roland Austin, *Supplement to the Bibliographer's Manual of Gloucestershire Literature*, pt. II (1916), pp. 505-572.

Michael A. Lofaro
University of Tennessee, Knoxville

JOHN WHITING (c. 1635-1689)

Works: *The Way of Israels Welfare* (1686).

Biography: John Whiting, the second son of the Honorable William and Susanna Whiting, was probably born in Eng. shortly before his parents came to America in the mid-1630s. His father, a wealthy merchant, served as assistant and treasurer of the young colony of Conn. Educated at Harvard College from which he obtained an A.B. in 1653 and an A.M. in 1655, Whiting remained in Cambridge until 1657, when he agreed to assist the aged and infirm Edward Norris, pastor of the First Church of Salem. Despite appeals from the Salem congregation that he remain as their minister, Whiting left Salem in 1659 and after a brief stay in Cambridge settled with his family in Hartford, Conn., in 1660. There he was ordained over the First Church, he and his wife having become members of the church by letter from their church in Cambridge. The selection of Whiting by the Hartford congregation was a tribute to the talent and potential of the young minister, for surely the congregation measured him against both the founder of the church, Thomas Hooker (q.v.), who had died in 1647, and the founder's colleague, Samuel Stone (q.v.), with whom Whiting would serve until 1663. In 1664 Joseph Haynes was selected to succeed Stone, and almost immediately, controversy broke out between Whiting and Haynes on the subject of baptism. The two challenged each other to public debate on the subject, but no record survives to indicate that either one accepted the challenge of the other. After several years of infighting, Whiting and his by-then minority party withdrew from the debate. Opposed to all attitudes on baptism (and church politics) save those in accord with the Cambridge Platform, Whiting and his party petitioned the General Court on Oct. 14, 1669, for the right to establish a new church in Hartford "according to such their Congregational principles." The organization of the Second or South Church in Hartford and Whiting's reordination as its pastor on Feb. 12, 1670, came none too soon, for by then Haynes and his party had brought the First Church into step with Presbyterianism. Except for service as chaplain of the Conn. militia in the mid-1670s, Whiting served with distinction both the Second Church and the interests of Congregationalism in the rapidly growing Hartford community until his death on Sept. 8, 1689. Married twice, first about 1654 to Sybil Collins of Cambridge, who bore him seven children, and then in 1673 to Phebe Gregson, who also bore him seven children, Whiting was survived by Phebe and an unknown number of children.

Critical Appraisal: Like many men of his time, John Whiting is noteworthy for his practical contributions as minister and public servant to the community at Hartford rather than for his literary or oratorical accomplishments. This observation is supported in Whiting's case by notice of the praise Cotton Mather (q.v.) lavished upon him in his *Magnalia Christi Americana*. There Mather linked Whiting with other important figures of early Conn. life and letters, citing him as one among the "most Worthy Men, wherewith *Connecticut*

Colony has been singularly favoured," men "never [to] be forgotten, till *Connecticut* Colony, do forget it self, and all Religion."

The General Council of Conn. recognized Whiting's contribution to the colony on two occasions during his life: first it offered him the chaplain's post noticed above, and then it invited Whiting to preach the election sermon for 1686. *The Way of Israels Welfare*, Whiting's only printed work, is the published version of the sermon he preached at the election on May 13, 1686. The sermon, which has claim to our attention as one of the earliest surviving examples of the Conn. election sermon, is significant for its restatement of declension themes and issues developed in Mass. election sermons of the 1670s and early 1680s by the younger Thomas Shepard (q.v.), Increase Mather (q.v.), and Samuel Torrey (q.v.), among others.

In Whiting's sermon, New Eng. is the new Israel nation of God's chosen people. But from auspicious beginnings wherein God and His people cooperated under the "Covenant" in the establishment of a "Kingdom of God" in the wilderness, New Eng., like Israel of old, has lost sight of its goal. Preaching out of II Chronicles 15:2 ("The Lord is with you while ye are with Him"), Whiting cautioned the audience that in its pursuit of secular ends, New Eng. had frustrated God's intentions and now ran the risk of God's lack of interest in New Eng.'s (Israel's) "Welfare." Thus he observed, "[We] have got nothing by wandring, so it is time to give it over." From Whiting's point of view, New Eng. must reform its ways, with the responsibility for instigating reform falling to its civil and ecclesiastic leaders. Lest the leaders doubt the quality of the reward to New Eng. for its reform and its renewal of the "Way," Whiting told them, "The recovery of first love and first works, would be our glory." In *The Way of Israels Welfare*, Whiting issued this command to the civil and ecclesiastic leaders and the people of New Eng.: "Let your hearts fall out with Sin, and fall in with God and Christ." For the particular edification of the leaders, he added, "Oh look to your work, and labour to do it well, and that is duty to God and man."

Although the sentiments expressed in this sermon became commonplace among New Eng.'s preachers by the end of the seventeenth century, that fact did not diminish the significance of Whiting's expression of them in Conn. in 1686. The presence of declension issues in *The Way of Israels Welfare* indicates that the declension phenomenon was not limited to the social, religious, or political condition of Mass. Additionally, one feature of the sermon suggests that Whiting understood better than some of his Mass. colleagues that New Eng.'s traditional orthodoxy eventually would have to give way to the approach of a cosmopolitan spirit in the eighteenth century. Unlike election sermons on similar subjects by his Mass. contemporaries, Whiting's sermon is not a jeremiad, and Whiting is definitely not a typical Puritan Jeremiah. Instead, the sermon, like many that appear in the early decades of the eighteenth century, is a relaxed and reasoned exercise, and the preacher is a calm and thoughtful spiritual father trying to impress his audience with the extremity of their situation and to move them, without benefit of harangue, to adopt a spirit of reform.

Suggested Readings: CCNE; Sibley-Shipton (I, 343-347). *See also* Cotton Mather, *Magnalia Christi Americana* (1702), Book IV.

Ronald A. Bosco
State University of New York at Albany

SAMUEL WHITING (1597-1679)

Works: *Oratio, Quam Comitijs Cantabrigiensibus* (1649); "Concerning the Life of the Famous Mr. Cotton, Teacher to the Church of Christ at Boston, in New-England" (w. c. 1653; pub. 1769, 1846); *A Discourse of the Last Judgement* (1664); *Abraham's Humble Intercession for Sodom* (1666).

Biography: Samuel Whiting was born in 1597 in Boston, Lincolnshire, Eng., where his father served as mayor (1600 and 1608). He attended Emmanuel College, Cambridge, falling under the influence of the great Puritan divines Richard Sibbes and John Preston and receiving an A.B. (1616) and an A.M. (1620). For three years, he was family chaplain to Sir Nathanael Bacon and to Sir Roger Townsend. After another three years as co-minister at Lynn Regis, he was prosecuted for nonconformity. He then took his ministry to Skirbeck, near Boston, where he enjoyed several years of peace until he was again charged with nonconformity.

Whiting sailed for New Eng. in Apr. 1636 with his son, daughter, and second wife, Elizabeth. After a wretched voyage, the Whitings landed on May 26; in Jun. they moved to Saugus, which was renamed Lynn in honor of Whiting's English pastorate, and on Nov. 8 he was installed as the town's minister, a position he filled until his death.

The New Eng. career of Samuel Whiting was distinguished: he was named an overseer of Harvard College (1654), delivered an Artillery Sermon (1660), is believed to have presided over the Synod of 1662, and was one of the ministers selected by the General Court in 1672 to lead a day of fasting and humiliation. Toward the end of his life, he was an outspoken opponent of civil encroachment in matters of ecclesiastical authority.

Although a prominent leader, Whiting was a tolerant man who declined to take part in the case against John Wheelwright (q.v.), discountenanced the law against celebrating Christmas, was averse to harsh treatment of Quakers, and befriended Indians. Although two of his sons remained on these shores as ministers, another returned to Eng. as an Anglican. Whiting loved to catechize children at his own home on the Sabbath. His humor and continual smile endeared him to his parishioners, one of whom, Obadiah Turner, left a diary describing Whiting as "a good liver" who kept "a noble garden": "Mr Whiting was of a quiet temper and not mch given to exstasies, but yet he would sometimes take a merrie part in pleasant companie." These same qualities, Turner implied, were the source of Samuel Whiting's authority: "In preaching he did not mch exercise his bodie.

But his clear voice and pleasant way were as potent to hold fast ye thoughts of old and young."

Critical Appraisal: Not a prolific writer, Samuel Whiting was nevertheless versatile. Harold Jantz cited evidence that he wrote some verse, and there is speculation that, as an accomplished scholar of Latin and Hebrew, he contributed to the *Bay Psalm Book*.

Whiting is best known today for his sketch "Concerning the Life of the Famous Mr. Cotton, Teacher to the Church of Christ at Boston, in New-England," published after Whiting's death. The "Life" focuses on John Cotton's (q.v.) education and ministry in Eng., reflecting Whiting's acquaintance with Cotton in Lincolnshire. But the narrative ends with Cotton's election sermon of May 1634, refers only generally to his preaching in New Eng., and completely ignores his role in the Antinomian controversy and his defense of the New Eng. Way. Whiting's purpose was to stress Cotton's long labor for the Puritan cause and the esteem in which he was held, so that "he may be a pattern to us all."

Modern scholars regard Whiting's "Life of. . .Cotton" as typical of the spiritual biographies that flourished around 1650. They were intended to ease New Eng.'s growing anxiety over the deaths of the founders, as well as the shortcomings of the new generation, and to enhance the image of the Congregational cause in Old and New Eng. Whiting, however, did not exploit Puritan biography nearly so much as did John Norton (q.v.) and Cotton Mather (q.v.), whose "Lives of Cotton" borrowed from Whiting's text.

A Discourse of the Last Judgement is intended to convince man of his unworthiness and to exhort him to repent. Although it warns about the "terrour" of damnation, it sees the Last Judgement as a time of "everlasting Consolation." As one of the "Lords Worthies" whose words can help men prepare, Whiting offered forty-two doctrines with reasons and uses. John Wilson (q.v.) and Jonathan Mitchel (q.v.) observed in the preface, *"The* Notes *are short, and concise, as being but the heads of what was prepared for preaching."* Although essentially an extended outline, *Last Judgement* reflects Whiting's gentleness in his urging that man be weaned of the world and look to heaven. He called for meditation and contemplation of God's grace, "that great Reward of Eternal Life."

A fuller glimpse of Whiting's vision and pastoral style is provided in *Abraham's Humble Intercession for Sodom*, which he offered as "the words of a dying man." (He did not die until thirteen years later.) The theme is the efficacy of prayer as a vehicle of faith, for Abraham was *"most renowned for his* Faith," and man can imitate Abraham: "When *faith* is most upon the wing in prayer, then are we ever nearest God." Whiting stressed the inwardness of devotion, but he also described prayer as an active drawing to God: being properly humble is "To besiege and beleaguer the Throne of Grace with suit after suit." Prayer is a personal *"Confession of sin"* as well as a selfless appeal for the welfare of other saints. He defined *prayer* by repeating key phrases in the "milde and winning wordes" that Obadiah Turner later recalled.

Whiting lacked the emotional range and psychological complexity of Thomas

Shepard (q.v.) and Thomas Hooker (q.v.). But he was, in Turner's words, "sound in doctrine, liberal in sentiment, and plain and practicall." He was a mild and compassionate Puritan who after 1650 hoped that his flock would remain true to New Eng.'s ideals.

Suggested Readings: CCNE; FCNEV; Sprague (I, 81-83). *See also* Edward J. Gallagher, Introduction, *Abel Being Dead Yet Speaketh*, by John Norton (1658; facs. ed., 1978), pp. xx-xxvii (examines Norton's elaboration on Whiting's "Life" of John Cotton); David D. Hall, *The Faithful Shepherd: A History of the New England Ministry in the Seventeenth Century* (1972), pp. 59, 136, 174, 179, 181; Zoltán Haraszti, *The Enigma of the Bay Psalm Book* (1956), p. 16; Babette May Levy, *Preaching in the First Half Century of New England History* (1945); Alonzo Lewis and James R. Newhall, *History of Lynn* (1865); Cotton Mather, *Magnalia Christi Americana* (1702), III, 156-161; William Whiting, *Memoir of Rev. Samuel Whiting, D.D.* (1872); Alexander Young, ed., *Chronicles of the First Planters of the Colony of Massachusetts Bay, from 1623 to 1636* (prints Whiting's "Life" of Cotton; 1846), pp. 419-431.

Wesley T. Mott
University of Wisconsin, Madison

EDWARD WIGGLESWORTH (1693-1765)

Works: "The Country-mans Answer," *Boston News-Letter*, April 18, 1720; *A Letter from One in the Country* (1720); *A Project for the Emission* (1720); *A Vindication* (1720); *Sober Remarks* (1724); *A Discourse Concerning the Duration* (1729); *The Blessedness of the Dead* (1731); *A Seasonable Caveat* (1735); *A Faithful Servant* (1737); *An Enquiry* (1738); *The Sovereignty of God* (1741); *A Letter to the Reverend Mr. George Whitefield* (1745); *Some Distinguishing Characters* (1754); *Some Evidences of the Divine Inspiration* (1755); *Some Thoughts* (1757); *The Doctrine of Reprobation* (1763).

Biography: Born in Malden, Mass., in early 1693, Edward Wigglesworth was the youngest son of Michael Wigglesworth (q.v.), author of *Day of Doom*, and his third wife, Sybil Avery. After attending the Boston Latin School, Edward entered Harvard, where he became Scholar of the House during his junior and senior years. Large grants from the Sprague funds enabled him to complete his bachelor's work in 1710. During the decade following his graduation, Wigglesworth taught school briefly at Casco Bay Fort, ushered regularly under Nathaniel Williams at the Boston Latin School, and preached on Sundays at Barnstable, Salem, and other vacant pulpits.

On Jan. 24, 1722, Harvard's Corporation unanimously selected Wigglesworth as the first Hollis professor of divinity. The Board of Overseers confirmed the appointment but required the corporation to test Wigglesworth's orthodoxy. Although he passed the examination, the Hollis professor quickly built a reputation for laying all sides of controversial issues before his students and letting them judge the weight of the evidence. Charles Chauncy (q.v.) remembered him as "one of the most candid men you ever saw; far removed from bigotry, no ways rigid in his attachment to any scheme, yet steady in his own principles, but at the same time charitable to others, though they widely differed from him." The Hollis professor eloquently demonstrated his steadfastness to Congregational principles in 1724 when attacked by John Checkley (q.v.), champion of Anglicanism.

Wigglesworth became a fellow of Harvard's Corporation in 1723 and, with the influence of newly appointed Governor Jonathan Belcher, received a doctorate in divinity from Edinburgh University in 1730. Increasing deafness compelled him to decline other positions such as the rectorship of Yale and membership in Scot.'s Society for Propagating Christian Knowledge. Although he served for some time as a commissioner for London's Society for Propagating the Gospel among Indians, deafness forced his resignation around 1755.

During the Great Awakening, Wigglesworth scorned New Light methods. He also became a vocal opponent of George Whitefield (q.v.) and other itinerant evangelists. After 1750 his writing evidenced a gradual compromise between orthodox Calvinism and Arminianism, which pointed toward Unitarianism.

Critical Appraisal: Wigglesworth's first published writings, which dealt with the ongoing currency debate of the early eighteenth century, established his opposition to land-bank advocates such as Oliver Noyes, John Colman, and Elisha Cooke, Jr. On May 11, 1720, Wigglesworth set forth his anticredit position in *A Letter from One in the Country*. The letter sparked an inflamed reply from Dr. Noyes. *A Vindication*, the "countryman's" coldly intelligent response to Noyes's heated passions, exhorted all New Englanders to confront the reality that consumption of more than they produced would lead to ruin unless the government called in all bills of credit, thereby preventing people from going further into debt. Instead of reverting to the jeremiad with its traditional emphasis on sins against the God of the covenant, Wigglesworth defended his conservative, hard-money viewpoint on the radically secular grounds chosen by his opponents.

At least one contemporary critic of Wigglesworth's essays on the money problem condemned the author for the circularity of his arguments. Elisha Cooke, Jr., attributed that circularity, as well as an apparent lack of clearheadedness, to academic isolation. He laughed at the Harvard instructor's mathematical demonstration that continued depreciation of provincial currency made zero value an easily approachable limit. Sharp-witted John Wise (q.v.) and other representatives of the rural debtor faction denounced members of the "court" faction, including Wigglesworth, for conspiring to preach frugality in order to enrich merchants and ministers at the common people's expense. Whatever motives underlay its composition, Wigglesworth's *Project for the Emission*, his final contribution to the currency debate, was a closely reasoned but pedantic essay. It possessed the readily observable characteristic of wordiness, proving that very early in his career the Harvard instructor had adopted the pattern that later prompted the overseers to direct him to be more concise in public lectures.

In 1724 Wigglesworth published *Sober Remarks*, a Congregationalist response to John Checkley's pro-Anglican tract titled *A Modest Proof*. Necessarily restating New Testament evidence cited by earlier advocates of the New Eng. Way, he calmly moved through general historical and doctrinal proofs to a systematic examination of each scriptural passage used by Checkley. One by one, Checkley's interpretive assertions crumbled beneath Wigglesworth's masterful blows. The defender of Congregationalism concluded that completion of the Scriptures, which provided an "infallible and perfect rule" for church government, alleviated any need for the "extraordinary" and "temporary" powers bestowed upon the first-century Apostles; in its minister or presbyter, each eighteenth-century congregation had its own bishop, who was both equal to and independent of all others. Although *Sober Remarks* could not resurrect the ecclesiastical order generated by similar sermons a century earlier, it became a tactical triumph in ongoing efforts to prevent Anglican infiltration of Harvard's governing board.

Over the twenty-year span encompassing the Great Awakening, Wigglesworth found evangelism as reproachable as Anglicanism. He addressed *A Seasonable Caveat, A Letter to the Reverend Mr. George Whitefield*, and *Some Distinguishing Characters* to the evangelistic pretenders. In the last of these three works, the Hollis professor thoroughly reviewed pertinent Scriptures and found evangelists "a Sort of Officers peculiar to the Apostolic Age." Since Whitefield and his fellow "Itinerants and Exhorters" could not possibly meet that qualification, they deserved the label of "Busy-bodies," who meddled in other congregations' affairs and neglected their own. The fiercest condemnation fell upon Whitefield, whom he perceived as engaging in the "uninstituted and very disorderly and pernicious practice" of casting unretracted errors upon people, thereby swaying them from God's truths.

Superficial reading of *A Discourse Concerning the Duration* seems to justify describing Wigglesworth as an uncompromising Calvinist whose style, like Cotton Mather's (q.v.), mingled traditional seventeenth-century plainness with colorful strokes of eighteenth-century flare. However, scrutinous comparison with Mather's works reveals distinct differences in tone and manner of presentation. The Matherians accused Wigglesworth and his supporters of preaching in a dull Anglican manner and of delivering what Increase Mather (q.v.) labeled "meer lectures of morality." Furthermore, *A Discourse Concerning the Duration* aggravated the Mathers and their followers, because it ignored covenant theology. Instead of insisting that the certainty of an omnipotent God's vengeance upon violators of the covenant deters wickedness, Wigglesworth focused on human free will and concluded that "rational expectation" of eternal punishment, which the Bible reveals possible, deters us from sinning.

An Enquiry into the Truth further illustrates Wigglesworth's departure from unconditional Calvinism. Using the format of dialog between a Calvinist and an Arminian, the author explored the doctrinal dispute over original sin. He found the strongest scriptural support for the Calvinist position but acknowledged that conditional Arminians were somewhat justified in recognizing man's independent will to sin and in pointing out the apparent inconsistency between original sin and divine perfection. Consequently, in confronting the controversial doctrine of original sin, no person should be so opinionated as to prejudice himself or others against weighing all sides.

Thirty-five years later, in *The Doctrine of Reprobation*, Wigglesworth reviewed sublapsarian, supralapsarian, and arminian differences concerning sin and salvation. Clearly distinguishing between God's effective decrees, which are morally good, and his permissive decrees, which may result in good or evil depending upon the exercise of human will, he concluded that no person is "under irresistable notions, either to good or evil." In fact, he said, the "bigger part" of those who gain salvation may be elected not by God's effective foreordination but by their own "diligent improvement of the means of grace, and earnest prayer for the aids of God's holy spirit." That recognition of the conditional nature of all salvation represented the culmination of Wigglesworth's gradual departure from unconditional Calvinism and signaled the approach of Unitarianism.

Suggested Readings: CCNE; DAB; Sibley-Shipton (V, 546-555); Sprague (I, 275-278). *See also* Perry Miller, *The New England Mind: From Colony to Province* (1961), pp. 315-328, 452-463, 472-476. Wigglesworth's "The Country-man's Answer" is reprinted in Andrew McFarland Davis, *Colonial Currency Reprints, 1682-1751* (1910), I, 409-412. *A Letter from One in the Country* appears in the same volume, pp. 416-442, and Wigglesworth's *A Project for the Emission* is in vol. II (1911), pp. 139-156.

Rick W. Sturdevant
University of California, Santa Barbara

MICHAEL WIGGLESWORTH (1631-1705)

Works: *Diary* (w. 1653-1657; pub. 1951); *The Day of Doom: Or, A Description of the Great and Last Judgment* (1662); *God's Controversy with New-England* (w. 1662; first pub. in PMHS; 1873); *Meat Out of the Eater, or Meditations Concerning the Necessity, End, and Usefulness of Afflictions unto Gods Children* (1670).

Biography: Michael Wigglesworth, pastor, physician, and poet of Malden, Mass., was born in Eng., probably in Yorkshire, on Oct. 18, 1631. The son of Edward and Esther (?) Wigglesworth, Michael arrived at Charlestown with his parents in 1638 and after a brief stay traveled with them to New Haven, Conn., where they settled in Oct. of that year. He was prepared for college by Ezekiel Cheever (q.v.), under whom he wrote Latin compositions before the age of 9. When his father became ill, young Wigglesworth was called upon to interrupt his education and return home to help support the family. In frail health himself, Wigglesworth remained at home for five years, and then at the age of 14, he resumed his studies. When he was 17, he entered Harvard College with the class of 1651, obtaining both an A.B. and A.M. there. From 1652 to 1654, he remained at Harvard as a fellow and a tutor of the college; Increase Mather (q.v.), Eleazer Mather (q.v.), John Eliot (q.v.), and Shubael Dummer were among his pupils at this time. Wigglesworth began to preach occasionally in 1653, and sometime during 1654 or 1655, he was invited to settle as minister at Malden. Formally ordained over the church at Malden on Sept. 7, 1656, he was able to discharge his duties only for a year or so. In 1657 he became the victim of a painful, lingering disease that lasted almost without interruption until 1686. During that thirty-year period, he shared (with limited success) authority over the Malden congregation with colleagues Benjamin Bunker (from 1663 to 1670), Benjamin Blackman (from 1674 to 1678), and Thomas Cheever, the son of Ezekiel Cheever (from 1681 to 1686). On Sept. 23, 1663, when his health had become so impaired that he had to suspend completely his pastoral labors, Wigglesworth sailed to Bermuda in the hope of a cure. That plan failing, he returned to Malden at the end of nine months and resumed his ministry as best he could. Although his ministry was drastically reduced during the period from 1663 to 1686, this was nevertheless a productive time for Wigglesworth, for he maintained a successful medical practice in Malden, and in addition to overseeing the printing of *The Day of Doom* (1662) in 1666 and 1670, he published *Meat Out of the Eater* in 1670. Although the matter has never been settled satisfactorily, it appears, according to the gist of a letter from Wigglesworth to Increase Mather in 1684, that the trustees of the Harvard Corporation invited Wigglesworth to assume the presidency of the college following the death of President John Rogers (q.v.), but the minister declined, saying, "I cannot think my bodily health and strength competent to undertake . . . such a weighty work as you mention. . . . Wherefore I hope the Colledge & Overseers will think of and apply themselves to a fitter person." However, by 1685, when the Malden church had become financially and administratively reduced to the point of public scandal, Wigglesworth made a startling recovery. At that time, according to Cotton Mather (q.v.), "It pleased God . . . wondrously to restore His *Faithful Servant*. He that had been for nearly Twenty years almost *Buried Alive*, comes abroad again." Thomas Cheever was dismissed from his position as Wigglesworth's colleague early in 1686, and by May Wigglesworth had so regained his health that he was able to preach the Mass. election sermon. A second testimony to the minister's pulpit talent came in 1696, when he was invited to preach the Artillery Election Sermon for that year. Neither sermon was ever published. Routinely preaching two or three times on a Sabbath and without concern for his personal comfort and working daily to preserve the spiritual as well as physical condition of his flock, Wigglesworth fulfilled his charge with uncommon vigor for the last twenty years of his life. He died on Jun. 10, 1705. Wigglesworth was married three times: first in 1655 to Mary Reyner of Rowley, Mass., his cousin, who died in 1659; then in 1679 to Martha Mudge, his "servant mayd . . . of obscure parentage," who died in 1690; and finally in 1691 to Sybil Sparhawk Avery of Cambridge, who survived him. Of the eight children he fathered during these marriages, three deserve notice: Mary, born in 1656, who married Samuel Belcher (q.v.); Samuel Wigglesworth (q.v.), born in 1689, who was widely known as physician and pastor of Hamilton, Mass.; and Edward Wigglesworth (q.v.), born in 1692 or 1693, who was the first Hollis professor of divinity at Harvard College.

Critical Appraisal: Although as a poet Michael Wigglesworth enjoyed a singularly high reputation during the colonial period, that reputation has diminished appreciably over the past century, in part because Wigglesworth's poetry suffers in comparisons between it and the poetry of contemporaries Anne Bradstreet (q.v.) and Edward Taylor (q.v.), in part because Wigglesworth's aesthetic bias, which was fashioned out of an appreciation of the Puritan plain style and a conviction of the rightness of New Eng.'s brand of Calvinism, strikes contemporary readers as more appropriate to the pulpit than to poetic stanzas. However, if we accept Cotton Mather's account of the reason that Wigglesworth took to poetry in the first place, we discover that Wigglesworth was aware of what today we consider to be the limitations of his poetry, and that from his point of view (and from the point of view of the several generations of colonials raised on the poetry), the intentional didactic or sermonic aspect, orthodox content, and plain style of his poetry were its very strengths. Referring to the period from 1657 to 1662, when Wigglesworth was first struck with his affliction, Mather wrote: "And that he might yet more *Faithfully* set himself to Do Good, when he could not *Preach*, he *Wrote* several Composures, wherein he proposed the Edification of such Readers, as are for Truth's dressed up in a *Plain Meeter*."

Without doubt, *The Day of Doom* is Wigglesworth's best-known work. In the prefatory lines to the poem, the poet acknowledged the Puritan bent of both his poem and his imagination:

> O Dearest Dread, most glorious King,
> I'le of thy justest Judgments sing:
> Do thou my head and heart inspire,
> To Sing aright, as I desire.
> *Thee, thee* alone I'le invocate,
> For I do much abominate
> To call the *Muses* to mine aid:
> Which is th' Unchristian use, and trade
> Of some that Christians would be thought,
> And yet they worship worse then nought.
> Oh! what a deal of Blasphemy,
> And Heathenish Impiety,
> In Christian Poets may be found. . . .
> Oh! guide me by thy sacred Sprite
> So to indite, and so to write,
> That I thine holy Name may praise,
> And teach the Sons of men thy wayes.

The first native American "best-seller," the poem was reprinted regularly until the end of the eighteenth century and was memorized by successive generations of New Eng. schoolchildren for whom the poem was an entertaining supplement to catechism and Bible. Filled with biblical allusion and direct reference and written in the ballad meter, the poem presents a vision of the judgment day wherein the reader, much like the reader of a Puritan sermon might be, is charged to look after his spiritual condition at the same time as he is urged to see the wisdom and justice of doctrines such as predestination and the final mercifulness of Calvin's God toward the saints.

God's Controversy with New-England, which was written in the same year that *The Day of Doom* was published, is probably the more genuinely "native" of the two poems for both its occasion and its style. Whereas *The Day of Doom* develops content that is universal and universally applicable, *God's Controversy* is directed at the condition of a fallen New Eng. Written at the time that New Eng. clergymen were first preaching against declension, the poem enlarged on the particular subject of "New-England Planted, Prospered, Declining, Threatned, Punished" for the particular edification of God's latest chosen people. *God's Controversy with New-England* is, then, a poetic jeremiad, cautioning New Englanders that the plight of a fallen Israel is theirs unless they return to the ideals of the founders and give up the path of worldliness and carnal security that they now follow. As it happens, the occasion for the poem was a drought that affected New Eng. in 1661-1662, a calamity that Wigglesworth interpreted as a punishment from God for New Eng.'s backsliding and a warning from God in which the final dissolution of New Eng. into a place of "barrenness," of "great & parching drought," is foreshadowed. Although the emotive impact of *The Day of Doom* is clearly more sustained than that of *God's Controversy with New-England*, the second poem reveals a deep love for New Eng. and a desire to see New Eng.'s potential fulfilled, leading one to wonder at the popularity this poem might have achieved if it had been printed in the seventeenth century. As much as *The Day of Doom* moved saints and sinners to consider their ways, sentiments such as this from the conclusion of *God's Controversy with New-England* might have moved some to repent and reform:

Ah dear New England! dearest land to me;
   Which unto God has hitherto been dear,
And mayst be more dear than formerlie,
   If to his voice thou wilt incline thine ear. . . .

Thou still hast in thee many praying saints,
   Of great account, and precious with the Lord,
Who dayly powre out unto him their plaints,
   And strive to please him both in deed & word.

Cheer on, sweet souls, my heart is with you all,
   And shall be with you, maugre Sathan's might:
And whereso'ere this body be a Thrall,
   Still in New-England shall be my delight.

Meat Out of the Eater, Wigglesworth's final major poetic effort, was completed in 1669 and published in 1670. The most introspective and, in that respect, personal of Wigglesworth's poetry, *Meat Out of the Eater* consists of a series of meditations and songs "about ye cross" written as much to console as to edify "enduring" Christians. By 1689, when this collection of poems was in its 4th edition, Wigglesworth had a secure following for his poetry, and as noticed above, he had resumed the challenges of his ministry. Although a few pieces of occasional verse have survived (they are listed in bibliographies prepared by John Sibley and Richard Crowder), Wigglesworth appears to have made no concentrated effort at poetry after 1670. Although unfair to judge, because there is no body of critical study to justify it, it seems likely that Wigglesworth's poetry will continue to rank third to that of Bradstreet and Taylor in studies of major colonial American poetry for some time to come.

Suggested Readings: CCNE; DAB; LHUS; Sibley-Shipton (I, 259-286); Sprague (I, 143-147); T₁. *See also* Deloraine P. Corey, *History of Malden* (1899); Richard Crowder, *No Featherbed to Heaven: A Biography of Michael Wigglesworth* (1962); John W. Dean, *Memoir of Rev. Michael Wigglesworth*, 2nd ed. (1871); Cotton Mather, *A Faithful Man Described and Rewarded* (a funeral sermon on Michael Wigglesworth; 1705); Edmund S. Morgan, ed., *The Diary of Michael Wigglesworth, 1653-1657: The Conscience of a Puritan* (1965); Kenneth B. Murdock, Editor's Introduction, *The Day of Doom* (1929).

Ronald A. Bosco
State University of New York at Albany

SAMUEL WIGGLESWORTH (1689-1768)

Works: *A Funerall Song...to the Memory of Mr Nathaniel Clarke* (w. 1707; pub. in Deloraine P. Corey, *History of Malden*, 1899); *A Funeral Elegy, upon Daniel Rindge* (1713); *The Excellency of the Gospel-Message* (1727); *The Pleasures of Religion* (1728); *A Religious Fear of God's Tokens Explained and Urged* (1728); *An Essay for Reviving Religion* (1733); *A View of the Inestimable Treasure of the Gospel* (1746); *The Blessedness of Such as Trust in Christ* (1755); *God's Promise to an Obedient People, of Victory Over Their Enemies* (1755).

Biography: Samuel Wigglesworth was born in Malden, Mass., on Feb. 4, 1689. His father was the Rev. Michael Wigglesworth (q.v.), Malden's pastor, physician, and poet, and his mother was Martha Mudge, Michael's second wife, who, according to a summary of gossip by Increase Mather (q.v.), was Michael's "servant mayd...of obscure parentage, & not 20 years old, & of no Ch[ur]ch, nor so much as Baptised." Samuel, establishing a fine reputation during his undergraduate years as an exemplary Christian and scholar, received an A.B. from Harvard College in 1707. He remained at Harvard for postgraduate study under Jonathan Remington, but he withdrew from the college in 1709, when he was charged and fined for his part in riotous disorders in Cambridge. Deciding that his now-tarnished reputation probably precluded a career in the ministry, he moved to Charlestown in Jun. 1709, where he served as apprentice-at-medicine under Thomas Greaves, his brother-in-law. The following spring, he left Charlestown and set up a practice at Ipswich Hamlet (now Hamilton), Mass. Whether the brevity of his preparation or, finally, a lack of interest in medicine as a career was the cause is unclear, but by the winter of 1710-1711, Wigglesworth had returned to his native Malden to teach, study theology, and, as necessary and opportune, practice medicine. During the early months of 1712, he returned in earnest to theological study, and on Jun. 20, 1712, he was offered a pulpit at Dracut on the frontier. Although he stayed in Dracut for a while, he was disinclined to settle there permanently, so after a brief stay at Groton, where he preached from Oct. 1713 to Jan. 1714, Wigglesworth returned to Ipswich Hamlet to preach to those over whom he once served as physician. On Oct. 12, 1714, the Third Church of Ipswich was organized, and on Oct. 27, 1714, Wigglesworth was ordained its pastor. During the next half-century, he tended to the spiritual needs of his flock and achieved a reputation throughout New Eng. as a defender of orthodoxy. Like his father before him and like Joseph Sewall (q.v.), his former classmate and closest friend, Wigglesworth was of the "old" New Eng. camp, keeping in sight always the original purpose for which New Eng. was established and the work to which that purpose called all men of faith. During the Great Awakening, he was a vocal supporter of New Light fundamentalism. Whether speaking to his congregation during the Awakening, or to the governor and other officials on election day, or to soldiers about to leave for Crown Point in 1755, Wigglesworth steadfastly maintained the simple, dogmatic faith of his ancestors. In recognition of his learning and his years of service to Congregationalism, he was invited to give the Dudleian Lectures in 1760. When he died on Sept. 3, 1768, he was mourned as a man of "a quick and clear Apprehension, lively fancy, fruitful Invention, sound Judgment, and tenacious Memory . . . mighty in Scripture—an enlightening & animating Preacher of the Truth . . . [who] not only preach'd the Truths and Duties of Christianity; but exemplarily exhibited them in his life." Married twice, first in 1715 to Mary Brintnall, who died in 1723 after bearing him four children, and then in 1730 to Martha Brown, who bore him ten more children, Wigglesworth was survived by Martha, four sons, and four daughters.

Critical Appraisal: Like the reputations of the younger Charles Chauncy (q.v.), Thomas Foxcroft (q.v.), and John Webb (q.v.)—men who represent the principal defenders of orthodoxy during the early and mideighteenth century— Wigglesworth's reputation rests largely on his ability to preach and support doctrines that day by day lost fashion during this period at the same time as he tried to accommodate those doctrines to the shifting attitudes of the time. Although they were thorough and energetic in their endeavors, Wigglesworth and the others were frustrated in their effort and had to witness the dissolution of the old New Eng. Way.

For all, the most effective medium through which to develop and advertise their position was the sermon. Wigglesworth was himself a popular preacher, and he maintained an active preaching schedule until the end of his life. These facts are not easily arrived at given the slight amount of sermonic material published by him; nevertheless, the sermons that were published remain as a record of the richness, power, and variety of his pulpit talent. Consistent with the Puritan tradition of preaching to occasion, among Wigglesworth's published sermons are an ordination sermon, a funeral sermon, a sermon to a young men's religious society, a humiliation day sermon, a fast day sermon, a sermon to soldiers about to engage in battle, and an election sermon. In all, there are repeated the themes and concerns of an earlier generation of New Eng. preachers. For instance, in *The Excellency of the Gospel-Message*, which was preached at the ordination of Josiah Dennis in 1727, Wigglesworth argued that ministers are God's "watchmen," who preserve the proper relation established between God and his people despite—or, perhaps, because of—the fact that his people have fallen into degenerate times. For our purpose, it is significant to notice that this was Wigglesworth's first published sermon, for it sets the tone and mood of sermons yet to come, and it likely summarizes the tone and mood out of which Wigglesworth had been preaching since 1712. Additionally, the sermon prepares us for Wigglesworth's use of the declension issue in his sermons and with it its attendant litany of the "sins of the land"; its accusation of the failure of the present generation to live up to the ideals of New Eng.'s fathers; its notice of the incursion of foreign doctrinal, political, and ethical influences into New Eng. Congregationalism (especially attacked are Catholicism and the French influence); and its call for reform.

These matters receive their fullest expression in *A Religious Fear of God's Tokens*, a humiliation sermon preached on Nov. 1, 1727, the morning after the famous earthquake struck New Eng., *The Blessedness of Such as Trust in Christ*, which was preached on Mar. 20, 1755, a day of public fast, *An Essay for Reviving Religion*, an election sermon preached on May 20, 1733, and *God's Promise to an Obedient People, of Victory over Their Enemies*, which was preached on May 25, 1755, to the Ipswich soldiers about to leave for Crown Point. All betray a distinctly conservative bias as Wigglesworth's sermonic voice ranged only from that of a forceful spiritual father, interpreting the relation between God and man, to that of a Puritan Jeremiah, stating the causes and legislating the solutions for the breakdown of that relation. In the fast and humiliation sermons, Wigglesworth argued that through secondary causes or events, God is making known his displeasure with man. Be it through drought, pestilence, or an earthquake, God is both cautioning his people against further backsliding and punishing them for their sins. Neither God's position nor Wigglesworth's appears to change between 1727 and 1755, although in the 1755 fast day sermon, a hopeful note is sounded as the preacher observes, "In Times of Drought, when the Heaven above is as Brass, the Earth under Foot as Iron, and the Rain of the Land Powder and Dust; He [the true believer] knowing from whose Hand the Affliction came, is assured also from whom the Deliverance must be look'd for." In *An Essay for Reviving Religion*, these concerns are stated for the edification of Mass.'s newly elected rulers, but instead of a hopeful message, Wigglesworth offered a prediction of the calamity that would befall New Eng. and its people once the interests of God and his religion were finally forgotten: "Their *Glory shall depart*; God will *cast them off*, and *abhor them; Remove the Hedge of his Providence*, and *take away his Kingdom from them;* whilst their Enemies who were won't to look upon their *Elevation* with *Envy*, shall behold their *ignominious Downfall* with *Scorn and Triumph*." In a fashion that suggests that Wigglesworth's predictions may have been on the verge of coming true, the possibility of a French victory and the emergence of a supreme Church of Rome are subjects addressed in *God's Promise to an Obedient People.* Although part of Wigglesworth's motive in addressing these subjects must have been to inspire the soldiers to courage and valor, we should not forget that the people to whom the following words were spoken were not, from the preacher's published point of view, particularly "Obedient":

> If the ambitious Designs of this proud insolent Nation [France] should succeed here, the least Evil we can expect, is . . . to sit under an arbitrary Government, & despotick Rule. . . . Your Houses and Lands would probably be taken from you. . . . And the French being Bigots to the Religion of . . . Rome . . . they will strenuously obtrude their monstrous Idolatries and detestable Errors, and even enforce them on us with Fire and Faggot, and all the other horrible Forms of Persecution.

The power of his mind, persuasiveness of his rhetoric, and depth of his religious conviction are easily discerned in the ideas and themes that Wigglesworth expressed in his sermons. For this reason, Wigglesworth's printed sermons as well as the ones that remain in manuscript at the Massachusetts Historical Society are worth the attention of the student of colonial American life and letters. In any future review of the position of the clergy during the final days of New Eng. Puritanism, Wigglesworth deserves study and comment.

Suggested Readings: CCNE; Sibley-Shipton (V, 406-412); T_1. *See also* Deloraine P. Corey, *History of Malden* (1899); Joseph B. Felt, *History of Ipswich, Essex, and Hamilton* (1834); John Langdon Sibley and Clifford K. Shipton, "Michael Wigglesworth" in *Biographical Sketches of Those Who Attended Harvard College* (1873), I, 259-286.

Ronald A. Bosco
State University of New York at Albany

ISAAC WILKINS (1742-1830)

Works: *Short Advice to the Counties of New-York* (1774); Speech Against Appointing Delegates to the Second Continental Congress (1775; pub. in Lorenzo

Sabine, *The American Loyalists*, 1847); *The Republican Dissected* (1775); *My Services and Losses in Aid of the King's Cause* (1785; pub. 1890); *A Sermon Preached in St. Peter's Church, in...Albany...1803* (1804); *The Truth, the Whole Truth* (1812).

Biography: Born in Jamaica, W. Ind., the son of a jurist, in 1742, Isaac Wilkins moved to N.Y. with his parents some six years later. Both parents died shortly thereafter. Wilkins was raised by an aunt and graduated from Columbia in 1760.

By 1772, despite early inclinations toward the ministry, Wilkins had become a representative from the West Chester borough to the N.Y. colonial Assembly, a post he filled until forced to leave the country in 1775. As an active leader of Loyalist resistance, he won temporary gains for his party and held his own in legislative debate against Philip Schuyler and George Clinton (q.v.). He also published at least two political pamphlets in defense of the Loyalist cause and won the dubious distinction of being satirized in John Trumbull's (q.v.) *M'Fingal*. Upon the outbreak of hostilities, he hid briefly in a secret room at his Castle Hill estate before removing to Eng. About a year later, he returned to America, settling on Long Island until the close of the war. He then began an interlude of farming and political service in Shelbourne, Nova Scotia.

When Wilkins again took up residence in N.Y., he had decided to prepare for the Episcopal ministry. In 1801 he was ordained a priest, assuming the rectorship of St. Peter's Church, West Chester. He had already been granted a life annuity from the British government and in 1811 received an honorary doctorate from Columbia. Maintaining his parochial charge into his 80s, Wilkins died at the rectory in West Chester in 1830.

Critical Appraisal: Although esteemed in his later role as a clergyman, Isaac Wilkins is more likely to be remembered for his political activities, speeches, and writings as a layman during the turbulent closing years of the colonial era. For some time, Wilkins was suspected of writing or collaborating in the author- ship of the four *Letters of a Westchester Farmer* (1774-1775). But there can now be little doubt that his close associate, Samuel Seabury (q.v.), was the "A. W. Farmer" solely responsible for the pamphlets. Wilkins probably did write *The Republican Dissected*, another pamphlet attributed to him, but the Sons of Lib- erty destroyed this piece before it ever left James Rivington's (q.v.) printing office. Present claims for Wilkins's writing, such as they are, must therefore rest mainly on the *Short Advice to the Counties of New-York*. Although its author announced himself only as "a country gentleman," this slim publication was almost certainly Wilkins's work, as established by the later testimony in *My Services and Losses*.

Like his generally eloquent—and apparently effective—speech before the N.Y. Assembly against sending delegates to the Second Continental Congress, Wil- kins's *Short Advice* sounds many of the same themes prevalent in the Seabury pamphlets. Both Seabury and Wilkins professed their attachment to true liberty; deplored what they took to be the undemocratic, coercive measures promoted by republican interests; and predicted a future of civil war or other calamities in the unlikely event an American rebellion succeeded in gaining independence. Both pled for prudence and "common sense" against the self-destructive willingness of some New Yorkers to forfeit such liberty and felicity as they already enjoyed. Thus far one can see how the Seabury pamphlets could have been connected to Wilkins.

But the address and rhetorical mood of the *Short Advice* place it otherwise in a category distinct from Seabury's *Letters*. Whereas Seabury's *persona* is a plain farmer who speaks "plain English," Wilkins's is a "country gentleman," the learned and presumably wise counselor who begins his elegantly turned discourse with a Latin motto and does not hesitate to cite Shakespeare and Classical sources. Seabury usually stressed the practical, material liabilities of republicanism in his address to farmers and merchants. Wilkins built instead on quasi-poetic myth, addressing a reader more readily engaged by ethical and philosophic concerns than monetary motives.

In Wilkins's telling of the American fable, the colonists inhabit a kind of enchanted island where they now flourish as "the freest people upon the globe, and if we were sensible of the blessing, I might add the happiest also." Far from plotting to enslave Americans, G.B. is the godly parent, the nurturing presence in union with whom "we may rise superior to the rest of the world, and set all the kingdoms of the world at defiance." Yet "mistaken or designing men" threaten to corrupt this Eden. If persuaded to follow their ungrateful leadings, the colonists' crime will be, predictably, one of pride and presumption: "but if we aim at too much, if we suffer ourselves to be led away with vain notions of *grandeur* and *independance*, we may lose the *substance* while we grasp at the *shadow*, and this our fair structure of liberty and happiness, which seems calculated to endure thro' a long succession of ages, will moulder into nothing, and like the *baseless fabric of a vision, leave not a wreck [sic] behind*."

Admitting the validity of some American grievances and some errors on Br.'s part, Wilkins found no warrant for open rebellion and no use for Revolutionary agreements "enforced by their High Mightiness the Mob." To attack Br. thus was "like the giants of old warring against heaven." There was the pathway to "slavery and destruction," a descent into unholy chaos, for "order is in every respect more eligible than confusion. 'Tis Heaven's first law, 'tis the *basis of liberty*." Wilkins's gentleman believed, however, that the order sustaining America's freedom and blessed happiness could yet be restored if the Assembly would accept its responsibility, and if the people would stand behind their duly chosen representatives.

This rhetorical disjunction between order and chaos kept its hold on Wilkins's imagination long after the demise of Loyalism. In his 1803 sermon on charity and the avoidance of schism, Wilkins displaced his earlier political vision onto the problem of church unity. In 1774 he was lamenting the political "confusion" ensuing when "every man is become a judge and ruler among us"; in 1803 he feared an ecclesial "confusion" and prideful dissension in which "every man . . . becomes his own Church, and his own lawgiver."

Suggested Readings: CCMC; Sprague (V, 462-470); T$_2$. *See also* Charles Evans, *American Bibliography* (1941), V, 215; Lorenzo Sabine, *The American Loyalists* (1847), pp. 692-705, with approximate version of Wilkins's speech reprinted on pp. 693-701.

John J. Gatta, Jr.
University of Connecticut

ELIZA YONGE WILKINSON (fl. 1779-1782)

Works: Caroline Gilman, ed., *Letters of Eliza Wilkinson* (w. c. 1779-1782; pub. 1839).

Biography: Little is known of the life of Eliza Yonge Wilkinson. Born to a prominent planter family named Yonge, resident at Yonge's Island in the Stono River district of S.C., she was "a young and beautiful widow" when she wrote her letters, according to her editor Caroline Gilman. She may have been the wife of Joseph Wilkinson who died in 1775. Her letters indicate that she was a spirited woman, happy to be a part of sea island planter society. Until the War for Independence, her major concerns reflected those of a plantation woman: management of her home while seeing to the physical and emotional well-being of all around her and accepting a dependence on the leading men of her society. This dependence would continue despite her assertion of women's ability to carry on political discourse.

Critical Appraisal: Eliza Wilkinson's patriotic reflections on the war and the occupation of S.C. provide a view of an occasional participant who was at times outspoken in her criticism of the British. Possibly not intended for a specific correspondent, her letters may have been a device to avoid the charge that she had committed, for that time and place, the unfeminine act of writing a history potentially for publication. Her description of war in the sea islands provides a primary account of the activities of female noncombatants: hiding possessions, fleeing approaching hostile forces, enduring pillage of goods, enduring romantic attentions of British officers, and coping with the ever-present confusion about troops, primarily because the uniforms of American forces were not standard.

Of greatest interest today is Eliza Wilkinson's assertion of political views and the right of women to hold such views. She was clearly aware of the unusual nature of her position that women had a right and an obligation to advance political opinions and not simply to limit themselves to talk of the latest fashions. Despite that admirable assertion, however, she did not challenge the expected female domestic role, nor did she exhibit any concern about the inconsistency of fighting to avoid enslavement by the British while she and other South Carolinians continued to enslave blacks who comprised a majority of the colony's population. In judging participants in the war, she assessed their worth on the basis of their male and female, free and unfree, devotion to independence, not by their devotion to the higher ideals set out in the Declaration of Independence. Although occasionally asserting the right of women to discuss politics, she remained a woman who willingly accepted her society as received.

Suggested Readings: T₂. *See also* Linda K. Kerber, *Women of the Republic: Intellect and Ideology in Revolutionary America* (1980); Mary Beth Norton, *Liberty's Daughters: The Revolutionary Experience of American Women, 1750-1800* (1980).

Arthur J. Worrall
Colorado State University

SAMUEL WILLARD (1640-1707)

Works: *Useful Instructions* (1673); *The Heart Garrisoned* (1676); *A Sermon Preached upon Ezek. 22* (1679); *The Duty of a People* (1680); *Ne Sutor Ultra Crepidam* (1681); *Covenant-Keeping* (1682); *The Fiery Tryal* (1682); *The Necessity of Sincerity* (1682); *The High Esteem* (1683); *The Child's Portion . . . Together with Several Other Sermons* (1684); *Mercy Magnified* (1684); *A Brief Discourse of Justification* (1686); *Heavenly Merchandize* (1686); *A Brief Discourse Concerning That Ceremony of Laying the Hand on the Bible in Swearing* (1689); *Principles of the Protestant Religion Maintained* (1690; with James Allen, Josua Moodey, and Cotton Mather); *The Barren Figtree's Doom* (1691); *The Danger of Taking God's Name in Vain* (1691); *The Mourner's Cordial* (1691); *Promise-Keeping* (1691); *The Sinfulness of Worshipping God with Men's Institutions* (1691); *Some Miscellany Observations on . . . Witchcrafts* (1692); *The Doctrine of the Covenant of Redemption* (1693); *Rules for the Discerning of the Present Times* (1693); *The Character of a Good Ruler* (1694); *The Law Established by the Gospel* (1694); *Reformation the Great Duty* (1694); *Impenitent Sinners Warned* (1698); *The Man of War* (1699); *Spiritual Desertions* (1699); *The Fountain Opened* (1700); *Love's Pedigree* (1700); *Morality Not to Be Relied on for Life* (1700); *The Peril of the Times Displayed* (1700); *A Remedy Against Despair* (1700); *The Truly Blessed Man* (1700); *The Best Priviledge* (1701); *The Checkered State of the Gospel Church* (1701); *The Christian's Exercise by Satan's Temptations* (1701); *The Fear of an Oath* (1701); *Prognostics of Impending Calamities* (1701); *Walking with God* (1701); *A Brief Reply to Mr. George Keith* (1703); *Israel's True Safety* (1704); *The Just Man's Prerogative* (1706); *A Thanksgiving Sermon* (1709); *Some Brief Sacramental Meditations* (1711); *A Compleat Body of Divinity* (1726); *Brief Directions to a Young Scholar* (1735); "A Briefe Account of a Strange & Unusual Providence of God Befallen to Elizabeth Knap of Groton" [w. 1672; pub. in CMHS, 4th ser., 8 (1868), 555-570].

Biography: Puritan clergyman, theologian, and leader, Samuel Willard was born in Concord, Mass., on Jan. 31, 1640. His father, Simon Willard, was one of Concord's first settlers. After graduation from Harvard in 1659, Willard continued his study of theology, eventually receiving his M.A. and becoming minister of the church at Groton, where he was ordained in July, 1664. After the Indian raid on Groton during King Philip's War, the town was temporarily abandoned, and Willard was called to preach at the Old South Church in Boston, where he shared the pulpit with the aging Thomas Thacher (q.v.). A learned and careful preacher, Willard was soon acclaimed throughout New Eng. for the education and dedication he brought to the Old South.

His policies, however, were not without controversy. A staunch defender of Puritan orthodoxy, Willard nonetheless was tolerant in pastoral matters, particularly issues concerning church membership, and as a result he was frequently criticized by other clergymen. During the tenure of Edmund Andros as governor of New Eng., it was Willard who was forced to open the doors of his meetinghouse for Anglican services, an occasion described with vituperation by Samuel Sewall (q.v.), who was among those left waiting in the street until the Anglicans had finished using the building. In 1692, when the witchcraft proceedings began at Salem, Willard was one of the few authorities to speak out against what was taking place, and it was he who later read Sewall's confession to the members of the Old South when the latter wished to be forgiven for his participation in the trials. From Jul. of 1700 until Aug. of 1707, Willard was vice-president of Harvard College, and for much of that time he assumed the duties of president as well. Throughout this period, he also continued his pastoral duties at the Old South, and he published several tracts and pamphlets.

Willard was twice married: to Abigail Sherman in 1664, and upon his first wife's death to Eunice Tynge in 1679. By his two wives, Willard fathered some eighteen children; among his many descendants was Joseph Willard, a president of Harvard. After a long and distinguished career, Samuel Willard died on Sept. 12, 1707, and was interred in the Old Granary Burial Ground. In the words of a contemporary, Willard was "a profound *Divine*, a very considerable *Scholar*, and an Heavenly *Christian*,...justly Esteem'd" after his death as "one of the *Wisest Men*, that has been known, of his *Order*, in Our Land."

Critical Appraisal: According to Ebenezer Pemberton (q.v.), who for a time shared the pulpit of the Old South with Samuel Willard and who preached his senior colleague's funeral sermon, Willard had "By his *Printed Works*...Erected himself a *Monument*, that will Endure when the *Famed* MAUSOLEUM's of the World shall moulder down, and be buryed in their own Ruines." Spoken from the perspective of the early eighteenth century, Pemberton's words of praise were hardly an exaggeration. With the exceptions of Increase Mather (q.v.) and Cotton Mather (q.v.), there were few individuals in New Eng. who could boast of Willard's written achievements. In addition to minor works such as prefaces and even a short poem, Willard had published, during his lifetime, some forty-five sermons, tracts, and essays. His greatest achievement, *A Compleat Body of Divinity* would remain in manuscript until nineteen years after its author's death, and upon its publication would be the longest single work issued up to that time by an American press.

Wide-ranging in scope and yet penetrating and exact in logic and information,

Willard's sermons and tracts encompassed the major issues of his day. In response to a pamphlet written by John Rogers (q.v.), Willard wrote *Ne Sutor Ultra Crepidam*, which helped to discredit the theology of the Anabaptists whom Willard believed were undermining the New Eng. system of thought as it was envisioned by the Puritan founders. According to Willard, "the design of our first Planters...was not Toleration." In fact, he states, they "were professed Enemies of it." When the former Quaker, George Keith (q.v.), questioned Willard's thought, Willard published his *Brief Reply*, in which he used Keith's own arguments against him. When the Salem investigations were intensifying and indictments were being issued with an alarming frequency, Willard published *Some Miscellany Observations*, which cautioned against the use of spectral evidence by the Salem courts as adequate proof for conviction on charges of witchcraft. According to Thomas Brattle (q.v.), had Willard's "notions and proposals been hearkened to and followed," the subsequent activities at Salem might very well have been avoided. Written along similar lines, Willard's "Briefe Account of...Elizabeth Knap of Groton" has been called "one of the best psychic investigations recorded in the witchcraft literature" of early New Eng.

Beyond a doubt, however, Willard's greatest achievement was his *Compleat Body of Divinity*. The product of a lifetime of meticulous thought and scholarship, Willard's *Compleat Body* consists of the monthly lectures delivered from 1688 to his death in 1707. In this massive work, Willard attempted to defend the New Eng. Way against the social and cultural forces which threatened to destroy it. Each of the "Two Hundred and Fifty Expository Lectures" in the *Compleat Body* explained a point in the Westminster Shorter Catechism. Read together, these lectures summarize Willard's thinking on the church and theology. According to Willard, man was a rational but flawed creature who was capable of knowing some aspects of divinity through his own intuitions and perceptions but who ultimately relied on God's grace and revelation for salvation. In the course of his lectures, Willard provided a systematic discussion of man's relationship with God in terms of covenant theology. Published by Thomas Prince (q.v.) and Joseph Sewall (q.v.) at the request of Willard's many admirers, *A Compleat Body of Divinity* is now considered "the fullest statement of the Puritan synthesis in American colonial history," and it remained a standard theological text until well into the nineteenth century.

Although Willard has been criticized for the technical difficulty of his prose style, he was a popular preacher who never lacked for an audience. His monthly lectures on the Westminster Catechism are said to have drawn "a large, permanent audience of the learned and the unlearned." His death was considered "an awful rebuke of heaven" upon New Eng., and on several occasions he was given the honor of preaching general election and artillery election sermons. Like his contemporaries, Increase Mather and Cotton Mather, Willard profoundly influenced the course of New Eng. thought during the critical period in its development. In the words of a biographer, "One strain of his systematic Puritanism gave sustenance to Enlightenment deism; another major emphasis led directly to the First Great Awakening."

Suggested Readings: CCNE; DAB; DARB; FCNEV; LHUS; Sibley-Shipton (II, 13-36); Sprague (I, 164-167); T_1. *See also* Chadwick Hansen, *Witchcraft at Salem* (1969); Joseph Haroutunian, *Piety Versus Moralism: The Passing of the New England Theology* (1932); H. A. Hill, *History of the Old South Church* (1890); Ernest Benson Lowrie, *The Shape of the Puritan Mind: The Thought of Samuel Willard* (1974); Perry Miller, *The New England Mind: The Seventeenth Century* (1939); idem, *The New England Mind: From Colony to Province* (1953); Norman Pettit, *The Heart Prepared: Grace and Conversion in Puritan Spiritual Life* (1966); Seymour Van Dyken, *Samuel Willard, 1640-1707: Preacher of Orthodoxy in an Era of Change* (1972).

James A. Levernier
University of Arkansas at Little Rock

ELISHA WILLIAMS (1694-1755)

Works: *Death the Advantage of the Godly* (1728); *Divine Grace Illustrious* (1728); *Essential Rights and Liberties of Protestants* (1744).

Biography: Elisha Williams was born in Hatfield, Mass., in 1694, a son of the Rev. William Williams (q.v.) and Elizabeth (Cotton) Williams and a great-grandson of John Cotton (q.v.) and Governor Simon Bradstreet. He was a brother of the younger William Williams (q.v.) and a half brother of Solomon Williams (q.v.) and the Loyalist Israel Williams. Graduating from Harvard in 1711, he afterwards studied theology with his father and read law. He preached to seamen in Nova Scotia and, from 1716 to 1719, taught Yale College students in his home. Ordained in 1722, he became the first pastor of the Newington Parish (Congregational) Church, Wethersfield, Conn., leaving in 1726 to assume the rectorship of Yale, where he remained until 1739.

From 1717 to 1722, Williams represented Wethersfield in the General Assembly and after leaving Yale was returned to the Assembly for the years 1740-1749. He was also a judge of the Conn. Supreme Court from 1740 to 1743 and served as a chaplain to the 1745 expedition against Louisbourg. He was appointed colonel and commander-in-chief of forces organized to conquer Can., an enterprise that was abandoned, and in 1754 was a delegate to the Albany Congress.

Williams married Eunice Carter in 1714. She died in 1750 while they were in Eng., and before Williams returned to Conn., he married Elizabeth Scott, a hymn writer. Williams, who was the father of six children, died in Wethersfield in 1755.

Critical Appraisal: Although the three published sermons of Elisha Williams reveal his erudition and deep religious concern and his success in rescuing Yale College from its doldrums and establishing it as a permanent school tell us much about his character, he is difficult to evaluate because of the controversy that occasionally engulfed him. Most eighteenth-century and later writers speak highly of his character, but several contemporary detractors painted him as insincere, ambitious, and self-interested. The issues they raised, as treated by Francis Parsons in *Six Men of Yale*, never have been settled definitively.

During the troubled years of Yale, Williams tutored a number of the college's students—including Jonathan Edwards (q.v.)—in his home, encouraging speculation that he belonged to a faction intent on moving the college from Saybrook to Hartford. There also must have been some dissatisfaction at his leaving the Newington Church for the Yale rectorship so soon after his appointment in 1722, when he had received a settlement of some 200 pounds. When Williams left Yale in 1739, citing poor health, an Anglican clergyman accused him of insincerity, claiming that his real motivation was an aspiration to the governorship of Conn. Williams's views of the relationship of church and state, expressed in the pamphlet *Essential Rights and Liberties of Protestants*, antagonized so many people that he failed in his reelection to the Supreme Court in 1743. In 1745 he was charged with enjoying the embarrassment of the Rev. Robert Breck, who was suspected of Arminianism and subjected to a public inquiry. As a "moderate supporter of the New Lights," Williams was also abused by Old Lights and those New Lights who indulged in excesses of revivalism and anti-intellectualism. Finally, near the end of his life, he seems to have scandalized some by remarrying less than a year after the death of his first wife.

Williams was ambitious and, as Francis Parsons pointed out, an unusually versatile man for eighteenth-century Conn. He was a gifted minister and lawyer, a successful teacher and educator, a scholar, and a man adept in military affairs and in dealing with worldly men. Although Benjamin Trumbull (q.v.) called him a "thorough Calvinist," he was liberal for his time and devoted to the exercise of reason in human affairs. His most famous work, *Essential Rights and Liberties*, invokes Locke as well as the Scriptures and states that "Reason teaches us that *all Men* are *naturally Equal* in Respect of *Jurisdiction* or *Dominion* one over another." Williams argued that God gave man understanding and freedom of the will as well as the liberty to act according to his own lights, within the bounds of law. The only qualifications on that liberty are found in the Scriptures and it is thus against the laws of God for a state to enforce nonbiblical religious requirements, such as whether to stand or kneel when praying. He presented the social-contract theory to explain how men came to have governments and insisted that governments were created to serve men. Although Christ's "officers" are to teach his laws, they "have no Warrant to make any Laws for men[,] nor are their Sentiments the rule to any Christians, who are commanded to *prove all Things*,...Whether they Be of God." Just as bishops and ministers have no power to create religious laws not sanctioned by Scripture, he reasoned, civil governments have "No Power to make or order Articles of Faith, Creeds, Forms of Worship, or Church Government."

This pamphlet, which puts a heavy stress upon both the liberties and duties of the conscience, was signed "Philalethes" but was assumed by most readers to be the work of Williams. It was occasioned by a 1742 law restricting ministers to preaching in their own parishes unless "expressly invited" into others. A minister who violated the law could be deprived of his livelihood. In effect the law also deprived laymen of the opportunity of hearing any clergymen except their own ministers, and Williams thus concluded that it was a violation of the Act of Tolerance, arguing that an American lost a right he would have had if he had lived in the mother country.

Divine Grace Illustrious, an earlier sermon addressed to the General Assembly, reveals an orthodox attitude toward grace, without which, Williams said, there is no chance of salvation. Man, who has a "deeply rooted" disposition to "advance Self in opposition to Grace," is unable to save himself without grace. All of God's children are fallen—all goodness "must issue from God." Yet, Williams argued in *Death the Advantage*, for one who has received grace and accepted God, death offers an "Inlet" to the joy of being with the Savior and a "Discharge from...Tabernacles of Clay." These two sermons, coming as he entered the prime of manhood, are articulate and persuasive, and although they are constructed along typical lines for Congregational sermons of the day, they have a suppleness that reveals a sophistication of mind. A fellow Wethersfield minister, quoted by Francis Parsons, said that Williams preached "chiefly on the great doctrines" and that his "diction and address were rational, nervous, and convincing to the understanding." Ezra Stiles (q.v.), who graduated from Yale during Williams's tenure, called him "a good classical scholar, well versed in logic, metaphysics, and ethics, and in rhetoric and oratory" who "delivered orations gracefully and with animated dignity."

As Francis Parsons has shown, Williams's New Light sympathies led him while in Eng. to solicit funds for the proposed College of New Jersey, although ostensibly he had gone there to persuade the British government to underwrite part of the expenses of the forces organized to invade Can. Despite his orthodox theological ideals, however, his attitude toward freedom of worship makes him seem modern. The best testimony to his commitment to this freedom appears in a letter addressed to him in Eng. by the Rev. Jonathan Parsons (q.v.), who complained about the oppression of Presbyterians in Conn. and appealed for Williams's help in securing relief for them. Presbyterians were being persecuted, because they refused to contribute to the salaries of Congregational ministers "on whose ministry they never attend." In a plea one hardly would address to an "insincere man," Parsons wrote, "I know your Attachment to Liberty too well, to think you would not do everything that appeared proper."

Suggested Readings: CCNE; DAB; Sibley-Shipton (V, 588-598); Sprague (I, 281-284). *See also* S. W. Adams and H. R. Stiles, *The History of Ancient Wethersfield* (1904); Isaac Backus, *A History of New England, with Particular Reference to the Denomination of Christians Called Baptists* (1871), II, 60; Alan Heimert and Perry Miller, eds., *The Great Awakening* (1967), pp. 323-339; Francis Parsons, *Six Men of Yale* (1939), pp. 3-31; Samuel H. Parsons, "Original Letter of the Rev. Jonathan Parsons," NEHGR, 12 (1858), 299-302; Chard Powers Smith, *Yankees and God* (1954); Benjamin Trumbull, *Complete History of Connecticut, Civil and Ecclesiastical . . . 1630-1742* (1797), II, 303.

Joseph H. Harkey
Virginia Wesleyan College

JOHN WILLIAMS (1664-1729)

Works: *Warning to the Unclean* (1699); *God in the Camp* (1707); *The Redeemed Captive, Returning to Zion* (1707); *Reports of Divine Kindness* (1707); *Several Arguments* (1721); *A Serious Word* (1729).

Biography: Born in 1664, John Williams grew up in Roxbury, Mass., where he was educated at Roxbury Latin School. Choosing not to follow his father's trade of shoemaking, he graduated from Harvard in 1683. Three years later, he became the Congregational minister at the frontier settlement of Deerfield, Mass., on the Connecticut River. During his first year at Deerfield, he married Eunice Mather, who was daughter of Eleazer Mather (q.v.) of Northampton, granddaughter of Richard Mather (q.v.) of Dorchester, niece of Increase Mather (q.v.) of Boston, and cousin of Cotton Mather (q.v.).

Williams prospered in Deerfield. The isolated town had been abandoned during King Philip's War, but it became a permanent settlement by the end of the seventeenth century. When Queen Anne's War broke out in 1702, Williams pleaded with Boston to send troops to protect the town from French and Indian raiding parties that often ventured into New Eng.'s backcountry. Although Governor Joseph Dudley (q.v.) dispatched twenty soldiers to Deerfield, the entire town was captured by a band of Canadian French and their Indian allies on Feb. 29, 1704. Many were killed inside the stockaded walls, including two of Williams's sons; the rest were marched through deep snow northward to Can., some dying of exhaustion along the way, including Williams's wife.

Williams remained a captive of the French until Oct. 1706, when he sailed to Boston with a shipload of "redeemed captives," leaving his daughter Eunice still in captivity. Cotton Mather noted Williams's arrival in his diary; Williams preached *Reports of Divine Kindness* from Mather's pulpit on Dec. 5, and the sermon was subsequently published as an addendum to Williams's *The Redeemed Captive*. Given forty pounds as compensation by the Mass. General Court, he returned to Deerfield and later married Abigail Bissell, who bore him five children. In 1707 his narrative of captivity was published in Boston. He served as chaplain of a New Eng. expedition against Port Royal in 1711 and later joined a delegation to Can. for the release of English prisoners. *The Redeemed Captive* received wide acclaim in New Eng., and a 2nd edition appeared in 1728. One year later Williams died.

Critical Appraisal: John Williams's fame rests on *The Redeemed Captive*. Although not anthologized so frequently as Mary Rowlandson's (q.v.) narrative of captivity, *The Redeemed Captive* is equally as important as the earlier narrative, which describes its author's experience during King Philip's War. Williams's narrative can be viewed in several ways: as a captivity narrative, as a jeremiad, as a work of historical value, and as an important anthropological document.

Although earlier literature of Spanish and English exploration in North America contained elements that dealt with Indian capture, New Englanders were the first to focus on the experience itself, thereby creating a unique American genre. Later American writers such as Cooper and Thoreau were to integrate the captivity theme into their literary works, and at the popular level, hack writers of dime novels continued its traditions until the end of the nineteenth century. *The Redeemed Captive* recorded the captivity experience of an entire town. Although Williams's own experience is of major concern, he faithfully recorded the tragic events that befell the members of his congregation and family.

As a Puritan minister, Williams was well acquainted with an older New Eng. genre, the jeremiad. Delivered from the pulpit and often later published, the jeremiad warned New Englanders not to ignore the first generation's errand of planting a New Israel in the American wilderness. By the time *The Redeemed Captive* was published in 1707, this tradition had been established for at least four decades. Williams underscored the symbolic nature of Deerfield's experience; he announced in the prolog to his narrative that the "history I am going to write proves that days of fasting and prayer, without reformation, will not avail to turn away the anger of God from a professing people." Williams, "animated to an heroical Christian resolution," tried to discern God's design behind the Deerfield Massacre, as it later came to be known.

Historians have relied upon *The Redeemed Captive* for information about frontier conditions during Queen Anne's War. Francis Parkman used it in his ambitious multivolume work *France and England in North America*, particularly in *A Half-Century of Conflict* (1892). Indeed, it gives us a glimpse of Canadian French-English affairs and Canadian French-Indian relations not readily found in other contemporary sources.

Anthropologically, *The Redeemed Captive* also tells us something about the nature of cultural conflict at the beginning of the eighteenth century. European misunderstanding of native American life can be seen particularly in the first third of the narrative; although not so virulently anti-Indian as his friend and relative-by-marriage Cotton Mather, Williams viewed his Abnaki and Caughnawaga Mohawk captors as "cruel and barbarous," yet capable of occasional kindness. The conflict between New Eng. Puritans and French Roman Catholics is also of major concern to Williams. Force-marched to a "popish country," Williams considered the Jesuits' efforts to convert members of his congregation (including his son Samuel) nothing short of satanic.

The Redeemed Captive is central to an understanding of the New Eng. Way as it occurred on the frontier and to an appreciation of how skillfully later American literary artists used the captivity experience to create a national identity and a sense of a unique past.

Suggested Readings: CCNE; DAB; FCNEV; Sibley-Shipton (III, 249-262); Sprague (I, 214-217); T$_1$. *See also* Edward W. Clark, ed., *The Redeemed Captive* (1976); Harrison T. Meserole, ed., *Seventeenth-Century American Poetry* (1968), pp. 480-481; Alden T. Vaughan and Edward W. Clark, eds., *Cups of Common Calamity: Puritan Accounts of Indian Captivity* (1981).

Edward W. Clark
Winthrop College

ROGER WILLIAMS (c. 1603-1683)

Works: *A Key into the Language of America* (1643); *The Bloudy Tenent of Persecution* (1644); *Conference Betweene Truth and Peace* (1644); *Mr. Cotton's Letter Lately Printed, Examined and Answered* (1644); *Queries of Highest Consideration* (1644); *Christenings Make Not Christians* (1645); *The Bloody Tenent Yet More Bloody* (1652); *The Examiner Defended* (1652); *Experiments of Spiritual Life and Health* (1652); *The Fourth Paper Presented by Major Butler* (1652); *The Hireling Ministry None of Christs* (1652); *George Fox Digg'd Out of His Burrowes* (1676).

Biography: The third of four children of James, a merchant tailor, and Alice Pemberton, Roger Williams was born, probably in 1603, in London and raised in the Smithfield district, a center of Separatist activity. His skill at shorthand drew the patronage of Sir Edward Coke (1617) who had him enrolled at Charterhouse (1621) and Pembroke Hall, Cambridge (1623). He received the B.A. in 1627 and proceeded to M.A. study, but having "forsaken the university," he did not take the degree, becoming in 1629 chaplain to Sir William Masham of Otes, Essex. In 1630 he married Mary Barnard; that summer as well, he met John Winthrop (q.v.), Thomas Hooker (q.v.), and John Cotton (q.v.). On Dec. 10, 1630, he and Mary sailed from Bristol for America on the *Lyon*.

On his arrival in Boston in Feb. 1631, he was offered a ministerial post in the church there but declined it on the grounds that the congregation was "unseparated." He accepted instead the office of assistant to the Rev. Samuel Skelton of Salem, but before leaving Boston, he attacked the magistrates for punishing breaches against the Sabbath, arguing that they had no right to enforce the First Table of the Decalogue. Thus began his famous running battle with the religious and civil authorities of the Massachusetts Bay colony, which centered upon his principle of the separation of church and state. Forced to leave Salem because of pressure from the Bay, he served as assistant at Plymouth (1631-1633). There his career as trader with and friend of the Indians began as did his enmity with

William Bradford (q.v.) resulting from his assertion that Christian kings did not have the right to dispose of Indian lands merely because they were "heathen." He also opposed the loyalty oaths of 1634 and 1635.

On Jul. 8, 1635, he was summoned to court and indicted on four charges. In Oct. he was banished from the Bay colony, and because he was about to be arrested, he fled in Jan. 1636 to the Narragansett country, where he attempted first to found a colony at Seekonk, and then, in May, he and four others founded Providence on land purchased from the Sachem Canonicus. Established as a political democracy, Providence quickly became a refuge for all kinds of dissenters, from Quakers to Jews, and this led to continuing disorder. Consequently, in Mar. 1643 Williams sailed to Eng., where he obtained a patent that incorporated Providence, Portsmouth, and Newport into Providence plantations and that recognized separation of church and state. He voyaged to Eng. again in Nov. 1651, returning in 1654 with a second patent that assured political stability. He was elected president of the General Assembly of R.I., a position he held until 1657. He held various public offices for most of the rest of his long life, continuing to oppose the wholesale grabbing of land by the colonies. In 1672 he engaged in a public debate with three Quakers that caused some to see him disavowing in his old age his earlier doctrine of religious toleration. Before the outbreak of King Philip's War in 1675, his last public duty was to act as negotiator with the Narragansetts in an effort to keep them out of the impending conflict. He failed in this as well as in his warnings to Providence. Both the tribe and the settlement were virtually destroyed. After a seven-year retirement imposed upon him by sickness, he died early in 1683.

Critical Appraisal: With the exceptions of *Experiments* and *George Fox*, all of Williams's writings date from the periods of his two voyages to Eng., and all are associated with the purpose of those voyages. His quarrels with the Boston theocracy—especially with John Cotton—and with the Plymouth colonists led him to seek patents for a colony of his own and to defend the need for such a colony. Consequently, Williams is best known as a controversialist on the side of what is now recognized as justice: political democracy, religious toleration, the separation of church and state. To his colonial contemporaries, however, he was a troublemaker bent upon destroying the colonial venture by impugning with the crown and later with Parliament the motives of the Mass. civil and religious leaders. Thus Cotton Mather (q.v.) could describe him as a man with a "windmill" in his head, and Vernon Parrington saw him as the lonely forerunner of Jeffersonian liberalism. As always, the truth lies somewhere in the middle.

Williams learned to be a controversialist at Cambridge where the medieval disputation was still an entrenched part of the curriculum. The disputation was concerned with rhetorical skill and the display of erudition, and Williams demonstrated that he was an apt student. His attacks and replies are ponderous and prolix, laced with biblical and Classical quotation and allusion, buttressed by arcane wordplay. *Mr. Cotton's Letter* or the *Bloody Tenent* books, for example, are not to be picked up for light reading, although they do contain rich veins of ore for the cultural historian or the serious student of literature. Written by a somewhat cantankerous septuagenarian, *George Fox* revealed, in addition to the historical and personal peculiarities of Williams's style, a crotchetiness and rigidity that do not blend well with the romanticized figure of the Providence monument.

The student wishing to encounter Williams with his controversialist guard down, however, will find *Experiments* and *A Key* both to be fascinating works. *Experiments* ("experiences") was written, as he told us, in the "very wild houses" of the Indians, when, on a trading mission, he heard of his wife's recent recovery from a serious illness and her resulting depression, which she interpreted as uncertainty about her spiritual condition. Addressed as it is to Mary and his children, the treatise gives us an intimate view of Williams's personal brand of Calvinism—by modern standards a ferociously gloomy kind of religion but one nevertheless tinged with his engaging personal concern for his "poor Companion and Yoak-fellow." In the epistle dedicatory, he revealed as well the totally organic interpenetration of his religion, his way of life, and his literary style. Concerned that the treatise, written as it was in the wilderness, would be too "rude and barbarous" for the genteel English reader, he asked: "An yet, is the Language plaine? it is the like Christs: Is the composure rude? such was his outward Beauty: Are the tryals (seemingly) too close? such is the two edged Sword of his most holy Spirit, which pierceth between the very Soul and Spirit, and bringeth every thought into the obedience of Christ Jesus." The ironic tone coupled with the stern statement of faith is characteristic as well.

For many years almost the exclusive possession of anthropologists and linguists, Williams's first book, *A Key*, is his most artistic. It follows in the tradition of the New Eng. prospectus-for-potential-colonists already well established by writers such as William Wood (q.v.) and Thomas Morton (q.v.), discussing in an almost predictable manner and order the climate, flora, fauna, and inhabitants of America, but it does so with unusual accuracy of observation, sensitivity of ear for the Narragansett language, and sympathy for the natural virtue of the Indian as expressed in his culture and harmonious relationship with nature. Running in counterpoint to the main theme are Williams's continuing satiric and ironic comparisons of barbaric virtue with "civilized" degeneracy, and the complementary near-tragic lamentation that, however admirable the Indians may be, they are pagans and, as such, damned. The dilemma, which Williams expressed here and which he elaborated a little later in *Christenings*, is that the Indian must be civilized before he can be Christianized but that in the civilizing process, his natural virtue is frequently destroyed. Consequently, in his epistle dedicatory, he objected to the wholesale baptisms reported by the Jesuits in New Fr. and Mex., because mere baptism cannot make a Christian of a pagan. But although he knew the Indians "are lost," at the same time he added, "I know not with how little *Knowledge* and *Grace* of Christ, the Lord may save, and therefore neither will *despaire*, nor *report* much."

The book is divided into thirty-two chapters, each of which deals with an aspect of Indian life, beginning with "Of *Salutation*" and ending, fittingly, with "Of Death *and* Buriall." Each chapter contains sections of vocabulary useful to the would-be trader or missionary—he called the method *"Implicite Dialogue"*— Narragansett on the left, English on the right. Each section of vocabulary is followed by an "Observation" on the vocabulary subject; for example, after a section ending, *"I have had a bad dream,"* he observed that "When they have a bad Dreame, which they conceive to be a threatning from God, they fall to prayer at all times of the night." Each chapter in turn ends with a *"generall* Observation" that draws spiritual and cultural conclusions; for example, that concluding the last chapter begins, "O, how terrible is the looke, the speedy and serious thought of death to all the sons of men?" The last part of each chapter is an emblematic poem, usually labeled "More particular," the poem taking the place of the more customary picture-emblem. The first stanza of the last poem provides a good example: *"The* Indians *say their bodies die,* / *Their soules they doe not die;* / *Worse are then* Indians *such, as hold* / *The soules mortalitie."* Contained in these concluding poems, perhaps too stridently for the modern reader, is Williams's entire tragic view of the colonial process and its effect upon the natives of North America. If it could ever have been said that in his religio-political writings Williams addressed not his own age but the eighteenth century, then surely in *A Key* he spoke not to his own age but to ours.

Suggested Readings: CCNE; DAB; DARB; DNB; LHUS; Sprague (VI, 8-21); T$_1$. *See also* Henry Chupack, *Roger Williams* (1969); *The Complete Writings of Roger Williams*, 7 vols. (1963); Wallace Coyle, *Roger Williams: A Reference Guide* (1977); Edmund S. Morgan, *Roger Williams: The Church and the State* (1967); John J. Teunissen and Evelyn J. Hinz, eds., *A Key Into the Language of America* (1973); idem, "Roger Williams, St. Paul, and American Primitivism," CRevAS, 4 (1973), 121-136; idem, "Roger Williams, Thomas More, and the Narragansett Utopia," EAL, 11 (1977), 281-295; Ola Elizabeth Winslow, *Master Roger Williams* (1957).

John J. Teunissen
University of Manitoba

SOLOMON WILLIAMS (1700-1776)

Works: *The Glorious Reward* (1730); *The Frailty and Misery of Man's Life* (1740); *A Firm and Immoveable Courage to Obey God* (1741); *The Comfort and Blessedness of Being at Home in God* (1742); *The More Excellent Way* (1742); *The Power and Efficacy of the Prayers* (1742); *The Surprizing Variety of the Acts of Divine Providence* (1742); *The Servants of the Lord* (1743); *Christ, the King* (1744); "A Letter...to the Rev. Mr. James Davenport" in *Two Letters from the Rev. Mr. Williams & Wheelock* (1744); *The Ministers of the Gospel* (1744); *The Business, Scope and End of Gospel Ministers* (1746); *A Vindication of the Gospel-Doctrine of Justifying Faith* (1746); *The Sad Tendency of Divisions and Contentions in Churches* (1751); *The True State of the Question* (1751); *The*

Vanity of Human Life (1754); *The Word of God* (1754); *The Duty of Christian Soldiers* (1755); *The Relations of God's People to Him* (1760); *The Duty of Christians* (1773); *The Greatness and Sovereignty of God* (1777).

Biography: Solomon Williams was born in Hatfield, Mass., on Jun. 4, 1700. His father, the senior William Williams (q.v.), was a distinguished minister, while his mother Christian, Williams's second wife, was a daughter of Solomon Stoddard (q.v.). His brothers included the younger William Williams (q.v.) and Elisha Williams (q.v.). After graduating from Harvard College in 1719, Williams returned to western Mass., where he taught for a year at the Hadley school and married Mary Porter of that town. On Dec. 5, 1722, he was ordained minister of the First Church at Lebanon, Conn., where he would serve for the remaining fifty-four years of his life.

One of the more distinguished ministers of his generation, Williams was known for his effectiveness in the pulpit (although he lacked a "strong commanding Voice"), his liberal theology, and his scholarship. He founded Lebanon's Philogrammatican Library, helped establish the town's grammar school, and was elected a trustee of Yale in 1749. Later named first professor of divinity at Yale, he declined that honor but in 1773 was awarded the college's first doctor of divinity degree. Although Williams supported the Great Awakening, he was a moderate New Light who had little sympathy for the Calvinism of his cousin Jonathan Edwards (q.v.). He vehemently opposed the enthusiastic excesses to which the Awakening frequently led.

Solomon Williams died at midnight on the evening of Feb. 28/29, 1776. Three of his sons graduated from Yale, while a fourth son, William Williams, graduated from Harvard and went on to become a signer of the Declaration of Independence and a member of the Continental Congress.

Critical Appraisal: Williams was a prolific publisher of sermons, and his writings illustrate most of the principal varieties of pulpit oratory. As a scholar, Williams gave more than the usual attention to the explications of his texts, but many of his sermons remain interesting, particularly for the light they shed on the dilemmas and vicissitudes that occasionally confronted an eighteenth-century minister. For example, two of Williams's published sermons were preached at the funerals of members of his congregation who had committed suicide. In *The Frailty and Misery of Man's Life*, Williams attempted to explain the actions of a Yale student who had become ill and jumped into a Lebanon millpond, drowning himself. In *The Greatness and Sovereignty of God*, Williams interpreted the suicide of Mrs. Faith Huntington, "a Daughter of the most respectable Family among us." The doctrines and applications of these sermons show Williams carefully defining the nature and limits of human reason and free will, as opposed to divine providence. These sermons may be compared to examples of the normal form of the funeral sermon, in which the minister's application stressed the exemplary qualities of the deceased. Thus, in *The Servants of the Lord, The Vanity of Human Life*, and *The Word of God*, Williams eulogized the lives of respected ministers. But in yet another funeral sermon, *The Surprizing Variety*, he emphasized the role of divine providence, since his subject was the death of a Yale student drowned while crossing the Haddam, Conn., ferry. A second student had narrowly escaped death in the same incident, and Williams himself had intended to accompany the unfortunate youth, but had been unable to locate his horse. Thus, he claimed, "The whole work of divine Providence is one perfect Plot & Design, laid in the eternal Counsel of divine Wisdom. The work of Providence in all the strange Variety of its particular Acts, is not in any part a Chance or Random Shot; but is all as God has made it." That Williams was considerably less assertive of the omnipresence of divine providence in his two sermons on suicides is evidence of the fine lines that ministers had to draw as they formed lessons from extraordinary occasions.

The Great Awakening and its associated enthusiastic upheavals presented Williams with even more delicate problems. Late in 1741, two children of Williams's congregation attended a tumultuous religious meeting and thereafter claimed to have seen a vision in which the Book of Life was revealed to them. Williams' name was printed in small letters at the bottom of a page. *The More Excellent Way*, Williams's attempt to quiet the resulting furor, offers a fascinating glimpse into the psychology of the Awakening and illuminates the dilemmas faced by moderate supporters of the Awakening such as Williams.

The Power and Efficacy of the Prayers records yet another unusual occasion. Eunice Williams, daughter of John Williams (q.v.), had returned from captivity in Can. to visit her brother Eleazar, minister at Mansfield, Conn. Preached at the Mansfield church, Williams's sermon developed an argument founded upon two interrelated themes: Eunice's decision to remain among her Mohawk captors for more than thirty-eight years, and her brother's effort to encourage the spread of the Awakening among his own congregation. Williams's contribution to this effort was to contrast Eunice's undoubted spiritual disadvantages with the supposed advantages of Eleazar's congregation: "It's to be feared there are great Numbers here present that are in an unconverted, unrenewed, unpardoned State...yet you now look with great Pity and Compassion on that *poor Captive*, for whom we have been now offering our *earnest Prayers* to God; who has been so long in such a pitiable and sorrowful Condition, and who is now in the Thickness of *popish* Darkness & Superstition." Although Williams rejected the fire and brimstone tactics of the more ardent awakeners, he preached in *The Power and Efficacy* one of the more effective sermons of "Prayer for the Revival of Religion."

Among Williams's remaining occasional writings are three sermons preached at ordinations (*The Business, Scope and End; The Glorious Reward*; and *The Ministers of the Gospel*) and two sermons on military events: *The Duty of Christian Soldiers*, preached to encourage a company setting out to fight the French in 1755, and *The Relations of God's People to Him*, celebrating the fall of Quebec in 1759. Williams also preached a Conn. election sermon (*A Firm and Immoveable Courage*) and in 1773 delivered *The Duty of Christians*, his half-century sermon. His purely doctrinal writings were less numerous, although in 1744 he published *Christ, the King*, a collection of seven sermons on the text of John 18:37.

Although most of Williams's publications were sermons, he wrote three additional texts significant for the study of the Great Awakening and its aftermath. His 1744 letter to James Davenport illuminates one of the more notorious instances of irresponsible religious enthusiasm during the Awakening. Davenport, a leading itinerant preacher, had incited a New London, Conn., mob to burn books and clothing that Davenport deemed offensive to piety. As the books included volumes by Benjamin Colman (q.v.), Increase Mather (q.v.), and Jonathan Parsons (q.v.) and the clothing included Davenport's own trousers, he was soon called upon to apologize for this "awful affair," as he termed it in a retraction that he forwarded to Williams. With the assistance of Eleazar Wheelock (q.v.), then minister of Lebanon's Second or North Society, Williams thereafter helped Davenport to become fully convinced of the error of his ways. Williams's letter carefully and moderately asserted the virtues of avoiding the "publick censuring of Ministers as unconverted, and promoting Separations from their Ministry," thus correcting Davenport's excesses and implicitly criticizing Gilbert Tennent (q.v.), whose famous Nottingham Sermon stated the revivalists' rationale for attacking "unconverted" ministers. Two years later, Williams again attacked New Light extremism in *A Vindication of the Gospel-Doctrine*, his reply to *What Is Christ to Me?*, a tract written by Andrew Croswell. Citing as his authorities Solomon Stoddard (q.v.) and Samuel Willard (q.v.), Williams severely criticized Croswell's Antinomian tendencies.

A moderate man living in immoderate times, Williams tried to steer a middle course during the Great Awakening. His trying experiences with Davenport, who was twice ruled insane, and with other unsavory aspects of the Awakening may account for the uncharacteristic severity of his attack on Croswell and his unfortunate treatment of his cousin Jonathan Edwards in *The True State of the Question*. Originally conceived by Williams's brother Elisha as a criticism of Edwards's writings on church membership, this tract was completed by Williams, published at the expense of the Northampton church from which Edwards had been dismissed, and distributed to every member of the congregation. This behavior displayed more than a trace of meanness, and Edwards's reply, *Misrepresentations Corrected*, was equally harsh. Yet the episode is probably best understood as evidence of the persistence of the passions aroused by the Awakening. Taken as a whole, Solomon Williams's sermons and tracts reveal that he was an impressive scholar, a more than competent stylist, and a master of pulpit oratory whose work deserves further study.

Suggested Readings: CCNE; Sibley-Shipton (VI, 352-361); Sprague (I, 321-326). *See also* Edwin Scott Gaustad, *The Great Awakening in New England* (1957), pp. 41, 146 n.54; Alan Heimert, *Religion and the American Mind* (1966), passim; Alan Heimert and Perry Miller, eds., *The Great Awakening* (1967), pp. 435-440, 516; Joseph Tracy, *The Great Awakening* (1842), pp. 249-253.

Douglas R. Wilmes
The Pennsylvania State University

WILLIAM WILLIAMS (1665-1741)

Works: *Cambridge Ephemeris. An Almanack of the Coelestial Motions, for. . .1685* (1685); *Cambridge Ephemeris. An Almanack. . .for. . .1687* (1687); *The Danger of Not Reforming Known Evill* (1707); *The Great Salvation Revealed and Offered in the Gospel Explained. . . .In Several Sermons* (1717); *A Painful Ministry: The Peculiar Gift of the Lord. . . .A Sermon at the Ordination of Mr. Stephen Williams* (1717); *A Plea for God, and an Appeal to the Consciences of a People Declining in Religion* (1719); *The Great Concern of Christians, and Especially of Ministers. . . .A Sermon. . .at the Ordination of. . .Warham Williams* (1723); *The Great Duty of Ministers to Advance the Kingdom of God. . .Preached at the Annual Convention of Ministers. . .May 26, 1726* (1726); *An Essay to Prove the Interest of the Children of Believers in the Covenant* (1727); *The Honour of Christ Advanced by the Fidelity of Ministers. . . .A Sermon. . .at the Ordination. . .of Nehemiah Bull, October 26. 1726* (1728); *The Death of a Prophet Lamented and Improved. . .Preach'd. . .on the Day of the Interment of Solomon Stoddard* (1729); *The Work of Ministers and the Duty of Hearers. . .Preached. . .upon the Ordination of Jonathan Ashley* (1733); *The Duty and Interest of a People, Among Whom Religion Has Been Planted* (1736).

Biography: William Williams was born in Newton, Mass., on Feb. 2, 1665, the third son and fourth child of Capt. Isaac Williams and his wife, Martha. Little is recorded about his formative years or college preparation. About 1679 he entered Harvard College from which he received the A.B. in 1683 and A.M. some years later. In 1685 he settled in Hatfield, Mass., where he was called to be minister of the church recently vacated by Nathaniel Chauncy (q.v.). Williams was ordained over the church in 1685 or 1686, and for more than a half-century, he faithfully served the needs of his Hatfield congregation. Although early in his career he appears to have had an interest in almanac writing, once he settled at Hatfield, Williams turned exclusively to developing his talent as a preacher. By the turn of the century, his reputation as a preacher was well established, and as the occasion for several of his published sermons indicates, he was frequently invited to give ordination sermons for ministers of neighboring towns—and for some distant relatives as well. The high point of his career came between 1719 and 1726, for in 1719 he was invited to preach before the governor and other officials at the Mass. election, and in 1726 he preached before the annual convention of ministers at Boston. Long sympathetic to the claims of Solomon Stoddard (q.v.) and others that the children of believers had a vested interest in the covenant, Williams began to preach to that effect in the late 1720s. During the 1730s, he rejoiced at the early signs of the Great Awakening and was an early champion of Jonathan Edwards (q.v.), whose efforts toward achieving a religious revival in Northampton Williams supported in print in an appendix to his *The Duty and Interest of a People* (1736). Williams died in Hatfield on Aug. 29, 1741. Although there is much obscurity and uncertainty in regard to facts concerning Williams's family affairs, it is generally reported that he was married twice, first in the mid-1680s to Elizabeth Cotton, who was the daughter of the Rev. Seaborn Cotton and who died in 1698, and then about the turn of the century to Christian (?) Stoddard, daughter of Solomon Stoddard. Of the eight children Williams is said to have fathered in these marriages, three are noteworthy: the younger William Williams (q.v.), who followed his father into the ministry and had a distinguished career at Weston, Mass., until he was dismissed from his pulpit for "gross Lasciviousness," Elisha Williams (q.v.), rector at Yale from 1722 to 1739; and Solomon Williams (q.v.), the distinguished minister of Lebanon, Conn., whose son William was a signer of the Declaration of Independence. It was a point of family pride that the senior Williams, his son Solomon, his grandson Eliphalet, and his great-grandson Solomon each preached sermons on his respective fiftieth anniversary in the ministry.

Critical Appraisal: Although William Williams has attracted no critical attention during the past two centuries, in the decades following his death, he was widely regarded as one of the leading figures of his generation, even by commentators with whom he likely would have had little in common. One such commentator, the younger Charles Chauncy (q.v.), reported in a letter to Ezra Stiles (q.v.),

> I have read all Mr. [Solomon] Stoddard's Writings, but was never able to see in them that strength of genius some have attributed to him. Mr. Williams of Hatfield, his son-in-law, I believe to have been the greater man, and I am ready to think greater than any of his own sons, though they were all men of more than common understanding.

Williams's talent as a thinker and preacher must have been the source of this appraisal, for in his spirited and sympathetic funeral sermon on Williams, Jonathan Edwards, who knew Williams personally, anticipated Chauncy's comment and supplied the necessary support for such grand claims. Edwards said of Williams,

> *Judiciousness and Wisdom* were eminently his Character. . . . In his *publick Ministry*, he mainly insisted on the most weighty and *important Things of Religion*; he was eminently an *evangelical* Preacher; evangelical Subjects seemed to be his Delight: Christ was the great Subject of his Preaching; and he much insisted on those Things that did nearly concern the *Essence and Power* of Religion. . . . His Sermons were none of them mean, but were all solid, wise Composures. His words were none of them vain, but all were weighty.

On the evidence of Williams's printed sermons, there appears to be no exaggeration in the assessment of his talent by Chauncy and Edwards. Williams clearly had a zest for both his Hatfield ministry and the contribution that that ministry might make toward the revival of New Eng.'s first interests. At Harvard during the 1670s and 1680s, Williams would have heard the assertions of Increase

Mather (q.v.), President Urian Oakes (q.v.), Samuel Willard (q.v.), and others to the effect that New Englanders had lost sight of the ideals of their fathers, which in turn had caused a breach between God and his latest chosen people. Of course, declension issues and such topics increased in intensity and took on new timeliness after the social and political upheavals of the 1680s and 1690s. Therefore, it is not surprising that in his earliest printed sermons, among which are ordination sermons and *A Plea for God, and An Appeal to...a People*, the aforementioned election sermon, Williams combined the counsel to his ministerial colleagues to be thankful for their call during times of great declension, for now they can conduct themselves as God's "watchmen," with appeals to both the ministers and all others in the audience to revive the work and interest of New Eng.'s founders.

Williams maintained this point of view throughout his career. As his last sermons make clear, the primary reason for his happy reception of the Great Awakening was his conviction that only through a mass renewal of the covenant terms upon which New Eng. was established could the original purpose of New Eng. as a religious plantation again prevail. Williams was not afraid of emotion or, as Edwards pointed out, of exploiting the emotive content of religion to achieve the humiliation and reformation of New Eng.'s people, for he believed that sermonic appeal to reason and revelation supported by the emotive content and language of religious experience was the principal posture through which man was to be led back to God. In this regard, preacher Williams achieved a compromise between seventeenth-century orthodoxy and eighteenth-century revivalism. As a man then who understood both the needs and the limitations of his time and whose expressions of that understanding elicited the admiration of friend and adversary alike, Williams deserves a critical review that is long overdue.

Suggested Readings: CCNE; Sibley-Shipton (III, 263-269); Sprague (I, 207-209). *See also* Jonathan Edwards, *The Resort and Remedy of Those That Are Bereaved by the Death of an Eminent Minister. A Sermon Preached...on the Day of the Interment of the Reverend Mr. William Williams* (1741).

Ronald A. Bosco
State University of New York at Albany

WILLIAM WILLIAMS (1688-1760)

Works: *The Duty of Parents to Transmit Religion to Their Children* (includes *The Duty of the Children of Gods Covenant People* and *The Obligations of Baptism and the Duties of Young Persons...to Take Their Parents Covenant*; 1721); *Divine Warnings...on Occasion of the Terrible Earthquake* (includes *True Wisdom...Persons in Their Youth...Renew'd Their Baptismal Covenant*; 1728); *The Office...Ordination of Mr. David Hall* (1729); *Martial Wisdom*

Recommended (1737); *The Serious Consideration...Execution of Philip Kennison* (1738); *God the Strength of Rulers* (1741); Preface and *A Discourse on Saving Faith* (pub. in *Four Sermons*; 1741); *Christ Living in the Saints...Death of Caleb Lyman* (1743); *The Divine Promises...Death of Hannah Williams* (1746).

Biography: William Williams was born May 11, 1688, to the Rev. William Williams (q.v.) and Elizabeth (Cotton) Williams of Hatfield, Mass. While pursuing the B.A. at Harvard, he kept a grammar school at Roxbury. In Feb. 1707/08 he was asked to preach to the village of Watertown Farms (later Weston), was formally called to be minister there in Aug. 1709, and was ordained Nov. 2, 1709. Williams received an M.A. in 1708 and married Hannah, the twelfth child of Solomon Stoddard (q.v.), on Jul. 6, 1710. He was once overseer for Harvard and accompanied as chaplain the Mass. commissioners to N.Y. in 1714-1715.

Although at one time the Weston Church found it necessary to remind its members that sleeping during sermons was "irreverent & indecent," Williams appears to have been a competent preacher; he was invited to deliver election sermons and preached at various times at other parishes. On Dec. 29, 1745, Hannah died and on Nov. 24, 1749, Williams made public his intention to marry Mrs. Mary Stone of Holliston. Evidently Williams's intentions and behavior were not well received, for on May 28, 1750, the Weston church met to consider "the awful reports going about of the heinous Miscarriages of their Pastor." On Oct. 16 the church deemed it necessary to call for a council of churches; interestingly, the formal results of the Council have been partially lost due to the "Over-officiousness & imprudence" of Williams in recording only part of the proceedings, resulting in an "imperfect Record."

Although the church voted to dissolve its pastoral relation to Williams (because of his "gross Lasciviousness" and "Immoral Conduct"), it yet accorded him the right to the "priviledges of Special ordinances." Evidently, the accusations were acccurate, for Williams wrote to his children that he had done "great Injury & wrong" to himself and his "dear Children." Although Williams longed to return to the ministry, he was forced to live by speculating in land until he died in Mar. 1760.

Critical Appraisal: William Williams appears to have been generally well respected throughout his early life and up to the death of his wife, Hannah. Most of his published sermons were requested by the "hearers," and Williams was evidently thought to be effective in convincing young people of their duties to take up their parents' covenant. Many of his early sermons in the 1720s are developed around the mutual obligations of parents to set proper religious examples and religious training while children must live up to the promises of their baptismal experience. He appealed to the parents' sense of responsibility and potential guilt, drawing scenes wherein parents see their children suffering in hell. In 1728 a Williams sermon was published advertising as part of its title that said sermon had resulted in many young people "renewing their Baptismal Covenant."

A useful catalog of the latest "intermixture of Mercy and Judgment" appears in his *Divine Warnings* sermon, in which Williams described the various political and physical manifestations (including the earthquake of 1727) of God's displeasure with the sinners of New Eng. In typical election and artillery sermons, he cautioned leaders to make their actions acceptable in God's eyes and, in a sermon at the occasion of a hanging, emphasized God's judgment for sins, in this case burglary. Elsewhere he provided useful if usual distinctions between "saving" and "common" faith and tried hard to define for his listeners and readers how a spirit could be "indwelling," yet not "personal." He was especially adept at the elegiac sermon; his sermon on the death of Caleb Lyman is a fine example of an "application." He surveyed Lyman's offices, accomplishments, and personality traits such as his "pleasing conversation."

Williams was most appealing in his last published sermon on the death of Hannah, his wife of thirty-five years. Preaching on the doctrine that promises are given to those who follow Christian example (Hannah, in this case), Williams admitted that not mourning seems "stoical and stupid," yet tried to "correct" himself to see her death as God's will. The sermon must have been touching to his listeners; at one point he stopped, saying, "Pity me, Pity Me, O ye my Friends. . . . Pray for me and mine." As a result of the scandal after Hannah's death, Williams lost his pulpit and most of his money through ill-advised investment. In his remaining days, he complained of a "Useless Life" and longed to return to the ministry but was afraid to do so for fear he might "Create Divisions and Disturbances." Although he remained a "peaceable parishioner," he essentially retired from public life, and no works were published in his last fifteen years of life.

Suggested Readings: CCNE; Sibley-Shipton (V, 295-300).

Dean G. Hall
Wayne State University

WILLIAM WILLIAMS (1727-1791)

Works: *Mr. Penrose, The Journal of Penrose, Seaman* (w. 1783; pub. 1815; rep., 1969).

Biography: William Williams was born and attended grammar school in Bristol, Eng., but while quite young went to sea. Even his first commander, Capt. Hunter, remembered him as a "drawer," so William seems early to have shown interest and talent as a visual artist. He jumped ship in Norfolk during his second voyage and made his way to the W. Ind., intending to make his living as a painter. By the time he was 20 in 1747, he had moved to Philadelphia and met Benjamin West, then a boy of 9. For the next thirteen years, West was a frequent visitor to Williams's home, reporting that Williams was "an excellent actor in taking off character" and attributing his choice of painting as a career to Williams.

Williams became America's first professional theatrical scene painter when employed by the Hallam Company in the Southwark Theatre in 1759. Then, in 1760-1761, Williams made another trip to the W. Ind. to commission portraits. Williams was married twice early; the two sons from his first marriage died in the American Revolution. His second marriage was to Mary Mare who bore him a son, William Joseph, who became a well-known portrait painter himself.

By 1769 Williams moved to New York City, supporting himself by painting and teaching. Disenchanted by the deaths of his second wife and sons, he returned to London in 1776 to paint for a patron who unfortunately died after only eighteen months. Eventually, Williams drifted back to his place of birth, where he married yet again. Evidently again quickly widowed, he was alone when Thomas Eagles supported him until Williams could be moved into the Merchants and Sailors' Almshouse, where he remained until his death in 1791.

Critical Appraisal: William Williams was a much more significant figure in the history of painting than in American literary history; he painted approximately 240 canvasses in his thirty-year stay in America. His literary reputation rests, however, on one work: his rendering of a fictitious sailor's journal, the history of Llewellin Penrose, which concentrates on Penrose's twenty-eight years spent abandoned on the Moskito Coast of South America. Because Williams could be considered American by virtue of his long stay in the country and because the work of fiction was completed by 1783, some grounds exist for calling Williams the first American novelist and the journal the first American novel.

Originally titled *Journal of Llewellin Penrose, a Seaman* in the bowdlerized 1st edition by Thomas Eagles, the journal was placed by Thomas's son, the Rev. John Eagles, with John Murray, publisher, of London in 1815. That edition is in four volumes. A pirated German edition followed in 1817 with extensive Greek and Latin footnotes added. Fortunately, Williams's manuscript survived, and the original is now available.

The journal itself relates in first person and in nearly chronological order Penrose's abandonment; his surroundings, including accurately detailed descriptions of plant, animal, and fish life; and his exposure to the native population into which he gradually ingratiated himself, marrying and raising his children there on the beach and in his cave. Because Williams's work was not reprinted until recently, most scholars and teachers have not treated it or included it in literature courses. The work, however, has much to recommend it: like *Robinson Crusoe*, the Penrose account is captivating as a tale of survival and human adaptation; like a natural history, it provides precise and realistic descriptions of unfamiliar social mores, plants, and wildlife; like fictions of Melville and Cooper, it examines the native peoples in their "happy state of Innocency"; and like most good works of literature, it reflects upon the human condition and society. Significantly, Williams's hero chooses to stay with his family, which grows beyond his wife and children to include a motley mix of castaways of several races, rather than return to civilization. Penrose is not rescued, and the final entries in the journal are made by his son Owen.

As David Dickason has pointed out, the work has several aspects that anticipate themes and techniques not dealt with or employed until much later in American literature. Williams's treatment of non-Christian blacks is sympathetic, usually rendering them more humane than their white Christian counterparts. In addition, Williams is one of the first to experiment with the use of "dialects and verbal mannerisms to distinguish and characterize many of his persons" and their deeds, without the sometimes burdensome descriptions and analyses characteristic of many eighteenth-century novels, are allowed to speak for themselves. Like many other early works that were not easily available to scholars and the public, Williams's one literary effort is yet generally unknown but is deserving of more attention.

Suggested Readings: David Howard Dickason, ed., *Mr. Penrose: The Journal of Penrose, Seaman* (1969); idem, *William Williams* (1970); John Eagle, "The Beggar's Legacy," BEM, 77 (Mar., 1855), 251-272; Thomas Flexner, "The Amazing William Williams," MagA, 37 (1944), 234-246, 276-278; William Sawitzky, "William Williams, First Instructor of Benjamin West," *Antiques*, 31 (1937), 240-242; John F. Williams, *William Joseph Williams: Portrait Painter and His Descendents* (1953).

Dean G. Hall
Wayne State University

JAMES WILSON (1742-1798)

Works: *Considerations on the Nature and the Extent of the Legislative Authority of the British Parliament* (w. 1768; pub. 1774); *Considerations on the Bank of North-America* (1785); *The Substance of a Speech* (1787); *A Charge Delivered...to the Grand Jury* (1791); *An Introductory Lecture to a Course of Law Lectures* (1791); Bird Wilson, ed., *The Works of the Honourable James Wilson*, 3 vols. (1804); *On the Improvement and Settlement of Lands in the United States* (1946).

Biography: Born in Fifeshire, Scot. on Sept. 14, 1742, James Wilson was the oldest son of William and Aleson (Landale) Wilson. Believing that their first son should enter the ministry, Wilson's devout parents arranged for his education at the University of St. Andrews. But William Wilson died young, and his son soon rejected a future career in a Scottish pulpit for the attractions of the New World. He emigrated in 1765 and by Feb. 1766, had become a Latin tutor at the College of Philadelphia, where he was awarded an honorary A.M. degree. But again Wilson broke from the confines of a career that promised too little scope for his ambition. After reading law under John Dickinson (q.v.), he was admitted to the bar in Nov. 1767. He found an appropriate profession in the law and politics, yet even these broad fields proved too small to contain his ambitious dreams, and this in the end led to tragedy.

An undeniably brilliant man who passionately desired to be both famous and rich, Wilson died disgraced and bankrupt. He remains a controversial figure, in part because analysts of his life and thought face the problem of where sympathy ends and apology begins. Yet his accomplishments were considerable by any standard. As a young lawyer, he quickly established a thriving and lucrative practice at Reading and Carlisle, Penn., and entered provincial politics. Elected to the Continental Congress, Wilson signed the Declaration of Independence, but his opposition to the Penn. constitution of 1776 led to his ouster from his congressional seat, although he was returned to Congress in the 1780s. He moved to Philadelphia in 1778, where he increased his already considerable legal reputation, although not always by defending popular causes. Because he represented Loyalists and formed business, legal, and social relationships with speculators such as William Duer (q.v.), his popular reputation was darkened, and in 1779 his house was attacked by rioters, with some loss of life. However, he was named a delegate to the Constitutional Convention of 1787, and played a prominent role in the deliberations and the effort to secure ratification of the Constitution in Penn. Thus Wilson became one of only six men to sign both the Declaration of Independence and the Constitution. In 1789, he was appointed associate justice of the Supreme Court, and in 1790 he oversaw the ratification of a new Penn. constitution of which he was the chief architect. Soon after his appointment as associate justice, he delivered a course of law lectures at the College of Philadelphia; the first session was attended by President George Washington (q.v.) and Vice-President John Adams (q.v.).

Wilson's career reached its peak in the years between 1787 and 1790. Thereafter he was faced by a rapid and seemingly irreversible decline in his fortunes. Throughout his adult life he had indulged in highly speculative business and land transactions, often financed with dubious credit arrangements. His financial position steadily worsened, and he vainly struggled to recoup his losses. His first wife, Rachel Bird, died in 1786, and in 1793 he married Hannah Gray. But he soon found that he could not support his young wife and his six children by his first marriage, and he was subsequently imprisoned for debt, although he retained his seat on the Supreme Court. In 1798 he moved to Edenton, N. C., where he died, owing huge sums of money, on Aug. 21, 1798.

Critical Appraisal: Much of Wilson's legal and political thought was notable both for its intellectual brilliance and for its prescience. He often anticipated the future development of American government in his arguments, and thus he often seemed out of step with his own time. In broad terms he stood for a democratic nationalism, believing that all power derived from the people's will and that the institutions of government should be tied as directly as possible to the democratic source of their authority. The local powers of the states therefore must be subordinate to the higher powers of the national government, since "the People" of the Constitution's Preamble are in essence a national rather than a local body politic. Yet Wilson was so adept at reconciling "rationally erected" theory with personal and political pragmatism that the exact nature of his democratic sympathies and his centralism remains debatable, as do certain aspects of his legal thought.

Although most of Wilson's writings were concerned with the affairs of the new nation, he made one notable contribution to the pre-Revolutionary pamphlet debates over America's proper relationship to Br. Wilson's arguments in *Considerations on...the British Parliament*, published in 1774 but written some years earlier, anticipated John Adams's analysis in *Novanglus* and the principles of the modern British Commonwealth. Wilson allowed a relationship of abstract "faith and obedience" to the British monarch, but he denied that the British Parliament had the power to govern the colonies. This radical argument was carried out by deduction: according to "the law of nature," a reciprocal relationship must exist between any people and their government. Since no such relationship existed between the colonists and the Parliament, which they had no voice in electing, it followed that the Parliament was irrelevant to American government.

Theoretically irrelevant as the British Parliament may have been, Wilson's arguments reached a dead end established by the increasingly common colonial perception that the British legislature had to be made practically irrelevant as well. Wilson approached the issue of outright independence hesitantly, although he was ultimately willing to sign the Declaration in 1776, unlike his mentor John Dickinson. Yet he would never again be so liberal as he was when he published his *Considerations*. His later writings reflect his attempts to make the legal and political doctrines of the new nation conform to the dictates of his intellect, and occasionally of his interest. This duality of intention appears in many of his actions, for intellectual substance and the appearance of propriety were often at odds in his life as he pursued his complex financial speculations. Thus Wilson's *Considerations on the Bank of North-America* presented a forceful if sometimes strained constitutional argument, claiming that under the Articles of Confederation a bank's national charter was proof against revocation of its state charter. Turning to the economic aspects of the case, he argued that the Bank of North America was not responsible for the depression then sweeping the country. Rather, foreign indebtedness was to blame: "we seemed to have forgot, that to pay was as necessary in trade as to purchase." Yet Wilson's many enemies in the Penn. Assembly could easily observe that such principles equally applied to Wilson himself, as he was then deeply in debt to the bank he so ably defended.

As one of the Supreme Court's six original justices, Wilson led a judicial career that was constrained by the realities of history. The principles of judicial review that might have allowed him to establish lasting precedents were not yet developed. His most famous ruling, in the case of *Chisholm* vs. *Georgia* (1793), has been said to anticipate John Marshall's arguments in *McCulloch* vs. *Maryland* (1819) and *Cohens* vs. *Virginia* (1821), but however the tangled provenances of jurisprudence are analyzed, Wilson's career on the bench clearly demonstrated the confounding of his aspirations by realities. That tragic theme underlies any estimation of Wilson's place in American history; more particularly, it informs a critical judgment of his greatest work, the law lectures that he delivered at the College of Philadelphia. Wilson believed that these lectures could become a cornerstone of American jurisprudence, yet he published only *An Introductory Lecture*. The complete course of lectures remained in manuscript until published by Wilson's son, Bird Wilson, in 1804. Many of the lectures were never even delivered, and the original design of the course was by no means carried out in Wilson's text. Thus his "Lectures on Law" were at best a flawed masterpiece, but they nevertheless deserve a wider readership than they have received. Wilson founded his analysis on a "law of nature" and derived from this principle a definition of American law that was explicitly related to the nature of the American body politic, which demanded "the consent of those whose obedience the law requires." In this he rejected William Blackstone's emphasis on the citizen's obligation to behave lawfully by virtue of the superiority of the law itself over the individual. In contrast, Wilson's definition posited an *agreement* to obey, an agreement based on a wide-ranging analysis of the nature of a free and democratic government.

James Wilson's writings reveal an optimism that often served him ill during his lifetime: "Let us suppose we have done nothing, while anything yet remains to be done." He proclaimed in his "Lectures on Law" that natural law itself "though immutable in its *principles*, will be progressive in its operations and effects." He was one of the more brilliant expositors of American confidence and optimism, and his instinct was always to look ahead. Thus he was intellectually and financially a speculator, but he loved ideas at least as well as he loved money. Although his writing suffered from occasional rhetorical grandstanding and a tendency to digress, he possessed a subtle and powerful mind. His prose was fully capable of giving form and substance to the ideas with which he so confidently speculated.

Suggested Readings: DAB; LHUS; T$_2$. *See also* Randolph G. Adams, ed., *Selected Political Essays of James Wilson* (1930); Richard E. Amacher, *American Political Writers: 1588-1800* (1979), pp. 145-147, 148; James De Witt Andrews, ed., *The Works of James Wilson*, 2 vols. (1896); Robert G. McCloskey, Introduction, *The Works of James Wilson*, 2 vols. (1967; reprints 1804 edition of the *Works*); Geoffrey Seed, *James Wilson* (1978); Charles Page Smith, *James Wilson: Founding Father* (1956).

Douglas R. Wilmes
The Pennsylvania State University

JOHN WILSON (c. 1588-1667)

Works: *A Song of Deliverance . . . with Poems Both Latin and English* (1626; 1st American ed., 1680); "Anagram . . . of Mrs. Abigail Tompson" (w.c. 1643; pub. 1840); "Upon the Death of . . . a Child" (frag. w. 1653; pub. 1702); "Johannes Harvardus, Anagr." (w. c. 1654; pub. 1702); "Claudius Gilbert, Anagram" (w. 1657; pub. 1944); "A Copy of Verses. . .on the Sudden Death of Mr. Joseph Brisco" (1657); four anagrams on Thomas Shepard (1663); three brief prefatory essays, "To the Christian Reader" (with Samuel Whiting, pub. in John Higginson, *The Cause of God*, 1663; with John Cotton, pub. in Richard Mather, *The Summe of Certain Sermons*, 1652; and with Jonathan Mitchell, pub. in Samuel Whiting, *A Discourse of the Last Judgement*, 1664); four anagrams on John Norton (1664); "Upon the Death of. . .Mr. William Tompson" (w. 1666; pub. 1927); *A Seasonable Watch-Word* (1677).

Biography: John Wilson, born in Windsor, Eng., about 1588, was one of the most revered and loved among the Puritan patriarchs of the Massachusetts Bay colony. Surviving associate ministers such as John Cotton (q.v.) and John Norton I (q.v.), Wilson served the First Church of Boston as teacher and then as minister from the church's inception in 1630 until shortly before his death in 1667, a period of thirty-seven years. In his *Memoria Wilsonia*, Cotton Mather (q.v.) called him "a father to the infant colonies of New-England" and later observed that any exact portrait must emphasize his great zeal for "testifying against every thing that he thought offensive unto God" and his great love, which caused him always to be "ready to help and relieve and comfort the distressed," but ever attendant upon his great love and zeal was his unflinching orthodoxy.

This reputation for orthodoxy Wilson earned early in his career. Although he was distinguished for scholarship and learning while at King's College, Cambridge, his inflexibility regarding a formality of ceremony (he refused to genuflect) eventually led to his refusal of a post as fellow at Cambridge. Falling under the influence of Puritan ministers such as Richard Rogers and William Ames, Wilson became increasingly dissatisfied with liberal Anglicanism and eventually determined to sail with John Winthrop (q.v.) to Massachusetts Bay in 1630. Having left his wife, the former Elizabeth Mansfield, in Eng., he returned for her the next year. They sailed back to New Eng. accompanied by many others whom he had persuaded to join the Congregational community. He also carried with him the news that his brother Edmund, who had only recently died, had bequeathed 1,000 pounds to the colony.

Shortly after his return in 1632, Wilson began to work toward the conversion of Mass.'s Indians. The story has often been told of how the Indian prince Sagamore John left the care of his only child to Wilson upon his death. In 1636 Wilson became heavily involved in the founding of Harvard College. He was named an overseer of the college, and Samuel E. Morison identified him as the architect of Old College, the institution's first building. However, even as he worked to establish Harvard, Wilson became embroiled in the Antinomian controversy, which concerned Anne Hutchinson. She publicly denounced "Wilson and other ministers as dangerous and unspiritual preachers." Consequently, she kept Wilson's congregation "constantly convulsed." In 1637 Hutchinson was summoned before a synod of churchmen and expelled from the colony.

Following this controversy, Wilson encountered vicissitudes common to a minister in the wilderness, but none so devisive or threatening to the unity of his congregation. He always opposed enthusiasm or fanaticism and interpreted Quakerism as a type of fanaticism, often preaching against this faith and others that departed from his Puritan orthodoxy. In 1647 he contributed ten volumes to a town library begun at Boston, and in the meantime, one of his daughters, Mary, had married the Rev. Samuel Danforth (q.v.). Mather related that people from far and wide sought out the famous Rev. Wilson "for the enjoyment of his patriarchal benedictions." At another point in his *Memoria*, he praised Wilson for his sincere humility, which he called "the top of all his other excellencies." Throughout Wilson's long service as minister, he also served his parishioners as indefatigable "anagrammatizer." For one so devoted to the form, it is apropos to close with an anagram on Wilson's name made by a gentleman who knew him; this anagram captures the essence of his individual vocation: "Wish no one ill."

Critical Appraisal: Although largely forgotten by today's anthologizers of American poetry, John Wilson enjoyed considerable fame in his own time as a poet, particularly for his anagrams. Most of Wilson's surviving anagrams are brief, no longer than the space comfortably occupying a broadside, and practically all of them treat the deaths of prominent Massachusetts Bay citizens. Some, however, evolve into the length of elegies. The anagram on John Norton I, "Into Honnor," for example, is composed of ninety-eight lines, each a fourteener in which the name of John Norton (often substituting "I" for "J") is spelled. (Note that the title "Into Honnor" also spells Norton's name.) The ingenuity of these lines alone—the anagram is perfect throughout—demands a measure of appreciation. Seizing the opportunity to praise Norton's orthodox opposition to new sects in New Eng., Wilson contrapuntally shaped an anagram on Norton's name at the expense of the Quakers: "Decrying every sect, but most / abhorring Quakerisme."

In a period that has forgotten not only the man but even the art of anagrammatizing, it is unlikely that Wilson will achieve more than casual acknowledgment for his accomplishments in this genre. As a poet of edificatory narrative, however, Wilson must be recognized, at least as the predecessor of Michael Wigglesworth (q.v.). One of his most celebrated poems for young people was the *Song of Deliverance for the Lasting Rememberance of Gods Wonderful Works*, written and printed in 1626 in Eng. but reprinted in Boston in 1680. This long poem renders into verse couplets, fourteeners again, the stories of the Spanish Armada's 1588 assault upon Eng.; the plague of 1603; the infamous Gunpowder Plot of 1605; a disastrous occurrence of 1623 in which most of the members of a Roman Catholic congregation were killed; and finally another plague of 1625. This couplet from the section on the Gunpowder Plot demonstrates that, contrary to some critical opinion, all does not become dross in Wilson's pen, even in a children's poem: "For as their powder was too dry. / (wherein they put their trust), / They saw it was but vanity, / to hope in fickle dust."

If John Wilson, Jr., could be believed when he wrote in the 1680 American edition of *The Song of Deliverance* that his father had composed such a quantity of poetry that it "would questionless make a large folio," then perhaps it is unfair to assess Wilson's poetry on the basis of what is extant. But no less an authority than Cotton Mather suggested that probably the pious would find Wilson's verse more interesting than those who would pass aesthetic judgment on it. Where Wilson appears to have had few equals, however, is in the construction of sermons. Regrettably, only a single example remains from a life in which thousands must have been produced. This single instance, nevertheless, indicates such a mastery of homiletic technique that it warrants extended commentary.

Cotton Mather appears to have been defensive when he related about Wilson's sermons that "In his younger time, he had been used unto a more methodical way of preaching," but later he "gave himself a liberty to preach more after the primitive manner," often performing "extempore sermons." But in one of his last sermons, *A Seasonable Watch-Word unto Christians Against Dreams* (w.1665), Wilson displayed complete command of the form. According to Thomas Thacher's (q.v.) introduction, the sermon was printed ten years after its delivery in response to alarming events perpetrated by several "Dreamers," two of whom were women claiming to have been commanded by God in dreams. One of these women walked through the streets of Cambridge stark naked, and the other seemed to cast evil spells on pregnant women. Some of these "Dreamers" were, said Thacher, Quakers.

In comparison to the lengthy, formal sermons of, say, Wilson's contemporary William Adams (q.v.), this sermon is brief and relatively unencumbered by the machinery of formality. Wilson made no divisions into introduction, doctrine, conclusions, or uses. Yet he clearly followed the prescribed order of homiletics for the day. He opened with the text of Jeremiah 29:8, "let not your Prophets and your Diviners...deceive you, neither hearken to your Dreamers." Next he proceeded to an explication of this text, observing that the people have permitted certain persons "to go about and give it out, as though they were Christ: and how many are ready to hearken to such." Among these persons, Wilson identified Quakers and Ranters as "those that trouble the Churches of God." Following his explication, he derived the doctrine that "Dreamers come, that shall be instrumental of the damnation of the souls of men." For the remainder of the sermon, he applied this doctrine to the members of his congregation in simple and plain metaphors such as the following: "the Lord hath pitty upon his poor people when he sees them thus taken in the net" and "these Dreamers have their soft Pillows to place under mens Elbows, that they may not be hurt by leaning thereon."

Throughout his argument, Wilson repeated the phrase "these and those" so that it becomes a sort of formulaic refrain, always signaling another reference to the false tales of "Dreamers" who are also, of course, false prophets. He employed this refrain first when he spoke of "these and those that would overturn all order among you." He concluded by admonishing his congregation to beware of God's ultimate power, which can and will ferret out all of those who do not love the truth of God's word (the hypocrites) and with an imperative that all repent. Discounting Wilson's religious intolerance, one may easily understand why this minister was held in such high esteem by his fellow New Englanders. His message was simple and straightforward, while the form in which he cast it reflected the maturity and independence of a man who was sure of his own commitment and who possessed the intellectual capacity and pastoral concern to make his message known to his congregation.

For those interested in the historical value of Wilson's sermon, it should be noted that this Puritan patriarch articulated succinctly the purpose for coming to New Eng.; in the center of this homily, Wilson stated, "we came not to separate from the Churches in Old England (God forbid) but we did indeed only separate from the polutions there" and so "that you might have the Ordinances of God in his Churches rightly gathered, and the holy Sacraments rightly administered." Wilson closed this reminder to his congregation with the simple but arresting exclamation: "I trow you did not come hither for the world, to scape the world." The spirit of this remark accords perfectly with that of the entire sermon and suggests Wilson's subtle design to awaken his parish to its shortcomings. Perhaps John Wilson, Sr., would be best remembered as a consummate artist of Puritan homiletics who loved to dabble in the making of poems.

Suggested Readings: CCNE; DAB; FCNEV; LHUS; Sprague (I, 12-15); T$_1$. See also Evert Duyckink and George Duyckinck, Cyclopaedia of American Literature (1881), I, 9n, 51, 64n; Thomas Hutchinson, The History of the Colony and Province of Massachusetts-Bay, ed. Lawrence S. Mayo (1765, 1936), I, 21, 23, 24, 50n, 51, 138, 161, 222, 231, 354, 357n, 393, 423; II, 372, 374, 378; Cotton Mather, Magnalia Christi Americana, ed. Thomas Robbins (1852), I, 79, 236, 247, 302-321; II, 33; Harrison T. Meserole, ed., Seventeenth-Century American Poetry (1968), pp. 217n, 368, 384-386, 389n; Perry Miller and Thomas H. Johnson, eds., The Puritans: A Sourcebook of Their Writings (1963), I, 127, 130-131; II, 499, 547, 549, 553-555, 667; Samuel Eliot Morison, The Founding of Harvard College (1935), pp. 113-115, 173-177, 193, 211n, 224-226, 258, 274, 277, 328, 331-332, 408, 423; idem, The Intellectual Life of Colonial New England (1936), pp. 125, 145, 152, 155n, 169, 212n; Kenneth B. Murdock, Handkerchiefs from Paul (1927), pp. xvi, xxxii, xxxiv, xli-lix, lxiii, lxv, lxxiii, 7-9, 12-14, 22-97, 116, 117, 120-130; Edward K. Rand, "John Wilson's Latin Verses on John Harvard," HGM, 42 (1933), 41-46; "Wilson, John," The National Cyclopaedia, XX, 98-99 (and in "Hutchinson, Anne," IX, 148). Jantz (FCNEV), Meserole, and Miller and Johnson print selections of Wilson's verse.

John C. Shields
Illinois State University

EDWARD MARIA WINGFIELD (c. 1560-c. 1613)

Works: A Discourse of Virginia (w. 1608; pub. 1860).

Biography: An experienced Elizabethan soldier and member of a prominent Catholic family in Eng., Edward Maria Wingfield was a leading figure in the group awarded the Va. charter in 1606. When the first 144 colonists sailed for

Va. in Dec. 1606, Wingfield, alone among the holders of the charter, accompanied them. Soon after the expedition reached Va., Wingfield was elected the first president of the Jamestown colony. His five-month tenure as president was marred by intrigue and strife among the colony's leaders, and he was removed from office by the Council, which included Capt. John Smith (q.v.). Although Wingfield and Smith shared a military background, they had little else in common. Lacking Smith's initiative and flair for action, Wingfield seems to have been a more gentle man who was out of place in the harsh environment of the New World. "I never desired to enamel my name in blood," he remarked in his *Discourse*. As president, Wingfield was an ineffectual leader faced by nearly insurmountable problems, including the colonists' own ineptitude, lack of food and supplies, widespread disease, and continual bickering. Nearly half of the colonists died during Wingfield's presidency. Returning to Eng. in 1608, Wingfield retained an interest in the Va. experiment. When the second charter of 1609 was granted, he was a substantial investor. He is last heard of in 1613, living in Stoneley, Eng.

Critical Appraisal: Most of *A Discourse of Virginia* consists of a journal describing the events at Jamestown between Jun. 1607 and Apr. 1608 and defending Wingfield's performance as president. A short preface, possibly written by someone other than Wingfield, and a concluding section in which Wingfield particularly defends himself against his detractors complete the work. Although written in Eng., the *Discourse* is probably based on a diary kept at Jamestown.

Wingfield's *Discourse* is of considerable historical interest, especially if read in conjunction with John Smith's more famous narratives. As a historian and a stylist, Wingfield was a cultured and well-informed observer and writer. In style and tone, his energetic self-defense reflects the peculiar mixture of pettiness and Elizabethan grandeur that characterized the Jamestown expedition, as well as the tensions in early seventeenth-century English society. A wealthy Catholic from a respectable family, Wingfield had to prove his equality in extremity (that is, "The corn was of the same which we all lived upon") and his patriotism to Protestant Eng. His defense, like his actions, ended in implicit confidence, as he noted that "the greatest monarchies of Asia and Europe," including Israel, Rome, Sp., and Eng., also began in hardship and strife. Thus the little colony of Jamestown, where, according to Wingfield, men quarreled over pocketknives and squirrel meat, is seen as a possible future seat of empire, and the grasp of imagination that eventually led to the settling of the West and the establishment of a national democracy became evident as early as 1608.

Suggested Readings: DAB; DNB; LHUS. *See also* Edward Arber and A. G. Bradley, eds., *Travels and Works of Captain John Smith*, 2 vols. (1910); Alexander Brown, *The Genesis of the United States* (1891), I, 170-172; II, 1055; Howard Mumford Jones, *The Literature of Virginia in the Seventeenth Century*, 2nd ed. (1968), pp. 21-23; Richard L. Morton, *Colonial Virginia* (1960), I, 4-14. The best edition of *A Discourse of Virginia* is in Philip L. Barbour, ed., *The Jamestown Colony Under the First Charter, 1606-1609* (1969), I, 213-234.

Douglas R. Wilmes
The Pennsylvania State University

EDWARD WINSLOW (1595-1655)

Works: *A Relation or Iournall of the Beginning and Proceedings of the English Plantation Setled at Plimoth in New England* (with William Bradford et al.; 1622), commonly known as *Mourt's Relation; Good Newes from New-England: Or, A True Relation of Things Very Remarkable at the Plantation of Plimoth* (1624); *Hypocrisie Unmasked by a True Relation of the Proceedings of the Governour and Company of the Massachusetts Against Samuel Gorton* (1646); *New-Englands Salamander, Discovered by an Irreligious and Scornfull Pamphlet, Called New-Englands Jonas Cast up at London* (1647); *The Glorious Progress of the Gospel, Amongst the Indians in New England* (1649).

Biography: Edward Winslow was born in Droitwich, Worcestershire, Eng., in 1595, of propertied and educated parents. Well-educated himself and resourceful, as his writings and accomplishments demonstrate, he was one of the four men—the others were Miles Standish, William Brewster, and William Bradford (q.v.)—to whom the survival of the Plymouth colony may be chiefly credited. While in Leyden, Hol., as a traveler, Winslow became associated with the group of English Separatists of whom John Robinson was pastor and among whom were a number of the future settlers of Plymouth. Remaining in Hol., Winslow found employment as a printer, and in 1618 he married Elizabeth Barker. In 1620 he sailed on the *Mayflower* to North America.

On the ship's arrival at Cape Cod, Winslow took part in the explorations that ended with the selection of Plymouth Harbor as the site of the permanent settlement. In Mar. 1621 Winslow's wife died, and the following May, he married the widow Susanna White—the colony's first marriage. During the first years after settlement, he proved eminently successful in dealings and negotiations with the Indians, upon whose friendliness the very existence of the colony depended. Many of these activities are recorded by Winslow himself in *Mourt's Relation* and in *Good Newes from New-England*, the latter of which he published in 1624 while on a visit to Eng. as agent for Plymouth Plantation. In 1624, also, he was elected one of the five assistants to Governor Bradford, a position he held until 1633 and during a number of years thereafter. In 1633, 1636, and 1644, he served as governor of the colony. Representing the interests of Plymouth and later Massachusetts Bay, he voyaged several more times to Eng., where on one occasion he was imprisoned by Archbishop Laud for having, as a layman, performed in the Plymouth church functions permissible only to ordained priests.

In 1646 Winslow, who had been instrumental in founding the New England Confederation, was induced to travel once again to Eng.—this time never to return—to defend the colony of Massachusetts Bay against accusations made against it by the religious radical Samuel Gorton (q.v.). During this controversy, he published in London *Hypocrisie Unmasked* (1646) and *New England's Salamander* (1647). In 1649, still in London, he published *The Glorious Progress of the Gospel Amongst the Indians in New England*. In his last years, he was in the service of Cromwell's government, being appointed, in 1655, chief commissioner of an expedition to seize the Spanish W.Ind. for the British. After a disastrous defeat at Santo Domingo, Winslow died of fever on shipboard and was buried at sea.

Critical Appraisal: Edward Winslow is best known today for his contributions to *Mourt's Relation* and for his *Good Newes from New-England*, books that provide accounts of the first two and a half years of Plymouth Plantation as observed and experienced by leading participants in the venture. In *Mourt's Relation* Winslow is generally recognized as the author of the promotional "A Letter from New England" (signed "E. W.") and of all of the narrative sections except the first, which is commonly attributed to William Bradford. The writing in both these books is fast paced, vivid, and—with the exception of occasional syntactical obscurities—as readable today as it must have been to interested Englishmen of the early seventeenth century. Winslow had two closely related purposes in these volumes. One was to satisfy the curiosity of his fellow countrymen concerning the progress of English colonization in America—to give "a full and true narration." But he was not content merely to record events; he also attempted to supply more general information. Thus in the concluding pages of *Good Newes*, he discussed the religion, customs, and manners of the Indians and described in surprisingly favorable terms the weather, soil, and "production" of New Eng. In these pages is reflected Winslow's second and, perhaps, main purpose—that of encouraging and reassuring prospective immigrants. Yet in this respect, Winslow was honest and realistic. His picture of living conditions in Plymouth during the first two and a half years was somewhat rosier than the facts warranted, but he did not conceal the threats of famine and Indian hostility, and he strongly emphasized that no one should expect to find an easy life and instant prosperity in New Eng. The would-be colonist should realize that the chief end of the American colonies was to enhance the glory of God and the honor of Eng. Financial profit, he assured his readers, was a possibility, but it should not be the main motive for emigration. Those who, like Thomas Weston of Wessagusset, made profit their sole motive would be sorely disappointed and would meet with probable failure.

After an interval of twenty-three years, during which no writing by Winslow appeared in print, his third book, *Hypocrisie Unmasked*, was published in London in 1646. Writing in refutation of charges made against Massachusetts Bay by Samuel Gorton in a pamphlet titled *Simplicities Defence Against Seven-Headed Policy* (1646), Winslow displayed skill and thoroughness as a controversialist. Gorton's grievances were that the Mass. government had illegally driven him from his lands in R.I. and had brought him to trial in Boston and sentenced him to prison for defying the magistrates and vilifying the clergy. Winslow answered the specific charges point by point, but his main concern, like that of his colonial sponsors, was Gorton's anticlericalism and his scorn of civil authority. Gorton was a religious sectarian, variously branded as an Antinomian, a Familist, and a Leveler, who expressed his frequently incoherent views vociferously and insultingly but whose following of a dozen or so in no way posed a threat to the governments of New Eng., which he correctly accused of a civil and political intolerance contrary to the laws of Eng. Winslow, who was of one mind with Governors John Winthrop (q.v.) and Bradford in deploring a burgeoning spirit of toleration in New Eng. in the 1640s, saw in Gorton an embodiment of forces destructive of the colonies' continued well-being. Thus his talents as a polemicist were employed in a cause with which most historians have had little sympathy. Indeed, the Puritan commissioners in Eng. who heard Gorton's case decided in his favor and restored his R.I. lands to him.

In 1647 Winslow again came to the defense of the New Eng. governments against accusations of intolerance and a disregard for the laws of Eng. In a brief tract, *New-Englands Salamander*, he wrote a spirited, if not entirely convincing, rejoinder to a pamphlet in which one John Child recorded the mistreatment of his brother and William Vassal by the magistrates and clergy of New Eng. Child not only dealt with specific instances but repeated Gorton's general strictures against the high-handedness of the Mass. and Plymouth authorities; in a postscript, he assailed Winslow's *Hypocrisie Unmasked*, in which he discerned "a deep and subtle Plot against the Lawes of *England*." Aside from the amusement provided by the vituperative ferocity with which the adversaries in this controversy attacked each other, these pamphlets make tedious reading. They have, however, historical value, and those of Gorton and Child are significant as evidence of an early stirring of the movement toward religious and civil liberty that was to burst forth in the next 175 years.

Winslow's final literary effort was the editing of *The Glorious Progress of the Gospel Amongst the Indians in New England*. The body of this booklet consists of four letters—one from Thomas Mayhew (q.v.) of Martha's Vineyard and three from John Eliot (q.v.) of Massachusetts Bay—and an appendix by an English clergyman identified by the initials "J. D." The letters contain accounts of successes in converting the Native Americans. The appendix applauds these successes and presents arguments in support of the belief, commonly held at that time, that the Indians were descended from the lost tribes of Israel. Winslow's contribution was a dedicatory epistle addressed to the English Parliament and introductory notes to the letters. This pamphlet shares, with several others published on the subject about the same time, the credit for the creation of the Society for the Propagation of the Gospel in New England, of which Winslow was one of the founders.

Suggested Readings: DAB; LHUS; T$_1$. *See also* William Bradford, *History of Plymouth Plantation*, ed. W. C. Ford (1912), passim; Jacob Bailey Moore, *Lives of the Governors of New Plymouth and Massachusetts Bay* (1851), pp. 93-138; Nathaniel Morton, *New-Englands Memoriall* (1669); Bradford Smith, *Bradford of Plymouth* (1951), passim; George F. Willison, *Saints and Strangers* (1945), passim.

Perry D. Westbrook
State University of New York at Albany

JOHN WINTHROP (1588-1649)

Works: "A Modell of Christian Charity" (1630); *A Short Story* (1644); *A Declaration of Former Passages* (1645); James Savage, ed., *The History of New England*, 2 vols. (1825-1826); Allyn B. Forbes, ed., *The Winthrop Papers*, 5 vols. (1929-1947).

Biography: In the spring of 1630, John Winthrop began his voyage to Mass. as part of what would come to be called "The Great Migration." The decision to leave Eng. had not come easily. Winthrop led a comfortable life as the squire of Groton, Suffolk, and had held a post in London as an attorney in the Court of Wards. However, perhaps during the years at Cambridge, he had become a Puritan, and the position of Puritans was becoming increasingly difficult. Meeting with other Puritan leaders at Tattershall Castle, Lincolnshire, Winthrop participated in the organization of the Massachusetts Bay Company and was later elected the first governor of the colony. About the time he began his voyage on the flagship *Arbella*, Winthrop, who had inherited the habit of diary keeping from his father, began a diary that he continued almost until his death. Winthrop served as governor or deputy governor of the colony for twelve of the nineteen years of the diary, and even when he did not hold such a post, he remained one of the most important men in Mass. Dealing with crises such as the Antinomian controversy, he played an important part in most of the major events in the colony and helped to set policies on government, economics, and religion. His legal and administrative skills contributed to the success of the colony and his opinions toward its early direction. As Winthrop represented the essential spirit of Puritan New Eng., it is fitting that Hawthorne should have chosen the night of his death for a central scene in *The Scarlet Letter*.

Critical Appraisal: One of Winthrop's most important pieces of writing is "A Modell of Christian Charity," a sermon that he wrote for delivery on board the *Arbella* on arrival at New Eng. This sermon stated certain crucial assumptions about the ideal social order and argued that the colonists had made a covenant with God to undertake what Perry Miller, borrowing from Samuel Danforth's (q.v.) 1670 election sermon, termed an "errand into the wilderness" to "establish a society in conformity with those assumptions. Winthrop believed that such a society could be a "city on a hill," a model for the rest of the world, and warned against the failure to fulfill this covenant. Some of Winthrop's assumptions, such as the perpetuation of the relatively stable hierarchical class system that had existed in Europe, did not hold up well on the New Eng. frontier; however, many of the ideas he expressed have been vital to American literature and intellectual history. For example, his ideas on charity appear again in the late nineteenth century in discussions of the stewardship of wealth; his warnings against deserting spiritual goals to seek material gain "for ourselves and our posterity" are reflected in the writings of the Transcendentalists; and the belief that American society should serve as a model for the world has long been a widespread belief.

Winthrop is now generally considered the probable author of most of *A Short Story of the Rise, Reign and Ruin of the Antinomians*, originally published anonymously with the note on the title page that it was "published...by one that was an eye and eare-witnesse." This work is composed of several sections including: "A Catalogue of...Erroneous Opinions" with a "confutation" for each of eighty-two "errors," a section on "Unsavory Speeches Confuted," an account of a "monstrous" fetus, and a defense of court proceedings. However, most of the material consists of accounts of the trials by the "Generall Court" and the church of Boston of Anne Hutchinson and others of her group. Derived from trial records, these accounts go beyond simple history. Winthrop seems to have relied heavily on transcripts of these events in creating his narrative, which sometimes presents a version of the dialog between Hutchinson and members of the court. Winthrop tried to present this material to support his own position against the Antinomians, but in remaining true to his materials, he produced a different result than he intended. Instead of warning Eng. against the dangers of Antinomianism, the book aided opponents of New Eng. Puritanism.

Winthrop's *Journal*, published under the title *The History of New England*, remains one of the most important American diaries. The entries are full and kept regularly for nearly two decades. One unusual feature of the diary is that Winthrop, probably to assume a pose of objectivity, usually referred to himself in the third person. This pose proved especially effective when Winthrop was treating the many controversies in which he was involved. Just as the Puritan spiritual journal might be kept as a way to examine one's life for evidence of salvation, so Winthrop's historical journal served to provide evidence of God's plan for New Eng. Winthrop used his entries to demonstrate how events revealed God's providential lessons and justice: A mouse that killed a snake was taken as a divine prophecy that the poor New Eng. Puritans would "overcome Satan here and dispossess him of his kingdom," and a drowning was declared to be God's punishment for sin. The great variety of such events showed Winthrop's conviction of the integration of all things in God's world; he found a place for minor actions alongside the affairs of state. In this way, Winthrop created a portrait of New Eng.'s spirit as well as its physical development.

Suggested Readings: DAB; DARB; LHUS; T₁. *See also* David D. Hall, ed., *The Antinomian Controversy* (1968); Steven E. Kagle, *American Diary Literature* (1979), pp. 143-147; Perry Miller, *Errand into the Wilderness* (1956), pp. 1-15, 141-152; idem, *The New England Mind* (1953); Edmund Morgan, *The Puritan Dilemma: The Story of John Winthrop* (1958); Samuel Eliot Morison, *Builders of the Bay Colony* (1930), pp. 51-104; Robert C. Winthrop, *The Life and Letters of John Winthrop*, 2 vols. (1864-1867). "A Model of Christian Charity" is included in Allyn B. Forbes, ed., *The Winthrop Papers* (1929-1947).

Steven E. Kagle
Illinois State University

JOHN WINTHROP, JR. (1606-1676)

Works: Except for letters, reports, and commentaries published much later as parts of certain edited "papers" and "collections," no fully substantiated works of the younger John Winthrop are available in printed form. He may never have produced anything with the intent of publication.

Biography: Born in Groton, Suffolk, Eng., in 1606, John Winthrop, Jr., was the eldest son of the better known John Winthrop (q.v.) (1588-1649). His formal education was extensive: at the King Edward VI School, Bury St. Edmunds; at Trinity College, Dublin; and at the Inner Temple, London. But he took no degree and was never admitted to the bar; he clearly suffered in his earlier years from a lack of staying power. However, after 1629, he proved an effective aide to his father in the development of the Massachusetts Bay Company, both in Eng. and America. In Mass. he served for a number of years as a member of the Council of Assistants and was delegated (1633-1634) to superintend the founding of the outlying settlement at Ipswich. He likewise oversaw (1643-1645) the establishment of the ill-starred ironworks at Braintree.

In 1646 he founded, on his own, New London, Conn., and beginning in 1657 served at Hartford as governor of the Conn. colony almost continuously until his death. A consummate politician, he negotiated (in Eng.) the extraordinarily liberal Conn. charter of 1662 and played an influential role in the English acquisition of New Neth. in 1664. Although the leader of a Puritan colony, he was fundamentally disinterested in religious controversy and concerned himself for many years with scientific matters; these matters included, in the fashion of the period, a wide variety of interests, such as medicine, astronomy, experimental agriculture, shipbuilding, botany, theories of money, weather phenomena, and what now is termed oceanography. He was the first colonial to be made a member of the Royal Society, enjoyed a wide correspondence with European *savants*, and developed a remarkable personal library. He died in harness, as Conn.'s representative to the United Colonies of New Eng., in Boston in 1676.

Critical Appraisal: John Winthrop, Jr., was an entrepreneur, an administrator, and a politician and also a devotee of natural philosophy, political and economic theory, and (sometimes) the occult. A good deal of his correspondence and appertaining documents are to be found in printed sources such as Allyn B. Forbes, ed., *Winthrop Papers* (Volumes II-V) and the *Collections* of the Massachusetts and Connecticut Historical Societies, but many more have not been published. (Most of them are at the Massachusetts Historical Society.) His writings, generally, served practical purposes—personal, public, and "scientific." He attempted no "belles-lettres." Winthrop's correspondence, both published and unpublished, is full of references to his activities as an amateur physician, in particular to his favorite prescription, a violent purgative he called "rubila." In his later years, he forwarded numerous reports to the Royal Society on the natural history of New Eng.

His comments upon public matters are of considerable historical interest. His "thought" was mixed. It was both progressive and traditional; he would have delighted Thomas Jefferson (q.v.), especially with his observations of natural phenomena and his unusual opinions upon military armaments (he advocated restraint) and the virtues of cheap money. Yet he was accepted in his own time by the European alchemical community. He was an acquaintance of Drs. Abraham and Johann Sibert Kuffler, whose real specialty was alchemy, but of even greater significance was his association with and sponsorship of a young "adept" named George Starkey (q.v.). It even has been proposed that Winthrop was the legendary "Eirenaeus Philalethes" (Peaceful Lover of Truth), who dominated the alchemical world of the midseventeenth century. His numerous reports to the Royal Society in London were often perceptive, sometimes imaginative, and occasionally naive.

Winthrop's aptitudes simply did not embrace theology: he accepted the orthodox Puritan position, but with a studied unconcern. In 1672, under pressure from the relentless R.I. Quaker William Coddington, he declared himself "in the firm belief of those truths of the holy Scriptures, which are not of any private interpretation," but there is no evidence that he ever personally participated in the theological arguments so beloved by the Puritan establishment. He rejected contemporary notions of witchcraft. On the other hand, he was never prepared to deny the existence of the supernatural: to the Royal Society he indicated, with a straight face, that the waterspouts of tropical latitudes were "blown up by some sea monster," and he suggested that the New Eng. wheat blight of the late 1660s might have been caused by "blasting from heaven."

In the area of politics, his papers reveal a man of extraordinary gifts. He instinctively recognized those things that were impracticable, was a genius of manipulation, and pushed home his policies (in particular, Conn.'s engulfment of New Haven and the English conquest of New Neth.) when the opposition was obviously helpless. Yet he abhorred violence and was of so genial a nature that he retained the goodwill of nearly all of those whom he had outwitted.

Suggested Readings: BDAS; DAB; T$_1$. *See also* Robert M. Benton, "The John Winthrops and Developing Scientific Thought in New England," EAL, 7 (1973), 272-280; Robert C. Black III, *The Younger John Winthrop* (1966); idem, "The Younger John Winthrop, Precursor of the Scientific Enlightenment" in *The Ibero-American Enlightenment*, ed. A. Owen Aldridge (1971); C. A. Browne, "Scientific Notes...of John Winthrop, Jr.," *Isis*, 11 (1928), 325-342; Richard S. Dunn, "John Winthrop, Jr., and the Narragansett Country," WMQ, 3rd ser., 13 (1956), 68-86; idem, *Puritans and Yankees, the Winthrop Dynasty of New England* (1962); E. N. Hartley, *Ironworks on the Saugus* (1957); Walter R. Steiner, M.D., "Governor John Winthrop, Jr.,...as a Physician," *The Connecticut Magazine*, 11 (1907), 25-42; R. S. Wilkinson, "The Alchemical Library of John Winthrop, Jr.," *Ambix*, 11 (1963), 33-51; idem, "The Problem of the Identity of Eirenaeous Philalethes," *Ambix*, 12; (1964), 24-43.

Robert C. Black III
Colorado Women's College

JOHN WINTHROP (1714-1779)

Works: *A Lecture on Earthquakes* (1755); *A Letter to the Publisher of the Boston Gazette* (1756); *Two Lectures on Comets* (1759); *Relation of a Voyage from Boston to New Foundland for the Observation of the Transit of Venus* (1761); *Two Lectures on the Parallax and Distance of the Sun* (1769).

Biography: Born in Boston on Dec. 19, 1714, and baptized by Cotton Mather (q.v.), John Winthrop was but one of the sixteen children of Adam and Anne (Wainwright) Winthrop. Adam Winthrop, a colonial magistrate, was the great-great-grandson of John Winthrop (1588-1649) (q.v.), first governor of the Massachusetts Bay colony. Several Winthrops shared John's interest in and affinity for science. His great-granduncle, also named John Winthrop (1606-1676) (q.v.), is considered to be the first American industrial chemist, became the first fellow of the Royal Society from America in 1663, and served as governor of Conn. Yet another John Winthrop, a cousin, was a geologist, paleontologist, and fellow of the Royal Society (elected 1734).

John Winthrop graduated from the Boston Latin School at the age of 14 in 1728 and entered Harvard College, leaving with an A.B. four years later. He spent the next six years at home, studying science until, in 1738, he became the second Hollis professor of mathematics and natural philosophy at Harvard. Candidates for professorship at that time had to undergo an examination by the overseers of the college. The committee usually investigated the candidate's religious devotion, but this issue was avoided at Winthrop's hearing, it being assumed that his views would be liberal and better left ignored. Winthrop, however, was no atheist. Years later, in his *Lectures on Comets*, he referred to God as the "All-wise Author of nature" who creates such effects as comets "to rouse mankind."

Winthrop held his professorship until his death over forty years later. During this time, he produced his great research in astronomy—publishing his findings in the *Philosophical Transactions of the Royal Society*, influencing both Benjamin Franklin (q.v.) and Count Rumford, and becoming recognized in both the colonies and in Eng. as an outstanding scientist and scholar. He not only instructed classes of Harvard students, but gave public lectures and demonstrations of the workings of the physical sciences as well.

Winthrop's first major project was a record of observations of sunspot activity made between Apr. 19 and 22, 1739. This is believed to be the first group of such studies made in Mass., if not in America, and the records are now kept at the Harvard Library. Winthrop supplemented information gathered from his own extensive scientific library with communications received from colleagues at the Royal Observatory at Greenwich and the Royal Society. During the transits of Mercury over the sun in 1740, 1743, and 1769, Winthrop studied the problems of determining the exact longitude between Cambridge (Mass.) and London, the equation of time, and the Newtonian laws of gravitation. In 1746 he set up the first laboratory for the study of experimental physics in America at Harvard. There he lectured on and demonstrated the laws of heat, light, and mechanics and the Newtonian doctrines of the movements of celestial bodies. It was also in this laboratory that Benjamin Thompson (later Count Rumford) attended Winthrop's lectures.

Winthrop made American mathematical history in 1751 by introducing "elements of fluxions" (now called differential and integral calculus) to the Harvard curriculum. His study of the New Eng. earthquake of Nov. 18, 1755 (*A Lecture on Earthquakes*), was attacked by Rev. Thomas Prince (q.v.) of Boston, who feared the clash between Winthrop's theories and orthodox theology. Winthrop's reply, *A Letter to the Publisher of the Boston Gazette*, denied any conflict between his observations and theistic religion. His theories on seismic activity are now regarded as being far ahead of their time.

In 1759, during a lecture, Winthrop made the first-known scientifically based prediction of the return of a comet. The comet was Halley's Comet, which had last appeared in 1682. Winthrop used as substantiation for his prediction an amalgam of Newton's theories from the *Principia*, Kepler's laws, and Halley's own observations. Then in 1761 he began elaborate preparations to observe the transits of Venus in that year and in 1769, including an expedition to St. John's, Newfoundland, jointly sponsored by Harvard and the colony of Mass., to observe and study the parallax of the sun. This was, if not the first organized scientific expedition in the colonies, certainly the first sponsored by a college or a colonial government.

John Winthrop's other scientific endeavors involved a wide range of scientific activity, including serving as a major support to Franklin in his studies of electricity, carrying on observations and studies of magnetism and meteorology for over twenty years, and studying the physical appearance of Venus, eclipses of Jupiter's satellites, partial solar eclipses, and the aberration of light. He was elected as a fellow of the Royal Society in 1766 and became a member of the American Philosophical Society in 1769. Although Winthrop was not a founder of the American Academy of Arts and Sciences in 1769, the idea for the organization is attributed to him. Among Winthrop's other honors are honorary doctor of laws degrees from the University of Edinburgh in 1771 and from Harvard in 1773. The Harvard degree was the first honorary doctor of laws given by that institution.

Winthrop was serving as probate judge of Middlesex County when, in 1769, he was appointed to the colony Council. He was removed by royal authorities for his opposition to granting colonial rights to Parliament. During the Revolution, Winthrop sided ardently with the Revolutionaries, numbering George Washington (q.v.) and Franklin among his friends. He died before the end of the war, on May 3, 1779, in Cambridge and was buried among other Winthrops in the Old King's Chapel Burying-Ground in Boston. He was hailed as a scientist widely honored in his fields—as a physicist, a mathematician, and America's first astronomer, seismologist, and Newtonian disciple. He pioneered the scientific method in America, contributing both his observations and experiments to the study of physics. He was also among the first to study the activity of comets and meteors. Finally, he established Harvard as a center for scientific research.

Winthrop married Rebecca Townsend in 1746. After her death in 1753, he married Hannah Fayerweather Tolman in 1756. She, along with several children from his first wife, survived him. Among these children was James Winthrop (1752-1821), eccentric Mass. jurist, Harvard librarian from 1772 to 1787, and author of *An Attempt to Translate Part of the Apocalypse of St. John into Familiar Language* (1794).

Critical Appraisal: John Winthrop's first published work was *A Lecture on Earthquakes*, a lecture given on Nov. 26, 1755, only eight days after an earthquake had suddenly rocked New Eng.'s pious Calvinists from their sleep in the middle of the night. Using both theories and quickly gathered observations (his own and others'), Winthrop attempted to explain what happened and why. He described earthquakes as being composed of both vertical and lateral motion of the earth and studied the nature of the New Eng. earthquake by measuring the distance falling bodies (such as church steeples) fell. Although he believed earthquakes were most frequent in areas of volcanic activity, due to their being caused by subterranean heat for the most part, any place was prone to them. He described in great detail his theories on the roles that such heat, along with electricity, and iron deposits might play in earthquakes and stated that they generally seem to travel from northwest to southeast. His deductions of seismic activity were perhaps primitive, but portions of them have been borne out by subsequent observations, and he is regarded as a pioneer in the field of seismology.

Winthrop's earthquake lectures prompted an attack by the Rev. Thomas Prince of Boston, who in 1727 had written *Earthquakes the Works of God and Tokens of His Just Displeasure*. Oddly enough, electricity entered into Rev. Prince's views also. He ascribed earthquakes to the prevalent and ungodly use of lightning rods that direct the electric current into the ground. Winthrop defended his premises and his own religious belief (God—not just the Deists' clockmaker, but a Present Force—is present in his scientific view) in his *A Letter to the Publisher of the Boston Gazette*. Winthrop's reconciliation of his religious and scientific views is well discussed by Louis Graham.

Winthrop's lectures on comets (including his Halley's Comet lecture) and the solar parallax and his account of his expedition to Newfoundland to observe the transit of Venus also exhibit a lively scholarly style without too much technicality that is understandable to the educated layman. His theories are sensible, often quaint and amusing in hindsight, but always valuable in serving as examples of the eighteenth-century scientific Enlightenment sprouting in the New World.

Suggested Readings: BDAS; DAB; Sibley-Shipton (IX, 240-264). *See also* E. Scott Barr, "Anniversaries in 1964 of Interest to Physicists," AJP, 32 (1964), 291-292; Robert M. Benton, "The John Winthrops and Developing Scientific Thought in New England," EAL, 7 (1973), 272-280; Louis Graham, "The Scientific Piety of John Winthrop of Harvard," NEQ, 46 (1973), 112-118; PMHS, 15 (1876), 11-13; Clifford K.

Shipton, *New England Life in the Eighteenth Century* (1973). See also the sermon by Samuel Langdon, the oration by Stephen Sewall, and the discourse by Edward Wigglesworth (q.v.) (all 1779) delivered upon Winthrop's death.

Randal Owen
St. Mary's Dominican College

WILLIAM WIRT (1772-1834)

Works: *The Letters of the British Spy* (1803); *The Rainbow; First Series* (1804); *The Old Bachelor* (1814); *Sketches of the Life and Character of Patrick Henry* (1817).

Biography: William Wirt, one of the best-known and best-liked lawyers of his day, rose from humble beginnings to become the friend and confidant of four presidents. Born in Bladensburg, Md., the youngest of six children of a Swiss immigrant tavern keeper and orphaned at 8 years of age, he received a Classical grammar school education, studied law, and moved at the age of 21 to Culpepper Court House in Va. to set up practice. In northern Va., the witty, charming, handsome young lawyer became the friend of important men such as James Madison (q.v.), James Monroe, and Thomas Jefferson (q.v.) and married Mildred, the daughter of the influential Dr. George Gilmer and sister of Francis Walker Gilmer. After Mildred's death in 1799, Wirt moved to Richmond and, in 1802, married Elizabeth Gamble, daughter of a wealthy merchant.

During the remainder of his career in Va., Wirt became one of the most notable of a remarkable group of Richmond lawyers and served in positions such as clerk of the House of Delegates, delegate, and chancellor for eastern Va., until Monroe appointed him attorney general of the U.S. in 1817—a post he held until Jackson entered the presidency in 1829. Wirt earned a wide reputation as an orator and lawyer during the famous James Callender libel trial of 1800 and the Aaron Burr trial of 1807, a reputation he increased in several landmark Supreme Court cases while attorney general. He was generally considered one of the greatest orators of his day. In fact, Congress invited him to deliver the eulogy for Jefferson and John Adams (q.v.) at their deaths in 1826. Wirt was Jefferson's choice to be the first president of the University of Virginia but declined the post.

A man who never liked public life because, as he put it, his "skin was too thin," Wirt retired in 1829 and settled in Baltimore, where he became an intimate friend of his future biographer, the novelist John Pendleton Kennedy. His strong opposition to Jackson's reelection prompted Wirt in 1832 to accept the presidential nomination of the Anti-Masonic party, but he carried only the state of Vt. He died two years later.

Critical Appraisal: The central figure among Va. writers between about 1803 and 1817, William Wirt was for many years regarded as perhaps the chief southern man of letters. He enjoyed a national reputation for his familiar essays and his biography of Patrick Henry, but he also wrote some poetry and at least one manuscript play, "The Path of Pleasure." In addition, his letters are excellent examples of the letter-writing art and vitally important sources of information about men and events of the period. Not only was Wirt recognized as one of the great orators of his day; he was also one of the three ablest southern writers of the period on the subject of American oratory or eloquence—along with Francis Walker Gilmer and St. George Tucker (q.v.). It might be well to note that Wirt's entire literary career spanned the brief period of fourteen years from 1803 to 1817, the year of his appointment as attorney general.

In a state that had bred prolific and skillful writers of the familiar essay for a hundred years, Wirt was the main stimulus of a group of professional men who were the best-known essayists of their period. Wirt was the moving force and chief contributor to three newspaper essay series that were republished in book form—*The Letters of the British Spy* (1803), *The Rainbow; First Series* (1804), and *The Old Bachelor* (1814). As an essayist, Wirt was clearly a transition figure, for he was attracted both to the sentiment, antiquarianism, and soaring rhetoric of Romanticism and to eighteenth-century rationalism, satire, and moral didacticism. The essays and the frame of a group of writers with tag names are modeled on the *Spectator*, but Wirt's style partakes of the new Romanticism. Indeed, one of the most dominant elements of the essays of this man who was moved to tears by certain musical sounds is the penchant toward sentimentality.

During Aug. and Sept. of 1803, Wirt published ten essays in the *Virginia Argus* using the persona of a British traveler writing letters to a friend in Eng. These essays were republished in book form the same fall under the title *The Letters of the British Spy*, a book that earned Wirt a national reputation and established the first southern reputation in belles lettres. The book had gone through ten editions by 1832, including a London edition, and had spawned several imitators as far away as Boston and Tennessee. Employing the letter form of the essay, the most popular form of the familiar essay in eighteenth-century southern gazettes, Wirt was writing in a tradition that eighteenth-century writers such as Montesquieu, Walpole, and Goldsmith had found useful for purposes ranging from moral instruction to polemics. Wirt's chief concern in the essays is Va.'s (read the South's) declining part in shaping the nation; he saw no new generation emerging that was equal to the Revolutionary giants. Throughout the ten essays he suggested, in reference to Va.'s past, what could be done to restore Va. to her former place of leadership in the nation—primarily through education, especially in eloquence. Such writing places Wirt firmly in one tradition in southern writing that has endured to our time, the abiding interest in the past and its relationship with the present and the regional patriotism that is prepossessed with the region and its place in contemporary America.

Soon after the *British Spy* appeared, Wirt and his friends organized the Rainbow Association, with ten members who, using pseudonyms, published a series of essays in the Richmond *Enquirer* between Aug. and Oct. 1804. Although the series continued, only ten essays appeared in book form. As in the *British Spy*, the main concern of the essays is the improvement of a new generation for the benefit of Va. The Rainbow essays are thoughtful, restrained, and generally competent.

Between Dec. 1810 and Dec. 1811, Wirt and his circle published twenty-eight essays in the *Enquirer*, with five more following in 1813 and all thirty-three appearing in book form in 1814. Again the group used pseudonyms with a central figure, Dr. Robert Cecil, the Old Bachelor. It is generally agreed that Wirt did the lion's share of the writing and that *The Old Bachelor* essays represent his best work, although they never were as popular as the *British Spy*. Indeed, Richard Beale Davis has cited this collection as the high watermark of the familiar essay in the early nineteenth century in Va. and in some respects in the whole nation. The purpose, again, was to instruct a rising generation to restore the fallen state of the intellect in Va., and the most frequent subjects are education and eloquence. In *The Old Bachelor*, Wirt's earlier nostalgic sentiments concerning Va.'s lost glory had developed into a pervasive sentimentalism, with an even stronger insistence that education, especially eloquence, was needed to restore Va. to its national leadership.

Unfortunately for his literary reputation, Wirt has been best remembered in the twentieth century for his *Sketches of the Life and Character of Patrick Henry* (1817), a biography that has been attacked, sometimes unjustly, by twentieth-century critics. As early as 1804, Wirt had expressed a desire to be "an American Plutarch" by writing a series of sketches of famous Virginians, including Patrick Henry. Over the years, however, Wirt settled on Henry as the model to hold up to contemporary youth, the American success story. The book enjoyed an instant popular success that continued for half a century, appearing in its 15th edition in 1859.

From a critical point of view, the book is not good biography, because a great deal is omitted and a great deal is distorted or slanted. If one considers Wirt's purpose in writing the book, however, it is a successful piece of literature and, in addition, not guilty of all of the sins of which it has been accused. John Taylor of Caroline (q.v.) pointed up the essential nature of the work when he called it "a splendid novel." Wirt's picture of colonial Va.'s aristocracy is far too grand; his portrait of Henry as a backwoods child of nature whose only real assets were a high moral character and a talent for oratory is not accurate. But Wirt wanted to develop the contrast that would show the humble, simple young man rising, largely through his eloquence, to lead a nation—an example for the youth of a fallen age.

The "Give Me Liberty or Give Me Death" speech has survived the rest of the book and has drawn the criticism that it is largely Wirt's speech presented as Henry's. Wirt took the speech from the accounts of eyewitnesses such as St. George Tucker and Thomas Jefferson and paraphrased all but the final paragraph, which he gave as direct quotation. Over the years, however, anthologists have given the entire speech as direct discourse, thus misrepresenting Wirt. In any case, the speech has become a vital part of the American myth. All in all, in an age in which Mason Locke Weems (q.v.) mythologized George Washington (q.v.) and others in his biographies, Wirt romanticized his subject to present his giant from Va.'s heroic age.

Suggested Readings: DAB; LHUS. *See also* Frank P. Caudle, "William Wirt and His Friends: A Study in Southern Culture, 1772-1834" (Ph.D. diss., Univ. of N.C., 1933); Peter Hoffman Cruse, "Biographical Sketch of William Wirt," *The Letters of the British Spy*, 10th ed. (1882); Richard Beale Davis, *Intellectual Life in Jefferson's Virginia, 1790-1830* (1964), 2nd ed. (1972); idem, "Poe and William Wirt," AL, 16 (1944), 212-220; idem, Introduction, *The Letters of the British Spy* (1970), pp.vii-xxii; Jay B. Hubbell, *The South in American Literature* (1954); idem, "William Wirt and the Familiar Essay in Virginia," WMQ, 23 (1943), 136-152; John Pendleton Kennedy, *Memoirs of the Life of William Wirt*, 2 vols. (1849, rev. ed. 1850); Joseph C. Robert, "William Wirt, Virginian," VMHB, 80 (1972), 386-441; W. R. Taylor, "William Wirt and the Legend of the Old South," WMQ, 14 (1957), 477-493.

Homer D. Kemp
Tennessee Technological University

JOHN WISE (1652-1725)

Works: *The Churches Quarrel Espoused* (c. 1710-1713); *A Vindication of the Government of New England Churches* (1717); *A Friendly Check from a Kind Relation* (1721); *A Word of Comfort to a Melancholy Country* (1721); "Instructions for the Emigrants from Essex County, Mass. to South Carolina, 1697" (1876); "The Narrative of Mr. John Wise" (w. c. 1691; pub. 1902).

Biography: Born Aug. 15, 1652, in Roxbury, Mass., John Wise graduated from Harvard College in 1673 and was ordained a Congregationalist minister. After serving first at Branford, Conn., and then as chaplain in a campaign against the Narragansetts, he took a second degree at Harvard (1676) and served briefly at a parish in Hatfield, Mass. He then married Abigail Gardner. In 1680 he accepted his call at Chebacco (now Essex) in Ipswich, Mass. Noted for being large and robust, Wise vigorously served the people of Chebacco for more than forty-five years. Shortly after revocation of the Mass. charter in 1684, Governor Andros attempted to raise money by an imposed tax. Wise led the rebellion against this tax, basing his stand on the Magna Charta. Consequently, he was arrested, tried, convicted, and even imprisoned for a short time. He also challenged the Salem witchcraft trials and petitioned the court in behalf of John and Elizabeth Proctor, although Mr. Proctor was eventually hanged. Wise spoke out for inoculation and argued the necessity of paper money despite the problems of inflation. An intelligent and vigorous defender of civil, religious, and humane liberties, Wise is best remembered for his two works defending the principles of religious freedom and the nature of Congregationalism as it developed in the American colonies.

Critical Appraisal: John Wise wrote four minor works, each occasional. His "Narrative" is an account of Sir William Phips's 1690 campaign against Quebec, for which Wise served as chaplain. Wise charged the officers with poor planning, saying their choice of a place to land and the want of provisions and ammunition contributed to the failure of the expedition that cost a thousand lives. As treasurer for an emigration project, he drafted "Instructions for the Emigrants" to gather information about living in S.C. In *A Friendly Check*, Wise ridiculed an attempt to block establishment of a paper currency, because such currency is vital for free trade by the colonies. *Word of Comfort* is also written in support of paper money.

But it is for two major works that Wise is best remembered. He has been called the "first man" in the colonies "to oppose taxation without representation," the "Father of American Independence," and "the first great American democrat" whose genius far exceeded that of better known contemporaries such as Increase Mather (q.v.) and Cotton Mather (q.v.). His public stand against Governor Andros's tax and his two works arguing against ministerial associations do much to legitimize these judgments about him. His writing is indeed clear, brilliant, compelling.

Wise published the first of his two major works in 1710 or at least by 1713. *The Churches Quarrel Espoused* was a "reply in satyre" to sixteen proposals first promulgated by Cotton Mather and others on Nov. 5, 1705. The delay between release of the proposals and Wise's reply supports Douglas H. Taylor's argument that Wise was contesting the authoritarian mentality behind the proposals as much as he was attacking the sixteen proposals themselves, which he recorded in his appendix. These proposals called for associations and councils of colonial ministers to serve as examiners of new ministers, arbiters of disputes between congregations and ministers, and interviewers of prospective ministers. Wise saw the proposals as contrary to the Cambridge Platform of 1648, contrary to the spirit of religious liberty maintained for sixty years in the colonies, and as the first steps toward an authoritarianism typical of the Roman papacy. In plain crisp metaphors (monetary, military, maritime, and legal), Wise prosecuted in the name of liberty those who would propose such associations. He called backers of the proposals drones who underestimated the good sense of the people and their commitment to independence.

In 1717, however, after Mather published his *Disquisition Concerning Ecclesiastical Councils*, Wise again attacked the sixteen proposals. *A Vindication of the Government of New England Churches* differs from *The Churches Quarrel* in that its tone is constructive and less satirical. This treatise presents first an argument from church history and then a fully developed argument from reason. Wise is perhaps the first in the colonies to argue that just as civil governments thrive and serve people best insofar as they operate by principles of democratic government, so too do churches thrive and serve people best insofar as they are independent and operating by democratic principles. Wise added additional arguments, but there is little doubt that *The Churches Quarrel* and *A Vindication* both depend on convictions spelled out in the Cambridge Platform. Yet neither is there doubt that Wise's primary argument in 1717 is from the "Light of Nature"; he insisted that democratic principles alone uphold the independence and liberty proper to new world government—civil or religious.

Suggested Readings: CCNE; DAB; DARB; LHUS; Sibley-Shipton (II, 428-441); Sprague (I, 188-189); T₁. See also Allan Cook, John Wise: Early American Democrat (1952); Sherwin L. Cooke, "John Wise, the Preacher of American Insurgency," PBosS (1925), 28-40; Paul S. McElroy, "John Wise: The Father of American Independence," EIHC, 81 (1945), 201-226; Clinton L. Rossiter, "John Wise: Colonial Democrat," NEQ, 22 (1949), 3-32; Douglas H. Taylor, "John Wise and the Development of American Prose Style" (Ph.D. diss., Univ. of Calif., Davis, 1967). "Instructions for Emigrants" is printed in NEHGR, 30 (1876), 64-67. "The Narrative" appears in PMHS, 2nd ser., 15 (1902), 281-296. A Vindication has been edited by Perry Miller (1958).

John F. Kuhn
Northern Michigan University

SALLY WISTER (1761-1804)

Works: *Sally Wister's Journal* (w. 1777-1778; pub. 1886); poems (untraced) signed "Laura" in the *Philadelphia Port Folio*.

Biography: Sally Wister was born in Philadelphia, Pa., on Jul. 20, 1761, of German and Welsh descent. Her parents were Quakers, and she attended a school for girls run by the notable Quaker philanthropist Anthony Benezet (q.v.). In Sept. 1777 the Wisters temporarily left war-ridden Philadelphia to live in Gwynedd (North Wales), Pa. There 16-year-old Sally kept "a sort of journal," structured partly in epistolary and partly in dialog form and addressed to her friend Deborah Norris, who had stayed in Philadelphia. When the family returned to the city ten months later, Sally kept her journal far more erratically. As an adult, Wister became more religious and apparently wrote poetry. She died unmarried at the age of 43 on Apr. 25, 1804.

Critical Appraisal: Covering the period from Sept. 1777 to Jul. 1778, the published portion of Sally Wister's journal is significant not so much because it documents Revolutionary history (in fact, the author omitted some important events), but because it reveals the everyday life of a typical Quaker teenage girl and contains nascent literary elements.

As Wister kept her journal, historic events such as the British capture of Philadelphia, the Battle of Germantown, the surrender of Burgoyne, and the winter at Valley Forge occurred. Although some figures who later assumed important positions stayed in the same country house as the Wisters, she concentrated on their human, not political, sides. For example, she wrote that Col. Wood, who became governor of Va., was "one of the most amiable of men; tall and genteel, [with] an agreeable countenance and deportment."

The journal is useful as a social document for its account of a Quaker girl's daily routine. Wister sewed, read, ironed, visited relatives, and chatted with the billeted officers. Absent is any kind of religious sensibility; since the journal is written to her friend Debby, perhaps the lack of such references is not so surprising.

The work's attraction lies in its mixture of drama (dialog), fiction (style, characterization, and narrative skill), epistle (direct references to Debby), and diary (self-examination and intimate revelation). Throughout, Wister showed her dramatic skill by capturing effective dialog exchanges. The work's main literary affinities, however, are with fiction. For instance, the style is sometimes consciously crafted, as in this brief entry: "Fifth-day, Sixth-day, and Seventh-day pass'd. The Gen'l still here; the Major still bashful." Like most teenage girls, Wister was very interested in the young officers quartered in her house, and her descriptions of her favorites—Maj. Stoddard, Mr. Tilly, and Capt. Dandridge— read like a novelist's description of three heroes. In addition to her character depictions, Wister effectively recounted certain episodes (for example, the joke played on Maj. Tilly in which fellow officers convinced him that a wooden dummy was a British grenadier). The journal sometimes resembles an epistolary novel, as Wister once significantly called herself "quite a heroine" and referred directly to her reader, Debby, especially in "created" conversations: "Oh, Debby; I have a thousand things to tell thee. I shall give thee so droll an account of my adventures that thee will smile. 'No occasion of that, Sally,' methinks I hear thee say, 'for thee tells me every trifle.'" Elsewhere, the work seems diarylike because of Sally's intimate confessions, especially concerning the young officers.

Finally, the journal has merit because the prose is still alive and frankly reflects its author. The following sketch illustrates her eye for detail, humor, and stylistic skill: "This eve came a parson belonging to the Army. He is (how shall I describe him?) near seven foot high, thin and meagre, not a single personal charm, and very few mental ones."

Suggested Readings: DAB. *See also* Wendy Martin, "Women and the American Revolution," EAL, 11 (1976-1977), 322-335, esp. p. 327; Albert Cook Myers, ed., *Sally Wister's Journal* (1902), notes and biographical introduction; notes and brief biographical introduction, *Journal of Miss Sally Wister*, PMHB, 9 (1885), 318-333, 463-478; 10 (1886), 51-60; Milton Rubincam, "The Wistar-Wister Family: A Pennsylvania Family's Contributions Toward American Cultural History," PennH, 20 (1953), 142-164.

Kathryn Zabelle Derounian
University of Arkansas at Little Rock

ICHABOD WISWALL (1637-1700)

Works: "Elegy on the Death of Governor Josiah Winslow" (1680); *A Judicious Observation of That Dreadful Comet, Which Appeared on November 18, 1680* (1683); "A Small Testimony of that Great Honour Due to That Honourable

Servant of God and His Generation John Alden Esq." (1687); "Upon the Death of That Reverend and Aged Man of God, Mr. Samuel Arnold" (1693).

Biography: Born in Eng. in 1637, Ichabod Wiswall immigrated with his family to New Eng. in 1642. He studied at Harvard for three years, but the college then added a fourth year to its curriculum, and Wiswall failed to graduate. Later, however, Wiswall was ordained to the ministry, and from 1676 until his death, he served as pastor of the church in Duxbury, Mass. Throughout his years in New Eng., he participated actively in Mass. civic affairs. About 1689 he served as agent of the colony in an attempt to prevent accession of Plymouth colony to Mass., but his efforts were foiled by Increase Mather (q.v.), Massachusetts Bay's representative. He died in 1700 in Duxbury.

Critical Appraisal: Although the author of several shorter elegies written in the tradition of the times, Ichabod Wiswall is best remembered for his 410-line poem on the comet written in 1680 and published three years later in London. In his *Judicious Observation of That Dreadful Comet*, Wiswall continued the pattern of the verse jeremiad popular in the late seventeenth century by describing this comet as portending "certain draughts of Joy and Pain, / Which mortal men must undergo." By claiming that the comet is a sign "Wherein is shewed the manifold Judgments that are like to attend upon most parts of the World," Wiswall stimulated and immediately kept the reader's interest.

Wiswall began his poem by suggesting that the lines written "In Heavens large folio, with the hand / Of him that doth all things command" apply to all men of New Eng. He traced the comet's path through the "Hemisphear" and described their fate: sailors ("Ye nimble Lads, who *Neptune* ride,... / Mind well your Helm; for you'l have oft / Salt breeming Waves, which will not burn") will be "drown'd in the deep," just as certainly as merchants will "lose their great Estates," husbandmen their "greater Cattel," and shepherds their "Sheep." Wiswall's poem succeeds in heightening his readers' awareness of their mortality by showing them that God's patience was wearing thin. Backsliding, for Wiswall and the other Puritans, had to be reversed, and in his poem on the comet, Wiswall made an emotional appeal to his listeners that was, if not effective, certainly popular.

Suggested Readings: CCNE; FCNEV; Sibley-Shipton (I, 560-561). *See also* Harrison T. Meserole, ed., *Seventeenth-Century American Poetry* (prints *A Judicious Observation*; 1968), pp. 443-445.

Jeffrey Walker
Oklahoma State University

JOHN WITHERSPOON (1723-1794)

Works: *Ecclesiastical Characteristics* (1753); *Justification and Holiness of Life* (1756); *A Serious Apology* (1756); *A Serious Enquiry into the Nature and Effects of the Stage* (1757); *The Absolute Necessity of Salvation Through Christ*

(1758); *The Trial of Religious Truth by Its Moral Influence* (1759); *The History of the Corporation of Servants* (1765); *Regeneration* (1765); *Practical Discourses* (1768); *An Address to the Inhabitants of Jamaica* (1772); *Considerations on the Nature and Extent of Legislative Authority of the British Parliament* (1774); *A Pastoral Letter from the Synod of New York and Philadelphia* (1775); *The Dominion of Providence Over the Passions of Men* (1776); *An Address to the Natives of Scotland Residing in America* (1778); *Some Truth, Much Wit . . . the Humble Confession . . . of Benjamin Towne* (1778); *The Druid* (1781); *A Letter from a Blacksmith* (1785); *A Draught of a Plan of Government and Discipline for the Presbyterian Church in North America* (1786); *An Essay on Money* (1786); *Christian Magnanimity* (1787); *An Address to the Senior Class of Students* (1788); *A Sermon on the Religious Education of Children* (1789).

Biography: John Witherspoon, son of a Calvinist Presbyterian minister, was born in Edinburgh in 1723. After receiving his divinity degree from the University of Edinburgh in 1743, he led congregations in Haddington, Ayrshire, and eventually Paisley. There he became allied with the Popular party, the conservative faction in a dispute over doctrinal purity. His sermons and satirical tracts in this cause soon earned him a reputation that spread as far as N.J., where in 1766 the trustees of the College of New Jersey (Princeton) elected him as the college's new president. After initially refusing, due to his own and his wife's misgivings, he finally accepted, arriving to fill his new post in 1768.

Witherspoon proved to be a popular and able college president. At Princeton he leavened the heavily theological curriculum by introducing courses in philosophy, history, oratory, and modern languages. He likewise became a leading figure in American Presbyterianism, helping to heal factional divisions and to strengthen ties with the Congregationalists and other churches. As the Revolution approached, Witherspoon became increasingly involved in politics. In 1766 he was elected to the Continental Congress and became a signer of the Declaration of Independence. With brief intermissions, Witherspoon remained an important and influential member of Congress until 1782, when, with the Revolution won, he returned to Princeton to work at restoring the war-shattered college. Despite his college duties, he was active in state politics until 1792, when he lost his sight and retired, dying two years later.

Critical Appraisal: Given his multiplicity of talents and the important positions he held, John Witherspoon was able to wield a formative influence in several areas of American life as the nation took shape. It is perhaps in politics that one finds the most obvious of his contributions. As a follower of John Locke, he wholeheartedly embraced the principles of liberty that underlay the movement for independence. With tracts such as *Considerations on the Nature and Extent of Legislative Authority of the British Parliament* (1774), he served the cause as an eloquent propagandist whose reputation for ecclesiastical conservatism gave his words a special weight. Less public, but more crucial, was his service in Congress at a time when the fundamental structures of the new country were being determined. Between 1776 and 1782, he was a member of more than

100 congressional committees, including some of the most important, such as those overseeing foreign policy and pursuit of the war. He likewise played a prominent role in the debates on the Articles of Confederation, in organizing the executive branch, in setting economic policy, and in drawing up instructions for the peace commissioners.

As a religious leader he was a major force in reconciling the bitterly divided Old Side and New Lights of the Presbyterian Church in America. Under his leadership, the newly united church flourished, and no single person was more instrumental than Witherspoon in determining the comprehensive reforms of catechisms, the directory of worship, the confessions of faith, and the forms of governance and discipline adopted by Presbyterians in 1788. In the related area of philosophy, Witherspoon was noted for his rejection of Berkeleyanism and his espousal of the empirical "common sense" approach that came to dominate American philosophical thought.

In his role as an educator, as in his religious orientation, Witherspoon combined a basic conservatism and a willingness to compromise with opposing viewpoints, so long as they did not violate what he considered essential principles. One of his first acts as president of Princeton was to increase both the size and range of the library, including in his acquisitions many of the authors with whom he had long disputed. During his presidency at Princeton, the curriculum was widened, the lecture system introduced, and enrollment increased—not just in numbers, but also in diversity of geographic origin, thus making Princeton much more of a national college than most others of the time.

Aside from his sermons, Witherspoon's writings were mostly occasional, often polemical, tracts on a variety of contemporary theological, political, and cultural questions. His prose style is generally sparing of rhetorical embellishment, in this respect resembling his pulpit manner, which was notable for its minimum of verbal and physical flourishes. He did, however, display a considerable talent for satire and irony. The dry wit and humor of works such as *Ecclesiastical Characteristics* and the *Corporation of Servants* led some to accuse him of a degree of levity unseemly in a clergyman (against which charge he defended himself by citing the Bible's use of humor as an instructional device). Of particular interest today among Witherspoon's writings is the series of 1781 essays collectively titled *The Druid*. They constitute the first orderly treatment of the ways in which the English language as used in America had begun to diverge from that of the mother country—a process that Witherspoon (a linguistic traditionalist, for all his political independence) mostly decried.

Suggested Readings: CCMC; DAB; DARB; LHUS; Sprague (III, 288-300); T_2. *See also* L. H. Butterfield, *John Witherspoon Comes to America* (1953); Varnum Collins, *President Witherspoon* (1925); A. L. Drummond, "Witherspoon of Gifford and American Presbyterianism," RSCHS, 12 (1958), 185-201; Leonard Kramer, "Muskets in the Pulpit: 1776-1783," JPHS, 31 (1953), 229-244; John Maclean, *History of the College of New Jersey* (1877); Thomas Wertenbaker, "John Witherspoon" in *The Lives of Eighteen from*

Princeton, ed. Willard Thorp (1946), pp. 68-85; D. W. Woods, *John Witherspoon* (1906).

Richard I. Cook
Kent State University

ROGER WOLCOTT (1679-1767)

Works: *Poetical Meditations, Being the Improvement of Some Vacant Hours* (1725); *Journal of Roger Wolcott at the Siege of Louisbourg* (w. 1745; pub. 1860); *Autobiography* (w. 1755; pub. 1881); *A Memoir for the History of Connecticut* (w. 1759; pub. 1895); "A Letter to the Freemen of Connecticut," *Connecticut Gazette* (Mar. 28, 1761); *A Letter to the Reverend Mr. Noah Hobart* (1761).

Biography: Youngest of the nine children of Simon and Martha Pitkin Wolcott, Roger Wolcott was born at Windsor, Conn., on Jan. 4, 1679. In his *Autobiography*, Wolcott related that he never was formally educated and when young was "extremely dull to learn," although his mother, talented and well educated, taught him to read and write when he was 11. At 15, he was apprenticed to a clothier, leaving at 20 to begin his own successful business. On Dec. 3, 1702, he married Sarah Drake, who bore him fifteen children—nine of whom reached adulthood—before her death on Jan. 21, 1748. Shortly after his marriage, he moved to South Windsor, where he set up a farm that "in a few years" was "made profitable."

Wolcott was chosen as a selectman of Windsor in 1707, thus beginning his public career. During 1709 he was admitted to the bar and chosen as a deputy to the General Assembly. He was elected as an assistant to the General Assembly from 1714 to 1741, when he became deputy governor. A member of various committees managing the important affairs of the colony, including boundary questions, Indian affairs, land matters, war, and monetary issues, Wolcott was also chosen as a representative of the colony before the Commissioners' Court in the Mohegan Indian controversy in 1738, 1742, and 1743. A justice of the peace until 1721, he then rose to judge of the Hartford County Court, superior court judge (1732), and chief justice (1741).

Besides his public service, Wolcott had a distinguished military career, beginning as commissary of the Conn. stores in Hovenden Walker's 1711 expedition against Quebec. Elected captain of one of the Windsor militia companies in 1722, he commanded one of the colony's standing companies a year later. In 1724 he was promoted to sergeant major of the Hartford County regiment and in 1739 became colonel of the First Regiment. Commissioned as major-general and second in command by Governor William Shirley (q.v.) of Mass. and Governor Law of Conn. in 1745, he joined the successful expedition against Cape Breton. There he wrote his *Journal of the Siege of Louisbourg*, which attributes the victory to God's providence and to the fact that "our soldiers were free-holders" and the defenders were mercenary troops.

In 1750 Wolcott was elected governor of Conn., serving until 1754, when he was defeated because of his alleged negligence in protecting the valuable cargo of a disabled Spanish ship that had put into New London. The British government exonerated him in 1755, and Wolcott lost that year's gubernatorial election by only 200 votes. Nonetheless, he viewed himself as "a discarded favorite" and retired to his farm, where he devoted his remaining years to studying church history and the Bible.

Wolcott died on May 17, 1767. As he had requested, he was buried without military honors or elaborate ceremony. His pastor, Joseph Perry, published a funeral sermon testifying to Wolcott's importance in the colony of Conn., *The Character of Moses Illustrated and Improved*.

Critical Appraisal: Roger Wolcott's principal contribution to American literature is his *Poetical Meditations* (1725), the first book of poetry published in Conn. The volume contains several meditations and commentaries on scriptural texts and a lengthy narrative in heroic couplets, "A Brief Account of the Agency of the Honourable John Winthrop." The "Account" describes John Winthrop's (q.v.) 1661 mission to obtain a charter for the colony of Conn. from King Charles II. Wolcott used the dramatic situation—Winthrop before the king and court dignitaries—to relate the early history of Conn., including the arrival of the first settlers, descriptions of the land and the Indians, the struggles of the colonists, and their firm religious ideals in establishing a Christian colony. The "Account" has intrinsic historical value, especially the passages on the Pequot wars and other Indian conflicts. Moreover, Wolcott captured the native beauty of Conn. and the colonists' sense of wonderment in the New World: "Clouds killing Pines in stately Man groves stand, / Firm *Oaks* fair *Branches* wide and large extend." Although the epic is influenced by the contemporary English Classic models, Wolcott frequently achieves vigor and fresh insight. In his meditation of Psalm LXIV, for example, Wolcott suggested that "the Curses Policies of Man" are so deeply hidden in the human heart that they can only be seen by a man of special vision: "He that can trace a Ship making her way, / Amidst the threatening Surges on the Sea; / . . . Or on a Rock find the Impressions there / Made by a Serpents Footsteps."

Wolcott's meditations retain the biblical resonance of earlier Puritan poetry, and he could evoke the Puritans' fervor and unique imagery. For example, in the meditation on Proverbs 18, Wolcott described Christ as "Impurpled in His Crucifixion." Wolcott's religious verse harks back to seventeenth-century poetry, but the "Account" of John Winthrop, with its heroic couplets and Classic influence, looks forward to the epics of David Humphreys (q.v.), Timothy Dwight (q.v.), Joel Barlow (q.v.), and John Trumbull (q.v.). Although there is disagreement about the aesthetic merit of Wolcott's verse, his *Poetical Meditations* represents a significant transition in American literature.

Besides his poetry, Roger Wolcott is important for his prose. After his defeat in the 1755 election, Wolcott wrote his *Autobiography*. A straightforward account of Wolcott's life, the work reveals his apparent religious faith. Throughout his life, Wolcott "made the Bible his test."

The *Memoir for the History of Connecticut* (1759), a brief history of the colony, reveals how Wolcott's faith and ideals influenced his public as well as private life. In 1759, President Thomas Clap (q.v.) of Yale, who was contemplating writing a history of Conn., requested Wolcott's own recollections of the early years of the colony. The *Memoir* begins with the year 1630, when the first house was built in Conn., and closes with the capture of Fort Duquesne in 1758. Emphasizing the legal proceedings that helped establish the colony as a cohesive political body and recounting the colonists' struggles with the Indians, the *Memoir* is written in direct, simple prose, with little detail or embellishment. Yet in spite of its factual nature, the *Memoir* displays Wolcott's character and integrity. He included a description of the affair of the Spanish ship—the reason he lost the governorship—although he later cancelled this section from the original manuscript. Although Wolcott downplayed the affair, his personal hurt was obvious: "At the next election the Governor was thrown down with a vengeance, and when down thought worthy of no more respect than a comon [sic] porter." However, such personal feelings rarely intrude in the *Memoir*. Instead, Wolcott vigorously demonstrated the wisdom that explains the trust placed in him. Typical is his analysis of public funds: "the public treasury is as the stomach to the body politick"; when "public men" supply it "in a due manner," the body will be healthy, but when "they look upon the public treasury as a source to feed and enrich themselves, a commonwealth as strong as that of the Romans will soon sink." Comparable statements throughout the *Memoir* suggest a tone of morality and integrity.

Although Wolcott was an able secular historian, his deepest interest was in church history. In *A Letter to the Reverend Mr. Noah Hobart* (1761), he argued that the best church government results from a mixture of laity and clergy, as opposed to Noah Hobart's (q.v.) contention that all power should reside in the minister. Written in clear and natural prose, Wolcott's detailed rebuttal demonstrates his knowledge of church history. Indeed, his strongest argument depends on the history of early Christianity. As does the *Memoir*, the *Letter* testifies to Wolcott's keen historical sense, as well as to his personal commitment to moral and religious ideals. Roger Wolcott's poetry and prose exemplify the religious beliefs and nature of thought prevalent during his lifetime. His primary contribution to American literature is the historical record he left in that poetry and prose.

Suggested Readings: DAB; LHUS; T$_1$. *See also* Albert C. Bates, "Sketch of Roger Wolcott," CHSC, 16 (1916), xxv-xxxv; idem, ed., "Wolcott Papers, 1750-1754," CHSC, 15, 16 (1915-1916); Robert Daly, *God's Altar: The World and the Flesh in Puritan Poetry* (1978), pp. 41-42; Jo Ella Ann Osborn Doggett, "Roger Wolcott's *Poetical Meditations*: A Critical Edition and Appraisal" (Ph.D. diss., Univ. of Tex. at Austin, 1974); Harrison T. Meserole, ed., *Seventeenth-Century American Poetry* (1968), pp. 498-499; Perry Miller and Thomas H. Johnson, eds., *The Puritans* (1938), pp. 551-552, 657-662; William Bradley Otis, *American Verse, 1625-1807* (1909), pp. 14-17, 63;

William J. Scheick and Jo Ella Doggett, *A Guide to Seventeenth-Century American Poetry* (1977). The *Autobiography* was published in Samuel Wolcott, *Memorial of Henry Wolcott* (1881). The *Memoir* was printed in CHSC, 3 (1895), pp. 321-336, and the *Journal* in CHSC, 1 (1860), 131-161.

Judith E. Funston
Michigan State University

WILLIAM WOOD (c. 1606-1639)

Works: *New-England's Prospect* (1634).

Biography: Partially because there are several William Woods in the history of seventeenth-century New Eng., few accurate biographical details are available. From what information does exist, we know that William Wood was born in Eng., probably in Lincolnshire County. He appears to have been well educated, most likely at Cambridge. Wood immigrated to Mass. in 1629 and settled near Boston. In 1633 he returned to Eng., and in 1634 his book *New-England's Prospect* was entered in the Stationer's Register in London. He booked return passage to New Eng. about 1635 and settled in Sandwich, where he became active in civil affairs. He died there in 1639.

Critical Appraisal: *New-England's Prospect*, a "True, Lively, and Experimental Description of That Part of America, Commonly Called New-England," is a descriptive-promotional account of Wood's New Eng. as he saw it between 1629 and 1633. Entertaining and accurate, Wood's narrative reflects his literary skill and his knowledge of nature.

The first half of the book contains twelve chapters that sketch the geographical features of New Eng.: the climate, soil, seasons, beasts, "fruits, woods, waters, and minerals"; the existing colonies; and a detailed account of the preparations that future travelers should make before immigrating to New Eng. The second half includes twenty chapters devoted to a description of the Indians: their homes, clothing, food, ornaments, worship, wars, and customs.

Wood's book is lively and well written, and it clearly indicates his literary training. His poetic descriptions, for instance, of trees ("Trees both in hills and plaines, in plenty be, / The long lov'd Oake, and mourneful Cypris tree"), birds ("The drosie Madge that leaves her day-lov'd nest, / And loves to rove when day-birds be at rest"), fish ("The luscious Lobster, with the Crabfish raw, / The Brinish Oister, Muscle, Periwiffe, / And Tortoise sought for by the Indian Aquaw"), and animals ("The kingly Lyon, and the strong arm'd Beare / The large lim'd Mooses, with the tripping Deare") are characterized by their scientific precision as well as by their poetic quality.

Extremely comprehensive and vivid in its portrayal of the topography of seventeenth-century America, *New-England's Prospect* no doubt did much to promote settlement in the New World. Like most promotional tracts written in the era, Wood's narrative strongly implied that the future colonial settler could be happy in this land of milk and honey. It is, of course, impossible to know the impact of Wood's narrative on New Eng. settlement, but its readers probably realized that the country could not, and did not, fulfill Wood's promises. As a document of natural history and description, however, *New-England's Prospect* stands atop the vast array of accounts written in the seventeenth-century because of its literary style and charm.

Suggested Readings: DAB; LHUS; T₁. *See also* Harrison T. Meserole, ed., *Seventeenth-Century American Poetry* (1968), pp. 399-402; *The National Cyclopaedia of American Biography* (1897), VII, 150. *New England's Prospect* has been edited by Alden T. Vaughan (1977).

Jeffrey Walker
Oklahoma State University

BENJAMIN WOODBRIDGE (1622-1684)

Works: *Church-Members Set in Joynt* (1648); "Upon the Author; by a Known Friend" (third prefatory poem, pub. in Anne Bradstreet, *The Tenth Muse*; 1650); *Justification by Faith* (1653); *The Method of Grace* (1656); "Upon the Tomb of the Most Reverend Mr. John Cotton" (lost broadside, pub. c. 1677; rep. in Cotton Mather, *Magnalia Christi Americana*, I, 258-259, 1703).

Biography: Born in 1622 at Stanton in Wiltshire, Eng., Benjamin Woodbridge was the son of the distinguished nonconforming minister John Woodbridge and his wife, Mary, daughter of the nonconformist author Robert Parker. He was first educated by Parker at Newbury in Berkshire and later attended Magdalen Hall, Oxford. He left Oxford in 1638; the next year, he followed his brother, John Woodbridge (q.v.), to New Eng., where he entered Harvard College and became its first graduate, receiving a B.A. in 1642. As Harvard's first graduate, Woodbridge was, states Cotton Mather (q.v.), "a *Star of the first Magnitude* in his constellation."

In 1647, Woodbridge returned to Eng. with John and enrolled at Oxford again, receiving an M.A. in 1648. Later that year, he was appointed rector at Newbury; while rector, he decided to conform and took holy orders from the bishop of Salisbury at Oxford in 1655. After the Restoration, he accepted the canonry at Windsor, became chaplain to Charles II, and was appointed a commissioner at the Savoy conference in 1661. Despite such cooperation, however, he was ejected from his post at Newbury in 1662 following the act of conformity. He then returned to nonconformist preaching privately, which resulted in his imprisonment despite the king's fondness for him. Between 1666 and 1669, when he returned to New Eng., Woodbridge was pastor of the church in Amesbury, Mass. After the indulgence of Mar. 1672, he began preaching more openly, and when the "popish plot" broke out in 1678, he preached every Sunday at Highclere in Hampshire. In 1683 he retired to Englefield in Berkshire, where he died on Nov. 1, 1684.

Critical Appraisal: Benjamin Woodbridge wrote two extant occasional poems, one a poem to Anne Bradstreet (q.v.), on the occasion of the publication in 1650 of her book *The Tenth Muse*, the other an elegy on John Cotton (q.v.). Both are written in closed heroic couplets and consist mainly of elaborate epideictic conceits in the manner of the early occasional verse of John Dryden. The poem to Bradstreet plays heavily on her femaleness. In her are united the Muses, the Virtues, and the Graces (all females); mankind no longer monopolizes perfection; the moon has eclipsed the sun. The elegy to Cotton is more interesting. Although not completely successful, it is certainly one of the most ambitious of the early colonial poems. Cotton's virtues are extolled in a number of ingenious, often paradoxical, conceits: Cotton, we are told, "Could wound at Argument without Division; / Cut to the quick, and yet make no Incision." Woodbridge's most interesting conceit, however, is the following: "O what a Monument of glorious worth, / When in a *New Edition* he comes forth / Without Errata's." This conceit, which was reprinted in Cotton Mather's *Magnalia*, is the probable source of Benjamin Franklin's (q.v.) famous epitaph on himself. In Woodbridge's poem, the conceit builds upon a previous one comparing Cotton to a "living breathing Bible," complete with index, title page, and a textual commentary. The conceit is not original with Woodbridge either, however; it has been traced as far back as to Francis Quarles, and it appears in enough sources to suggest that it was part of the stock-in-trade of seventeenth-century poets. Most modern readers would find the "wit" of the Woodbridge poem to be relentlessly strained, its lines relentlessly end-stopped, and its rhythms awkward; but the poem does possess a degree of intellectual strength and vigor.

Suggested Readings: CCNE; FCNEV; Sibley-Shipton (I, 20-27; Sprague (I, 129-131). *See also* Edmund Calamy, *The Non-Conformists Memorial* (1775); Burton Stevenson, *The Home Book of Quotations* (1967), pp. 571-572; Carl Van Doren, ed., *Benjamin Franklin's Autobiographical Writings* (1945), pp. 28-29.

Michael P. Clark
University of Michigan
and
Robert K. Diebold
Husson College

JOHN WOODBRIDGE (1613-1695)

Works: "To My Dear Sister, the Author of These Poems" (2nd of the introductory poems to Anne Bradstreet's *The Tenth Muse* [1650]; rep. in subsequent editions); *Severals Relating to the Fund* (1682).

Biography: John Woodbridge was born in Eng. at Stanton, Wiltshire, in 1613, the son of John and Sarah Woodbridge, and the brother of Benjamin

Woodbridge (q.v.), another New Eng. poet and divine. Because he refused to take the oath of conformity, Woodbridge was forced to leave Oxford before graduation and to complete his education privately. In 1634 Woodbridge accompanied his uncle, Thomas Parker (q.v.), to New Eng., where they took up residence at Newbury. Parker was ordained the pastor of Newbury, and Woodbridge served the town in a variety of official capacities. Sometime around 1640, Woodbridge married Mercy Dudley, the daughter of Governor Thomas Dudley (q.v.) and the sister of Anne Bradstreet (q.v.). Together with the Dudleys and the Bradstreets, Woodbridge helped to found Andover, on the banks of the Merrimack River, where he was ordained pastor.

In 1647, apparently at the request of friends, Woodbridge resigned his position at Andover and returned to Eng., where he served as minister and public official. In 1663, with the return to the British throne of Charles II, Woodbridge once again left Eng. for Mass., settling this time at Newbury, where he assisted his uncle as pastor until 1672, when difficulties concerning the administration of the Newbury congregation resulted in Woodbridge's forced resignation. Throughout the remainder of his life, Woodbridge was active in local and regional politics. He died on Mar. 17, 1695, approximately four years after his wife, and he was survived by eleven children. According to Cotton Mather (q.v.), Woodbridge was "a great reader, a great scholar, a great Christian, and a pattern of goodness in all the successive stations, wherein the Lord of Hosts had placed him."

Critical Appraisal: Upon his return to Eng. in 1647, John Woodbridge brought with him a manuscript of incalculable importance to the literary history of North America. This manuscript consisted of several poems by his sister-in-law Anne Bradstreet. Chief among the "friends" whom Bradstreet was later to call "less wise than true," Woodbridge presented the Bradstreet manuscript to the London publisher Stephen Bowtell, who in 1650 printed the poems under the title *The Tenth Muse Lately Sprung up in America*. Bowtell had earlier published Nathaniel Ward's (q.v.) *The Simple Cobler of Aggawam*, and it has been suggested that Ward may have recommended Bowtell to Woodbridge as a potential publisher for Bradstreet's poetry.

The exact nature of Woodbridge's involvement with the manuscript of *The Tenth Muse* after it was given to Bowtell will probably never be known for certain. It is generally believed, however, that Woodbridge probably acted as the emissary for Bradstreet's husband and father when he authorized the publication of her book, and that he probably undertook responsibility for any editorial problems relating to the publication of the manuscript, possibly including the arrangement of the poems themselves and the correction of proof. Prefacing the volume were a short epistle to the reader about the author and her poems and a series of poems by various writers attesting to the author's genius. Woodbridge is generally credited with having written the epistle and one of the introductory poems and with having solicited the other poems from admirers of Bradstreet's verse. Among these poems were one by his brother Benjamin and another by Nathaniel Ward. The remaining poems seem to have been written by British writers with whom Woodbridge was likely to have had some acquaintance while he was at Oxford and who probably had read the manuscript of Bradstreet's poems at Woodbridge's personal request.

Woodbridge's prefatory note to *The Tenth Muse* and his poem "To My Dear Sister, the Author of These Poems" are significant because they provide contemporary insights, by someone who knew her well, into Bradstreet's attitude toward the publication of her first volume of poems. From the preface, for example, it is known that Woodbridge published the volume in part because he feared that others might publish, "to the Authors prejudice," a volume of pirated or "broken pieces," and that Bradstreet herself did not yet wish to see her poetry published, probably because she had still to revise her poems to her complete satisfaction: "This only I shall annex, I feare the displeasure of no person in the publishing of these Poems but the Authors, without whose knowledge, and contrary to her expectations, I have presumed to bring to publick view what she resolved should never in such a manner see the Sun." From the preface it is also known that Bradstreet was regarded as "a Woman, honoured, and esteemed where she lived, for her gracious demeanour, her exact diligence in her place, and discreet managing of her family occasions" and that the "Poems are the fruit but of some few houres, curtailed from her sleep, and other refreshments."

The probability that Bradstreet had not yet finished revising her poems when Woodbridge brought them to press is further mentioned in his poem "To My Dear Sister": "'Tis true, it doth not now so neatly stand, / As ift 'twere pollisht with your owne sweet hand." Nonetheless, Woodbridge believed that the extraordinary quality of Bradstreet's poems spoke for itself and that the pleasure and edification her poems would give the world more than counterbalanced any "shame" she might experience, or "blame" he might incur, from their too hasty publication. Comparing Bradstreet's poems to "an infant" whose mother "will blush" and "complaine" when people admire its beauty, Woodbridge stated that in his opinion Bradstreet's poems were far too "rare," too "faire," and too "delightfull" to deprive the world of their charms for the sake of a mother's "modest minde." Woodbridge's poem is also noteworthy for the descriptions it provides of Bradstreet herself: "There needs no painting to that comely face, / That in its native beauty hath such grace." No other such description of the famous poet exists. Bradstreet, once she had had time to pursue her poems in print, was apparently pleased with her brother-in-law's poetic tribute, for she extended the metaphor of motherhood into the poem she herself later wrote on her famous "Book."

Woodbridge's only other published work was a short pamphlet titled *Several Relating to the Fund*, a work which has been praised as "the first American tract on currency and banking extant." Woodbridge's wife, Mercy Woodbridge, also wrote a verse epistle to her sister Anne, but no copy of her poem seems to have survived.

Suggested Readings: DAB; DNB; FCNEV; Sprague (I, 129-131). *See also* John Harvard Ellis, ed., *The Works of Anne Bradstreet* (1897), pp. xxxv-xxli, 83-89; Joseph R.

McElrath, Jr., and Allen Robb, eds., *The Complete Works of Anne Bradstreet* (1981), pp. xi-xlii; Josephine K. Piercy, *Anne Bradstreet* (1965), pp. 17, 76, 111; Ann Stanford, *Anne Bradstreet: The Worldly Puritan* (1970), pp. 7, 71-74, 77; Elizabeth Wade White, *Anne Bradstreet: "The Tenth Muse"* (1971), pp. 222-225, 253-292.

James A. Levernier
University of Arkansas at Little Rock

CHARLES WOODMASON (c. 1720-c. 1776)

Works: "Horace, Ode iv, Book 1, Imitated," *Gentleman's Magazine*, 23 (May 1753), 240-241; "C. W. in Carolina to E. J. at Gosport," *Gentleman's Magazine*, 23 (Jul. 1753), 337-338; "To Benjamin Franklin, Esq; of Philadelphia, on His Experiments and Discoveries," *Gentleman's Magazine*, 24 (Feb. 1754), 88; "Horace, Ode iii, Book I, Imitated," *Gentleman's Magazine*, 24 (Aug. 1754), 381; "The Art of Manufacturing Indigo in Carolina," *Gentleman's Magazine*, 25 (May and Jun. 1755), 201-203, 256-259; "A Political Problem," *South Carolina Gazette and Country-Journal*, Mar. 28, 1769; Richard J. Hooker, ed., *The Carolina Backcountry on the Eve of the Revolution: The Journal and Other Writings of Charles Woodmason, Anglican Itinerant* (1953).

Biography: Retrospective references to Woodmason's early life gleaned from his American journal suggest that he emigrated from Eng. for economic reasons and that he had at one time lived in London, was a devout Anglican, and considered himself a gentleman. In 1752, in his early 30s, he sailed from Gosport, Eng. (perhaps his birthplace), for S.C., leaving his wife and young son behind. He bought land and slaves and set himself up as a planter and merchant in Prince Frederick Parish, the Peedee River region near the coast. There he prospered and held local civic, military, and church offices. In 1756 he agreed to conduct religious services temporarily for his parish, a task he continued until 1762, when he appears to have returned to Eng., probably because of the death of his wife. He was in Charleston again within a year, where he was soon appointed a justice of the peace, clerk to several committees of the colonial legislature, and commissioner of streets, among other public offices. In 1765 he was described to the bishop of London as the "principal acting Magistrate" of the city. But when he sought to be appointed stamp distributor under the Stamp Act, he encountered popular disapproval. The same year, likely because of his religious zeal and his restlessness, he applied for the position of "itinerant minister" in the immense backwoods parish of St. Mark's and left for London to be ordained. He began his ministry the following summer. His parish consisted of about one-third of the entire province, an irreligious and lawless region, the haven of outlaws and dissenting religious sects. Vigilantes, calling themselves "Regulators," were attempting to bring law and order. In addition to undertaking his missionary labors (he traveled on horseback 3,000 miles each year), he became their leading spokesman, seeking redress for their main grievances—the lack of legal protection and inadequate representation in the legislative bodies—and tempering their violence. By 1772, in poor health and no longer young and disheartened by his failure to hold the line against the "sectarians," he left S.C. for Va. and Md., where he is known to have preached. He returned to Eng. in 1774 and preached occasionally in Bristol, and he applied to the bishop of London for assistance as a Loyalist refugee in 1776. The place and date of his death, like those of his birth, are not known.

Critical Appraisal: Shortly after his arrival in S.C., Woodmason began to send verse to the London *Gentleman's Magazine*, a periodical hospitable to American contributions. They appeared in respectable but unexciting company among the "Poetical Essays." Competence, lack of originality, and some touches of wit characterized this section of the magazine generally and Woodmason's "essays" in particular. He was, after all, an Englishman just removed to America and presumably followed the literary fashions. In form and diction, his Horatian imitations are like countless others. His poetic epistle to "C. W. in Carolina to E. J. at Gosport" belongs to the popular genre of topographical verse, and his tribute to Benjamin Franklin (q.v.) may be compared to other occasional tributes to scientific discovery. Yet his verses are exceptional in one respect: despite their conventionality, they show the impress of the American scene. The theme of his first contribution, a Horatian ode, is *carpe diem*, and he employed Arcadian names like Chloe and Phillis, but he referred to distinctive characteristics of the landscape such as its rice fields and the "smok'd huts" of Negro slaves, and his neo-Classic language is salted with Americanisms. The topographical poem is his most memorable literary accomplishment. It is what Samuel Johnson, in describing John Denham's *Cooper's Hill*, called "local poetry, of which the fundamental subject is some particular landscape." In Woodmason's case, there is an additional reason for localizing. He was writing a letter to a friend at home about the novelties and particularities of the American setting. His procedure, in 128 lines of heroic couplet, was to relate for his friend a catalog of the names of Carolina rivers, often of Indian origin, and the gentry who established plantations on their banks. This, in turn, provided an opportunity to hold forth on the "endless beauty" of the terrain and the distinctions of its inhabitants and their "delightful villas." But to his British eyes, nature was "bounteous in excess" and uncertain, and he noted the presence of a specific serpent in Eden, the rattlesnake. So despite the novelty of his material and his adequacy as a versifier, the poem ends lamely, affirming the priority of his native Eng. and the "Stella" he has left there. "To Benjamin Franklin" is also localized. Woodmason contended that America is the place "Where most the hostile elements contend" and hence it is appropriate that an American provide relief from them, and he described "tremendous thunders" that drive a fearful menagerie of American animals—bears, wolves, alligators, and rattlesnakes included—to their wilderness lairs and the damage done by lightning to the principal church of the town. In Charleston Woodmason might well have known Dr. John Lining, Franklin's friend, who replicated the kite experiment in 1753, the date of Woodmason's poem.

Woodmason's personal journal, according to Richard J. Hooker who edited it, "is probably the fullest extant account of any American colonial frontier." It is certainly vivid and vehement, and it validates his authority as the foremost spokesman for the "Regulators." On their behalf in 1767, he wrote a powerful "Remonstrance" to the Commons House of Assembly, arguing logically and eloquently that the backcountry settlers should have the same civil and religious rights as the people of the prosperous and cultivated coast. His attacks on the New Light Baptists and other sectarians, although shamefully biased, convey a delight in his satiric skills. He did not boggle at heavy sarcasm or ribald allusion. His sermons were forthright and, because they are usually topical, are a lively record of frontier society. Nor did he take his office so seriously that he could not write, for purposes of controversy, a burlesque sermon that still carries a sting.

Suggested Readings: CCV. *See also* Hennig Cohen, "A Colonial Topographical Poem," *Names*, 1 (1953), 252-258; Claude E. Jones, "Charles Woodmason as a Poet," SCM, 59 (1958), 189-194; *A Poetical Epistle from Charles Woodmason Esq., to Benjamin Franklin, Esq.* with foreword by L. H. Butterfield and note on Franklin's electrical experiments by Whitfield J. Bell, Jr.

Hennig Cohen
University of Pennsylvania

JOHN WOOLMAN (1720-1772)

Works: *Some Considerations on the Keeping of Negroes* (Pt. I; 1754); *An Epistle of Tender Love and Caution* (1755); *Considerations on Keeping Negroes* (Pt. II; 1762); *Considerations on Pure Wisdom and Human Policy* (1769); *A First Book for Children* (1769); *Considerations on the True Harmony of Mankind* (1770); *An Extract from John Woolman's Journal* (1770); *Epistle to the Quarterly and Monthly Meeting of Friends* (1772); *A Journal of the Life, Gospel Labours, and Christian Experiences of That Faithful Minister of Jesus Christ, John Woolman* (1774); *Remarks on Sundry Subjects* (1774); *Works* (1774); *A Plea for the Poor* (1793).

Biography: John Woolman was born on Oct. 19, 1720, in Rancocas in Burlington County, N.J. His family, which included thirteen children, were Quakers, and at an early age, Woolman developed a profound respect for God and the Quaker religion. Although he had little formal education, Woolman valued learning and, as his writings attest, was widely read. In 1749 Woolman married Sarah Ellis, whom he described in his *Journal* as "a well inclined damsel." The couple had two children, but only one, a daughter named Mary, survived infancy. By trade a tailor and a merchant, Woolman found it necessary to curtail his business activities when, shortly after his marriage, he felt a calling to the public ministry. Occasionally, he taught school, but for the most part, he restricted his activities to working on his farm, which included several hundred acres and a large orchard, and to preaching.

A kind and gentle individual whom people instinctively respected, Woolman journeyed thousands of miles, at a time when travel was difficult at best, in the hopes of bringing the Quaker religion and spirit to those who might benefit from them. During the course of some thirty years, Woolman's travels took him to New Eng. and to the South, where he preached against slavery, which he denounced through much of his later life as a "dark gloominess hanging over the land." At the close of the French and Indian War, he visited the Indians of western Pa., whose rights he championed upon his return home, and in 1772 he felt a calling to preach in Eng., where he died of smallpox on Oct. 7, 1772, just a few months after his arrival. Although the effects of Woolman's teachings were not particularly far-reaching during his own lifetime, his many writings on behalf of the poor and oppressed, particularly his strong abolitionist statements, have made him perennially popular among nineteenth- and twentieth-century reformists.

Critical Appraisal: John Woolman is best remembered today for the *Journal* he wrote intermittently between 1756 and his death in 1772, which was posthumously published by the Society of Friends in 1774. Although many devout Quakers kept journals, Woolman's *Journal* excels all others in clarity of expression, devotion to truth, and general piety; for this reason, popular interest in his *Journal* has never slackened, despite the fact that those of his contemporaries are for the most part forgotten, except by scholars knowledgeable in the field. The British Romantic Charles Lamb once remarked, for example, that Woolman's *Journal* was "the only American book I ever read twice." On this side of the Atlantic, the nineteenth-century poet John Greenleaf Whittier, also a Quaker, admitted a deep moral indebtedness to the *Journal*, which he edited with an introduction in 1871, and which was widely read during the Civil War for its statements on abolition.

But Woolman's *Journal* is much more than a cultural document about the life and wisdom of a remarkable man who labored untiringly and unselfishly to rectify injustice and establish social harmony. The lasting appeal of the *Journal* ultimately rests in the fact that its self-effacing humility and genuine expression of human love transcend the limitations of time and space and teach, as few other works do, what it means to be fully human and truly compassionate. Among other things, Woolman's *Journal* captures and conveys the essence of Quaker humanism at the moment in history when it was perhaps most intensely practiced and expressed, whether among the poor and destitute or on the frontier among the "heathen." Because Woolman's love for mankind crossed over barriers of sex, race, and religion, few people can read his *Journal* without being moved by it, and nearly all who read it feel emotionally and spiritually uplifted by the fact that it is humanly possible for mankind to achieve the moral stature and integrity of someone like John Woolman.

As an American book, Woolman's *Journal* also deserves attention, for it is the progenitor of classic accounts of the American personality such as Benjamin Franklin's (q.v.) *Autobiography*, Thoreau's *Walden*, Whitman's *Leaves of Grass*, and Henry Adams's *Education*. Like Woolman, Whitman was a Quaker who advocated inner harmony and spiritual contentment, and, also like Woolman, Thoreau was a reformer who called for a life of greater simplicity and peace. In fact, so effective is Woolman's *Journal* as autobiographical literature that Ellery Channing called it "the sweetest and purest autobiography in the language."

Although Woolman's other works do not achieve the literary universality of his *Journal*, they are nonetheless well worth reading for the information they provide about Woolman and his times. Especially noteworthy are his *Considerations on the Keeping of Negroes* (Part I and Part II), in which Woolman argued, with considerable force, for the abolition of slavery on the grounds that the institution demoralized and enslaved slaveholders as well as slaves, and *A Plea for the Poor* (1793), in which he maintained that everyone is morally accountable for the evils of poverty and that everyone is responsible for working toward its elimination. Along with Samuel Sewall's (q.v.) *The Selling of Joseph* (1700) and the tracts of Anthony Benezet (q.v.) and Samuel Fothergill (q.v.), Woolman's *Considerations* are numbered among the first American writings advocating the abolition of slavery in America and are responsible for much of the abolitionist activities carried on in America during the latter part of the eighteenth century.

Suggested Readings: DAB; DARB; DNB; LHUS; T₂. *See also* Edwin H. Cady, *John Woolman* (1966); Thomas E. Drake, *Quakers and Slavery in America* (1950); Amelia Mott Gummere, ed., Introduction, *The Journal and Essays of John Woolman* (1922); William L. Hedges, "John Woolman and the Quaker Utopian Vision," in *Utopias: The American Experience*, ed. Gairdner B. Moment and Otto F. Kraushaar (1980) pp. 87-102; Howard William Hintz, *The Quaker Influence in American Literature* (1940), pp. 26-34; Rufus M. Jones, *Quakers in the American Colonies* (1911); Edith Keen Livesay, "John Woolman: Persona and Person" (Ph. D. diss., Univ. of Del., 1976); Frank Morley, *The Tailor of Mount Holly: John Woolman* (1926); Phillips P. Moulton, ed., Introduction, *The Journal and Major Essays of John Woolman* (1971); idem, "The Influence of the Writings of John Woolman," QH, 60 (1971), 3-13; idem, "John Woolman: Exemplar of Ethics," QH, 54 (1965), 81-93; idem, "John Woolman's Approach to Social Action—as Exemplified in Relation to Slavery," CH, 35 (1966), 399-410; Catherine O. Peare, *John Woolman: Child of Light* (1954); Paul Rosenblatt, *John Woolman* (1969); Daniel B. Shea, Jr., *Spiritual Autobiography in Early America* (1968), pp. 3-86; Shore Teignmouth, *John Woolman: His Life and Our Times* (1913); F. B. Tolles, "'Of the Best Sort of Pain': The Quaker Esthetic," AQ," (1959), 484-502; Janet Whitney, *John Woolman: American Quaker* (1942).

James A. Levernier
University of Arkansas at Little Rock

TUNIS WORTMAN (d. 1822)

Works: *An Oration on the Influence of Social Institution upon Human Morals and Happiness* (1796); *A Solemn Address to Christians and Patriots,* *upon the Approaching Election of a President of the United States* (1800); *A Treatise Concerning Political Enquiry, and the Liberty of the Press* (1800); *An Address, to the Republican Citizens of New-York, on the Inauguration of Thomas Jefferson* (1801).

Biography: Nothing is known of Tunis Wortman's early life. He emerges from the records in the 1790s as a young New York City lawyer and Jeffersonian politician within a circle of intellectuals that included the physician and author Elihu Hubbard Smith (q.v.), law professor James Kent, and novelist Charles Brockden Brown (q.v.). Especially close to Smith, the group's leader, Wortman may have modeled his expository style after the debates among these students of the Enlightenment.

Wortman was an early proponent of the modern Revolutionary faith: overthrow of traditional authority will bring forth a perfect secular order. A cosmopolite, he identified with advancing stages of the French Revolution, presupposed an interplay between the revolutions in America and Fr., assumed the irreversibility of each depended upon the success of the other, and viewed them together as the incipient death of monarchy and the birth of universal peace. Mankind was perfectible, remaining sinful out of willfulness and circumstance, not original depravity. Wortman became disillusioned, however, with Napoleon's imperialist Fr. In 1801 he said, "Our every hope and every sentiment was ardently engaged" with the French; perhaps this was "imprudent," but the emotions arose from "the best of motives, which heaven will forgive."

Wortman combined idealism with practical politics. First secretary of the New-York Democratic Society and member of the state's Manumission Society, he was also a leader in politicizing the Tammany Society, turning this traditional association into a wing of the Jeffersonian party. Ideologically committed to his party, he viewed Federalists as antirepublican Anglophiles. The War of 1812 and Federalist opposition to it led Wortman in 1813 to start a short-lived newspaper, the *Standard of Union* (NYC), dedicated to supporting James Madison's (q.v.) administration. His life after the war until he died in New York City on Sept. 19, 1822, remains unrevealed.

Critical Appraisal: One scholar has called Wortman's major work, his *Treatise*, the book Thomas Jefferson (q.v.) ought to have written. Defending freedom of the press, it effuses a spirit of liberality in fact more advanced than typical of most Jeffersonians. The approach is axiomatic as arguments flow from elementary propositions and their counterpropositions. Wortman deductively examined reasons for and against restraining the press and concluded with firm support for absolute freedom of expression. The mere absence of prior restraint would not encompass this freedom; liberty of the press required that there be no prosecution for seditious libel.

Unlike the works of other political ideologues of the Early National Period, the *Treatise* confronts the question of secrecy in government. Here Wortman backed off from an absolute stand. He sought to minimize the use of secrecy, but admitted its practical necessity at times. Yet he deserves great credit for having faced an issue ignored by even the greatest among his contemporaries. For the time, his work was a unique proposal for an investigative society and a leading expression of the belief that truth must overcome falsehood in a free play of ideas.

Wortman's writings exhibit a thoroughgoing environmentalism (more typical of the age), a rejection of the well-embedded notion of mankind's innate sinfulness, and a sense of human perfectibility. These views underpin his millennialist expectation of a golden age when republican government spreads over the earth. "Persecution and superstition, vice, prejudice and cruelty will take their eternal departure from the earth. National animosities and distinctions will be buried in eternal oblivion." This is the message of his *Oration* on social institutions.

His other works are especially political and narrowly partisan in the Jeffersonian party's cause. In newspaper editorials, his last extant writings, he abandoned his own liberal creed and assurance of the inviolability of truth, accusing America's first wartime political opposition (1812-1814) of harboring subversive inclinations and having aided the British enemy, a smear meant to stifle open debate.

Suggested Readings: Isaac Q. Leake, *Memoir of the Life and Times of General John Lamb* (1850); Leonard W. Levy, *Legacy of Suppression: Freedom of Speech and Press in Early American History* (1960); Eugene P. Link, *Democratic-Republican Societies, 1790-1800* (1942); Henry F. May, *The Enlightenment in America* (1976); Jerome Mushkat, *Tammany: The Evolution of a Political Machine, 1789-1865* (1971); Elihu Hubbard Smith, *Diary*, ed. James E. Cronin (1973).

Nelson S. Dearmont
The Papers of Robert Morris

Z

JOHN PETER ZENGER (1697-1746)

Works: Editor and publisher of the *New-York Weekly Journal* (1733-1746); *A Brief Narrative of the Case and Tryal of John Peter Zenger* (1736).

Biography: Born in Ger. in 1697, John Peter Zenger immigrated to N.Y. sometime between 1710 and 1711. Zenger's importance to the development of American letters is best discussed in light of his career as publisher and editor. Apprenticed in 1711 to William Bradford (q.v.), the official printer of the crown in the N.Y. colony, Zenger formed a partnership with Bradford in 1725. But Zenger dissolved the partnership the following year and went to work for himself, publishing several theological texts in Dutch and English and a version of Venema's *Arithmetica* (1730), the first arithmetic text printed in N.Y. Zenger lived an uneventful life until 1733, when he decided to edit the *New-York Weekly Journal*. Employing several satiric mediums, the publication repeatedly attacked the administration of William Cosby, the royal governor of N.Y. Although Zenger did not actually write the articles himself, as publisher he was held responsible for them. Consequently, he was arrested in 1734 and charged with criminal libel. In 1735 he was acquitted in a landmark case. After his release, Zenger became the public printer for N.Y. in 1737 and N.J. in 1738. He died in N.Y. in 1746.

Critical Appraisal: John Peter Zenger was an unlikely hero. To some extent, he was more a passive symbol than an active participant in the history-making process. His contribution to the American heritage resulted from a trial in which he and his newspaper were accused of plotting the overthrow of the government. Under eighteenth-century English law, criminal libel statutes protected the king as well as his appointed administrators—even those who worked in the colonies. Any publication, whether true or false, that criticized the government or its officials was considered as an attempt to provoke insurrection and subject to prosecution.

In 1734 several of Zenger's friends financed and organized the *New-York Weekly Journal*. Zenger's knowledge of printing made him the logical choice for editor. Established as a critical voice against Governor Cosby's political indiscretions and as a vehicle for encouraging popular unrest against his administration, the newspaper was intended to apply pressure on the ministry in London and force it to recall Cosby. The *Journal* attacked the governor through a series of satiric essays and cartoon advertisements. Apparently, Cosby believed that the paper posed a real danger to his position and continued public support. Thus he had Zenger incarcerated and stressed issues 7, 47, 48, and 49 as significant illustrations of the *Journal's* threat to the "stability of government."

Zenger spent ten months in jail awaiting his trial. His first two lawyers, James Alexander and William Smith, both active supporters of the *Journal*, attacked two of the judges assigned to Zenger's case, labeling them as Cosby's "political henchmen." As if in confirmation of these accusations, both lawyers were immediately disbarred. Facing a legal machine that seemed deliberately set against him, Zenger's position looked hopeless. By a stroke of good fortune, however, the disbarred Alexander managed to obtain the services of Andrew Hamilton, reputedly the best lawyer in America. Fully documented in Zenger's *A Brief Narrative of the Case and Tryal of John Peter Zenger*, Hamilton's defense was founded on the theory that individual citizens have the right to criticize their rulers. According to Hamilton, Zenger's press was simply the mouthpiece for individual men to exercise their freedom. The state, the lawyer contended, exists to serve and protect the liberties of every man, and consequently, when a state administrator fails in his professional duties, citizens are obligated to criticize and even disobey the official: "It is a right which all freemen claim, and are entitled to complain when they are hurt; they have a right publicly to remonstrate the abuses of power, in the strongest terms, to put their neighbors upon their guard against the craft or open violence of men in authority."

Hamilton's impassioned defense greatly influenced the jury, and it awarded a "not guilty" verdict for Zenger. This was, essentially, the first victory for the freedom of the press in the American colonies. Thus the unheroic Zenger, through the assistance of his articulate attorney, has come to symbolize the principle of democratic freedom. It was the legal theory behind the Zenger case—that individual men possess the right to criticize their government—that eventually led to the reality of the American Revolution several decades later.

Suggested Readings: DAB; LHUS. *See also* C. R. Hildeburn, *A List of the Issues of the Press in New York* (1889); idem, *Sketches of Printers and Printing in New York* (1895); J. B. McMaster, "A Free Press in the Middle Colonies," PRev (Jan. 1886); Livingston Rutherford, *John Peter Zenger: His Press, His Trial, and a Bibliography of Zenger Imprints* (1904); L. R. Schuyler, *The Liberty of the Press in the American Colonies Before the Revolutionary War* (1905).

Anthony S. Magistrale
University of Vermont

JOHN JOACHIM ZUBLY (1724-1781)

Works: *Leichenpredigt* (1746); *Eine Leicht-Predigt* (1747); *Eine Predigt welche ein Schweitzer* (1749); *Evangelisches Zeugnuss* (1751); *The Real Chris-*

tians Hope in Death (1756); *The Stamp-Act Repealed* (1766); *An Humble Enquiry into the Nature and Dependency of the American Colonies upon the Parliament of Great-Britain* (1769); *A Funeral Sermon on the Death of the Rev. George Whitefield* (1770); *A Letter to the Rev. Samuel Frink* (1770); *The Wise Shining on the Brightness of the Firmament* (1770); *Calm and Respectful Thoughts* (1772); *The Nature of That Faith Without Which It Is Impossible to Please God* (1772); *The Faithful Minister's Course Finished: A Funeral Sermon* (1773); *The Law of Liberty* (1775); *Letter to Mr. Frink* (1775); *Pious Advice* (1775); *To the Grand Jury of the County of Chatham, State of Georgia* (1777).

Biography: Born in St. Gall, Switz., in 1724 and educated in the gymnasium there, John Joachim Zubly came to S.C. in 1744 and joined his family who had emigrated in 1736. After serving as an assistant pastor and in several temporary positions in S.C. and Ga., Zubly became pastor of the Independent Presbyterian Church of Savannah in 1760. In 1770 the College of New Jersey awarded him an honorary A.M. and in 1774, a doctor of divinity degree. He amassed a considerable fortune in land and slaves and was active in the politics of church and state. After serving in the Provincial Congress of Ga., he was elected in 1775 as one of Ga.'s five delegates to the Continental Congress. Zubly was prominent in the debates but became disturbed by the growing trend toward independence. He irritated John Adams (q.v.) and a number of other delegates, particularly Samuel Chase (q.v.), who charged that Zubly wrote a letter informing Ga. Governor James Wright of the Congress's Revolutionary intent. The charge was never substantiated, but Zubly, blaming illness, departed suddenly from Philadelphia on Nov. 10, 1775. In 1777 the patriots then controlling Savannah accused him of treason, banished him from Ga., and confiscated half of his estate. He spent two years in S.C. with Loyalist friends and then returned to Ga. when the royal government was reinstated. He partially resumed his pastoral duties in Savannah, where he died in 1781.

Critical Appraisal: Because of his colorful personality and energetic life, most of the studies of author, preacher, and politician J. J. Zubly have been biographical, but he was one of colonial Ga.'s most impressive literary figures. His early writings are clearly the work of a Protestant divine brought up and trained in Europe. Not only are they written in German—Zubly was the master of six languages, ancient and modern—but they also reflect the sentimental pietistic turn of the eighteenth-century continental imagination. In these early works, as opposed to his later, more mechanical and conventional funeral sermons, Zubly betrayed an intense preoccupation with death. *The Real Christians Hope in Death*, his first English work, is a collection of deathbed scenes from the lives of pious Christians, most of them Swiss or German. Their experiences at the point of death range from simple bravery to near miracle. Some see Christ or talk to him as they expire; others fall into trances and sing psalms with an unearthly sweetness; all are cheerful and even long for death.

As Zubly accumulated wealth and power in the 1760s and 1770s, his writings became political and thus recognizably American. The best example of his writings on church politics is *A Letter to the Reverend Samuel Frink* (1770) in which he asserted the full ecclesiastical rights of dissenters in Savannah. But the conflicts portrayed in Zubly's pamphlets on church politics now seem localized and even personal. The content of his sermons and tracts on colonial government, on the other hand, are memorable and significant. Indeed, he was Ga.'s most important author in the dispute between G.B. and her colonies.

Based on the principle that Christian duty has a political side, *The Stamp-Act Repealed; A Sermon Preached in the Meeting at Savannah in Georgia, June 25th, 1766* celebrates the repeal of "an unhappy ill-advised act" that had been passed by a Parliament "who wanted America ruled with a rod of iron." Zubly offered thanks to "our great and good king" as well as "thanks unto God, that our invaluable privileges are preserved, that our land is not become a land of slaves, nor our fields a scene of blood." He drew analogies between the British empire and the tribes of Israel when, having conquered their enemies, they were on the verge of civil war. He compared the British king to several biblical kings who realized that "gaining the affection of loyal subjects" is a greater security than forced submission. Zubly's enthusiasm over the repeal of the Stamp Act in 1766 was, however, dampened by the almost simultaneous passage of the Declaratory Act designed to secure Parliament's jurisdiction over the colonies. In *An Humble Enquiry into the Nature of the Dependency of the American Colonies upon the Parliament of Great-Britain, and the Right of Parliament to Lay Taxes on the Said Colonies* (1769), Zubly laid aside his pastoral cloak, remained anonymous, and styled himself a "free-holder of South Carolina." He argued that the liberties of Englishmen depend on the British Constitution, which limits Parliament's power. Since the charter of S.C. makes the colony subject immediately to the crown, the Declaratory Act, which binds the colonies to Parliament "in all cases whatsoever," is unconstitutional. The charter, moreover, gives the colonial Assembly the right to levy taxes, but the Declaratory Act makes this right subordinate to Parliament's and thus nullifies the power of the local Assembly in which the colonists are truly represented. Zubly complained that "the words IN ALL CASES WHATSOEVER are so exceeding extensive, that. . .even hewing of wood, and drawing of water, might be argued to be included in them." He nevertheless reasserted his loyalty to the king and claimed that most Americans reject the idea of independence. He returned to these themes in his last important political sermon, *The Law of Liberty. A Sermon on American Affairs, Preached at the Opening of the Provincial Congress of Georgia* (1775). He advised caution on both sides. In the sermon proper, based on the text "So speak ye, and so do, as they that shall be judged by the law of liberty" (James 2:12), Zubly told the members of the Provincial Congress that although they have the right to seek political liberty, they should remember the responsibilities of liberty and the judgment they will ultimately face before God. Likewise, the British ministers should respect their countrymen's rights and remember their own Christianity. In a prefatory address to the earl of Dartmouth, Zubly charged the British ministry, in somewhat stronger language than that of the sermon, to secure the rights of

Americans, repeal the Declaratory Act, control such military violence as had occurred in New Eng., and beware of the colonists who have taken "Death or Freedom" as their "general motto." As if to underscore his warning, Zubly included as an appendix "A Short and Concise Account of the Struggles of Swisserland [sic] for Liberty," in which the violent fervor of the Swiss patriots is emphasized.

The rhetoric of the prefatory address to Dartmouth is as impressive as any of the Revolutionary period. But the radical rhetoric is deceptive. Zubly's words were more a warning than a threat, and at the Continental Congress, he remained loyal to the crown and opposed independence. A republic, he cautioned his fellow delegates in 1775, is "little better than government of devils."

Suggested Readings: CCV; DAB; Sprague (III, 219-222); T_2. *See also* Thomas R. Adams, *American Independence: The Growth of an Idea: A Bibliographical Study of the American Political Pamphlets Printed Between 1764 and 1776 Dealing with the Dispute Between Great Britain and Her Colonies* (1965), pp. 32-34, 55-57, 68, 150; Richard E. Amacher, "John Joachim Zubly (1724-1781)" in *Southern Writers: A Biographical Dictionary*, ed. Robert Bain, J. M. Flora, and Louis D. Rubin (1979), pp. 514-515; Kenneth Coleman, *Colonial Georgia, A History* (1976), pp. 153, 158, 223-234, 273-275; idem, ed., *Revolutionary Tracts by John Joachim Zubly* (1972); Marjorie Daniel, "John Joachim Zubly—Georgia Pamphleteer of the Revolution," GHQ, 19 (1935), 1-16; Jay B. Hubbell, *The South in American Literature, 1607-1900* (1954), pp.165-166, 974; Roger A. Martin, "John J. Zubly: Preacher, Planter, and Politician" (Ph.D. diss., Univ. of Ga., 1976); William E. Pauley, Jr., "Tragic Hero: Loyalist John J. Zubly," JPH, 54 (1976), 61-81; Eunice R. Perkins, "John Joachim Zubly, Georgia's Conscientious Objector," GHQ, 15 (1931), 313-323; Paul H. Smith, "John Joachim Zubly" in *The Encyclopedia of Southern History*, ed. D. C. Roller and R. W. Twyman (1979), p. 1371; Paul H. Smith, ed., *Letters of Delegates to Congress, 1774-1789*, vol. II (1976).

M. Jimmie Killingsworth
New Mexico Institute of Mining and Technology

APPENDIX A
Year of Birth

This appendix provides a listing of entries according to year of birth. A separate category (Not Known) contains the names of those individuals for whom precise information remains unavailable.

NOT KNOWN

Allen, John (fl. 1764-1788)
Ashe, Thomas (fl. 1680-1682)
Aston, Anthony (fl. 1682-1747)
Atkins, Josiah (fl. 1781)
Bannerman, Mark (d. 1727)
Beete, John (fl. 1795-1797)
Bland, Edward (d. 1653)
Breintnall, Joseph (d. 1746)
Brereton, John (fl. 1590-1602)
Brewster, Martha Wadsworth (fl. 1725-1757)
Budd, Thomas (fl. 1678-1698)
Cockings, George (fl. 1760-1802)
Denton, Daniel (fl. 1656-1696)
Dumbleton, Joseph (fl. 1740-1750)
Fenno, Jenny (fl. 1791)
Frame, Richard (fl. 1692)
Gray, Robert (fl. 1609)
Gutridge, Molly (fl. 1778)
Hammon, Briton (fl. 1747-1760)
Hammond, John (fl. 1634-1663)
Harris, Benjamin (fl. 1673-1711)
Hepburn, John (fl. 1715-c.1745)
Holme, John (fl. 1685-1701)
Howard, Martin, Jr. (fl. 1730-1781)

Howell, Rednap (fl. 1750-1787)
Huit, Ephraim (fl. 1611-1644)
Hunter, Robert (fl. 1714-1734)
Johnson, Robert (fl. 1600-1621)
Lawson, Deodat(e) (fl. 1660-1715)
Lawson, John (d. 1711)
Leacock, John (fl. 1776)
Long, John (fl. 1768-1791)
Lyon, Richard (fl. 1620-1651)
Markland, John (fl. 1721-1735)
Micklejohn, George (d. 1817)
Mixer, Elizabeth (fl. 1707-1720)
Moorhead, Sarah Parsons (fl. 1741-1742)
Morrell, William (fl. 1623-1625)
Paxton, Robert (d. 1714)
Pead, Deuel (d. 1727)
Reid, James (fl. 1768-1769)
Rich, Richard (fl. 1609-1610)
Robinson, J. (fl. 1792)
Tailfer, Patrick (fl. 1734-1741)
Taylor, Jacob (d. 1746)
Tillam, Thomas (d. after 1668)
Wheeler, Thomas (fl. 1640-1676)
White, Elizabeth (d. 1669)
Wilkinson, Eliza Yonge (fl. 1779-1782)
Wortman, Tunis (d. 1822)

1530

Lane, Ralph

1560

Hariot, Thomas
Wingfield, Edward Maria (c. 1560)

1566

Gorges, Sir Ferdinando (c. 1566)

1571

Lowell, Percival

1572

Pory, John
Strachey, William

1575

Archer, Gabriel
Purchas, Samuel
Rosier, James
Ruggle, George
White, John

1576

Dudley, Thomas

1577

West, Thomas, Baron de la Warr

1578

Sandys, George
Ward, Nathaniel (c. 1578)

1579

Cushman, Robert (c. 1579)
Morton, Thomas (c. 1579)
White, Andrew, S.J.

1580

Percy, George
Smith, Captain John

1582

Knott, Edward, S.J.

1583

Bulkeley, Peter

1584

Cotton, John

1585

Morton, George
Rolfe, John (c. 1585)
Whitaker, Alexander

1586

Hooker, Thomas

1587

Higginson, Francis

1588

Wilson, John (c. 1588)
Winthrop, John

1590

Bradford, William
Lechford, Thomas (c. 1590)
Pynchon, William (c. 1590)

1592

Chauncy, Charles (c. 1592)
Gorton, Samuel (c. 1592)
Wheelwright, John (c. 1592)

1593

Phillips, George

1595

Parker, Thomas
Spelman, Henry (c. 1595)
Welde, Thomas
Winslow, Edward

1596

Mather, Richard

1597

Davenport, John
Underhill, John (c. 1597)
Whiting, Samuel (1597)

1598

Peter, Hugh

1599

Gardiner, Lion
Johnson, Edward (c. 1599)

1600

Mason, John (c. 1600)
Vincent, Philip

1601

Hooke, William

1602

Maverick, Samuel (c. 1602)
Moxon, George
Stone, Samuel

1603

Williams, Roger (c. 1603)

1604

Eliot, John

1605

Shepard, Thomas

1606

Norton, John
Winthrop, John, Jr.
Wood, William (c. 1606)

1608

Berkeley, Sir William (c. 1608)
Cobbet, Thomas
Fisker, John
Josselyn, John (c. 1608)
Noyes, James
Pierson, Abraham (c. 1608)

1609

Clap, Roger
Clarke, John
Dunster, Henry
Oxenbridge, John

1610

Somerby, Anthony

1612

Bosworth, Benjamin (c. 1612)
Bradstreet, Anne (c. 1612)
Dane, John (c. 1612)
Gookin, Daniel (c. 1612)

1613

Morton, Nathaniel
Woodbridge, John

1614

Bulkeley, Edward
Firmin, Giles (c. 1614)

1615

Cheever, Ezekiel
Norwood, Henry
Steendam, Jacob

1616

Higginson, John

1617

Folger, Peter

1618

Hinckley, Thomas
Scottow, Joshua (c. 1618)
Walley, Thomas

1620

Thacher, Thomas

1621

Hubbard, William (c. 1621)
Mayhew, Thomas, Jr. (c. 1621)

1622

Arnold, Samuel
Fitch, James
Woodbridge, Benjamin

1624

Easton, John (c. 1624)
Hull, John
Mitchel, Jonathan

1626

Danforth, Samuel
Saffin, John
Starkey, George (c. 1626)

1627

Morton, Charles (c. 1627)

1630

Hoar, Leonard (c. 1630)
Mather, Nathaniel
Perry, Edward
Rogers, John

1631

Oakes, Urian (c. 1631)
Rowlandson, Joseph (c. 1631)
Stoughton, William
Weld, Edmund
Wigglesworth, Michael

1632

Allen, James
Burt, Jonathan (c. 1632)

Chamberlain, Richard
Torrey, Samuel

1633

Bradstreet, Samuel (c. 1633)
James, John (c. 1633)
Moodey, Joshua

1634

Nowell, Samuel

1635

Hooker, Samuel
Rowlandson, Mary (c. 1635)
Shepard, Thomas
Whiting, John (c. 1635)

1636

Alsop, George (c. 1636)
Bulkeley, Gershom
Hale, John
Selyns, Henricus

1637

Mather, Eleazer
Wiswall, Ichabod

1638

Keith, George (c. 1638)
Tulley, John

1639

Brigden, Zechariah
Chauncy, Nathaniel
Cheever, Samuel
Chester, Stephen
Church, Benjamin
Danckaerts, Jasper

Mather, Increase
Saltonstall, Nathaniel (c. 1639)

1640

Belcher, Samuel (c. 1640)
Cotton, John
Cotton, John, of Queen's Creek (c. 1640)
Hammond, Lawrence (c. 1640)
Savage, Thomas
Willard, Samuel

1641

Goodhue, Sarah

1642

Russell, Daniel
Taylor, Edward (c. 1642)
Tompson, Benjamin
White, Henry (c. 1642)

1643

Bulkeley, Peter, II
Steere, Richard
Stoddard, Solomon

1644

Chauncy, Israel
Lederer, John (c. 1644)
Penn, William

1645

Dunster, David (1645)
Maule, Thomas (c. 1645)

1647

Bacon, Nathaniel
Calef, Robert (c. 1647)
Dudley, Joseph

Noyes, Nicholas
Pain, Philip (c. 1647)
Richardson, John

1648

Foster, John
Hayden, Anna Tompson
Hobart, Nehemiah
Mayhew, Matthew
Rogers, John
Shepard, Jeremiah

1650

Adams, William
Drake, Francis (c. 1650)
Gookin, Daniel, Jr.
Mathew, Thomas (c. 1650)

1651

Fitzhugh, William
Norton, John, II
Pastorius, Francis Daniel

1652

Fiske, Sarah Symmes
Leeds, Daniel
Sewall, Samuel
Wise, John

1655

Blair, James (c. 1655)
Henchman, Richard (c. 1655)
    1656)

1657

Clayton, John
Payson, Edward

1658

Brattle, Thomas
Bray, Thomas (c. 1658)
Capen, Joseph
Makemie, Francis

1659

Dunton, John
Rawson, Grindall
Russell, Noadiah

1660

Danforth, John

1661

Paine, John
Thomas, Gabriel

1662

Brattle, William

1663

Bradford, William
Dickinson, Jonathan
Mather, Cotton
Trott, Nicholas
Walter, Nehemiah

1664

Williams, John

1665

Makin, Thomas
Penhallow, Samuel
Williams, William

1666

Danforth, Samuel
Knight, Sarah Kemble
Lynde, Benjamin
Saltonstall, Gurdon
Tompson, Edward

1667

Cooke, Ebenezer (c. 1667)

1668

Gibbs, Henry

1670

Story, Thomas (c. 1670)
Wadsworth, Benjamin

1671

Buckingham, Thomas
Jones, Hugh
Knapp, Francis
Morgan, Joseph
Morris, Lewis
Stephens, William

1672

Bowers, Bathsheba (c. 1672)
Pemberton, Ebenezer

1673

Beverley, Robert (c. 1673)
Church, Thomas
Coleman, Benjamin
Coxe, Daniel
Mayhew, Experience
Morgan, Abel

1674

Byrd, William, of Westover
Logan, James
Niles, Samuel

1675

Chalkley, Thomas
Dudley, Paul

1676

Spotswood, Alexander

1677

Adams, Eliphalet
Eells, Nathaniel
Henchman, Daniel

1678

Brooke, Henry
Gyles, John (c. 1678)
Symmes, Thomas

1679

Blackamore, Arthur (c. 1679)
Boylston, Zabdiel
Bulkley, John
Wolcott, Roger

1680

Checkley, John

1681

Barnard, John
Dummer, Jeremiah

1682

Attwood, Peter, S.J.
Loring, Israel

1683

Boehm, John Philip
Catesby, Mark
Monis, Judah

1684

Burnham, William
Hanson, Elizabeth

1685

Berkeley, George
Dulany, Daniel, the Elder
Eliot, Jared
Garden, Alexander (c. 1685)
Hansford, Charles (c. 1685)
Marsh, Jonathan
Mather, Azariah

1686

Bradford, Andrew
Fox, John (c. 1686)

1687

Cooke, Samuel
Leeds, Felix
Prescott, Benjamin
Prince, Thomas
Webb, John

1688

Colden, Cadwallader
Keimer, Samuel
Sewall, Joseph

Thacher, Peter
Williams, William

1689

Shurtleff, William
Wigglesworth, Samuel

1690

Beissel, Johann Conrad
Thomson, John (c. 1690)

1691

Douglass, William (c. 1691)
Frelinghuysen, Theodorus Jacobus

1692

Allin, James

1693

Appleton, Nathaniel
Carew, Bampfylde-Moore
MacSparran, James
Sauer, Christopher, I
Wigglesworth, Edward

1694

Clark, Peter
Clayton, John
Cooper, William
Graham, John
Lord, Benjamin
Shirley, William
Williams, Elisha

1695

Dickinson, Moses
Doolittle, Benjamin
Rose, Aquila
Wetmore, James

1696

Checkley, Samuel
Gay, Ebenezer
Johnson, Samuel
Oglethorpe, James Edward
Walter, Thomas

1697

Foxcroft, Thomas
Franklin, James
Stiles, Isaac
Townsend, Jonathan
Zenger, John Peter

1698

Dock, Christopher (c. 1698)
Gee, Joshua
Paine, Solomon
Parks, William (c. 1698)
Peabody, Oliver
Smith, Michael

1699

Bartram, John
Coleman, Elihu
Hall, Clement (c. 1699)
Leeds, Titan
Martyn, Benjamin

1700

Bacon, Thomas (c. 1700)
Beach, John
Dale, Thomas
Emerson, Joseph
Evans, Lewis (c. 1700)
Fitch, Thomas
French, David
Kil(l)patrick, James (c. 1700)
Lewis, Richard (c. 1700)
Pickering, Theophilus
Rand, William
Tennent, John (c. 1700)

Von Zinzendorf, Nicholas Ludwig, Count
Williams, Solomon

1701

Antill, Edward
Sterling, James

1702

Greenwood, Isaac
Hancock, John
Hooper, William
Prentice, Thomas
Turell, Ebenezer

1703

Beckwith, George
Beveridge, John
Chase, Thomas (c. 1703)
Clap, Thomas Stephen
Edwards, Jonathan
Parkman, Ebenezer
Tennent, Gilbert

1704

Dawson, William
Dunbar, Samuel
Mercer, John
Smith, Josiah
Spangenberg, Augustus Gottlieb

1705

Adams, John
Alison, Francis
Chauncy, Charles
Churchman, John
Gist, Christopher
Green, Joseph (c. 1705)
Jewett, Jedidiah (c. 1705)
Parsons, Jonathan
Ralph, James (c. 1705)
Tennent, William, II
Walker, Timothy

1706

Callender, John
Franklin, Benjamin
Hobart, Noah
Mather, Samuel
Seccombe, Joseph

1707

Byles, Mather
Ferris, David
Hopkins, Stephen
Stith, William

1708

Ames, Nathaniel, II
Seccomb, John
Stanton, Daniel
Turell, Jane Colman
Webb, George (c. 1708)

1709

Adair, James (c. 1709)
Cooke, Samuel
Robbins, Philemon

1710

Bland, Richard
Brickell, John (c. 1710)
Carter, Landon
Carver, Jonathan
McGregore, David
Sergeant, John

1711

Cole, Nathan
Hammon, Jupiter
Hutchinson, Thomas
Mitchell, John
Muhlenberg, Henry Melchior
Wheelock, Eleazar

1712

Ashley, Jonathan
Blair, Samuel
Green, Jonas
Hamilton, Dr. Alexander

1713

Ashbridge, Elizabeth
Benezet, Anthony
Hayden, Esther (c. 1713)
Hunter, George, S.J.
Oliver, Peter
Todd, Jonathan

1714

Hall, Elihu
Osborn, Sarah
Parker, James (c. 1714)
Whitefield, George
Winthrop, John

1715

Beatty, Charles Clinton
   (c. 1715)
Curwen, Samuel
Finley, Samuel
Fothergill, Samuel
Gray, Ellis
Norton, John

1716

Barnard, Thomas
Buell, Samuel
Burr, Aaron
Schlatter, Michael
Waller, Benjamin

1717

Bass, John
Frothingham, Ebenezer (c. 1717)

1718

Brainerd, David
Camm, John
Cradock, Thomas
Eliot, Andrew
Maury, James
Sandeman, Robert
Welles, Noah

1719

Bellamy, Joseph
Hitchcock, Gad
Thacher, Oxenbridge

1720

Mayhew, Jonathan
Woodmason, Charles (c. 1720)
Woolman, John

1721

Hopkins, Samuel

1722

Adams, Samuel
Auchmuty, Samuel
Bradford, William, "the third"
Briant, Lemuel
Cleaveland, John
Dorr, Edward
Dulany, Daniel, the Younger
Green, Jacob
Marshall, Humphry
Pinckney, Eliza Lucas (c. 1722)
Smith, John

1723

Davies, Samuel
Hart, Oliver
Livingston, William
Occom, Samson

Owen, Goronwy
Witherspoon, John

1724

Backus, Isaac
Campbell, Isaac (c. 1724)
Emerson, Joseph
Gadsden, Christopher
Husband, Herman
Johnson, Stephen
Rivington, James
Zubly, John Joachim

1725

Cooper, Samuel
Mason, George
Otis, James

1726

Badger, Stephen
Bowdoin, James
Chandler, Thomas Bradbury
Fletcher, Bridget Richardson
Gaine, Hugh
Macpherson, John (c. 1726)
Pattillo, Henry
Webster, Pelatiah

1727

Bordley, John Beale
Griffitts, Hannah
Haven, Samuel
Loudon, Samuel
Rogers, Robert (c. 1727)
Smith, William
Stiles, Ezra
Williams, William

1728

Adams, Amos
Gordon, William
Nicholas, Robert Carter

Sewall, Jonathan
Smith, William
Warren, Mercy Otis

1729

Seabury, Samuel
Thomson, Charles

1730

Barton, Thomas
Garden, Dr. Alexander
Johnson, Susannah Willard (Hastings)
Sherwood, Samuel
Street, Nicholas
Terry, Lucy
Timberlake, Henry
West, Benjamin
Whitaker, Nathaniel

1731

Bailey, Jacob
Banneker, Benjamin
Galloway, Joseph (c. 1731)

1732

Burr, Esther Edwards
Dickinson, John
Duffield, George
Lee, Richard Henry
Morris, Thomas
Shippen, Joseph
Washington, George

1733

Apthorp, East
Chaplin, Ebenezer
Cleaveland, Benjamin
Fiske, Nathan
Haven, Jason
Howard, Simeon
Jarratt, Devereux
Noble, Oliver
Prime, Benjamin Young

1734

Church, Benjamin
Drinker, Elizabeth Sandwith
Inglis, Charles (c. 1734)
Smalley, John

1735

Adams, John
Carroll, John
Crèvecoeur, Michel Guillaŭme Jean de
Dana, James
Hall, Prince (c. 1735)
Hemmenway, Moses
Peters, Samuel A.
Rugeley, Rowland (c. 1735)
Schaw, Janet (c. 1735)
Trumbull, Benjamin

1736

Godfrey, Thomas
Jones, David
Montrésor, John
Stockton, Annis Boudinot

1737

Carroll, Charles, of Carrollton
Cooper, Myles
Deane, Silas
Fergusson, Elizabeth Graeme
Hopkinson, Francis
Munford, Robert (c. 1737)
Odell, Jonathan
Paine, Thomas

1738

Allen, Ethan
Bolling, Robert
Boucher, Jonathan
Duché, Jacob
Eddis, William
Goddard, Mary Katharine
Hart, Levi
Viets, Roger

1739

Adams, Zabdiel
Allen, James
Bartram, William
Clinton, George
Maylem, John

1740

Hewat, Alexander (c. 1740)
Lee, Arthur
Leonard, Daniel
Martin, Alexander
Meigs, Return Jonathan
Stansbury, Joseph
Tennent, William, III

1741

Arnold, Benedict
Chase, Samuel
Digges, Thomas Atwood
Niles, Nathaniel
Sherburne, Henry
Warren, Joseph

1742

Bland, Theodorick
Drayton, William Henry
Evans, Nathaniel
Hunt, Isaac (c. 1742)
Reese, Thomas
Wilkins, Isaac
Wilson, James

1743

Allen, Thomas
Claggett, Thomas John
Jefferson, Thomas
Thomas, John

1744

Adams, Abigail
Belknap, Jeremy

Brockway, Thomas (c. 1744)
Burke, Thomas (c. 1744)
Gerry, Elbridge
Henley, Samuel
Hitchcock, Enos
Moody, James
Quincy, Josiah, Jr.

1745

Asbury, Francis
Edwards, Jonathan, Jr.
Emmons, Nathaniel
Equiano, Olaudah (c. 1745)
Hazard, Ebenezer
Jay, John
Rush, Benjamin
Seixas, Gershom Mendez

1746

Billings, William
Bradford, Ebenezer
Fitch, Elijah
Jones, Absalom
McClurg, James
McCorkle, Samuel Eusebius
Spring, Samuel

1747

Coombe, Thomas
Duer, William
Evans, Israel
Filson, John (c. 1747)
Fithian, Philip Vickers
Forrest, Thomas

1748

Alline, Henry
Brackenridge, Hugh Henry
Hicks, Elias
Martin, Luther
Murdock, John (c. 1748)
Sewall, Jonathan Mitchell
Strong, Nathan
Tufts, Henry

1749

Backus, Charles
Perkins, Nathan
Ramsay, David
Sampson, Ezra
Thomas, Isaiah

1750

Daboll, Nathan
Hopkins, Lemuel
Trumbull, John
Tucker, Nathaniel

1751

Dodge, John
Fenno, John
Iredell, James
Ledyard, John
Madison, James
Morton, Perez
Murray, Judith Sargent
Scott, Job
Smith, Samuel Stanhope

1752

Bleecker, Anne Eliza
Clark, George Rogers
Crawford, Charles
Dwight, Timothy
Freneau, Philip
Graydon, Alexander
Humphreys, David
Markoe, Peter (c. 1752)
Morris, Gouverneur
Smith, John
Tappan, David
Thacher, Peter
Tucker, St. George

1753

Haynes, Lemuel
Howe, John
Randolph, Edmund

Senter, Isaac
Taylor, John, of Caroline

1754

Barlow, Joel
Imlay, Gilbert (c. 1754)
Leland, John
Parke, John
Thacher, James
Wheatley, Phillis (c. 1754)

1755

Adams, Hannah
Butler, James
Clarke, John
Coxe, Tench
Marrant, John

1756

Lee, Henry
Smith, Anna Young

1757

Beckley, John James
Hamilton, Alexander
Livingston, (Henry) Brockholst
Meigs, Josiah
Pinckney, Charles
Smith, Eunice
Tyler, Royall

1758

Lee, Charles
Minot, George Richards
Porter, Eliphalet
Smith, William Loughton
Webster, Noah

1759

Blair, John Durbarrow
Cooper, Thomas

Foster, Hannah Webster
Morton, Sarah Wentworth
Weems, Mason Locke

1760

Allen, Richard
Bruce, David (c. 1760)
Carey, Mathew
Duane, William
Johnson, Thomas (c. 1760)
Marshall, Humphrey
Murray, William Vans
Wells, Helena (c. 1760)

1761

Alsop, Richard
Cogswell, Mason Fitch
  (c. 1761)
Gallatin, Albert
Morse, Jedidiah
Wister, Sally

1762

Bend, Joseph Grove John
  (c. 1762)
Roane, Spencer
Rowson, Susanna Haswell

1763

Bidwell, Barnabas
Cobbett, William
Griswold, Stanley
Holmes, Abiel
Kinnan, Mary
Livingston, Anne Home

1764

Dwight, Theodore
Ladd, Joseph Brown
Meigs, Return Jonathan
Palmer, Elihu

1765

Brown, William Hill (c. 1765)
Burroughs, Stephen
Low, Samuel

1766

Barton, Benjamin Smith
Dunlap, William
Hodgkinson, John (c. 1766)
Thomas, Robert Bailey
Toulmin, Harry

1768

Dennie, Joseph

1769

Bache, Benjamin Franklin
Emerson, William
Odiorne, Thomas

1770

Everett, David

1771

Brown, Charles Brockden
Faugeres, Margaretta V. Bleecker
Lathy, Thomas Pike
Mann, Herman
Smith, Elihu Hubbard

1772

Burk, John Daly (c. 1772)
Cliffton, William
Wirt, William

1773

Paine, Robert Treat

1774

Branagan, Thomas
Story, Isaac

1775

Allen, Paul
Elliot, James
Munford, William

1776

Relf, Samuel

1777

Day, Thomas M.
Linn, John Blair

1778

Shaw, John

1783

Payson, Edward

APPENDIX B
Place of Birth

This appendix provides an alphabetical listing of entries according to place of birth. The appendix consists of three general categories: those persons for whom no certain information is available; those individuals who were born in the geographical locale of what is now the United States; and those persons born in other lands and countries. Names for individuals born in the United States are further categorized according to separate states. Names for individuals born outside the United States are subdivided according to country or region. When ascertainable, a year of birth is provided within parentheses following each name. For those entries for whom no year of birth is known, date of death or other identifying years are supplied.

NOT KNOWN

Atkins, Josiah (fl. 1781)
Fenno, Jenny (fl. 1791)
Fletcher, Bridget Richardson (1726)
Gutridge, Molly (fl. 1778)
Hall, Prince (c. 1735 [or 1748])
Hammon, Briton (fl. 1747-1760)
Monis, Judah (1683)
Moorehead, Sarah Parsons (fl. 1741-1742)
Pain, Philip (c. 1647)
Savage, Thomas (1640)
Taylor, Jacob (d. 1746)
Wortman, Tunis (d. 1822)

UNITED STATES

Connecticut

Adams, William (1650)
Allen, Ethan (1738)

Alsop, Richard (1761)
Arnold, Benedict (1741)
Backus, Charles (1749)
Backus, Isaac (1724)
Barlow, Joel (1754)
Beach, John (1700)
Beckwith, George (1703)
Bellamy, Joseph (1719)
Bradford, Ebenezer (1746)
Brainerd, David (1718)
Brewster, Martha (fl. 1725-1757)
Brockway, Thomas (c. 1744)
Buckingham, Thomas (1671)
Buell, Samuel (1716)
Bulkley, John (1679)
Burnham, William (1684)
Burr, Aaron (1716)
Chandler, Thomas Bradbury (1726)
Chaplin, Ebenezer (1733)
Cheever, Samuel (1639)
Chester, Stephen (1639)

Cleaveland, Benjamin (1733)
Cleaveland, John (1722)
Cogswell, Mason Fitch (1761)
Cole, Nathan (1711)
Cooke, Samuel (1687)
Daboll, Nathan (1750)
Day, Thomas M. (1777)
Deane, Silas (1737)
Dodge, John (1751)
Doolittle, Benjamin (1695)
Dorr, Edward (1722)
Edwards, Jonathan (1703)
Eells, Nathaniel (1677)
Eliot, Jared (1685)
Emmons, Nathaniel (1745)
Ferris, David (1707)
Fitch, Elijah (1746)
Fitch, Thomas (1700)
Goddard, Mary Katharine (1738)
Griswold, Stanley (1763)
Hall, Elihu (1714)
Hart, Levi (1738)
Haynes, Lemuel (1753)
Holmes, Abiel (1763)
Hopkins, Lemuel (1750)
Hopkins, Samuel (1721)
Humphreys, David (1752)
Johnson, Samuel (1696)
Ledyard, John (1751)
Lord, Benjamin (1694)
Mather, Azariah (1685)
Meigs, Josiah (1757)
Meigs, Return Jonathan (1740)
Meigs, Return Jonathan (1764)
Morgan, Joseph (1671)
Morse, Jedidiah (1761)
Noble, Oliver (1733)
Norton, John (1715)
Occom, Samson (1723)
Palmer, Elihu (1764)
Perkins, Nathan (1749)
Peters, Samuel A. (1735)
Rogers, John (1648)
Russell, Noadiah (1659)
Seabury, Samuel (1729)
Sherwood, Samuel (1730)
Smalley, John (1734)
Smith, Elihu Hubbard (1771)
Stiles, Ezra (1727)
Stiles, Isaac (1697)
Street, Nicholas (1730)
Strong, Nathan (1748)
Todd, Jonathan (1713)

Trumbull, Benjamin (1735)
Trumbull, John (1750)
Viets, Roger (1738)
Webster, Noah (1758)
Webster, Pelatiah (1726)
Welles, Noah (1718)
Wetmore, James (1695)
Wheelock, Eleazar (1711)
Wolcott, Roger (1679)

Delaware

Davies, Samuel (1723)
French, David (1700)
Jones, Absalom (1746)
Jones, David (1736)
Parke, John (1754)

Maine

Gyles, John (c. 1678)
Howard, Simeon (1733)

Maryland

Banneker, Benjamin (1731)
Bordley, John Beale (1727)
Carroll, Charles, of Carrollton (1737)
Carroll, John (1735)
Chase, Samuel (1741)
Claggett, Thomas John (1743)
Dickinson, John (1732)
Digges, Thomas Atwood (1741)
Dulany, Daniel, the Younger (1722)
Galloway, Joseph (c. 1731)
Gist, Christopher (1705)
Husband, Herman (1724)
Murray, William Vans (1760)
Shaw, John (1778)
Thomas, John (1743)
Weems, Mason Locke (1759)
Wirt, William (1772)

Massachusetts

Adams, Abigail (1744)
Adams, Amos (1728)
Adams, Eliphalet (1677)
Adams, Hannah (1755)
Adams, John (1705)
Adams, John (1735)
Adams, Samuel (1722)
Adams, Zabdiel (1739)
Allen, James (1739)
Allen, Thomas (1743)
Allin, James (1692)
Ames, Nathaniel, II (1708)

Appleton, Nathaniel (1693)
Apthorp, East (1733)
Ashley, Jonathan (1712)
Auchmuty, Samuel (1722)
Badger, Stephen (1726)
Bailey, Jacob (1731)
Barnard, John (1681)
Barnard, Thomas (1716)
Bass, John (1717)
Belcher, Samuel (c. 1640)
Belknap, Jeremy (1744)
Bidwell, Barnabas (1763)
Billings, William (1746)
Bowdoin, James (1726)
Bowers, Bathsheba (c. 1672)
Boylston, Zabdiel (1679)
Bradstreet, Samuel (c. 1633)
Brattle, Thomas (1658)
Brattle, William (1662)
Briant, Lemuel (1722)
Brigden, Zechariah (1639)
Brown, William Hill (c. 1765)
Bulkeley, Gershom (1636)
Bulkeley, Peter, II (1643)
Burr, Esther Edwards (1732)
Byles, Mather (1707)
Callender, John (1706)
Capen, Joseph (1658)
Carver, Jonathan (1710)
Chauncy, Charles (1705)
Chauncy, Israel (1644)
Chauncy, Nathaniel (1639)
Checkley, John (1680)
Checkley, Samuel (1696)
Church, Benjamin (1639)
Church, Thomas (1673)
Clap, Thomas Stephen (1703)
Clark, Peter (1694)
Clarke, John (1755)
Coleman, Elihu (1699)
Colman, Benjamin (1673)
Cooke, Samuel (1709)
Cooper, Samuel (1725)
Cooper, William (1694)
Cotton, John (1640)
Curwen, Samuel (1715)
Dana, James (1735)
Danforth, John (1660)
Danforth, Samuel (1666)
Dennie, Joseph (1768)
Dickinson, Moses (1695)
Dudley, Joseph (1647)
Dudley, Paul (1675)

Dummer, Jeremiah (1681)
Dunbar, Samuel (1704)
Dunster, David (1645)
Dwight, Theodore (1764)
Dwight, Timothy (1752)
Edwards, Jonathan, Jr. (1745)
Eliot, Andrew (1718)
Elliot, James (1775)
Emerson, Joseph (1700)
Emerson, Joseph (1724)
Emerson, William (1769)
Everett, David (1770)
Fenno, John (1751)
Fiske, Nathan (1733)
Fiske, Sarah Symmes (1652)
Foster, Hannah Webster (1759)
Foster, John (1648)
Foxcroft, Thomas (1697)
Franklin, Benjamin (1706)
Franklin, James (1697)
Frothingham, Ebenezer (c. 1717)
Gay, Ebenezer (1696)
Gee, Joshua (1698)
Gerry, Elbridge (1744)
Gibbs, Henry (1668)
Goodhue, Sarah (1641)
Gookin, Daniel, Jr. (1650)
Gray, Ellis (1715)
Green, Jacob (1722)
Green, Jonas (1712)
Green, Joseph (c. 1705)
Greenwood, Isaac (1702)
Hale, John (1636)
Hammond, Lawrence (c. 1640)
Hancock, John (1702)
Haven, Jason (1733)
Haven, Samuel (1727)
Hayden, Anna Tompson (1648)
Hayden, Esther (c. 1713)
Hemmenway, Moses (1735)
Henchman, Daniel (1677)
Henchman, Richard (c. 1655)
Hitchcock, Enos (1744)
Hitchcock, Gad (1719)
Hobart, Nehemiah (1648)
Hobart, Noah (1706)
Hooker, Samuel (1635)
Hutchinson, Thomas (1711)
Jewett, Jedidiah (c. 1705)
Johnson, Susannah Willard (Hastings) (1730)
Knight, Sarah Kemble (1666)
Leland, John (1754)
Leonard, Daniel (1740)

Loring, Israel (1682)
Lynde, Benjamin (1666)
Mann, Herman (1771)
Marsh, Jonathan (1685)
Mather, Cotton (1663)
Mather, Eleazer (1637)
Mather, Increase (1639)
Mather, Samuel (1706)
Mayhew, Experience (1673)
Mayhew, Jonathan (1720)
Mayhew, Matthew (1648)
Maylem, John (1739)
Minot, George Richards (1758)
Mixer, Elizabeth (fl. 1707-1720)
Morton, Perez (1751)
Morton, Sarah Wentworth (1759)
Murray, Judith Sargent (1751)
Norton, John, II (1651)
Nowell, Samuel (1634)
Noyes, Nicholas (1647)
Oliver, Peter (1713)
Otis, James (1725)
Paine, John (1661)
Paine, Robert Treat (1773)
Paine, Solomon (1698)
Parkman, Ebenezer (1703)
Parsons, Jonathan (1705)
Payson, Edward (1657)
Peabody, Oliver (1698)
Pemberton, Ebenezer (1672)
Pickering, Theophilus (1700)
Porter, Eliphalet (1758)
Prentice, Thomas (1702)
Prescott, Benjamin (1687)
Prince, Thomas (1687)
Quincy, Josiah, Jr. (1744)
Rand, William (1700)
Rawson, Grindall (1659)
Richardson, John (1647)
Robbins, Philemon (1709)
Rogers, Robert (c. 1727)
Russell, Daniel (1642)
Saltonstall, Gurdon (1666)
Saltonstall, Nathaniel (c. 1639)
Sampson, Ezra (1749)
Seccomb, John (1708)
Seccombe, Joseph (1706)
Sewall, Jonathan (1728)
Sewall, Jonathan Mitchell (1748)
Sewall, Joseph (1688)
Shepard, Jeremiah (1648)
Shurtleff, William (1689)
Smith, Eunice (1757)

Smith, John (1752)
Spring, Samuel (1746)
Stoddard, Solomon (1643)
Story, Isaac (1774)
Stoughton, William (1631)
Symmes, Thomas (1678)
Tappan, David (1752)
Thacher, James (1754)
Thacher, Oxenbridge (1719)
Thacher, Peter (1688)
Thacher, Peter (1752)
Thomas, Isaiah (1749)
Thomas, Robert Bailey (1766)
Tompson, Benjamin (1642)
Tompson, Edward (1666)
Townsend, Jonathan (1697)
Turell, Ebenezer (1702)
Turell, Jane Colman (1708)
Tyler, Royall (1757)
Wadsworth, Benjamin (1670)
Walker, Timothy (1705)
Walter, Thomas (1696)
Warren, Joseph (1741)
Warren, Mercy Otis (1728)
Webb, John (1687)
West, Benjamin (1730)
Wheeler, Thomas (c. 1640)
Wigglesworth, Edward (1693)
Wigglesworth, Samuel (1689)
Willard, Samuel (1640)
Williams, Elisha (1694)
Williams, John (1664)
Williams, Solomon (1700)
Williams, William (1665)
Williams, William (1688)
Winthrop, John (1714)
Wise, John (1652)

New Hampshire

Burroughs, Stephen (1765)
Clarke, John (1755)
Drake, Francis (c. 1650)
Hanson, Elizabeth (1684)
Odiorne, Thomas (1769)
Payson, Edward (1783)
Senter, Isaac (1753)
Sherburne, Henry (1741)
Tufts, Henry (1748)

New Jersey

Dunlap, William (1766)
Fithian, Philip Vickers (1747)
Howell, Rednap (fl. 1750-1787)

Imlay, Gilbert (c. 1754)
Johnson, Stephen (1724)
Leeds, Felix (1687)
Leeds, Titan (1699)
Martin, Alexander (1740)
Martin, Luther (1748)
Moody, James (1744)
Odell, Jonathan (1737)
Parker, James (c. 1714)
Sergeant, John (1710)
Smith, John (1722)
Tennent, William, II (1740)
Woolman, John (1720)

New York

Antill, Edward (1701)
Bend, Joseph Grove John (c. 1762)
Bleecker, Anne Eliza (1752)
Clinton, George (1739)
Duane, William (1760)
Faugeres, Margaretta V. Bleecker (1771)
Freneau, Philip (1752)
Hammon, Jupiter (1711)
Hicks, Elias (1748)
Jay, John (1745)
Livingston, (Henry) Brockholst (1757)
Livingston, William (1723)
Low, Samuel (1765)
Marrant, John (1755)
Morris, Gouverneur (1752)
Morris, Lewis (1671)
Prime, Benjamin Young (1733)
Seixas, Gershom Mendez (1745)
Smith, William (1728)
Whitaker, Nathaniel (1730)

Pennsylvania

Allen, Richard (1760)
Bache, Benjamin Franklin (1769)
Barton, Benjamin Smith (1766)
Bartram, John (1699)
Bartram, William (1739)
Blair, John Durbarrow (1759)
Bradford, Andrew (1686)
Bradford, William, "the third" (1722)
Breintnall, Joseph (d. 1746)
Brown, Charles Brockden (1771)
Churchman, John (1705)
Cliffton, William (1772)
Coombe, Thomas (1747)
Coxe, Tench (1755)
Drinker, Elizabeth Sandwith (1734)
Duché, Jacob (1738)

Duffield, George (1732)
Evans, Israel (1747)
Evans, Nathaniel (1742)
Fergusson, Elizabeth Graeme (1737)
Filson, John (c. 1747)
Forrest, Thomas (1747)
Godfrey, Thomas (1736)
Graydon, Alexander (1752)
Griffitts, Hannah (1727)
Hart, Oliver (1723)
Hazard, Ebenezer (1745)
Hopkinson, Francis (1737)
Leacock, John (fl. 1776)
Linn, John Blair (1777)
Livingston, Anne Home (1763)
McCorkle, Samuel Eusebius (1746)
Marshall, Humphry (1722)
Murdock, John (1748)
Ralph, James (c. 1705)
Ramsay, David (1749)
Reese, Thomas (1742)
Rush, Benjamin (1745)
Shippen, Joseph (1732)
Smith, Anna Young (1756)
Smith, Samuel Stanhope (1751)
Stanton, Daniel (1708)
Stockton, Annis Boudinot (1736)
Wister, Sally (1761)

Rhode Island

Allen, Paul (1775)
Alline, Henry (1748)
Church, Benjamin (1734)
Hopkins, Stephen (1707)
Howard, Martin, Jr. (fl. 1730-1781)
Ladd, Joseph Brown (1764)
Niles, Nathaniel (1741)
Niles, Samuel (1674)
Scott, Job (1751)

South Carolina

Drayton, William Henry (1742)
Gadsden, Christopher (1724)
Pinckney, Charles (1757)
Smith, Josiah (1704)
Smith, William Loughton (1758)
Wells, Helena (c. 1760)
Wilkinson, Eliza Yonge (fl. 1779-1782)

Virginia

Beverley, Robert (c. 1673)
Bland, Richard (1710)
Bland, Theodorick (1742)

Bolling, Robert (1738)
Byrd, William, of Westover (1674)
Carter, Landon (1710)
Clark, George Rogers (1752)
Cotton, John, of Queen's Creek (c. 1640)
Fox, John (c. 1686)
Hansford, Charles (c. 1685)
Jarratt, Devereux (1733)
Jefferson, Thomas (1743)
Johnson, Thomas (c. 1760)
Kinnan, Mary (1763)
Lee, Arthur (1740)
Lee, Charles (1758)
Lee, Henry (1756)
Lee, Richard Henry (1732)
McClurg, James (1746)
Madison, James (1751)
Marshall, Humphrey (1760)
Mason, George (1725)
Mitchell, John (1711)
Munford, Robert (c. 1737)
Munford, William (1775)
Nicholas, Robert Carter (1728)
Randolph, Edmund (1753)
Relf, Samuel (1776)
Roane, Spencer (1762)
Stith, William (1707)
Taylor, John, of Caroline (1753)
Timberlake, Henry (1730)
Waller, Benjamin (1716)
Washington, George (1732)
White, Henry (c. 1642)

OTHER COUNTRIES

Africa

Equiano, Olaudah (c. 1745)
Spotswood, Alexander (1676)
Terry, Lucy (1730)
Wheatley, Phillis (c. 1754)

Bermuda

Starkey, George (c. 1628)
Tucker, Nathaniel (1750)
Tucker, St. George (1752)

England

Allen, James (1632)
Allen, John (fl. 1767-1788)
Alsop, George (c. 1636)
Archer, Gabriel (1575)

Arnold, Samuel (1622)
Asbury, Francis (1745)
Ashbridge, Elizabeth (1713)
Ashe, Thomas (fl. 1680-1682)
Aston, Anthony (fl. 1682-1747)
Attwood, Peter, S.J. (1682)
Bacon, Nathaniel (1647)
Bacon, Thomas (c. 1700)
Beckley, John James (1757)
Beete, John (fl. 1795-1797)
Berkeley, Sir William (c. 1608)
Blackamore, Arthur (c. 1679)
Bland, Edward (d. 1653)
Bosworth, Benjamin (c. 1612)
Boucher, Jonathan (1738)
Bradford, William (1590)
Bradford, William (1663)
Bradstreet, Anne (c. 1612)
Bray, Thomas (c. 1658)
Brereton, John (fl. 1590-1602)
Brooke, Henry (1678)
Budd, Thomas (fl. 1678-1698)
Bulkeley, Edward (1614)
Bulkeley, Peter (1583)
Burt, Jonathan (c. 1632)
Butler, James (1755)
Calef, Robert (c. 1647)
Camm, John (1718)
Carew, Bampfylde-Moore (1693)
Catesby, Mark (1683)
Chalkley, Thomas (1675)
Chamberlain, Richard (1632)
Chase, Thomas (c. 1703)
Chauncy, Charles (c. 1592)
Cheever, Ezekiel (1615)
Clap, Roger (1609)
Clarke, John (1609)
Clayton, John (1657)
Clayton, John (1694)
Cobbet, Thomas (1608)
Cobbett, William (1763)
Cockings, George (fl. 1760-1802)
Cooke, Ebenezer (c. 1667)
Cooper, Myles (1737)
Cooper, Thomas (1759)
Cotton, John (1584)
Coxe, Daniel (1673)
Cradock, Thomas (1718)
Cushman, Robert (c. 1579)
Dale, Thomas (1700)
Dane, John (c. 1612)
Danforth, Samuel (1626)
Davenport, John (1597)

Dawson, William (1704)
Denton, Daniel (fl. 1656-1696)
Dudley, Thomas (1576)
Duer, William (1747)
Dumbleton, Joseph (fl. 1740-1750)
Dunster, Henry (1609)
Dunton, John (1659)
Eddis, William (1738)
Eliot, John (1604)
Firmin, Giles (c. 1614)
Fiske, John (1608)
Fitch, James (1622)
Fitzhugh, William (1651)
Folger, Peter (1617)
Fothergill, Samuel (1715)
Frame, Richard (fl. 1692)
Gardiner, Lion (1599)
Gookin, Daniel (c. 1612)
Gordon, William (1728)
Gorges, Sir Ferdinando (c. 1566)
Gorton, Samuel (c. 1592)
Gray, Robert (fl. 1609)
Hall, Clement (c. 1699)
Hammond, John (fl. 1634-1663)
Hariot, Thomas (1560)
Harris, Benjamin (fl. 1673-1711)
Henley, Samuel (1740)
Higginson, Francis (1587)
Higginson, John (1616)
Hinckley, Thomas (1618)
Hoar, Leonard (c. 1630)
Hodgkinson, John (c. 1766)
Holme, John (fl. 1685-1701)
Hooke, William (1601)
Hooker, Thomas (1586)
Howe, John (1753)
Hubbard, William (c. 1621)
Huit, Ephraim (fl. 1611-1644)
Hull, John (1624)
Hunter, George, S.J. (1713)
Iredell, James (1751)
James, John (c. 1633)
Johnson, Edward (1599)
Johnson, Robert (fl. 1600-1621)
Jones, Hugh (1670)
Josselyn, John (c. 1608)
Keimer, Samuel (1688)
Knapp, Francis (1671)
Knott, Edward, S.J. (1582)
Lane, Ralph (1530)
Lathy, Thomas Pike (1771)
Lawson, Deodat(e) (fl. 1660-1715)

Lawson, John (d. 1711)
Lechford, Thomas (c. 1590)
Leeds, Daniel (1652)
Long, John (fl. 1768-1791)
Lowell, Percival (1571)
Lyon, Richard (fl. 1620-1651)
Makin, Thomas (1665)
Markland, John (fl. 1721-1735)
Marshall, Humphry (1722)
Martyn, Benjamin (1699)
Mason, John (c. 1600)
Mather, Nathaniel (1630)
Mather, Richard (1596)
Mathew, Thomas (c. 1650)
Maule, Thomas (c. 1645)
Maverick, Samuel (c. 1602)
Mayhew, Thomas, Jr. (c. 1621)
Micklejohn, George (d. 1817)
Mitchel, Jonathan (1624)
Moodey, Joshua (1633)
Morrell, William (fl. 1623-1625)
Morris, Thomas (1732)
Morton, Charles (c. 1627)
Morton, George (1585)
Morton, Thomas (c. 1579)
Moxon, George (1602)
Norton, John (1606)
Norwood, Henry (1615)
Noyes, James (1608)
Oakes, Urian (c. 1631)
Oglethorpe, James Edward (1696)
Osborn, Sarah (1714)
Oxenbridge, John (1609)
Paine, Thomas (1737)
Parker, Thomas (1595)
Parks, William (c. 1698)
Pead, Deuel (d. 1727)
Penhallow, Samuel (1665)
Penn, William (1644)
Percy, George (1580)
Perry, Edward (1630)
Peter, Hugh (1598)
Phillips, George (1593)
Pierson, Abraham (c. 1608)
Pory, John (1572)
Purchas, Samuel (1575)
Pynchon, William (c. 1590)
Rich, Richard (fl. 1609-1610)
Rivington, James (1724)
Robinson, J. (fl. 1792)
Rogers, John (1630)
Rolfe, John (c. 1585)
Rose, Aquila (1695)

Rosier, James (1575)
Rowlandson, Joseph (c. 1631)
Rowlandson, Mary (c. 1635)
Rowson, Susanna Haswell (1762)
Rugeley, Rowland (c. 1735)
Ruggle, George (1575)
Saffin, John (1626)
Sandys, George (1578)
Scottow, Joshua (c. 1618)
Sewall, Samuel (1652)
Shepard, Thomas (1605)
Shepard, Thomas (1635)
Shirley, William (1694)
Smith, Captain John (1580)
Somerby, Anthony (1610)
Spelman, Henry (c. 1595)
Stansbury, Joseph (1740)
Steere, Richard (1643)
Stephens, William (1671)
Stone, Samuel (1602)
Story, Thomas (c. 1670)
Strachey, William (1572)
Taylor, Edward (c. 1642)
Tennent, John (c. 1700)
Thacher, Thomas (1620)
Tillam, Thomas (d. after 1668)
Torrey, Samuel (1632)
Toulmin, Harry (1766)
Trott, Nicholas (1663)
Tulley, John (1638)
Underhill, John (c. 1597)
Vincent, Philip (1600)
Walley, Thomas (1618)
Ward, Nathaniel (c. 1578)
Webb, George (c. 1708)
Weld, Edmund (1631)
Welde, Thomas (1595)
West, Thomas, Baron de la Warr (1577)
Wheelwright, John (c. 1592)
Whitaker, Alexander (1585)
White, Andrew, S.J. (1579)
White, Elizabeth (d. 1669)
White, John (1575)
Whitefield, George (1714)
Whiting, John (c. 1635)
Whiting, Samuel (1597)
Wigglesworth, Michael (1631)
Williams, Roger (c. 1603)
Williams, William (1727)
Wilson, John (c. 1588)
Wingfield, Edward Maria (c. 1560)
Winslow, Edward (1595)
Winthrop, John (1588)

Winthrop, John, Jr. (1606)
Wiswall, Ichabod (1637)
Wood, William (c. 1606)
Woodbridge, Benjamin (1622)
Woodbridge, John (1613)
Woodmason, Charles (c. 1720)

France

Benezet, Anthony (1713)
Crèvecoeur, Michel Guillaŭme Jean de (1735)

Germany

Beissel, Johann Conrad (1690)
Boehm, John Philip (1683)
Dock, Christopher (c. 1698)
Frelinghuysen, Theodorus Jacobus (1691)
Lederer, John (c. 1644)
Muhlenberg, Henry Melchior (1711)
Pastorius, Francis Daniel (1651)
Sauer, Christopher, I (1693)
Spangenberg, Augustus Gottlieb (1704)
Von Zinzendorf, Nicholas Ludwig Count (1700)
Zenger, John Peter (1697)

Holland

Danckaerts, Jasper (1639)
Montrésor, John (1736)
Morton, Nathaniel (1613)
Selyns, Henricus (1636)
Steendam, Jacob (1615)

Ireland

Adair, James (c. 1709)
Alison, Francis (1705)
Barton, Thomas (1730)
Beatty, Charles Clinton (c. 1715)
Berkeley, George (1685)
Blair, Samuel (1712)
Branagan, Thomas (1774)
Brickell, John (c. 1710)
Bruce, David (c. 1760)
Burk, John Daly (c. 1772)
Burke, Thomas (c. 1744)
Carey, Mathew (1760)
Colden, Cadwallader (1688)
Dulany, Daniel, the Elder (1685)
Finley, Samuel (1715)
Gaine, Hugh (1726)
Inglis, Charles (c. 1734)
Logan, James (1674)
Loudon, Samuel (1727)
McGregore, David (1710)
MacSparran, James (1693)

Makemie, Francis (1658)
Maury, James (1718)
Mercer, John (1704)
Smith, Michael (1698)
Sterling, James (1701)
Tennent, Gilbert (1703)
Tennent, William, II (1705)
Thomson, Charles (1729)
Walter, Nehemiah (1663)

Scotland

Bannerman, Mark (d. 1727)
Beveridge, John (1703)
Blair, James (c. 1655)
Brackenridge, Hugh Henry (1748)
Campbell, Isaac (c. 1724)
Douglass, William (c. 1691)
Garden, Alexander (c. 1685)
Garden, Dr. Alexander (1730)
Graham, John (1694)
Hamilton, Dr. Alexander (1712)
Hepburn, John (fl. 1715-c. 1745)
Hewat, Alexander (c. 1740)
Hooper, William (1702)
Hunter, Robert (fl. 1714-1734)
Keith, George (c. 1638)
Kil(l)patrick, James (c. 1700)
Macpherson, John (c. 1726)
Pattillo, Henry (1726)
Paxton, Robert (d. 1714)

Reid, James (fl. 1768-1769)
Sandeman, Robert (1718)
Schaw, Janet (c. 1735)
Smith, William (1727)
Tailfer, Patrick (fl. 1734-1741)
Thomson, John (c. 1690)
Wilson, James (1742)
Witherspoon, John (1723)

Switzerland

Gallatin, Albert (1761)
Schlatter, Michael (1716)
Zubly, John Joachim (1724)

Wales

Easton, John (c. 1624)
Evans, Lewis (c. 1700)
Lewis, Richard (c. 1700)
Morgan, Abel (1673)
Owen, Goronwy (1723)
Thomas, Gabriel (1661)

West Indies

Crawford, Charles (1752)
Dickinson, Jonathan (1663)
Hamilton, Alexander (1757)
Hunt, Isaac (c. 1742)
Markoe, Peter (c. 1752)
Pinckney, Eliza Lucas (c. 1722)
Wilkins, Isaac (1742)

APPENDIX C
Principal Place(s) of Residence

This appendix provides an alphabetical listing of the entries according to principal place or places of residence. Since many writers moved frequently, this list is by no means exhaustive or complete regarding every place where every writer lived. Rather, it is an attempt to group early American writers according to those places where they spent the most substantial portions of their adult lives. With only a few exceptions, no more than three places of residence are given for any one writer. A year of birth or other appropriate identifying years appear in parentheses after each name.

UNITED STATES

No Fixed Residences

Asbury, Francis (1745)
Carew, Bampfylde-Moore (1693)
Fothergill, Samuel (1715)
Scott, Job (1751)
Whitefield, George (1714)

Alabama

Toulmin, Harry (1766)

Connecticut

Adams, Eliphalet (1677)
Alsop, Richard (1761)
Arnold, Benedict (1741)
Atkins, Josiah (fl. 1781)
Backus, Charles (1749)

Backus, Isaac (1724)
Barlow, Joel (1754)
Bass, John (1717)
Beach, John (1700)
Beckwith, George (1703)
Bellamy, Joseph (1719)
Beveridge, John (1703)
Bradford, Ebenezer (1746)
Brainerd, David (1718)
Brewster, Martha (fl. 1725-1757)
Brockway, Thomas (c. 1744)
Buckingham, Thomas (1671)
Buell, Samuel (1716)
Bulkeley, Gershom (c. 1636)
Bulkeley, Peter, II (1643)
Bulkley, John (1679)
Burnham, William (1684)
Chaplin, Ebenezer (1733)
Chauncy, Israel (1644)
Chauncy, Nathaniel (1639)

Cheever, Ezekiel (1615)
Chester, Stephen (1639)
Clap, Thomas Stephen (1703)
Cleaveland, Benjamin (1733)
Cogswell, Mason Fitch (1761)
Cole, Nathan (1711)
Cooke, Samuel (1687)
Daboll, Nathan (1750)
Dana, James (1735)
Davenport, John (1597)
Day, Thomas M. (1777)
Deane, Silas (1737)
Dickinson, Moses (1695)
Dorr, Edward (1722)
Dwight, Theodore (1764)
Dwight, Timothy (1752)
Edwards, Jonathan (1703)
Edwards, Jonathan, Jr. (1745)
Eliot, Jared (1685)
Fitch, James (1622)
Fitch, Thomas (1700)
Frothingham, Ebenezer (c. 1717)
Gardiner, Lion (1599)
Graham, John (1694)
Griswold, Stanley (1763)
Hall, Elihu (1714)
Hammon, Jupiter (1711)
Hart, Levi (1738)
Haynes, Lemuel (1753)
Higginson, John (1616)
Hobart, Noah (1706)
Holmes, Abiel (1763)
Hooke, William (1601)
Hooker, Samuel (1635)
Hooker, Thomas (1586)
Hopkins, Lemuel (1750)
Hopkins, Samuel (1721)
Huit, Ephraim (fl. 1611-1644)
Humphreys, David (1752)
James, John (c. 1633)
Johnson, Samuel (1696)
Johnson, Stephen (1724)
Knight, Sarah Kemble (1666)
Lederer, John (c. 1644)
Ledyard, John (1751)
Lord, Benjamin (1694)
Marsh, Jonathan (1685)
Mason, John (c. 1600)
Mather, Azariah (1685)
Meigs, Josiah (1757)
Meigs, Return Jonathan (1740)
Mitchel, Jonathan (1624)
Morgan, Joseph (1671)

Morse, Jedidiah (1761)
Niles, Nathaniel (1741)
Noble, Oliver (1733)
Norton, John (1715)
Occom, Samson (1723)
Paine, Solomon (1698)
Parsons, Jonathan (1705)
Perkins, Nathan (1749)
Peters, Samuel A. (1735)
Pierson, Abraham (c. 1608)
Prime, Benjamin Young (1733)
Robbins, Philemon (1709)
Rogers, John (1648)
Rowlandson, Joseph (c. 1631)
Rowlandson, Mary (c. 1635)
Russell, Daniel (1642)
Russell, Noadiah (1659)
Saltonstall, Gurdon (1666)
Sampson, Ezra (1749)
Sandeman, Robert (1718)
Seabury, Samuel (1729)
Sherwood, Samuel (1730)
Smalley, John (1734)
Smith, Elihu Hubbard (1771)
Steere, Richard (1643)
Stiles, Ezra (1727)
Stiles, Isaac (1697)
Stone, Samuel (1602)
Street, Nicholas (1730)
Strong, Nathan (1748)
Tennent, William, III (1740)
Todd, Jonathan (1713)
Trumbull, Benjamin (1735)
Trumbull, John (1750)
Tulley, John (1638)
Underhill, John (c.1597)
Viets, Roger (1738)
Vincent, Philip (1600)
Webster, Noah (1758)
Welles, Noah (1718)
Wetmore, James (1695)
Wheelock, Eleazar (1711)
Whitaker, Nathaniel (1730)
Whiting, John (c. 1635)
Williams, Elisha (1694)
Williams, Solomon (1700)
Winthrop, John, Jr. (1606)
Wolcott, Roger (1679)

Delaware

Alison, Francis (1705)
Brooke, Henry (1678)

Cobbett, William (1763)
Dickinson, John (1732)
Ferris, David (1707)
French, David (1700)
Inglis, Charles (c. 1734)
Parke, John (1754)
Tennent, Gilbert (1705)
Thomas, Gabriel (1661)
Thomson, John (c. 1690)

Georgia

Burroughs, Stephen (1765)
Holmes, Abiel (1763)
Marrant, John (1755)
Meigs, Josiah (1757)
Oglethorpe, James Edward (1696)
Palmer, Elihu (1764)
Stephens, William (1671)
Tailfer, Patrick (fl. 1734-1741)
Zubly, John Joachim (1724)

Illinois

Dodge, John (1751)
Griswold, Stanley (1763)

Kentucky

Clark, George Rogers (1752)
Filson, John (c. 1747)
Gist, Christopher (1705)
Imlay, Gilbert (c. 1754)
Johnson, Thomas (c. 1760)
Marshall, Humphrey (1760)
Toulmin, Harry (1766)

Louisiana

Meigs, Return Jonathan (1764)

Maine

Bailey, Jacob (1731)
Beveridge, John (1703)
Brereton, John (fl. 1590-1602)
Gallatin, Albert (1761)
Gyles, John (c. 1678)
Hemmenway, Moses (1735)
Josselyn, John (c. 1608)
Montrésor, John (1736)
Morton, Thomas (c. 1579)
Payson, Edward (1783)
Prentice, Thomas (1702)
Rosier, James (1575)
Story, Isaac (1774)
Tufts, Henry (1748)
Tyler, Royall (1757)
Whitaker, Nathaniel (1730)

Maryland

Allen, Paul (1775)
Alsop, George (c. 1636)
Attwood, Peter, S.J. (1682)
Bacon, Thomas (c. 1700)
Banneker, Benjamin (1731)
Bend, Joseph Grove (c. 1762)
Bordley, John Beale (1727)
Boucher, Jonathan (1738)
Bray, Thomas (c. 1658)
Bruce, David (c. 1760)
Campbell, Isaac (c. 1724)
Carroll, Charles, of Carrollton (1737)
Carroll, John (1735)
Chalkley, Thomas (1675)
Chase, Samuel (1741)
Chase, Thomas (c. 1703)
Claggett, Thomas John (1743)
Cooke, Ebenezer (c. 1667)
Cradock, Thomas (1718)
Danckaerts, Jasper (1639)
Digges, Thomas Atwood (1741)
Dulany, Daniel, the Elder (1685)
Dulany, Daniel, the Younger (1722)
Eddis, William (1738)
Gist, Christopher (1705)
Goddard, Mary Katharine (1738)
Green, Jonas (1712)
Hamilton, Dr. Alexander (1712)
Hammond, John (fl. 1634-1663)
Howell, Rednap (fl. 1750-1787)
Hunter, George, S.J. (1713)
Husband, Herman (1724)
Jones, Hugh (1671)
Lederer, John (c. 1644)
Lewis, Richard (c. 1700)
Martin, Luther (1748)
Murray, William Vans (1760)
Parks, William (c. 1698)
Pead, Deuel (d. 1727)
Rowson, Susanna Haswell (1762)
Shaw, John (1778)
Smith, William (1727)
Sterling, James (1701)
Thomas, John (1743)
Weems, Mason Locke (1759)
White, Andrew, S.J. (1579)

Massachusetts

Adams, Abigail (1744)
Adams, Amos (1728)
Adams, Eliphalet (1677)

Adams, Hannah (1755)
Adams, John (1705)
Adams, John (1735)
Adams, Samuel (1722)
Adams, William (1650)
Adams, Zabdiel (1739)
Allen, James (1632)
Allen, James (1739)
Allen, John (fl. 1764-1788)
Allen, Thomas (1743)
Allin, James (1692)
Ames, Nathaniel, II (1708)
Appleton, Nathaniel (1693)
Apthorp, East (1733)
Arnold, Samuel (1622)
Ashley, Jonathan (1712)
Backus, Isaac (1724)
Badger, Stephen (1726)
Barnard, John (1681)
Barnard, Thomas (1716)
Belcher, Samuel (c. 1640)
Belknap, Jeremy (1744)
Bidwell, Barnabas (1763)
Billings, William (1746)
Bosworth, Benjamin (c. 1612)
Bowdoin, James (1726)
Bowers, Bathsheba (c. 1672)
Boylston, Zabdiel (1679)
Bradford, Ebenezer (1746)
Bradford, William (1590)
Bradstreet, Anne (c. 1612)
Bradstreet, Samuel (c. 1633)
Brainerd, David (1718)
Brattle, Thomas (1658)
Brattle, William (1662)
Briant, Lemuel (1722)
Brigden, Zechariah (1639)
Brown, William Hill (c. 1765)
Bulkeley, Edward (1614)
Bulkeley, Gershom (c. 1636)
Bulkeley, Peter (1583)
Burk, John Daly (c. 1772)
Burr, Aaron (1716)
Burr, Esther Edwards (1732)
Burroughs, Stephen (1765)
Burt, Jonathan (c. 1632)
Byles, Mather (1707)
Calef, Robert (c. 1647)
Callender, John (1706)
Capen, Joseph (1658)
Carver, Jonathan (1710)
Chauncy, Charles (c. 1592)
Chauncy, Charles (1705)

Checkley, John (1680)
Checkley, Samuel (1696)
Cheever, Ezekiel (1615)
Cheever, Samuel (1639)
Church, Benjamin (1639)
Church, Benjamin (1734)
Church, Thomas (1673)
Clap, Roger (1609)
Clark, Peter (1694)
Clarke, John (1755)
Cleaveland, John (1722)
Cobbet, Thomas (1608)
Cockings, George (fl. 1760-
  1802)
Coleman, Elihu (1699)
Colman, Benjamin (1673)
Cooke, Samuel (1709)
Cooper, Samuel (1725)
Cooper, William (1694)
Cotton, John (1584)
Cotton, John (1640)
Curwen, Samuel (1715)
Cushman, Robert (c. 1579)
Dane, John (c. 1612)
Danforth, John (1660)
Danforth, Samuel (1626)
Danforth, Samuel (1666)
Davenport, John (1597)
Dennie, Joseph (1768)
Doolittle, Benjamin (1695)
Douglass, William (c. 1691)
Drake, Francis (c. 1650)
Dudley, Joseph (1647)
Dudley, Paul (1675)
Dudley, Thomas (1576)
Dummer, Jeremiah (1681)
Dunbar, Samuel (1704)
Dunster, David (1645)
Dunster, Henry (1609)
Dunton, John (1659)
Dwight, Timothy (1752)
Edwards, Jonathan (1703)
Eells, Nathaniel (1677)
Eliot, Andrew (1718)
Eliot, John (1604)
Emerson, Joseph (1700)
Emerson, Joseph (1724)
Emerson, William (1769)
Emmons, Nathaniel (1745)
Everett, David (1770)
Fenno, Jenny (fl. 1791)
Fenno, John (1751)
Firmin, Giles (c. 1614)

Fiske, John (1608)
Fiske, Nathan (1733)
Fiske, Sarah Symmes (1652)
Fitch, Elijah (1746)
Fletcher, Bridget Richardson (1726)
Folger, Peter (1617)
Foster, Hannah Webster (1759)
Foster, John (1648)
Foxcroft, Thomas (1697)
Franklin, Benjamin (1706)
Franklin, James (1697)
Frothingham, Ebenezer (c. 1717)
Gallatin, Albert (1761)
Gay, Ebenezer (1696)
Gee, Joshua (1698)
Gerry, Elbridge (1744)
Gibbs, Henry (1668)
Goodhue, Sarah (1641)
Gookin, Daniel (c. 1612)
Gookin, Daniel, Jr. (1650)
Gordon, William (1728)
Gorton, Samuel (c. 1592)
Gray, Ellis (1715)
Green, Jacob (1722)
Green, Joseph (c. 1705)
Greenwood, Isaac (1702)
Griswold, Stanley (1763)
Gutridge, Molly (fl. 1778)
Hale, John (1636)
Hall, Prince (c. 1735)
Hammon, Briton (fl. 1747-1760)
Hammond, Lawrence (c. 1640)
Hancock, John (1702)
Harris, Benjamin (fl. 1673-1711)
Haven, Jason (1733)
Hayden, Anna Tompson (1648)
Hayden, Esther (c. 1713)
Haynes, Lemuel (1753)
Hemmenway, Moses (1735)
Henchman, Daniel (1677)
Henchman, Richard (c. 1655)
Higginson, Francis (1587)
Higginson, John (1616)
Hinckley, Thomas (1618)
Hitchcock, Enos (1744)
Hitchcock, Gad (1719)
Hoar, Leonard (c. 1630)
Hobart, Nehemiah (1648)
Hobart, Noah (1706)
Holmes, Abiel (1763)
Hodgkinson, John (c. 1766)
Hooker, Thomas (1586)
Hooper, William (1702)

Hopkins, Samuel (1721)
Howard, Simeon (1733)
Howe, John (fl. 1753-1812)
Hubbard, William (c. 1621)
Hull, John (1624)
Hutchinson, Thomas (1711)
James, John (c. 1633)
Jewett, Jedidiah (c. 1705)
Johnson, Edward (1599)
Johnson, Susannah Willard (Hastings) (1730)
Josselyn, John (c. 1608)
Knight, Sarah Kemble (1666)
Lathy, Thomas Pike (1771)
Lawson, Deodat(e) (fl. 1660-1715)
Lechford, Thomas (c. 1590)
Leland, John (1754)
Leonard, Daniel (1740)
Loring, Israel (1682)
Lowell, Percival (1571)
Lynde, Benjamin (1666)
Lyon, Richard (fl. 1620-1651)
Mann, Herman (1771)
Marrant, John (1755)
Mason, John (c. 1600)
Mather, Cotton (1663)
Mather, Eleazer (1637)
Mather, Increase (1639)
Mather, Nathaniel (1630)
Mather, Richard (1596)
Mather, Samuel (1706)
Maule, Thomas (c. 1645)
Maverick, Samuel (c. 1602)
Mayhew, Experience (1673)
Mayhew, Jonathan (1720)
Mayhew, Matthew (1648)
Mayhew, Thomas, Jr. (c. 1621)
Minot, George Richards (1758)
Mitchel, Jonathan (1624)
Mixer, Elizabeth (fl. 1701-1720)
Monis, Judah (1683)
Montrésor, John (1736)
Moodey, Joshua (1633)
Moorhead, Sarah Parsons (fl. 1741-1742)
Morrell, William (fl. 1623-1625)
Morse, Jedidiah (1761)
Morton, Charles (c. 1627)
Morton, George (1585)
Morton, Nathaniel (1613)
Morton, Perez (1751)
Morton, Sarah Wentworth (1759)
Morton, Thomas (c. 1579)
Moxon, George (1602)
Murray, Judith Sargent (1751)

Niles, Samuel (1674)
Noble, Oliver (1733)
Norton, John (1606)
Norton, John, II (1651)
Norton, John (1715)
Nowell, Samuel (1634)
Noyes, James (1608)
Noyes, Nicholas (1647)
Oakes, Urian (c. 1631)
Odiorne, Thomas (1769)
Oliver, Peter (1713)
Otis, James (1725)
Oxenbridge, John (1609)
Pain, Philip (c. 1647)
Paine, John (1661)
Paine, John (1773)
Paine, Robert Treat (1773)
Parker, Thomas (1595)
Parkman, Ebenezer (1703)
Parsons, Jonathan (1705)
Payson, Edward (1657)
Peabody, Oliver (1698)
Pemberton, Ebenezer (1672)
Perry, Edward (1630)
Peter, Hugh (1598)
Phillips, George (1593)
Pickering, Theophilus (1700)
Pierson, Abraham (c. 1608)
Porter, Eliphalet (1758)
Prentice, Thomas (1702)
Prescott, Benjamin (1687)
Prince, Thomas (1687)
Pynchon, William (c. 1590)
Quincy, Josiah, Jr. (1744)
Rand, William (1700)
Rawson, Grindall (1659)
Richardson, John (1647)
Rogers, John (1630)
Rowlandson, Joseph (c. 1631)
Rowlandson, Mary (c. 1635)
Rowson, Susanna Haswell (1762)
Russell, Daniel (1642)
Saffin, John (1626)
Saltonstall, Nathaniel (c. 1639)
Sampson, Ezra (1749)
Sandeman, Robert (1718)
Savage, Thomas (1640)
Scottow, Joshua (c. 1618)
Seccomb, John (1708)
Seccombe, Joseph (1706)
Sergeant, John (1710)
Sewall, Jonathan (1728)
Sewall, Joseph (1688)

Sewall, Samuel (1652)
Shepard, Jeremiah (1648)
Shepard, Thomas (1605)
Shepard, Thomas (1635)
Shirley, William (1694)
Shurtleff, William (1689)
Smith, Eunice (1757)
Somerby, Anthony (1610)
Spring, Samuel (1746)
Starkey, George (c. 1626)
Stiles, Isaac (1697)
Stoddard, Solomon (1643)
Story, Isaac (1774)
Stoughton, William (1631)
Symmes, Thomas (1678)
Tappan, David (1752)
Taylor, Edward (c. 1642)
Terry, Lucy (1730)
Thacher, James (1754)
Thacher, Oxenbridge (1719)
Thacher, Peter (1688)
Thacher, Peter (1752)
Thacher, Thomas (1620)
Thomas, Isaiah (1749)
Thomas, Robert Bailey (1766)
Tillam, Thomas (d. after 1668)
Tompson, Benjamin (1642)
Tompson, Edward (1666)
Torrey, Samuel (1632)
Townsend, Jonathan (1697)
Tulley, John (1638)
Turell, Ebenezer (1702)
Turell, Jane Colman (1708)
Tyler, Royall (1757)
Underhill, John (c. 1597)
Wadsworth, Benjamin (1670)
Walker, Timothy (1705)
Walley, Thomas (1618)
Walter, Nehemiah (1663)
Walter, Thomas (1696)
Ward, Nathaniel (c. 1578)
Warren, Joseph (1741)
Warren, Mercy Otis (1728)
Webb, John (1687)
Webster, Pelatiah (1726)
Weld, Edmund (1631)
Welde, Thomas (1595)
West, Benjamin (1730)
Wheatley, Phillis (c. 1754)
Wheeler, Thomas (fl. 1640-1676)
Wheelwright, John (c. 1592)
Whitaker, Nathaniel (1730)
White, Elizabeth (d. 1669)

Whiting, John (c. 1635)
Whiting, Samuel (1597)
Wigglesworth, Edward (1693)
Wigglesworth, Michael (1631)
Wigglesworth, Samuel (1689)
Willard, Samuel (1640)
Williams, John (1664)
Williams, Roger (c. 1603)
Williams, William (1665)
Williams, William (1688)
Wilson, John (c. 1588)
Winslow, Edward (1595)
Winthrop, John (1588)
Winthrop, John, Jr. (1606)
Winthrop, John (1714)
Wise, John (1652)
Wiswall, Ichabod (1637)
Wood, William (c. 1606)
Woodbridge, Benjamin (1622)
Woodbridge, John (1613)

Michigan

Carver, Jonathan (1710)
Dodge, John (1751)
Griswold, Stanley (1763)
Meigs, Return Jonathan (1764)
Morris, Thomas (1732)
Rogers, Robert (c. 1727)
Trumbull, John (1750)

Mississippi

Adair, James (c. 1709)
Toulmin, Harry (1766)

New Hampshire

Belcher, Samuel (c. 1640)
Belknap, Jeremy (1744)
Burroughs, Stephen (1765)
Chamberlain, Richard (1632)
Clarke, John (1609)
Dennie, Joseph (1768)
Evans, Israel (1747)
Everett, David (1770)
Hanson, Elizabeth (1684)
Haven, Samuel (1727)
Johnson, Susannah Willard (Hastings) (1730)
McGregore, David (1710)
Moodey, Joshua (1633)
Noble, Oliver (1733)
Odiorne, Thomas (1769)
Payson, Edward (1783)
Penhallow, Samuel (1665)
Rogers, Robert (c. 1727)

Sandeman, Robert (1718)
Seccombe, Joseph (1706)
Sewall, Jonathan Mitchell (1748)
Sherburne, Henry (1741)
Shurtleff, William (1689)
Smith, John (1752)
Stiles, Ezra (1727)
Thomas, Isaiah (1749)
Tufts, Henry (1748)
Underhill, John (c. 1597)
Walker, Timothy (1705)
Wheelock, Eleazar (1711)
Wheelwright, John (c. 1592)

New Jersey

Antill, Edward (1701)
Benezet, Anthony (1713)
Blair, Samuel (1712)
Bradford, Ebenezer (1746)
Bradford, William (1663)
Brainerd, David (1718)
Budd, Thomas (fl. 1678-1698)
Burr, Aaron (1716)
Burr, Esther Edwards (1732)
Chandler, Thomas Bradbury (1726)
Coxe, Daniel (1673)
Davies, Samuel (1723)
Dickinson, Moses (1695)
Drake, Francis (c. 1650)
Duffield, George (1732)
Dunlap, William (1766)
Edwards, Jonathan (1703)
Evans, Nathaniel (1742)
Finley, Samuel (1715)
Fithian, Philip Vickers (1747)
Frelinghuysen, Theodorus Jacobus (1691)
Freneau, Philip (1752)
Green, Jacob (1722)
Hart, Oliver (1723)
Hepburn, John (fl. 1715-c.1745)
Holme, John (fl. 1685-1701)
Howell, Rednap (fl. 1750-1787)
Hunter, Robert (fl. 1714-1734)
Imlay, Gilbert (c. 1754)
Jones, David (1736)
Kinnan, Mary (1763)
Leeds, Daniel (1652)
Leeds, Felix (1687)
Leeds, Titan (1699)
Livingston, (Henry) Brockholst (1757)
Livingston, William (1723)
Moody, James (1744)
Morgan, Joseph (1671)

Morris, Lewis (1671)
Norwood, Henry (1615)
Odell, Jonathan (1737)
Parker, James (c. 1714)
Seabury, Samuel (1729)
Smith, John (1722)
Smith, Samuel Stanhope (1751)
Stockton, Annis Boudinot (1736)
Tennent, Gilbert (1703)
Tennent, William, II (1705)
Tennent, William, III (1740)
Tufts, Henry (1748)
Witherspoon, John (1723)
Woolman, John (1720)

New York

Adair, James (c. 1709)
Ashbridge, Elizabeth (1713)
Auchmuty, Samuel (1722)
Bend, Joseph Grove John (c. 1762)
Bleecker, Anne Eliza (1752)
Bradford, Andrew (1686)
Bradford, William (1663)
Brown, Charles Brockden (1771)
Buell, Samuel (1716)
Burk, John Daly (c. 1772)
Burroughs, Stephen (1765)
Clinton, George (1739)
Cobbett, William (1763)
Colden, Cadwallader (1688)
Cooper, Myles (1737)
Coxe, Tench (1755)
Crèvecoeur, Michel Guillaûme Jean de (1735)
Denton, Daniel (fl. 1656-1696)
Duer, William (1747)
Dunlap, William (1766)
Dwight, Theodore (1764)
Dwight, Timothy (1752)
Edwards, Jonathan (1703)
Edwards, Jonathan, Jr. (1745)
Faugeres, Margaretta V. Bleecker (1771)
Fenno, John (1751)
Freneau, Philip (1752)
Gaine, Hugh (1726)
Gallatin, Albert (1761)
Gardiner, Lion (1599)
Hamilton, Alexander (1757)
Hammon, Jupiter (1711)
Haynes, Lemuel (1753)
Hicks, Elias (1748)
Hodgkinson, John (c. 1766)
Hunter, Robert (fl. 1714-1734)
Inglis, Charles (c. 1734)
Jay, John (1745)

Johnson, Samuel (1696)
Linn, John Blair (1777)
Livingston, Anne Home (1763)
Livingston, (Henry) Brockholst (1757)
Livingston, William (1723)
Long, John (fl. 1768-1791)
Loudon, Samuel (1727)
Low, Samuel (1765)
Martin, Luther (1748)
Maverick, Samuel (c. 1602)
Maylem, John (1739)
Meigs, Josiah (1757)
Monis, Judah (1683)
Montrésor, John (1736)
Morgan, Joseph (1671)
Morris, Gouverneur (1752)
Morris, Lewis (1671)
Morris, Thomas (1732)
Norwood, Henry (1615)
Occom, Samson (1723)
Odell, Jonathan (1737)
Paine, Thomas (1737)
Palmer, Elihu (1764)
Parker, James (c. 1714)
Peters, Samuel A. (1735)
Prime, Benjamin Young (1733)
Rivington, James (1724)
Robinson, J. (fl. 1792)
Rogers, Robert (c. 1727)
Sampson, Ezra (1749)
Seabury, Samuel (1729)
Seixas, Gershom Mendez (1745)
Selyns, Henricus (1636)
Smith, Elihu Hubbard (1771)
Smith, William (1727)
Smith, William (1728)
Stansbury, Joseph (1740)
Steendam, Jacob (1615)
Steere, Richard (1643)
Taylor, Jacob (d. 1746)
Tennent, William, III (1740)
Tyler, Royall (1757)
Underhill, John (c. 1597)
Webster, Noah (1758)
Wetmore, James (1695)
Wilkins, Isaac (1742)
Williams, William (1727)
Wortman, Tunis (d. 1822)
Zenger, John Peter (1697)

North Carolina

Adair, James (c. 1709)
Ashe, Thomas (fl. 1680-1682)
Bartram, William (1739)

Brickell, John (c. 1710)
Brown, William Hill (c. 1765)
Burke, Thomas (c. 1744)
Catesby, Mark (1683)
Gist, Christopher (1705)
Godfrey, Thomas (1736)
Hall, Clement (c. 1699)
Hariot, Thomas (1560)
Howard, Martin, Jr. (fl. 1730-1781)
Howell, Rednap (fl. 1750-1787)
Husband, Herman (1724)
Iredell, James (1751)
Jarratt, Devereux (1733)
Lane, Ralph (1630)
Lawson, John (d. 1711)
McCorkle, Samuel Eusebius (1746)
Martin, Alexander (1740)
Micklejohn, George (d. 1817)
Pattillo, Henry (1726)
Reese, Thomas (1742)
Schaw, Janet (c. 1735)
Smith, Michael (1698)
Spangenberg, Augustus Gottlieb (1704)
Thomson, John (c. 1690)
White, Henry (c. 1642)
Wilson, James (1742)

Ohio

Beatty, Charles Clinton (c. 1715)
Dodge, John (1751)
Everett, David (1770)
Gist, Christopher (1705)
Jones, David (1736)
Meigs, Return Jonathan (1740)
Meigs, Return Jonathan (1764)
Morris, Thomas (1732)

Pennsylvania

Alison, Francis (1705)
Allen, Paul (1775)
Allen, Richard (1760)
Ashbridge, Elizabeth (1713)
Bache, Benjamin Franklin (1769)
Barton, Benjamin Smith (1766)
Barton, Thomas (1730)
Bartram, John (1699)
Bartram, William (1739)
Beatty, Charles Clinton (c. 1715)
Beete, John (fl. 1795-1797)
Beissel, Johann Conrad (1690)
Benezet, Anthony (1713)
Beveridge, John (1703)
Blair, Samuel (1712)
Boehm, John Philip (1683)

Bordley, John Beale (1727)
Bowers, Bathsheba (c. 1672)
Brackenridge, Hugh Henry (1748)
Bradford, Andrew (1686)
Bradford, William (1663)
Bradford, William, "the Third" (1722)
Brainerd, David (1718)
Branagan, Thomas (1774)
Breintnall, Joseph (d. 1746)
Brooke, Henry (1678)
Brown, Charles Brockden (1771)
Bruce, David (c. 1760)
Budd, Thomas (fl. 1678-1698)
Butler, James (1755)
Carey, Mathew (1760)
Chalkley, Thomas (1675)
Churchman, John (1705)
Cliffton, William (1772)
Cobbett, William (1763)
Colden, Cadwallader (1688)
Coombe, Thomas (1747)
Cooper, Thomas (1759)
Coxe, Tench (1755)
Crawford, Charles (1752)
Dennie, Joseph (1768)
Dickinson, John (1732)
Dickinson, Jonathan (1663)
Dock, Christopher (c. 1698)
Drinker, Elizabeth Sandwith (1734)
Duane, William (1760)
Duché, Jacob (1738)
Duffield, George (1732)
Elliot, James (1775)
Equiano, Olaudah (c. 1745)
Evans, Israel (1747)
Evans, Lewis (c. 1700)
Evans, Nathaniel (1742)
Fenno, John (1751)
Fergusson, Elizabeth Graeme (1737)
Ferris, David (1707)
Filson, John (c. 1747)
Finley, Samuel (1715)
Forrest, Thomas (1747)
Frame, Richard (fl. 1692)
Franklin, Benjamin (1706)
Freneau, Philip (1752)
Gadsden, Christopher (1724)
Gallatin, Albert (1761)
Galloway, Joseph (c. 1731)
Gist, Christopher (1705)
Goddard, Mary Katharine (1738)
Godfrey, Thomas (1736)
Graydon, Alexander (1752)
Green, Jonas (1712)

Griffitts, Hannah (1727)
Hart, Oliver (1723)
Hazard, Ebenezer (1745)
Hobart, Noah (1706)
Hodgkinson, John (c. 1766)
Holme, John (fl. 1685-1701)
Hopkinson, Francis (1737)
Hunt, Isaac (c. 1742)
Husband, Herman (1724)
Inglis, Charles (c. 1734)
Jones, Absalom (1746)
Jones, David (1736)
Keimer, Samuel (1688)
Keith, George (c. 1638)
Leacock, John (fl. 1776)
Linn, John Blair (1777)
Livingston, Anne Home (1763)
Logan, James (1674)
Macpherson, John (c. 1726)
Makin, Thomas (1665)
Markoe, Peter (c. 1752)
Marshall, Humphry (1722)
Martin, Alexander (1740)
Montrésor, John (1736)
Morgan, Abel (1673)
Morris, Gouverneur (1752)
Muhlenberg, Henry Melchior (1711)
Murdock, John (c. 1748)
Paine, Thomas (1737)
Palmer, Elihu (1764)
Parker, James (c. 1714)
Pastorius, Francis Daniel (1651)
Penn, William (1644)
Ralph, James (c. 1705)
Ramsay, David (1749)
Relf, Samuel (1776)
Rose, Aquila (1695)
Rowson, Susanna Haswell (1762)
Rush, Benjamin (1745)
Sauer, Christopher I (1693)
Schlatter, Michael (1716)
Seixas, Gershom Mendez (1745)
Shippen, Joseph (1732)
Smith, Anna Young (1756)
Smith, Elihu Hubbard (1771)
Smith, John (1722)
Smith, Josiah (1704)
Smith, William (1727)
Spangenberg, Augustus Gottlieb (1704)
Stansbury, Joseph (1740)
Stanton, Daniel (1708)
Story, Thomas (c. 1670)
Taylor, Jacob (d. 1746)

Tennent, Gilbert (1703)
Thomas, Gabriel (1661)
Thomson, Charles (1729)
Thomson, John (c. 1690)
Von Zinzendorf, Nicholas Ludwig Count (1700)
Webb, George (c. 1708)
Webster, Pelatiah (1726)
Williams, William (1727)
Wilson, James (1742)
Wister, Sally (1761)
Witherspoon, John (1723)

Rhode Island

Adams, John (1705)
Allen, Paul (1775)
Bass, John (1717)
Berkeley, George (1685)
Callender, John (1706)
Checkley, John (1680)
Church, Benjamin (1639)
Church, Benjamin (1734)
Church, Thomas (1673)
Clarke, John (1609)
Easton, John (c. 1624)
Franklin, James (1697)
Goddard, Mary Katharine (1738)
Gorton, Samuel (c. 1592)
Hitchcock, Enos (1744)
Hopkins, Samuel (1721)
Hopkins, Stephen (1707)
Howard, Martin, Jr. (fl. 1730-1781)
MacSparran, James (1693)
Mann, Herman (1771)
Maylem, John (1739)
Morton, Thomas (c. 1579)
Niles, Samuel (1674)
Osborn, Sarah (1714)
Scott, Jobb (1751)
Senter, Isaac (1753)
Stiles, Ezra (1727)
West, Benjamin (1730)
Williams, Roger (c. 1603)

South Carolina

Adair, James (c. 1709)
Ashe, Thomas (fl. 1680-1682)
Aston, Anthony (fl. 1682-1747)
Beete, John (fl. 1795-1797)
Catesby, Mark (1683)
Cooper, Thomas (1759)
Cotton, John (1640)
Dale, Thomas (1700)
Drayton, William Henry (1742)

Dumbleton, Joseph (fl. 1740-1750)
Gadsden, Christopher (1724)
Garden, Alexander (c. 1685)
Garden, Dr. Alexander (1730)
Hart, Oliver (1723)
Henchman, Daniel (1677)
Hewat, Alexander (c. 1740)
Hodgkinson, John (c. 1766)
Kil(l)patrick, James (c. 1700)
Ladd, Joseph Brown (1764)
Pinckney, Charles (1757)
Pinckney, Eliza Lucas (c. 1722)
Ramsay, David (1749)
Reese, Thomas (1742)
Rugeley, Rowland (c. 1735)
Smith, Josiah (1704)
Smith, Michael (1698)
Smith, William Loughton (1758)
Stephens, William (1671)
Tailfer, Patrick (fl. 1734-1741)
Tennent, William, III (1740)
Trott, Nicholas (1663)
Tucker, Nathaniel (1750)
Webb, Thomas (c. 1708)
Wells, Helena (c. 1760)
Wilkinson, Eliza Yonge (fl. 1779-1783)
Woodmason, Charles (c. 1720)
Zubly, John Joachim (1724)

Vermont

Allen, Ethan (1738)
Bosworth, Benjamin (c. 1612)
Elliot, James (1775)
Haynes, Lemuel (1753)
Niles, Nathaniel (1741)
Terry, Lucy (1730)
Tyler, Royall (1757)

Virginia

Archer, Gabriel (1575)
Atkins, Josiah (fl. 1781)
Bacon, Nathaniel (1647)
Bannerman, Mark (d. 1727)
Beckley, John James (1757)
Berkeley, Sir William (c. 1608)
Beverley, Robert (c. 1673)
Blackamore, Arthur (c. 1679)
Blair, James (c. 1655)
Blair, John Durbarrow (1759)
Bland, Edward (d. 1653)
Bland, Richard (1710)
Bland, Theodorick (1742)
Bolling, Robert (1738)

Boucher, Jonathan (1738)
Burk, John Daly (c. 1772)
Burke, Thomas (c. 1744)
Byrd, William, of Westover (1674)
Camm, John (1718)
Carter, Landon (1710)
Catesby, Mark (1683)
Clark, George Rogers (1752)
Clayton, John (1657)
Clayton, John (1694)
Cotton, John, of Queen's Creek (c. 1640)
Davies, Samuel (1723)
Dawson, William (1704)
Dumbleton, Joseph (fl. 1740-1750)
Equiano, Olaudah (c. 1745)
Fithian, Philip Vickers (1747)
Fitzhugh, William (1651)
Fox, John (c. 1686)
Gist, Christopher (1705)
Gookin, Daniel (c. 1612)
Hammond, John (fl. 1634-1663)
Hansford, Charles (c. 1685)
Hariot, Thomas (1560)
Henley, Samuel (1744)
Humphreys, David (1752)
Jarratt, Devereux (1733)
Jefferson, Thomas (1743)
Johnson, Robert (fl. 1600-1621)
Johnson, Thomas (c. 1760)
Jones, Hugh (1671)
Kinnan, Mary (1763)
Lane, Ralph (1530)
Lederer, John (c. 1644)
Lee, Arthur (1740)
Lee, Charles (1758)
Lee, Henry (1756)
Lee, Richard Henry (1732)
Leland, John (1754)
McClurg, James (1746)
McCorkle, Samuel Eusebius (1746)
Madison, James (1751)
Makemie, Francis (1658)
Markland, John (fl. 1721-1735)
Marshall, Humphrey (1760)
Mason, George (1725)
Mathew, Thomas (c. 1650)
Maury, James (1718)
Mercer, John (1704)
Micklejon, George (d. 1817)
Mitchell, John (1711)
Munford, Robert (c. 1737)
Munford, William (1775)
Nicholas, Robert Carter (1728)

Norwood, Henry (1615)
Owen, Goronwy (1723)
Parks, William (c. 1698)
Pattillo, Henry (1726)
Paxton, Robert (d. 1714)
Pead, Deuel (d. 1727)
Percy, George (1580)
Pory, John (1572)
Randolph, Edmund (1753)
Reid, James (fl. 1768-1769)
Rich, Richard (fl. 1609-1610)
Roane, Spencer (1762)
Rolfe, John (c. 1585)
Sandys, George (1578)
Smith, Captain John (1580)
Smith, Samuel Stanhope (1751)
Spelman, Henry (c. 1595)
Spotswood, Alexander (1676)
Stith, William (1707)
Strachey, William (1572)
Taylor, John, of Caroline (1753)
Tennent, John (c. 1700)
Thomson, John (c. 1690)
Timberlake, Henry (1730)
Tucker, St. George (1752)
Waller, Benjamin (1716)
Washington, George (1732)
Weems, Mason Locke (1759)
West, Thomas, Baron de la Warr (1577)
Whitaker, Alexander (1585)
Wingfield, Edward Maria (c. 1560)
Wirt, William (1772)

Wisconsin

Carver, Jonathan (1710)
Long, John (fl. 1768-1791)

OTHER COUNTRIES

Canada

Alline, Henry (1748)
Bailey, Jacob (1731)
Bidwell, Barnabas (1763)
Burroughs, Stephen (1765)
Cleaveland, Benjamin (1733)
Foster, Hannah Webster (1788)
Inglis, Charles (c. 1734)
Long, John (fl. 1768-1791)
Marrant, John (1755)
Moody, James (1744)
Odell, Jonathan (1737)
Seccomb, John (1708)
Smith, William (1728)
Viets, Roger (1738)
Wilkins, Isaac (1742)

England

Gorges, Sir Ferdinando (c. 1566)
Gray, Robert (fl. 1609)
Knapp, Francis (1671)
Knott, Edward, S.J. (1582)
Martyn, Benjamin (1699)
Purchas, Samuel (1575)
Ruggle, George (1575)
White, John (1575)

APPENDIX D
Chronology

1492   Christopher Columbus reaches American shores.

1497   John Cabot claims North America for England.

1507   New World first called "America."

1513   Juan Ponce de León discovers Florida.
Vasco Nuñez de Balboa reaches Pacific Ocean.

1519   Hernando Cortés begins conquest of Aztecs in Mexico.

1522   Ferdinand Magellan completes circumnavigation of globe.

1535   Jacques Cartier claims Gulf of St. Lawrence for France.

1536   John Calvin publishes *Institutes*.

1539   Hernando de Soto begins exploring interior of North America.

1558   Elizabeth I ascends throne of England.

1565   Pedro Menéndez de Avilés heads first permanent North American settlement at St. Augustine, Florida.

1576   Martin Frobisher explores North American coastline.

1580   Francis Drake becomes first Englishman to complete circumnavigation of globe.

1582   Richard Hakluyt, *Divers Voyages Touching the Discovery of North America*

1585   British establish colony at Roanoke Island in Virginia.

1587   Birth of Virginia Dare, English colonial, at Roanoke.
Walter Raleigh unable to discover whereabouts of British colonists at Roanoke.

1588   British destroy Spanish Armada.
Thomas Hariot, *Briefe and True Report*

1602   Bartholomew Gosnold becomes first Englishman to set foot on New England soil.

1603   Samuel de Champlain explores New France.
James I ascends British throne.

1605   James Rosier, *True Relation*

1606   Separatists establish congregation at Scrooby, England.
        James I charters London and Plymouth Companies.
        London Company authorizes colonization of Virginia.

1607   First permanent English settlement established at Jamestown in Virginia.
        Capt. John Smith reputedly captured by Indians and saved from death through intercession
        of Pocahontas, daughter of Powhatan.
                George Percy, *Discourse of the Plantation of the Southern Colony in Virginia*

1608   Samuel de Champlain founds Quebec.
        Capt. John Smith elected leader at Jamestown.
        First European women arrive in Jamestown.
                Captain John Smith, *True Relation*

1609   Henry Hudson explores Hudson River.
                William Strachey, *True Reportory*

1610   British ships save Jamestown settlers from starvation.

1611   Henry Spelman, *Relation of Virginia*

1612   Virginia Company colonizes Bermuda.
                Captain John Smth, *Map of Virginia*

1613   Pocahontas converts to Christianity.
        Dutch establish fort on Manhattan Island.
                Samuel Purchas, *Purchas His Pilgrims*
                Alexander Whitaker, *Good Newes from Virginia*

1614   Capt. John Smith maps coast of New England.
        John Rolfe and Pocahontas marry.
        Virginia begins exporting tobacco.

1616   Pocahontas visits England, where she dies.
                Captain John Smith, *Description of New England*

1617   Plague ravages Indian tribes of New England.

1619   First African captives brought to Virginia and sold into slavery.
        House of Burgesses convenes in Virginia.

1620   Virginia Company authorizes Pilgrims to colonize North America.
        Mayflower arrives in New England.
        Mayflower Compact is ratified and signed by Pilgrim colonists.
        Plymouth Colony established on December 26th.
                Captain John Smith, *New England's Trials*

1621   John Carver dies, and William Bradford is elected governor of Plymouth colony.
        Pilgrims obtain grant to New England lands.
        Pilgrims celebrate first Thanksgiving.
        New Amsterdam founded.

1622   Indians massacre English settlers in Virginia.
                George Morton, *Mourt's Relation*
                William Bradford and Edward Winslow, *Relation*

1623   Dutch settle New Amsterdam.

1624   Captain John Smith, *Generall Historie of Virginia*
                Edward Winslow, *Good Newes from New-England*

1625   Charles I ascendes throne of England.
        Jesuits arrive in Quebec.
                William Morrell, *Nova Anglia*

1626   Dutch purchase Manhattan Island from Indians.
                George Sandy's translation of Ovid's *Metamorphosis*

1627   Thomas Morton establishes settlement at Merrymount.

1628   Myles Standish attacks Merrymount.
        Thomas Morton deported to England.
        John Endicott establishes Massachusetts Bay colony at Salem.

1629   Parliament dissolved.
        Congregationalism introduced at Salem.
        John Winthrop becomes governor of Massachusetts Bay colony.

1630   Great Migration of Puritans to Massachusetts Bay begins.
        John Winthrop arrives in New England aboard *Arbella*.
        Boston established on banks of Charles River.
                John Cotton, *God's Promise to His Plantation*
                Francis Higginson, *New England's Plantation*
                Captain John Smith, *True Travels*

1631   Roger Williams arrives in Salem.
                Captain John Smith, *Advertisements for the Inexperienced Planters*

1632   Lord Baltimore granted charter for Maryland.
                Thomas Hooker, *Souls Preparation*

1633   John Cotton and Thomas Hooker arrive in New England.
        William Laud becomes archbishop of Canterbury.

1634   English Catholics settle Maryland.
        First tavern opens in Boston.
                William Wood, *New-Englands Prospect*

1635   General Court banishes Roger Williams from Massachusetts Bay colony.
        Boston Latin School founded.
        Puritans settle Connecticut River Valley.
        Richard Mather arrives in Boston.

1636   Roger Williams founds Providence in Rhode Island.
        General Court authorizes founding of Harvard College.
        Peter Bulkeley settles Concord, Massachusetts.

1637   Pequot War in Connecticut.
        General Court banishes Anne Hutchinson and John Wheelwright from Massachusetts Bay
        on grounds of Antinomianism.
                Thomas Morton, *New English Canaan*

1638   John Wheelwright settles Exeter, New Hampshire.
        Anne Hutchinson settles in Rhode Island.
        New Sweden founded.
                An Almanack for...1639, Calculated for New England
                John Underhill, *News from America*

1639   Roger Williams founds Baptist Church in America.
        First printing press established at Cambridge, Massachusetts.
        Massachusetts Bay begins regular postal service.

1640   End of Great Migration.
        Boston Commons established for public use.
                Bay Psalm Book

1641   Massachusetts Bay codifies its laws.
        Star Chamber abolished in England.
                John Cotton, *Way of Life*
                Thomas Shepard, *Sincere Convert*

1642   Civil War (1642-1649) erupts in England.
        French found Montreal.
        Sir William Berkeley becomes governor of Virginia.
                Thomas Lechford, *Plain Dealing*

1643   Virginia exiles nonconformist ministers.
        Massachusetts, Connecticut, and Plymouth colonies form alliance agreement for mutual
        defense.
        Indian mission established on Martha's Vineyard.
                Richard Mather, *Church-Government and Church-Covenant*
                Roger Williams, *Key into the Language of America*

1644
        Indian uprising in Virginia.
        John Winthrop defeated in election for governor of Massachusetts Bay.
        General court banishes Baptists from Massachusetts Bay.
                John Cotton, *Keys of the Kingdom of Heaven*
                Roger Williams, *Bloudy Tenent of Persecution*

1645   Execution of Archbishop Laud in England for treason.
        Roxbury Latin School established.

1646   John Winthrop elected governor of Massachusetts Bay.
        John Eliot begins ministry to Indians of Massachusetts.
                Peter Bulkeley, *Gospel-Covenant*
                John Cotton, *Milk for Boston Babes*

1647   Towns in Massachusetts required by law to employ teachers of reading and writing.
        Peter Stuyvesant becomes director of New Netherland.
                John Cotton, *Bloudy Tenent Washed*
                Nathaniel Ward, *Simple Cobler of Aggawam*

1648   Cambridge Platform.
                John Cotton, *Way of the Congregational Churches*
                Thomas Hooker, *Survey of the Summe of Church Discipline*

1649   Charles I executed in England.
        Beginning of Oliver Cromwell's Commonwealth in England.
        British establish Society for the Propagation of the Gospel in Foreign Parts.
        Maryland passes Toleration Act protecting all Christian sects.
                John Eliot, *Glorious Progress of the Gospel Among the Indians*
                Henry Norwood, *Voyage to Virginia*

1650   Anne Bradstreet, *Tenth Muse*
                William Pynchon, *Meritorious Price of Our Redemption*

1651   First Navigation Act.

1652   Rhode Island enacts antislavery laws.
        Boston establishes mint.
        First bookstore opens in Boston.
        Massachusetts Bay colony annexes Maine.

1653   Virginia colonists begin settlement of Carolinas.
Edward Johnson, *Wonder-Working Providences*
John Eliot, *Catechism in the Indian Language*

1654   John Norton, *Orthodox Evangelist*

1655   New Netherland annexes New Sweden.

1656   Public library opens in Boston.
Massachusetts Bay banishes Quakers from colony.
John Hammond, *Leah and Rachel*

1658   Death of Oliver Cromwell.
Richard Cromwell appointed Protector of Realm.
John Norton, *Abel Being Dead Yet Speaketh*

1659   Charles Chauncy, *Plain Doctrine of Justification*
John Eliot, *Christian Commonwealth*

1660   Mary Dyer executed in Boston for Quaker beliefs.
Regicide judges arrive in New England.
John Eliot establishes Indian congregation at Natick, Massachusetts.
Stuarts (Charles II) restored to throne of England.
Almshouse opens in Boston.
Parliament enacts Navigation Acts granting monopolies on colonial trade.

1661   Virginia institutionalizes slavery.
New England recognizes Charles II as king of England.
Governor John Endicott ends persecution of Quakers in New England.
John Davenport, *The Saint's Anchor-Hold*

1662   Half-Way Covenant.
Charles Chauncy, *Anti-Synodalia*
Michael Wigglesworth, *Day of Doom*

1664   New Netherlands surrenders to British.
New Amsterdam becomes New York.

1665   First dramatic production performed in North America.
Great Plague ravages London.

1666   Great Fire in London.
George Alsop, *Character of the Province of Maryland*
John Eliot, *Indian Grammar*

1668   French establish fort at Sault Ste. Marie.
Treaty of Aix-la-Chapelle.
Philip Pain, *Daily Meditations*
Thomas Shepard, *Wine for Gospel Wantons*

1669   Old South Church founded in Boston.
Hudson Bay Company organized.
John Eliot, *Indian Primer*
Nathaniel Morton, *New England's Memoriall*
Michael Wigglesowrth, *Meat Out of the Eater*

1670   British settle South Carolina.
First section of House of Seven Gables built in Salem, Massachusetts.
Daniel Denton, *Brief Description of New York*
John Mason, *Brief History of the Pequot War*
Increase Mather, *Life and Death of Richard Mather*

1671   French establish claim to North American interior.
       John Eliot, *Indian Dialogues*
       Jonathan Mitchel, *Nehemiah on the Wall in Troublesome Times*

1672   First American copyright law enacted by Massachusetts General Court.
       George Fox travels through British colonies in North America.
       John Josselyn, *New England's Rarities*
       John Lederer, *Discoveries of John Lederer*

1673   Marquette and Jolliet explore Mississippi River.

1675   John Foster begins printing in Boston.
       King Philip's War (1675-1678) begins.
       Quakers settle New Jersey.
       Indian massacre at Deerfield, Massachusetts.
       Benjamin Tompson, *New Englands Crisis*

1676   Bacon's Rebellion.
       Mary Rowlandson taken captive by Indians who sack Lancaster, Massachusetts.
       King Philip executed.
       Peter Folger, *Looking-Glass for the Times*
       Increase Mather, *Brief History of the Warr*
       Roger Williams, *George Fox Digged Out of His Burrows*

1677   Massachusetts Bay colony supports British Navigation acts.
       William Hubbard, *Narrative of the Troubles with the Indians in New England*
       Increase Mather, *Relation of the Troubles in New England*
       Urian Oakes, *Elegy on the Rev. Mr. Thomas Shepard*

1678   Smallpox epidemic ravages New England.
       End of King Philip's War.
       Popish Plot in England.
       France claims upper Mississippi River Valley.
       Anne Bradstreet, *Several Poems*

1679   Fire ravages Boston.

1680   French Huguenots settle Charlestown, South Carolina.
       New Hampshire separates from Massachusetts.
       Increase Mather, *Divine Right of Infant-Baptism*

1681   Charles II grants William Penn a charter to colonize Pennsylvania.

1682   LaSalle explores Mississippi River.
       Governor William Berkeley suppresses printing in Virginia.
       William Penn arrives in Pennsylvania.
       Philadelphia founded.
       Cotton Mather, *Ornaments for the Daughters of Zion*
       William Penn, *Brief Account*
       Mary Rowlandson, *Soveraignty and Goodness of God*

1683   Mennonites settle Germantown, Pennsylvania.
       William Penn ratifies treaty with Indians of Pennsylvania.
       Increase Mather organizes scientific society in Boston.

1684   Charles II revokes charter for Massachusetts Bay Company.
       Increase Mather, *Essay for the Recording of Illustrious Providences*

1685   James II ascends throne of England.
       William Bradford sets up printing press in Philadelphia.

1685   French Huguenots migrate to North America.
           Thomas Budd, *Good Order Established in Pennsylvania*

1686   Sir Edmund Andros appointed governor of New England and northern colonies.
       Anglican services held in Boston.
           Samuel Willard, *Discourse of Justification*

1687   Andros dissolves governments of Rhode Island and Connecticut.
           William Penn, *Excellent Privilege of Liberty of Property*

1688   Increase Mather travels to England to negotiate for new charter for Massachusetts.
       James II is deposed.
           Increase Mather, *New-England Vindicated*

1689   William and Mary ascend British throne in "Glorious Revolution."
       Massachusetts overthrows Governor Andros.
       King William's War (1689-1697) begins.
       Parliament passes Toleration Act.
       James Blair appointed commissary of Virginia.
           Cotton Mather, *Memorable Providences Relating to Witchcrafts and Possessions*

1690   French and Indian war parties raid British settlements throughout New England.
       Sir William Phips captures Port Royal, Nova Scotia.
       William Rittenhouse builds paper mill at Germantown, Pennsylvania.
       Benjamin Harris publishes *Public Occurrences*, first American newspaper, in Boston.
           New England Primer

1691   Pennsylvania grants independent status to Delaware.

1692   Witchcraft hysteria erupts at Salem, Massachusetts.
       Postal system established for North American colonies.
       Massachusetts receives new charter.
           Increase Mather, *Cases of Concience Concerning Evil Spirits*

1693   College of William and Mary established in Virginia.
           Cotton Mather, *Wonders of the Invisible World*

1694   Joshua Scottow, *Narrative of the Planting of the Massachusetts Colony*

1695   Christ Church founded in Philadelphia, Pennsylvania.
           Thomas Maule, *Truth Held Forth and Maintained*

1696   French and Indians attack Pemaquid Fort in Maine.
           Increase Mather, *Angelographia*

1697   French and Indians attack Haverhill, Massachusetts; Hannah Dustan taken captive.
       Treaty of Ryswick concludes King William's War.
       Plague ravages Charleston, South Carolina.

1698   "Old Swedes" (Gloria Dei) Church founded in Philadelphia.
       Beginning of triangular slave trade.
           Gabriel Thomas, *Historical and Geographical Account of the Province and Country of Pennsylvania and New Jersey*

1699   Williamsburg becomes capital of Virginia.
       William Penn returns to Pennsylvania.
       French settle Louisiana and Illinois Territories.
           Jonathan Dickinson, *God's Protecting Providence*
           Cotton Mather, *Decennium Luctuosum*

1700   Yale College founded in Connecticut.
                        Robert Calef, *More Wonders of the Invisible World*
                        Samuel Sewall, *Selling of Joseph*
                        Samuel Willard, *Peril of the Times*

1701   French establish fort at Detroit.
                        Cotton Mather, *Magnalia Christi Americana*

1702   Queen Anne ascends throne of England.
        Queen Anne's War (1702-1713) begins.
                        John Hale, *Modest Inquiry*
                        Increase Mather, *Ichabod*

1704   Deerfield massacre.
        Madame Sarah Kemble Knight journeys from Boston to New York.
        Boston News-Letter, first regularly published American newspaper, begins publication.

1705   Robert Beverley, *History and Present State of Virginia*
                        John Rogers, *Epistle to Quakers*

1706   French and Spanish attack Charlestown, South Carolina.
                        George Keith, *Journal of Travels*
                        Cotton Mather, *Negro Christianized*
                        Increase Mather, *Discourse on Earthquakes*

1707   Act of Union unites England, Scotland, and Wales into United Kingdom of Great Britain.
                        John Williams, *Redeemed Captive*

1708   Connecticut adopts Saybrook Platform.
                        Ebenezer Cooke, *Sot-Weed Factor*

1709   New York and New England plan but later abandon joint attack on Quebec and Montreal.
        Quakers build meeting house in Boston.
                        Ezekiel Cheever, *Short Introduction to Latin Tongue*
                        John Lawson, *New Voyage to Carolina*

1710   German migration to America begins.
                        Cotton Mather, *Bonifacius, or, Essays to Do Good*
                        John Wise, *Churches Quarrel Espoused*

1711   Tuscarora Indian War (1711-1713) begins in North Carolina.
        British fleet fails in attempted capture of Quebec.
        Fire ravages Boston.

1712   Slaves revolt in New York City.
        Pennsylvania bans importation of African slaves.

1713   Treaty of Utrecht concludes Queen Anne's War.

1714   George I ascends British throne.
                        Robert Hunter, *Androboros*
                        Cotton Mather, *Duodecennium Luctuosum*
                        Solomon Stoddard, *Guide to Christ*

1715   Yemassee Indian uprising in South Carolina.
                        Joseph Morgan, *History of the Kingdom of Basaruah*

1716   First American playhouse built in Williamsburg, Virginia.
                        Thomas Church, *Entertaining Passages Relating to King Philip's War*

1717   Mississippi Bubble.
                John Wise, *Vindication of Government of New England Churches*

1718   Beginning of Scot-Irish migration to Pennsylvania.
        Spain establishes outpost at San Antonio, Texas.
        French establish New Orleans.
                Samuel Keimer, *Brand Pluck'd from the Burning*

1719   James Franklin begins publication of *Boston Gazette*.
        Andrew Bradford begins publication of *American Weekly Mercury*.
                Benjamin Wadsworth, *Some Consideration about Baptism*

1720   South Sea Bubble.

1721   James Franklin begins publication of *New England Courant*.
        Cotton Mather and Zabdiel Boylston begin smallpox inoculation in Boston.
                Cotton Mather, *Christian Philosopher*

1722   Lovewell's War (1722-1725) begins.
        Daniel Coxe designs first plan for colonial union in North America.
                James Blair, *Our Savior's Divine Sermon on the Mount*
                Benjamin Franklin, *Silence Dogood Papers*

1723   Benjamin Franklin leaves Boston for Philadelphia.

1724   Hugh Jones, *Present State of Virginia*
                Cotton Mather, *Parentator*

1725   Lovewell's Fight.
        New York Gazette begins publication.
        Nathaniel Ames begins publication of *Astronomical Diary and Almanac* (1725-1775).
                Thomas Symmes, *Lovewell Lamented*
                Roger Wolcott, *Poetical Meditations*

1726   British establish Fort Oswego on Lake Ontario.
        Tennents open "Log College" at Neshaminy, Pa.
                Samuel Penhallow, *History of the Wars of New-England with the Eastern
                Indians*

1727   Benjamin Franklin founds Junto Club in Philadelphia.
        Maryland Gazette begins publication.
        George II ascends throne of England.
                Cadwallader Colden, *History of the Five Indian Nations*
                Thomas Prince, *Earthquakes*

1728   William Byrd surveys boundary between North Carolina and Virginia.

1729   Baltimore founded in Maryland.
        North and South Carolina separate.
        Benjamin Franklin begins publishing *Pennsylvania Gazette*.
        George Berkeley arrives in America.
                Benjamin Franklin, *Modest Inquiry into the Nature and Necessity of a Paper-
                Currency*
                Isaac Greenwood, *Arithmetick, Vulgar and Decimal*
                Samuel Mather, *Life of the Very Reverend and Learned Cotton Mather*

1730   Printing press set up in Charlestown, South Carolina.
        Benjamin Franklin establishes Library Company of Philadelphia.

1730   John Bartram founds Botanical Gardens in Pennsylvania.
        Paper mill built in Massachusetts.

1731   Mark Catesby, *Natural History of Carolina, Florida, and the Bahama Islands*
                               Thomas Prince, *Vade Mecum for America*

1732   *South Carolina Gazette* begins publication.
        Rhode Island Gazette begins publication.
        James Oglethorpe granted permission to settle Georgia.
        Benjamin Franklin begins publication of *Poor Richard's Almanac* (1732-1757).
        Johan Conrad Beissel establishes Seventh-Day Adventist community at Ephrata, Pennsylvania.
                               William Cooper, *Three Discourses*

1733   John Peter Zenger begins publication of *New York Weekly Journal*.
        Georgia settled.
        Molasses Act passed by Parliament.
        Richmond founded in Virginia.

1734   Beginning of Great Awakening.
                               Jonathan Edwards, *Divine and Supernatural Light*

1735   Scarlet fever epidemic in New England.
        John Peter Zenger acquitted in trial for libel against governor of New York.

1736   William Parks begins publication of *Virginia Gazette*.
        William Tennent founds "log college" on his New Jersey farm.
                               William Douglass, *Practical History of a New Epidemical Eruptive Miliary
                               Fever*
                               Thomas Prince, *Chronological History of New-England*

1737   Jonathan Edwards, *Narrative of the Surprising Conversions*
                               John Peter Zenger, *Brief Narrative of the Case and Tryal of John Peter
                               Zenger*

1738   George Whitefield visits America.

1739   Methodists open churches in American colonies.
                               John Callender, *Civil and Religious Affairs of Rhode Island*

1740   Faneuil Hall built in Boston.
                               Aquila Rose, *Poems*
                               Gilbert Tennent, *Danger of an Unconverted Ministry*

1741   Great Awakening divines Presbyterians into "Old Light" and "New Light" groups.
        Moravians settle in Pennsylvania.
        Andrew Bradford begins publishing *American Magazine* in Philadelphia.
        Benjamin Franklin begins publishing *General Magazine* in Philadelphia.
                               Jonathan Edwards, *Sinners in the Hands of an Angry God*
                               Patrick Tailfer, *True and Historical Narrative of the Colony of Georgia*

1742   Count Zinzendorf visits America.
                               Jonathan Edwards, *Some Thoughts Concerning the Present Revival of Reli-
                               gion in New England*

1743   Benjamin Franklin establishes American Philosophical Society in Philadelphia.
                               Charles Chauncy, *Seasonable Thoughts on the State of Religion in New
                               England*

1744   King George's War (1744-1748) begins.
        George Whitefield visits America.
                               Mather Byles, *Poems*

1745   British capture Louisburg, on Cape Breton Island, from French.

1746   College of New Jersey (later Princeton University) founded.
        Jonathan Edwards, *Treatise Concerning Religious Affections*

1747   Colonial plans to capture Montreal and Quebec fails.
        William Livingston, *Philosophic Solitude*
        William Stith, *History of the First Discovery and Settlement of Virginia*

1748   Treaty of Aix-la-Chapelle concludes King George's War.

1749   Academy of Philadelphia (later University of Pennsylvania) founded.
George II grants charter to Ohio Company.
        Thomas Chalkley, *Journal*
        Jonathan Edwards, *Life of David Brainerd*
        Ebenezer Turell, *Life and Charater of the Reverend Benjamin Colman*

1750   Jonathan Edwards dismissed from pulpit of Northampton, Massachusetts.
        Jonathan Mayhew, *Discourse Concerning Unlimited Submission*

1751   John Bartram, *Observations on American Plants*

1752   Great Britain adopts Georgian calendar.

1753   French authorize establishing forts from Lake Erie to Ohio River.
George Washington sent to investigate French expansion into western territories.

1754   French and Indian War (1754-1763) begins.
William Braddock appointed commander in chief of British forces in North America.
French erect Fort Duquesne on Allegheny and Monangahela Rivers.
Washington surrenders to French at Fort Necessity.
Albany Congress convenes to discuss Indian problem.
Benjamin Franklin drafts Albany Plan of Union.
King's College (now Columbia University) founded in New York.
        Samuel Blair, *Works*
        Jonathan Edwards, *On the Freedom of the Will*
        John Woolman, *Some Considerstions on the Keeping of Negroes* (Part I)

1755   Sir William Johnson establishes Fort William Henry on Lake George.
French Acadians deported from Nova Scotia to British colonies.
Connecticut Gazette begins publication.
        Lewis Evans, *Geographical, Historical, Political, Philosophical, and Mechanical Essays*

1756   Quakers withdraw from Pennsylvania legislature.
Fort Oswego captured by the French.
General Montcalm assumes control of French forces in Canada.
New Hampshire Gazette begins publication.

1757   William Pitt begins directing war against France.
Gen. Montcalm captures Fort William Henry.
        Martha Brewster, *Poems*
        William Smith, *History of the Province of New York*

1758   British capture Louisburg, Fort Frontenac, and Fort Duquesne.
Gen. Montcalm defeats British forces at Battle of Ticonderoga.
Jonathan Edwards appointed President of College of New Jersey.
        Jonathan Edwards, *Great Christian Doctrine of Original Sin Defended*
        Benjamin Franklin, *Way to Wealth*

1758   John Maylem, *Conquest of Louisbourg*
               Thomas Prince, *Psalms, Hymns, and Spiritual Songs*

1759   British victory over French on Plains of Abraham; Wolfe and Montcalm are killed.
        British capture Quebec.
        Cherokee Indian War (1759-1761) begins.

1760   French defeat British in second battle at Plains of Abraham.
        George III ascends British throne.
        British capture Montreal.

1761   James Otis opposes Writs of Assistance.

1762   Great Britain and Spain declare war.
        France gives Louisiana to Spain.
        St. Louis founded.
               James Otis, *Vindication of the Conduct of the House of Representatives*
               John Woolman, *Considerations on the Keeping of Negroes* (Part II)

1763   Treaty of Paris concludes French and Indian War.
        Pontiac's Rebellion (1763-1764).
        Royal Proclamation of 1763 limits colonial expansion westward of Alleghenies.
        Mason-Dixon survey (1763-1767).

1764   Sugar Act replaces Molasses Act of 1733.
        Rhode Island College (later Brown University) founded.
        Colonists boycott British goods.
               Thomas Hutchinson, *History of the Colony of Massachusetts Bay*
               James Otis, *Rights of the British Colonies Asserted and Proved*
               Oxenbridge Thacher, *Sentiments of a British American*

1765   Parliament passes Stamp Act and Quartering Act.
        Stamp Act Congress convenes in New York City.
        Colonists adopt nonimportation agreements.
               Samuel Adams, *Resolutions*
               John Dickinson, *Late Regulations Respecting the British Colonies*
               Thomas Godfrey, *Prince of Parthia*
               Martin Howard, *Letter from a Gentleman at Halifax*

1766   Parliament repeals Stamp Act.
        Queen's College (later Rutgers University) founded.
               Robert Rogers, *Ponteach*

1767   Townshend Revenue Acts passed by Parliament.
               John Dickinson, *Letters of an American Farmer*

1768   Treaty of Fort Stanwix.
        Great Britain dissolves Massachusetts legislature.
        British seize John Hancock's ship, *Liberty*, on grounds of smuggling.

1769   Dartmouth College founded in New Hampshire.
        Whitefield's final visit to America.
        Daniel Boone explores Kentucky.
               Alexander Martin, *America, a Poem*
               John Winthrop, *Lectures*

1770   Boston Massacre.
        Lord North becomes Prime Minister of England.
        Repeal of Townshend Revenue Acts, except for taxation on tea.

1770   Robert Munford, *Candidates*
        John Woolman, *Considerations on the True Harmony of Mankind*

1771 House of Burgesses opposes Protestant bishop for North American colonies.
        Timothy Dwight, *America*
        Philip Freneau and Hugh Henry Brackenridge, *Rising Glory of America*
        John Macpherson, *Pennsylvania Sailor's Letters*

1772 Committees of Correspondence organized.
    Francis Asbury becomes leader of American Methodists.
        John Trumbull, *Progress of Dulness* (Part I)

1773 Tea Act passed in Great Britain.
    Boston Tea Party.
        John Allen, *American Alarm*
        John Dickinson, *Two Letters on the Tea Tax*
        Phillis Wheatley, *Poems on Various Subjects*

1774 Parliament passes Coercive Acts.
    Boston Port Act closes Boston harbor.
    Quebec Act extends borders of Quebec to Ohio River.
    First Continental Congress convenes in Philadelphia.
    Congress passes Declaration of Rights and Grievances.
    Connecticut and Rhode Island end slave trade.
        Jacob Duché, *Caspipina's Letters*
        Francis Hopkinson, *A Pretty Story*
        Thomas Jefferson, *Summary View of the Rights of British America*
        Arthur Lee, *Appeal to the Justice and Interests of the People of Great Britain*
        Josiah Quincy, Jr., *Observations on the Act of Parliament*
        Samuel Seabury, *Free Thoughts on the Proceedings on the Continental Congress*
        John Woolman, *Journal*

1775 Siege of Boston and battles of Lexington, Concord, and Bunker Hill begin Revolutionary War.
    Ethan Allen captures Ticonderoga and Crown Point from British.
    Second Continental Congress convenes in Philadelphia.
    Gen. Washington appointed commander of Continental Army.
    Congress establishes American Navy.
    Congress appoints Committee on Foreign Correspondence.
    George III declares American colonies in state of official rebellion.
        James Adair, *History of the American Indians*
        Daniel Leonard, *Massachusettensis*
        John Trumbull, *M'Fingal* (Canto I)
        Mercy Otis Warren, *The Group*

1776 Congress adopts Declaration of Independence.
    Virginia passes Bill of Rights.
    British evacuate Boston.
    Nathan Hale executed by British for espionage.
    Washington attacks British at Trenton after crossing Delaware River.
    Phi Beta Kappa Society founded in Virginia.
        John Adams, *Thoughts on Government*
        Thomas Paine, *Common Sense*
             American Crisis

1777 Congress adopts Articles of Confederation.
    Loyalist estates are confiscated by Congress.

1777   Gen. Burgoyne surrenders to Continental Army.
        Washington winters at Valley Forge.
                Robert Munford, *The Patriots*

1778   British evacuate Philadelphia and Congress returns.
        France recognizes American independence.
        Cherry Valley Massacre.
        Wyoming Valley Massacre.
        George Rogers Clark explores Illinois territory.
                Hugh Henry Brackenridge, *Six Political Discourses*
                Devereux Jarratt, *Brief Narrative of the Revival of Religion in Virginia*
                Jonathan Carver, *Travels*

1779   George Rogers Clark captures Vincennes.
        John Paul Jones's *Bonhomme Richard* defeats the British ship *Serapis*.
                Ethan Allen, *Narrative of...Captivity*
                Gouverneur Morris, *Observations on the American Revolution*

1780   Benedict Arnold plots to surrender West Point to British.
        Maj. André is hanged for spying.
                Anthony Benezet, *Short Account of the People Called Quakers*

1781   American troops victorious at Yorktown.
        Cornwallis surrenders.
        Congress appoints commission to draw up treaty with England.
        Last state ratifies Articles of Confederation.
                Philip Freneau, *The British Prison Ship*
                Samuel Peters, *General History of Connecticut*

1782   Provisional peace treaty drawn up in Paris.
        Lord North resigned as prime minister of England.
        Congress adopts Great Seal.
                Michel Guillaüme Jean de Crévecoeur, *Letters from an American Farmer*

1783   Congress proclaims official end to Revolutionary War.
        Continental Army disbands.
        Treaty of Paris ratified.
        Vermont Gazette begins publication.
                Samuel Low, *Glory of America*

1784   Spain prohibits American navigation on Mississippi River.
        China trade begins.
        Samuel Seabury becomes first Episcopal bishop for America.
                Ethan Allen, *Reason the Only Oracle of Man*
                Jeremy Belknap, *History of New-Hampshire* (Vol. 1)
                Jedidiah Morse, *Geography Made Easy*

1785   Land Ordinance of 1785.
                Timothy Dwight, *Conquest of Canaan*
                John Marrant, *Narrative of the Lord's Wonderful Dealings*

1786   Ohio Company established.
        Shays's Rebellion.
        United States mint established.
                Joel Barlow, John Trumbull, David Humphreys, and Lemuel Lemuel
                Hopkins, *The Anarchiad*
                Philip Freneau, *Poems*

1787 Congress drafts Constitution.
      John Fitch invents steamboat.
                  John Adams, *Defence of Constitutions*
                  Joel Barlow, *Vision of Columbus*
                  Alexander Hamilton, James Madison, and John Jay, *The Federalist*
                  Peter Markoe, *Algerine Spy*
                  William Vans Murray, *Political Sketches*

1788 States ratify Constitution.
                  Timothy Dwight, *Triumph of Infidelity*
                  Philip Freneau, *Miscellaneous Works*
                  Thomas Jefferson, *Notes on the State of Virginia*
                  Richard Henry Lee, *Letters from the Federal Farmer*
                  George Richards Minot, *History of the Insurrections in Massachusetts*

1789 George Washington elected first president of United States.
      First United States Congress convenes in New York.
      University of North Carolina established.
      French Revolution begins.
      Congress adopts Bill of Rights.
      First Tariff Act.
      First Thanksgiving.
                  William Hill Brown, *Power of Sympathy*
                  Olaudah Equiano, *Interesting Narrative*
                  David Ramsay, *History of the American Revolution*

1790 First American copyright law is passed.
      Thomas Jefferson appointed secretary of state.
      John Carroll appointed bishop of Baltimore.
                  David Humphreys, *Miscellaneous Works*
                  Susanna Haswell Rowson, *Charlotte Temple*
                  Royal Tyler, *The Contrast*
                  Mercy Otis Warren, *Poems*

1791 National Bank Act.
      Massachusetts Historical Society established.
      Bill of Rights enacted.
      Vermont enters Union as 14th state.
                  William Bartram, *Travels*
                  Thomas Paine, *Rights of Man* (Parts I and II)
                  Benjamin Young Prime, *Columbia's Glory*

1792 George Washington elected to second term as president.
      Federalist and Republican parties emerge.
      New York Stock Exchange organized.
                  Joel Barlow, *Advice to the Privileged Orders* (Part I)
                  Hugh Henry Brackenridge, *Modern Chivalry*
                  Thomas Odiorne, *Progress of Refinement*

1793 Eli Whitney invents cotton gin.
      Fugitive Slave Act.
      Yellow fever epidemic in Philadelphia.
      France and England declare war; America remains neutral.
      Citizen Genêt travels to North America.
                  Ann Eliza Bleecker, *Posthumous Works*
                  Samuel Hopkins, *System of Doctrine*

1794   Whiskey Rebellion in Pennsylvania.
        Battle of Fallen Timbers.
        Jay's Treaty.
        Congress authorizes Post Office Department.
        Congress ends slave trade with foreign nations.
                Joel Barlow, *Advice to the Privileged Orders* (Part II)
                Timothy Dwight, *Greenfield Hill*
                Thomas Paine, *Age of Reason* (Part I)

1795   First railroad built in United States.
        Yazoo scandal.
        Pinckney's Treaty.
                Philip Freneau, *New Poems*
                John Blair Linn, *Miscellaneous Works*

1796   John Adams elected second president of United States.
        George Washington delivers his "Farewell Address."
        Beginning of Greek Revival in United States.
                Joel Barlow, *Hasty Pudding*
                Thomas Paine, *Age of Reason* (Part II)

1797   XYZ Affair.
                Jonathan Boucher, *View of the Causes and Consequences of the American Revolution*
                Hannah Webster Foster, *The Coquette*
                Herman Mann, *The Female Review*
                Sarah Wentworth Morton, *Beacon Hill*
                Samuel Relf, *Infidelity*
                Benjamin Trumbull, *History of Connecticut* (Part I)
                Royal Tyler, *Algerine Captive*

1798   Yellow fever epidemic erupts in Philadelphia.
        Alien and Sedition Acts passed.
        Virginia and Kentucky Resolutions passed.
        Eleventh Constitutional Amendment.
                Charles Brockden Brown, *Wieland*
                William Dunlap, *Major André*
                William Munford, *Plays and Poems*
                Susannah Haswell Rowson, *Reuben and Rachel*

1799   Napoleon rises to power.
                Hannah Adams, *Summary History of New-England*
                Charles Brockden Brown, *Edgar Huntly*
                                        Arthur Mervyn (Part I)
                                        Ormond
                Mathew Carey, *Porcupiniad*

1800   Washington, D.C., becomes capital of the United States.
        Library of Congress established.
        Tuesday Club convenes for first time.
                Joel Barlow, *Letters from Paris*
                Henry Sherburne, *Oriental Philanthropist*
                Mason Locke Weems, *Life of Washington*

Index

Act of Uniformity, 29, 867, 1097, 1115
Adair, James, *3–4*, 121, 605
Adams, Abigail, *4–7*, 16, 1521
Adams, Amos, *7–9*
Adams, Charles Francis, 5, 6, 7, 608
Adams, Eliphalet, *9–11*, 21, 756, 757, 1266
Adams, Hannah, *11–13*
Adams, Henry, 17, 1662
Adams, John (1705–1740), *13–16*
Adams, John (1735–1826), 5, *16–18*, 23, 80, 81, 85, 96, 104, 159, 208, 238, 296, 299, 381, 398, 436, 467, 479, 489, 552, 555, 557, 623, 626, 642, 645, 646, 674, 697, 731, 778, 796, 822, 827, 828, 882, 885, 894, 895, 896, 955, 1041, 1052, 1072, 1073, 1113, 1126, 1201, 1256, 1257, 1299, 1416, 1435, 1456, 1480, 1493, 1521, 1522, 1524, 1544, 1622, 1623, 1640, 1667
Adams, John Quincy, 628, 1073
Adams, Joseph, 106
Adams, Matthew, 611
Adams, Percy G., 210
Adams, Samuel, *18–20*, 149, 174, 184, 381, 645, 810, 881, 885, 1126, 1456, 1519
Adams, William, 9, *20–23*, 1627
Adams, Zabdiel, *23–24*, 296
Addison, Joseph, 50, 138, 274, 289, 401, 435, 437, 574, 598, 609, 611, 623, 680, 780, 803, 850, 899, 1037, 1070, 1122, 1137, 1219, 1270, 1301, 1335, 1481, 1521, 1523
African Colonization Movement, 37
African Methodist Episcopal (AME) Church, 37
Akenside, Mark, 1102
Alamance Creek, battle of, 787, 789, 804, 1010
Albany Board of Indian Commissioners, 361
Albany Congress, 777, 778, 781, 1603
Albany Plan, 1357
Aldridge, William, 944
Alexander, William, 1322
Alien and Sedition Laws, 238, 383, 385, 467, 468, 827, 882, 883–84, 949, 1065
Alison, Francis, *24–27*, 845, 1349, 1456
Alleine, Richard, 364
Allen, Ethan, *27–29*, 63, 305, 674, 774, 1165, 1433
Allen, James (1632–1710), *29–30*, 42, 425
Allen, James (1739–1808), *30–32*
Allen, John, *32–34*
Allen, Paul, *34–36*
Allen, Richard, *36–38*, 841
Allen, Thomas, *38–40*
Allerton, Isaac, 409

Allibone, Samuel, 30, 1145
Allin, James, *40–42*
Alline, Henry, *42–44*
Almanacs: calculators of, 49–50, 96,
    211–12, 307, 315–16, 411–13, 459,
    594, 682, 756, 887, 888, 889, 890–
    91, 1260, 1310, 1414, 1454–55,
    1487–88, 1554–55; printers of, 189,
    190, 606–7, 609, 611, 625, 652–53,
    848, 1275, 1449; verse in, 193, 200,
    303, 308–10, 316, 422, 424, 425,
    595, 891, 1224, 1258–59
Almon, John, 453, 1006
Alsop, George, *45–46*, 71, 441
Alsop, Richard, *46–48*, 221, 358, 500,
    774, 1329
American Academy of Arts and Sciences,
    174, 381, 1012, 1183, 1434, 1439,
    1554, 1638
American Antiquarian Society, 738,
    1136, 1360, 1451
American Baptist Historical Society, 619
American Bible Society, 823, 1041, 1042
American Board of Commissioners for
    Foreign Missions, 1041, 1042
American Colonization Society, 1042
American Company of Comedians, 590
American Episcopate Controversy, 57,
    79, 292–93, 305, 343, 379, 400,
    517, 737, 815, 1286
American Ethnological Society, 628
American Friend, The, 545
American Jewish Historical Society, 1293
American Magazine, The (1741), 182
American Magazine, The (1787–1788),
    825, 915, 1531, 1532, 1535–37
*American Magazine and Monthly Chroni-
    cle, The*, 300, 780, 1320, 1350
American Mercury, The, 774
American Minerva, 1532, 1537–38
American Museum, The, 273, 274, 898,
    922, 1217, 1450, 1536
American Philosophical Society: founders
    of, 111, 607, 1256, 1456; members
    of, 89, 109, 113, 280, 338, 383,
    479, 637, 922, 951, 1319, 1335,
    1349, 1638; paper delivered before,

1346; seal of, 779; *Transactions* of,
    51
American Quarterly Review, 630
American Register, The, 215
American Remembrancer, 1006
American Republic, The, 949
American Tract Society, 194, 510, 1042
American Weekly Mercury, 182, 188,
    214, 849, 897, 898, 1525
American Whig Society, 1388
Ames, Fisher, 49
Ames, Nathaniel, II, *48–50*, 887, 1555
Ames, William, 579, 1134, 1168, 1625
Amherst, Jeffrey, 356, 650, 1003, 1038
Amory, Katherine, 406
Anchor Club, 343
Anderson, Hugh, 1408
Anderson, Quentin, 985
André, Maj. John, 63, 1434
Andrews, Jedidiah, 14, 758
Andrews, William D., 1349
Andros, Edmund, 130, 153, 230, 231,
    419, 471, 707, 1295, 1310, 1398,
    1601, 1643, 1644
Annapolis Convention, 397, 697, 961,
    1211
Anne I (queen of England), 77, 396,
    499, 824, 1086, 1364
Anthology Club, 531, 861
Antill, Edward, *51–53*
Antinomian controversy, 232, 331, 332,
    389, 391, 426, 532, 567, 1092,
    1168, 1548, 1549, 1565, 1566–67,
    1585, 1625, 1633, 1634
Antinomianism, 119, 209, 232, 566,
    568, 665, 1393, 1495, 1614
Antinomian Synod, 232, 770
Aplin, John, 932
Appleton, Nathaniel, *53–57*, 641–42, 648
Apthorp, East, *57–59*
Apthorp, Fanny, 218, 1051
Arbuthnot, John, 138, 780
Archdale, John, 959
Archer, Gabriel, *59-62*, 205
Argall, Samuel, 1253, 1557
Arminianism: advocates of, 23, 116, 304,
    305, 454, 488, 573, 635, 765, 783,
    986, 996, 1139, 1208, 1376, 1387,

1506, 1587, 1588–89, 1604; opponents of, 228, 327, 386–87, 511, 535, 567, 719, 1078, 1140, 1340
Arnold, Benedict, *62–65*, 212, 434, 493, 549, 625, 1005, 1006, 1020, 1021, 1024, 1101, 1172, 1192, 1296, 1297, 1367, 1369
Arnold, Samuel, *65–66*, 1442
Arthur, T.S., 91
Articles of Confederation: critics of, 463, 465, 698, 1180, 1542–43; debates on, 778, 1649; drafting of, 1456; provisions of, 1542–43, 1623; ratification of, 1127; signers of, 645–46; supporters of, 956
Arundell, Thomas, 1243
Asbury, Francis, 37, *66–68*, 820
Ashbridge, Elizabeth, *68–70*
Ashe, Thomas, *70–72*
Ashley, Jonathan, *72–73*, 454
Associates of Dr. Bray, 202, 203
Aston, Anthony, *74–75*
Atkins, Josiah, *75–76*
Atkins, Samuel, 887
Attwood, Peter, S.J., *76–78*, 801, 1573
Auchmuty, Samuel, *78–80*, 815
Audubon, John James, 115
Aurora, 81, 436, 467, 842, 1537
Austin, Samuel, 416

Bach, Johann Sebastian, 571
Bache, Benjamin Franklin, *81–82*, 122, 238, 273, 467, 553, 555, 558, 1537
Backus, Charles, *83–84*
Backus, Isaac, *84–87*, 619
Bacon, Francis, 159, 334, 355, 424, 833, 861, 887, 899, 1105, 1160
Bacon Nathaniel, *87–88*, 141, 142, 239, 394–95, 986, 987
Bacon's Rebellion, 87–88, 141, 144, 239, 372, 394–95, 986–87
Bacon, Thomas, *88–90*, 679, 700
Badger, Stephen, 54, 56, 90–92
Bailey, Jacob, *92–95*, 1482
Bailey, Samuel, 1224
Baillie, Robert, 1803
Bailyn, Bernard, 40, 807
Baine, Rodney M., 1061, 1062

Baker, David, 356
Balance, The, 1269
Baldwin, William, 108, 113
Ballads, 99, 788, 1445
Bancroft, George, 631
Bank of North America, 397, 1125, 1623
Bank of the United States, 1212
Banks, Joseph, 283
Banneker, Benjamin, *95–98*
Bannerman, Mark, *98–100*
Barbadoes Gazette, 849, 850
Barbour, James, 1229
Barbour, Philip, 61, 1244
Barclay, Robert, 418, 561, 852
Barlow, Joel, 47, 96, *100–102*, 213, 214, 438, 500, 501, 773, 900, 1004, 1007, 1129, 1329, 1349, 1380, 1535, 1536, 1651
Barnard, John, 10, *103–4*, 105, 314, 315, 1135, 1505, 1527
Barnard, Thomas, *105–6*
Barrett, Samuel, 577
Barrett, William, 1395
Barrow, Isaac, 117
Barrow, Robert, 446, 447
Barth, John, 371
Barthélémy, Jean-Jacques, 13
Barton, Andrew. *See* Forrest, Thomas
Barton, Benjamin Smith, *107–8*, 113, 114, 115
Barton, Thomas, *108–10*, 1350
Barton, William P., 113
Bartram, John, *110–12*, 113, 337, 360, 541, 542, 637, 638, 906, 951, 952, 1016
Bartram, William, 108, 111, *112–15*, 337, 397, 951
Bass, John, *115–17*
Baxter, Joseph, 648
Baxter, Richard, 364, 567, 975
Bayle, Pierre, 138
Bayley, Josiah, 106
Beach, John, *117–19*, 448, 759, 1550, 1558
Beadhall, James, 801
Beatty, Charles Clinton, *119–21*, 479, 1423
Beckford, William, 737

Beckley, John James, *121–23*
Beckwith, George, *123–24*, 676
Bedini, Silvio, 98
Bee, The, 898
Beecher, Lyman, 504
Beete, John, *125–26*
Behn, Aphra, 88, 152
Beissel, Johann Conrad, *126–28*, 1274, 1275
Belarmine, Robert, S.J., 793
Belcher, Jonathan, 243, 244, 245, 254, 680, 1192, 1298, 1321, 1322, 1587
Belcher, Samuel, *128–29*, 1590
Belknap, Jeremy, *129–31*, 707, 725, 731, 1536
Bellamy, Joseph, *131–33*, 416, 513, 718, 719, 759–60, 1077, 1326, 1367
Bend, Joseph Grove John, *133–34*
Benét, Stephen Vincent, 1056
Benezet, Anthony, *134–37*, 322, 365, 466, 1645, 1662
Benjamin, Park, 1301
Bennington, battle of, 39
Bentley, William, 753
Berkeley, George, *137–40*, 262, 520, 1213
Berkeley, William, 87–88, *140–42*, 144, 145, 157, 394, 876, 986, 1088
Berkenmeyer, Christoph Wilhelm, 1059
Berkshire "Constitutionalists," 39
Bernard, Francis, 173, 320, 807
Berni, Francesco, 48
Beveridge, John, *142–43*, 376, 673, 1350
Beverley, Robert, *143–46*, 158, 585, 845, 899
Biddle, Nicholas, 35
Bidwell, Barnabas, *146–48*
Bigelow, William, 1450
Billings, William, *148–50*, 256, 1516
Bill of Rights, 347, 826, 934, 956, 962
Bill of Rights Society, 880
Bird, Robert Montgomery, 690
Blackamore, Arthur, *150–52*
Blackfriars Theatre, 1399
Blacklock, Thomas, 142
Blacks, education of, 79, 135, 202, 695, 696, 841, 1042, 1216
Blackstone, William, 1624

Blackwell, Edward, 1137
Blair, Francis P., 650
Blair, James, 144, 151, *152–54*, 430, 844, 846
Blair, John Durbarrow, *154–55*, 166
Blair, Samuel, *155–57*, 429, 1418, 1427, 1459
Blake, William, 1483, 1580
Bland, Edward, *157–59*
Bland, Richard, *159–61*, 264–66, 1061, 1385, 1387
Bland, Theodorick, *161–63*, 1211
Bleecker, Anne Eliza, *163–64*, 547, 714
Boehm, John Philip, *164–66*, 1280
Boel, Henricus, 613
Boerhaave, Hermann, 52, 458
Bolingbroke, Henry St. John, 466, 929
Bolles, Joseph, 695
Bolling, Robert, *166–68*
Bolton, Ann, 174, 176
Bonoeil, John, 1253, 1254
Boone, Daniel, 274, 563, 813, 814, 950, 1239
Boone, Thomas, 622
Bordley, John Beale, *168–69*, 1066
Boscawen, Edward, 536, 1003
Boston Athenaeum, 12, 531
Boston Centinel, 435
Boston Chronicle, 1448
Boston Evening Post, 1177, 1448
Boston Gazette, 18, 58, 182, 454, 601, 1113
Boston Gazette and Country Journal, 1448
Boston Magazine, 149, 150, 220
Boston Massacre: accounts of, 174, 661, 912, 1520; aftermath of, 807; causes of, 20; commemorations of, 321, 1051, 1080, 1081, 1141, 1440, 1449, 1571; poems on, 31, 1559; trial, 16, 1107, 1201
Boston News Letter, 312, 313, 435, 1085, 1147, 1448
Boston Patriot, 7, 545
Boston Port Act, 1076, 1107, 1201, 1202, 1449
Boston Post Boy, 712
Boston Public Library, 739, 1194

Boston Tea Party, 507, 808, 894, 1076, 1171, 1189, 1202, 1227
Boston Weekly Magazine, 1250
Boswell, James, 1104
Bosworth, Benjamin, *169–71*
Boucher, Jonathan, *171–73*, 298, 990, 1287
Boudinot, Elias, 3
Bouquet, Henry, 650, 1351
Bourne, Edward Gaylord, 284
Bowdoin, James, *173–74*, 1440, 1520, 1521
Bowen, Daniel, 1004
Bowers, Bathsheba, *174–76*
Bownas, Samuel, 713
Bowtell, Stephen, 1656
Boyle, Robert, 336, 975, 978, 1045, 1160, 1372
Boylston, Zabdiel, *177–78*, 458, 459–60, 682, 1526
Brackenridge, Hugh Henry, *178–81*, 221, 553, 1163, 1349, 1482
Braddock, Edward, 108, 109, 179, 650, 1009, 1020, 1192, 1350, 1356, 1457
Bradford, Andrew, *181–83*, 188, 189, 677, 849, 887, 889, 890, 891, 1241, 1413
Bradford, Ebenezer, *183–84*
Bradford, William (1590–1657), *185–87*, 408, 791, 831, 963, 1046, 1047, 1048, 1049, 1050, 1055, 1175, 1462, 1609, 1630, 1631, 1632
Bradford, William (1663–1752), 176, 182, *187–89*, 605, 887, 889, 890, 891, 1132, 1665
Bradford, William, "the third" (1722–1791), 188, *189–90*, 1350
Bradstreet, Anne, *190–92*, 193, 207, 476, 498, 594, 656, 921, 1086, 1234, 1235, 1246, 1263, 1265, 1517, 1591, 1593, 1655, 1656, 1657
Bradstreet, Samuel, *192–93*
Bradstreet, Simon, 191, 192, 326, 419, 476, 656, 1083, 1263, 1517, 1603
Brady, Nicholas, 149, 517
Brahe, Tycho, 978
Brainerd, David, 120, *193–95*, 510, 1564
Brainerd, John, 1564

Branagan, Thomas, *195–96*
Brandywine, battle of, 161, 240, 590, 953, 1020, 1021
Brant, Joseph, 539
Brattle Street Church, 9, 73, 197, 199, 368, 381, 386, 926, 976, 1391, 1439, 1489
Brattle, Thomas, *197–99*, 200, 201, 261, 472, 1602
Brattle, William, 53, *199–201*, 261, 269, 472, 1153
Bray, Thomas, *201–3*, 1104, 1581
Brayley, William, 218
Breintnall, Joseph, *203–4*, 214, 897, 1414, 1525
Bremner, James, 1350
Brereton, John, 61, *205–6*, 1243
Brewster, Martha Wadsworth, *206–8*
Brewster, William, 185, 408, 1046, 1630
Briant, Lemuel, *208–9*
Brickell, John, *210–11*, 872
Brigden, Zechariah, *211–12*
Brightman, Thomas, 793
Brinsley, John, 314
Briscoe, Nathaniel, 1174
British Museum, 113, 338, 611, 716, 739, 992
Brockway, Thomas, *212–13*
Brooke, Henry, *213–14*, 1243
Brooks, Charles, 1489
Broughton, Thomas, 12
Brown, Alexander, 60–61
Brown, B. Gratz, 650
Brown, Charles Brockden, 35–36, *215–17*, 239, 436, 439, 493, 900, 1067, 1330, 1331, 1663
Brown, Herbert Ross, 592
Brown, Richard, 1174
Brown, William Hill, *217–20*, 1051, 1052, 1221
Bruce, David, *220–22*
Brunhouse, Robert, 1207
Bryant, Jacob, 13
Bryant, William Cullen, 283
Buchanan, John, 154
Buckingham, Thomas, *222–23*, 241, 242, 966
Buckminster, Joseph, 12

Budd, Thomas, *224–25*, 605
Buell, Samuel, *225–28*
Bulkeley, Edward, *228–29*
Bulkeley, Gershom, *230–31*, 235
Bulkeley, Peter (1583–1659), *232–33*, 391, 527, 528, 1084
Bulkeley, Peter, II (1643–c. 1688), *233–35*
Bulkley, John, *235–37*
Bull, William, 741
Bullfinch, Charles, 1052
Bunker Hill, battle of, 32, 179, 238, 1020, 1051, 1052–53, 1389, 1519
Bunyan, John, 819, 1030, 1136, 1451
Burgoyne, John, 163, 547, 625, 1522, 1645
Burk, John Daly, *237–39*
Burke, Edmund, 353, 438, 818
Burke, Thomas, *240–41*, 953
Burnham, William, *241–43*
Burns, Robert, 99, 221
Burr, Aaron (1716–1757), *243–45*, 246, 1192, 1318, 1430
Burr, Aaron (1756–1836), 238, 697, 882, 948, 949, 955, 1213
Burr, Esther Edwards, 244, *245–47*, 529, 1430
Burrington, George, 210
Burroughs, George, 868, 869
Burroughs, Stephen, *247–49*
Burt, Jonathan, *250–51*
Burton, Robert, 1518,
Bushy Run, battle of, 1351
Butler, James, *252–54*
Butler, Samuel, 50, 94, 371, 899, 1009
Buxtehude, Dietrich, 571
Byles, Mather, 15, 32, 149, *254–57*, 311, 642, 680, 1290
Byrd, William, I, 144, 146, 585
Byrd, William, II (of Westover), 140, 144, 146, 151, *257–59*, 285, 397, 598, 858, 1015, 1146, 1219, 1365, 1386, 1424
Byrd, William, III, 166, 167

Caldwell, John, 926
Calef, Robert, *260–62*, 975
Calhoun, Daniel, 1535

Calhoun, John, 656, 1417
Callender, James Thomson, 122
Callender, John, *262–63*
Callister, Henry, 90
Cambridge Platform, 666, 983, 1582, 1644, 1645
Cambridge Synod (1648), 392, 1082
Camm, John, 160, *263–66*, 282, 989
Campbell, Charles, 161–62
Campbell, Isaac, *266–68*
Campion, Thomas, 424
Capen, Joseph, *268–70*
Carew, Bampflyde-Moore, *270–72*
Carey, Mathew, 37, 122, *272–75*, 922, 1251, 1536, 1544
Carleton, Guy, 1101
Carlisle, David, Jr., 436, 438
Carlson, C. Lennart, 14, 849, 850
Carlyle, Joseph, 766
Caroline I (queen of England), 256, 352
Carroll, Charles (of Carrollton), 78, *275–77*, 483, 801
Carroll, John, 276, *277–79*
Carter, Landon, 167, 264–66, *279–82*
Carter, Robert, 583, 584
Carteret, Philip, 419
Carver, Jonathan, 4, *282–85*, 337, 652, 1171, 1238
Castine Gazette, 1395
Castle William, 985, 1021, 1324, 1527
Caswell, Richard, 953
Catesby, Mark, 111, *285–87*, 337, 338, 474, 638
Causton, Thomas, 1409
Cave, Edward, 182
Censor, The, 807
Cervantes, Miguel de, 179, 1494
Chalkley, Thomas, *287–89*, 1371
Chamberlain, Richard, *289–91*
Chambers, Ephraim, 849
Champion, The, 1205
Chandler, Thomas Bradbury, 79, *291–95*, 1354
Chaplain, Abraham, 564
Chaplin, Ebenezer, *295–97*
Chapman, George, 714
Chapman, Nathaniel, 923
Charles I (king of England), 475, 523,

1043, 1088, 1092, 1170, 1273, 1518, 1550

Charles II (king of England), 22, 45, 87, 140, 376, 396, 582, 795, 974, 1057, 1082, 1089, 1134, 1159, 1375, 1522, 1572, 1651, 1654, 1656

Chase, Richard, 219

Chase, Samuel, 276, *297–99*, 882, 954, 955, 1667

Chase, Thomas, 133, 297, *299–300*

Chateaubriand, François, 114, 283

Chatterton, Thomas, 861, 900

Chaucer, Geoffrey, 425, 654, 1160

Chauncy, Charles (c. 1592–1672), *301–3*, 304, 306, 307, 310, 754, 1262, 1441

Chauncy, Charles (1705–1787), 85, 235, 293, 294, 302, *303–6*, 331, 334, 491, 502, 504, 561, 600, 602, 642, 997, 998, 1188, 1210, 1290, 1506, 1551, 1563, 1587, 1594, 1616

Chauncy, Elnathan, 308, 310

Chauncy, Israel, 301, *306–7*

Chauncy, Nathaniel, 301, *307–10*, 1514, 1515, 1615

Checkley, John, *310–12*, 611, 1514, 1587, 1588

Checkley, Samuel, *312–13*

Cheever, Ezekiel, 311, *313–15*, 487, 657, 1469, 1589, 1590

Cheever, Samuel, *315–16*

Cheever, Thomas, 1590

Chester, Stephen, *316–17*

Chesterfield (fourth earl of), 259, 1580

Chesterton, G. K., 353, 355, 930

Chestnut Street Theatre (Philadelphia), 274

Child, Josiah, 1105

Child, Lydia Maria, 1056

Child, Robert, 988, 992, 1372, 1373

Childs, Francis, 552

Chiswell, John, 167

Christanna, Fort, 1365

Christian History, 42, 926, 1139, 1428, 1437, 1438

Church, Benjamin (1639–1718), 230, *317–19*, 321–22

Church, Benjamin (1734–1778), *319–21*, 1520

Church, Thomas, 318, *321–22*, 1562

Churchill, Charles, 435, 774

Churchman, John, *322–24*

Church Street Theatre (Charleston), 125

Church Times, 133

Cibber, Colley, 75, 678

Cicero, Marcus Tullius, 52, 159, 623, 899, 907, 1086, 1116, 1196

Claggett, Thomas John, 324–25

Clap, Nathaniel, 13

Clap, Roger, *326–27*

Clap, Thomas Stephen, *327–28*, 667, 759, 1163, 1651

Clark, George Rogers, *328–29*, 814, 843, 909, 961

Clark, Peter, *330–31*

Clarke, John (1609–1676), *331–33*, 348

Clarke, John (1755–1798), *333–35*

Clarke, Mary Bayard, 953

Clarkson, Thomas, 136, 537

Classis of Amsterdam, 613

Classis of Emden, 612

Clay, Henry, 628, 630, 948, 949

Clayton, John (1657–1725), *335–37*, 338, 845

Clayton, John (1694–1774), 111, 121, *337–39*, 637, 1015, 1016

Cleaveland, Benjamin, 339-41

Cleaveland, Ebenezer, 1177

Cleaveland, John, *341–43*, 1177

Clemens, Samuel, 840, 1067, 1172

Clifford's Inn, 1054

Cliffton, William, *343–45*

Clinton, George, *345–47*, 1355, 1597

Clinton, Henry, 63, 1287

Cobbett, Thomas, 333, *347–49*, 790, 1234

Cobbett, William, 221, 274, 343, *349–55*, 436, 1214, 1249, 1537

Cockings, George, *355–57*

Coddington, William, 262, 505

Coercive Acts, 808

Coetus of Pennsylvania, 1279

Cogswell, James, 910

Cogswell, Mason Fitch, 47, *358–59*, 774, 1329

Colden, Cadwallader, 111, *359–62*, 459, 541, 637, 1016, 1037, 1079, 1354, 1355
Cole, Charles, 678
Cole, Nathan, *362–65*
Coleman, Elihu, *365–66*
Colerick, John, 221
Coleridge, Samuel Taylor, 114, 122, 283, 440, 1196, 1483
Collier, J. Payne, 670
Collins, William, 378, 861
Collins, Zaccheus, 113
Collinson, Peter, 111, 112, 113, 115, 204, 338, 897, 1016
Colman, Benjamin, 9, 197, 199, 200, *366–70*, 386, 460, 472, 600, 642, 648, 976, 977, 979, 1154, 1239, 1290, 1339, 1456, 1489, 1490, 1491, 1527, 1614
Colonial agents, 258, 487, 488, 975, 1167, 1168, 1169, 1273, 1548, 1549, 1630
Columbian Centinel, 220, 1052, 1395
Columbian Herald, 861
Columbian Magazine, 130, 167, 273, 557, 560, 780
Columbian Minerva, 939
Columbus, Christopher, 101, 409, 833
Comets, 49, 594, 978, 1637, 1638, 1647
Comfort, William, 1160
Commager, Henry Steele, 1534
Commercial Advertiser, 1532, 1538
Commissioners for the Propagation of the Gospel among the Indians, 425
Committees of Correspondence, 19, 94, 159, 255, 433, 443, 810, 893, 904, 1112, 1431, 1448
Committees of Safety, 799, 960, 961, 1446, 1519
Common Sense, 1205
Compton, Henry, 153
Concord, battle of, 531, 784, 785, 1328
Conestoga Treaty, 1456
Congregational Fund Board, 981
Congregational Library, 718
Congress (U.S.), 298, 552, 1180, 1358, 1359, 1480, 1640. *See also* House of Representatives; Senate

Congressional Journal, 632
Congressional Register, 552
Connecticut Courant, 500, 956, 1132, 1269, 1270, 1326, 1531, 1535
Connecticut Evangelical Magazine, 533, 718, 1326, 1403
Connecticut General Assembly: acts and deliberations of, 235, 242, 581, 947; appeals to, 1124; members of, 222, 580, 694, 1603, 1650; sermons delivered before, 514, 966
Connecticut General Association, 718
Connecticut General Court, 770, 962, 963, 1198, 1582
Connecticut Historical Society, 230, 358, 363, 432, 914
Connecticut Journal, 1401
Connecticut Medical Society, 358, 773
Connecticut Mirror, 500
Connecticut Missionary Society, 718, 1164, 1403
Connecticut Society for the Abolition of Slavery, 1381
Connecticut Society for the Promotion of Freedom, 500
Connecticut Wits: influence of, 525, 764; members of, 47, 100, 358–59, 500, 501, 773, 797, 1329, 1330, 1481; precursors of, 214, 1102, 1380
Connors, Donald F., 1055
Constitution (U.S.), 555, 623, 628, 882, 884, 1214, 1301
Constitution (U.S.), ratification of: advocates of, 443, 444–45, 397–98, 478, 673, 698, 817–18, 824–26, 883, 935, 948–49, 1004, 1212, 1403, 1447, 1450, 1531; opponents of, 161, 345, 346, 627, 730, 880, 885, 955–56, 962, 1213, 1229
Constitutional Convention: accounts of, 698, 934; delegates to, 443, 607, 646, 732, 818, 934, 955, 961, 1033, 1180, 1211, 1523, 1622; deliberations of, 647, 961-62, 1543; proposals to convene, 697
Continental Congress: acts and deliberations of, 28, 632, 633, 823, 881, 1446, 1564; chaplains of, 469, 479;

criticism of, 294–95, 634, 1299,
    1597; delegates to, 5, 16, 19, 159,
    161, 240, 275, 297, 345, 397, 433,
    443, 463, 478, 607, 621, 632, 645,
    697, 773, 778, 779, 822, 880, 883,
    885, 904, 933, 955, 1033, 1206,
    1211, 1256, 1523, 1622, 1648,
    1667; proposals to, 85, 213, 464,
    776, 1228; secretary of, 1456
Conway, Moncure, 1213
Cook, Capt. James, 877, 878, 879
Cooke, Ebenezer, 88, *370–72*, 401, 597,
    1137, 1482
Cooke, George Frederick, 493
Cooke, John Esten, 923
Cooke, Nicholas, 35
Cooke, Samuel (1687–1747), *372–73*
Cooke, Samuel (1709-1783), *374–76*
Cooley, Timothy, 729
Coombe, Thomas, *376-78*
Cooper, James Fenimore, 215, 322, 493,
    690, 814, 1007, 1068, 1607, 1620
Cooper, Myles, *379-81*
Cooper, Samuel, *381-83*
Cooper, Thomas, *383-85*, 1477
Cooper, William, 73, 381, *385-87*, 460,
    680, 1209, 1339
Copernicus, Nicolaus, 212
Copley, Thomas, S.J., 1572
Cornwallis, Charles, 75, 540, 625, 1004,
    1434
Corporation for Promoting the Gospel of
    Jesus Christ in New England, 1169
Corporation for the Relief of Widows and
    Children of Clergy, 79
Cosby, William,1036, 1665, 1666
Cotton, John (1584–1652), 66, 232, 370,
    374, *387–92*, 393, 426, 427, 448,
    475, 491, 497, 666, 746, 769, 770,
    847, 968, 976, 983, 1014, 1049,
    1057, 1082, 1083, 1084, 1093,
    1116, 1314, 1470, 1511, 1514,
    1585, 1603, 1608, 1609, 1625, 1655
Cotton, John (1640-1699), *393–94*, 1393
Cotton, John (of Queen's Creek, c.
    1640– after 1678), 88, *394–95*
Cotton, Joshua, 1475
Cotton, Seaborn, 1471

Court of St. James, 5, 16
Cowie, Alexander, 1481
Cowley, Abraham, 1160, 1191
Cowper, William, 1580
Coxe, Daniel, *395–97*
Coxe, Tench, 221, *397–99*, 1066
Cradock, Thomas, 300, *399–401*
Crandall, John, 332-33
Cranfield, Thomas Hinckley, 1022
Crashawe, William, 1568
Craven, Wesley F., 1222
Crawford, Charles, *401–3*
Crèvecoeur, Michel Guillaüme Jean de,
    46, 299, *403–6*, 420, 470, 676, 813,
    814, 1007
Crisp, Tobias, 569, 1393
Crocker, Josiah, 1438
Crockett, David ("Davy"), 948
Cromwell, Oliver, 45, 77, 140, 332,
    348, 657, 766, 980, 1037, 1089,
    1090, 1097, 1169, 1214, 1631
Cronin, James E., 1330
Croswell, Andrew, 602, 635, 1027,
    1186, 1614
Crowder, Richard, 1593
Crukshank, Joseph, 96
Culpepper, Thomas, 145
Cummings, Abraham, 535
Curwen, Samuel, *406–7*
Cushman, Robert, *408–10*, 1047
Custis, John, 1015
Cutler, Manasseh, 478
Cutler, Timothy, 117, 1557
Cutter, Benjamin, 375

Daboll, Nathan, *411–13*
Daily Advertiser (Albany, N.Y.), 500
Daily Advertiser (New York City), 346,
    552, 616
Daily Advertiser (Pa.), 555
Daily American Advertiser, 555
Daily Courant, 1205
Dale, Samuel, 285
Dale, Thomas, *413–15*, 854
Dana, Eleutheros, 1004
Dana, James, *415–17*, 448, 759, 1464
Dana, Samuel, 416
Dancing, criticism of, 721

Danckaerts, Jasper, *417–19*
Dane, John, *419–21*
Dane, Nathan, 420
Danforth, John, *421–23*, 425
Danforth, Samuel (1626–1674), *423–24*,
    425, 595, 1116, 1215, 1316, 1626,
    1633
Danforth, Samuel (1666–1727), 422,
    423, *424–26*, 1224
Danton, George-Jacques, 468
Darlington, William, 108, 111, 952
Darnall, Henry, 1138
d'Aumont, J. B., 384
Davenport, James, 305, 668, 669, 709,
    1026, 1027, 1189, 1422, 1506,
    1563, 1614
Davenport, John, 347, 373, *426–28*, 638,
    766, 1169, 1176, 1177, 1178
Davies, Samuel, *428–30*, 566, 675, 990,
    1144, 1217, 1220, 1342, 1350,
    1352, 1387, 1419, 1420
Davis, Emerson, 1190
Davis, James, 693
Davis, Jefferson, 1533, 1534
Davis, John, 436
Davis, Richard Beale, 1642
Dawson, William, *430-31*, 941, 1137,
    1385
Day, Jeremiah, 431
Day, Stephen, 920
Day, Thomas M., *431–33*
Dean, James, 1564
Deane, Samuel, 868
Deane, Silas, *433–34*, 478, 880
DeArmond, Anna, 849
de Bry, Theodor, 715
Decatur, Stephen, 253
Declaration of Independence: advocates
    of, 19, 492; drafting of, 826, 827,
    1456; effects of, 39; opponents of,
    64, 443, 469, 808; precursors of,
    464, 609, 1436; publishing of, 652;
    signers of, 297, 645, 778, 1256,
    1622, 1623, 1648
Declaratory Act, 1668, 1669
Defoe, Daniel, 130, 265, 271, 440, 574,
    849, 930, 1043, 1417, 1451
Deism: advocates of, 29, 203, 237, 334,

    362, 566, 609, 683, 765, 928, 949,
    1129–30, 1138, 1387, 1552; oppo-
    nents of, 90, 138, 184, 228, 236,
    400, 417, 439, 502, 545, 774, 818,
    924–25, 1145, 1217, 1302, 1344,
    1410, 1560
de Labadie, Jean, 417, 418
de Lahontan, Baron, 146
DeLancey, James, 1356, 1357
de La Potherie, Le Roy de Bacqueville,
    361
Dell, William, 665
Delphian Club, 35
Denham, John, 502, 548, 1659
Dennie, Joseph, 35, 344, 352, 353, *435–
    40*, 557, 558, 900, 1330, 1331,
    1395, 1447, 1449, 1450, 1451,
    1493, 1534
Denton, Daniel, *441–42*
Derham, William, 682
Desaguliers, John, 682
de Sales, Francis, 276
Descartes, René, 138, 198, 200, 715,
    1045
de Tocqueville, Alexis, 130
de Vattel, Emmerich, 478
De Witt, John, 1105
Dexter, Franklin Bowditch, 447
Dialogs, 50, 139, 147, 364, 412, 432,
    523, 694, 700, 739–40, 807, 1332,
    1336–38, 1547, 1558, 1588
Diary, or Loudon's Register, The, 914
Dickason, David, 1621
Dickens, Asbury, 436, 439
Dickens, Charles, 407
Dickinson, Emily, 191, 579
Dickinson, John (1732–1808), 273, *442–
    45*, 676, 807, 823, 873, 881, 928,
    929, 930, 931, 1286, 1335, 1457,
    1621, 1623
Dickinson, Jonathan (1663–1722), *445–
    47*
Dickinson, Jonathan (1688–1747), 118,
    243–44, 447, 448, 1101, 1419,
    1422, 1558
Dickinson, Moses, *447–49*, 581, 582,
    1430
Digges, Thomas Atwood, 218, *449–50*

Dillenius, Johan Jacob, 111, 1016
Dinwiddie, Robert, 281, 650, 1009, 1385, 1510, 1523
Disbrow, Mary, 231
Dixon, John, 712
Dock, Christopher, *450–52*
Dod, John, 475
Dodge, John, *452–54*
Dodsley, Robert, 1352
Donne, John, 714, 1117, 1118, 1184, 1333
Doolittle, Benjamin, *454–56*
Dorchester Company, 1577
Dorchester Heights, battle of, 39
Dorr, Edward, 242, *456–58*
Douglass, David, 74, 357, 654, 1408
Douglass, William, 177, *458–61*, 611, 682
Dove, David James, 672, 673
Drake, Francis, *461–62*
Drake, Joseph Rodman, 344
Drake, Samuel Gardner, 455
Draper, Lyman C., 329
Drayton, William Henry, *462–64*, 622, 623, 720, 1431
Drinker, Elizabeth Sandwith, *465–66*
Dryden, John, 50, 214, 274, 344, 560, 861, 1122, 1123, 1273, 1521, 1655
Duane, William, 122, 436, *466–69*, 842
Dublin Gazette, 89
Dublin Mercury, 89
Duché, Jacob, 25, *469–71*, 1350
Dudleian Lectures, 8, 23, 54, 375, 473, 518, 601, 642–43, 753, 783, 1551, 1594
Dudley, Joseph, 316, *471–73*, 474, 476, 976, 1263, 1527, 1606
Dudley, Paul, 472, *473–75*
Dudley, Thomas, 190, 471, 473, *475–77*, 657, 770, 918, 1168, 1234, 1656
Duels: criticism of, 155, 1304, 1368, 1545; participants in, 238, 240, 273, 697, 861, 948, 949
Duer, William, *477–79*, 1622
Duffield, George, 120, *479–80*
Dulany, Daniel, "the elder" (1685–1753), *480–82*, 699, 897, 1137, 1138

Dulany, Daniel, "the younger" (1722–1797), *482–83*
Dumbleton, Joseph, *483–86*, 1138
Dummer, Jeremiah, 835, *486–90*
Dummer, Shubael, 1590
Dummer, William, 1406
Dunbar, Samuel, *490–92*
Dunlap, John, 555
Dunlap, William, 31, 36, 147, 215, 238, *492–94*, 760, 761, 915, 1067, 1068, 1329, 1330, 1331, 1451
Dunmore, John, 161, 162, 1211
Dunmore's War, 328
Dunster, David, *494–96*
Dunster, Henry, 301, 310, 495, *496–98*, 920, 921, 1014
Dunton, John, *498–99*
Dupin, Louis, 330
Duquesne, Fort, 108, 1319, 1652
Dury, John, 1372
Dutch West India Company, 417, 1294, 1373
Dwight, Theodore, 47–48, 221, 358, *500*, 774, 1329, 1330
Dwight, Timothy, 47, 101, 213, 431, 493, *500–504*, 534, 796, 900, 1005, 1007, 1329, 1331, 1403, 1411, 1450, 1536, 1537, 1651

Eagle; or, Dartmouth Centinel, The, 435, 438
Eames, John, 683
Earthquake of 1727, 41, 223, 368, 603, 1147–48, 1304, 1595, 1619
Earthquake of 1755, 1638, 1639
Earthquakes, 897, 978, 1195, 1295, 1340
East India Company, 833, 1196, 1456
Easton, John, *505–6*
Easty, Mary, 261
Eaton, Theophilus, 1178, 1179
Echo, The, 1329
Eddis, William, *506–7*
Eden, Robert, 506
Edes, Benjamin, 555
Edwards, Daniel, 456-57
Edwards, Fort, 549
Edwards, Jonathan (1703–1758), 8, 39, 41, 72, 73, 91, 103, 124, 131–33,

193–94, 225, 226, 243, 245, 304,
305, 330, 342, 368, 373, 386, 387,
416–17, 429, 448, 459, 488, 490,
500, 501, 503, 504, *507–12*, 513,
534, 565, 591, 675, 718, 719, 721,
729, 732, 775, 776, 777, 829–30,
912, 913, 946, 996, 1011, 1136,
1139, 1140, 1141, 1149, 1154,
1164, 1208, 1209, 1286, 1291,
1304, 1313, 1340, 1371, 1383,
1385, 1390, 1391, 1404, 1405,
1419, 1421, 1430, 1563, 1564,
1604, 1612, 1614, 1615, 1616
Edwards, Jonathan, Jr. (1745–1801),
416, *513–15*, 1404
Eells, Nathaniel, *515–16*, 644, 645,
1188, 1465
Ehret, George, 115, 338
Eliot, Andrew, 105, 294, *516–19*, 1527,
1528
Eliot, Jared, *519–21*
Eliot, John, 3, 393, 394, 419, 423, 425,
519, *521–24*, 579, 594, 657, 658,
659, 920, 997, 1000, 1001, 1178,
1179, 1513, 1546, 1590, 1632
Elizabeth I (queen of England), 293, 662,
834, 862, 1161, 1556
Ellicott, Andrew, 96, 652, 653
Ellicott, Clark, 411
Ellicott, Elias, 96
Elliott, James, *524–26*
Ellis, John, 1093
Emerald, 220
Emerson, Joseph (1700–1767), *526–28*
Emerson, Joseph (1724–1775), *528–30*
Emerson, Mary Moody, 531
Emerson, Ralph Waldo, 527, 528, 531–
32, 985, 1103, 1347
Emerson, William, *530–33*, 861
Emmons, Nathaniel, *533–36*, 732, 1369
Endecott, John, 332, 639, 640, 770, 962,
1054, 1056, 1167
English Civil War, 663, 665, 667, 859,
1169, 1518
Ephrata Cloister, 127, 1274
Equiano, Olaudah, *536–39*
Erskine, John, 121
Essex Gazette, 343

*Essex Journal, and Merrimack Packet,
The*, 1446
Evans, Charles, 42, 1017, 1251
Evans, Israel, *539–41*
Evans, Lewis, *541–43*, 1356
Evans, Nathaniel, *543–44*, 559, 560,
654, 1350
Everard, Richard, 210
Everett, David, *544–46*
Ewing, John, 26
Eyre, John, 611

Fairfax Resolves, 961
Fairfax, Thomas, 962
Farish, Hunter Dickinson, 584
Farmer's Weekly Museum, 436, 438,
439, 557, 558, 686, 1330, 1395,
1447, 1449, 1451
Farquhar, George, 414
Fauchet, Claude, 1212–13
Faugeres, Margaretta, 164, *547–49*
Faulkner, William, 1220
Federal Orrery, 1121
*Federal Republican and Baltimore Tele-
graph*, 35
Federal Street Theatre (Boston), 864,
1071
Fénelon, François, 560, 861
Fennell, James, 125
Fenno, Jenny, *550–51*
Fenno, John, 274, 343, 436, 439, *551–
59*, 673, 1329, 1330, 1537
Fenno, John Ward, 554, 558
Fergusson, Elizabeth Graeme, *559–60*,
684, 1328, 1350
Fergusson, Robert, 828
Ferrar, Nicholas, 1255
Ferris, David, *560–62*
Fessenden, Thomas, 438
Fiedler, Leslie, 219
Fielding, Henry, 130, 272, 274, 700,
818, 1205, 1580
Filmer, Robert, 172, 265
Filson, John, *562–64*, 813, 950
Fink, Mike, 179
Finley, Samuel, 562–63, *564–66*, 730,
1339, 1418, 1421, 1422–23
Firmin, Gyles, *567–69*, 1093

Fisher, Hugh, 1339, 1340
Fiske, John, *569–73*
Fiske, Nathan, *573–75*
Fiske, Samuel, 1187–88
Fiske, Sarah Symmes, *575–76*
Fitch, Elijah, *576–78*
Fitch, James, *578–80*
Fitch, Thomas, *580–83*
Fitch, William, 788
Fithian, Philip Vickers, *583–84*
Fitzhugh, William, *585–87*
Fleet, Thomas, 611
Fletcher, Bridget Richardson, *587–88*
Flint, Josiah, 21, 22, 422
Folger, Abiah, 589, 606
Folger, Peter, *588–89*
Folklore, 101, 248, 401, 563, 699, 1172,
   1366, 1545
Foote, Samuel, 1580
Forbes, James, 108
Forbes, John, 769
Ford, Worthington Chauncey, 688
Forrest, Thomas, *589–91*
Forten, James, 841
"Fort Fight" (1675), 230
Foster, Hannah Webster, *591–93*
Foster, John, 269, *593–95*
Fothergill, John, 111, 113, 283, 359,
   596, 907, 951
Fothergill, Samuel, *595–97*, 1662
Fox, George, 188, 665, 887, 888, 1282,
   1610
Fox, John, *597–99*
Foxcroft, Thomas, 304, 386, *599–604*,
   1465, 1594
Foxe, John, 364, 1092
Frame, Richard, *605*, 938, 1414
Franciscans, 76
Francke, August Hermann, 452, 1500
Franklin, Ann, 611
Franklin, Benjamin, 25, 49, 81, 94, 109,
   111, 120, 142, 174, 180, 182, 183,
   188, 189, 202, 203, 204, 269, 273,
   274, 276, 325, 360, 362, 377, 381,
   396, 404, 405, 420, 425, 433, 439,
   443, 449, 477, 487, 541, 542, 543,
   559, 581, 589, *606–10*, 611, 632,
   637, 652, 654, 674, 677, 682, 693,
   777, 780, 796, 797, 799, 808, 822,
   826, 845, 848, 849, 850, 857, 873,
   880, 887, 891, 895, 897, 906, 938,
   950, 951, 954, 959, 968, 1004,
   1007, 1015, 1016, 1026, 1030,
   1101, 1125, 1126, 1132, 1137,
   1138, 1159, 1160, 1201–2, 1204,
   1205, 1218, 1242, 1256, 1275,
   1348, 1350, 1351, 1352, 1371,
   1381, 1414, 1415, 1420, 1425,
   1454, 1455, 1456, 1457, 1460,
   1461, 1515, 1524, 1525, 1526,
   1544, 1545, 1554, 1555, 1580,
   1637, 1638, 1655, 1659, 1662
Franklin, Deborah, 142, 606, 608
Franklin, James, 49, 177, 311, 459, 606,
   610–12, 873, 1515
Franklin, William, 559, 606, 608
Free African Society, 37, 841
Freeman, Douglas Southall, 555
Freeman's Journal, 273, 525, 616
Free Negro Convention Movement, 37
Frelinghuysen, Theodorus Jacobus, *612–
   14*, 1419, 1427
French and Indian (Seven Years') War:
   chaplains in, 108, 123, 342; clergy
   in, 108, 120, 429, 430; in essays,
   430, 990, 1350; finances of, 582;
   histories of, 1351, 1356; journals of,
   246, 626, 650, 1021, 1238–39,
   1322–23; persecution of Catholics
   during, 801; in plays, 356–57; in
   poems, 207, 357, 470, 1003; in sermons, 244, 429, 566, 1384, 1423,
   1595, 1613; soldiers in, 63, 282,
   345, 356, 654, 764, 1020, 1061,
   1238, 1322
French and Indian Wars: campaigns during, 734, 762, 1276–77, 1644,
   1650; chaplains in, 222, 223; histories of, 1079; propaganda during,
   453, 1087. *See also* King George's
   War; King William's War; Queen
   Anne's War
French, David, *614–15*
French Revolution: critics of, 84, 297,
   344, 350, 439, 557, 817, 1042–43,
   1213, 1359, 1411, 1532; histories

of, 467–68, 1034; supporters of, 102, 383, 384, 548, 1410–11, 1663

Freneau, Philip, 32, 81, 122, 179, 238, 344, 438, 552, 553, 555, 556, *615–17*, 626, 900, 916, 942, 1007, 1163, 1227, 1330, 1349, 1485, 1535, 1538

Friendly Club, 1329

Frothingham, Ebenezer, 363, *617–20*, 694, 1125

Fuller, Samuel, 1175

Fuller, Thomas, 609, 693

Fuseli, Henry, 812

Gadsen, Christopher, 19, *621–24*

Gage, Thomas, 784, 785, 1481

Gaine, Hugh, *624–26*, 1357

Gale, Theophilus, 330

Gallatin, Albert, 221, 467, *626–31*

Galloway, Joseph, 109, *631–34*

Galt, John, 673

Garden, Alexander (c. 1685–1756), *634–36*, 1340

Garden, Alexander, Dr. (1730–1791), 111, 112, 286, *636–38*, 1016

Gardiner, Harvey, 646, 647

Gardiner, Lion, *638–41*, 964, 1499

Garrick, David, 1580

Gates, Horatio, 549, 1024

Gates, Thomas, 60, 1557

Gaustad, Edwin Scott, 1078, 1188, 1189, 1210, 1325

Gay, Ebenezer, 306, *641–44*, 998

Gay, John, 74, 590, 929

Gay, Peter, 831

Gazette de Leide, 552–53

Gazetteer, 880, 881

Gazette of the United States, 436, 439, 440, 552, 553, 554, 555, 556, 557, 558, 673, 929, 1330, 1359

Gee, Joshua, *644–45*, 985, 1188

General Advertiser, 81, 467, 553

General Land Office, 1004, 1005

General Magazine, 182, 214, 607, 1026

Genêt, Edmond, 81, 557, 1033, 1212

Gentleman's Magazine, 182, 286, 380, 483, 898, 899, 1525, 1659

Genzmer, George, 848

George I (king of England), 313, 499, 1364

George II (king of England), 382, 618, 958, 1192, 1423

George III (king of England), 65, 256, 319, 350, 377, 407, 412, 465, 537, 559, 823, 1020, 1189, 1402, 1423, 1440

Georgia Provincial Congress, 1667, 1668

Germantown, battle of, 1645

Gerry, Elbridge, *645–47*, 956

Gessner, Solomon, 943

Gibbs, Henry, 55, *648–49*

Gilliard, Thomas, 356

Gillon, Alexander, 623

Girardin, Louis, 238

Girty, Simon, 179

Gist, Christopher, *649–51*

Glorious Revolution, 77, 464, 716

Goddard, Mary Katharine, *651–53*

Goddard, William, 651, 652, 653

Godfrey, Thomas, 590, *653–55*, 1242, 1350

Godwin, William, 215, 239, 812, 1129

Goen, C. C., 619, 1210

Goldsmith, Oliver, 99, 344, 377, 435, 437, 440, 1104, 1463, 1483, 1641

Gooch, William, 941

Goodhue, Sarah, *655–57*

Gookin, Daniel (c. 1612–1687), 461, 579, *657–59*, 999, 1244

Gookin, Daniel, Jr. (1650–1718), 657, *659–60*

Gordon, Thomas, 905

Gordon, William, *660–61*

Gore, Christopher, 551

Gorges, Sir Ferdinando, *661–64*, 847, 992, 1031, 1054, 1055

Gorges, Robert, 662

Gorton, Samuel, 476, *664–66*, 1630, 1631

Gosnold, Capt. Bartholomew, 59, 61, 205, 1243

Gosse, Étienne, 48

Gothicism, 163, 217, 239, 1221

Graham, John, *666–68*

Graham, Louis, 1639

Grant, James, 621, 622

Gray, Ellis, *668–70*

Gray, Robert, *670–72*, 1223

Gray, Thomas, 378, 1483

Graydon, Alexander, 143, *672–74*

Gray's Inn, 87, 290, 1399

Great Awakening: attacks on Calvinism of, 208–9; attacks on "unconverted" ministers, 1421–22; defense of "unconverted" ministers, 668–69, 708; conversions during, 85, 1099, 1288, 1613; criticism of emotionalism of, 25, 41, 72–73, 105, 195, 304, 305, 368–69, 455, 520, 635–36, 772, 947, 991, 1136, 1176–77, 1188–89, 1208, 1209–10, 1291, 1383, 1384, 1459–60, 1490; itinerant ministers, 131, 225, 944, 1420, 1563, 1579–80; criticism of itinerant ministers, 73, 491, 515–16, 709–11, 758, 912–13, 932, 1078, 1150, 1186, 1506–7, 1587, 1588; moderates during, 54, 103, 335, 528, 642, 829, 910, 1059, 1140, 1303, 1612, 1614; narratives of, 116, 156, 363–64, 804, 1428–29, 1438; origins of, 613–14, 1390, 1405, 1406, 1419; poems about, 207, 340–41, 680, 1026–27, 1420; supporters of, 386, 429, 509, 511, 565, 601, 602, 644, 645, 926, 1109, 1139–40, 1194, 1325, 1340–41, 1419–20, 1421–23, 1427–29, 1437–38, 1527, 1529, 1570, 1594, 1615, 1617. *See also* New Lights; New Side; Old Lights; Old Side; Wallingford Controversy

Great Swamp Fight (1675), 1090

Green, Frederick, 268

Green, Jacob, 124, 183, *674–77*

Green, Jonas, *677–79*

Green, Joseph, 15, 32, *679–81*, 1096, 1290

Green, Samuel, 411

Green, Timothy, III, 411, 412

Greene, M. Louise, 619

Greene, Nathanael, 674, 796, 883

Greenfield Gazette, 525

Greenleaf, Joseph, 1448, 1449

Greenleaf, Thomas, 555, 1537

Green Mountain Boys, 27, 1433

Greenough, Horatio, 1131

Green Spring, battle of, 75

Greenwood, Isaac, *681–83*

Grenville, Richard, 714, 862

Griffitts, Hannah, *684–85*

Griswold, Fort, 718

Griswold, Rufus, 214, 1319

Griswold, Stanley, *685–87*

Gronovius, John Frederick, 111, 338, 360, 637, 908, 1016

Grotius, Hugo, 591

Guardian, The, 574

Guilford Court House, battle of, 1484

Gutridge, Molly, *688–89*

Gwatkin, Thomas, 737

Gyles, John, *689–90*, 1088

Hakluyt, Richard, 59, 61, 205, 206, 396, 715, 863, 1184, 1196

Hale, Edward Everett, 631, 863

Hale, James, 1017, 1018

Hale, John, *691–92*

Half-Way Covenant: advocates of, 306, 747, 974, 981, 983, 1014, 1175, 1389–90, 1392, 1506; opponents of, 132, 302, 426, 427, 618, 768, 970, 1094, 1095, 1115; provisions of, 124

Halifax, Fort, 1021

Halifax Gazette or Weekly Advertiser, 1445

Halifax Journal, 218

Hall, Clayton, 45

Hall, Clement, *692–94*

Hall, David, 607

Hall, Elihu, *694–95*

Hall, John, 436

Hall, Prince, *695–96*, 945

Hallam, Lewis, 74, 760

Hallenbeck, Chester T., 560

Hamilton, Alexander (1757–1804), 122–23, 161, 346, 347, 379, 398, 439, 478, 552, 553, 555, 556, 557, 629, 674, *697–98*, 824, 827, 903, 934, 935, 956, 1041, 1212, 1358, 1416, 1537, 1538, 1543

Hamilton, Alexander, Dr. (1712–1756), 89, 300, 678, 679, *698–701*, 858
Hamilton, Andrew, 1666
Hamilton, Henry, 328, 452, 453
Hammon, Briton, 539, *701–3*
Hammon, Jupiter, *703–5*, 946, 1165
Hammond, John, *705–6*
Hammond, Lawrence, *706–8*
Hamor, Ralph, 1240
Hanchet, Daniel, 598
Hancock, John (1702–1744), 54, *708–11*, 1422
Hancock, John (1737–1793), 19, 381, 382, 645, 709, 1440, 1448, 1449, 1456, 1520
Hansen, Chadwick, 869
Hansford, Charles, *711–12*, 1509, 1510, 1511
Hanson, Elizabeth, *712–14*
Haraszti, Zoltán, 17, 919, 921, 1548
Harbinger, 949
Harding, Chester, 12
Hariot, Thomas, *714–16*, 862
Harlem Heights, battle of, 672
Harley, Robert, 987
Harper, Francis, 114, 115
Harris, Benjamin, *716–17*
Harrison, Benjamin, III, 144
Hart, Levi, *717–19*, 764
Hart, Oliver, *719–22*, 1431
Hart, William, 1570
Harte, Bret, 1068
Hartford Church Controversy, 1392
Hartford Convention, 1164
Hartley, David, 12, 449, 1102, 1103
Harvard University Press, 1020
Hastings, George Everett, 1320
Hastings, Selina, 944
Hauksbee, Francis, 682
Haven, Jason, 490, *722–24*
Haven, Samuel, *724–26*
Haw, James, 300
Hawkesworth, John, 878, 1065
Hawthorne, Nathaniel, 130, 215, 216, 220, 1056, 1633
Hayden, Anna Tompson, *726–27*
Hayden, Esther, *727–28*
Hayes, Edward, 205

Haymarket Theatre (Boston), 220
Haynes, Lemuel, *728–30*
Hazard, Ebenezer, 661, *730–31*, 1041
Heath, Robert, 396
Heimert, Alan, 618, 1571
Heller, Joseph, 198
Hemmenway, Moses, 534, 535, *731–33*
Henchman, Daniel, *733–34*, 735
Henchman, Richard, 733, *734–36*, 757
Henderson, Jacob, 1138
Henderson, Richard, 814
Hendrick, Fort, 1038
Henley, Samuel, *736–38*, 1075
Hennipen, Louis, 146
Henry, Fort, 157
Henry, John, 760
Henry, Patrick, 160, 265, 280, 281, 789, 884, 934, 962, 989, 1074, 1214, 1229, 1641, 1642
Hepburn, John, *738–40*
Herbert, George, 118, 609, 1284, 1412, 1549
Herrick, Robert, 431, 1056, 1265
Hewat, Alexander, *740–42*
Hewitt, Richard, 712
Hibbins, William, 1168
Hibernian Journal, The, 273
Hicks, Elias, *742–44*
Hicks, William, 1320
Higginson, Francis, *745–46*
Higginson, John, 745, *746–48*, 790, 1096
Hilliard, Timothy, 55
Hinckley, Thomas, *748–49*, 1194
Hitchcock, Enos, *749–52*, 1221
Hitchcock, Gad, *752–53*
Hoar, Leonard, *753–55*, 1097, 1234
Hobart, Jeremiah, 269
Hobart, Joshua, 519
Hobart, Nehemiah, 736, *755–58*,
Hobart, Noah, 118, 119, 583, *758–60*, 1550, 1551, 1558, 1652
Hobbes, Thomas, 642–43
Hodgkinson, John, 125, *760–61*, 1329, 1330
Hodgson, William, 449
Holbrook, Samuel, 551
Holdsworth, Edward, 897, 1137, 1193

Hollis, Thomas, 368, 519, 682, 683, 975, 1503
Holly, Israel, 124
Holme, John, *761–63*, 938, 1414
Holmes, Abiel, *763–66*, 1410
Holmes, Obediah, 332–33
Holmes, Oliver Wendell, 764, 765, 1494
Holmes, Thomas J., 977
Holyoke, Edward, 54
Homer, 241, 714, 861, 899, 1217, 1510
Homony Club, 506
Hooke, William, *766–67*
Hooker, Samuel, *767–69*
Hooker, Thomas, 232, 233, 364, 389, 391, 427, 522, 568, 569, 570, 747, 767, *769–71*, 983, 1014, 1083, 1084, 1168, 1304, 1314, 1392, 1393, 1504, 1517, 1548, 1582, 1586, 1608
Hooper, William, *771–73*
Hopkins, Lemuel, 47–48, 358, 500, *773–74*, 1004, 1329
Hopkins, Samuel, 83, 184, 416, 513, 534, 719, 732, *774–77*, 1110, 1367, 1368, 1404, 1570
Hopkins, Stephen, *777–79*, 781, 782, 1112
Hopkins Foundation, 53
Hopkinson, Francis, 32, 142, 143, 149, 273, 469, 559, 560, 654, *779–81*, 1310, 1350, 1494
Horace (Quintus Horatius Flaccus), 14, 15, 167, 241, 424, 431, 615, 623, 918, 957, 1057, 1131, 1380, 1492
Hornberger, Theodore, 606, 1320
Horsfield, Thomas, 108
Horton, Douglas, 1083
House of Representatives (U.S.), 122, 162, 525, 627, 628, 646, 827, 884, 934, 1051, 1077
Howard, Leon, 1102, 1103, 1117
Howard, Martin, Jr., 777, 778, 779, *781–82*, 1111, 1112
Howard, Simeon, *782–84*
Howe, John, *784–86*
Howe, Robert, 674
Howe, William, 274, 350, 397, 407, 559, 577, 625, 633, 634, 1020

Howell, James, 609
Howell, Rednap, *787–89*
Hubbard, William, 229, 506, 594, 658, *789–92*, 965, 1234, 1264, 1310, 1467, 1562
Hubbell, Jay B., 941, 1062
Hudson, Samuel, 1393
Huit, Ephraim, *792–94*
Hull, Isaac, 253
Hull, John, 659, 754, *794–96*, 1305
Hull, William, 686
Hume, David, 276, 347, 417, 1521, 1580
Humphreys, David, 101, 500, 501, 773, 774, *796–98*, 1004, 1071, 1329, 1450, 1651
Humphry, John, 476
Hunt, Isaac, 672, *798–800*
Hunt, Leigh, 440, 799
Hunter, George, S.J., 78, *800–802*, 1573
Hunter, Robert, 359, 396, *802–3*, 1036
Huntington, Joseph, 1404
Husband, Herman, 787, *803–6*
Huss, John, 1500
Hutchins, John, 625
Hutchinson, Thomas, 57, 173, 314, 406, 476, *806–11*, 894, 985, 1012, 1106, 1108, 1201, 1322, 1355, 1446, 1448, 1449, 1451, 1522
Hutchinson, Anne, 389, 391, 476, 531, 532, 569, 666, 806, 1082, 1168, 1548, 1565, 1567, 1625, 1634
Hutchinsonian Synod. *See* Antinomian Synod
Huxham, John, 637
Huygens, Christian, 361, 907
Hymns, 23, 37, 42, 127, 149, 256, 339–41, 400, 429, 430, 531, 532, 548, 587, 588, 704, 725, 921, 1057–58, 1099, 1217, 1275, 1281, 1362, 1403, 1405, 1406, 1515–16

Imlay, Gilbert, *812–14*
Independent Chronicle, 436
Independent Journal, 824
Independent Reflector, The, 904, 905, 1132, 1354, 1357
Independent Whig, The, 905

Indians: anthropology of, 107, 336, 631, 658, 683, 878, 1607, 1610–11; belief in cannibalism of, 250, 446; converted to Christianity, 92, 522, 523, 657, 658, 1001–2, 1150, 1155; as descendants of Welsh, 564; descriptions of, 112, 145, 158, 239, 259, 271, 442, 638, 650, 715, 813, 843, 846, 872, 876–77, 986, 995, 999, 1038–39, 1099, 1105, 1246, 1363–64, 1463, 1573, 1631, 1653; belief in inevitable destruction of, 263, 293, 959; early encounters with, 61, 62, 206, 662, 671, 715, 863, 1047, 1089, 1162, 1197, 1240, 1243–44, 1333, 1334, 1363–64, 1400, 1568, 1572, 1577–78, 1630; education of, 79, 109, 202, 658, 1298, 1365, 1563, 1564, 1571; in fiction, 163; language of, 393, 425, 909, 995, 1179, 1215, 1573–74, 1610–11; as Lost Tribe of Israel, 3, 121, 605, 1632; in plays, 1239, 1337–38; in poetry, 938, 1032, 1052, 1065, 1273, 1308, 1374, 1380, 1433, 1468, 1651; property rights of, 236–37, 360, 478, 664, 860, 906; sympathizers with, 136, 419, 452, 453, 457, 505, 526, 809, 1039, 1042, 1054, 1055, 1150, 1275, 1365, 1499, 1584, 1608–9; warfare with, 88, 140, 307, 328, 349, 453, 488, 525, 547, 589, 648, 978, 1079, 1155–56, 1238, 1244–45, 1351, 1407, 1433, 1480, 1562. *See also* French and Indian Wars; King Philip's War; Missions and missionaries; Paxton Riots; Pequot War

Indian captivity narratives, 48, 163, 349, 446, 453, 689–90, 702–3, 712–14, 838–39, 855–56, 945, 946, 1003, 1087–88, 1156, 1245, 1246–47, 1496, 1606–8

Indian tribes: Abnaki, 838, 1607; Catawba, 3; Cherokee, 3, 113, 621, 944, 945, 1005–6, 1463; Chickasaw, 3; Chippewa, 283, 908, 909; Choctaw, 4; Coree, 871; Creek, 113, 144, 249, 733; Dakota (Sioux), 283, 908; Delaware, 120, 843, 855, 1456; Housatonic, 509, 1298; Iroquois, 361, 539, 540, 908, 909; Mohawk, 361, 815, 1607, 1613; Mohegan, 9, 579, 909, 995, 1098, 1266, 1650; Montauk, 393; Narragansett, 263, 393, 506, 995, 1090, 1246, 1467, 1609, 1610, 1643; Niantic, 9, 393; Nipmuck, 230, 1562; Occaneechee, 157; Ojibway, 908; Oneida, 1042, 1099; Patuxent, 1572; Penobscot, 1243; Pequot, 9, 503, 639, 963, 995; Piscataway, 1572, 1573–74; Seneca, 288; Shawnee, 288, 843, 855, 909, 1351; Stockbridge, 1042; Susquehanna, 46, 877; Tuscarora, 158, 871; Wampanoag, 318, 322, 393, 1000, 1001, 1225

Ingersoll, Jared, 581, 582
Inglis, Charles, *815–17*
Inner Temple, 166, 894, 1477
Inns of Court, 473, 874, 880
Insurance Company of North America, 730
Intolerable Acts, 464, 1520
Iredell, James, *817–18*
Irving, Charles, 537
Irving, Washington, 405, 493, 1007, 1056, 1295
Italicus, Silius, 300
Ives, Eli, 108

Jackson, Andrew, 892, 893
James I (king of England), 662, 1161, 1196, 1240, 1253, 1254, 1386, 1387, 1556
James II (king of England), 153, 464, 465, 498, 973, 974, 975, 1151, 1152
James, Henry, 216, 985
James, John, *819–20*
Jantz, Harold, 30, 66, 231, 234, 310, 495, 571, 869, 917, 918, 1023, 1057, 1095, 1117, 1143, 1148, 1224, 1360, 1595

Jarratt, Devereux, *820–21*
Jay, John, 345, 347, 478, 698, 774, *822–25*, 902, 934, 948, 956, 1041, 1212, 1537
Jay Treaty, 81, 274, 352, 468, 774, 822, 903, 948, 949, 1212, 1359
Jefferson, Thomas, 6, 18, 39, 81, 88, 96, 104, 108, 122, 123, 145, 160, 161, 239, 281, 286, 350, 383–84, 385, 398, 404, 439, 464, 467, 469, 534, 546, 552–53, 554, 556, 557, 609, 616, 628, 629, 650, 674, 686, 764, 773, 780, 796, 797, 822, 823, *825–28*, 878, 879, 885, 892, 893, 903, 922, 933, 934, 951, 955, 961, 990, 991, 1004, 1063, 1075, 1076, 1127, 1180, 1212, 1214, 1218, 1219, 1220, 1229, 1256, 1257, 1358, 1359, 1386, 1387, 1410, 1474, 1477, 1509, 1521, 1524, 1535, 1536, 1537, 1636, 1640, 1642, 1663
Jemison, Mary, 839
Jennings, Samuel, 887, 888
Jeremiads: ambivalence in, 426; decline of, 198; in response to earthquake of 1727, 41, 223, 1147, 1304; in election sermons, 223, 579, 768, 967, 1098, 1398–99, 1473; in execution sermons, 603–4; in fast and humiliation sermons, 517, 979; in histories, 1284; influence on secular oratory, 1520; in Indian captivity narratives, 1245, 1607; in response to materialism, 325, 409; in poems, 170, 187, 250, 462, 1592, 1647; precursors of, 427; in sermon by Nehemiah Hobart, 757; in sermon by Grindall Rawson, 1216; in sermon by Ebenezer Turell, 1490; in thanksgiving sermons, 229
Jersey Chronicle, 616
Jesuits, 76, 277, 278, 418, 793, 800–801, 859–60, 1289, 1572–74, 1607
Jewett, Jedidiah, *829–30*
Johnson, Edward, 293, 664, *831–32*, 993, 1095, 1168–69, 1312
Johnson, Marmaduke, 1116

Johnson, Nathaniel, 733
Johnson, Robert, *832–34*, 1223
Johnson, Samuel (1696–1772), 57, 117, 118, 139, 292, 360, 379, 488, 667, 759, *834–36*, 1348, 1354, 1557, 1558
Johnson, Samuel (1709–1784), 274, 377, 542, 1104, 1122, 1270, 1335, 1538, 1539, 1580, 1659
Johnson, Stephen, *836–37*
Johnson, Susannah Willard (Hastings), *837–39*
Johnson, Thomas, *839–40*
Johnson, Thomas H., 858
Johnson, William, 3, 79, 109, 293, 1354, 1356, 1457, 1564
John Street Theatre (New York), 238, 900
Jones, Absalom, 37–38, *840–42*
Jones, Bassett, 1372
Jones, David, *842–44*
Jones, Howard Mumford, 62
Jones, Hugh, *844–46*
Jones, Samuel, 844
Jones, Skelton, 238
Jones, William, 13
Jonson, Ben, 714, 1184, 1185, 1273
Josselyn, John, *846–47*
Journal of the Times, 35
Juliana Library Company, 109
Juvenal (Decimus Junius Juvenalis), 241, 623, 957

Kaiser, Leo, 303, 1057
Kalm, Peter, 541
Kaplan, Sidney, 945
Kean, Thomas, 74
Keats, John, 215, 344
Keene, Richard Raynall, 957
Keimer, Samuel, 204, 606, 609–10, *848–50*, 889, 890, 1242, 1414, 1524
Keith, George, 188, 224, 418, *850–53*, 887, 935, 936, 937, 1602
Keithian schism, 188, 224, 852
Kemp, James, 324, 325
Kendrick, William, 939
Kennedy, John Pendleton, 1640
Kent, James, 1663

Kentucky Gazette, 839
Kepler, Johannes, 714, 978, 1638
Kettell, Samuel, 862
Key, Francis Scott, 325, 1307
Kil[l]patrick, James, 414, *853–55*
King, Robert, 536
King, Rufus, 551, 1537
King George's War, 455, 529
King Philip's War: chaplains in, 1023,
    1090–91; Council of War during,
    1048; covenant renewals during,
    579; destruction of Lancaster during,
    1244–45; efforts to prevent, 1609;
    financing of, 794; histories of, 263,
    790, 974, 978, 1268; influence on
    elegies, 317; Martha's Vineyard dur-
    ing, 999; narratives of, 318–19,
    321–22, 326, 505–6, 1246–47,
    1561–62; persecution of Christian
    Indians during, 522, 657, 658; per-
    secution of Quakers during, 1166; in
    poems, 1467–68; in sermons, 229,
    768, 791, 1098, 1224, 1225, 1245;
    surgeons in, 230; towns abandoned
    during, 1601, 1606; relief of victims
    of, 981. *See also* Fort Fight; Great
    Swamp Fight
King's College controversy, 625, 904,
    905, 1286, 1348, 1352, 1354, 1357,
    1558
King William's War, 318, 689, 690,
    1475
Kinnan, Mary, 838, *855–56*, 1088
Kittredge, George, 1454
Klein, Walter, 127
Knapp, Francis, *856–57*, 898
Knapp, Samuel, 862
Knight, Russell, 646, 647
Knight, Sarah Kemble, 223, *857–59*,
    1504
Knott, Edward, S.J., *859–60*, 1574
Kraus, Michael, 1012

Labadists, 417–19, 1294
Ladd, Joseph Brown, *861–62*, 1003
Lafayette, Marquis de, 75, 221, 273,
    539, 1521
Lahontan, Louis-Armand, 361

Lake George, battle of, 1356
Lamb, Charles, 1661
Lancaster, Bruce, 361
Lake George, battle of, 1356
Lamb, Charles, 1661
Lancaster, Bruce, 329
Lane, Ralph, *862–63*
Langdon, Samuel, 1272
Lathy, Thomas Pike, *864–67*
Latrobe, Benjamin, 278
Laud, William, 232, 476, 663, 745, 754,
    769, 792, 1055, 1115, 1167, 1311,
    1517, 1548, 1577, 1630
Laurens, Henry, 622, 623, 1125, 1206
Law, Jonathan, 589, 1650
Law, William, 43
Lawrence, D. H., 404, 405, 608
Lawson, Deodat[e], *867–71*
Lawson, John, 146, 210, 259, *871–73*
Lay Preacher's Magazine, The, 436
Leacock, John, *873*
Leary, Lewis, 31, 32, 556, 942
LeBoeuf, Fort, 650
Lechford, Thomas, *874–76*, 1092
LeConte, John, 115
Lederer, John, *876–77*
Ledyard, John, *877–79*
Lee, Arthur, 140, 433, *879–82*, 929
Lee, Charles, 140, *882–83*
Lee, Henry, 140, 553, *883–84*
Lee, Richard Henry, *884–86*
Lee, Robert E., 883
Leeds, Benjamin, 317
Leeds, Daniel, 594, *886–88*, 889, 890,
    1414, 1555
Leeds, Felix, *888–90*
Leeds, Titan, 848, 889, *890–91*, 1555
Leigh, Benjamin Watkins, 1064
Leigh, Egerton, 464
Leisler, Jacob, 471
Leland, John, *891–93*
Lemay, J. A. Leo, 45, 46, 300, 699,
    818, 857, 899, 941, 1320, 1573
Lemmon, Robert, 956
Lennox, Charlotte, 218
Leonard, Daniel, 17, *893–96*
Leverett, John, 53, 54, 199, 304, 370,
    472, 912, 1019, 1097, 1153, 1469

Levy, Babette, 302, 985
Lewis and Clark Expedition, 35, 951, 952
Lewis, Richard, 151, 857, *896–99*, 1137
Lewis, R. W. B., 985
Lexington, battle of, 23, 63, 376, 786, 1020, 1328, 1520
Libbertus, Sibrandus, 1134
Library Company of Burlington, 1335
Library Company of Philadelphia, 203, 204, 607, 608, 682, 907, 1335
Library of Congress, 430, 701
Lilly, George, 143
Lincoln (4th earl of), 190, 191, 475
Lincoln's Inn, 942, 1516
Linn, John Blair, *899–901*
Linnaeus, Carolus, 111, 338, 360, 361, 637, 1015
Lisle, John, 754
Literary Magazine, The, 215
Literary Magazine and Universal Review, 542
Littlepage, Lewis, 823
Livingston, Anne Home, *901–2*
Livingston, (Henry) Brockholst, *902–4*
Livingston, William, 542, 822, 902, *904–5*, 1330, 1348, 1354, 1356, 1357, 1550, 1558
Lloyd, Henry, 703
Lloyd, John, 704–5
Lloyd, Joseph, 703, 1165
Lloyd, Thomas, 552
Locke, John, 8, 20, 28, 138, 159, 172, 237, 267, 276, 334, 347, 511, 518, 642–43, 753, 835, 861, 1077, 1102, 1103, 1127, 1217, 1290, 1648
Logan, Deborah, 684
Logan, James, 214, 360, 845, *906–8*, 938, 1241, 1335, 1413
Loggins, Vernon, 946
London Company, 663
London Magazine, 898, 1006
London *Post*, The, 717, 848
Long, John, *908–9*
Longfellow, Henry Wadsworth, 1056, 1482,
Long Island, battle of, 672, 796, 1020
Lord, Benjamin, *910–11*, 1163

Lord, Joseph, 733
Loring, Israel, *911–14*
Lost Colony, 833
Loudon, Samuel, *914–15*
Louis XVI (king of France), 557
Louisburg, capture of: during French and Indian War, 356, 491, 1003, 1020, 1021, 1038, 1191, 1279; during King George's War, 368, 406, 529, 712, 1079, 1186–87, 1322–23, 1423, 1603, 1650–51
Louisiana Purchase, 827, 934, 1416
Lovelace, Francis, 998
Low, Samuel, *915–16*
Lowance, Mason I., Jr., 977
Lowell, Amy, 916
Lowell, James Russell, 916
Lowell, Percival, *916–18*
Lowell, Robert, 916, 1056
Loyalists: Anglicans as, 79, 109, 171–72, 264, 292, 324, 377, 379, 469, 815, 1101, 1171, 1285, 1497, 1658; attacks on, 255, 276, 298, 324, 377, 379, 404, 463, 464, 672, 781, 799, 807, 905, 1226, 1278, 1299, 1317, 1401, 1431, 1497, 1522, 1571, 1667; attacks on patriots by, 842, 1216, 1445; advocates of compassion for, 621, 773, 1063; attempted neutrality of, 397, 559, 624, 625, 1227, 1355; patriots falsely accused of being, 31, 1063, 1622; as refugees, 93, 109, 292, 379, 406, 463, 469, 637, 663, 680, 694, 741, 781, 799, 808, 815, 894, 1101, 1107, 1171, 1211, 1228, 1285, 1299, 1355, 1369, 1497, 1551, 1597, 1659; writings of, 172–73, 294–95, 379–80, 405, 406–7, 464, 633–34, 781–82, 800, 810, 816, 894–95, 1024–26, 1076, 1101–2, 1107–9, 1171–72, 1278, 1286–87, 1299–1300, 1369–70, 1497–98, 1597–98
Ludlow Post Man, The, 1136
Lynde, Benjamin, *918–19*
Lyon, Richard, 497, *919–21*

Maccarty, Thaddeus, 1209

McClurg, James, *922-23*
McCorkle, Samuel Eusebius, *923-25*
Maccovius, Johannes, 1134
McCrea, Jane, 549
McCreery, John, 239
McGregore, David, *925-27*
McHenry, James, 96, 97
Machiavelli, Niccoló, 236, 1105, 1160
McKean, Thomas, 351, 354, 673, 1130
Mackenzie, John, 622
McLoughlin, William, 86
McMurtrie, Douglas, 1525
MacPherson, John, *927-31*
MacSparran, James, *931-33*
Madison, James, 81, 100, 122, 147, 161,
    162, 329, 347, 467, 478, 553, 629,
    646, 686, 698, 824, 827, 884, 892,
    903, 922, *933-35*, 956, 961, 962,
    1034, 1212, 1214, 1229, 1415,
    1474, 1484, 1531, 1537, 1543, 1640
Madoc (king of Wales), 560
Maecenas, Gaius, 15
Makemie, Francis, 155, *935-37*
Makin, Thomas, *937-39*
Malebranche, Nicholas, 138
Malthus, Thomas Robert, 352
Mangan, John, 1310
Manifest destiny, 9, 213, 1007
Mann, Herman, *939-40*
Marbois, Barbé, 135
Marie Antoinette (queen of France), 468
Marion, Francis, 1545
Markland, John, *940-42*, 1137
Markoe, Peter, *942-44*
Marlowe, Christopher, 714
Marrant, John, 539, *944-46*
Marsh, Jonathan, *946-48*
Marshall, Humphrey (1760-1841), *948-50*
Marshall, Humphry (1722-1801), *950-52*
Marshall, John, 426, 646, 882, 903, 948,
    1212, 1229, 1230, 1416, 1545, 1623
Marshall, Moses, 951
Martin, Alexander, 237, 250, *952-54*
Martin, Luther, *954-57*
Martyn, Benjamin, *957-60*, 1104
Mary I (queen of England), 570, 862
Maryland Gazette, 268, 276, 281, 300,

507, 677, 678-79, 699, 700, 897,
    898, 899, 955, 1137, 1138
Maryland General Assembly, 77, 400,
    801, 896, 955, 1136-37, 1151,
    1303, 1453
Maryland Historical Magazine, 678
Maryland Historical Society, 133, 268,
    300, 400, 1701
Maryland House of Delegates, 297, 481
Maryland Journal The, 651, 652, 956
Maryland Society for the Abolition of
    Slavery, 96
Mason, George, 140, 328, 818, *960-62*,
    1211
Mason, John, 578, 629, 640, 663, *962-
    65*, 1499
Mason, Robert, 290
Masons, 89, 396, 607, 680, 695-96, 783,
    841, 915, 944, 945, 1050, 1051,
    1343, 1519
Massachusetts Bay Company, 745, 769,
    1031, 1090, 1167, 1198, 1577,
    1633, 1635
Massachusetts Bible Society, 1183
Massachusetts Centinel, 551, 555
Massachusetts Constitution, 85, 382
Massachusetts Constitutional Convention,
    19, 40, 130, 173, 752, 1439
Massachusetts, Fort, 455, 1087
*Massachusetts Gazette and Boston
    Weekly News-Letter*, 296, 1107
Massachusetts Gazette and Post Boy, 894
Massachusetts General Association, 1367-
    68
Massachusetts General Court: actions of,
    665, 790, 791, 794, 864, 912, 1083,
    1092, 1168, 1174, 1283, 1450,
    1565, 1566, 1584, 1606; chaplains
    of, 660, 1439; debates of, 808, 809,
    810; members of, 18, 192, 326,
    645, 657, 707, 893, 918, 1198,
    1263, 1305; records of, 495; ser-
    mons delivered before, 1504, 1528,
    1529; speeches before, 348; propos-
    als to, 315, 497, 874, 1166
Massachusetts Historical Society, 6, 92,
    130, 174, 425, 531, 639, 707, 791,

914, 1012, 1023, 1045, 1136, 1385, 1393, 1439, 1490, 1596, 1635
Massachusetts House of Representatives, 18, 105, 162, 173, 645, 646, 1012, 1106, 1527
Massachusetts Magazine, 220, 574, 1052, 1069, 1070, 1071, 1121, 1122, 1447, 1450-51, 1537
Massachusetts Missionary Magazine, 533, 1042, 1367
Massachusetts Missionary Society, 533, 1367
Massachusetts Provincial Congress, 173, 645, 1519
Massachusetts Society for the Propagation of Christian Knowledge, 8, 53, 517, 1042
Massachusetts Spy, 80, 555, 1445-46, 1447-49, 1450, 1451
Massachusetts State Library, 187
Mather, Azariah, *965-67*
Mather, Cotton, 3, 15, 30, 54, 65, 154, 170, 177, 187, 195, 197, 199, 250-51, 254, 260-61, 274, 301, 303, 314, 315, 325, 347, 368, 370, 386, 389, 393, 423, 458, 495-60, 462, 472, 473, 475, 476, 481, 487, 490, 491, 496, 497, 503, 527, 570, 579, 589, 600, 601, 611, 642, 644, 645, 677, 682, 692, 747, 754, 756, 780, 854, 920, 921, 965, 966, *967-70*, 975, 976, 977, 979, 983, 984, 985, 988, 989, 994, 1013, 1014, 1022, 1084, 1094, 1095, 1096, 1120, 1133, 1142, 1148, 1149, 1153, 1154, 1174, 1215, 1216, 1234, 1262, 1264, 1266, 1295, 1296, 1303, 1304, 1312, 1393, 1406, 1441, 1467, 1469, 1488, 1513, 1514, 1515, 1527, 1582, 1585, 1588, 1590, 1591, 1601, 1602, 1606, 1607, 1609, 1625, 1627, 1637, 1644, 1654, 1655, 1656
Mather, Eleazer, *970-71*, 983, 1389, 1590, 1606
Mather, Increase, 30, 54, 170, 197, 199, 229, 254, 260-61, 291, 315, 348, 349, 368, 370, 386, 389, 393, 459,

459-60, 471, 472, 473, 476, 488, 499, 506, 578, 594, 600, 601, 611, 658, 747, 790, 936, 963, 967, 968, 970, 971-80, 983, 984, 985, 1019, 1043, 1148, 1153, 1234, 1389, 1390, 1406, 1411, 1473, 1478, 1488, 1513, 1514, 1527, 1583, 1588, 1590, 1593, 1601, 1602, 1606, 1614, 1617, 1644, 1647
Mather, Nathaniel, *980-82*
Mather, Richard, 124, 389, 593, 594, 920, 970, 973, 974, 980, *982-84*, 985, 1013, 1014, 1169, 1389, 1472, 1546, 1548, 1606
Mather, Samuel, *984-86*, 1393, 1394
Mathew, Thomas, *986-87*
Maule, Thomas, *987-89*
Maury, James, 265, *989-92*
Maury, Matthew Fontaine, 990
Maverick, Samuel, *992-93*
Mayflower Compact, 185
Mayhew, Experience, 393, 394, *994-96*, 997
Mayhew, Jonathan, 54, 58-59, 208, 293, 304, 305, 306, 320, 342, 642, 681, 783, 994, *996-98*
Mayhew, Matthew, *998-1000*
Mayhew, Thomas, Jr., 523, 589, 998, *1000-1002*, 1632
Maylem, John, *1002-3*
Mead, Robert, 1549
Mecom, Benjamin, 581
Medical Repository, The, 1329, 1331
Meigs, Josiah, *1003-5*
Meigs, Return Jonathan (1740-1823), 1004, *1005-6*
Meigs, Return Jonathan (1764-1825), *1006-7*
Melville, Herman, 216, 220, 420, 474, 878, 1620
Mencken, H.L., 1540
Mercer, John, *1008-9*
Mercury and New England Palladium The, 1042
Meredith, Hugh, 606
Merry, Robert, 900
Meserole, Harrison T., 495, 496, 117, 1142, 1143, 1258

Meserve, Walter J., 432, 1066, 1068, 1233
Messer, Asa, 412
Methodist Publishing House, 67
Micklejohn, George, *1010-11*
Middle Temple, 258, 443, 894, 1072, 1161, 1525
Middleton, Thomas, 621-22
Mifflin, Thomas, 144, 674, 1066
Mill, John Stuart, 139
Millennialism, 132, 213, 267, 502, 511, 1284, 1411
Miller, Arthur, 198
Miller, Perry, 369, 472, 579, 611, 613, 791, 831, 858, 913, 1044, 1045, 1284, 1304, 1325, 1633
Milns, William, 125
Milton, John, 99, 159, 213, 223, 234, 274, 344, 352, 431, 532, 550, 729, 861, 899, 957, 1372, 1376, 1395, 1436, 1483, 1510, 1549
Miner, Ward, 1132
Minerva, The, 939
Ministerium of Pennsylvania, 1059
Minot, George Richards, *1011-13*
Minutemen, 8, 728, 1328
Missions and missionaries: Anglican, 311, 543; on frontier, 514, 583, 729, 843, 1164, 1345, 1459, 1658; to Indians, 9, 21, 90, 120, 193, 194, 293, 393-94, 423, 479, 497, 513, 522, 523, 579, 589, 657-59, 718, 842, 843, 860, 994-95, 999-1002, 1042, 1099, 1178, 1179, 1215, 1280, 1289, 1298, 1303, 1312, 1362, 1392, 1467, 1475, 1563, 1564, 1570-71, 1573, 1625; of Jesuits, 860, 1289; of Quakers, 1396; of Moravians, 195, 1361, 1500-1501; at Natick, 90, 522, 1150; of SPCK, 193, 201, 1289; of SPG, 58, 118, 931-32, 1171, 1285, 1342-43; of SPGNE, 994-95
Mitchel, Jonathan, 228, 461, 462, *1013-15*, 1097, 1098, 1264, 1309, 1398, 1585
Mitchell, John, *1015-17*
Mix, Stephen, 241, 242

Mixer, Elizabeth, *1017-18*
Moliére (Jean Baptiste Poquelin) 1494, 1521
Molina, Giovanni, 48
Monis, Judah, *1018-20*
Monroe, James, 122, 162, 467, 934, 990, 1212, 1640
Montcalm, Louis Joseph, 403, 491
Montesquieu, Baron de La Brède et de, 274, 276, 346, 347, 519, 956, 1217, 1641
Monthly Anthology, 531, 1538
Monthly Magazine (N.Y.), 215
Monthly Magazine and British Register, 1330
Monthly Recorder, The, 344
Monthly Review, 741, 909, 1205
Montrésor, John, 63, 64, 80, *1020-22*, 1297
Moodey, Joshua, 330, *1022-24*, 1472
Moody, James, *1024-26*
Moody, Samuel, 527, 528
Mooney, James, 30
Moorhead, Sarah Parsons, *1026-27*
Moravians, 165, 195, 566, 1059, 1275, 1361, 1362, 1420, 1500-1501
More, Hannah, 353
More, Thomas, 1160
Morgan, Abel, *1027-29*
Morgan, Joseph, 130, *1029-31*, 1427
Morison, Samuel Eliot, 309, 1043, 1045, 1046, 1134, 1135, 1198, 1199, 1322, 1625
Morning Chronicle, 35
Morning Post, 35
Morning Ray, 435, 438
Morrell, William, *1031-32*, 1273
Morris, Gouverneur, *1032-35*, 1212
Morris, Lewis, 51, 1033, *1035-37*
Morris, Thomas, *1038-39*
Morse, Jedidiah, 12, *1039-42*, 1410, 1411
Morton, Charles, *1043-46*, 1155
Morton, George, 185, *1046-47*
Morton, Nathaniel, 169, 462, 790, 1046, *1047-50*, 1264, 1442
Morton, Perez, 149, 218, *1050-51*, 1052
Morton, Sarah Wentworth, 32, 218,

1051-53, 1071, 1121, 1122, 1330, 1451

Morton, Thomas, 663, 847, 988, 1049, 1053-56, 1610

Motley, John, 1056

Mott, Frank Luther, 1450, 1536

Mott, Lucretia, 466

Mount Vernon, 796, 1131, 1453, 1523

Mount Vernon Convention, 961

Moxon, George, *1056-58*, 1198

Muhlenberg, Henry Melchior, 113, *1058-61*, 1280, 1501

Munford, Robert, *1061-64*, 1067, 1068

Munford, William, 1062, *1064-65*

Murdock, John, *1065-68*

Murdock, Kenneth B., 977

Murfee, Mary Noailles, 1463

Murphy, Henry C., 1374

Murray, John, 305

Murray, Judith Sargent, 1052, *1068-72*, 1450

Murray, Walter, 74

Murray, William Vans, *1072-73*

Napoleon I (emperor of France), 100, 102, 228, 467, 1663

Nash, Francis, 953

National Academy of Design, 493

National Gazette, 81, 553, 555, 556, 557, 616, 1220, 1485

Navigation Act, 142, 992

Neal, John, 35, 36, 215

Necker, Jacques, 467-68

New American Magazine, 1132

New Divinity movement, 131-32, 501, 513, 514, 775-77, 1403

New England Chronicle, 80

New England Company, 1167, 1215

New England Courant, 177, 311, 606, 609, 611, 612

New England Historical and Genealogical Society, 420

New England Magazine, 273

New England Tract Society, 1041

New England Weekly Journal, 14, 254, 898, 899

New Hampshire Gazette, 1445

New Hampshire Historical Society, 1508

New Hampshire Journal; or, Farmer's Weekly Museum. See *Farmer's Weekly Museum*

New Hampshire Provincial Assembly, 1564

New-Haven Gazette, The, 1004

New Haven General Court, 1495

New Jersey Provincial Congress, 675, 1101

New Lights: attacks on, 373, 491, 758, 800, 1176, 1177, 1209, 1384-85, 1387, 1459, 1587, 1660; attacks on ministers by, 105; attacks on religious liberalism by, 342, 732, 1604; beliefs of, 565; education of, 429, 491; emotionalism of, 304, 334; influence of, 718-19, 804; supporters of, 193, 601, 642, 644, 667, 829, 926, 1139, 1140, 1163, 1303, 1594, 1604, 1605, 1612; unrest caused by, 10, 327, 416, 910, 1124, 1383, 1475, 1649; verse attacks on, 680, 1026-27

Newport Mercury, 781, 861, 1002, 1559

New Side, 25, 156, 1419, 1429, 1430

New Theatre, Southwark (Philadelphia), 125, 590, 654, 1066, 1067, 1620

Newton, Isaac, 197, 334, 360-61, 682

Newton, John, 548, 835, 861, 899, 1530, 1638

New World, 1301

New York Advertiser, 500

New York Democratic Society, 1663

New York Gazette, 188, 625, 815, 897

New York Historical Society, 188, 628, 688, 1434

New York Journal, 346, 1537

New York Magazine, 163, 547, 900

New York Manumission Society, 822, 1331, 1663

New-York Mercury, 440, 542, 625, 1357, 1756

New York Packet, 1535

New York Post, 1269

New York Provincial Assembly, 345, 1597

New York Provincial Congress, 1033

New York State Assembly, 903

New-York Weekly Journal, 1665-66
New York Weekly Post-Boy, 1132
Niagara, Fort, 1356
Nicholas, Robert Carter, 737, *1074-76*, 1211
Nicholson, Francis, 144, 145, 153, 598, 599, 802, 803
Niles, Nathaniel, *1076-77*
Niles, Samuel, 116, 209, *1078-80*
Noble, Oliver, *1080-82*
Norcott, John, 524
Norris, Isaac, 443
North Carolina Assembly, 804
North Carolina Provincial Congress, 1144
Northumberland Gazette, 385
Northwest Ordinance, 1456
Northwest Passage, 878, 1380
Norton, John (1606-63), 973, *1082-85*, 1093, 1314, 1472, 1585, 1625, 1626
Norton, John, II (1651-1716), 21, *1085-87*
Norton, John (1715-1778), *1087-88*
Norwood, Henry, *1088-90*
Nott, Samuel, 718
Novels, 93-94, 130, 151-52, 179-81, 183-84, 215-17, 218-20, 252-53, 449-50, 493, 591-93, 750-51, 813-14, 864-65, 939-40, 942-43, 1030-31, 1220-22, 1248-50, 1317-18, 1487, 1493, 1552, 1620-21
Nowell, Samuel, *1090-92*
Noyes, James, *1092-94*, 1134
Noyes, Joseph, 759
Noyes, Nicholas, *1094-96*
Noyes, Oliver, 1587
Nurse, Rebecca, 1094
Nuttall, Thomas, 108, 113

Oakes, Urian, 659, 748-749, 754, 755, *1097-98*, 1215, 1234, 1571, 1472, 1617
Occasional Reverberator, 1357
Occom, Samson, 226, 430, *1098-1101*, 1337, 1560, 1563, 1569
Odell, Jonathan, *1101-2*, 1369
Odiorne, Thomas, *1102-3*
Ogle, Samuel, 1380
Oglethorpe, James Edward, 361, 899,

941, 959, *1103-6*, 1377, 1378, 1408, 1409
Ohio Company, 478, 650, 1005, 1008
Old American Company, 760, 761, 1232
Old England; or, The Constitutional Journal, 1205
Old Lights: attacks on George Whitefield by, 644; rationalism of, 305, 520; supporters of, 416, 601, 680, 758, 1150, 1208, 1290, 1383, 1384-85, 1459-61, 1464, 1506; at Yale College, 373
Oldmixon, John, 145
Old North Church, 968, 984, 985
Old Side, 25, 1419, 1420, 1649
Old South Church, 18, 30, 386, 754, 867, 1153, 1194, 1244, 1283, 1303, 1441, 1601
Olive Branch Petition, 881
Oliver, Andrew, 407, 807
Oliver, Peter, 810, *1106-9*, 1201
Oliver, Thomas, 1049
Onderdonk, James, 849
Ord, George, 113
Ortelius, Abraham, 1185
Osborn, Sarah, *1109-11*
Osborne, John, 354
Osgood, David, 184
Ossian, 861, 900, 1065
Otis, James, 381, 646, 778, 781, 782, 810, 895, 929, 1108, *1111-13*, 1435, 1448, 1521
Ovid (Publius Ovidius Naso), 307, 483, 899, 1061, 1242, 1273
Owen, Goronwy, *1113-14*
Oxenbridge, John, *1114-16*

Paca, William, 298
Pacifism, 26, 136, 566, 597, 684, 713, 744, 804, 946, 1275, 1335, 1423
Packet, The, 914
Paget, John, 427
Pain, Phillip, *1117-19*
Paine, Elisha, 339
Paine, John, *1119-21*
Paine, Robert Treat, 218, 1052, *1121-23*, 1330
Paine, Solomon, 618, *1123-25*

Paine, Thomas, 34, 104, 190, 241, 351, 402, 445, 468-69, 545, 555, 609, 623, 676, 684, 800, 861, 915, 925, 1004, 1034, *1125-28*, 1129, 1256, 1401, 1436
Palfrey, John, 231
Palmer, Elihu, *1128-30*
Paltsits, Victor Hugo, 441, 1132
Panoplist, The, 1041, 1042, 1533
Parke, John, 614-15, *1130-32*
Parker, James, 624, *1132-33*, 1357
Parker, Theodore, 602
Parker Thomas, 1092, 1094, *1133-35*, 1656
Parkhurst, Thomas, 498
Parkman, Ebenezer, *1135-36*
Parkman, Francis, 186, 1156, 1607
Parks, William, 371, 483, 484, 897, 898, 941, *1136-38*, 1424
Park Theatre (N.Y.), 760
Parliament: attacks on powers of, 19, 160, 376, 464, 482, 778, 1076, 1189, 1192, 1202, 1436, 1623; colonial acceptance of powers of, 581, 778, 781, 809, 810, 1112, 1113, 1287; colonial lobbyists at, 880; expulsion of John Wilkes from, 33; independence of colonial legislatures from, 802; members of, 352, 1104, 1184, 1556; reform of, 384; sermons preached before, 1517; testimony before, 633, 634; tracts addressed to, 332, 958, 959, 1517-18
Parrington, Vernon Louis, 774, 1417, 1609
Parris, Samuel, 261
Parsons' Cause, 989
Parsons, Hugh, 250
Parsons, Jonathan, *1138-41*, 1605, 1614
Parsons, Moses, 829
Parsons, Theophilus, 1121, 1122
Pastorius, Francis Daniel, 937, *1141-43*
Pattillo, Henry, *1144-45*
Paxton Riots, 109, 799, 1060
Paxton, Robert, *1145-47*
Payson, Edward (1657-1732), *1147-48*
Payson, Edward (1783-1827), *1148-49*
Peabody, Oliver, 7, 54, 91, *1149-51*

Pead, Deuel, *1151-52*
Peale, Rembrandt, 279
Pearce, Roy Harvey, 838, 855
Pemberton, Ebenezer, *1153-55*, 1303, 1304, 1430, 1527, 1601
Pemberton, James, 96
Pemberton, Samuel, 1520
Penhallow, Samuel, *1155-56*
Penn, John, 142
Penn, Thomas, 272
Penn, William, 3, 418, 605, 762, 849, 887, 906, 938, 950, 1105, 1142, *1156-60*, 1335, 1396, 1442, 1443, 1545
Pennsylvania Assembly, 607, 632, 1142, 1623
Pennsylvania Chronicle, 443, 444, 651, 652, 1335
Pennsylvania Constitution, 627, 628, 1622
Pennsylvania Defense Association, 607
Pennsylvania Gazette, 143, 357, 606, 610, 614, 848, 850, 897, 898, 931, 938, 1034, 1138
Pennsylvania Herald, 273
Pennsylvania Historical Society, 1066, 1297
Pennsylvania Journal, 189
Pennsylvania Land Company, 1396
Pennsylvania Magazine, 780
Pennsylvania Packet, The, 470
Pennsylvania Society for the Abolition of Slavery, 96, 274, 607, 704
Pepys, Samuel, 1306
Pequot War, 639-41, 962-65, 1049, 1050, 1392, 1492-96, 1499-1500, 1651
Percy, George, *1160-62*
Percy, Henry, 714
Percy, Thomas, 99
Perkins, Nathan, *1162-65*, 1530
Perkins, William, 793, 1568
Perrin, William H., 949
Perry, Edward, *1165-66*
Peter, Hugh, 638, *1166-70*, 1173, 1548
Peters, Samuel A., 815, *1170-73*

Petiver, James, 872
Pettit, Norman, 569
Phi Beta Kappa Society, 122, 1128, 1229
Philadelphia Evening Post, 1369
Philadelphia Gazette, 1220
Philadelphia Journal of the Medical and Physical Sciences, 923
Philadelphia Medical and Physical Journal, 107
Philadelphia Society for Promoting Agriculture, 168
Philadelphia Zeitlang, 1352
Phillips, George, *1173-75*
Phillips, Samuel, 1147, 1148, 1174
Philosophical Society of Boston, 974
Phips, Spencer, 382
Phips, William, 261, 691, 733-34, 735, 968, 975, 1276, 1644
Pickering, Theophilus, 467, *1175-77*
Pickering, Thimoty, 436, 439
Pickman, Benjamin, 406
Pierson, Abraham, 579, 657, *1178-79*
Pietism, 613, 1059, 1142, 1361, 1500, 1667
Pilot, The, 545
Pinckney, Charles, *1179-81*
Pinckney, Eliza Lucas, *1181-82*
Pindar, 241
Piracy, 1477
Pirtle, Henry, 329
Pistole Fee controversy, 159, 280, 281, 1385, 1387
Pitt, William, 1171, 1192, 1344
Pittsburgh Gazette, 221
Plan of Union (1754), 777
Plan of Union (1801), 514
Plantation Covenant, 314
Plato, 14, 694
Playford, John, 1516
Playhouse Bill, 75
Plowden, Charles, 279
Plutarch, 958
Plymouth Company, 662, 663
Plymouth General Court, 748, 1166
Poe, Edgar Allan, 215, 217, 273, 548
Polar Star and Boston Daily Advertiser, 237
Political Gazette, 1395

Political Magazine, The, 1172
Political Observatory, The, 686
Political Register, The, 351, 353, 354, 355
Polyanthus, 1493
Pomeroy, Benjamin, 1563
Pomfret, John, 320, 578, 905
Pontiac's War, 1020, 1021, 1038, 1238, 1239
Poor, Enoch, 539, 540
Pope, Alexander, 50, 99, 138, 159, 214, 255, 265, 274, 344, 369, 414, 431, 502, 525, 560, 623, 654, 678, 680, 700, 854, 855, 861, 899, 929, 958, 1009, 1122, 1123, 1205, 1219, 1273, 1380, 1483, 1510, 1521, 1523, 1525, 1560, 1580
Porcupine, The, 531
Porcupine's Gazette and Daily Advertiser, 221, 350, 353
Porter, Dorothy, 945
Porter, Eliphalet, *1182-84*
Porter, John, 209
Port Folio, The, 35, 436, 437, 438, 439, 560, 673, 1073, 1450, 1493, 1538
Portico, 35
Port Royal expedition, 103, 222, 472
Portsmouth Mercury and Weekly Advertiser, 1445
Pory, John, *1184-85*
Potter, Henry, 941
Powell, John Wesley, 631
Pownall, Thomas, 491, 541, 542, 1111, 1356
Pratt, Richard Henry, 1564
Premillenarianism, 618
Prentice, Thomas, *1186-87*
Presbyterian General Assembly, 718
Presbyterian Ministers' Fund, 25
Presbyterian Schism of 1741, 25, 26, 669, 1419, 1420, 1429
Presbytery of Donegal, 1458
Presbytery of Letterkenny, 25
Presbytery of Morris County, 183, 675
Presbytery of New Brunswick, 564, 1420, 1430
Presbytery of New York, 924

Presbytery of Philadelphia, 1419, 1427, 1428-29, 1430, 1458
Prescott, Benjamin, *1187-90*
Preston, John, 389, 1584
Price, Richard, 610
Priestley Joseph, 12, 13, 353, 384, 610, 900
Prime, Benjamin Young, *1190-93*
Prince, Sarah, 246, 247
Prince, Thomas, 42, 187, 460, 601, 963, *1193-95*, 1437, 1438, 1465, 1472, 1475, 1602, 1638, 1639
Prince, Walter, 1172
Prince, William, 1485
Princeton, battle of, 189
Prior, Matthew, 679
Privateering, 249, 928
Promotional literature, 45, 70-72, 141, 146, 157-58, 205-6, 210, 224, 259, 396, 409, 441-42, 563, 605, 670-71, 706, 715, 745-46, 762-63, 833-34, 872, 876, 958-59, 1031, 1047, 1055, 1105, 1159, 1223, 1240-41, 1243-44, 1253-54, 1443, 1568-69, 1653-54
Prospect; or, View of the Moral World, The, 1129
Protestant Post-Boy, The, 717
Protester, The, 1205
Providence Gazette, 651, 778
Prynne, William, 874
Public Advertiser, 880
Public Occurrences, 716
Purchas, Samuel, 59, 61-62, 441, 1159, 1161, *1195-97*, 1240, 1243, 1363
Purdie, Alexander, 881
Purry, Jean Pierre, 959
Pusey, Caleb, 887, 888
Putnam, Israel, 674, 796
Pynchon, William, 1057, 1083, *1197-1200*

Quaker journals, 69, 175-76, 288-89, 323-24, 446, 561-62, 596-97, 743-44, 1166, 1282, 1335, 1370-71, 1396-97, 1661-62
Quaker sermons, 596, 743, 852

Quarles, Francis, 847, 887, 1118, 1225, 1265, 1655
Quarry, Robert, 144
Quarterly Review, 673, 764
Quebec Act, 823
Queen Anne's War, 318, 471, 1155, 1364, 1606, 1607
Quincy, Edmund, 709
Quincy, Josiah, Jr., 12, 369, 1050, *1201-3*, 1435
Quinn, Arthur Hobson, 432
Quintilian (Marcus Fabius Quintilianus), 899
Quisenberry, A.C., 949

Racine, Jean Baptiste, 440
Radcliffe, Ann, 526
Rainbow Association, 1641-42
Raleigh Register, 788
Raleigh, Walter, 205, 206, 670, 714, 715, 862, 863, 1185, 1196
Ralph James, *1204-6*
Ramsay, Allan, 98, 99
Ramsay, David, 661, 741, 1182, *1206-8*, 1346
Ramsay, William, 120
Ramsey, Paul, 416
Ramus, Petrus, 497
Rand, William, *1208-11*
Randall, Benjamin, 44
Randolph, Edmund, 122, 140, 1074, *1211-15*, 1229
Randolph, John, 162, 166, 430, 1076
Ravenscroft, Thomas, 1549
Rawson, Grindall, *1215-16*
Ray, John, 285
Rayner, John, 1023
Read, John, 311
Reading Mercury, The, 1136
Redwood Library, 1381
Reese, Thomas, *1216-18*
Reforming Synod of 1679, 974, 1097, 1473
Regulator movement, 787-89, 804-5, 1010, 1144, 1658, 1660
Reid, James, *1218-20*
Relf, Samuel, *1220-22*
Relf's Gazette, 1220

Religious Intelligencer, 1533
Remembrancer, 1205
Restoration, 45, 140, 767, 795, 974, 993, 1057, 1082, 1134, 1372, 1398, 1511, 1654
Revere, Paul, 1448, 1450
Revolutionary War: in almanacs, 412, 1554; Anglican supporters of, 266, 1010; blacks in, 695, 945, 1433; British occupation during, 225, 633, 703, 783, 915, 1191, 1292, 1388; causes of, 380, 800, 1107; chaplains in, 8, 39, 130, 179, 342, 479, 539, 750, 752, 836, 842, 1080, 1269, 1367, 1403, 1479; confidential agents during, 449; Congregational church during, 295; Deist interpretation of, 1129; essays on, 676; finances of, 961, 1034, 1542; histories of, 465, 660-61, 673-74, 808-10, 884, 1207; journals of, 75-76, 130, 328-29, 452-53, 466, 584, 626, 673-74, 784-86, 909, 1006, 1021, 1024-26, 1060, 1182, 1296-97, 1382, 1434-35, 1486, 1599, 1645-46; land warrants issued to veterans of, 563; Methodist church during, 67; millennial view of, 502; ministers' support of, 374, 381, 724, 842, 1216, 1279, 1318-19, 1339, 1401-2, 1431, 1439, 1569, 1571; missionaries during, 91, 1564; newspapers during, 624, 625, 652, 1226-27; in novels, 939-40; opponents of, 72, 79, 109, 118, 136, 320, 397, 404, 405, 406, 469, 507, 559, 632, 642, 694, 800, 1326, 1352, 1355, 1369, 1497; in plays, 179, 873, 1063, 1072, 1521-22; in poems, 503, 616, 684, 688, 780, 797, 1053, 1077, 1101-2, 1192, 1300, 1369-70, 1536; prisoners of war, 28, 453, 616, 621, 672; propaganda during, 1125, 1126, 1172, 1457, 1521; Quakers during, 744; Regulator movement as precursor of, 805; satire concerning, 609, 905, 1063, 1101-2, 1369-70, 1521; sermons

commemorating, 23, 212-13, 479-80, 540, 577, 718, 721, 730, 1183, 1352-53; soldiers in, 39, 75, 154, 212, 590, 672, 694, 697, 796, 812, 882, 883, 902, 908, 928, 948, 1005, 1020-21, 1024, 1061, 1130, 1211, 1296, 1484, 1486, 1531; surgeons in, 922, 1206, 1256, 1434, 1544; treaty with France, 433, 434. *See also* Loyalists; Pacifism
Reynolds, Joshua, 377, 1463
Rhode-Island Gazette, 612
Rhode Island General Assembly, 332, 777, 778, 1609
Rhode Island Historical Society, 1264
Rich, Richard, *1222-23*
Richardson John, 303, 310, *1223-25*
Richardson, Lyon N., 1450, 1536
Richardson, Samuel, 152, 218, 246, 609, 623, 673, 750, 814, 818, 865, 930, 1380
Richmond Enquirer, 1229, 1230, 1641, 1642
Richmond Standard, 923
Rickman, John, 878
Riley, Isaac, 47
Rind, William, 677, 679, 880, 881
Ripley, Ezra, 531
Rising glory of America theme, 24, 179, 180, 1349
Rittenhouse, David, 96, 108, 652, 1319
Rivers, James, 741
Rivington, James, *1125-28*, 1597
Rivington's New York Gazette and Universal Advertiser, 1226
Rivington's New-York Gazetteer, 1226
Rivington's New York Loyal Gazette, 1226, 1227, 1228
Rivington's Royal Gazette, 1101, 1226, 1227, 1228, 1369
Roane, Spencer, *1228-31*
Robbins, Philemon, *1231-32*
Roberts, Kenneth, 63, 1021, 1239, 1296, 1297
Robertson, William, 741
Robinson, J., 125, *1232-33*
Roby, Luther, 786
Roche, Mary, 413-14

Rogerenes, 676, 1236
Rogers, John (1630-1684), 53, 191, 755, 1022, *1233-36*, 1590
Rogers, John (1648-1721), 579, 676, *1236-38*, 1376, 1602
Rogers, Nathaniel, 347, 1517
Rogers, Robert, 282-83, 1021, *1238-39*, 1338
Rogue histories, 248-49, 270-72, 1486-87
Rolfe, John, 1196, *1239-41*, 1253
Romanticism, 196, 699, 1641
Rose, Aquila, 849, *1241-43*
Rosier, James, *1243-44*
Ross, Robert, 566
Rossiter, Clinton, 608
Rousseau, Jean Jacques, 17, 221, 627, 929, 957, 1129
Rowe, Elizabeth Singer, 246, 550
Rowland, John, 1418, 1423
Rowlandson, Joseph, 230, *1244-45*, 1246
Rowlandson, Mary, 163, 229, 230, 689, 713, 855, 1244, *1245-47*, 1607
Rowson, Susanna Haswell, 592, *1247-50*
Royal American Magazine, 1446, 1449-50
Royal College of Physicians, 178
Royal Society of Arts, 51, 637
Royal Society of Arts and Sciences at Upsala, 637
Royal Society of Edinburgh, 637
Royal Society of London: lectures before, 177, 360; members of, 174, 177, 199, 258, 285, 286, 336, 395, 474, 607, 637, 638, 652, 682, 733, 797, 968, 969, 1016, 1424, 1469, 1635, 1637, 1638; as model for Philosophical Society of Boston, 974; papers contributed to, 111, 204, 336, 338, 473-74, 683, 897, 907, 951, 1045, 1636
Royal Society of Sciences at Göttingen, 607
Rugeley, Rowland, *1250-52*
Ruggle, George, *1252-55*
Rule, Margaret, 260
Rural Moralist, The, 526
Rush, Benjamin, 97, 107, 136, 273, 274, 350-51, 354, 873, 1015, 1066, 1206, *1255-58*, 1329, 1330, 1331
Rush-Light, The, 351
Rusk, Ralph, 840
Russell, Benjamin, 551
Russell, Daniel, *1258-59*
Russell, Noadiah, *1260-61*
Rutherford, Samuel, 771

Sabin, Joseph, 30, 1026, 1251
Saffin, John, 496, *1262-65*
Sag Harbor, battle of, 1005
St. Clair, Arthur, 252, 813, 834, 1064-65
Salem Gazette, 375
Salem Register, 1394
Salmon, Thomas, 1105
Saltmarsh, John, 665, 666, 1393
Saltonstall, Gurdon, 9, 101, *1265-67*
Saltonstall, Nathaniel, *1267-69*
Sampson, Deborah, 939
Sampson, Ezra, *1269-71*
Sandeman, Robert, 760, *1271-72*
Sanderson, Robert, 794
Sandys, George, *1272-74*
Saratoga, battle of, 63, 540, 549, 1434
Sargeant, Winthrop, 380
Satire: in almanacs, 50, 303, 412, 1414, 1455, 1488; in novels, 130, 179-81, 219, 943; in plays, 591, 701, 802, 873, 894, 1062-63, 1066-67, 1521-22; in poems, 32, 46, 47, 94, 102, 144, 221, 241, 256, 300, 303, 319, 320, 343, 344, 352, 359, 431, 560, 626, 678, 680, 774, 780, 788, 797, 840, 857, 861, 903, 904, 905, 1002, 1003, 1009, 1037, 1064, 1101-2, 1122-23, 1131, 1163, 1244, 1264, 1288, 1299, 1344, 1369, 1376, 1395, 1414, 1467-68, 1481, 1510, 1521, 1597; in non-fictional prose, 119, 142, 149, 150, 160, 167, 249, 259, 265, 280, 414, 425, 436, 546, 598, 609, 611, 678, 679, 680, 699, 700, 729, 778, 799, 957, 959, 1009, 1056, 1219, 1244, 1359, 1372, 1408-9, 1510, 1517-18, 1550, 1644, 1648, 1649, 1660, 1665, 1666
Saturday Evening Herald, 35

Sauer, Christopher, I, *1274-76*, 1352
Savage, Edward, 764
Savage, James, 868
Savage, Thomas, *1276-77*
Saybrook, Fort, 746-47, 963
Saybrook Platform, 581, 583, 910, 1266, 1390
Scarlet fever, 460
Schaw, Janet, *1277-78*
Schlatter, Michael, *1279-81*, 1352
Schuyler, Philip, 672, 674, 697, 914, 1597
Scioto Land Company, 478
Scott, Charles, 948
Scott, Job, *1281-83*
Scott, John Morin, 904, 905, 1348, 1354, 1357
Scott, Jonathan, 43
Scott, Thomas, 864
Scottish Charitable Society, 459
Scottow, Joshua, *1283-85*
Seabury, Samuel, 118, *1285-87*, 1348, 1354, 1597, 1598
Seagood, George, 151
Searle, John, 1141
Sears, Isaac, 1227
Seccomb, John, *1287-89*
Seccombe, Joseph, *1289-91*
Secker, Thomas, 57-58, 379
Second Great Awakening, 502, 1368, 1403, 1533
Sedgwick, Maria, 1056
Seifert, Shirley, 329
Seixas, Gershom Mendez, *1291-94*
Selyns, Henricus, *1294-96*
Senate (U.S.), 275, 1416
Seneca, Lucius, Annaeus, 945, 1160
Senter, Isaac, *1296-97*
Sentman, George, 329
Sergeant, John, *1298*, 1564
Sericulture, 1254-55
Serle, Ambrose, 625
Sermons: artillery election, 54, 228, 256, 313, 330, 600, 641, 648, 649, 668, 723, 752, 756, 783, 979, 1023, 1091, 1098, 1153, 1472, 1528, 1584, 1590, 1602, 1619; election, 10, 23, 30, 39, 54, 66, 106, 128-29, 223, 228, 235-36, 242-43, 313, 316, 330, 368, 375, 381, 382, 427, 457, 519, 579, 641, 648, 660, 691-92, 723, 725, 747, 753, 758, 768, 783, 791, 912, 947, 966-67, 974, 979, 1023, 1115-16, 1153, 1310-11, 1314-16, 1384, 1398-99, 1404, 1410, 1465-66, 1472, 1473, 1511-12, 1528, 1551, 1583, 1585, 1590, 1602, 1613, 1615, 1617, 1618, 1619; execution, 11, 313, 603, 1100, 1325; fast and humiliation, 212, 377, 380, 534, 800, 837, 842, 892, 974, 1404, 1442, 1465, 1517, 1566, 1595; funeral, 10, 54, 226, 244-45, 269, 313, 373, 454, 456-57, 530, 579, 602, 603, 649, 683, 686, 709, 720, 723, 725, 783-84, 820, 829, 910, 966, 1141, 1154, 1165, 1195, 1304, 1341, 1347, 1421, 1423, 1465, 1476, 1513, 1515, 1528, 1550, 1551, 1571, 1595, 1601, 1612, 1616, 1619, 1651; half-century, 226, 227-28, 1165, 1613; ordination, 23, 54, 106, 120, 184, 212, 244, 256, 454, 518, 527, 667, 669, 708, 722, 723, 725, 758-59, 783, 784, 829, 830, 966, 1081, 1165, 1195, 1209, 1231, 1325, 1403, 1423, 1489-90, 1514, 1550, 1563, 1570, 1571, 1595, 1613, 1615; thanksgiving, 10, 212, 382, 530, 577, 721, 841, 1183, 1186-87, 1195, 1293, 1404
Seven Years' War. *See* French and Indian War
Severn, battle of, 705, 706
Sewall, Jonathan, 894, *1298-1300*
Sewall, Jonathan Mitchell, *1300-1302*
Sewall, Joseph, 600, 601, 1153, 1194, 1289, 1290, *1303-5*, 1505, 1594, 1602
Sewall Samuel, 21, 22, 169, 195, 197, 269, 365, 381, 386, 473, 487, 496, 648, 733, 735, 736, 756, 794, 913, 918, 1023, 1044, 1120, 1134, 1148, 1224, 1263, 1268, 1300, 1303,

1305-7, 1310, 1412, 1438, 1472, 1478, 1513, 1601, 1662

Shaffer, Arthur, 1214

Shaftesbury (first earl of), 159

Shakespeare, William, 148, 191, 274, 344, 352, 415, 532, 654, 784, 865, 899, 900, 1039, 1161, 1185, 1222, 1240, 1399, 1400, 1483, 1549

Sharp, Granville, 136, 537

Shaw, John, *1307-9*

Shaw, Lemuel, 545

Shays's Rebellion, 174, 774, 1012-13, 1450, 1493

Shelley, Mary, 215, 812

Shelley, Percy, 215, 344

Shepard, Jeremiah, 40, *1309-11*

Shepard, Thomas (1605-1649) 195, 232, 233, 389, 391, 392, 427, 497, 568, 659, 748-49, 770, 913, 967, 983, 1013, 1014, 1082, 1083, 1084, 1116, 1149, 1174, 1309, 1311-13, 1314, 1315, 1391, 1392, 1442, 1471, 1586

Shepard, Thomas (1635-1677), 1097, 1309, *1313-16*, 1583

Sherburne, Henry, *1316-18*

Sherman, John, 1310

Sherwood, Samuel, *1318-19*

Shipley, William, 637

Shippen, Joseph, *1319-21*, 1350

Shipton, Clifford, K., 30, 642, 668, 829, 1079, 1209

Shirley, William, 57, 542, *1321-24*, 1356, 1650

Short fiction, 163, 1450

Shumway, Henry, 295

Shurtleff, William, *1324-25*

Sibbes, Richard, 389, 1584

Sibley, John, 234, 375, 977, 1310, 1593

Sidney, Algernon, 265

Sidney, Philip, 190, 1264, 1549

Simmons, Menno, 1237

Simms, William Gilmore, 4, 690, 741

Sinclair, Harold, 329

Skelton, Samuel, 745, 1608

Skelton, Thomas, 707

Slavery, defense of, 384, 399, 401-2, 635, 1263-64, 1408

Slavery, opposition to: by blacks, 37, 96, 97, 537-39, 704-5, 730, 841, 945, 946, 1560; by Catholics, 276; through colonization efforts, 1042; in England, 383; in Georgia, 959, 1104, 1408; during Great Awakening, 635; by Thomas Jefferson, 827; by Methodists, 67; in New Jersey, 675; in Pennsylvania, 1142, 1257; in poetry, 196, 1039, 1053, 1560; in prose, 135-36, 196, 239, 274, 365-66, 384, 402, 416, 419, 500, 514, 562, 584, 609, 676-77, 730, 739-40, 743, 776, 777, 813, 880-81, 962, 1203, 1263, 1306-7, 1318, 1346, 1485, 1532, 1662; by Quakers, 135-36, 288, 323, 365, 561, 562, 739-40, 740, 1371, 1661, 1662; as result of Revolutionary War, 76; in Rhode Island, 130; as a cause of sectionalism, 1035; at Yale College, 1530, 1532

Slaves: freeing of, 95, 652, 695, 829, 840, 949, 1433, 1465, 1559; narratives by, 38, 537-39, 702-3, 946; in plays, 1067-68; religious instruction of, 89, 1096, 1144, 1216, 1558; trading in, 445, 536, 585, 818, 880, 1374, 1508; white fear of, 763, 880

Sloane, Hans, 111, 638, 1424

Sluyter, Peter, 417, 418, 419

Smalley, John, 533, *1326-27*

Smallpox: deaths caused by, 606, 650, 1087, 1236, 1258, 1281, 1314, 1558, 1661; deaths caused by inoculations for, 246, 510, 1436; epidemics, 199, 458, 836, 853, 1262, 1266, 1441-42, 1528; among Indians, 959, 1049, 1310; inoculation controversies, 177-78, 368, 386, 458-60, 611, 682, 700, 853-54, 968, 984, 1194, 1304-5, 1514, 1526; medical text on, 1442; treatment controversies, 413, 414, 854

Smith, Adam, 629, 930

Smith, Anna Young, *1328*

Smith, Caleb, 245

Smith, Elihu Hubbard, 47, 215, 358,
    493, 774, 1052, *1328-31*, 1663
Smith, Eunice, *1331-32*
Smith, Henry Nash, 283
Smith, Hezekiah, 1507
Smith, Capt. John (1580-1631), 59-62,
    71, 146, 158, 205, 206, 271, 441,
    663, 670, 845, 847, 1055, 1159,
    1161, *1332-34*, 1363, 1386, 1387,
    1400, 1536, 1629
Smith, John (1722-1771), *1334-35*, 1371
Smith, John (1752-1809), *1336-38*
Smith, Joshua, 340
Smith, Josiah, *1338-42*
Smith, Michael, *1342-44*
Smith, Samuel Stanhope, *1345-47*
Smith, Sydney, 344
Smith, Thomas, 833
Smith, William (1727-1803), 25, 543,
    544, 654, 845, *1347-53*, 1420
Smith, William (1728-1793), 542, 904,
    905, 1348, *1353-57*
Smith, William Loughton (1758-1812),
    1358-59
Snyder, Simon, 383
Society for the Education of Parochial
    Schoolmasters, 1348
Society for the Encouragement of Learn-
    ing, 958
Society for the Encouragement of the
    Arts, Manufactures, and Commerce,
    520
Society for the Furtherance of the Gos-
    pel, 1361
Society for Promoting the Gospel, 517
Society for the Promotion of the Knowl-
    edge of God among the German in
    America, 1279
Society for the Propagation of Christian
    Knowledge (SPCK), 193, 194, 201,
    517, 680, 1099, 1186, 1289, 1587
Society for the Propagation of the Gospel
    among the Indians, 1041, 1042,
    1439, 1587
Society for the Propagation of the Gospel
    in Foreign Parts (SPG), 57, 78, 117,
    852, 931, 993, 997, 999, 1001,
    1171, 1285, 1342-43, 1348, 1477,
    1558
Society for the Propagation of the Gospel
    in New England (SPGNE), 658,
    994, 1632
Society of Antiquaries, 737
Society of Jesus. *See* Jesuits
Society of United Irishmen, 237
Somerby, Anthony *1359-60*
Sons of Liberty, 18, 173, 189, 190, 379,
    381, 621, 873, 912, 1069, 1192,
    1202, 1226, 1228, 1326, 1355,
    1446, 1448
*South-Carolina and American General
    Gazette*, 741, 1251, 1445
South Carolina Assembly, 414, 621, 622,
    1105, 1206, 1431, 1432
South Carolina Gazette, 414, 463, 464,
    483, 484, 622, 635, 899, 1252,
    1339, 1343, 1359
South Carolina Provincial Congress,
    1251, 1430
Southern Literary Messenger, 151, 273,
    1241
Southey, Robert, 1463
South Sea Company, 958
Southwell, Robert, 258
Sowle, Daniel, 188
Spangenberg, Augustus Gottlieb, *1360-
    63*, 1501
Sparks, Jared, 878
Sparrow, Thomas, 677, 679
Spectator, The, 574, 609, 611, 905,
    1264, 1461
Spelman, Henry, *1363-64*
Spenser, Edmund, 310, 425, 1259
Spinoza, Benedict, 138, 417
Spotswood, Alexander, 144, 151, 153,
    259, 598, 844, *1364-66*
Spotswood, William, 435
Sprague, William Buell, 30, 369, 447
Spring, Samuel, *1366-69*
Stamp Act: defenses of, 8, 360, 782,
    1106; protests against, 171, 189,
    281, 282, 297, 298, 320, 321, 443,
    482, 519, 580, 581, 582, 679, 778,
    837, 989-90, 997, 1132, 1192,
    1349, 1355, 1456, 1510, 1658; ef-

fect on colonial press, 190, 1445; popular unrest caused by, 1012, 1021; refusals to enforce, 168; repeal of, 19, 241, 293, 530, 1559, 1668
Stamp Act Congress, 443, 621, 622; 1111
Standard of Union, 1663
Standish, Miles, 1054, 1056, 1630
Stanford, Donald, 303
Stannard, David, 579
Stansbury, Joseph, 1011, *1369-70*
Stanton, Daniel, *1370-71*
Starkey, George, *1371-73*, 1636
State Gazette, 555
Steele, Richard, 138, 265, 574, 609, 611, 849, 850, 1137, 1270, 1335
Steendam, Jacob, *1373-75*
Steere, Richard, 496, *1375-77*
Steiner, Bernard, 371
Stephens, Leslie, 608
Stephens, Thomas, 1104, 1377
Stephens, William, 960, 1105, *1377-78*
Sterling, James, 857, 1350, *1379-81*
Sterne, Laurence, 218, 438, 559, 623, 818, 957, 1203
Stewart, George, 611
Stiles, Ezra, 123, 303, 416, 501, 619, 686, 764, 765, 766, 778, 912, 1004, 1036, 1110, 1163, 1260, 1326, 1329, *1381-83*, 1430, 1465, 1605, 1616
Stiles, Isaac, *1383-85*
Stillman, Samuel, 945
Stith, William, 266, 430, 1137, *1385-88*
Stockton, Annis Boudinot, 249, *1388-89*
Stoddard, Solomon, 124, 197, 509, 1093, 1310, *1389-92*, 1412, 1612, 1614, 1615, 1616, 1618
Stokes, Richard L., 1056
Stone, Albert E., 404
Stone, Samuel, 228, 229, 578, 747, 769, 770, *1392-94*, 1582
Stony Point, battle of, 1005
Storey, Enoch, Jr., 114
Story, Isaac, *1394-95*
Story, Thomas, *1396-97*

Stoughton, William, *1397-99*, 1472, 1473
Stowe, Harriet Beecher, 777
Strachey, William, 1363, *1399-1400*
Street, Nicholas, *1401-2*
Strong, Nathan, *1402-5*
Stuart, John, 741
Suffolk Resolves, 294, 295, 1520
Sugar Act, 443, 778, 781, 782
Suicide, 363, 421, 432, 703, 812, 894, 1051, 1165, 1612, 1613
Sullivan, John, 1024
Summers, George, 1222
Sumner, Increase, 1440
Supreme Court (U.S.), 297, 298, 818, 903, 1230, 1416, 1433, 1622, 1623
Swedenborg, Emanuel, 1483
Swedish Royal Academy of Science, 338
Swift, Jonathan, 50, 130, 138, 139, 159, 265, 271, 274, 414, 609, 623, 667, 780, 802, 803, 891, 929, 1037, 1328, 1450, 1581, 1550, 1554
Sydenham, Thomas, 458, 1442
Symmes, Thomas, *1405-7*, 1515
Symonds, William, 1363
Synod of Dort, 1134
Synod of New York, 244, 1419
Synod of Philadelphia, 25, 1419, 1458, 1459, 1460
Synod of Philadelphia and New York, 1423, 1430
Synod of 1643, 1134
Synod of 1662, 302, 427, 974, 981, 1014, 1134, 1175, 1584
Synod of Ulster, 1458

Tablet, The, 435, 437, 438, 439
Tacitus, Publius Cornelius, 236, 654, 899, 1160
Tailfer, Patrick, 959, 960, 1104, 1377, 1378, *1408-9*
Talbot, William, 867
Talleyrand-Perigord, Charles Maurice de, 646, 647
Tammany Society, 1663
Tanner, John, 839
Tappan, David, 184, 1368, *1409-11*
Tasso, Torquato, 167

Tate, Nahum, 149, 517
Tatler, The, 574
Taylor, Edward, 15, 21, 207, 243, 487,
    496, 579, 580, 910, 1057, 1095,
    1224, 1259, 1383, 1385, *1411-13*,
    1471, 1491, 1493
Taylor, Jacob, 214, 848, 887, *1413-15*,
    1525
Taylor, John, 117
Taylor, John (of Caroline), *1415-17*,
    1642
Taylor, Nathaniel, 686, 687
Temperance literature, 49, 91, 136, 274,
    493, 1213, 1340, 1545
Temple of Reason, The, 1129
Tennent, Gilbert, 26, 246, 429, 564,
    565, 566, 613, 669, 675, 709-11,
    720, 1026, 1027, 1060, 1078, 1164,
    1189, 1217, 1335, 1339, 1342,
    1350, 1352, *1417-23*, 1427, 1428,
    1430, 1431, 1437, 1438, 1459,
    1460, 1490, 1506, 1614
Tennent, John, *1424-26*
Tennent, William, I (1673-1746), 120,
    156, 564, 565
Tennent, William, II (1705-1777), 613,
    720, 1060, 1164, 1217, 1342, 1418,
    1419, 1420, *1426-29*, 1430
Tennent, William, III (1740-1777), 720,
    1427, *1429-32*
Terrick, Richard, 736
Terry, Lucy, *1433-34*
Tertullianus, Quintus, Septimius Florens,
    693, 1290
Thacher, James, *1434-35*
Thacher, Oxenbridge, 1201, *1435-37*,
    1439, 1440
Thacher, Peter (1688-1744), *1437-38*,
    1527
Thacher, Peter (1752-1802), 1436, *1437-
    38*, 1527
Thacher, Peter (1752-1802), 1436, *1439-
    41*, 1476
Thacher, Thomas, 754, *1441-42*, 1472,
    1601, 1627
Thayer, Alexander Wheelock, 150
Theological Magazine, The, 513
Thomas, Gabriel, 224, 605, *1442-43*

Thomas, George, 1380
Thomas, Isaiah, 182, 436, *1443-52*,
    1455, 1537
Thomas, John, *1452-53*
Thomas, Robert Bailey, 413, *1453-55*
Thomas's Massachusetts Spy, 1447
Thomson, Adam, 700
Thomson, Charles, *1455-58*
Thomson, James, 241, 431, 1102
Thomson, John, 1419, *1458-61*
Thoreau, Henry David, 404, 744, 1347,
    1607, 1662
Thorowgood, Thomas, 3
Thucydides, 159, 1160
Thurloe, John, 1090
Ticonderoga, Fort, 27, 39, 63, 531, 728,
    843, 1434
Tiffin, Edward, 686
Tillam, Thomas, 918, *1461-62*
Tillotson John, 117, 209, 400, 643, 1580
Timberlake, Henry, *1463-64*
Time-Piece, The, 238, 616
Timothy, Peter, 1252
Tindal, Matthew, 1229, 1145
Tinkcom, Harry M., 385
Todd, Jonathan, 760, *1464-66*
Tolles, Frederick B., 907
Tompson, Benjamin, 726, *1466-69*, 1470
Tompson, Edward, *1470-71*
Tompson, Joseph, 726, 727
Torrey, Samuel, 21, 967, *1471-74*, 1583
Toulmin, Harry, *1474-75*
Townsend, Jonathan, *1475-76*
Townshend Acts, 18, 463, 622, 807,
    881, 1107, 1456
Transcendentalism, 29, 1633
Treat, Robert, 307
Treaty of San Lorenzo, 1212
Treaty of Utrecht, 1156
Tree of Liberty, The, 179
Trenchard, John, 905
Trenton, battle of, 189, 274, 1127
Trott, Nicholas, *1477-78*
Trumbull, Benjamin, 47, 211, 231, *1478-
    80*, 1604
Trumbull, John, 101, 214, 358, 438,
    500, 501, 773, 799, 894, 900, 1004,

1052, 1251, 1329, *1480-82*, 1597, 1561

Trumbull, Jonathan, 1171, 1172, 1173

Tryon, William, 787, 788, 1010, 1144

Tucker, Josiah, 407

Tucker, Nathaniel, *1482-83*

Tucker, St. George, 923, 1482, 1483, *1484-85*, 1641, 1642

Tuesday Club of Annapolis, 89, 677-78, 700-701

Tuesday Club of Philadelphia, 436, 440

Tufts, Henry, *1485-87*

Tufts, John, 1406

Tull, Jethro, 169, 521

Tulley, John, 594, 796, 891, *1487-88*

Turell, Ebenezer, 13, 14, 368, 369, *1489-91*

Turell, Jane Colman, 14, 368, 1489, 1490, *1491-92*

Turner, Frederick Jackson, 504, 1035

Twain, Mark. *See* Clemens, Samuel

Two-Penny Act controversy, 159, 264-65, 280, 281, 282, 989, 1075

Tyler, Moses Coit, 49, 161, 441, 745, 762, 873, 920, 965, 983, 1086, 1095, 1286, 1319, 1352, 1437, 1548

Tyler, Royall, 435, 437, 525, 729, 798, 1067, 1068, 1071, 1394, *1493-94*

Tyson, Martha E., 98

Underhill, John, 639, 963, 964, *1495-96*, 1499

United States Magazine, The, 179

Universal Asylum, The, 560

Universal Instructor, 848, 849

Universal Spectator, The, 1205

University of Virginia Press, 1241

Upham, Charles 869

Valley Forge, 63, 750, 1130, 1545, 1645

VanDerBeets, Richard, 856

Vassa, Gustavus. *See* Equiano, Olaudah

Vaughan, Alden, 1254

Vergil (Publius Vergilius Maro), 376, 400, 424, 483, 678, 861, 899, 1086, 1251, 1416, 1510

Vespucci, Amerigo, 409

Viets, Roger, *1497-98*

Villiers, George, 802

Vincent, Philip, 639, 964, *1499-1500*

Virginia Argus, 1641

Virginia Company, 157, 833, 834, 1240, 1253, 1386, 1387, 1399

Virginia Declaration of Rights, 933, 960-61

Virginia Evangelical and Literary Magazine, The, 155

Virginia Gazette, 159, 162, 166, 167, 241, 408, 430, 483, 484, 712, 737, 880, 881, 1009, 1075, 1137, 1138, 1219, 1229, 1424

Virginia General Assembly, 122, 1424

Virginia Herald, 555

Virginia Historical Register, 1241

Virginia Historical Society, 1213

Virginia House of Burgesses, 144, 159, 161, 162, 166, 258, 280, 585, 597, 705, 737, 826, 844, 884, 885, 989, 1062, 1074, 1075, 1137, 1365, 1385, 1387, 1424, 1509, 1523

Virginia House of Delegates, 161, 880, 885, 934, 1061, 1064, 1074, 1229, 1416, 1640

Virginia Medical Society, 922

Virginia Plan, 961, 1211, 1213

Virginia Society for the Advancement of Useful Knowledge, 338

Virginia State Constitution, 826, 933

Viticulture, 51

Voltaire, François, 167, 221, 402, 814, 861, 929

Volunteers Journal, 273

von Goethe, Johann Wolfgang, 218

von Graffenried, Christopher, 871

von Zinzendorf, Count Nicholas Ludwig, 165, 1059, 1275, 1361, *1500-1502*

Wadsworth, Benjamin, 30, 54, 222, 600, *1503-5*

Wadsworth, Daniel, 456

Waldron, William, 668

Walker, Hovenden, 488

Walker, Timothy, *1505-8*

Walker, Williston, 1369

Walker, Zechariah, 306-7

Wallace, David Duncan, 741

Waller, Benjamin, 711, *1508-11*
Waller, Edmund, 241, 431, 1510
Walley, Edward, 766
Walley, John, 296
Walley, Thomas, 748, *1511-12*
Wallingford controversy, 416-17, 448, 759-60, 1464-65
Walpole, Robert, 259, 930, 1641
Walter, Nehemiah, 600, *1512-13*, 1514
Walter, Thomas, 311, *1513-16*
Walton, George, 290-91
Wanderer, The, 598
Ward, John, 797
Ward, Nathaniel, 395, 567, 1093, *1516-19*, 1656
Ward, Samuel, 777
Wards, Artemas, 551
Ware, Henry, 765
Warham, John, 326, 792
War of 1812, 253, 325, 525, 628, 784, 785, 814, 843, 865, 934, 1006, 1033, 1164, 1292, 1663
War of Jenkins' Ear, 1104
Warren, Austen, 854
Warren, James, 646-47
Warren, Joseph, 31, 238, 578, 1050, 1051, 1389, 1448, *1519-21*
Warren, Mercy Otis, 17, 646-47, 894, 1451, *1521-23*
Warren, Peter, 712
Warton, Thomas, 378
Washington, Fort, 449, 672
Washington, George, 16, 47, 48, 63, 64, 76, 81, 82, 96, 155, 159, 161, 168, 171, 184, 190, 196, 212, 221, 273, 274, 278, 299, 398, 412, 449, 453, 466, 468-69, 540, 550, 552, 553, 554, 555, 557, 578, 650, 672, 674, 697, 718, 724, 732, 750, 780, 796, 797, 798, 804, 813, 815, 818, 825, 826, 873, 882, 883, 884, 922, 943, 948, 953, 954, 955, 961, 1004, 1007, 1024, 1033, 1041, 1053, 1062, 1072, 1125, 1127, 1130, 1131, 1183, 1192, 1193, 1211, 1212, 1213, 1214, 1238, 1256, 1292, 1300, 1302, 1346-47, 1368, 1404, 1434, 1453, 1486, 1521,

1423-24, 1531, 1538, 1571, 1622, 1638, 1643
Washington, Martha, 1523
Wasp, 1269
Waters, Daniel, 1395
Waters, Henry, 992
Watkins, Tobias, 36
Watson, John F., 873
Watts, Isaac, 44, 149, 246, 255, 340, 364, 550, 729, 944, 981, 1298
Wayne, Anthony, 674, 684, 842, 843, 1005, 1024
Wayne, Caleb, 436
Webb, George, 214, *1524-26*
Webb, John, 517, 601, 1465, *1526-29*, 1594
Webb, Nathan, 296
Webster, John, 1185
Webster, Noah, 412, 825, 915, 1164, 1329, 1331, *1529-41*
Webster, Pelatiah, 460, 1514-43
Webster, Samuel, 331
Weekly Register, 897, 1205
Weems, Mason Locke, 798, 1302 *1543-46*, 1643
Wegelin, Oscar, 705, 1251
Weiser, Conrad, 127, 541, 542
Weld, Edmund, *1546-47*
Welde, Thomas, 832, 920, 1168, 1169, 1546, *1547-49*, 1567
Welles, Noah, 118-19, 758, 759, *1549-51*
Wellman, James, 296
Wells, Helena, *1551-53*
Wells, Robert, 741, 1251, 1252, 1445
Welsteed, William, 668
Wertenbaker, Thomas, 303
Wesley, Charles, 44, 339-40, 429, 1579
Wesley, John, 43, 67, 68, 136, 194, 339-40, 407, 429, 1144, 1579
West, Benjamin (1730-1813), *1553-55*
West, Benjamin (1738-1820), 492, 494, 654, 799, 1319, 1350
West, John, 597
Western Telegraphe and Washington Advertiser, 221
Western World, 949

Westminster Assembly, 770, 1083, 1134, 1135, 1199

West, Samuel, 435

West, Stephen, 416, 1367

West, Thomas (Baron De La Warr), 60, 1162, 1223, *1555-57*

Weston, Thomas, 408, 1631

Wetmore, James, 759, 1348, 1354, 1383, *1557-59*

Weymouth, George, 662, 1243

Wharton, Charles, 278

Whately, Thomas, 808

Wheatley, Phillis, 403, 537, 538, 703, 944, *1559-61*

Wheeler, Thomas, 229, *1561-62*

Wheelock, C. Webster, 1191

Wheelock, Eleazar, 1099, 1100, 1326, 1336, 1337, 1479, *1562-65*, 1569, 1614

Wheelwright, John, 569, 666, 1548, *1565-67*, 1584

Whipple, John, 655, 656

Whiskey Rebellion, 179, 180, 221, 525, 590, 628, 629, 674, 804, 883, 1213

White, William, 25

Whitefield, George, 54, 105, 132, 156, 246, 272, 304, 305, 320-21, 339, 363, 368, 386, 429, 515, 516, 536, 538, 564, 565, 601, 613, 622, 635-36, 642, 644, 645, 668, 675, 709, 725, 729, 829, 912, 944, 1060, 1078, 1136, 1139, 1140, 1177, 1189, 1194, 1290, 1325, 1339, 1340, 1419, 1420, 1422, 1428, 1439, 1459, 1490, 1506, 1527, 1559, 1563, 1570, *1578-81*, 1587, 1588

White Plains, battle of, 39

Whiting, John, 1392, *1582-84*

Whiting, Samuel, 347, 1469, *1584-86*

Whitman, Elizabeth, 591

Whitman, Samuel, 242

Whitman, Walt, 91, 571, 762, 985, 1662

Whittier, John Greenleaf, 289, 1056, 1142, 1661

Whitwell, William, 106

Whitworth, Richard, 283

Wigglesworth, Edward, 54, *1586-89*, 1591

Wigglesworth, Michael, 128, 170, 234, 314, 496, 527, 683, 704, 1014, 1057, 1118, 1305, 1473, 1586, *1589-93*

Wigglesworth, Samuel, 1590-91, *1593-96*

Wightman, Valentine, 235

Wignell, Thomas, 125, 1248

Wildes, Harry Emerson, 1159

Wilkes, John, 880

Wilkins, Isaac, *1596-99*

Wilkinson, Eliza Yonge, *1599-1600*

Wilkinson, James, 328, 812, 814

Willard, Samuel, 30, 370, 579, 1154, 1303, 1393, 1472, 1473, *1600-1603*, 1614, 1617

William III (king of England), 77, 717, 801, 973, 975

William IV (king of England), 704

William Henry, Fort, 1003, 1192

Williams, Elisha, 1139, *1603-6*, 1612, 1616

Williams, John, 460, 682, 689, 713, *1606-8*, 1613

Williams, Roger, 3, 263, 331, 332, 389, 392, 393, 394, 476, 481, 505, 594, 664, 665, 770, 853, 963, 1050, 1168, 1169, 1237, 1376, 1511, 1548, *1608-11*

Williams, Solomon, 759, 1603, *1611-14*, 1616

Williams, William (1665-1741), 1603, 1612, *1615-17*, 1618

Williams, William (1688-1760), 1288, 1612, 1616, *1617-19*

Williams, William, (1727-1791), *1619-21*

Williamson, Hugh, 109

Wills, Gary, 827

Wilson, Alexander, 113

Wilson, James, 464, *1621-24*

Wilson, John, 389, 422, 423, 427, 571, 1014, 1082, 1092, 1215, 1264, 1442, 1469, 1585, *1624-28*

Wilson, Matthew. *See* Knott, Edward, S.J.

Windham, Willam, 351

Wing, Vincent, 212, 424

Wingate, Edmund, 1008
Wingfield, Edward Maria, 60, *1628-29*
Winship, George, 303
Winslow, Edward, 185, 409, 665, 1001, 1047, *1630-32*
Winslow, John, 701, 702
Winslow, Josiah, 748
Winslow, Ola, 1134
Winthrop, Fitz-John, 222, 317, 1226, 1469
Winthrop, John (1588-1649), 90, 308, 317, 321, 348, 389, 473, 475, 476, 663, 691, 746, 770, 791, 831, 847, 875, 876, 917, 963, 992, 1054, 1056, 1084, 1093, 1108, 1120, 1168, 1173, 1174, 1198, 1372, 1389, 1421, 1549, 1558, 1565, 1566, 1567, 1608, 1625, 1632, *1633-34*, 1635, 1637, 1651
Winthrop, John, Jr. (1606-1676), 473, 639, 640, 656, 1167, 1372, 1373, 1469, *1635-36*, 1637
Winthrop, John (1714-1779), 1350, 1521, *1637-40*
Winthrop, Wait, 317, 1304
Wirt, William, *1640-43*
Wise, John, 747, 1093, 1176, 1570, 1587, *1643-45*
Wister, Sally, *1645-46*
Wiswall, Ichabod, 65-66, *1646-47*
Witchcraft: almanac essays on, 49; hysteria of 1690s, 197-98, 231, 260-61, 315, 648, 691, 790, 868-69, 912, 968-69, 975, 988, 1022, 1023, 1094, 1267-68, 1305, 1306, 1310, 1398, 1601, 1602, 1643; practiced by Indians, 1100; laws concerning, 1477; Parsons trial, 250, 1199; tracts and letters on, 260-61, 290-91, 691-92, 868-69, 969, 975, 988, 1434, 1442, 1490, 1602
Wither, George, 887
Witherspoon, John, 25, 583, 830, 933, 1164, 1345, 1346, 1367, *1647-50*
Wolcott, Henry, 792
Wolcott, Roger, 236, 760, *1650-53*
Wolfe, James, 356, 357, 382, 491, 536, 953, 1003, 1020

Wollstonecraft, Mary, 215, 466, 467, 526, 812, 813, 1552
Wood, Abraham, 157
Wood, William, 847, 1055, 1561, 1610, *1653-54*
Woodbridge, Benjamin, 1093, 1245, *1654-55*, 1656
Woodbridge, John, 1134, 1245, 1654, *1655-58*
Woodbridge, Mercy, 1657
Woodbridge, Timothy, 222, 241, 242
Woodmason, Charles, 120, *1658-60*
Woolman, John, 135, 322, 365, 366, 676, 744, 1371, *1660-62*
Worcester Magazine, The, 1447, 1450
Wordsworth, William, 99, 114, 283, 378, 440, 900, 1103, 1196
Workman, John, 754
Wormeley, Ralph, 144
Worsley, Benjamin, 1372
Wortman, Tunis, *1662-64*
Wotton, Henry, 1264
Wragg, William, 622, 623
Wright, Louis B., 45, 144
Wright, Lyle, 1222
Wright, Susanna, 685
Wroth, Lawrence, 371, 1002, 1003, 1525
Wyatt, Edith Franklin, 812, 814
Wythe, George, 826, 961, 1064, 1229, 1509

XYZ Affair, 81, 82, 469, 646, 647, 1072

Yale, Elihu, 487
Yellow Fever: deaths caused by, 81, 120, 393, 547, 1329; epidemics, 393, 558, 1015, 1329; Philadelphia epidemic of 1793, 37, 466, 554, 841, 1015, 1129, 1257; treatments of, 350, 1015
Yorktown, seige of, 539, 1484
Young Arthur, 168, 169
Young, Edward, 246, 330, 378, 578, 729
Young, Thomas, 29

Zenger, John Peter, 188, 1354, *1665-66*
Zoets, Jan, 1375
Zubly, John Joachim, 722, *1666-69*

About the Editors

JAMES A. LEVERNIER is Director of American Studies and teaches English, American literature, and American Studies at the University of Arkansas at Little Rock. He specializes in early American literature. His book-length publications include *The Indians and Their Captives* (Greenwood Press, 1977), and *Soldiery Spiritualized: Nine Sermons Preached before the Artillery Companies of New England, 1674-1774*.

DOUGLAS R. WILMES, formerly chairman of the English Department at Alliance College, teaches American literature and American Studies at The Pennsylvania State University. A specialist in early American literature, particularly the satire of the period, Professor Wilmes is editor of *Studies in Contemporary Satire*.